Collins

Scot land the best

PETER IRVINE

HarperCollins Publishers
Westerhill Rd, Bishopbriggs Glasgow G64 2QT

www.collins.co.uk

First published in Great Britain in 1993
by Mainstream Publishing Company (Edinburgh) Ltd

First published by HarperCollins Publishers in 1997

This edition published in 2001
Revised 2002

© Peter Irvine, 1993, 1994, 1996, 1997, 1998, 1999, 2000, 2001, 2002 (text)
© HarperCollins Publishers, 1999, 2000, 2001 (maps on pp. 324-327)
© Bartholomew Ltd, 1999, 2000, 2001 (maps on pp. 328-345)

ISBN 0 00 712199 7 (paperback edition)
     0 00 714083 5 (hardback edition)

Printed in Italy by Amadeus, S.p.A.

CONTENTS

INTRODUCTION

Welcome to the latest edition of *Scotland the Best*! The style of the book is to be reductive and concise so I'll start as I mean to continue and keep this introduction short. In the following pages you'll find all (and only) the best things about Scotland, each conveyed in a few lines. The guide is subjective and impressionistic but it gives you the facts (see below); it is the inside track. Unlike other guides, I don't include things simply because they are there, but only if they above the ordinary and beyond the mediocre. It's like a digest of many other guides – about food, walking, pubs, history, of many other opinions and loads of feedback from you, the reader. But nobody mentioned in these pages has paid to be included and purposefully, we carry no ads or sponsorship and there is no series editor influencing the content. For helping me compile and evaluate the huge amounts of info and disinfo, I must thank my intrepid researcher Keith Davidson, my long suffering PA Penny, and once again, Georgia.

Given its selective nature, *Scotland the Best* is a kind of barometer of what's going on in Scotland. At the time of going to print, events throughout the UK, like foot-and-mouth, and in the USA have had a huge impact on the tourism industry and in all kinds of ways that are yet to be revealed. Consequently, as I write many of the places that I recommend are going through difficulties and some may not survive; I can only hope that in our small way, all the people associated with, and included in, this book are helping to make things better. There is strength in the diversity you will find in these pages – especially when we work together. Enjoy us!

Peter Irvine
Edinburgh, October 2001

A DECLARATION

Scotland the Best is a handbook of information about all the 'best' places in Scotland. 'Best' you will understand is a subjective term; it means 'best' according to what I think. Needless to say, there seem to be a lot of readers who agree with my judgement and even if you don't, you may see that I and my associates have gone to some efforts to reach our assertions. It's intended to be obvious that I am conveying opinions and impressions. They're true because the motives are true; we believe in what we are saying. We take no bribes and and have no vested interest in any of the places recommended, other than that we do talk things up and shamelessly proclaim the places we like or admire.

Along with observations, every 'item' conveys factual information; I hope it's plain where the facts end and the opinions begin. In guide books this is not always the case. However, it's with 'the facts' that inconsistencies may appear. We try to give accurate and clear directions explaining how to find a place and basic details that might be useful. This information is gleaned from a variety of sources and may be supplied by the establishment concerned. We do try to verify everything usually by visiting, but the process of acquiring and transcribing information is tricky when there's so much of it. Things change and because nowhere we mention has solicited their inclusion (or if they have, it has made little difference), nor been invited to check what we say … well, mistakes can be made. With this density of information it's impossible to run it past proprietors, and they might not like what we say because it's our opinion, not theirs. So I'm sorry if we get a number wrong. We hope there aren't any mistakes, but we may not find out until you let us know. Please do so we can fix it.

This admission is therefore made in advance. I hope you haven't gone up the glen with no cash to find that after all they don't accept credit cards, or arrive at the golf club to find that you've booked into a sauna parlour. My cringing excuse is that we are merely human. This guide is made by fallible humans like me for fallible humans, of which I hope you are one. However, be clear of one thing, this book is more than about searching for something better, it is actually about striving for perfection.

HOW TO USE THIS BOOK

There are three ways to find things in this book:

1. There's an index at the back.

2. The book can be used by category, e.g. you can look up the best restaurants in the Borders or the best scenic routes in the whole of Scotland. Each entry has an item number in the outside margin. These are in numerical order and allow easy cross-referencing.

3. You can start with the maps and see how individual items are located, how they are grouped together and how much there is that's worth seeing or doing in any particular area. Then just look up the item numbers. If you are travelling round Scotland, I would urge you to use the maps and this method of finding the best of what an area or town has to offer.

   The maps correspond to the recognisable regions of Scotland. There's also an overall map to show how the regions fit together. The list of maps is on p.321 and the map section is at the back of the book.

   All items have a code which gives (1) the specific item number; (2) the map on which it can be found; and (3) the map co-ordinates. For space reasons, items in Glasgow and Edinburgh are not marked on Maps A and B, although they do have co-ordinates in the margin to give you a rough idea of the location. City maps are readily available from any tourist office or newsagent.

TICKS FOR THE BEST THERE IS

Although everything listed in the book is notable and remarkable in some way, there are places that are outstanding even in this superlative company. Instead of marking them with a rosette or a star, they have been 'awarded' a tick.

 Amongst the very best in Scotland

 Amongst the best (of its type) in the UK

 Amongst the best (of its type) in the world, or simply unique

Listings generally are not in an order of merit although if there is one outstanding item it will always be at the top of the page and this obviously includes anything which has been given a tick.

Hotels and restaurants are also grouped according to price and this is why a cross-marked place may appear further down the page (ticks also indicate exceptional value for money).

A NOTE ON CATEGORIES

Edinburgh and Glasgow, the destinations of most visitors and the nearest cities to more than half of the population, are covered in the substantial Sections 2 and 3. Both have been extended from the last edition mainly to cover the proliferation and diversification of restaurants. You will probably need a city map to get around, although Maps A and B should give you the rough layout.

For the purposes of maps, and particularly in Section 4 (Regional Hotels and Restaurants), I have used a combination of the subdivision of Scotland based on the current standard political regions along with the historical ones, e.g. Argyll, Clyde Valley. From Sections 5 to 12, categories are based on activities, interests and geography and refer to the whole of Scotland. Section 13 covers the islands, with a page-by-page guide to the larger ones.

Section 14 is intended to give a comprehensive and concise guide to the best of the major Scottish towns in each area. Some of the recommended hotels and restaurants will be amongst the best in the region and will have been referred to in Section 4, or even amongst the best in Scotland and referred to in Sections 5 to 13, but otherwise they have been selected because they are the best there is in the town or the immediate area.

There are some categories like Bed and Breakfasts, Fishing Beats, Antique Shops that haven't been included because they are impracticable to assess (there are too many of them, are too small, or they change hands too often). Fishing places would be spoiled if too many people knew about them, and for similar reasons I've declined to draw attention to (for example) places to see birds of prey. In this edition there are several new categories that might be useful like places to take kids camping and venues suitable for hosting house parties.

If there are other categories that you would like to see in future editions, please let us know (*see p. 14*).

THE CODES

1.   The Item Code

At the outside margin of every item is a code which will enable you to find it on a map. Thus **1269** MAP 1 *C2* should be read as follows: **1269** is the item number, listed in simple consecutive order; MAP 1 refers to the Argyll/Ayrshire/Clyde Valley – the map section is at the back of the book; *C2* is the map co-ordinate, to help pinpoint the item's location on the map grid. A co-ordinate such as *xC1* indicates that the item can be reached by leaving the map at grid reference *C1*.

2.   The Hotel Code

Below each hotel recommended is a band of codes as follows:

20RMS   JAN-DEC   T/T   PETS   CC   KIDS   TOS   LOTS

20RMS means the hotel has 20 bedrooms in total. No differentiation is made as to the type of room. Most hotels will offer twin rooms as singles or put extra beds in doubles if required. This code merely gives an impression of size.

JAN-DEC means the hotel is open all year round. **APR-OCT** means approximately from the beginning of April to the end of October.

T/T refers to the facilities: **T/** means there are direct-dial phones in the bedrooms while **/T** means there are TVs in the bedrooms.

PETS means the hotel accepts dogs and other pets, probably under certain conditions (e.g. pets should be kept in the bedroom). It's usually best to check first.

XPETS indicates that the hotel does not generally accept pets.

CC means the hotel accepts major credit cards (e.g. Access and Visa).

XCC means the hotel does not accept credit cards.

KIDS indicates children are welcome and special provisions/rates may be available.

XKIDS does not necessarily mean that children are not able to accompany their parents, only that special provisions/rates are not usually made. Check by phone.

TOS means the hotel is part of the Taste of Scotland scheme and has been selected for having a menu which features imaginative cooking using Scottish ingredients. The Taste of Scotland produces an annual guide of members.

TR Top Rooms – the best rooms in the house!

GF means the establishment is gay-friendly.

LOTS Rooms which cost more than £75 per night per person. The theory is that if you can afford over £150 a room, it doesn't matter too much if it's £150 or £175.

Other price bands are:

EXP Expensive: £55-75 per person.

MED.EX Medium (expensive): £40-55.

MED.INX Medium (inexpensive): £32-40.

INX Inexpensive: £25-32.

CHP Cheap: less than £25.

Rates are per person per night. They are worked out by halving the published average rate for a twin room in high season and should be used only to give an impression of cost. They are based on 1999 prices. Add between £2 to £5 per year, though the band should stay the same unless the hotel undergoes improvements.

3.   The Restaurant Code

Found at the bottom right of all restaurant entries. It refers to the price of an average dinner per person with a starter, a main course and dessert. It doesn't include wine, coffee or extras.

EXP Expensive: more than £30.

MED Medium: £20-30.

INX Inexpensive: £12-20.

CHP Cheap: under £12.

These are based on 2001 rates. With inflation, the relative price bands should stay about the same. Where a hotel is notable also for its restaurant, there is a restaurant line below the hotel entry and a separate code in the corner.

SD indicates the signature dish of the chef.

4.   The Walk Code

A great number of walks are described in the book, especially in section 9. Found at bottom-right corner of item:

2-10km   CIRC   BIKE   1-A-1

2-10km means the walk(s) described may vary in length from 2km to 10km.

CIRC means the walk can be circular, while **xCIRC** shows the walk is not circular and you must return more or less the way you came.

BIKE indicates the walk has a path which is suitable for ordinary bikes.
xBIKE means the walk is not suitable for, or does not permit, cycling.
mtBIKE means the track is suitable for mountain or all-terrain bikes.

The **1-A-1** Code

First number **(1, 2 or 3)** indicates how easy the walk is.
1 the walk is easy.
2 medium difficulty, e.g. standard hillwalking, not dangerous nor requiring special knowledge or equipment.
3 difficult: care and preparation and a map are needed.

The letters **(A, B or C)** indicate how easy it is to find the path.
A the route is easy to find. The way is either marked or otherwise obvious.
B the route is not very obvious, but you'll get there.
C you will need a map and preparation or a guide.

The last number **(1, 2 or 3)** indicates what to wear on your feet.
1 ordinary outdoor shoes, including trainers, are probably okay unless the ground is very wet.
2 you will need walking boots.
3 you will need serious walking or hiking boots.

Apart from designated walks, the **1-A-1** code is employed wherever there is more than a short stroll required to get to somewhere, e.g. a waterfall or a monument.

LIST OF ABBREVIATIONS

As well as codes and because of obvious space limitations, a personal shorthand and ad hoc abbreviation system has had to be created. I'm the first to admit some may be annoying, especially 'restau' for restaurant, but it's a long word and it comes up often. The others which are used are …

Aber	Aberdeen	no smk	no smoking
accom	accommodation	nr	near
adj	adjacent		
admn	admission	o/look	overlook(s)/ing
app	approach	opp	opposite
approx	approximately	o/side	outside
atmos	atmosphere		
av	average	pl	place
AYR	all year round	poss	possible
		pt	point/port
bedrms	bedrooms		
betw	between	R	river
br	bridge	rep	reputation
BYOB	bring your own bottle	r/bout	roundabout
		road	rd
cl	closes/closed	refurb	refurbished/ment
contemp	contemporary	restau	restaurant
cotts	cottages	ret	return
		rm(s)	room(s)
dining-rm	dining room	RSPB	Royal Society for the Protection of Birds
E	east	rt	right
Edin	Edinburgh		
esp	especially	S	south
excl	excluding or excellent	SD	signature dish
exhib(s)	exhibition(s)	self/c	self-catering
exp	expensive	sq	square
		st	street
facs	facilities	stn	station
ft	fort	SYHA	Scottish Youth Hostel Association
gdn(s)	garden(s)	☕	Worth going to for the tearoom alone
GF	gay-friendly		
Glas	Glasgow	TDH	Table d'hôte
gr	great	TGP	Time of going to print
		TIC	Tourist Information Centre
HS	Historic Scotland		
hr(s)	hour(s)	TO	tourist office
		TR	top rooms
incl	including	t/away	take-away food
inexp	inexpensive	t/off	turn off
info	information	trad	traditional
		tratt	trattoria
j/tie	jacket and tie		
jnct	junction	univ	university
L	loch	v	very
LO	last orders	vegn	vegetarian
min(s)	minute(s)	W	west
mt(s)	mountain(s)	w/end(s)	weekend(s)
N	north	yr(s)	years
NTS	National Trust for Scotland		

YOUR HELP NEEDED
(AND WIN GOOD WHISKY)

Scotland the Best wouldn't be the best if I didn't receive feedback and helpful suggestions from so many people. It really has become an interactive book because so many of you seem to know what sort of places are likely to fit. With each new edition I believe I get closer to the definitive best guide including everywhere in Scotland that's any good. It bothers me if I miss something – a new restaurant might be forgiveable, but there may be an established one that I've omitted from this edition. There are pubs for example that have been doing great food for years and as each edition passes I get closer to knowing all of them. This completeness is because people write to tell me. And I hope very much that they will continue to do so. *Scotland the Best* is supposed to follow the inside track to Scotland and you who live here, or are experiencing it as a visitor, are on it. Send me the word!

Write and let me know whether you have found the information helpful and accurate and whether you agree or disagree with my selections. Have places lived up to your expectations and, in particular, are there any superlative places that ought to have been mentioned? Even if it's your own place and you think it deserves wider attention, let me know. Everywhere you recommend will be checked out for the next edition in 2003/2004. Please send your comments or suggestions to:

> Peter Irvine/*Scotland the Best*
> Reference Department
> HarperCollins Publishers
> Westerhill Rd
> Bishopbriggs
> Glasgow
> G64 2QT

For sharing this information, HarperCollins will be happy to share out some good whisky and cheese. A bottle of malt (any from the list of my suggestions on p.188) together with a drum of Tobermory cheddar will be presented at the launch of the next edition, to the best three suggestions received by 30 September 2003. Recommendations can be for any category or for any number of categories, and anywhere that you recommend will be included next time, if it checks out. Please give reasons for your recommendation and specific directions if it is difficult to find.

You can also contact me on the internet through the *Scotland the Best* website which is sponsored by Famous Grouse whisky. The address is

www.s1play.com

SECTION 1

The Likes of You and Me

THE BIG ATTRACTIONS

Amongst the 'top 10' (paid admn) and the 'top 10' (free) visitor attractions, these are the ones really worth seeing. Find them under their item nos.

EDINBURGH CASTLE; HOLYROOD PALACE; EDINBURGH ZOO; THE NATIONAL GALLERY; DYNAMIC EARTH: 377/379/385/384/383/MAIN ATTRACTIONS.

KELVINGROVE ART GALLERY; THE BURRELL COLLECTION; SCIENCE CENTRE: 727/728/731/MAIN ATTRACTIONS.

THE MUSEUM OF TRANSPORT; THE GLASGOW BOTANICS; THE GALLERY OF MODERN ART: 734/735/736/OTHER ATTRACTIONS.

THE PEOPLE'S PALACE, GLASGOW: 730/MAIN ATTRACTIONS.

THE EDINBURGH BOTANICS: 388/OTHER ATTRACTIONS.

CULZEAN CASTLE; STIRLING CASTLE: 1695/1692/CASTLES.

ABERDEEN ART GALLERY: 2127/PUBLIC GALLERIES.

THE BIG IDEA, IRVINE: 1644/KID-FRIENDLY.

OTHER UNMISSABLES ARE:

1
MAP 6
B3
LOCH LOMOND: App via Stirling and A811 to Drymen or from Glas, the A82 Dumbarton rd to Balloch. Britain's largest inland waterway and a trad playground, especially for Glaswegians; jet-skis, show-off boats.

W bank Balloch-Tarbert is most developed: marinas, cruises, ferry to Inchmurrin Island. Luss is tweeville, like a movie set (it is used in the Scottish TV soap High Road) but has ok tearm (1381/TEAROOMS). Rd more picturesque beyond Tarbert to Ardlui (1165/HOSTELS); see 1265/BLOODY GOOD PUBS for the non-tourist/real Scots experience of the Drover's Inn at Inverarnan. New mega vis centre & Imax opening 2002 at Balloch.

E bank more natural, wooded; good lochside and hill walks (1884/MUNROS). Rd winding but picturesque beyond Balmaha towards Ben Lomond.

2
MAP 2
B3
THE CUILLINS, SKYE: This hugely impressive mt range in the S of Skye, often shrouded in cloud or rain, is the romantic heartland of the Islands. The Red Cuillins are smoother and nearer the Portree-Broadford rd; the Black Cuillins gather behind and are best approached from Glen Brittle (1898/SERIOUS WALKS; 1555/WATERFALLS). This classic, untameable mt scenery has attracted walkers, climbers and artists for centuries. It still claims lives regularly. For best views apart from Glen Brittle, see 1585/SCENIC ROUTES; 1601/VIEWS. Vast range of walks and scrambles (see also 1615/PICNICS).

3
MAP 4
C3
DUNDEE, CITY of DISCOVERY: No you Scots people, this is not a joke. Dundee, often derided, usually missed by tourists is worth a visit. Esp for DCA (2128/GALLERIES) & Verdant Works (2100/MUSEUMS) & the *Discovery* itself: the tall-masted ship, built in Dundee for the 1901 Antarctica expedition with Scott and Shackleton. 10am-5pm (till 4pm Nov-Mar), opens 11am on Sun. The frigate **UNICORN** further along in dockland, is the oldest British warship afloat. ADMN

4
MAP 2
C3
LOCH NESS: Most visits start from Inverness (2249/INVERNESS) at the N end via the R Ness. Ft Augustus is at the other end, 56km S. L Ness is part of the still-navigable Caledonian Canal linking the E and W coast to Ft William. Many small boats line the shores of the R Ness, and one of the best ways to see the loch is on a cruise from Inverness (Jacobite Cruises 01463 233999) or Drumnadrochit (L Ness Cruises 01456 450202). Most tourist traffic uses the main A82 N bank rd converging on Drumnadrochit where the L Ness Monster industry gobbles up your money. If you must, the 'official' L Ness Monster Exhibition is the one to choose. On the A82 you can't miss Urquhart Castle (1729/RUINS). But the two best things about L Ness are: the S rd (B862) from Ft Augustus back to Inverness (1591/SCENIC ROUTES; 1566/WATERFALLS); and the detour from Drumnadrochit to Cannich to Glen Affric (20-30km) (1541/GLENS; 1904/GLEN AND RIVER WALKS; 1553/WATERFALLS). Younger Botanic Gardens/Inverewe/Crathes/Logan/Dawyck: 1471/1472/1473/1475/1477/GARDENS/ VILLAGES/BEACHES/WATERFALLS/LOCHS/VIEWS/CASTLES/RUINS/HILLS p. 193-270.

5 **WEMYSS BAY-ROTHESAY FERRY:** Calmac 01475 650100. The g
MAP 1 stn at Wemyss Bay is the railhead from Glas (60km by rd on the A7. ...d has
C3 the atmos and vitality of an age-old terminus. The frequent ferry (Calmac) has
all the Scottish traits and sausage rolls you can handle, and Rothesay (with its
winter gdn and castle and period seaside mansions) appears out of blood-
smeared sunsets and rain-sodden mornings alike, a gentle watercolour from
summer holidays past. Go to the (Victorian) toilet when you get there and Mt
Stuart (1755/HOUSES). Both are superb.

6 **LOCH ETIVE CRUISES:** 01866 822430, though booking not essential. From
MAP 1 Taynuilt (Oban 20km) through the long narrow waters of one of Scotland's
C1 most atmospheric lochs, a 3hr journey in a small cruiser with indoor and outdoor seating. Pier is 2km from main Taynuilt crossroads on A85. Easter-mid
Oct. Leaves 2pm (and 10am & 12 noon in summer not Sat/Sun). Travel into the
heart of the Highlands, the loch sides inaccessible by car; deer and golden
eagles may attend your journey.

7 **GLENELG-KYLERHEA:** The shorter of the 2 remaining ferry journeys to Skye,
MAP 2 and definitely the best way to get there if you're not pushed for time. The drive
B3 to Glenelg from the A87 is spectacular (1582/SCENIC ROUTES) and so is this 5min
crossing of the deep Narrows of Kylerhea. Apr-Oct (frequent) 9am-5.45pm and
Sun in summer (from 10am). 01599 511302.

8 **CORRAN FERRY:** From Ardgour on A861-Nether Lochaber on the A82 across
MAP 2 the narrows of L Linnhe. A convenient 5min crossing which can save time to
C3 pts S of Mallaig and takes you to the wildernesses of Moidart and
Ardnamurchan and which is a charming and fondly regarded journey in its
own rt. Runs continuously until 8.50pm summer, 7.50pm winter.

9 **THE MAID OF THE FORTH CRUISE TO INCHCOLM ISLAND:** 0131 331 4857.
MAP 7 The wee boat (though they say it holds 225 people) which leaves every day at
A1 different times (phone for details) from Hawes Pier in S Queensferry (15km
Central Edin via A90) opp the Hawes Inn, just under the famous railway br
(378/MAIN ATTRACTIONS) and also from the pier at N Queensferry (summer
only). 45min trips under the br and on to Inchcolm, an attractive island with
walks and an impressive ruined abbey. Much birdlife and also many seals. 1hr
30mins ashore. Tickets at pier.

10 **THE WEST HIGHLAND LINE:** Rail info: 08457 484950. One of the most pic-
MAP 2 turesque railway journeys in Europe and quite the best way to get to Skye
from the S. Travel to Ft William from Glas, then relax and watch the stunning
scenery, the Bonnie Prince Charlie country (MARY, CHARLIE AND BOB, p. 239) and
much that is close to a railwayman's heart go past the window. Viaducts and
tunnels over loch and down dale. Also possible to make the same journey
(from Ft William to Mallaig and/or return) by steam train on certain days.
Journey time just under 2hrs. Check on 01463 239026 or 01524 732100. For
anyone interested in trains, there's a museum in the restored stn at
Glenfinnan. Trains for Mallaig leave from Glas Queen St about 3 times a day
and take about 5hrs.

11 **FROM INVERNESS:** Info on 08457 484950. Two less-celebrated but mes-
MAP 2 merising rail journeys start from Inverness. The journey to Kyle of Lochalsh no
longer has an observation car in the summer months, so get a window seat
and take an atlas; the last section through Glen Carron and around the coast
at Loch Carron is especially fine. There are 3 trains a day and it takes 2hrs
30mins. Inverness to Wick is a 3hr 50min journey. The section skirting the E
coast from Lairg-Helmsdale is full of drama and is then followed by the trans-
fixing monotony of the Flow Country (it's the best way to see it). There are 3
trains a day in summer.

12 **THE PLANE TO BARRA:** Most of the island plane journeys pass over many
MAP 2 smaller islands (e.g. Glas-Tiree, Glas-Stornoway, Wick-Orkney) and are fascinating on a clear day, but BA's daily flight from Glas to Barra is doubly special
because the island doesn't have an airport and you land on Cockleshell Beach
in the N of the island (11 km from Castlebay) after a splendid app. The Otter
holds only 12 passengers and leaves and lands according to the tide. 08457
733377.

FICTION

Iain Banks, *The Wasp Factory*; *The Crow Road*

Christopher Brookmyre, *One Fine Day In The Middle Of The Night*

George Douglas Brown, *The House with the Green Shutters*

George Mackay Brown, *Greenvoe*; *The Masked Fisherman*

John Buchan, *The 39 Steps/Short Stories*

Lewis Grassic Gibbon, *Sunset Song*

Neil Gunn, *Highland River*; *The Silver Darlings*

Alasdair Gray, *Lanark*

Archie Hind, *The Dear Green Place*

James Hogg, *Confessions of a Justified Sinner*

Robin Jenkins, *The Cone Gatherers*

James Kelman, *How Late It Was, How Late*

A L Kennedy, *Night Geometry and the Garscadden Trains*

William McIlvanney, *Docherty*

Nancy Brysson Morrison, *The Gowk Storm*

Ian Rankin, The Rebus Collection Latest: *Set In Darkness*

Bess Ross, *A Bit of Crack and Car Culture*

Sir Walter Scott, *The Heart of Midlothian*; *The Two Drovers and Other Stories*; *Old Mortality*

Ian Crichton Smith, *Consider The Lilies*

Alan Spence, *Its Colours They Are Fine*

Robert Louis Stevenson, *Kidnapped*; *Master of Ballantrae*; *Catriona*; *Dr Jekyll and Mr Hyde*

Muriel Spark, *The Prime of Miss Jean Brodie*

Alexander Trocchi, *Cain's Book*; *Young Adam*

Alan Warner, *Morvern Callar*; *The Sopranos*

Irvine Welsh, *Trainspotting*; *Maribou Stork Nightmares*

NON-FICTION

Boswell and Johnson, *Journey to the Western Islands*

Derek Cooper, *Skye*

Jim Crumley, *A High And Lonely Place*

Tom Devine, *The Scottish Nation: 1700–2000*

Raymond Eagle, *Seton Gordon: A Highland Gentleman*

Antonia Fraser, *Mary Queen of Scots*

George MacDonald Fraser, *The Steel Bonnets*

Douglas Gifford, ed, *Scottish Literature*

Elizabeth Grant of Rothiemurchus, *Memoirs of a Highland Lady*

Phillip Hills, *Appreciating Whisky*

Osgood Mackenzie, *100 Years in the Highlands* (out of print but still available at Inverewe Gdns)

Charles Maclean, *The Story of St Kilda*

Cameron McNeish, *The Munros*

Gavin Maxwell, *Ring of Bright Water*

Edwin Muir, *Scottish Journey*

William Poucher, *The Magic of Skye*

John Prebble, *1000 Years of Scotland's History*; *The Lion in the North*; *The Highland Clearances*; *Culloden*; *Glencoe*

TC Smout, *A History of the Scottish People*

Nigel Tranter, *The Story of Scotland*

George Way and Romilly Squire, *The Collins Scottish Clan & Family Encyclopedia*

Christopher Whyte, ed, *Gendering The Nation: Studies In Modern Scottish Literature*

The West Highland Way: Official Guide

POETRY

Robert Burns, *Collected Songs and Poems*

Robert Fergusson, *Selected Poems*

Sorley Maclean, *Collected Poems*

Norman McCaig, *Collected Poems*

Edwin Morgan, *New Selected Poems*

A FEW THINGS THE SCOTS GAVE THE WORLD

The population of Scotland has never been much over 5 million and yet we discovered, invented or manufactured for the first time the following quite important things.

The decimal point

Logarithms

The Bank of England

The overdraft

Cannabis (the active principle)

Documentary films

Colour photographs

Encyclopaedia Britannica

Postcards

The gas mask

Theory of Combustion

The advertising film

The bus

The steam engine

The locomotive

The fax machine

The photocopier

Video

The telephone

Television

Radar

Helium

Neon

The telegraph

Street lighting

The lawnmower

Kinetic energy

Electric light

The alpha chip

The Thermos flask

The hypodermic syringe

Finger-printing

The kaleidoscope

Anaesthesia

Antiseptics

Golf clubs

The 18-hole golf course

Tennis courts

The bowling green

Writing paper

The thermometer

The gravitating compass

The threshing machine

Insulin

Penicillin

Interferon

The pneumatic tyre

The pedal bicycle

The modern road surface

Geology

Artificial ice

Morphine

Ante-natal clinics

Bovril

Marmalade

The fountain pen

The Mackintosh

Gardenias

Dolly, the cloned sheep

Not bad is it?

13 UP HELLY AA: Info: 01595 693434. Traditionally on the 24th day after Christmas, but now always the last Tues in Jan. A mid-winter fire festival based on Viking lore where 'the Guizers' haul a galley thro the streets of Lerwick and burn it in the park; and the night goes on.   JAN

14 CELTIC CONNECTIONS, GLASGOW: Tickets and info: 0141 353 8000. A huge
MAP B festival of Celtic music from round the world held in the Royal Concert Hall
D3 and other city venues over 3 weeks. Concerts, ceilidhs, workshops.   JAN

15 BURNS NIGHT: The National Bard celebrated with supper. No single major event (tho plans are afoot).   JAN 25TH

16 GLASGOW ART FAIR, GLASGOW: Info: 0141 552 6027. Britain's most signifi-
MAP B cant commercial art fair o/side London held in mid-April in tented pavilions
D3 in George Sq with selected galleries from Scotland and UK.   APRIL

17 MELROSE SEVENS: Info TIC 01896 822555. Border town of Melrose com-
MAP 8 pletely taken over by tournament in their small is beautiful rugby ground. 7-
C2 a-side teams from all over incl international. It's just a good place to go, fanat-
ical or not. *See p. 121* for accom and eats.   APRIL

18 FIFE POINT TO POINT, LEVEN, FIFE: 01333 360229. Major 'society' i.e. county
MAP 5 set, get-together at Balcormo Mains Farm. Sort of Scottish equivalent of
C3 Henley with horses organised by Fife Fox and Hounds. Range Rovers, ham-
pers, Hermès and what's left of the Tories in Scotland.   APRIL

19 PAPS OF JURA HILL RACE, ISLE OF JURA: Details from the hotel 01496
MAP 1 820243. The amazing hill race up and down the 3 Paps or distinctive peaks
B2 (total of 7 hills altogether) on this large remote island (2193/MAGICAL ISLANDS).
About 150 runners take part on the 16 mile challenge from the distillery in
Craighouse, the village.   MAY

19a BURNS AND A' THAT, AYR & AYRSHIRE: Info 01292 678100. Fledgling festival
MAP 1 (the first outing in 2002 was a big critical success and looks set to be annual)
C3 mainly in Ayr and Alloway with flagship open-air classical concert at Culzean
Castle. Celebrates the bard but programme focuses on contemporary music
and theatre.   MAY

19b BIG IN FALKIRK, FALKIRK: Info 0141 552 6027. Held mainly in Callander Park
MAP 6 outside town centre so a delightful, almost rural setting for 'Scotland's
D3 International Street Arts Festival'. Street theatre usually incl one big finale
show with fireworks. Gala-day feel to daytime family programme.   MAY

20 FLOWER SHOWS, INGLISTON & AYR: Many Scottish towns hold flower
MAP A shows, mainly in the autumn, but the big spring show at the Royal Highland
xA3 Centre by Edinburgh Airport (Ingliston) is well worth a look. Call 0131 335
MAP 1 6200 for info. Meanwhile the annual show in Ayr in early August is huge!
C3 Check local TIC for details.   SPRING & AUG

21 COMMON RIDINGS, BORDER TOWNS: Info Jedburgh TIC 01835 863435. The
MAP 8 Border town festivals. Similar formats over different weeks with 'ride-outs' (on
B2, C2 horseback to outlying villages etc) ,'shows', dances and games, culminating on
the Fri/Sat. Total local involvement. Hawick is first, then Selkirk, Peebles/
Melrose, Gala, Jedburgh, Kelso and Lauder end of July.   MAY-JULY

22 ROYAL HIGHLAND SHOW, INGLISTON SHOWGROUND, EDINBURGH: 0131
MAP A 335 6200. The premiere agricultural show (over 4 days) in Scotland and for the
xA3 farming world, the event of the year. Animals, machinery, food, crafts and
shopping. Compulsive for some, big day out for the masses.   JUNE

23 BARRA LIVE, BARRA: Contact Hector MacInnes 01871 810270. A massive
MAP 2 ceilidh with strong Irish flavour, the high point of the summer on this fabulous
A3 island. Everybody comes. Held in a marquee on Tangusdale Machair by the
beach.   JULY

24 SCOTTISH GAME CONSERVANCY FAIR, PERTH: Held in the rural and histor-
MAP 4 ical setting of Scone Palace, a major Perthshire day out and gathering for the
C3 hunting, shooting, fishing and of course, shopping brigade. Details: 01738
552300.   JULY

25
MAP 3
C1
SCOTTISH TRADITIONAL BOAT FESTIVAL, PORTSOY: Perfect little festival in perfect little Moray coast town nr Banff over a w/end in late June/early July. Old boats in old and new harbours, open-air ceilidhs, great atmos. 01261 842951.
JULY

26
MAP 4
C4
T IN THE PARK, BALADO AIRFIELD nr KINROSS: Scotland's highly successful pop festival with all that is current in Britpop and beyond. The T stands for Tennents, the sponsors who are much in evidence. Not as lifestyle-affirming as Glastonbury, but among the best fests in the UK.
JULY

27
MAP B
E5
GIG ON THE GREEN, GLASGOW: Big-scale festival/all-day concerts in middle of Glasgow. 2000: Oasis, 2001: Eminem, 2002: Prodigy and Slipknot – you get the idea?
AUG

28
MAP A
EDINBURGH INTERNATIONAL FESTIVAL, EDINBURGH: 0131 473 2000. The 3 week 'biggest arts festival in the world' with the Military Tattoo and major opera/music/drama. The big fireworks are on the final Saturday. Incorporates The Fringe Festival with hundreds of events every night; Fringe Sunday on the second w/end. Also the International Film Festival, Jazz Festival and (mainly for delegates on a bit of a jolly) the TV festival. Edin is full. (459/ESS. EDIN CULTURE)
AUG

29
MAP B
E5
EDINBURGH INTERNATIONAL BOOK FESTIVAL: 0131 228 5444. A tented village in Charlotte Sq Gardens. Same time as the above but deserving of a separate entry because it is so uniquely good. (459/ESS. EDIN CULTURE)
AUG

30
MAP B
E5
THE WORLD PIPE BAND CHAMPIONSHIPS, GLASGOW: 0141 221 5414. Unbelievable numbers (3-4000) of pipers from all over the world competing and seriously doing their thing on Glasgow Green.
AUG

31
MAP 5
C2
LEUCHARS AIR SHOW, LEUCHARS nr ST ANDREWS: Info: 01334 839000. Major air-show held over one day in RAF airfield with flying displays, exhibitions, classic cars etc.
SEPT

32
MAP 5
C2
THE PEDAL FOR SCOTLAND GLASGOW-TO-EDINBURGH BIKE RIDE: Fun, charity fund-raiser annual bike event. From George Sq to Meadowbank with a pasta party at the halfway point.
SEPT

33
MAP 1
B1
TOUR OF MULL RALLY, ISLE OF MULL: Info Tobermory TO 01688 302182. The highlight of the national rally calendar is this raging around Mull w/end. Though drivers enter from all over the world, the overall winner has often been a local man (well plenty time for practice). There's usually a waiting list for accom, but camping ok and locals put you up.
OCTOBER

34
MAP 5
B3
SCOTTISH WILDLIFE & COUNTRYSIDE FAIR, VANE FARM: 0131 311 6500. Scotland's largest and wildest conservation event held over 2 days at the RSPB nature reserve (1689/WILDLIFE RESERVES). Displays, demos, talks, crafts & retail stands. Esp gr for kids.
SEPT

35
ST ANDREWS NIGHT: Not such a big deal, but dinners etc and cultural ID.
NOV 30TH

36
MAP A
EDINBURGH'S HOGMANAY, EDINBURGH: Everywhere gets booked up, but call TIC for accom, 0131 557 3990 for info. One of the world's major winter events. Launched with a Torchlight Procession through the city centre and with a full, largely populist programme. Main event is the Street Party on 31st; you need a wrist-band. You have to hope that everyone will be good as well as happy. It's my party and I'll cry if I want to, but I'm usually just amazed. (459/ESS EDIN CULTURE)
DEC/JAN

SEVEN THINGS TO DO BEFORE YOU DIE

37 **LOCHNAGAR ON THE LONGEST DAY:** Nr Ballater via L Muick. Leave evening
MAP 3 before and camp/keep your vigil kind of thing. 4hrs to get up. Take map, good
B4 boots, food, dram etc. From first light across the Cairngorm Plateau, the Dee
Valley, Morvern, Bennachie appear; and God, if you're lucky. Later, in Aug the
Royal Family are beneath you (1889/MUNROS).

38 **SANDWOOD BAY, KINLOCHBERVIE:** Another place to go in the long light of
MAP 2 summer days. It's a fair trek from the N (Cape Wrath) or even (more usually)
C1 the southern app via Balchrick and Kinlochbervie (1524/BEACHES). Take a tent,
some beers and wine; a few friends. Sit in the long sunset and/or the dawn.
The summer will pass; and the winter.

39 **A WEEKEND AWAY WITH GOOD FRIENDS OR SOMEONE YOU LOVE:** As
long as it's sympatico, does it really matter where? There are plenty suggestions in the following pages (*see esp pp. 149-56, and p. 157*, GET-AWAY-FROM-IT-
ALL). But for that special pampering **KINNAIRD, CROMLIX, ISLE OF ERISKA
RAEMOIR** are among the v best country hotels in Britain. The food, the service; the grounds are yours (1136/COUNTRY-HOUSE HOTELS) or **THE HOUSE
OVER-BY** in faraway Skye – the treat retreat (1180/ISLAND HOTELS).

40 **THE TRESHNISH ISLANDS:** Go especially when the puffins are there too. The
MAP 1 trip to the Treshnish (from Ulva Ferry on Mull) on a summer's day is a voyage
A1 of discovery (incl Staffa). Go in July, walk amongst these enchanting creatures
before they disappear back into the cold Atlantic. Purify the soul. (1665/BIRDS.)

41 **ST KILDA:** The most westerly islands in the UK, 110 miles into the Atlantic.
MAP 2 Remote, symbolic, superlative in every way, ingrained deep in the spiritual
xA2 heart of the Scots. The community evacuated in 1930 represented the last in
an age of innocence and freedom now gone forever; life was hard but perfectly attuned to this dramatically beautiful place. Highest sea cliffs in UK, premier sea bird breeding stn. Village of Hirta conserved. NTS (0131 226 5922)
arrange 'working parties' (May-Aug, 14-day trips from Oban) or boat charter
from Oban 3 times a yr (0831 121156), 10-day cruises or *MV Kuma*, a former
research vessel out of Uig on Lewis: 01851 672381.

42 **THE AONACH EAGACH or THE CLUANIE RIDGE:** Two awe-inspiring ridges;
MAP 2 in good weather among the most exhilarating walks in the world. The first is
C4/C3 definitely not for the faint-hearted, but most of us could do them once in a
lifetime. So do them before you're too doddery. And go with someone who's
done them before or knows hillwalking. Just go with somebody good
(1794/1796/SERIOUS WALKS).

43 **SUMMER PICNICS:** It's a warm, dry summer's day (ok it hasn't been a common occurrence recently): you stock up from one of the great delis on pp.
182–83 like Valvona in Edinburgh (1429/DELIS) or the wonderful Ndebele
(267/CAFÉS) or Heart & Buchanan (104/T/AWAY) or Delizique (1436/DELIS) in
Glasgow and head for the river. There's a lot of good river picnic sites listed on
p. 104. Most are places that the locals know and have gone for generations
(when those summer's days were longer and somehow, better). But you find
your spot with your family or your mates, maybe light a fire, and cool off in
the pool. It's best to take old sandals or trainers and of course take care.
Afterwards, a game of rounders. There may be midgies, there may be showers, but to my mind this is the most blissful way to spend a summer's day in
Scotland.

SECTION 2

Edinburgh

The telephone code for Edinburgh is 0131
Refer to MAP A, *unless otherwise stated*

44
D2 ✓ ✓ **THE BALMORAL:** 556 2414. Princes St at E end above Waverley Stn. Capital landmark with its clock always 2 min fast (except at Hogmanay) so you don't miss your train. The old pile especially dear to Sir Rocco Forte's heart. Exp for a mere tourist but if you can't afford to stay there's always afternoon tea in the refurbished Palm Court. Few hotels anywhere are so much in the heart of things. Good business centre, fine sports facs; luxurious and distinctive rms with some ethereal views of the city. Main restau, Number One Princes Street (111/BEST RESTAUS), excellent and less formal brasserie, Hadrian's (good power b/fast venue). Even the non-pretentious bar, NB works (occ has music). **TR:** the 3 'Royal' suites – Presidential, Balmoral & Glamis. 188RMS JAN-DEC T/T PETS CC KIDS LOTS

45
C3 ✓ ✓ **THE CALEDONIAN HILTON:** 459 9988. Princes St, W End. Edin institution – former stn hotel built in 1903. Now in Hilton hands & upgrading continues to reinforce 5-star status. Good business hotel with all facs you'd expect (tho not in all rms). 'Living Well' spa with not large pool. Endearing lack of uniformity about the rms. Executive rms on fifth floor (and deluxe rms elsewhere) have gr views. Capital kind of place in every respect. Main restau, The Pompadour, for fine and très formal dining. Brasserie on ground floor. Cally Bar a famous rendezvous. **TR:** the Caledonian Suite. 249RMS JAN-DEC T/T XPETS CC KIDS TOS LOTS

46
C3 ✓ ✓ **THE SHERATON GRAND:** 229 9131. Festival Sq on Lothian Rd and Conference Centre, this city-centre business hotel won no prizes for architecture when it opened late 1980s, but now both Festival Sq & the newly emerged Conference Sq behind one part of the shiny new financial district & Edin looks like a real city at last. This is a reliable stopover with excellent service. Larger rms and castle views carry premiums, but make big difference. Terrace restau adequate, but 'The Grill' menu prepared under the supervision of Nicolas Laurent is elegant, Scottish and innovative (108/BEST RESTAUS) and Santini also excl (152/BEST ITALIAN). The health club 'One' is the best in the city with gr pool. **TR:** the 2 'Diplomatic Suites'. 261RMS JAN-DEC T/T PETS CC KIDS TOS LOTS

47
xE4 ✓ **PRESTONFIELD HOUSE:** 668 3346. Off Priestfield Rd, 3km S of city centre. The Heilan' coos in the 14-acre grounds tell you this isn't your average urban bed for the night. A romantic, almost other-worldly 17th-century building with period features still intact. Architect Sir William Adam, responsible for the ceiling in the Tapestry Rm, also 'did' the ornamental ceilings in Holyrood Palace. Bulk of rms recently refurb, though older ones have more character. Most rms are small with small TVs but luxurious beds. Dining-rm elegant but gets mixed reviews. **TR:** 5/6/16/17. 29RMS JAN-DEC T/T PETS CC XKIDS LOTS

48
B2 ✓ **CHANNINGS:** 315 2226. S Learmonth Gdns, parallel to Queensferry Rd after Dean Br. tasteful alternative to hotel chain hospitality. 5 period town houses joined to form a quietly elegant West End hotel. Efficient and individual service incl 24-hr rm service. Gr views from top-floor rms, incl the Prime Minister's alma mater – Fettes College. **TR:** 12/14/16 & 20 good enough for Sean/Elton/David Coulthard so prob good enough for the rest of us. Brasserie has 2 AA rosettes. 46RMS JAN-DEC T/T XPETS CC KIDS TOS LOTS

49
E2 **ROYAL TERRACE:** 557 3222. 18 Royal Terr. Romanesque plunge pool, other sports facs, multi-level terraced gdn out back, deceptively large number of rms and town house décor a tad on the Baroque side. In other words, fabulous darling! Well … a good business bet. Bar/restau not so notable among the natives. We do like the terrace. **TR:** Aberlour Suite. 108RMS JAN-DEC T/T XPETS CC KIDS TOS LOTS

50
D3 **HOLIDAY INN CROWNE PLAZA:** 557 9797. 80 High St. Modern but sympathetic building on the Royal Mile, handy for everything. Good facs but some say service lacking. Thin walls, not gr views. Another **HOLIDAY INN** out west nr the Zoo (08704 009026) with acres of rms leisure facs & 2 restaus is a superior bed box. **TR:** 429. 238/303RMS JAN-DEC T/T PETS CC KIDS TOS LOTS

51 **THE GEORGE:** 225 1251. George St (betw Hanover St and St Andrew Sq). An
C2 Inter-Continental Hotel but Robert Adam-designed and dating back to late 18th century. Good views to Fife from the top 2 floors. Pricey, but you pay for the location and the Georgian niceties (and extra for the views). Carvery plus good restau, the Chambertin (198/SCOTTISH RESTAUS). Good Festival & Hogmanay Hotel close to the heart of things (taken over by luvvies during TV fest). **TR:** Stewart or Melville (quieter) suites.

195RMS JAN-DEC T/T PETS CC KIDS LOTS

INDIVIDUAL & BOUTIQUE HOTELS

52 ✓ ✓ **THE SCOTSMAN:** 556 5565. North Bridge. De-luxe boutique hotel in
D2 landmark building (the old offices of *The Scotsman* newspaper group) converted into chic, highly individual accom with every modern fac: internet, flat-screen TV, privacy locker in all rms. Labyrinthine lay-out (stairs & firedoors everywhere) & slow lifts apart, this is the coolest hotel in town (2002). Nice art, whisky bar & brasserie (114/BISTROS), & excl leisure facs – Escape – with sexiest hotel pool in town. **TR:** Penthouse & Director's suites.

68RMS JAN-DEC T/T XPETS CC KIDS LOTS

53 ✓ ✓ **THE HOWARD:** 315 2220. 34 Gr King St in the heart of the Georgian
C1 New Town. 3 townhouses in splendid st imbued with quiet elegance tho only 5 mins Princes St. No bar or restau but restful drawing rm & 15 spacious individual rms, sympatico with architecture but not old-fashioned. 3 new suites (**TR**) downstairs have own entrances for discreet liaisons or just convenience & own drawing rm for entertaining. A very Edinburgh accommodation.

15RMS+3SUITES JAN-DEC T/T XPETS CC XKIDS LOTS

54 ✓ ✓ **THE MALMAISON:** 468 5000. Tower Pl, Leith, at the dock gates.
xE1 Award-winning, praise-laden and still expanding designer hotel with individual and rather natty rms. All facs we smart, young, modern people expect eg CD players in each chambre (borrow CDs from reception). **TR** have harbour views & 4-poster beds. Brasserie and café-bar have stylish ambience too (134/BEST BISTROS) and there are many other caffs nearby in this water-front quarter. Pity about the new flats outfront, but Leith still onwards & upwards.

101RMS JAN-DEC T/T PETS CC KIDS EXP

55 ✓ ✓ **THE POINT:** 221 5555. 34 Bread St. You'd never guess this used to be
C3 a Co-operative department store. Space and colour combinations manage to look simultaneously rich and minimal, some castle views. **TR**, the suites (LOTS), come with side-lit Jacuzzis. Once mentioned as one of the gr designery hotels in the world and on the cover of *Hotel Design*. Café-bar Monboddo and restau have modern and spacious, mid-Euro feel. Good places to meet Edinburgers. Conference Centre adj with gr penthouse often used for cool Edin launches & parties.

140RMS JAN-DEC T/T PETS CC KIDS EXP

56 ✓ ✓ **THE BONHAM:** 226 6050. 35 Drumsheugh Gdns. Discreet town-
B3 house in quiet W End cres. Cosmo service and ambience a stroll from Princes St. Owned by same people as the Howard and Channings (48/BEST HOTELS). Rms stylish but not minimalist. Elegant dining in calm, spacious restau (esp end table by back window). Chef Michel Bouyer. Simple wine-list. No bar.

42RMS JAN-DEC T/T XPETS CC XKIDS GF LOTS

57 ✓ **EDINBURGH RESIDENCE:** 226 3380. 7 Rothesay Terr. Another town
B3 house affair but on extravagant scale. Several Georgian town houses have been joined into an elegant residencia (or v upmarket time-share). Usually rms (or suites available), but no cheap, as they say. No restau either but 24 hr room service. Big bathrms, views of Dean Village. Drawing rm if you're feeling lonely. Quiet W End but nr nightlife and shops. In receivership at TGP but likely to continue.

21RMS (8 SUITES) JAN-DEC T/T XPETS CC KIDS LOTS

58 ✓ **ROYAL GARDEN APARTMENTS:** 625 1234. York Buildings, Queen St opp
D2 Nat Portrait Gallery (389/ATTRACTIONS) nr Playhouse Theatre and funky Broughton St. Self-cat v well turned-out apts with coffee-shop on grd floor & access to private gdns. Gr views esp top floor. Avail nightly let (3 days' min at peak periods).

9RMS JAN-DEC T/T XPETS CC XKIDS MED.EX

59 **RICK'S:** 622 7800. 55 Frederick St. Very city centre hotel and bar/restau in
C2 downtown location a stone's throw from George St. By same people who
have Indigo Yard (369/HIP BARS) so the bar is full-on esp late. Restau
(130/BISTROS) has (loud) contemporary dining. Rms upstairs surprisingly quiet.
Modern, urban feel eg DVD players as standard. Same rate single or twin.
Don't let the rms above the bar thing put you off. Go as high as you can –
these rms among the best in the centre at this price.

10RMS JAN-DEC T/T XPETS CC XKIDS MED.INX

60 **BOROUGH:** 668 2255. 72 Causewayside. V urban & self-consciously hip hotel
xD4 in conversion of former snooker hall/warehouse on s side. Notable designer
Ben Kelly (of the legendary Hacienda) somehow fails to warm this place up or
excite. Stark look & cold lighting. Rms small & furnishings not gr, but this is still
a fairly cool place to say. Bar & restau (above) more
buzzy & cheaper.   9RMS JAN-DEC T/T XPETS CC XKIDS MED.EX

61 **HANOVER HOTEL:** 226 7576. 37 Rose St slap in the middle of town (betw
C2 Hanover & Frederick St) opp Yo Sushi & Easyeverything. Central & serviceable
hotel one-up from a travel-lodge tho no b/fast (tray in rm). Does have ground
floor coffee shop.   43RMS JAN-DEC T/T XPETS CC XKIDS MED.EX

62 **PARLIAMENT HOUSE:** 478 4000. 15 Calton Hill. Good central location, only
E2 200m from E end of Princes St and adj to Calton Hill (417/BEST VIEWS), although
tucked away. Small bar in residents lounge and restau for b/fast, even meals –
but OK town house-style décor. About half the rms have views – so you know
where to go.   53RMS JAN-DEC T/T XPETS CC KIDS EXP

63 **WEST END HOTEL:** 225 3656. 35 Palmerston Pl. Capital haunt for Highlanders
B3 and Islanders who feel like a blether in Gaelic or a good folk music session in
the bar (decent measures). Popular with folkie non-guests too. Spacious rms –
no sae cheap anymore, but real.   8RMS JAN-DEC T/T XPETS CC KIDS MED.EX

64 **CANON COURT APARTMENTS:** 474 7000. Canonmills at foot of New Town
C1 and nr Botanics (388/ATTRACTIONS). Self-cat 1 & 2 bedrm aptms often avail for
short lets even 1 night. No café, but an inx stopover. Cable TV. some rms o/look
water of Leith. The gas station over the rd is a social hub esp middle of the
night.   43APTMS JAN-DEC T/T PETS CC KIDS MED.INX

65
C3 ✓✓ **INNER SANCTUM** and the **OLD RECTORY** at the **WITCHERY:** 225 5613. Castlehill. 2 highly individual rms and an apartment above the Witchery restau (109/BEST RESTAUS) at the top of the Royal Mile. Prob the most exceptional and atmospheric in town – designed by owner James Thomson and Mark Rowley – fairly camp/theatrical, OTT and v sexy. Go with somebody good. More rms & apts imminent at TGP. Watch this Old Town space for one of the most urbane stopovers in town.

2+1 APT JAN-DEC T/T XPETS CC XKIDS GF LOTS

66
B1 ✓✓ **19 ST BERNARDS CRES:** 332 6162. In leafy and elegant New Town crescent (the one that's often used in period movies), an exemplary Georgian townhouse stuffed with antiques and the impeccable good taste of its owner, one William Balfour. All niceties are here incl lovely bathrms (tho not en suite) and b/fast in the dining rm. A not-so-wee gem.

3RMS JAN-DEC X/X XPETS XCC XKIDS GF MED.INX

67
C1 ✓ **SAXE COBURG HOUSE:** 332 2717. 24 Saxe Coburg Pl, a Georgian house in a quiet bit of Stockbridge with one of Edin's gr old swimming baths on the corner. Can't be objective about this place because prop Gillian Glover, restau critic has always been kind about this book, but by all accounts this is a v superlative B&B with nice decor & detail. One might expect a v good b/fast.

5RMS FEB-DEC X/T XPETS CC KIDS MED.INX

68
xE4 ✓ **SOUTHSIDE:** 668 4422. 8 Newington Rd. On main st in s side with many hotels/GH stretching halfway to Dalkeith, a surprisingly civilised haven. Careful attention to decor & detail & excl b/fast. 'Café South' operates in on-street dining rm in summer. Some traffic noise, but upstairs rms double-glazed. Nice prints. Parking nearby.

7RMS JAN-DEC X/T XPETS CC KIDS GF MED.INX

69
xE1 ✓ **ARDMOR HOUSE:** 554 4944. 74 Pilrig St which is off Leith Walk & with lots of other B&Bs – this the top spot. Individual, contemporary and relaxed – & that's just the proprietors Colin and Robin & their gorgeous wee dog, Lola.

5RMS JAN-DEC X/T PETS CC KIDS GF MED.INX

70
C2 **24 NORTHUMBERLAND ST:** 556 8140. A definitive New town B&B. Georgian townhouse in mid-New Town full of antiques (owner a notable dealer). Only 3 rms so often booked.

3RMS JAN-DEC X/X XPETS CC XKIDS MED.EXP

71
C2 **17 ABERCROMBY PLACE:** 557 8036. Another plush and private Georgian town house; discreet lack of signage. Once abode of the New Town's architect, Playfair, now belongs to advocate Eirlys Lloyd. No smk. Lovely st with gdns opp. A Wolsey Lodge.

10RMS JAN-DEC T/T XPETS CC KIDS MED.EXP

72
B1 **SIX ST MARY'S PLACE:** 332 8965. Vegn-friendly GH on main st of Stockbridge (St Mary's Pl part of Raeburn Pl) and busy main rd out of town for Forth Rd Br and N, this is a tastefully converted Georgian town house. Informal, friendly, well-cared-for accom popular with academics and people we like. No smk. Vegn breakfast in conservatory. Jolly; nice people.

8RMS JAN-DEC T/T XPETS CC KIDS GF MED.INX

73
D1 **STUART HOUSE:** 557 9030. 12 E Claremont St. Nr the corner of main rd and pleasant walk up to Princes St (1.5km). Residential New Town st and family house decorated with taste and attention to detail – bonny flower gdn out front. Book well in advance. No smk.

5RMS JAN-DEC T/T XPETS CC KIDS MED.EXP

74
xD4 **TEVIOTDALE HOUSE:** 667 4376. 53 Grange Loan, towards E end. Fecund flower gdn out front in suburban southside house & comfortable better than your av B&B within. Mostly big beds (some 4-posters) & famously big b/fasts. New owners since last edn.

7RMS JAN-DEC T/T XPETS CC KIDS MED.INX

THE BEST 'ECONOMY' HOTELS AND TRAVEL-LODGES

Hotels/B&Bs below are included on grounds of price, convenience or just because we like them for some idiosyncratic reason.

75 **APEX INTERNATIONAL:** 300 3456. 31-35 Grassmarket. Once part of Heriot-
C3 Watt Univ, a determined conversion resulted in a central hotel with contemporary Euro-bland façade. Civilised although a tad characterless, this is a good location esp at Festival time. Rms with castle view, are more exp, but worth the extra. Ground-floor bar/restau **METRO** (140/BISTROS) is a fairly fashionable watering hole. Another Apex (474 3456) nr Haymarket with 68 rms and a restau called Tabu (mixed reviews) is ... more merely a bed-box.

168RMS JAN-DEC T/T XPETS CC KIDS EXP

76 **HILTON EDINBURGH AIRPORT:** 519 4400. At the airport, 10km W of city cen-
xA3 tre. No way 'economy', but a reliable travellers' tryst. An L-shaped box high-class transit camp; charming staff. You can virtually roll out of bed and check in. That smell over the airport by the way is due to some unconscionable thing they do to chickens in their concentration camp nearby. Stay indoors and don't have the fricassee! 150RMS JAN-DEC T/T PETS CC KIDS LOTS

77 **TRAVEL INN:** 228 9819. 1 Morrison Link, nr Haymarket Stn. One of 5 in the city
B3 (at TGP) & see below. Likeable for the fact it makes no pretence to be anything other than a bed factory. Big, office-block dull but v cheap – as norm, flat charge. 7 rms specially adapted for wheelchair users.

281RMS JAN-DEC X/T XPETS CC KIDS CHP

78 **TRAVEL INN, LEITH:** 555 1570. Newhaven Pl which means off Commercial Rd,
xE1 along from Royal Yacht Britannia (signed) & behind Harry Ramsden's. Regular box, but: easy parking, quiet location, sports complex adj (Next Generation incl open-air pool – get trial ticket) and for half of the rms a 'sea-view'. Otherwise formula incl Beefeater restau out front. 44RMS JAN-DEC X/T PETS CC KIDS MED.INX

79 **PREMIER LODGE:** 220 2299. 94-96 Grassmarket. Basic and boisterously locat-
C3 ed accom next to Biddy Mulligan's which is open to 1am, but levels 4/5 or at the back best. The Grassmarket is fairly full-on, so good for party animal business types on a budget. 44RMS JAN-DEC X/T PETS CC KIDS MED.INX

80 **IBIS:** 240 7000. Hunter Sq. First in Scotland of the Euro budget chain (one
D3 other in Glas 511/LESS EXP HOTELS). Dead central behind the Tron so good for Hogmanay (or not). Serviceable and efficient. For tourists doing the sights, this is best bed box for location. 99RMS JAN-DEC T/T PETS CC KIDS MED.INX

81 **ST CHRISTOPHER INN:** 0207 407 1856. 9-13 Market St, behind Waverley Stn.
D3 Some good views from upper floors to Princes St. Couldn't be handier for the stn or city centre. This (with sister place in London) a hostel rather than hotel with bunk rms tho' there are 4 tw/dbl rms & 1 single. Price depends on no sharing (£11–20 at TGP). Belushi's café-bar on ground floor open till 1am. A cheap, v central option, better than most other hostels (facs are en-suite).

24RMS JAN-DEC X/X XPETS XCC XKIDS CHP

82 **HOTEL JAVA:** 467 7527. Constitution St, Leith, next to the estimable Port O'
xE1 Leith (308/UNIQUE EDIN PUBS). Friendly, contemporary bar with v basic but inexp rms in Leith nr docks and with many of the city's best bars and restaus nearby. Rms at back and round courtyard.

9RMS JAN-DEC X/T PETS CC KIDS CHP

83 **TAYLORS HALL:** 622 6800. Cowgate. If you don't mind the racket (or want to
D3 be part of it), this is a clubby/young thing kind of hotel in the heart of the throbbing Cowgate area and above the hugely popular 3 Sisters pub. 3 bars to choose from, 24 hr licence for residents. Can do 4 in a rm. Rms not above the courtyard best. 42RMS JAN-DEC T/T PETS CC XKIDS MED.EX

84 **TRAVEL LODGE:** 557 6281 (or central booking 0800 850950). 33 St Mary's St.
E3 Edin central version of national (often roadside) chain. All usual, formulaic facs but inx and nr Royal Mile (Holyrood end) and Cowgate for late-night action.

193RMS JAN-DEC T/T XPETS CC KIDS INX

Edin has some YHA hostels (nae drinking) and independents (young and Hoochy, open 24 hrs), also some handy univ halls of residence to let o/side term time. With all the independent hostels, it's best to turn up around 11/11.30am if you haven't booked. The SYHA is the Scottish Youth Hostels Association. 01786 891400.

85
D3, C3
✔ ✔ **ROYAL MILE BACKPACKERS:** 557 6120. 105 High St. On the Royal Mile, nr the Cowgate with its late-night bars. Ideal central cheap 24 hr crash-out dormitory accom with all the facs for itinerant youth seeking a capital experience. The same company (who also run Mac backpackers tours) have the original hostel, **THE HIGH ST HOSTEL** (8 Blackfriars St): 557 3984, and the **CASTLE ROCK**, 15 Johnston Terr (225 9666) in the old Council Environmental Health HQ. Is huge (190 beds in various dorms, but no singles/doubles) and some gr views across the Grassmarket or to the castle which is just over there. Same folk (Mr Backpacker himself, Peter Macmillan) also have places in Ft William, Inverness, Oban, Pitlochry & Skye. CHP

86
A3
✔ ✔ **S.Y. HOSTEL, EGLINTON:** 337 1120. 18 Eglinton Cres. From the stained glass over the main door to the tartan and wood entrance foyer, you know you're not in a typical hostel. Grand late-Victorian pile (shame about the lighting) in a quiet W End st with 150 beds – majority in dorms but some rms for 4 (single sex dorms). Members only but you can join at reception. Booking recommended. Open 24 hrs. CHP

87
A2
✔ **BELFORD HOSTEL:** 225 6209. Douglas Gdns, nr Gallery of Modern Art (excellent café, 199/BEST TEAROOMS) and quaint Dean Village, but still fairly central. Bizarre concept – 98 beds in partitioned-off (un-soundproofed) 'rms' of 6-10 in a converted church. Top-bunk berth gets you a view of the vaulted wooden ceiling way above. Nice stained glass. Games rm, bar, MTV. Sister establishment **EDINBURGH BACKPACKERS HOSTEL**, 65 Cockburn St (220 1717), is closer to action. CHP

88
D2
PRINCES ST BACKPACKERS EAST: 556 6894. 5 W Register St. Behind Burger King at E end of Princes St. Incredibly central for cheap accom. Basic and attracts the usual international crowd. Same people have **PRINCES ST WEST**, 3 Queensferry St (226 2939), the city's biggest (accom for 250+) with a bar, café, shop. CHP

89
xC4
S.Y. HOSTEL, BRUNTSFIELD: 447 2994. 7 Bruntsfield Cres. S of Tollcross about 10 min walk from W End. Reliable and secure hostel accom in a verdant corner of Bruntsfield. 130 beds but booking 2-3 months in advance essential at peak times. Again, members only, join at reception. Doors cl 2am. CHP

90
D3
From July-Sep, SYHA also opens a temporary hostel in **ROBERTSON'S CLOSE** off Cowgate. Phone HQ for info 01786 891400.

91
xA2
QUEEN MARGARET COLLEGE: 317 3310. Clerwood Terr. Way out, midway betw main rds W to Glas and N to Forth Br; about 10km, so transport probably essential (or bus). Campus facs, e.g. refectory, laundry, bank, good sports. Shared bathrms, etc. and a bit dreary, so not exceptional value, but a private and well-equipped refuge from uptown hassles. Phone first. Also self-catering flats. May-Aug only. CHP

92
xD4
ARGYLE BACKPACKERS HOTEL: 667 9991. 14 Argyle Pl, in Marchmont area of up-market student flats. Quiet area though Argyle Pl the most happening st. 2 km to centre across 'The Meadows' (not advised for women at night). Nice gdn. CHP

THE BEST HOTELS OUTSIDE TOWN

See Lothians map on pages 340–341.

93
MAP 7
B1
✔ ✔ **GREYWALLS, GULLANE:** 01620 842144. On coast 36km E of Edin off A198 just beyond golfers' paradise of Gullane. Prob best co house retreat o/side town. Full report 908/LOTHIANS.

94
MAP 7
A1
✔ ✔ **CHAMPANY INN:** 01506 834532. On A904, 3km Linlithgow on rd to Forth Rd Bridge and S Queensferry. Exemplary restau with rms some o/looking gdn & a parrot called Friday. Legendary restau for steaks and seafood (240/RESTAUS FOR BURGERS AND STEAKS). B/fast in cosy dining kitchen excl with nice bacon. Extraordinary wine-list with dinner. Veggies should not venture here. 16RMS JAN-DEC T/T XPETS CC KIDS LOTS

95
MAP 7
B2
✔ **BORTHWICK CASTLE, NORTH MIDDLETON:** 01875 820514. On B6367, 3km off the A7, 18km bypass, 26km SE of centre. So this is a real Border castle, a big red one. Walls 30m high, this magnificent tower house knocks you off your horse with its authenticity – Mary Queen of Scots was blockaded here once and at night you expect to see her swishing up the spiral stairs. 8 rms in castle, 2 in gatehouse, the (v) grand banqueting hall is impressive, dinner (EXP) a big disappointment (food not changed much since medieval times). 10RMS MAR-DEC T/X PETS CC KIDS LOTS

96
MAP A
xA3
✔ **NORTON HOUSE, INGLISTON:** 333 1275. Off A8 v close to airport, 10km W of city centre. Baronial country house hotel atmos with urban clientele, close to airport. Pleasant grounds to roam, good service and excellent food in Conservatory Restaurant (2AA Rosettes). Also informal bistro. 47RMS JAN-DEC T/T XPETS CC KIDS TOS LOTS

97
MAP 7
B2
JOHNSTOUNBURN HOUSE, HUMBIE: 01875 833696. On B6457 2km from A68 and 25km SE of centre. Bypass 22km. Country class in this 17th-century manor with relaxed and friendly service. Some rms in its coach house, all have that upbeat frilliness. Public areas v cool, esp the panelled 18th-century dining-rm. Mavis Hall park adj offers clay pigeon shooting, fishing, off-road, etc., so it's an excellent all-round centre v close to the city. Hotel on market (as private house) so ring first. **2002 UPDATE: NOW CLOSED** 20RMS JAN-DEC T/T PETS CC KIDS TOS LOTS

98
MAP 7
A1
DALHOUSIE CASTLE, BONNYRIGG: 01875 820153. Just off B704 2km from the A7, 15km from bypass and 23km S of centre. The castle that tries too hard? It looks fantastic in its setting and some bits date way back to the 13th century otherwise ersatz tho ideal for weddings. (Previous guests incl Edward I, Cromwell, Queen Victoria, some rock stars.) Another 5 rms in adj Victorian lodge. 34RMS JAN-DEC T/T PETS CC KIDS TOS LOTS

99
MAP 7
A1
HOUSTOUN HOUSE, UPHALL: 01506 853831. On A899 at end of Broxburn/Uphall Main St, 8km from r/bout at the start of the M8 Edin–Glas motorway. Airport 10km, 18km W of centre. Bits of this tower house date to the 16th century, in sharp contrast to shiny leisure facs (inc pool) which attracts local patronage. 4-posters in some rooms, blazing fires and 2 restaus all in extensive greenery. Only quite posh hotel in barren hinterland of W. Lothian. Stuffed with farmers during Royal Highland Show week. Sports facs, incl a pool. 72RMS JAN-DEC T/T XPETS CC KIDS TOS LOTS

100
MAP 7
A1
DALMAHOY, KIRKNEWTON: 333 1845. On A71 (Kilmarnock rd) on edge of town – bypass 5km, 15km W of centre, airport 6km. Georgian house with distinctive rms and big modern annexe (6 turret suites best). Two internationally rated courses make this a golfing mecca. Plenty of other sports facs to while away the hours or improve your handicaps generally. V elegant surroundings. Part of the Marriott chain. 215RMS JAN-DEC T/T XPETS CC KIDS TOS LOTS

OPEN ARMS, DIRLETON: Report 911/LOTHIANS.

TWEEDDALE ARMS, GIFFORD: Report 913/LOTHIANS.

THE BEST RESTAURANTS

101
xE1
✔ ✔ **MARTIN WISHART:** 553 3557. 54 The Shore. Discreet waterside frontage for one of Edinburgh's most notable foody experiences. Small if not cramped room designed on simple lines & uncomplicated menu & wine-list. Michelin chef Martin & AA restau of the yr raise expectation here, but prep, cooking & presentation are demonstrably a cut above the rest. Martin just has that touch that we don't have that turns a French bean into a fine French bean. Iain Mellis cheeses. **SD**: Ravioli of lobster and truffle; Buccleuch beef. Lunch Tues-Fri, Dinner Tues–Sat. LO 9.30pm   EXP

102
C3
✔ ✔ **ROGUE:** 228 2700. 63 Morrison St thro très discreet, hardly marked door in the corner of the Scottish Widows building. The inimitable Dave Ramsden's new uptown bar & restau fêted for food (Richard Alexander) & design (Sam Booth) as soon as it opened in summer 2001. Both menu & decor combine classic & modern elements; the whole effect is understated style tho some may find the rm too cool & corporate. Michelin surely on the way for extensive Mod-British menu with Conran approach – it's all Easily Eaten. **SD**: Buccleuch beef with rosti, jelly & fruit. 7 days. lunch & LO 11pm.
MED

103
C3
✔ ✔ **THE ATRIUM:** 228 8882. Foyer of the Traverse Theatre (453/CULTURE), Cambridge St off Lothian Rd. Can it really be 10 yrs since the Atrium opened and immediately became the top meal in town? Andrew Radford's breakthro restau still one of the most stylish venues in town for biz lunch or supper with atmos. Many chefs have come & gone (& opened their own restaus), but the kitchen & outfront combo of inspiration & efficiency was still among the slickest in town at TGP. **SD**: Lamb and pork, pithiviers, confits. EXP

104
D3
✔ ✔ **THE TOWER:** 225 3003. Corner of Chambers St and George IV Br above the Museum of Scotland. Restaurant supremo James Thompson's top end and top floor restau in the distinctive 'tower' on the corner of the new museum building. Benefits from the much-admired grand design and detail of Gordon Benson's architectural vision. Décor has been described as retro-futurist; it feels that it could be anywhere except for Edin rooftops and castle skyline outside the windows (and in summer, the terr). Gr private dining-rm in the tower itself. Kitchens far below in Prehistoric Scotland, but food everything one would expect – Scottish slant on modern British. The steaks are good. 7 days. Lunch and dinner. LO 11pm. W/end booking essential. Smokers to the balcony!
EXP

105
C2
✔ ✔ **OLOROSO:** 226 7614. 33 Castle St. Unassuming entrance and lift to this rooftop restau renowned for its terrace with views of the castle, the New Town and Fife. Bar snacks are the best deal; main dining room exp but chef Tony Singh excels esp with the meatier dishes. **SD**: Highland beef carpaccio. Lunch and dinner 7 days. LO 10.30pm. Bar till 1am   EXP

106
xE1
✔ **(FITZ)HENRY:** 555 6625. 19 Shore Pl. Famous formerly as Dave Ramsden's restau (see Rogue, above) which made it into Michelin territory. Hard act to follow for Alan Morrison & Valerie Faichney, but chef Hubert Lamort is still there & the ambience in this warehousey room off the waterfront in Leith has barely changed. Perhaps it's calmer now since Alan has a more discreet presence. Open fire is nice in winter. Foodies fortunate to have this as well as Martin Wishart (above) in this corner of Leith. Lunch Mon-Fri, Dinner Mon-Sat, LO 10pm.
MED

107
C2
✔ **FISHER'S IN THE CITY:** 225 5109. 58 Thistle St. New (2001), shiny, buzzy, uptown version of one of Leith's longest best eateries (179/SEAFOOD) & this place works on all its levels. Fisher fan staples ('favourites') all here – the fishcakes, the soup & the blackboard specials, excl wine-list combined with gr service Some vegn & meat (steaks a special). Open all day (reduced menu late aft). **SD**: fishcakes of course.
MED

108
C3
✔ **THE GRILL ROOM at the SHERATON:** 229 9131. The fine dining rm at Edin's most corporate of top hotels. Sits alongside The Terrace which has the view (of Festival Sq) and Santini's, the Italian place out back (on Conference Sq). Not much 'Grill' about it, but a serious dining-out experience with an accoladed menu by long-standing chef Nicolas Laurent. Atmos

minimal, food presentation minimalist (4 scallops, big plate loadsamoney starters), but much of the clientele are on expenses. Nevertheless, even for locals this is an estimable chef at the height of his powers. 7 days lunch Mon-Fri & LO 10.30pm (cl Sun). **SD:** Lamb, scallops, lovely puds. MED

109 ✔ **THE WITCHERY:** 225 5613. Castlehill. At the top of the Royal Mile where
C3 the tourists come, many will be unaware that this is one of the city's best restaus and certainly its most stylishly atmospheric. 2 salons, the upper more witchery; in the 'secret gdn' downstairs, a converted school playground, James Thompson has created a more spacious ambience for the (same) elegant Scottish menu. 7 days. The cooking, which has always played second string in the symphony of the whole experience here, has improved of late & meets the gastronomic expectations of the menu. The wine-list is exceptional. Lunch and dinner LO a v civilised 11.30pm. (275/LATE-NIGHT RESTAUS) EXP

110 ✔ **MARTIN'S:** 225 3106. 70 Rose St N Lane. Quiet lane behind busy shop-
C2 ping precinct nr Princes St – odd place to find a decent restau but this is one of Edin's longstanding top eateries. Exemplary service, v high standard of contemporary cooking, delicate desserts and an unsurpassed (incl unpas-teurised) Celtic cheeseboard. Good on game and Martin knows his wines. 3 AA rosettes. Lunch Tue-Fri, dinner Tue-Sat. LO 10pm. EXP

111 ✔ **NUMBER ONE PRINCES STREET, BALMORAL HOTEL:** 556 2414. Address
D2 with a certain ring for the principal restau of the Balmoral (44/BEST HOTELS) entered through lobby or off st. Based apparently on the Mandarin Grill, Hong Kong, these opulent subterranean salons have ample space around the tables, but the lighting and lacquering do little to cosify the ritzi-ness. Chef Jeff Bland ensures that **HADRIAN'S BRASSERIE,** a peppermint lounge at st level, complements well. Cl Sat/Sun lunch. LO 10.30pm. EXP

112 **THE MARQUE:** 466 6660. 19 Causewayside. Discreet southside bistro/restau
xD4 owned by chefs Glyn Stevens and John Rutter which in 2001 spawned a satel-lite in Grindlay St nr the Lyceum called **MARQUE CENTRAL** (118/BISTROS) – John chefs there. The orig Marque seems more grown-up & restau-like tho' for atmos & lighter bites we prefer Central. This Marque still hits the mark for a posher night out with (or just like) your parents. And the wine-list is superb. Lunch & LO 10pm (11pm w/ends). Cl Mon. MED

113 **RHODES & CO:** 220 9190. 3 Rose St opp M & S and Jenners of which it is a part.
C2 Totally professional dining out experience from Gary, the Rhodes boy. High expectation so not always entirely realised. Stark, modern rm upstairs and bar by big windows on the street. Perhaps a bit soulless, but the fairly plain fare is generally impeccably prepared and presented without fuss (but not by Gary who long since moved on). Mashed potatoes, for example, and sticky toffee pud rarely come better than this. Lunch 7 days. Dinner Mon – Sat. LO 10.30pm. **2002 UPDATE: NOW CLOSED**

114
D2 ✔ ✔ **NORTH BRIDGE:** 622 2900. 20 North Bridge. The brasserie of the Scotsman Hotel (52/INDIVIDUAL HOTELS) with separate entrance directly on to main rd. Formerly the foyer & public counter of the *Scotsman* newspaper converted into excl bar/brasserie. Surrounding balcony reached by rather intrusive metal staircase, but overall v sympathetic ambience for exemplary brasserie-type menu which incl sushi. Toilets are a find when you find them. 7 days, all day LO 10.30pm. MED

115
C3 ✔ ✔ **BLUE:** 221 1222. Cambridge St. Upstairs in the Traverse Theatre building. From the makers of The Atrium (103/BEST RESTAUS), a lighter, more informal menu which continues all day till late. Still one of most fashionable places in town to graze, you can still eat for under a tenner; the menu, which changes seasonally, tempts you to more. Sound levels high, but partly because it's full of people with something to say. 12noon-3pm and 6pm-11pm daily. Set snacks only in the afternoon, bar open to 1am daily. Cl Sun. Others come & go but Blue is still the coolest shade of blue. INX

116
xE1 ✔ ✔ **SKIPPERS:** 554 1018. 1a Dock Pl. In a corner of Leith off Commercial Rd by the docks. Look for Waterfront (see below) and bear left into adj cul-de-sac. The pioneer restau in Leith before it was a restau quarter. Quite the best real bistro in town. V fishy, v quayside intimate and friendly. Look no further out to sea. Lunch & dinner 7 days, LO 10pm. MED

117
C4 ✔ ✔ **THE APARTMENT:** 228 6456. 7 Barclay Pl, up from the King's Theatre. Hugely popular contemporary eating-out experience pressing all the right buttons. Big helpings of 'chunky, healthy' food, famously good salads. Malcolm Innes will attend your grazings & ravings. New venture on its way at TGP. We will be there. 7 days, dinner. Lunch Fri/Sat only; LO 11pm. Best to book. INX

118
C3 ✔ **MARQUE CENTRAL:** 229 9859. 30b Grindlay St adj (& part of) the Lyceum. This Marque is offshoot of the original (112/RESTAUS), but we prefer it. Central of course (though in a site that has been curiously difficult to make work), but it's more informal here & the tone of everything esp the food & the pricing (v good value lunch & pre-theatre menu) is just right. Some big tables, mellow atmos. Lunch & LO 10pm (11pm w/ends). Cl Sun. CHP/MED

119
xC4 ✔ **HOWIE'S:** 221 1777. 208 Bruntsfield Pl on the way to Morningside & 225 1721 at 10 Victoria St, certainly one of the best in this st of many bistros. Both are flagship outposts in Howie's urban village chain which serve the locals, but are worth coming across the city for. Unpretentious, inexpensive, contemp Scottish food. Can't say better than that. Bruntsfield is converted church. All 7 days, lunch and dinner. LO 10/10.30pm. Cl Mon lunch. BYOB (with corkage) or unpretentious wine list. Also: INX

120
B1 ✔ **HOWIE'S STOCKBRIDGE:** 225 5553. Glanville Pl by the br in Stockbridge.
D2 David Howie Scott's latter venture which turned a white elephant site into an instant success. Similar approach and menu to other Howies and not exactly a canteen, more a buzzy bistro with good value contemporary food. 7 days, lunch & LO 10pm. **HOWIE'S WATERLOO:** 556 5766. 29 Waterloo Pl. 200 m east end of Princes St (The Balmoral). Similar fare and service in beautiful lofty rm. Easier to get tables than those above. 7 days LO 10.30pm. Also BYOB. INX

121
xC4 ✔ **SWEET MELINDA'S:** 229 7953. 11 Roseneath St which is in deepest Marchmont but round the corner from Argyle Pl where all the good shops are. Single not large rm on st with nice pics, catering v much for the neighbourhood clientele, ie students not short of a bob or two. On Tues you can pay 'what you think the meal is worth' – they wouldn't do this in Leith. Mainly fish, but meat & vegn. Home-made bread & gr touches. Everybody always goes back. Good wines & fizz. Lunch & LO 10pm. Cl Sun/Mon. MED

122
E4 ✔ **BLONDE:** 668 2917. 75 St Leonard's St. Tucked away in the s side a former Howie's restau (see above) that almost outdoes Howie's with a v similar menu & approach. (Owner Andy Macgregor used to be a Howie's chef, so who knows he may have invented that version of the Banoffie Pie.) Pale wood & spartan ie blonde set of rms & easy-eat food with quaffable wine. We do keep going back here. Lunch & LO 10pm. 7 days. INX

123 ✓ **THE SHORE:** 553 5080. 3 The Shore, Leith. Bar (often with live light folk or
xE1 jazz) where you can eat from the same menu as the dining-rm/restau.
Real fire and large windows looking out to the quayside – strewn with bods
on warm summer nights. Food, listed on a blackboard, changes daily but is
consistently good. Lots of fish, some meat, some vegn. No smk in restau/OK in
bar. 7 days, LO 10pm. (343/PUB FOOD) MED

124 ✓ **THE NEW BELL:** 668 2868. 233 Causewayside. Way down Causewayside
xD4 in the s side, the New Bell is upstairs from the Old Bell; you may walk thro'
the pub to find it. And it is a find! Woody, warm pubby atmos, nice rugs etc.
Richard & Michelle Heller have got the rm and the Mod-British menu just
right. Food & v decent vino well-priced for this sound quality & smart delivery.
Dinner only. 7 days LO 10.30pm. INX

125 ✓ **NICOLSON'S:** 557 4567. 6a Nicolson St, opp Festival Theatre which
D3 makes this upstairs spacious room a good rendezvous pre- & après. But
in any case it's one of the best Mod-British meals on the south side. Gr staff.
Window seats, where once J.K. Rowling hatched her plot to take over the
world, best. 7 days. Lunch & LO 10.30pm. Cl Sun. MED

126 **THE VINTNER'S ROOM:** 554 6767. 87 Giles St, Leith. Cobbled courtyard to
xE1 wine bar, with woody ambience and open fire. Vaults, formerly used to store
claret (Leith was an important wine pt), also incl a restaurant lit by candlelight.
Bar and restau have same evening menu (French tone using fresh Scottish
produce), but cheaper options at lunch in the bar and less formal. Excellent
cheeseboard and wine list. Mon-Sat lunch and 6.30-10pm. MED

127 **PODRICIOUS … THE BISTRO:** 225 2208. 192 Rose St at the W End where
C2 'nobody goes' ie anyone looking for good food. But hopefully somebody (&
now you) will stumble on this place, a simple & crisp bistro run by energetic
couple (his dad's nickname was 'Podricious'). Excl value & good detail (except
the pictures). Tues-Sat lunch & LO 10pm. MED

128 **INDIGO YARD:** 220 5603. 7 Charlotte Lane. Food in bar area and in restau
B3 upstairs in converted and glazed-over yard behind the W End. Enormously
popular, always buzzing & noisy later (you may not hear your wine pop nor
your coin drop in the condom machine). Earlier therefore better for food.
Contemp fusion food is better than café-bar standard. 7 days, b/fast, lunch
and evening menu LO 10pm. (369/HIP) INX

129 **MONTPELLIERS:** 229 3115. 159 Bruntsfield Pl. Same ownership as above and
C4 similar buzz and noise levels, but more accent on food. From b/fast menu to
late supper, they've thought of everything. All the contemp faves. Gets v busy.
7 days. LO 10pm. INX

130 **RICK'S:** 622 7800. 55a Frederick St. Basement bar/restau of Rick's Hotel
C2 (59/HOTELS) by same people as Indigo Yard & Montpelliers (above). Food more
ambitious here and usually works. Later on prob too noisy to enjoy food, so
choose table carefully. Go-for-it crowd not as hip as they think (Nouveau
Ricks?). Good cocktails. 7 days all day. LO 11pm Bar 1am. MED

131 **BROWNS:** 225 4442. 131 George St nr Charlotte Sq. First Scottish venture of
C2 this carefully-run small chain. One of the most successful packaging of the
late 90s Menu-U-Like, this is a reliable meal out. Can be noisy but excellent
service. 7 days, noon-11.30pm. INX

132 **THE WATERFRONT:** 554 7427. 1c Dock Pl. In this foody corner of the water-
xE1 front, The Waterfront conservatory o/looks the backwater dock. It's *the* place
to head in summer, but the warren of rms is cosy in winter. Food has wavered
a bit over the yrs (but v good when last we tried – autumn 2001). Site, setting
and gr friendly service are mostly what you come for. 7 days, Lunch & LO
9.30/10pm. MED

133 **BOUZY ROUGE:** 225 9594. 1 Alva St, nr corner with Queensferry St. Edin
B3 branch of the foody empire of the Brown family (def more style & integrity
than most – see Roman Camp, Callendar, Bouzy Rouge & Rococo, Glasgow
872/CENTRAL HOTELS, 555/BISTROS, 537/GLAS RESTAUS). This Mediterraneo space
is well thought out; accessible dining with some flair for the money (well you
know what I mean). This basement can seem cramped (esp the seats), but reliable, contemporary and inx. 7 days, lunch and dinner, LO 9.30pm (Fri/Sat
10.30pm). INX

134 **MALMAISON BRASSERIE:** 555 6969. Tower Pl at Leith dock gates. Restau and
xE1 café-bar of Malmaison (54/INDIVIDUAL HOTELS). Authentic brasserie atmos and
menu, as in all Malmaisons, the expanding chain, with linen cloths, big windows & Paris meets NYC menu. Separate **CAFÉ MAL** with snackier food, is less
successful but is now the best it's been. 7 days. Lunch and dinner.   MED.INX

135 **ORTEGAS:** 557 5754. 38 St Mary's St. Old Town bistro by folk who started
D3 Food Plantation (300/TAKEAWAYS). A bit tucked away but v close to Royal Mile.
Excl innovative and eclectic menu eg mushroom & nettle nachos, Brazilian
warm beet salad. Interesting wines. This place a bit of an Edin secret. Lunch &
LO 10pm. Cl Sun/Mon.   INX

136 **THE DORIC:** 225 1084. 15 Market St. Opp the Fruitmarket Gallery and the
D3 back entrance to Waverley Stn. Upstairs boho bistro. Only locals know that
this is quintessential Edinburgh & tho the food is neither remarkable nor
cheap, we must still climb those creaking stairs for time to time for a civilised
supper & a v excl bottle of vino. 7 days, lunch & LO 10pm.   MED

137 **LE SEPT:** 225 5428. 7 Old Fishmarket Close. The cobbled close winds steeply
D3 off the High St below St Giles. Wee o/side terr in summer and narrow woody
rm inside for nonsmokers (but smokey rm too). Crêpes, omelettes, plats du
jour and Franco-bistro food. Cheerful, busy rendezvous with well-regarded
staff. 7 days: Lunch & LO 10.30pm (Sat 11, Sun 10pm).   INX

138 **THE DIAL:** 225 7179. 44-46 George IV Br. Modern Scottish with an interna-
D3 tional spin in this subterranean designer eaterie. Some swear by this place,
but some drawbacks, e.g. v basementy, variable service. But then it looks cool,
does a bargain pre-theatre menu and much effort has gone into the aes-
thetics, edible or otherwise. Good vegn choice (8 starters, 3 mains). 7 days,
lunch & LO 10pm.   MED

139 **A ROOM IN THE TOWN:** 225 8204. 18 Howe St, corner of Jamaica St. No one
C2 can work out why they didn't call it 'A Room in the New Town' which is better
and describes where it is. Not sure about the mural either. However, good
bistro menu and friendly service. Predom Scottish menu with twists. Their
wicked banoffee pie however is as it comes. Same folk have **A ROOM IN THE
WEST END** (226 1036) in William St with an upstairs bar **TEUCHTERS** (they
love to be outsiders) & the restau downstairs. Similar menu. 7 days lunch & LO
10pm.   INX

140 **METRO:** 474 3466. Grassmarket. In Apex Hotel (75/ECONOMY HOTELS) on
C3 ground floor on main drag but doesn't feel like hotel restau. Big windows and
spacious - echoes of Conran. Contemporary British menu. Bar on mezzanine.
7 days. LO 10pm, bar midnight.   INX

THE BEST FRENCH RESTAURANTS

141
E3
✔ ✔ **PLAISIR DU CHOCOLAT:** 556 9524. 251 Canongate. Tho' principally a tearm, this Royal Mile gem also serves excl pâtés, omelettes & onion soup. And the bread! Full Report: 251/TEAROOMS.

141a
D3
✔ **LA GARRIGUE:** 557 3032. 31 Jeffrey St. Recent (2002) addition to league of authentic French restaus in city, this more Languedoc than Left Bank. Light space and view of Calton Hill (tho building developments opp afoot). Simple food with flair and unusual touches. Best to book. Mon-Sat, lunch and LO 10pm   MED

142
B2
✔ **LAFAYETTE:** 225 8678. 9 Randolph Pl upstairs (pre-drinks down) in unusual mock Tudor building in corner of the W End. Tall windows, fairly formal setting, you don't come for the fun but for the food. Chef Fabrice Bouteloup has the je ne sais quoi – this is a gastronomic outpost of the nearby French Institute. Lunch & LO 10pm. Cl Sun.   EXP

143
C1
✔ **DUCK'S AT LE MARCHE NOIR:** 558 1608. 2-4 Eyre Pl. Malcolm Duck presides with meticulous attention to detail in his bistro/restau at the lower end of the New Town. In a residential neighbourhood, an easy-going but still business-like atmos. The French (Toulouse sausages), très Ecossais ingredients on the whole. Good-value wine list. Dinner 7 days, lunch Mon-Fri. LO 10-10.30pm (earlier Sun).   EXP

144
C2
✔ **CAFÉ SAINT-HONORÉ:** 226 2211. 34 Thistle St Lane, betw Frederick St and Hanover St. Suits a-plenty, New Town regulars and occasional lunching ladies all to be found in this busy, shiny bistro-cum-restau which oozes & even smells like Paris. Go on a rainy day when it feels esp warm & sweet & comforting. Luch Mon-Fri, LO 10pm. Cl Sun. Veggies phone ahead.   EXP

145
xC4
✔ **JACQUES:** 229 6080. 8 Gillespie Pl, Bruntsfield. Endearing French staff and atmos. Hard-working wee rustic eaterie close to the King's Theatre. Has all those French dishes and their estimable Plateau des Fruits de Mer. Excl affordable French wine list. Loyal following, book ahead. Lunch and LO 11pm.   INX

146
C2
✔ **CAFÉ MARLAYNE:** 226 2230. 76 Thistle St. The third in the triumvirate of excl & authentic French eateries within 100m of another (Café St-Honoré, La P'tite Folie), this the most recent (2000) & a wee gem (we do mean wee). Personal, intimate & v v French. Food generally fab (tho not gr for veggies). Isla & Baub will draw you in & you'll think of it like the spot you found on your holidays (one that's not in any guide books). Lunch & LO 10pm. Cl Sun/Mon.

147
xE1
DANIEL'S: 553 5933. 88 Commercial Quay, off Dock Pl. Versatile with small deli, takeaway and bistro. Main eaterie is housed in conservatory at back of old bonded warehouse in 'restaurant row'. Clean lines, modern look and v popular. Offers contemporary French menu with Alsace and external influences that pack us in esp for 'tarte flambé' & casseroles (169/PIZZAS). Also tables by the water 7 days, 10am-10pm.   INX

148
B3
FRENCH CORNER BISTRO: 226 1890. 17 Queensferry St upstairs & on corner of Alva St. 3 high-ceilinged Georgian rms usually full of people & buzz. This took the elements of the Pierre Victoire formula & does all of it better. Food accessible French bistro fare, with good steaks, crêpes & cheese for example. You come back here, it's like a club. Lunch & LO 10.30/11pm. Cl Sun.   INX

149
D3
MAISON BLEU: 226 1900. 36 Victoria St. Contemp & unique spin on inx French food in restau (& chain) expanding as we speak. Grazing menu of 'bites' to mix 'n' match. Gr choice, très reasonable prices, but food often excl. Gr value set lunch (2 bites & pud <£5). Lunch & LO 10.30pm. BYOB (not w/ends).   INX

150
C2
LA P'TITE FOLIE 225 7983. 61 Frederick St. The word is unpretentious – mis matched furniture, inx French *plat du jour*. Relaxed eating-out in single New Town rm. Cheap lunch. 7 days. LO 10/11pm. Cl Sun lunch.   INX

151
B2
CAFÉ D'ODILE: 225 5366. 13 Randolph Cres. A secret gdn and small cafeteria downstairs at the French Institute. Lunch only but can be booked for parties at night (BYOB). Gr views over the New Town, simple French home-cooking, patronised by ladies who lunch and students. Tue-Sat. A more central d'Odile upstairs at the Stills Gallery, Cockburn St. Excl lunch venue. Same hrs   CHP

152
C3 ✓ **SANTINI:** 221 7788. Conference Sq by Conference Centre & back of the Sheraton (of which it is a part, below the excl health club). Seriously well-thought out Italian restau & bistro created by Mr Santini himself who has brought the same clean lines & stylish eating-out experience to London & Milan. Waiters & ingredients v Italia. You can eat long or light. Pizza oven not arrived at TGP, but reputed to be the business. Meantime, the smartest pasta in town. Lunch & dinner LO 10.30pm. Cl Sun. MED/INX

153
B3 ✓ **SCALINI:** 220 2999. 10 Melville Pl. Downstairs (*the scalini*) bistro restau in a low-ceilinged sliver of a basement with a straightforward and personal approach to Italian cooking – Silvio will tell you what's good tonight and he'll be right. They have an amazing collection of vintage Barberas, probably one for your birthday. Smoking upstairs. Cl Suns. MED

154
E1 ✓ **VALVONA & CROLLA:** 556 6066. 19 Elm Row. Cafe at the back of the leg-endary deli, and with all the flair and attention to detail that you would expect. First-class ingredients, produce shipped in from Italy (fresh veg from Milan markets) and gr Italian domestic cooking. One of the best & healthiest b/fasts in town & fabuloso lunch (any wine in the shop for £3 corkage is a deal) tho not chp. This place is a treat without the trappings. May be queues. No smk. Mon-Sat 8am-5pm. INX

155
C2 ✓ **CAFFE D.O.C.:** 220 6846. 49a Thistle St. Caff counter at the window, but up back this is most def a restau & one of the best Italians in town. Alison & Massimo combine Scottish ingredients & Italian culinary flair. Lunch lighter, dinner a bit of a treat. Lunch & 7-10pm. Cl Sun/Mon. MED

156
C2 ✓ **COSMO:** 226 6743. 58 N Castle St (a no through rd). V much in the old, dis-creet style for those with some time and cash on their hands. Has been the up-market Italian restau for yrs. The lighting and the music are soft, the service impeccable and the (Italian) wine list exemplary. Menu pragmatically brief; allow time to enjoy it in this not unpleasant time-warp. Cl Sun and Sat lunch. EXP

157
E1 ✓ **TINELLI:** 652 1932. 139 Easter Rd. Small and neat restau with unassum-ing frontage on unfashionable st that was serving carpaccio & proper Italian food long before the pasta explosion. Still simple & uncompromising. This is the real tiramisù. Lunch and LO 11pm. Cl Sun/Mon. MED

158
C2 **EST EST EST:** 225 2555. 135 George St at W End. One of a triumvirate of chain super-restaurants at the w end of George St. This prob the best for design value; the biggest & busiest. You don't have to like it, but the crowds do! Food & service can be off-hand, but it has the buzz. This corporate invention does get that right. Smile it's a Blair New World. Lunch & LO 11.00pm (10.30pm Suns). INX

159
C2 **LIBRIZZI'S:** 226 1155. Corner N Castle St and Queen St. Central under-estimated ristorante one block from George St. Sicilian chef and influence on usual and unusual Italian fare. Esp good fish of the day. Good service and well selected wines. Lunch & LO 10.30pm. Cl Sun. MED

160
D2 **BELLINI:** 476 2602. Corner Abercromby Pl & Dublin St. Very New Town address & ambience in this once again, underestimated & underused Italian restau with estimable chef & good service. Some home-made pastas & specials always interesting. Menus quite diverse. Nice cheese. Lunch Tues-Fri, Dinner Tues-Sun LO 10pm. MED

THE TRUSTY TRATTS

161
B3 ✓ **BAR ROMA:** 226 2977. 39 Queensferry St. One of Edin's long-standing fave Italians, now revamped and hurtled into the 90s and beyond. Almost looks like a Pizza Express from the outside. Inside always bustling (this includes the menu) with Italian rudeboy waiters as the floor show. 7 days, all day. LO 11.30pm. INX

162 ✓ **GIULIANO'S:** 556 6590. 18 Union Pl, top of Leith Walk nr the main r/bout,
D2 opp Playhouse Theatre. No change at Giuli's but something sets it apart as it's usually heaving with happy punters, many birthdays! It's just pasta and pizza but in a no-nonsense menu that appeals. The food is great, the din is loud. Lunch and LO 2am daily – Giuli's is always late 'n' live. Also another 'on the shore' in Leith (554 5272) which is esp good for kids (246/KID-FRIENDLY); see below.   INX

163 **LAZIO:** 229 7788. 95 Lothian Rd. One of the prerequisites of a 'Trusty Tratt' is
C3 that they're there where you want them to be. This W End stalwart is nr Usher Hall, Filmhouse & many other destinations Best on these blocks. Report 282/LATE NIGHT RESTAUS.   INX

164 **LA LANTERNA:** 226 3090. 83 Hanover St. One of several tratts sub street level
C2 in this block all family-owned. But this gets our vote. For 20 yrs the Zaino family have produced this straight-down-the-line Italian menu from their open kitchen at the back of their no-frills restau with American soundtrack. 80% of their customers are regulars and wouldn't go anywhere else. Well chosen wine-list. Lunch & LO10pm. Cl Sun.   INX

165 **PIATTO VERDE:** 228 2588. 7 Dundee Terr along from Fountain Park cinema
B4 complex & opp 'Victor Paris'. Not obvious but a v decent neighbourhood tratt & the place to head for round here after the movies. Simple home cooking from Roberto Verde who came for his hols in '93 & never went home. Usual fare & blackboard specials. He called the lasagne after his mum – now that is nice! Good inx vino. Dinner only, LO 11pm. Cl Tues.   INX

UMBERTO'S: 554 1314. Off Bonnington Rd. (244/KID-FRIENDLY PLACES).

GORDON'S TRATTORIA: 225 7992. 231 High St. (280/LATE-NIGHT RESTAUS).

GIULIANO'S ON THE SHORE: 554 5272. 1 Commercial St (246/KID-FRIENDLY).

VITTORIA: 556 6171. Brunswick St (271/CLASSIC CAFFS).

THE BEST PIZZA

166 ✓ **PIZZA EXPRESS:** 332 7229. 1 Deanhaugh St, Stockbridge. Ubiquitous
B1 national chain, same formula everywhere, but what-the-hell, it's great design & great pizza. Stockbridge branch best; award for architecture, in refurbed bank with Water of Leith gurgling below. Simple, no-nonsense, affordable pizza with good service. Edin W End branch, 225 8863, 32 Queensferry St. Both open till 12 midnight daily. Also North Br, adj Calton Highland Hotel – these 2 branches have the best vibes. Newest branch on shore in Leith. No booking.   INX

167 ✓ **L'ALBA D'ORO:** 557 2580. 5-11 Henderson Row. The t/away pizza section
C1 of the estimable fish 'n' chip shop, but this is def a slice above the rest. 3 sizes (incl indiv 7") & infinite toppings to go. Not thin but crispy/crunchy. Also pasta, wine, fresh OJ. No ordinary chip shop! 7 days lunch & LO 12.   CHP

168 **MAMMA'S:** 225 6464. 30 Grassmarket. Also corner of Broughton Pl &
C3 Broughton St (558 8868) & 1 Howard St, Canonmills (558 7177). Brash, American-style with informal booking system and tacky decor/layout which is the antithesis of Pizza Express. Some alternatives to pizza, but you come to mix 'n' match – haggis, calamari and BBQ sauce and 40 other toppings piled deep so a cheap & filling meal. Diff hrs, but Broughton St open earliest & Grassmarket latest. All 7 days.   INX

169 **DANIEL'S BISTRO:** 553 5933. 88 Commercial St on 'restaurant row' in Leith. Gr
xE1 for the Tarte Flambé – v like a thin thin pizza made from milk bread dough topped with onions, crème fraîche & lardons – an Alsace & house speciality. There are other thin pizzas too (146/FRENCH RESTAUS). 7 days 10am-10pm. INX

THE BEST MEDITERRANEAN FOOD

170
D3

✓ **IGG'S:** 557 8184. 15 Jeffrey St, nr Royal Mile. Since 1989 this has been a corner of Spain in Scotland & one of the consistently best restaus in the city. Warm south v much reflected in the excl wine-list, but food from well-sourced Scottish ingredients more cosmo than merely Med. Some tapas but see below. Good biz lunch spot. Lunch & LO 10.30. Cl Sun.   MED

171
D3

✓ **BARIOJA:** 557 3622. 19 Jeffrey St. And after Iggs the restau, the tapas bar next door – they are joined together in the basement. Small tables and not much room to move upstairs; more space, less ambience down. Fairly authentic tapas menu but no sideboard or counter full as in San Sebastian; Spanish waiters and vino. 11am – 12pm. 7 days.   INX

172
D2

✓ **CAFÉ MEDITERRANEO:** 557 6900. 73 Broughton St. Fairly discreet frontage to small, bright rms on busy little Broughton St. Family feel (the Crollas, scions of the V and C – 1429/DELIS) to this cafe/bistro/restau serving not unsurprisingly Mediterranean snacks and meals c/o creative chef Neil O'Brian (but not pasta). Deli counter, various coffees. Nice for b/fast incl Suns (248/SUN B/FAST). 7 days till 6pm and Fri-Sat LO 10pm.   INX/MED

173
C2

✓ **NARGILE:** 225 5755. 73 Hanover St. Not so much Mediterranean, most definitely Turkish. This is where to go to mess with the meze. All east of the Med fares from houmous to shashlik with lots for veggies & good fish choice. Some tables cramped but this is a night out with the mates or mate kind of place. Buzbag as expected & fair selection of other Turkish & non Turkish wines. Lunch & LO 10.30pm (11pm Fri/Sat). Cl Sun.   INX

174
D2

✓ **TAPAS TREE:** 556 7118. 1 Forth St. Party night-out kind of restau with upbeat Spanish staff, gypsy/Cajun soundtrack & Flamenco live on Thurs. Starter/main/pud is the heavier option but 3 well-chosen tapas (veg, fish and something else) with some robust bread and a bottle of house red makes for a v decent meal. Snappy service. Tapas in the £2 to £5 range, so not a pocket buster. 11am-11pm. 7 days.   INX

175
D4

PHENECIA: 662 4493. 55-57 W Nicolson St, on corner nr Edin Univ. N African Mohammed Sfina's unfussy and demonstrably yellow N African/Spanish eaterie with couscous, lots of grilled meats and wide vegn choice. Poss to eat v cheaply at lunch-time. Goodly portions. Regular clientele (hard to get bored with this long & widespread menu). Lunch Mon-Sat & LO 10.30pm. They have the Château Musar.   INX

176
C1

TAPAS OLÉ: 556 2754. 8-10 Eyre Pl and 225 7069, 4 Forrest Rd, nr the Univ. Tapas restau/bar. Meat/vegn/seafood menus and the usual vinos. Good value & authentic with Spanish proprietor and waiters. Live music sometimes, live clientele always. An inx night out! We prefer Eyre Pl, the room is better. 7 days, lunch and LO 10.30 pm.   INX

THE BEST SEAFOOD RESTAURANTS

177
xE1
✓ ✓ **SKIPPERS:** 554 1018. 1a Dock Pl, Leith. Bistro with truly maritime atmos; mainly seafood. Best to book. Many would argue Skippers *is* still the best place to eat seafood in this town. Full report: 116/BEST BISTROS.

178
C2
✓ ✓ **FISHERS in the CITY:** 225 5109. 58 Thistle St. Separate entry to sister restau (below). Bigger & buzzier & one of the best all-rounders in the aforesaid city. (107/BEST RESTAUS). MED

179
xE1
✓ ✓ **FISHERS:** 554 5666. Corner of The Shore and Tower St, Leith. At the foot of an 18th-century tower opp Malmaison Hotel and rt on the quay (though no boats come by). Seafood cooking with flair and commitment in boat-like surroundings where trad Scots dishes get an imaginative twist. Hugely popular, some stools around bar and tables o/side in summer (can be a windy corner). Often all are packed. Cheeseboard has some gr Brits if you have rm for a third course. 7 days. 12noon-10.30pm. MED

180
D3
✓ **CREELERS:** 220 4447. 3 Hunter Sq. Tim & Fran's restau & smoke house near Brodick is also called Creelers. this corner of Arran in the city behind the Tron Church is just a short cast from the Royal Mile (tables alfresco in summer). One of the best seafood spots in town (but with 2 meat & 1 vegn dish). Nice paintings, good atmos, not exp. Bistro at front, restau at back. Lunch and LO 10.30/11pm (Cl Sun in winter). MED

181
C2
✓ **THE MUSSEL INN:** 225 5979. 61 Rose St and in Glas (630/SEAFOOD RESTAUS). In the heart of the city centre where parking ain't easy, a gr little seafood bistro specializing in mussels and scallops (kings and queens) which the proprietors rear/find themselves. Also 'catch of the day' and a non-fish pasta option. Good chips. Lunch and dinner. LO 10pm. INX

182
D2
✓ **CAFÉ ROYAL OYSTER BAR:** 556 4124. W Register St. One of the city's best rms & here forever but still a place for a flourish of indulgence or just to impress. Beluga caviar followed by Homard Newburg with a bottle of Bolly will cost you an arm and a leg. But you can also snack. Higher celeb quotient here for the classy surroundings with spillover atmos from adj bar. Tiles, linen, dark wood, v Victorian. Visitors usually find it all v groovy; locals lament that it ain't what it was. Lunch and LO 10pm. 7 days. EXP

THE BEST FISH 'N' CHIPS

183
C1
✓ **L'ALBA D'ORO:** Henderson Row, nr corner with Dundas St. Large selection of deep-fried goodies, incl many vegn savouries. It's a lot more than your usual fry-up – as several plaques on the wall attest (incl *Scotland the Best!*) and the pasta/pizza counter next door is a real winner (167/PIZZAS). Open till 12midnight. CHP

184
D2
✓ **THE RAPIDO:** 77 Broughton St. Fine chips. Popular with late-nighters stumbling back down the hill to the New Town, and the flotsam of the 'Pink Triangle'. Open till 1.30am (3.30am Fri-Sat). CHP

185
E1
✓ **THE DEEP SEA:** Leith Walk, opp Playhouse. Open late and often has queues but these are quickly dispatched. The haddock has to be 'of a certain size'. Trad menu. Still one of the best fish suppers you'll ever feed a hangover with. Open till 2am (-ish) (3am Fri-Sat). CHP

186
D3
✔ ✔ **BANNS:** 226 1112. 5 Hunter Sq, just off Royal Mile at the Tron Church. David Bann's breakthrough restau elevates vegn food into the top end of cuisine. Even die-hard carnivores would be happy here – the food is that good. No hint of hessian or sandals, no dodgy stodge. Stylish decor, open kitchen cosmo menu, creative take on round the world dishes. Excl organic wine & beer list, open v late at w/ends with mellow DJs. All day 11am-11pm (3am w/ends). INX

187
D4
✔ **SUSIE'S DINER:** 667 8729. 51-53 W Nicolson St. Cosy, neighbourhood (the univ) self-service diner. Nice people behind and in front of the counter. Mexican and Middle-Eastern dishes. Occasional live music and belly dancing nights (sic). Lotsa choice menu incl. Licensed, also BYOB. Mon 9am-8pm, Tue-Sat 9am-9pm. Cl Sun. CHP

188
C2
✔ **HENDERSON'S:** 225 2131. 94 Hanover St. Edin's original and trail-blazing basement vegn self-serve café-cum-wine bar. Canteen seating to the left (avoid), candles and live piano or guitar downstairs to the rt (better). Happy wee wine list and organic real ales. Good cheese & choc mousse goes on forever. 8am-10.30pm. Cl Sun. Also has the Farm Shop upstairs with a deli and takeaway and the more bar-like **HENDERSON'S BISTRO** round the corner in Thistle St. NOTE: Henderson's (organic) oatcakes are *the* best. CHP

189
D3
✔ **BLACK BO'S:** 557 6136. 57 Blackfriars St. Now long-est proper vegn restau ie waiter service, foody approach to the food with some unpredictable often inspired vegn ideas and combos. Intimate & woody, laid-back set-up. Adj bar has been cool for yrs. Food less fruity than formerly and not so stodgy. Lunch Fri/Sat only. Dinner 7 days. LO 10.30pm. INX

190
D4
✔ **KALPNA:** 667 9890. 2-3 St Patrick Sq. They say 'you do not have to eat meat to be strong & wise' & are they of course right. Maxim taken seriously in this long-est Indian restau on the s side nr the Odeon Cinema. Thali gives a good overview while bargain Wed buffet features regional cuisine. Special Gujarati menu on Sun evens (6-10pm). Lunch Mon-Fri, dinner Mon-Sat, LO 10.30pm. (218/INDIAN RESTAUS). No smk. INX

191
D4
✔ **ANN PURNA:** 662 1807. 45 St Patrick Sq. Excellent vegn restau nr Edin Univ with genuine Gujarati/S Indian cuisine. Good atmos – old customers are greeted like friends by Mr & Mrs Pandya. Indian beer, some suitable wines. Lunch Mon-Fri, dinner 7 days, LO 11pm. (220/INDIAN RESTAUS) INX

192
E4
ENGINE SHED CAFÉ: 662 0040. 19 St Leonard's Lane. Hidden away off St Leonard's St, this is a lunch-oriented vegn café where much of the work is done by adults with learning difficulties on training placements, so worth supporting. Simple, decent food and gr bread – baked on premises, for sale separately. Nice stopping-off point after a tramp over Arthur's Seat. Mon-Thu 10.30am-3.30pm, Fri 10.30am-2.30pm, Sat 10.30am-4pm, Sun 11am-4pm. CHP

193
C3
CORNERSTONE CAFÉ: 229 0212. Underneath St John's Church at the corner of Princes St and Lothian Rd. V central and PC self-service coffee shop in church vaults. Home-baking and hot dishes at lunchtime. Some seats outside in summer (in graveyard!) and market stalls during the Festival. One World Shop adj is full of Third World-type crafts and v good for presents. A respite from the fast-food frenzy of Princes St. Open 9.30am-4pm (later in Festival). Cl Sun. CHP

194
E4
ISABEL'S: 662 4014. 83 Clerk St (in basement of Nature's Gate wholefood shop). Compact café (5 tables) & menu. V healthy, v still. Mon-Sat 11.30am-6.30pm. (Cl earlier Tues/Sat). Cl Sun. CHP

194a
D3
LEGUME: 667 1597. 11 S College St. Off 'the Bridges', behind Univ old Quad building, discreet restau serving seriously good vegn menu with French cuisine skill. Brief but exemplary menu & service. Lunch & LO 9pm (9.30pm w/ends). MED

194b
D3
SURUCHI: 556 6583. 14a Nicolson St. Excl Indian, esp good for vegn dishes. Report 216/INDIAN RESTAUS.

195
C2
✓ **WINTER GLEN:** 477 7060. 3a1 Dundas St, which is on the rt going down-hill opp the Scottish Gallery. Comfortable, intimate basement restau. Pleasing name comes not from sentiment, but from the surnames of the own-ers (Brian Winter cooks). Nevertheless this mainly Scottish menu originates from glen and loch and bay; Scotland's first-class ingredients featured and presented with panache. Smart service, urbane atmos. In most of the other guides that count – 2 AA rosettes. Cl Sat lunch & Sun.   MED

196
D3
✓ **DUBH PRAIS:** 557 5732. 123b High St. Slap bang (but downstairs) on the Royal Mile opp the Holiday Inn. Only 9 tables and a miniature galley kitchen from which proprietor/chef James McWilliams and his team produce a remarkably reliable à la carte menu & specials from sound and sometimes surprising Scottish ingredients. Haggis is panfried, smoked haddock comes with Ayrshire bacon. Athol Brose is as good as it gets. V regular clientele & even some lucked-out tourists in this outpost of culinary integrity on the Royal Mile. Cl Sun-Mon. LO 10.30pm. Pron 'Du Prash'.   MED

197
xE4
✓ **FENWICK'S:** 667 4265. 15 Salisbury Pl. Tucked away in the depths of Newington tho with plenty students and tourists from the drab hotel belt to attract, this 90s kind of restau is an honest-to-goodness treat. Excl value. The cooking, with assorted international manoeuvres, offers local pro-duce turned out with style and honesty. Excl affordable wine-list (from estimable Villeneuve), but can BYOB. Lunch and LO 10.30pm.   INX

198
C2
✓ **CHAMBERTIN:** 225 1251. 21 George St. Despite French title, a v Taste of Scotland menu in discreet, v professionally run main restau of George Hotel (51/BEST HOTELS) an opulent salon where suits dine at lunch time and other members of the Edin establishment compare chips (on the shoulder). More relaxed in the eves. Lunch Mon-Fri, LO 10pm Mon-Sat. Cl Sun.   EXP

199
D2
HALDANE'S: 556 8407. 39 Albany St. In basement of The Albany. Fine dining nr Brougton St and prob the best proper meal in the area. Scottish by nature rather than hype. Everything done in a country house style, tho menu unpre-tentious. Lunch Mon-Fri, LO 9.30pm. Cl Sun.   MED

200
D3
OFF THE WALL: 558 1497. 105 High St. Not so much off the wall, but in the wall – a doorway off the tartan & tat Royal Mile & stairs up to this calm first-floor rm. A discreet bistro often missed by the ravening foodies (but not Gillian Glover of *Scotland on Sunday* who loved it … and if it's good enough for her …). Short, simple menu with Scottish stalwarts (salmon, venison, beef – and always haggis) all nicely concocted with contemporary ingredients and twist. Mon-Sat, lunch and LO 10pm.   MED

201
D3
JACKSONS: 225 1793. 209 High St. In the midst of the Mile, Jacksons plays the Scottish card big time. Here for almost 20 yrs, this is a v TOS experience. In the cellar so to speak, but tables o/side in summer. Not sure about the haggis tim-bale thing, but Lyn MacKinnon I like and she's so … well, very Scottish. 7 days, lunch and dinner.   MED

202
C3, D2
STAC POLLY: 229 5405. 8a Grindlay St. Opp Lyceum Theatre and not far from Usher Hall, Traverse and cinemas. Dark wood and tartan interior is quietly smart; service, too. Scottish beef, salmon, game well sourced. Cheeses come from Iain Mellis. There's another basement **STAC POLLY** at 29-33 Dublin St in the New Town (556 2231). Similar menu but it feels clubbier. V fine. Both: lunch Mon-Fri. Dinner 7 days LO 10pm (Grindlay St 11 pm).   MED

203
D3
THE GRAIN STORE: 225 7635. 30 Victoria St. Regulars climb the stairs for the pigeon, salmon or guinea fowl – perhaps the vegn alternative – then hang around this laid-back first-floor eaterie drinking wine or coffee. An informal and welcoming stone-walled labyrinth. Perhaps more 'mod Brit' than simply 'Scottish'. Lunch and dinner LO 10 (11pm Fri/Sat). 7 days.   MED

THE BEST MEXICAN (AND CENTRAL AMERICAN) RESTAURANTS

205 ✓ **VIVA MEXICO:** 226 5145. Anchor Close, Cockburn St. Since 1984 the pre-
D3 eminent Mexican bistro in town. Judy Gonzalez's menu still throws in
something innovative now and again, although all the expected dishes are
here and originals like Mole Poblano (chicken in chocolate sauce) remain.
Reliable venue for those times when nothing else fits the mood but sour
cream, fajitas and limey lager; nice atmos downstairs. Lunch (not Sun) and LO
10.30pm (Sun 10pm). INX

206 ✓ **MOTHER'S:** 662 0772. 107-109 St Leonard's St. Gr wee neighbourhood
E4 restau that manages to do the basics well (unlike many other Tex/Mexi-
cans in town). Burgers, excl fajitas and one or two departures. Simple décor,
good staff, proper coffee, home-made desserts. Bit of a southside institution
this place. Dinner 6-10pm Tue-Thu and Sun, 6-10.30pm Fri-Sat. Cl Mon. INX

207 **PANCHO VILLA'S:** 557 4416. 240 Canongate. This spartan cantina remains a
E3 reliable exponent of what we've come to regard as Mexican cooking with
nosh of the 'chilada, 'ajita, 'ichanga school. Plain décor, decent edibles, happy
place for parties. Lunch 12noon-2.30pm Mon-Sat, dinner 6-10.30pm daily. INX

208 **CUBA NORTE:** 221 1430. Morrison St (W End nr Haymarket Stn). Yes, we know
B3 it's not Mexican and perhaps not Cuban either, but this bar/restau with Latin
vibes has been a success since it opened late '98 (despite the pundits poo-
pooing that a cool place could be this far W). Bar at front, tables upstairs
through back serving Cuba-style cuisine (though we know they don't have
any food, never mind a cuisine) incl tapas & cocktails. Some tango, flamenco
and DJ salsa (various w/end nights) may drown out the flava later on, but a
better attempt at Havana than most. 7 days lunch and LO 10.30pm. INX

209 **MARIACHI:** 538 0022. 72 Commercial Quay (the line of restaus off Dock Pl in
xE1 Leith, looking over to the Scottish Exec office – and car park). This place one of
the best is mostly, but not all Mexican (much like Mexico). However there are
Mexican waiters. Good for seafood variants. 7 days, LO 10.30pm/11pm. INX

THE BEST JAPANESE & FUSION RESTAURANTS

210 ✓ **YO SUSHI:** 220 6040. 66 Rose St. Two of best 'Japanese' places in town are
D2 chains (see below). This the full singing, dancing Edin version of the
London lot. Street-level conveyor sushi & downstairs club room full of cool
gimmicks (karaoke waiters, DJs, massage, etc). Authentic sushi/sashimi all
rolled & precisely arranged in front of you. Assorted sets & bentos to go (free
delivery under 2 miles). 7 days 12-11pm, club till 1am. INX

211 ✓ **BONSAI:** 668 3847. 46 W Richmond St on discreet st on southside a Jap
D3 caff/bistro (formerly Kelly's) where Andrew & Noriko Ramage show a deft
hand in the kitchen. Freshly made sushi/yakitori & teppanyaki. No conveyor
belt in sight. Teriyaki steaks, salads & crème brûlée – yes, crème brûlée! 7 days
noon-11pm. INX

212 **WOK WOK:** 220 4340. 37 George St. W end in row of restau – all chains, but
C2 this one best. Asian fusion mix so not Japanese but Chinese/Thai/Vietnamese
mix. We love those chilli king prawns & to sit outside during the Book Festival.
You can eat light and late. 7 days all day LO 11pm (w/ends midnight at least,
Sun 10pm). INX

213 **YUMI:** 337 2173. 2 W Coates (continues from Haymarket Terr, W End). The
B3 classier and more polite of the capital's Japanese restaus – definitely old-style.
This is where visiting Japanese businessmen go (& stay, it is actually a hotel).
Many miles & yen away from Yo Sushi so not a lot of fun, but the real deal, com-
plete with tea ceremony & tatami room. Dinner only. LO 9.30pm. 7 days. EXP

214 **TAMPOPO:** 220 5254. 25a Thistle St. Not a restau but a gr wee Japanese noo-
C2 dle bar where you pick up a ramen to go or one of those meal-on-a-tray
things. The original & still the best noodle in town. Bentos in lacquered boxes,
sushi platters with green tea. Lunch and 6-9pm. Cl Sun/Mon. CHP

THE BEST INDIAN RESTAURANTS

215
xE1 ✔ **BRITANNIA SPICE:** 555 2255. 150 Commercial St on developing end of Leith nr Ocean Terminal & Britannia (the Royal Yacht). Widespread menu from the sub-continent served by mainly Nepali waiters in modern maritime setting. Some awards, some suits. 7 days, lunch LO 11pm.   MED

216
D3 ✔ **SURUCHI:** 556 6583. 14a Nicolson St. Upstairs opp Festival Theatre and 121 Constitution St, Leith (554 3268). Owner from Jaipur called Mr Rodriguez plus chefs from Bengal, Delhi and S India equals eclectic Indian menu written touchingly in Scots dialect (potatoes are tatties). Unfussy décor and food with light touch attracts students/academics from nearby univ as well as theatregoers. Loads for veggies. Better than av wines but can BYOB. Monthly food fests. Leith new at TGP. This place is routinely praised to the skies; mostly we agree. Lunch and LO 11.30pm daily.   INX

217
D3 ✔ **KEBAB MAHAL:** 667 5214. 7 Nicolson Sq. Nr Edin Univ and Festival Theatre. Gr vegetable biryani and delicious lassi for under a fiver? Hence high cult status. Late-night Indo-Pakistani halal caff that attracts Asian families as well as students and others who know. Kebabs, curries and excellent sweets. One of Edin's most cosmopolitan restaus. Sun-Thu 12noon-12midnight, Fri-Sat 12noon-2am. Prayers on Fri (1-2pm). No alcohol zone.   CHP

218
D4 ✔ **KALPNA:** 667 9890. St Patrick Sq. The original Edin Indian veggie restau and still the business. Lighter, fluffier and not as attritional as so many tandooris. Wed buffet a bargain & Sun even Gujarati menu. Report: 190/VEGN RESTAUS.   INX

219
xE1 **THE RAJ:** 553 3980. 89 Henderson St on S corner of The Shore, Leith. Nice location for Tommy Miah's airy Indian/Bangladeshi restau here some yrs now, but still bustling. Regular events (Bangladeshi New Year and Food/Culture Fest) add to the jollity; jars of things available to buy and take home, also recipe books. Sun-Thu still does food 'at 1983 prices'. Tables best on the raised front area. Totally Raj, in the non-Irvine Welsh sense (in-joke for Edin readers). Lunch and LO 11.30pm, 7 days.   INX

220
D4 **ANN PURNA:** 662 1807. 45 St Patrick Sq. Friendly and family-run Gujarati/S Indian veggie restau with seriously value-for-money business lunch. Report: 191/VEGN RESTAUS.   INX

221
B3 **INDIAN CAVALRY CLUB:** 228 3282. Athol Pl, W End, just off the main Glas rd, about 250m from Princes St the upmarket one tho'. Bargain business lunch attracts the suits. Another restau you'll like if you go for the retro colonial style. We don't esp – but no quibbles about the nibbles or the mainly excl main dishes. This seems an unlikely carry-out place, but they do, and it's one of the best in town. Lunch and LO 11.30pm daily.   INX

222
C4 **SHAMIANA:** 228 2265. 14 Brougham St, Tollcross. Recommended by everyone from Egon Ronay (not a recommendation we'd rely on) to Gordon Brown our dear Chancellor. 25 yrs in this spot, once stylish now just reliably good. The only exclusively N Indian/Kashmiri cuisine in town. Open curiously short hrs, dinner only. Proprietors, the Britt brothers have never compromised & this, as always, is laudable. Closes (not LO) 10pm (9pm Sun, i.e. it's only open 4 hrs). MED

223
D3 **KHUSHI'S:** 556 8996. 16 Drummond St. Long regarded as the only real Indian kitchen, this basic Punjabi café (no restau twiddly bits) has been drawing in students and others for cheap eats since Nehru was in his collar, or at least in the news. It's just round the corner from Edin Univ's Old College. Short no-nonsense menu, cheap no-nonsense prices. Unique, this is the stripped-down curry. Lunch Mon-Sat, dinner Mon-Thu 5-9pm, Fri-Sat 5-9.30pm. Cl Sun.   CHP

224
D2 **ZEST:** 556 5028. 115 N St Andrew St, close to St Andrew Sq and soon to be Harvey Nix. Light, modern Indian caff by the same people who have Eastern Spices (305/TAKEAWAYS). Also do home delivery (on orders above £10) so handy for New Town couch potatoes (or Aloos) 7 days lunch, LO 11pm   INX

225
xD4 **NAMASTE:** 41 W Preston St. New (& no phone number) at TGP, but clearly a room (on the southside) & a restau we will like. Nomads' tent kind of decor & N Indian cuisine, tho many usual dishes. Nice light naans. Good presentation. Dinner 7 days. LO 10pm.

THE BEST THAI RESTAURANTS

226
C3
✓ **THAI ORCHARD:** 228 4438. 44 Grindlay St. Opp Lyceum nr Filmhouse so handy location for excl Thai food in bright green room with one of the best waiters in town (working the whole place singlehanded when we were there). A family affair as is often best. Good seafood. Lunch Mon-Fri, dinner 7 days. LO 11.30pm.   INX

227
D2
✓ **ERAWAN ORIENTAL:** 556 4242. 14 S St Andrews St. The more upmarket of the Erawan dynasty (see below), betw Princes St and the soon-to-come Harvey Nix. Location the thing, but large brasserie-type rm with competent Thai cuisine mainly business at lunch and pleasure at night. Prob the nicest place to eat Thai in town. 7 days. LO 10.45pm.   MED

228
C2
SIAM ERAWAN: 226 3675. 48 Howe St. On corner of Stockbridge area, the first proper Thai to arrive in Edin and still thought by many to be the best – manages that quiet Eastern elegance v well. Same people also have **ERAWAN EXPRESS**, 220 0059, 176 Rose St, a kind of Thai canteen but not quite as inspired as its big sis. Both lunch Mon-Sat, dinner daily, LO 11pm.   INX

229
C1, B3
SONGKRAN: 225 4804. 8 Gloucester St (behind Oddbins at the end of St Stephen St) and 225 7889 24a Stafford St in West End. Latter in basement so Stockbridge best for ambience. Food varies; the chefs alternate – you want to get 'auntie'. Fresh prep & authentic – even the fishcakes are OK. Lunch (not Sun) and LO 11pm.   INX

230
D3, C4
AYUTTHAYA: 556 9351. 14b Nicolson St, opp Festival Theatre. Decent prospect pre- or post-show. Long, thin, a bit claustrophobic restau, but attentive (and if necessary speedy) service, good vegn selection and a steady hand in the kitchen. Under the same ownership is **SUKHOTHAI:** 229 1537. 23 Brougham Pl, Tollcross. Funkier eaterie with relaxed atmos tho dire decor. Food adequate. Ayutthaya best. Both 7 days lunch & LO 10.30pm.   INX

231
MAP 7
B1
LANNA THAI CAFÉ, MUSSELBURGH: 653 2788. 32 Bridge St opp Brunton Hall. Unexpected Thai corner of city suburbs. Big local following so must book w/ends. Not bad bet if you're at the UCI cinema. Lunch, LO 10.30pm.   INX

232 ✓ **JASMINE:** 229 5757. 32 Grindlay St opp Lyceum. Rel new Chinese restau
C3 with growing rep. Pre-post-theatre menus & good service to match.
Seafood a speciality (Cantonese style). BYOB at TGP. Often may need to book
or queue in tiny doorway. Mon-Fri lunch, LO 11.30pm (12.30 on w/end, 11pm
Sun). MED

233 ✓ **JOANNA'S CUISINE:** 554 5833. 42 Dalmeny St. For yrs this was the
xE1 'Dalmeny St place', now it's the delightful & decorative eponymous
Joanna's. Tiny dining rm on ground floor of tenement off Leith Walk, nevertheless produces a menu of 200 Peking dishes. Home-made stocks rather
than MSG & other touches like specially imported teas make this a place people swear by, so book. Dinner only. LO 10.30pm (11.30 w/ends). Cl Tues. MED

234 ✓ **KWEILIN:** 557 1875. 19 Dundas St. The long-established New Town
C2 choice with imaginative Cantonese cooking (and other regions); v good
seafood and genuine dim sum in pleasant but somewhat uninspired setting.
Excl wine-list. No kids allowed in the evening – somewhere for grown-ups to
eat their quail in peace. Book. LO 10.45pm. Cl Mon. MED

235 ✓ **DRAGON WAY:** 668 1328. 74 S Clerk St. Décor gloriously OTT in a
xE4 Crouching Tiger not so Hidden Dragon kind of a way and often described
as 'Hollywood film set'. Good food mind you, and service, so one of the more
interesting Chinese nights out. Cantonese with Peking & Szechuan as we like.
Lunch Mon-Fri and LO 10.30. INX

236 ✓ An easily (but definitely not to be) missed mini-Chinatown, comprising:
B3 **ORIENTAL DINING CENTRE:** 221 1288. 8 Morrison St, nr Lothian Rd
RAINBOW ARCH, the restau with excl rep, a dim sum basement bar and
HO HO MEI NOODLE SHACK, a stripped-down canteen upstairs, cash only
(279/LATE RESTAUS) – cheap eats & a beer under the bright lights – Mon-Sat
5.30pm-1.30am. The Rainbow Arch is best by far in this neck of the W End.
Clarissa Dickson Wright can oft be seen ploughing thro' plates of unmention-
able animal parts all deliciously & authentically prepared. 12noon-midnight
daily. INX

237 ✓ **LOON FUNG:** 556 1781. 2 Warriston Pl, Canonmills. Upstairs (and down
C1 when it's crowded) the famous lemon chicken and crispy duck go round
for ever. Now there's also crispy monkfish in honey. Good dim sum. Mon-Fri
noon-midnight, Sat 2pm-1am, Sun 2pm-midnight. INX

238 **NEW EDINBURGH RENDEZVOUS:** 225 2023. 10a Queensferry St. This old
B3 Chinese dining rm is easy to miss (upstairs, next door to travel agents) but it's
the real McCoy and serves dishes you won't find in any other Scottish Chinese
restaus, e.g. shredded sea blubber. Sound nice? Diehards say nobody does
better Peking food in this town. 7 days. Lunch and LO 11pm Mon-Sat, 1-11pm
Sun. INX

239 **LEE ON:** 229 7732. 3-5 Bruntsfield Pl. Through purple porthole-effect win-
C4 dows, a restau popular with the Chinese community. Feels a bit *Man From
UNCLE*, but food fine. 7 days. Lunch (not Sun) and dinner. LO 12midnight. INX

THE BEST RESTAURANTS FOR BURGERS AND STEAKS

240
xA2
✔✔ **CHAMPANY'S:** 01506 834532. On A904, Linlithgow to S Queensferry rd (3km Linlithgow), but nr M9 at jnct 3. Accolade-laden restau (and 'Chop and Ale House') different from others below because it's out of town (and out of some pockets). Both surf 'n' turf with live lobsters on premises. Famously good Aberdeen Angus beef. Good service, huge helpings (Americans may feel at home). Top wine-list. Chop House 7 days, lunch and LO 10pm; restau lunch (not Sat) and LO 10pm. Cl Sun. Hotel rms adj (94/HOTELS O/SIDE TOWN) INX.EXP

241
C1
✔ **BELL'S DINER:** 225 8116. 7 St Stephen St, Stockbridge. Edin's small, but celebrated burger joint, the antithesis of the posh nosh. Now legendary, nothing has changed in almost 30 yrs except the annual paint job. Burgers, steaks, shakes and coincidentally, the best veggie (nut) burger in town. Mon-Fri 6-10.30pm, Sat-Sun 12noon-10.30pm. INX

242
D4, B1
✔ **BUFFALO GRILL:** 667 7427. 12-14 Chapel St opp Appleton tower on the univ campus, and 1 Raeburn Pl, Stockbridge (332 3864). Although this diner trades on its reputation for steaks and such-like, there are some Mexican concessions to veggies. Both gr spots for easy-going nights out with chums so book and BYOB Lunch Mon-Fri, LO 10.15pm (Sun 10pm). INX

243
D2
SMOKE STACK: 556 6032. 53-55 Broughton St. From the makers of The Basement (262/GR EDIN PUBS) came something across the rd – a burgundy and blue diner rather than an orange and blue bar. Modish décor has a soothing effect. Loads of burgers (Scottish beef or vegn), seared salmon, etc. jollied along by a gr staff. Proper menu available lunch and dinner, but food of some sort all day. Lunch Mon-Sat, 7 days LO 10.30pm. INX

244
xE1
✔ **UMBERTO'S:** 554 1314. Bonnington Rd Lane off Bonnington Rd to E of Newhaven Rd jnct. Whitewashed coach house hidden away in a v unlikely part of Leith. In contrast to some other 'kiddie' places, grown-ups would actually want to eat here too. Downstairs is a civilised restau, upstairs a theme area for kids where some booths form part of a big toy train and mobile youngsters can run in and out of the Wendy house. Excl Italian cooking with a Scottish twist. Upstairs open Mon-Sat 12noon-2pm then 5-10pm, Sat 12noon-7.30pm, Sun 12noon-6pm. INX

245
xC4
✔ **LUCA'S:** 446 0233. 16 Morningside Rd. The ice cream kings (1321/ICE CREAM) from Musselburgh opened this modern ice-creamerie and caff where kids with dads will enjoy their spag and their sundae. Big cups of capp. Crowded if not claustrophobic upstairs but no style police. 7 days. INX

246
xE1
✔ **GIULIANO'S ON THE SHORE:** 554 5272. 1 Commercial St, by the br. With its checked tablecloths, accented waiters and cheerful pizza/pasta menu, this is almost a cartoon version of an Italian restau – no slight intended – and kids love it. Always a birthday party happening at w/ends. Lunch and LO 10.30/11pm. Now sells Luca's ice-cream (see above). INX

247
xC1
YE OLDE PEACOCK INN: 552 8707. Newhaven Rd nr Newhaven Harbour and opp Harry Ramsden's (a more obvious place to take kids perhaps, *see below*), but this has been one of Edin's unsung all-round family eateries for yrs – you can take gran as well as the bairns. The fish here really is fresh, the menu is more adventurous than you'd think with lots that wee kids and we kids like. High tea is a treat. Lunch and LO 9.45pm. 7 days. CHP

248
xA3
BRIDGE INN, RATHO: 333 1320. Canal Centre, Ratho, W Lothian. 14km W of centre via A71, turning rt opp Dalmahoy Golf Club. Well worth the drive for an afternoon on, or by, the Union Canal. The Pop Inn Restau has special menus for kids, play areas and numerous distractions. Sailings and walks. LO food 9pm, bar open 12noon-11pm (12midnight Fri-Sat). (357/PUB FOOD) INX

249
xA2
CRAMOND BRIG HOTEL: 339 4350. At the R Almond as you hit Edin on the dual carriageway from the Forth Rd Br. This inn has put a lot of effort into attracting families with its indoor/outdoor play areas (Funky Forest). If you've driven for hrs with a whingeing child and want steak and chips while the kids play themselves into a stupor then this is convenient. The decor, however, is ghastly. Lunch and LO 9.30pm, 7 days. Open from lunch straight through to close on Sat-Sun. INX

250
xD1
HARRY RAMSDEN'S: 551 5566. Newhaven Rd. Edin branch of national chain. Bright, tacky, predictable menu, but nice location by harbour nr *Britannia* and the other new big developments. With seats o/side. All day, 7 days. LO 10pm – eg you might go here after using the open-air pool at Next Generation. CHP

251
E2
✔✔ **PLAISIR DU CHOCOLAT:** 556 9524. 257 Canongate at bottom end of Royal Mile on tourist trek, but this is a real find. Chocolate yes but definitely connoisseurs' teas (no coffee) and patisserie. Also excl salads, omelettes, pâtés and innovative cuisine. The famous Polane bread direct from the bakeries in Paris is exquisitely delish with soup or just olive oil (they also sell by quarter-loaf). Tables on the terrace and inside an Art Nouveau-ish rm. A top spot for that reviving cuppa. Tues-Sun 10am–6pm.

252
A2
✔✔ **GALLERY OF MODERN ART CAFÉ:** Belford Rd. Unbeatable on a fine day when you can sit out on the patio by the grass, with sculptures around, have some wine and a plate of Scottish cheese and oatcakes. Hot dishes are excellent – always 2 soups, meat/fish/vegn dish. Coffee and cake whenever. Then it's back to the art. Oh well! Mon-Sat 10am-4.30pm, Sun 2-4.30pm. (390/OTHER ATTRACTIONS). Lunch dishes usually gone by 2.30pm.

253
C2
✔✔ **QUEEN STREET CAFÉ:** National Portrait Gallery (389/OTHER ATTRAC-TIONS), Queen St, betw Hanover and St Andrew's Sq. And through the arched window … a civil slice of old Edin gentility. Serving seriously good light meals (same people as **GOMA**, above), tasteful sandwiches, coffee and cake – best scones in town, among other things. Mon-Sat 10am-4.30pm, Sun noon-4.30pm.

254
D3
✔ **FRUITMARKET CAFÉ:** 226 1843. 29 Market St. Attached to the Fruitmarket Gallery, a cool spacious place for coffee, cake or a light lunch. Big salads & creative snacks, but they're not beyond potato wedges. Big windows to look out; good mix of tourists, Edin faithfuls and art seekers – the latter go upstairs. Mon-Fri 11am-3pm, Sat till 4, Sun 12-5.

255
C1
AU GOURMAND: 624 4666. 1 Brandon Terr at foot of Dundas St at Canonmills. V. French, v. New Town deli counter and caff in back with big windows onto garden. A secret haven. Deli selection small but exquisite. Gr coffee. Mon–Sat 9am–6pm.

256
D3,C4
FAVORIT: 220 6880. 20 Teviot Pl, nr Univ. and 30 Leven St nr King's Theatre (221 1800). By people who brought us Indigo Yard (369/STYLE BARS) and Iguana nearby (373/STYLE BARS). All-day, all-round drop-in café in contemporary style reminiscent of City Café. They've thought of everything. Great late (277/LATE BARS). Both: 7 days, 8.30am/8am-3am. We think Leven St best.

257
D3, C2
CAFÉ FLORENTIN: 225 6267. 8 St Giles St. A true Edin-Franco original, this place is no longer what it was. Once they turned an entire generation of Edimbourgeois on to almond croissants and wicked tartelettes. Trading perhaps on past glory but still a funky caff where advocates rub shoulders with student grunge queens over a blast of caffeine. Open 7am-10pm daily (till 6pm in wint). The other **FLORENTIN** at 5 NW Circus Pl, has diff ownership. It's nicely Stockbridge. 7am-7pm daily.

258
xD4
KAFFE POLITIK: 446 9873. 146-148 Marchmont Rd. All black and white and wood and middle-Euro chic at another converted bank in the heart of student flat land. Damn fine cup of coffee, sodas, juice, soup 'n' sandwiches and unfussy hot dishes. Small choice of v good breakfasts (288/SUN BREAKFAST). Some o/side tables. 10am-10pm daily.

259
D3
BLACK MEDICINE COFFEE SHOP: 622 7209. 2 Nicolson St, corner of Drummond St. Funky American-style coffee shop by the same people as Nicolson's (125/BEST BISTROS) on busy Southside corner opp Festival Theatre and Univ Old Quad. Good place to take your book from Thins; get a window seat! Good smell. Big bagels, cookies & smoothies. 7 days. 8am-8pm (Suns from 9am).

260
E2
CLARINDA'S: 557 1888. 69 Canongate. Nr the bottom of the Royal Mile nr the Palace (and the new Parliament building). A small tearoom with hot dishes and snacks that may seem more of a sit-down stop on the tourist trail but has some of the best home-baking in town (esp the apple pie). V reasonable prices; run by good Edinburgh folk who slave over that stove. T/aways poss (I know I do). 7 days 10am-4.45pm (from 12noon Sun).

261 **THE ELEPHANT HOUSE:** 220 5355. 21 George IV Br. Nr libraries and Edin Univ,
D3 a rather self-conscious but big-time and well-run coffee shop with light snacks and big choice. Counter during day, waitress service evens. Big smoking section. Cakes/pastries are bought in but can be taken out. 7 days 8am-11pm (9am from Sat/Sun). Same people have **ELEPHANTS & BAGELS** at Nicolson Sq. Soup 'n' a bagel t/away and sit-in. 7 days 8.30am-7pm (w/ends 10am-5pm).

262 **G&T (GLASS & THOMPSON):** 557 0909. 2 Dundas St. Patrician New Town cof-
C2 fee shop and deli with contemporary food and attitude. A Clarissa Dickson-Wright kind of place: they love food. Gr *antipasti*, salads, sandwiches to go; and some cakes! 8.30am-5.30pm, Sun 11am-4.30pm. (296/TAKEAWAYS)

263 **BOTANIC GARDENS CAFETERIA:** By 'the House' (where there are regular
xB1 exhibs), within the gdns (388/OTHER ATTRACTIONS). For café only, enter by Arboretum Pl. Disappointing catering style food (in fact it can be ghastly) but the o/side tables & the view of the city is why we come. And the squirrels. 10am-5pm.

264 **CAFFE SARDI:** 220 5553. 18-20 Forrest Rd. More a restau perhaps with all the
D3 expected dishes but also serves a mean Danish pastry and espresso. Coffee machine is a Big Gold Dream and with waitresses from the old country and Italian television on cable, a hint, just a hint, of Soho's Bar Italia. Mon-Sat 10am-11/12pm. Cl Sun.

265 **CAFÉ GRANDE:** 228 1188. 182-184 Bruntsfield Pl. Coffee shop during the day,
xC4 more adventurous bistro menu at night (INX). In among assorted coffees and herbal teas, Bovril can be had. Occasional lapses (not all puds home-made) but a nice restful alternative to brash Montpeliers opp. 9am-11pm, till 12midnight Thu-Sat. Sun 10am-10pm.

266 **CALIFORNIA COFFEE CO:** 228 5001. Kiosks not caffs! By the Odeon cinema
E4, D3, (Clerk St), top of Middle Meadow Walk (opp Forrest Rd) and outside John
D2 Lewis' dept store and St Andrew's cathedral. Caffeine kiosks in former police boxes. Similar fare to Starbucks and Costas but these are home-grown and have in their way, reclaimed the streets. Hrs vary but early-late. Gr coffee to go.

267
C4

✓ ✓ **NDEBELE:** 221 1141. 59 Home St, Tollcross. The Ndebele are a southern African people, but this café has dishes from all over the continent so get your ostrich, mielie bread and moi moi here – or just have a coffee. Loads of sandwiches, light meals and a good groovalong soundtrack. Brill for vegns. Africa distant and usually hot, this delightfully chilled. Daily 10am-10pm. T/away and sit-in.

268
D2

✓ **BLUE MOON CAFÉ:** 557 0911. 1 Barony St on corner of Broughton St. Broughton St. Longest-established gay café Scotland and still evolving (2156/GAY EDIN). Straight-friendly & a good place to hang out from b/fast-late. Home-made cakes by Clark's mum, all day b/fast. Female staff efficient, boys more spacey. Free condoms in the gents for the impecunious or impatient. Mon-Fri 11am-10pm, Sat/Sun 9.30am-10pm. LO 40 min before close.

269
xC4

✓ **LUCA'S:** 446 0233. 16 Morningside Rd. In town version of legendary ice cream parlour in Musselburgh (1444/ICE CREAM). Ice cream and snacks d/stairs, more family food parlour up. Cheap and cheerful. Gr for kids. 7 days.

270
D1

LOST SOCK DINER: 557 6097. Corner of E London St/Broughton St, adj Sundial laundrette. An innovation and caused a whirl when it opened – a café/restau attached to a laundrette where you could eat well while your washing spun. Several changes of chef and food policy since, still a cool place to snack with or without your powder. 7 days. LO 4pm Mon, 10pm Tue-Sat. Sun 10am-5pm. Seats o/side in summer.

271
E1

VITTORIA: 556 6171. Brunswick St, corner of Leith Walk. May get forgotten in the foody guides or the Italian round-up but Vittoria is one of the best, least pretentious Scottish-Italian scrans in town. Great fry-ups, omelettes and full Italian carbo variants. Some o/side tables on interesting corner. 7 days. 10am-11pm. Recovering after a recent fire at TGP.

272
C3

WEB 13: 229 8883. 13 Bread St. The city's most homely Internet boutique, many terminals. At quieter times, bloke who looks much more attuned to messing around with motherboards will muck in to make you a sandwich. Again, all the usual facs for web, e-mail, etc. Quarter- and half-hr rates, dozen PCs, colour scanning, printing and all that jazz. E-mail: queries@web13.co.uk. Excl 3-egg omelette & the breakfast *sc(ram)bled* egg and mushroom baguette are recommended. Mon-Fri 9am-8pm, Sat 10am-6pm, Sun noon-6pm.

273
xE1

CANASTA: 554 5190. 10 Bonnington Rd, nr corner with Gr Jnct St, Leith. Café for locals, not one of your downtown cappuccino numbers. Best omelettes in the burg, and usual café grub (haddock and chips, grills) and cakes home-made before you (I) get up. Tea in a mug. Takeaway. We should honour these people though caff sadly for sale at TGP. Cl Sun.

KEBAB MAHAL: 667 5214. Nicolson Sq. Cult I. Report: 217/INDIAN.

KHUSHI'S: 556 8996. 16 Drummond St. Cult II. Report: 223/INDIAN.

THE BEST LATE-NIGHT RESTAURANTS

274
D3
✓ ✓ **BANN UK:** 226 1112. 5 Hunter Sq on Royal Mile by the Tron. Excl vegn eaterie (186/VEGN RESTAUS) that's so good you wouldn't notice. Lots organic so late night nosh, excl beer & wine-list without the toxin overload. Fri/Sat also have light tapas menu & mellow DJs. Perfect. **Till 11pm & 3am Fri/Sat.**   MED

275
C3
✓ ✓ **THE WITCHERY:** 225 5613. Castlehill, top of Royal Mile nr the Castle. Not open v late, but does take bookings up till 11.30pm, that crucial half hr beyond 11 that allows you to eat after the movies. Special after-theatre menu from 10.30pm has 2 courses for a tenner, a v good deal from one of the best restaus in town (109/BEST RESTAUS). 7 days, lunch and **LO 11.30pm.**

276
B1, B3
✓ **PIZZA EXPRESS:** Best branches in Stockbridge 332 7229. 1 Deanhaugh St and W End at 32 Queensferry St (225 8863). **Open till midnight** and no booking policy, so a good bet. New Leith branch on the shore (554 4332), prob best chance of food after 11 in Leith. Report 166/BEST PIZZA.

277
D3, C4
✓ **FAVORIT:** 220 6880. 20 Teviot Pl and 30 Leven St (221 1800). New York diner type café/restau – salads, pasta, wraps, Ben and Jerry's from dawn till almost dawn (256/BEST TEAROOMS). **7 days, 8.30am-3am.**   MED

278
E1
✓ **GIULIANO'S:** 556 6590. 18 Union Pl, Leith walk opp Playhouse. Buzzing Italian tratt day and night. Report 162/TRUSTY TRATTS. **Handily open till 2am (2.30 w/ends).**

279
B3
NOODLE SHACK: 221 1288. 8 Morrison St. 50m Lothian Rd corner opp rebuilt cinema complex. Upstairs from Rainbow Arch, a big bowl of noodles in a bright canteen. Limited booze, cash only. A post modern midnight. **Till 1am (cl Sun).**   INX

280
D3
GORDON'S TRATTORIA: 225 7992. 231 High St. Although some late-night visitors mistake this for a kebab house, it's v definitely Italian. Best late-night spag in the Old Town. **Sun-Thu LO 12midnight, Fri-Sat 3am**.   INX

281
B3
BAR ROMA: 226 2977. 39a Queensferry St, nr W End of Princes St. Buzzing day and night. An Edin institution even better after revamp. All the old standbys snappily served & lots of late night Italian jive. Best wine-list you'll find in W End after midnight. (See 161/TRUSTY TRATTS). **12noon-12midnight Sun-Thu; 12.45am Fri-Sat**.   INX

282
C3
LAZIO: 229 7788. 95 Lothian Rd. Best of the Lothian Rd bunch by far, tho' you'd never know. Totally genuine Italian family restau (163/TRUSTY TRATTS). There's one guy always there eating at 1 in the morning when we're there. Now that's regular irregular. **Till 1.30am, 3am Fri/Sat.**   INX

283
D2 ✓ **HADRIAN'S:** 557 5000. 2 North Bridge, corner of & brasseries restau of Balmoral (44/HOTELS). Good daily (power) brunch place, but also Suns. **From 7.30am.** Not chp, but light (or lavish) & laid-back.

✓ **SCOTSMAN HOTEL:** 556 5565. 20 N. Bridge. B/fast in Edin's top new boutique hotel (52/HOTELS), a late addition to this b/fast menu so no   item number. Many refs to the morning paper this hotel replaces in the building & an excl repas.

284
D2 ✓ **MEDITERRANEO:** 557 6900. 73 Broughton St. On busy st for b/fast (see below), this is the best choice for the non fry-up & easy start to the day. From coffee/croissants to olive oil lunch in light surroundings (172/MED RESTAUS). **From 11am.**

285
D2 ✓ **BLUE MOON CAFÉ:** 556 2788. 1 Barony St. Also on/off Broughton St the straight-friendly gay caff with all day b/fast (all variations). **From 10am.** People may notice who you come in with.

286
C4 **FAVORIT:** 221 1800. 30 Leven St. The hip all-rounder. **Open 7 days from 8am.** Report: 256/BEST TEAROOMS and 277/LATE-NIGHT RESTAUS.

287
D3 **NEGOCIANTS:** 45-47 Lothian St. Nr univ. Gr all-round pub (350/PUBS WITH GOOD FOOD), open v late and pretty early for Sun breakfast. **From 10am (brunch till 6pm).**

288
xD4 **KAFFE POLITIK:** 446 9873. 146-148 Marchmont Rd. Quite possibly the best scrambled eggs with Emmenthal and chives on toast in town. And good coffee in serenely cerebral surroundings. **From 10am.** (2581/BEST TEAROOMS)

289
D3 **CITY CAFE:** Blair St. It's been here so long, it's easy to take for granted … but for that 'BIG' breakfast (carnivore or veggie), few places in the city beat the content or American diner atmos. **From 11am.**

290
xE1 **KING'S WARK:** 554 9260. 36 The Shore on busy corner for traffic, but calm & comforting inside. Dining rm or bar. No early start (**12.30pm**), but a civilised brunch.

291
D3 **BLACK MEDICINE COFFEE SHOP:** 622 7209. 2 Nicolson St. Gr atmos American-style coffee with bagels/muffins type start to Sundays. 259/COFFEESHOPS. From **9am.**

292
D3 **ELEPHANT HOUSE:** 220 5355. 21 George IV Bridge. Another (this time extensive) coffee-house nr the univ that's open early for caffeine & sustenance. 261/COFFEE SHOPS. **From 9am.**

293
D2, D1 **THE BROUGHTON ST BREAKFAST:** As well as top spots (see above), there's lots of choice in the main st of Edin's East Village. From the top down: **MATHER'S** the no-compromise drinking den does the trad fry-up from **12.30pm,** as does **THE OUTHOUSE** down the lane but with veggie variants (& outside courtyard) & until 4pm. **BAROQUE** also kicks in from **12.30pm** with similar nosh (slightly more expensive). **THE BASEMENT** also does Tex-Mex brex from **noon** tho' it is a basement. Further down on corner with people-watching windows is **THE BARONY** with b/fast & the papers from 12.30-3.30 (gr live music Sun late aft). **THE LOST SOCK DINER** is at the bottom and round the corner. Neighbourhood caff **from 10am** (they also do laundry – see 270/CAFÉS).

294
D3 **CAFÉ FLORENTIN:** St Giles St, off Royal Mile opp Cathedral. The first to open for a civilised start (or finish). The authentically French coffee shop with croissants/pain au chocolat and whirly pastries. Caff now feels a bit rundown, perhaps like you do if you're still running on Sat night. **From 7am.** (257/BEST TEAROOMS)

295 ✓ **ROWLAND'S:** 225 3711. 42 Howe St. And still after the food-to-go explo-
C2 sion, the top-notch New Town takeaway. Creative hot dishes change daily. Interesting sandwich rolls, excellent cheeses, bread, cakes and other carefully selected fare. Also does o/side catering. Mon-Fri 8am-5pm. Cl Sat-Sun.

296 ✓ **G&T (GLASS & THOMPSON):** 557 0909. 2 Dundas St. Deli and coffee
C2 shop on main st in New Town, but also takeaway sandwiches/rolls in infi-nite formats using their drool-making selection of quality ingredients (breads, cheeses, salamis, etc.). Take away to office, gdns or dinner party. Excellent sit-in area and small terr for whiling away Edinburgh days. Mon-Fri 8.30am-6.30pm, Sat 8.30am-5.30pm, Sun 11am-4.30pm. (262/BEST TEAROOMS)

297 ✓ **EMBO:** 652 3880. 29 Haddington Pl. Half way down Leith Walk & one of
E1 the reasons for going that far. Bespoke sandwiches & esp wraps. Excl cof-fee & smoothies. 'Panino Bar' & a couple of tables o/side the door. Good to know. Mon-Fri 7.30am-3.30pm, Sat 9am-4pm. Cl Sun.

298 ✓ **STIR:** 228 6139. 63 Lothian Rd down from Usher Hall & 248 Morrison St
C3 (221 1155) betw EICC & Haymarket Station. Latter uptown/busier & longer opening hrs but both serve 10 great soups (can sample), stews & real salads. Daytime only, Morrison St cl Sun & at 3pm Mon-Sat. More Stirs stirring at TGP.

299 ✓ **THE GLOBE:** 558 3837. 42 Broughton St. A bright spot on the corner in
D2 the middle of the East Village. Open all day till 3/4pm for sand-wiches/rolls and toasted focaccia. Big window for people-watching. Branches at 23 Henderson Row and Castle St and George IV Bridge. Henderson Row branch the best for real b/fast. Cl Sun.

300 **FOOD PLANTATION:** High St. Friendly takeaway with homemade feel (all the
D2 baking is fresh incl well chunky muffins). Sandwiches to go and to order, wraps, crêpes and interesting soups. The best food-to-go on the tourist strip, tho under new ownership at TGP. Cl Sun.

301 **TWO THIN LADDIES:** 229 0653. 103 High Riggs, Tollcross. More sit-in than
C3 takeaway than orig place in Grassmarket. Gr name & v much the opp of the Two Fat Ladies food odyssey. Muesli to tortillas with s/wiches & wraps aplen-ty in betw. Cakes home-made but not their smoothies. Only one thin laddie left at TGP. 7 days 8am-8pm (5pm in winter).

302 **PRET À MANGER:** Shandwick Pl, Castle St, St Andrews Sq (& spreading like
B3, C2 mayo). Pity they sold out to McDonald's.

303 **IT'S ORGANIC:** 228 9444. 15 Bread St & also at 7 William St. Healthy happy eat-
C3, B3 ing both in (not many seats) & to-go. Soups, juices, smoothies in all combos. S/wiches, wraps etc. Organic coffee & tea. Mon-Sat 8am-6pm. Cl Sun.

304 **THE DELTA:** 346 8973. 27 Roseburn Terr. Seriously good Indian t/away in the
xA3 west of the city. Good fish and vegn choice. Huge selection, so t/away the menu. Some delivery. 7 days, 5pm-11pm.

305 **EASTERN SPICES:** 558 3609. 2 Canonmills Br, by the clock. On the grapevine,
C1 this place is better than most – phone in your order or turn up and wait. Also home delivery. Full Indian menu from pakora to pasanda and meals for one. 5-11.30 7 days.

306 **TASTE GOOD:** 313 5588. 67 Slateford Rd. At last a 21st cent Chinese t/away
C1 unfortunately far from centre (they do deliver). Contemp look & presentation. Tastes good too (also seating). 7 days 4.30-12midnight.

307 **L'ALBA D'ORO:** 557 2580. 5-11 Henderson Row. Excl pizza, pasta, wine as well
C1 as fish 'n' chips. Report 167/PIZZAS.

307a **DUCK'S DE LA GARE:** 557 8887. Waverley Steps (off Princes St into the
D2 station). Best takeaway in Princes Mall & station precinct by people who have notable French restau Marché Noir (143/FRENCH RESTAUS). Usual fare, just better than what's around. Some seats. 7 days.

308 ✓ ✓ ✓ **PORT O' LEITH:** 58 Constitution St. The legendary Leith bar on busy
xE1 rd to what used to be the docks. The incorrigible & incorruptible
Mary Moriarty still puts up the odd sailor but it's mainly the rest of us from the
sea of life who frequent this unchanging neighbourhood pub full of warmth,
chat, good music & all the things we left behind. Truly a port in the storm. Go
find it. Till 12.45am.

309 ✓ **CAFÉ ROYAL:** Behind Burger King at the E end of Princes St, one of Edin's
D2 longest celebrated pubs. Unrelated to the London version, though there
is a similar Victorian/Baroque elegance. Through the partition is the Oyster
Bar (182/SEAFOOD RESTAUS). Central counter and often standing rm only. Open
to 11pm (later at w/ends).

310 ✓ **BENNET'S:** Leven St, by King's Theatre. Just stand at the back and watch
C4 light stream through the stained glass on a sunny day as it always did.
Same era as Café Royal and similar ambience, mirrors and tiles. Decent food at
lunch (348/PUB FOOD). Till 11.30pm Mon-Wed, 12.30am Thu-Sat, 11pm Sun.

311 ✓ **THE POND:** 467 3815. 2 Bath Rd, off Seafield Rd, Leith. Cool Edin bar on
xE1 the edge of dead dockland. They don't make 'em as understated as this,
anywhere except Amsterdam. Till 1am. (366/HIP BARS).

312 **BARONY BAR:** 81 Broughton St. Real-ale venue with a mixed clientele & good
D2 vibe. Belgian and guest beers. Newspapers to browse over a Sun afternoon
b/fast or a (big) lunchtime pie. Bert's band on Sun aft/evens one of the best
pub nights in town. Till 12midnight Mon-Thu, 12.30am Fri-Sat, 11pm Sun.

313 **THE BASEMENT:** 109 Broughton St. Much-imitated, still crucial, this is a
D3 chunky, happening sort of, er, basement where you can have Mex-style food
during the day served by laaarvely staff in Hawaiian shirts. At night, the punters are well up for it – late, loud and lively. Till 1am daily.

314 **SHEEP'S HEID:** 656 6952. The Causeway, Duddingston Village. Not central, but
xE4 a pleasant and dramatic drive away behind Arthur's Seat in the Queen's Park.
Old coaching inn with good crack, some locals & ok grub in courtyard patio
(346/PUB FOOD). Food till 8.30pm, pub 11pm (12midnight Fri-Sat).

315 **KAY'S BAR:** 39 Jamaica St. The New Town – incl Jamaica St – sometimes gives
C2 the impression that it's populated by people who were around in the late
18th century. It's an Edinburgh thing (mainly male). They care for the beer
(338/REAL-ALE PUBS). Until 11.45pm (11pm Sun).

316 **MATHER'S:** 1 Queensferry St. Edin's W End has a complement of 'smart' bars
B3 that cater for people with tight haircuts and schedules. The alternative is here
– a stand-up space for old-fashioned pubbery, slack coiffure and idle talk
(330/'UNSPOILT' PUBS). Till 12midnight Mon-Thu, 1am Fri-Sat, 11pm Sun.

317 **ROBBIE'S:** Leith Walk, on corner with Iona St. Some bars on Leith Walk are
E1 downright scary – but not this one. Tolerant, good range of beer, TV will have
the football on (or not). Wild mix of Trainspotters, locals and the odd dodgy
character or 3, even a stray social worker (HQ is nearby). Always has 'it' factor.
(328/'UNSPOILT' PUBS). Till 12midnight Mon-Sat, 11pm Sun.

318 **CITY CAFÉ:** 220 0127. 19 Blair St. Seems ancient, but 13 yrs on, the retro
D3 Americana chic has aged gracefully. Pool tables, all-day food, decent coffee. A
hip Edin bar that has stood the test of mind-altering time. Music downstairs
w/ends courtesy of guest DJs (289/SUNDAY BREAKFAST). 11am-1am daily.

319 **BELUGA BAR:** 624 4545. 30a Chambers St. Token hip (well up to a point) &
D3 new bar (at TGP) in this section. Restau upstairs but we don't rate food. Down
designery staircase is vast cavern for drinking, debauchery, pub-grub etc.
Places like this everywhere, but this one used to be a dental hospital.

320 **THREE SISTERS:** Cowgate. Of the many booming bars in the Cowgate, we
D3 may as well select this one – one of Edinburgh's busiest bars. Nothing v special but good conversion of old warehouse and better than your av super bar
(3 atmospheres to choose from). Also has rms. 7 days, 11am-1am.

321 **THE DOME:** 624 8624. 14 George St. Finally Edin's first megabar but not a
C2 chain. Former bank and grandiose in the way that only a converted temple to
Mammon could be. Main part sits 15m under elegant domed roof with island
bar and raised platform at back for determined diners. Staff almost impeccable, pricey menu; you come for the surroundings more than the victuals (MED).
Lunch and LO dinner 10pm daily. Also snack menu for casual diners away
from roped-off posh nosh area. Adj real-ale Art Deco bar Frazers is separate,
more intimate, better for a blether. 'Garden' patio bar at back (in good weather) – enter via Rose St. Final bit, downstairs: Why Not?, a nightclub for over-25s
still lookin' for lurvv. Main bar Sun-Thu till 11.30pm, Fri-Sat till 1am.

322 **THE DORIC:** 225 1084. 15 Market St. More a bistro/restau than a mere pub, but
D3 the smaller rm by the bar is Edin in a nutshell (136/BISTROS) & **THE HEBRIDES**
on the ground floor is also the real McCoy.

THE BEST OLD 'UNSPOILT' PUBS

*Of course it's not necessarily the case that when a pub's done up, it's spoiled, or
that all old pubs are worth preserving, but some have resisted change and that's
part of their appeal. Money and effort are often spent to 'oldify' bars and contrive
an atmos. The following places don't have to try.*

323 ✓ **THE DIGGERS:** 1 Angle Park Terr. (Officially the Athletic Arms.) Jambo
xA4 pub *par excellence*, stowed with the Tynecastle faithful before and after
games. Still keeps a gr pint of McEwan's 80/-, allegedly the best in Edin. The
food is basic ie pies. Till 11pm/midnight Mon-Sat, 6pm Sun.

324 ✓ **THE ROYAL OAK:** Infirmary St. Tiny upstairs and not much bigger down.
D3 During the day, pensioners sip their pints (couple of real ales) while the
cellar opens till 2am. Music up and down. Hell for non-smokers but they definitely don't make 'em like this any more. Gold carat pubness.

325 ✓ **ROSEBURN BAR:** 1 Roseburn Terr, on main Glas rd out W from Haymarket
xA3 and one of the nearest pubs to Murrayfield Stadium. Wood and grandeur
and red leather, bonny wee snug, fine pint of McEwan's and wall-to-wall rugby
of course. Heaving before internationals. Till 11pm (midnight w/ends).

326 ✓ **CLARK'S:** 142 Dundas St. A couple of snug snugs, red leather, brewery
C2 mirrors and decidedly no frills. Good McEwan's – just the place to pop in
if you're tooling downhill from town to Canonmills. A local you would learn to
love. Till 11pm (11.30pm Thu-Sat).

327 **BLUE BLAZER:** 2 Spittal St opp Point Hotel. No frills, no pretensions, just
C3 wooden fixtures and fittings, pies and toasties in this fine S&N-owned howf
that usually carries half a dozen real ales. More soul than any of its competi-
tors nearby. All day till 12/12.30. Sun 12.30pm-11pm.

328 **ROBBIE'S:** Leith Walk, on corner of Iona St. Real ales and new lagers in a neigh-
xE1 bourhood howf that tolerates everyone from the wifie in her raincoat to multi-
pierced yoof of indeterminate gender. More rough than smooth of course, but
with the footy on the box, a pint and a packet of Hula Hoops – this is a bar to
save or savour life. Till 12midnight Mon-Sat, 11pm Sun. (317/UNIQUE EDIN PUBS)

329 **OXFORD BAR:** 8 Young St, downhill from George St. No time machine need-
C2 ed – just step in the door to see an Edin that hasn't changed since yon times.
Careful what you say; this is an off-duty cop shop. Some real ales but they're
beside the point as the pies. Till 1am (midnight Sun).

330 **MATHER'S:** 1 Queensferry St. Not only a reasonable real-ale pub but almost
B3, D2 worth visiting just to look at the ornate fixtures and fittings – frieze and bar
esp – they don't make 'em like that these days. Unreconstructed in every
sense. Till 12midnight Mon-Thu, 1am Fri-Sat, 11pm Sun. (316/UNIQUE PUBS)
There's another, unrelated, **MATHER'S** in Broughton St which is managing to
keep its head above water in the city's grooviest thoroughfare by remaining
pub-like and unpretentious.

331 **STEWART'S:** 14 Drummond St on the S Side off S Bridge. Lino, beer, pension-
D3 ers and folk who sing when in their cups. Few concessions to anything that
has happened to the licensed trade since the 1960s. Till midnight Mon-Sat,
11pm Sun.

THE BEST REAL-ALE PUBS

332 ✓ **THE CUMBERLAND BAR:** Cumberland St, corner of Dundonald St. After
C1 work this New Town bar attracts its share of suits, but later the locals
reclaim it and Camra (Campaign for Real Ale) supporters seek it out too. Av of
12 real ales on tap. Nicely appointed, decent pub lunches, unexpected beer
gdn. Mon-Wed till 12am, Thu-Sat to 1am. Sun 12.30-10pm.

333 ✓ **STARBANK INN:** 64 Laverockbank Rd, Newhaven. On the seafront rd W of
xC1 Newhaven harbour. Usually 8 different ales on offer. Gr place to sit with
pint in hand and watch the sun sink over the Forth. The food is good (351/PUB
FOOD). Bar till 11pm Sun-Wed, 12midnight Thu-Sat.

334 ✓ **THE BOW BAR:** 80 W Bow, halfway down Victoria St. They know how to
D3 treat drink in this excellent wee bar. For a whisky & ale – a fair few available. One of the few places in the Grassmarket area an over 25-year-old might
not feel out of place. Bliss. Till 11.30pm Mon-Sat, 11pm Sun.

335 ✓ **THE GUILDFORD ARMS:** 1 W Register St. Behind Burger King at E end of
D2 Princes St (opp Balmoral Hotel) on same block as the Café Royal
(309/UNIQUE PUBS). Lofty, ornate Victorian hostelry with loadsa good ales.
There are some you won't find anywhere else in the city. Pub grub available
on 'gallery' floor as well as bar. Sun-Wed till 11pm, Thu-Sat till 12midnight.

336 **BERT'S:** 29 William St. Rare ales, a suit and supersec crowd after work but a fair
B3, B1 mix at other times in this *faux* Edwardian bar. Decent pies for carnivores or
veggies alike and a good place to escape from office neurosis. Till 11pm Sun-
Thu, 12midnight Fri-Sat. More local **BERT'S** at 2 Raeburn Pl, Stockbridge.

337 **THE CANNY MAN:** 237 Morningside Rd. Officially known as the Volunteer
xC4 Arms, but everybody calls it the Canny Man. Good smorrebrod at lunch time
& evens (345/PUB FOOD), and wide range of real ales. Casual visitors may feel
that management have an attitude (problem).

338 **KAY'S BAR:** 39 Jamaica St, off India St in the New Town. Go on an afternoon
C2 when gentlemen of a certain age talk politics, history and rugby over pints of
real ale. The bow-tied barman patiently serves. All red and black and vaguely
distinguished with a tiny snug – The Library. Till midnight (11pm Sun).
(315/UNIQUE PUBS)

339 **CASK & BARREL:** 115 Broughton St. Wall-to-wall distressed wood, gr selection
D1 of real ales and mixed crowd at the bottom of groovy Broughton St. Don't
hold that against it. Till 12.30am Sun-Wed, 1am Thu-Sat.

340 **CLOISTERS:** 26 Brougham St, Tollcross. Nine real ales on tap in this simple and
C4 unfussy bar with its wooden panelling and laid-back app. Same owners as
Bow Bar (*see above*). Basic pub grub at lunchtimes, bar closes 12midnight
(12.30am Fri-Sat).

341 **CALEY SAMPLE ROOM:** 5-8 Angle Park Terr. Half-owned by the nearby (inde-
A4 pendent) Caledonian Brewery, the CSR sells all the expected Caledonian real
ales and a couple of guests besides. A neighbourhood bar most of the time, a
haven for home and away fans before and after games at Tynecastle. Basic
pub lunches Mon-Fri, drink served till 12midnight Sun-Thu, 1am Fri-Sat.

342 **CALEDONIAN BEER FESTIVAL:** An annual event held around the first w/end
A4 in June at Edin's own – and independent – Caledonian Brewery, a red-brick
Victorian pile at 42 Slateford Rd (on rt-hand side going out of town). It's a gr
site, 50 real ales from Adnams to Whitbread on tap, food and music (esp jazz)
on Fri & Sat evenings and Sun afternoon in a marquee and the brewery's own
'Festival Hall', a refurbed barley store. See local press for details or call 623
8066. The 'Festival Hall' also hosts ceilidhs most Sats. (466/CEILIDHS)

PUBS WITH GOOD FOOD

343 ✓ **THE SHORE:** 553 5080. 3 The Shore. A bistro/restau but the same (black-
xE1 board) menu faster and friendlier in the bar (where you can smoke). Light
meat dishes, lots of fish and always something vegn. Lunch and LO 10pm.
(123/BEST BISTROS)

344 ✓ **KING'S WARK:** 554 9260. 36 The Shore, on the corner of Bernard St.
xE1 Woody, candlelit, comfortable. A business haunt at lunchtimes and a
good informal restau-cum-bar in the evenings. Scottish slant on the menu,
incl excellent fish in beer batter and chips; also food at the bar and real ales.
Lunch and LO10pm. Bar open to 11pm, 12midnight Fri-Sat.

345 ✓ **THE CANNY MAN:** 447 1484. 237 Morningside Rd (aka The Volunteer
xC4 Arms) on the A702 via Tollcross, 7km from centre. Idiosyncratic renowned
eaterie with a certain hauteur. Carries a complement of malts as long as your
arm and a serious wine list. Excellent smorrebrod lunches (12noon-3pm, not
Sun) & evens 6.30-9.30pm. Salads & desserts with Luca's ice-cream (& alcohol).
No loonies or undesirables are welcome (you may be tested) but this is a
civilised pub; you could be in the Cotswolds. Till 12midnight Mon-Sat, 11pm
Sun. (337/REAL-ALE PUBS)

346 **SHEEP'S HEID:** 656 6952. Causeway, Duddingston Village. An 18th-century
xE4 coaching inn 10km from centre behind Arthur's Seat and reached most easily through the Queen's Park. OK grub incl alfresco dining when poss. The village and the nearby wildfowl loch should be strolled around if you have time.
Atmos rather than food is why we go. Food Lunch & 6.30-9.30.

347 **CRAMOND INN, CRAMOND VILLAGE:** 336 2035. Go west and down to the
xA1 sea. Appeal mainly in this (398/WALKS) but low ceilings, log fires, real ales make
this a good escape from the city. Lotsa fish. Can snack or pack. Lunch and LO
9.30pm, 7 days.

348 **BENNET'S:** 229 5143. 8 Leven St, next to the King's Theatre. An Edin standby,
C4 listed for several reasons (310/UNIQUE PUBS), not least for its honest-to-goodness (and cheap) pub lunch. À la carte (sausage, fish, steak pie, etc.) and daily
specials under the enormous mirrors. Lunch only, 12noon-2pm.

349 **THE ABBOTSFORD:** 225 5276. 3 Rose St. A doughty remnant of Rose St drink-
C2 ing days of yore, and still the best pub lunch nr Princes St. Fancier than it used
to be but still grills and bread & butter pudding. Huge portions. LO in bar
2.30pm. Restau upstairs serves food in evening too – LO 9.45pm. Bar till 11pm.
Cl Sun.

350 **NEGOCIANTS:** 225 6313. 45-47 Lothian St. (Pron 'Nigoshunts' by locals.)
D3 Mirrors, food, space and shooters (non-lethal variety) upstairs; dancefloor, DJs
(every night), drink and more drink down. Range of clients from civilised
bagel-nibblers mid-morning to Chimayed-out dance fiends in the wee small
hrs. Zanier and less pretentious than Iguana next door,– but just as studenty.
Table service lacks pace – but hey! LO food 2.30am. Open 9am-3am daily.
(483/ESS CULTURE/CLUBS)

351 **STARBANK INN:** 552 4141. 64 Laverockbank Rd, the seafront rd in Newhaven.
xC1 Long - est family pub with real ales (333/REAL ALE PUBS) and excl value food, with
big helpings. Gr seafood platter as well as mince 'n' tatties. 7 days lunch and dinner LO 9pm (Sun all day menu).

352 **OLD CHAIN PIER:** 552 1233. 1 Trinity Cres, on the Forth just W of Newhaven
xD1 Harbour. Rt on the waterfront, nr Ocean Terminal. Well-kept real ale, gr bar
snacks (Stilton with oatcakes, interesting toasties) and excellent-value bar
meals. Some delays at busy times so be prepared to watch the sunset. LO food
8pm. Bar 12noon-11pm Sun-Wed, till 12midnight Thu-Sat.

OUTSIDE TOWN

Refer to Lothians map on pages 340–341.

353 ✓ **THE WATERSIDE, HADDINGTON:** 01620 825674. 28km from town off
MAP 7 A1. Longest, landmark pub food watering hole. On riverside, esp ambient
B1 in summer. Can feel like England. Upstairs restau and labyrinthine and v pub-
like downstairs. Big helpings. Excellent food. Lunch and supper. LO 10pm.

354 ✔ **DROVER'S INN, EAST LINTON:** 01620 860298. 5 Bridge St. Off the A1,
MAP 7   35km E of city. Fair way to go for eats, but don't think about the A1, think
B1   about this welcoming pub with notable food (they run a courtesy bus if it
goes on too long). A classic village pub with warmth and delicious meals in
bistro beside bar or restau up top. Beer gdn out back is o/looked and trains
whoosh by, but on a sunny day, partake their excellent lunch here. Lunch and
dinner (6-9.30pm) daily.

355 ✔ **HORSESHOE INN, EDDLESTON nr PEEBLES:** 01721 730225.
MAP 7   35km SW on A703. Roadside hostelry (has 8rms), but more a restau than
A2   a pub. 7 days, 12noon-3pm and evenings to 9/9.30pm. All day Sun, incl their
estimable roasts.

356 **THE SUN INN, LOTHIANBURN:** 663 2456. On a bend of the A7 nr t/off for
MAP 7   Newtongrange, under mega viaduct, 18km S of city centre. Happy, homely
A2   pub in the unfashionable netherlands of Midlothian. Bistro-style food, lunch
and LO 9pm (9.30 pm w/ends). Popular family spot (book w/ends).

357 **THE BRIDGE INN/THE POP INN, RATHO, W LOTHIAN:** 333 1320. 16km W of
MAP 7   centre via A71, turning rt opp Dalmahoy Golf Club. Large choice of comfort-
A1   ing food in canalside setting. Has won various awards, incl accolades for its
kids' menu. Restau, bar food and canal cruises with nosh. Pop Inn 12noon-9pm
daily. Restau lunch daily and LO 9pm Mon-Sat. Bar till 11pm, 12midnight Fri-
Sat. (248/KID-FRIENDLY)

358 **GOBLIN HA', GIFFORD:** 01620 810244. 35km from town in neat E Lothian
MAP 7   village. One of two hotels, this has the pub grub cornered. Lunch and supper
B1   (6-9pm, 9.30pm Fri-Sat). Gdn gets v busy in summer. Nice for kids.

THE BEST PLACES TO DRINK OUTDOORS

359 **THE HUB:** 473 2067. Castlehill. The café-bar of the International Festival
C3   Centre mixed reviews for food but enclosed terrace for people-watching.
Brollies & heaters extend the possibilities.

360 **THE SHORE:** 553 5080. 3 The Shore, Leith. Excellent place to eat (123/BEST
xE1   BISTROS), some tables just o/side the door, but it's fine to wander over to the
dock on the other side of the st and sit with your legs over the edge. Do try
not to fall in. From 11am daily.

361 **THE WATERFRONT:** 554 7427. 1c Dock Pl. Another v good Leith eaterie
xE1   (132/BEST BISTROS) but with waterside tables and adj barge for those who
fancy a float. Gr wine list. From 12noon Mon-Sat, 12.30pm Sun.

362 **PEAR TREE:** 667 7533. 38 W Nicholson St. Adj to parts of Edin Univ so real stu-
D4   dent style with big (surprisingly floral) beer gdn and refectory-style food.
From noon Mon-Sat, 12.30pm Sun. Round the corner on main drag, the oppor-
tunistically named **HUMAN BE-IN** spills out onto the wide pavement.

363 **THE OUTHOUSE:** 557 6668. 12a Broughton St Lane. Large enclosed patio out
D2   back, home to summer Sun afternoon barbecues. No view except of other
people. (368/HIP)

364 **THE PLEASANCE:** In The Pleasance. Open during the Festival only, this is one
E3   of the major Fringe venues, and has a large open courtyard. If you're here,
you're on the Fringe, so to speak.

365 **POPROKIT** 556 4272. 2 Picardy Pl. Catwalk café becomes sidewalk café in
D1   warm weather. Busy corner on major r/bout, but also the apex of the pink triangle and a traffic light system that never seems to go green so big people-
watching potential. (376/HIP)

General locations: **GREENSIDE PL** (**THEATRE ROYAL** and **CAFÉ HABANA**),
bars in **THE GRASSMARKET**, and **IGUANA** and **NEGOCIANTS** (321/322/373/
HIP/350/PUBS WITH GOOD FOOD) on **LOTHIAN ST**. All make a stab at pavement
café culture when the sun's out.

366 **OPAL LOUNGE:** 226 2275. 51a George St. Basement mid-fashion mile for lat-
C2 est and most ambitious 'lifestyle' project from the Indigo Yard stable (see below). Sunken and sexy lounges incl dancefloor and restau (you would eat here without having gone to eat). Gr staff know how to serve cocktails. Big door presence. Admn and queue after 10pm. Open till 3am 7 days (food till 10pm).

367 **PO NA NA:** 226 2224. 43b Frederick St. Still popular N African theme bar – part
C2 of the chain but not obtrusively. Functions as a bar till 11pm, then it's more of a club with entry charge and DJs, and maybe a queue to get in. 7 days till 3am. The fag machine is covered in zebra skin. Used to be almost decadent, who knows now? (483/ESS CULTURE/CLUBS).

368 **THE OUTHOUSE:** 557 6668. 12a Broughton St Lane. Happily mixed & unob-
D2 trusive modern bar off Broughton St 'in the lane' off the 'pink triangle'. Modish food available 12noon-4pm for self-conscious business diners and a regular Sun barbecue on the patio (not the greatest of views). One of the few bars in the UK doing the absinthe thing – drink more than 2 at your peril. Till 1am.

369 **INDIGO YARD:** 220 5603. 7 Charlotte Lane, off Queensferry St. Tucked away in
B3 the W End, this spacious designer café-bar offers exposed brickwork, balcony tables, booths and babes in blue of both genders serving good food and drink. More Med than Mex cuisine with flexible menu, but poss too loud later on for serious dining (128/BEST BISTROS). Bar till 1am daily. Same people have **IGUANA** (*see below*), **FAVORIT** (256/BEST TEAROOMS) & **RICK'S** (*see below*).

370 **RICK'S:** 622 7800. 55a Frederick St. New Town variant of the above. Another
C2 café-bar-restau but this time also with rms (59/HOTELS). Same problem with the eating experience here as the others viz too much noise from the bar, tho' prob best on this page. Bar service good & they know how to make cocktails. Rocks from 10 onwards (till 1am).

371 **OXYGEN:** 557 9997. Infirmary St. By the people who brought us Baroque in
D3 Broughton St and The Water Shed (*see below*). This slightly off campus, off Grassmarket bar is cool but not too cool – it's also the complete antithesis of The Oak next door (324/UNSPOILT PUBS).

372 **THE POND:** Corner of Bath Rd and Salamander St, Leith. Turn rt at the foot of
xE1 Constitution St past the warehouses. This bar is so cool it's the complete opposite of a style bar, a million miles from George St (& hard to find). Run by the people who do clubs like Soft (& formerly Going Places), Edinburgh Beige Cricket Team and the fanzine, *Shavers Weekly*, The Pond is where you'll find the people who don't want to be cool; they want to watch fish & swing in the bas-ket chair. Open when you are.

373 **IGUANA:** 220 4288. 41 Lothian St. From the makers of Indigo Yard (*see above*)
D3 comes this self-consciously clubby café-bar over the road from Edin Univ's Bristo Sq buildings – so v studenty in term time. DJs (Wed-Sun) play ambi-ent/dub/dance later on. During the day people eat, drink or sip coffee in calm, cool surroundings. LO food 10pm. Bar 9am-1am. (483/ESS CULTURE/CLUBS)

374 **THE WATER SHED:** 220 3774. 44 St Stephen St. Neighbourhood café-bar with
C1 *de rigueur* light wood, blue and orange décor. Coffee/food served 10am-7pm (yes, Med-Mex inevitably), really kicks in as a bar later on – open till 1am daily. Share a cocktail or some cheap Chardonnay with Stockbridge's shiny happy people.

375 **CITY CAFÉ:** 220 0127. 19 Blair St. A true original that went from *the* hippest,
D3 to nowhere, and now back again with the cool night people. Buzzing at the w/end, downstairs the DJs play all kinds depending on the night. Pool tables never stop. 11am-1am daily.

376 **POPROKIT:** 556 4272. 2 Picardy Pl. Corner glass box at the top of Broughton
D2 St and pink triangle for a be-seen crowd though, with DJs in the basement open decks etc. Till 1am daily. Tables o/side but much human and traffic traf-fic. (365/DRINK OUTDOORS)

377
C3 ✓✓✓ **EDINBURGH CASTLE:** 225 9846. Go to Princes St and look up. The main attraction; extremely busy AYR. Tartan tea cosies on sale in the shop rake in the bawbees. And yet. St Margaret's 12th-century chapel is simple and beautiful, the rolling history lesson that leads up to the display of Scotland's crown jewels is fascinating; the Stone of Destiny is a big deal to the Scots (though others may not see why). And, ultimately, the Scottish National War Memorial is one of the most genuinely affecting places in the country – a simple, dignified testament to shared pain and loss. Last ticket 45 min before closing. Apr-Sep 9.30am-6pm, Oct-Mar 9.30am-5pm. HS

378
xA1 ✓✓✓ **THE FORTH BRIDGE:** S Queensferry, 20km W of Edin via A90. First turning for S Queensferry from dual carriageway; don't confuse with signs for road br. Or train from Waverley to Dalmeny, and walk 1km. Knocking on now and showing its age, the br was 100 in 1990. But still … Can't see too many private finance initiative wallahs rushing in to do anything of similar scope these days – who would have the vision? An international symbol of Scotland, it should be seen, but go to the N side, S Queensferry's v crowded & sadly, very tacky these days.

379
E2 ✓✓ **PALACE OF HOLYROOD HOUSE:** 556 1096. Foot of the Royal Mile. Queenie's N Brit time-share – she's here for a wee while late June/early July every yr. Large parts of the palace are dull (Duke of Hamilton's loo, Queen's wardrobes) so only a dozen or so rms are open, most dating from 17th century but a couple from the earlier 16th-century bit. Lovely cornices abound. Anomalous Stuart features, adj 12th-century abbey ruins quite interesting. Upper-class souvenir shop. Apr-Oct: 9.30am-5.15pm (last ticket), daily. Nov-Mar: 9.30am-3.45pm (last ticket) daily. HS

380
C3 ✓✓ **THE ROYAL MILE:** The High St, the medieval main thoroughfare of
D3 the capital following the trail from the volcanic crag of Castle Rock
E3 and connecting the 2 landmarks above. Heaving during the Festival but if on
E2 a winter's night you chance by with a frost settling on the cobbles and there's no one around, it's magical. Always interesting with its wynds and closes (Dunbar's Close, Whitehorse Close, the secret gdn opp Huntly House), but lots of tacky tartan shops too. Central block cl to traffic during Festival Fringe to create best street performance space in UK. See it on a walking tour – there are several esp at night (ghost/ghouls/witches, etc.). Some of the best actually take you under the st. Mercat Tours (557 6464) and Witchery (225 6745) are pretty good.

381
D3 ✓✓ **ROYAL MUSEUM:** 247 4219. Chambers St. From the skeletons to archaeological artefacts, stuffed animal habitats to all that we have done. Humankind and its interests encapsulated (and displayed) here. Building designed by Captain Francis Fowkes, Royal Engineers, and completed in 1888. Impressive atrium with well, spacious coffee-shop – often hosts dinners and parties. Mon-Sat 10am-5pm, Sun 12noon-5pm. Open till 8pm on Tue. FREE

382
D3 ✓✓ **MUSEUM OF SCOTLAND:** Chambers St. The story of Scotland from geological beginnings to Kirsty Wark's Saab Convertible, all housed in a marvellous new building by Gordon Benson and Alan Forsyth. Opened in Dec '98, both it and the Royal (above) had admissions abolished in April 2001. World-class space with resonant treasures like St Filian's Crozier and the Monymusk Reliquary, said to contain bits of St Columba. Early peoples to v recent ones. Mon-Sat 10am-5pm, Sun 12noon-5pm. Open till 8pm on Tue and from 4.30-8pm it's free. **TOWER RESTAURANT** (own entrance) is on the top floor (104/RESTAURANTS). ADMN

383
E3 ✓✓ **OUR DYNAMIC EARTH:** 550 7800. Foot of Holyrood Rd. Edin's Millennium Dome, an interactive museum/visitor attraction, made with Millennium money and a huge success since it opened summer '99. Salisbury Craigs rise above, the universe and everything below. Vast restau, outside an amphitheatre. Apr-Oct: 10am-6pm daily. Nov-Mar: 10am-5pm Wed-Sun. ADMN

384 ✓ ✓ **NATIONAL GALLERY OF SCOTLAND:** 624 6200. The Mound.
C3 Neoclassical buildings housing a superb collection of Old Masters in a series of hushed salons. Many are world famous, but you don't emerge goggle-eyed as you do from the National in London – more quietly elevated. At TGP, the building in front, Royal Scottish Academy, is closed for refurbishment so expect a building site around whole area. Should be impressive when it finally re-opens. Mon-Sat 10am-5pm, Sun 12-5pm. Extended hours during Festival.   FREE

385 ✓ ✓ **EDINBURGH ZOO:** 334 9171. Corstorphine Rd. 4km W of Princes St,
xA3 buses from Princes St Gdns side. Whatever you think of zoos, this one is highly respected and its serious zoology is still fun for kids (organised activities in Jul/Aug). The penguins waddle out at 2pm daily and the sad, accusing eyes of the wolves connect with onlookers in a profoundly disconcerting manner. Open Open AYR 7 days, 9am-4.30pm (till 5pm, Mar). 9am-6pm Easter onwards, but times set to change 2002 so check first. (1633/KIDS)   ADMN

386 ✓ **ROYAL COMMONWEALTH POOL:** 667 7211. Dalkeith Rd. Hugely suc-
xE4 cessful pool complex which includes a 50m main pool, a gym, sauna/ steam rm/suntan suites and a jungle of flumes. Goes like a fair, morning to night. Some people find the water overtreated and over noisy, but Edin has many good pools to choose from; this is the one that young folk prefer. Some lane swimming. Mon-Fri 9am-9pm, Wed 10am-9pm. Sat-Sun 10am-4pm.

387 ✓ **ROYAL YACHT BRITANNIA:** 555 5566. Ocean Dr, Leith, in the docks, enter
xE1 by Commercial St at end of Gr Junction St. Now finally berthed outside Conran's shopping mall, the Ocean Terminal (incl average shopping experience & 3 disappointing Conran food outlets). Done with ruling the waves, the royal yacht has found a permanent home as a tourist attraction (and prestigious corporate night out). Close up, the Art Deco lines are surprisingly attractive, while the interior was one of the sets for our best-ever soap opera. Jun-Sept 9.30am-4.30pm; Oct-Mar 10am-3.30pm; Apr-May 9.30am-4pm. Booking advised in Aug.   ADMN

THE OTHER ATTRACTIONS

388 ✓ ✓ ✓ **ROYAL BOTANIC GARDEN:** 552 7171. Inverleith Row, 3km from
C1 Princes St. Enter from Inverleith Row or Arboretum Pl. 70 acres of ornamental gdns, trees and walkways; a joy in every season. Tropical plant houses, landscaped rock and heath gdn and enough space just to wander. Chinese Gdn coming on nicely, precocious squirrels everywhere. The 'Botanics' have talks, guided tours, events (info 552 5339). They also look after other impt outstanding gdns throughout Scotland. Gallery with occasional exhibs and café with outdoor terrace for serene afternoon teas (263/BEST TEAROOMS). Total integrity and the natural high. Open 7 days 9.30am-4pm (Nov-Jan), 5pm (Feb & Oct), 6pm (Mar & Sept), 7pm (Apr-Aug).   FREE

389 ✓ ✓ **NATIONAL PORTRAIT GALLERY:** 624 6200. 1 Queen St. Sir Robert
D2 Rowand Anderson's fabulous and custom-built neo-Gothic pile houses paintings and photos of the good, great and merely famous. Danny McGrain hangs out next to the Queen Mum and Nasmyth's familiar pic of Burns is here. Good venue for photo exhibs, beautiful atrium with star-flecked ceiling and frieze of (mainly) men in Scottish history from a Stone-Age chief to Carlyle. Splendid. Gr café (253/BEST TEAROOMS). Mon-Sat 10am-5pm, Sun 12-5pm. Extended hrs during Festival.   FREE

390 ✓ **NATIONAL GALLERY OF MODERN ART:** 624 6200. Belford Rd. Betw
A2 Queensferry Rd and Dean Village (nice to walk through). Best to start from Palmerston Pl and keep left or see below (Dean Gallery). Former school with permanent collection from Impressionism to Hockney and the Scottish painters alongside. An intimate space where you can fall in love (with paintings or each other). Important temporary exhibs. The café is excellent (252/BEST TEAROOMS). Mon-Sat 10am-5pm, Sun 12-5pm. Extended hrs during Festival.   FREE

391 **DEAN GALLERY:** 624 6200. Belford Rd. Across the (busy) rd from GOMA.
A2 Relatively new (1999) addition to Edin art and life – sexy, intimate spaces,

communal coffee shop, gdns to wander. Superb 20th-century collection; many surreal moments. Gr way to app both galleries is by Water of Leith Walkway (396/WALKS IN THE CITY). Mon-Sat 10am-5pm, Sun 2-5pm. Extended hrs during Festival. FREE

392 **MUSEUM OF CHILDHOOD:** 529 4142. 42 High St. Local authority-run shrine
D3 to the dreamstuff of tender days where you'll find everything from tin soldiers to Lady Penelope on video. Full of adults saying, 'I had one of them!' Child-size mannequins in upper gallery can foment an *Avengers*-era spookiness if you're up there alone. Mon-Sat 10am-5pm. July & Aug Sun 12-5pm. (1633/KIDS)
FREE

393 **ST GILES' CATHEDRAL:** 225 9442. Royal Mile. Not a cathedral really, although
D3 it was once – the High Kirk of Edinburgh, Church of Scotland central and heart of the city since the 9th century. The building is mainly medieval with Norman fragments and all encased in a Georgian exterior. Lorimer's oddly ornate Thistle chapel and the 'big new organ' are impressive. Simple, austere design and bronze of John Knox set the tone historically. Holy Communion daily and other regular services. Atmos coffee shop in the crypt. Summer: Mon-Fri 9am-7pm, Sat 9am-5pm, Sun 1-5pm. Winter: Mon-Sat 9am-5pm, Sun 1-5pm.   FREE

394 **THE GEORGIAN HOUSE:** 226 3318. 7 Charlotte Sq. Built in the 1790s, this
B2 town house is full of period furniture and fittings. Not many rms, but the dining-rm and kitchen are drop-dead gorgeous – you want to eat and cook there. Delightful ladies from the National Trust for Scotland answer your queries. Moderator of the General Assembly of the Church of Scotland bides up the stair. Mar-Oct Mon-Sat 10am-5pm, Sun 2-5pm; Nov-Dec Mon-Sat 11am-4pm, Sun 2-4pm. Last admn 4.30pm. NTS

395 **LAURISTON CASTLE:** 336 2060. Cramond Rd S. 9km W of centre by A90, turn-
xA1 ing rt for Cramond. Elegant architecture and gracious living from Edwardian times. A largely Jacobean tower house set in tranquil grounds o/looking the Forth. The liveability of the house and the preoccupations of the Reid family make you wish you could poke around for yourself, but there are valuable and exquisite decorative pieces and furniture and it's guided tours only. You could always continue to Cramond for the air (398/WALKS IN THE CITY). Apr-Oct 11am-5pm (cl lunch, cl Fri); Nov-Mar 2-4pm, w/ends only. ADMN

BUTTERFLY FARM, NR DALKEITH: Report: 1634/KIDS.

DEEP SEA WORLD, NORTH QUEENSFERRY: Report: 1639/KIDS.

ARTHUR'S SEAT: Report: 397/WALKS IN THE CITY.

THE PENTLANDS: Report: 400/WALKS OUTSIDE THE CITY.

THE SCOTT MONUMENT/CALTON HILL: Report: 419/417/BEST VIEWS.

See page 11 for walk codes.

396
A2
B2
B1
C1
D1

✓ ✓ **WATER OF LEITH:** The indefatigable wee river that runs from the Pentlands through the city and into the docks at Leith can be walked for most of its length, though obviously not by any circular route. (A) The longest section from Balerno 12km o/side the city, through Colinton Dell to the Tickled Trout pub car park on Lanark Rd (4km from city centre). The 'Dell' itself is a popular glen walk (1-2km). All in all a superb urban walk.

START: (A) A70 to Currie, Juniper Green, Balerno; park by High School. (B) Dean Village to Stockbridge: enter through a marked gate opp Menzies Hotel on Belford Rd (combine with a visit to the art galleries) (390/391/ATTRACTIONS). (C) Warriston, through the spooky old graveyard, to The Shore in Leith (plenty of pubs to repair to). Enter by going to the end of the cul-de-sac at Warriston Cres in Canonmills; climb up the bank and turn left. Most of the Walkway (A, B and C) is cinder track & good cycling.   12KM (OR LESS) XCIRC BIKE 1-A-1

397
xE3

✓ ✓ **ARTHUR'S SEAT:** Of many walks, a good circular one taking in the wilder bits, the lochs and gr views (418/BEST VIEWS) starts from St Margaret's Loch at the far end of the park from Holyrood Palace. Leaving the car park, skirt the loch and head for the ruined chapel. Pass it on your rt and, after 250m in a dry valley, the buttress of the main summit rears above you on the rt. Keeping it to the rt, ascend over a saddle joining the main route from Dunsapie Loch which appears below on the left. Crow Hill is the other peak crowned by a triangular cairn – both can be slippery when wet. From Arthur's Seat head for and traverse the long steep incline of Salisbury Crags. Paths parallel to the edge lead back to the chapel. (Incidentally, nae mt bikes off tarmac or the polis will have words.)

PARK: There are car parks beside the loch and in front of the palace (paths start here too, across the rd).   5-8KM CIRC MT BIKE (RESTRICTED ACCESS) 2-B-2

START: Enter park at palace at foot of the High St and turn left on main road for 1km; the loch is on the rt.

398
xA1

CRAMOND: This is the charming village (not the suburb) on the Forth at the mouth of the Almond with a variety of gr walks. (A) To the rt along the 'prom'; the trad seaside stroll. (B) Across the causeway at low tide to Cramond Island (1km). Best to follow the tide out; this allows 4 hrs (tides are posted). People have been known to stay the night in summer, but this is discouraged. (C) Cross the mouth of the Almond in the tiny passenger boat which comes on demand (summer 9am-7pm, winter 10am-4pm) then follow coastal path to Dalmeny House which is open to the public in the afternoons (May-Sep, Sun-Thu); or walk all the way to S Queensferry (8km). (D) Past the boathouse and up the R Almond Heritage Trail which goes eventually to the Cramond Brig Hotel on the A90 and thence to the old airport (3-8km). Though it goes through suburbs and seems to be on the flight path of the London shuttle, the Almond is a real river with a charm and ecosystem of its own. The Cramond Bistro (312 6555) on the riverside is not a bad wee bistro and awaits your return. BYOB. Lunches & even meals. 7 days. **CRAMOND INN** (347/PUB FOOD) is another gr place to recharge.   1/3/8KM XCIRC BIKE 1-A-1

START: Leave centre by Queensferry Rd (A90), then rt following signs for Cramond. Cramond Rd N leads to Cramond Glebe Rd; go to end.

PARK: Large car park off Cramond Glebe Rd to rt. Walk 100m to sea.

399
xA2

CORSTORPHINE HILL: W of centre, a knobbly hilly area of birch, beech and oak, criss-crossed by trails. A perfect place for the contemplation of life's little mysteries and mistakes. Or walking the dog. It has a radio mast, a ruined tower, a boundary with the wild plains of Africa (at the zoo) and a vast redundant nuclear shelter that nobody's supposed to know about. See how many you can spot. If it had a tearoom in an old pavilion, it would be perfect.

START: Leave centre by Queensferry Rd and 8km out turn left at lights, signed Clermiston. The hill is on your left for the next 2km.

PARK: Park where safe, on or nr this rd (Clermiston Rd).   1-7KM CIRC XBIKE 1-A-1

NEWHAILES HOUSE: Report 1758a/COUNTRY HOUSES.

EASY WALKS OUTSIDE THE CITY

Refer to Lothians map on pages 340–341.

400
MAP 7
A2

✓ **THE PENTLANDS:** A serious range of hills rising to almost 600m, remote in parts and offering some fine walking. There are many paths up the various tops and round the lochs and reservoirs. (A) A good start in town is made by going off the bypass at Colinton, follow signs for Colinton Village, then the left fork up Woodhall Rd. Second left up Bonaly Rd (signed Bonaly Scout Camp). Drive/walk as far as you can (2km) and park by the gate leading to the hill proper where there is a map showing routes. The path to Glencorse is one of the classic Pentland walks. (B) Most walks start from signposted gateways on the A702 Biggar Rd. There are starts at Boghall (5km after Hillend ski slope); on the long straight stretch before Silverburn (a 10km path to Balerno); from Habbie's Howe about 18km from town; and from the village of Carlops, 22km from town. (C) The most popular start is probably from the visitor centre behind the Flotterstone Inn, also on the A702, 14km from town (decent pub lunch and 6-10pm, all day w/ends); trailboard and ranger service. The remoter tops around Loganlea reservoir are worth the extra mile.

1-20KM CAN BE CIRC MTBIKE 2-B-2

401
MAP 7
A2

HERMITAGE OF BRAID: Strictly speaking, still in town, but a real sense of being in a country glen and from the windy tops of the Braid Hills there are some marvellous views back over the city. Main track along the burn is easy to follow and you eventually come to Hermitage House info centre; any paths ascending to the rt take you to the ridge of Blackford Hill. In winter, there's a gr sledging place over the first br up to the left and across the main rd.

START: Blackford Glen Rd. Go S on Mayfield to main T-jnct with Liberton Rd, turn rt (signed Penicuik) then hard rt.   1-4KM CAN BE CIRC XBIKE 1-A-1

402
MAP 7
A1

ROSLIN GLEN: Special: spiritual, historical and enchanting, with a chapel (1783/CHURCHES), a ruined castle and woodland walks along the R Esk.

START: A701 from Mayfield or Newington (or bypass, t/off Penicuik, A702 then fork left on A703 to Roslin). Some parking at chapel (1783/CHURCHES), 500m from corner of Main St/Manse Rd, or follow B7003 to Rosewell (also marked Rosslynlee Hospital) and 1km from village the main car park is to the left.

1-8km XCIRC BIKE 1-A-1

403
MAP 7
A1

ALMONDELL: A country park to W of city (18km) nr (and one of the best things about) Livingston. A deep, peaceful woody cleft with easy paths and riverine meadows. Fine for kids, lovers and dog walkers. Visitor centre with teashop. Trails marked.

START: Best app from Edin by A71 via Sighthill. After Wilkieston, turn rt for Camp (B7015) then follow signs. Or A89 to Broxburn past start of M8. Follow signs from Broxburn.   2-8KM XCIRC BIKE 1-A-1

404
MAP 7
A1

BEECRAIGS AND COCKLEROY HILL: Another country park SW of Linlithgow with trails and clearings in mixed woods, a deer farm and a fishing loch. Gr adventure playground for kids. Best is the climb and extraordinary view from Cockleroy Hill, far better than you'd expect for the effort. From Ben Lomond to the Bass Rock; and the gunge of Grangemouth in the sky to the E.

START: M90 to Linlithgow (26km), through town and left on Preston Rd. Go on 4km, park is signed, but for hill you don't need to take the left turn. The hill, and nearest car park to it, are on the rt.   2-8KM CIRC MTBIKE 1-A-1

405
MAP 7
B2

BORTHWICK AND CRICHTON CASTLES: Takes in 2 impressive castles, the first a posh hotel (95/HOTELS O/SIDE TOWN) and the other an imposing ruin on a ridge o/looking the Tyne. A walk through dramatic Border Country steeped in lore. Tricky route obvious at first in either direction, then peters out, but the castle you're going to is always in view. Nice picnic spots nr Crichton.

START: From Borthwick: A7 S for 16km, past Gorebridge, left at N Middleton; signed. From Crichton: A68 almost to Pathhead, signed then 3km.

7KM XCIRC XBIKE 1-B-2

WOODLAND WALKS NR EDINBURGH

Refer to Borders map on pages 342–343 and Lothians map on pages 340–341.

406 **DAWYCK GARDENS, nr STOBO:** 01721 760254. 10km W of Peebles on B712
MAP 8   Moffat rd. Outstn of the Edin Botanics; a 'recent' acquisition, though tree plant-
A2   ing here goes back 300 yrs. Sloping grounds around the Scrape Burn which trickles into the Tweed. Landscaped woody pathways for meditative walks. Famous
for shrubs and blue Himalayan poppies. Mar-Nov 9.30am-6pm. 7 days. ADMN

407 **HUMBIE WOODS:** 25km SE by A68 t/off at Fala. Follow signs for church. Most
MAP 7   open woods (beech) beyond car park, through paddock. The churchyard is as
B2   reassuring a place to be buried as you could wish for; if you're set on cremation, come here and think of earth. Deep in the woods with the burn besides;
after-hrs the sprites and the spirits must have a hell of a time.

408 **SMEATON GARDENS, EAST LINTON:** 2km from village on N Berwick rd
MAP 7   (signed Smeaton). Up a drive in an old estate is this walled gdn going back to
B1   the early 19th century. An additional pleasure is the Lake Walk halfway down
the drive through a small gate in the woods. A 1km stroll round a secret finger lake in magnificent woodland. Gdn hrs Mon-Fri 9am-4.30pm, Sat from
10am, Sun from 11.30am; cl w/ends Jan and Feb. (2085/GARDEN CENTRES).

409 **WOODHALL DENE, NR DUNBAR:** A1 Dunbar bypass, E to Spott then rd to
MAP 7   left, 5km. Small car park in river hollow. Follow river to important ancient
B1   woodland site (2km). Can be damp. Few folk.

410 **DALKEITH COUNTRY PARK:** 15km SE by A68. The wooded policies of
MAP 7   Dalkeith House; enter at end of Main St. Surprisingly extensive area so close to
B1   town and conurbation. Along the river banks and under these stately deciduous trees, carpets of bluebells, daffs and snowdrops, primroses and wild garlic
according to season. Adventure playground for kids, natural playground for
the rest of us.

411 **VOGRIE COUNTRY PARK, NR GOREBRIDGE:** 25km S by A7 then B6372 6km
MAP 7   from Gorebridge. Small country park well organised for 'recreational pursuits'.
B1   9-hole golf course, tearoom and country ranger staff. May be busy on Sun, but
otherwise a corral of countryside on the v edge of town.

412 **CARDRONA FOREST/GLENTRESS, NR PEEBLES:** 40km S to Peebles, 8km E
MAP 8   on B7062 and similar distance on A72. Cardrona on same rd as Kailzie Gdn.
B2   Tearoom (Apr-Oct) is excl. Forestry Commission woodlands so mostly regimented firs, but Scots pine and deciduous trees up the burn. Set trails incl mt
bikes. Nice in late autumn and winter. Some dark mysterious bits.

THE BEST BEACHES

Refer to Lothians map on pages 340–341 & Fife map on pages 336–337.

413 ✓ **SEACLIFF:** The best beach, least crowded/littered; perfect for picnics,
MAP 7   beachcombing, and gazing into rock pools. Harbour good for swimming.
B1   50km from Edin, Seacliff is off the A198 out of N Berwick, 3km after Tantallon
Castle (1727/RUINS). At a bend in the rd and a farm (Auldhame) there is an
unsigned rd off to the left. 2km on there's a barrier, costing £1 coin to get car
through. Car park 1km then walk. From A1, take E Linton t/off, go through
Whitekirk towards N Berwick, then same.

414 **PORTOBELLO:** Edin's town beach, 8km from centre by London Rd. When
MAP 7   sunny – chips, lager, bad ice cream. When miserable – soulful dog walkers.
B1   Arcades, mini-funfair, long prom and pool (423/SPORTS FACS). Maybe the
Evening News may shame the council enough to reinstate its former glory.

415 **YELLOWCRAIGS:** Nearest decent beach (35km). A1 or bypass, then A198
MAP 7   coast rd. Left o/side Dirleton for 2km, park and walk 100m across links to fair-
B1   ly clean strand and sea. Gets busy, but big enough to share. Hardly anyone
swims, but you can. Scenic. **GULLANE BENTS**, a sweep of beach, is nearby and
reached from village main st. Connects westwards with Aberlady Reserve.

416 **SILVER SANDS, ABERDOUR:** Over Forth Br on edge of charming Fife vill
MAP 5 (1516/COASTAL VILLS). Can go by train from Edin. Caff, cliff walk. Nice.
B4

THE BEST VIEWS OF THE CITY

417 ✓ ✓ **CALTON HILL:** Gr view of the city easily gained by walking up from
E2 E end of Princes St by Waterloo Pl, to the end of the buildings and
then up stairs on the left. The City Observatory and the Greek-style folly lend
an elegant backdrop to a panorama (unfolding as you walk round) where the
view up Princes St and the sweep of the Forth estuary are particularly fine. At
night, the city twinkles. Popular cruising area for gays – take care.

418 ✓ ✓ **ARTHUR'S SEAT:** W of city centre. Best app through Holyrood Park
xE3 from foot of Canongate by Holyrood Palace. The igneous core of an
extinct volcano with the precipitous sill of Salisbury Crags presiding over the
city and offering fine views for the fit. Top is 251m; on a clear day you can see
100km. Surprisingly wild considering proximity to city. (397/WALKS IN THE CITY)

419 **SCOTT MONUMENT:** 529 4068. East Princes St. Design inspiration for
D2 Thunderbird 3. This 1844 Gothic memorial to one of Scotland's best-kent literary sons rises 61.5m above the main drag and provides scope for the ver-
tiginous to come to terms with their affliction. 287 steps mean it's no cake-
walk; narrow stairwells weed out claustrophobics too. Those who make it to
the top are rewarded with fine views. Underneath, a statue of the mournful Sir
Walter gazes across at Jenners. Mar-May & Oct 9am-6pm; June-Sept 9am-
8pm; Nov-Feb 9am-4pm. All Suns 10am-6pm.   ADMN

420 **CAMERA OBSCURA:** 226 3709. Castlehill, Royal Mile. At v top of st nr castle
C3 entrance, a tourist attraction that, surprisingly, has been there for over a century. You ascend through a shop, photography exhibs and holograms to the
viewing area where a continuous stream of small groups are shown the effect
of the giant revolving periscope thingie. All Edin life is visible – amazing how
much fun can be had from a pin-hole camera with a focal length of 8.6m. Apr-
Oct 9.30am-6pm, sometimes later. Nov-Mar 10am-5pm.   ADMN

421 **NORTH BERWICK LAW:** The conical volcanic hill, a beacon in the E Lothian
MAP 7 landscape. **TRAPRAIN LAW** nearby is higher, tends to be frequented by rock-
B1 climbers, but has major prehistoric hillfort citadel of the Goddodin and a def-
inite aura.   BOTH 1-A-1

THE PENTLANDS/HERMITAGE: Reports: 400/401/WALKS O/SIDE CITY.

CASTLE RAMPARTS: Report: 377/MAIN ATTRACTIONS.

THE BEST SPORTS FACILITIES

SWIMMING AND INDOOR SPORTS CENTRES

422 ✓ ✓ **ROYAL COMMONWEALTH POOL:** 667 7211. Dalkeith Rd (386/MAIN
xE4 ATTRACTIONS). The biggest, but Edin has many others. Recommended
xD4 are **WARRENDER** (447 0052), Thirlestane Rd 500m beyond the Meadows S of
xE1 centre; **LEITH VICTORIA** (555 4728), in Jnct Pl off the main st in Leith complete
C1 with crèche facilities; **GLENOGLE** (343 6376) in Stockbridge, the New Town
choice, v friendly. All these pools are old and tiled, 25yd long, seldom crowded and excellent for lane swimming – at certain times. Also all have Pulse centres & fitness classes. Different sessions, phone to check.

423 **PORTOBELLO:** 669 6888. Portobello Esplanade (414/BEACHES). Similar to oth-
xE1 ers above. Recently refurbed, excellent Turkish baths still there, ladies-only,
gents-only and mixed days. Phone for details.

424 **AINSLIE PARK:** 551 2400. Pilton Dr, off Ferry Rd, N of centre, 5km from Princes
xC1 St. Has serious keep-fit side but all the usual spa, sauna, steam too. Mon-Fri
xE1 10am-10pm; Sat & Sun 9am-6pm.

425 **NEXT GENERATION:** 554 5000. Newhaven Harbour. V much part of the regen-
xD1 eration of the waterfront, this sportsarama complex in the David Lloyd stable
(in fact son of, hence naff name). Courts, gym, 2 pools incl one outdoor o/look-

ing Forth (only in non-wet weather). Not cheap, but not as exp as some in town. 7 days till 11.30pm. Members only.

426 **MEADOWBANK:** 661 5351. London Rd. City athletics stadium with courts for
xE2 squash and badminton (often booked), Pulse centre, weights room, 13m indoor climbing wall, all-weather football/hockey pitches and velodrome. No pool.

427 **MARCO'S:** 228 2141. 51 Grove St. Labyrinthine commercial centre with aero-
B3 bic classes, gym, squash and snooker. No pool. Little Marco's will look after your kids while you sweat.

428 **UNIVERSITY GYM:** 650 2585. The Pleasance. No-nonsense complex, v cheap.
E3 The best in town for weights (all the right machinery) and circuit training. Squash, badminton, indoor tennis, etc. Membership required (can be short-term) but not during the quiet vac periods. For a reasonable fee, the Fitness and Sports Injury Centre (FASIC) is an excellent alternative to the 'take 2 aspirin and go away' school of GP. Few fake suntans.

429 **EDINBURGH CLUB:** 556 8845. 2 Hillside Cres. Probably the most civilised of
E1 non-hotel-type clubs. Usually members only, longer-stay visitors may be able to negotiate a rate. Good weights (mainly Universal), sauna/steam/sun/bistro. Good aerobics classes. And spinning, apparently. No pool.

430 **DRUMSHEUGH BATHS CLUB:** 225 2200. 5 Belford Rd, W End. Private swim-
A2 ming club in elegant building above Dean Village that costs a fortune to join and has a waiting list (although it's only a matter of weeks). But gorgeous Victorian pool with rings and trapeze over the water, sauna, multigym and bistro. Frequented by the quality. If you're chums with New Town lawyer, get him to sign you in as a guest.

431 **BALMORAL SPA, BALMORAL HOTEL:** 556 2414. Health club for residents
D2 (44/HOTELS), members and visitors (half-day tickets). Pool, sauna, steam, gym.

432 **ONE SPA, SHERATON HOTEL:** 229 9131. Actually a separate 4-storey building
C3 behind hotel. Opened Sept 2001, offering the height of luxury with usual pool, spa, gym to more exotic hydrotherapy, whole-body mud encasement & treatments for anything & everything. Emphasis on pampering rather than sport. Treat yourself to a day or half-day ticket.

433 **ESCAPE, SCOTSMAN HOTEL:** 556 5565. Enter thro' hotel or from Market St.
D2 Metallic, modern health club with all facs & excl service. Low-lit pool, floor of machinery. Sexy, almost cruisy. Look good!

GOLF COURSES

There are several municipal courses (see phone directory under City of Edin Council) and nearby, esp down the coast, some famous names that aren't open to non-members. Refer to Lothians map on pages 340–341.

434 **BRAID HILLS:** 447 6666. Braid Hills app. 2 18-hole courses (no. 2 summer
MAP A only). Thought to be the best in town. Never boring; exhilarating views.
xC4 Booking usually not essential, except evenings & w/ends. Women welcome (and that ain't true everywhere round here).

✓✓ **GULLANE NO. 1:** 01620 842255. The best of 3 courses in pretty vil-lage. Report: 1945/GOLF COURSES.

✓✓ **GLEN GOLF CLUB (AKA NORTH BERWICK EAST):** 01620 892726. 36 km from Edin, worth the drive. Report: 1946/GOLF COURSES.

MUSSELBURGH: 665 6981. Original home of golf. Report: 1947/GOLF COURSES.

GIFFORD: 01620 810591. Off the beaten track. Report: 1972/GOLF IN GREAT PLACES.

OTHER ACTIVITIES

435 **TENNIS:** There are lots of private clubs though only the **GRANGE** (332 2148)
xD4 has lawn tennis and you won't get on there easily. There are places you can
slip on (best not to talk about that), but the municipal centres (Edin resi-
dents/longer-stay visitors should get a Leisure Access card (661 5351) allowing advance reservation) are: **THE MEADOWS:** (NE corner by Univ Library).
Just turn up. Many courts; **SAUGHTON:** 444 0422. Stevenson Dr. 8km W of city
centre. 2 astroturf courts and one other. Also used for football & hockey, so
phone to book; **CRAIGLOCKHART:** 444 1969. Colinton Rd. 8km SW of centre
via Morningside and Colinton Rd. 6 indoor courts, 7 outdoor and a 'centre
court' – best to check/book by phone. Other separate sports facs incl squash,
badminton and gym, 443 0101. Centre open Mon-Thu 9am-11pm, Fri 10am-
11 pm, Sat-Sun 9am-10.30pm.

436 **WORLD OF FOOTBALL:** 443 0404. Part of the 'Newmarket Leisure Village'
xA4 complex at the Corn Exchange, off Chesser Avenue. Newest of its type. 8 covered pitches. Can be booked between 9am-10.30pm daily.

437 **SKIING:** Artificial slopes at **HILLEND** on A702, 10km S of centre. 445 4433.
xC4 Excellent fac with various runs. The matting can be bloody rough when you
fall and the chairlift is a bit of a dread for beginners, but once you can ski here,
St Anton is all yours. Tuition every evening (not Thu) and w/ends. Open till
10pm in winter, 9pm in summer. Snowboarders welcome but it ain't Whistler.

438 **PONY-TREKKING: LASSWADE RIDING SCHOOL:** 663 7676. Lasswade exit
xE4 from city bypass then A768, rt to Loanhead 1km and left to end of Kevock Rd.
Full hacking and trekking facs and courses for all standards and ages.

439 **PENTLAND HILLS TREKKING CENTRE:** 01968 661095. At Carlops on A702
xE4 (25km from town) has sturdy, steady Icelandic horses who will bear you good-
naturedly into the hills. Exhilarating stuff.

440 **ICE-SKATING: MURRAYFIELD ICE RINK:** 337 6933. Riversdale Cres, just off
xA3 main Glas Rd nr zoo. Cheap, cheerful and chilly. It has been here forever and
feels like a gr 1950s B movie … go round! Sessions daily from 2.30pm. Also …
WINTER WONDERLAND: E Princes St Gardens. Big open-air ice rink in the
gdns below the Scott Monument. Open late Nov-early Jan. 7 days. Mass fun!

441 **ALIEN ROCK:** 552 7211. Old St Andrew's Church, Pier Pl, Newhaven. Indoor
xD1 rock climbing in a converted kirk. Laid back atmos, bouldering rm and interesting 12m walls of various gnarliness to scoot up. Daily; phone for sessions.
Have a pint after in **THE STARBANK** or **THE OLD CHAIN PIER** nearby
(351/352/PUB FOOD).

442 ✓ ✓ **THE ADVENTURE CENTRE, RATHO:** 229 3919. S Plate Hill, Ratho.
xA2 Follow signs from the M8 and A71. Still under construction at TGP
but open April 2002. Ambitious and exciting facility designed to appeal to Joe
Public and elite athletes alike. Will incl: urban sports prk (BMX, skateboards,
etc), air park (a kind of assault course with ropes & trusses), National Judo
Academy, mountain bike tracks, scuba-diving pool and state-of-the-art
adventure sports gym, not to mention the NRCC (below). Oh and there's a
300-seater restau, internet café, 220-seater lecture/film theatre, corporate
facs, crèche & retail sector (incl the excl Tiso). Think big. Open 7 days. Times &
prices to be confirmed at time of gong to press. Call for details.

443 ✓ ✓ **NATIONAL ROCK CLIMBING CENTRE:** Main feature of above com-
xA2 plex. 'The biggest indoor climbing arena in the world!' Essentially a
roofed-over quarry so a unique mix of natural & artificial rock. Beginners' walls
to major permanent international competition walls for the expert.
Bouldering area and 5000 sq m of outdoor rock (free to climb). Huge, impressive, important. Non-climbers can ogle.

THE BEST GALLERIES

444 **CITY ART CENTRE:** 529 3993. Market St. This is the place the populist block-
D3 buster exhibs come to as well as excellent social/educational displays.
Sensibly curated city asset. Convenient and carefully run café.

445 **THE FRUITMARKET GALLERY:** 225 2383. Across the rd in Market St, a small-
D3 er, more warehousey space for more contemporary work, retrospectives,
installations. Always interesting. Café (254/BEST TEAROOMS) highly recommended for meeting and eating, watching the world go by.

446 **THE COLLECTIVE GALLERY:** 220 1260. 22 Cockburn St. Installations of
D3 Scottish and other young contemporary trailblazers. Members' work won't
break the bank.

447 **INGLEBY GALLERY:** 556 4441. 6 Calton Terr. Important, chic gallery in a pri-
E2 vate house backing onto Calton Hill. Often shows work by significant contemporary UK artists.

448 **THE SCOTTISH GALLERY:** 558 1200. 16 Dundas St. Guy Peploe's influential
C2 New Town gallery on 2 floors. Where to go to buy something painted, sculpt-
ed, thrown or crafted by up-and-comers or established names – everything
from affordable jewellery to original Joan Eardleys. Or just look.

449 **OPEN EYE GALLERY:** 557 1020. 75-79 Cumberland St and **12** (558 9872) opp.
C1 Excellent small galleries in residential part of New Town. Always worth checking out for accessible contemporary painting and ceramics. Almost too accessible (take cheque book).

450 **THE PRINTMAKERS' WORKSHOP AND GALLERY:** 557 2479. 23 Union St, off
D1 Leith Walk nr London Rd r/bout. Workshops that you can look over. Exhibs of
work by contemporary printmakers and shop where prints from many of the
notable names in Scotland are on sale at reasonable prices. Bit of a treasure.
Also run courses.

451 **DOGGERFISH:** 558 7110. 11 Gayfield Sq. Suzanna Beaumont's cutting edge
D1 gallery in a converted garage in the heart of the 'East Village'. Not much wall
space but always worth seeing what's on it. W/end viewing. Good openings.

452 **PHOTOGRAPHY:** Edin is blessed with 2 contemporary photo-art venues.
D1, D3 **STILLS:** 622 6200, 23 Cockburn St, with a café. **PORTFOLIO:** 220 1911, 43
Candlemaker Row, is a small 2-floor space in what used to be the city's left-
wing bookshop.

ESSENTIAL CULTURE

*For the current programmes of the places recommended below and all other
venues, consult* The List *magazine, on sale at most newsagents.*

UNIQUE VENUES

453 **THE TRAVERSE:** 228 1404. Small but influential, dedicated to new work
C3 (though mainly touring companies) in modern Euro, v architectural 2-theatre
premises in Cambridge St (behind Lyceum & Usher Hall). Good rendezvous
café-bar in theatre (115/BEST BISTROS) plus excellent adj restau (103/BEST
RESTAUS).

454 **DANCE BASE:** 225 5525. 14-16 Grassmarket. Scotland's national centre for
C3 dance, now in its new, purpose-built location. Classes & workshops AYR but
check *The List* for dance performance in its larger studio. State of the art building, worth a visit on its own.

455 **THE CAMEO:** 228 4141. Home St in Tollcross. 3 screens showing important
C4 new films and cult classics. Some late movies at w/ends. Good snug bar.

456 **FILMHOUSE:** 228 2688. Lothian Rd, opp Usher Hall. 3 screens with everything
C3 from first-run art-house movies to subtitled obscurities and retrospectives.
Home of the annual Film Festival; café-bar (till 11.30pm Sun-Thu, 12.30am Fri-
Sat) is a haven from the excesses of Lothian Rd. Open to non-cinephiles.

457 **THE QUEEN'S HALL:** 668 2019. Clerk St. Converted church with good atmos
E4 and v varied prog. Your best bet if you want to go somewhere for decent
music. Café-bar & art exhibitions. Diverse (choral, jazz, art pop). Good atmos.

458 **THE FESTIVAL THEATRE:** 529 6000. Nicolson St. Edin's showcase theatre re-
D3 created from the old Empire with a huge glass frontage of bars and a stage and screen dock large enough to accommodate the world's major companies. Eclectic programme AYR.

THE FESTIVALS

459 ✓ ✓ ✓ Edinburgh invented arts festivals (more than 50 years ago) &
D3 now can truly be called a Festival City. Many of the festivals listed below are world leaders.

EDINBURGH INTERNATIONAL FESTIVAL: 473 2000. Last 3 weeks of Aug.

EDINBURGH FESTIVAL FRINGE: 226 5138. 3 weeks in Aug.

EDINBURGH INTERNATIONAL FILM FESTIVAL: 229 2550. 2 weeks in Aug.

EDINBURGH INTERNATIONAL BOOK FESTIVAL: 228 5444. 2 weeks in Aug.

EDINBURGH MILITARY TATTOO: 225 1188. 3 weeks in Aug.

EDINBURGH INTERNATIONAL JAZZ & BLUES FESTIVAL: 467 5200. 1-2 weeks, end Jul/beginning Aug.

EDINBURGH INTERNATIONAL SCIENCE FESTIVAL: 530 2001. 1-2 weeks Apr.

SCOTTISH INTERNATIONAL CHILDREN'S FESTIVAL: 225 8050. 1 week end May/beginning Jun.

EDINBURGH MELA: 557 1400. 2 days early Sept.

EDINBURGH'S CAPITAL CHRISTMAS: 557 3900. 4 weeks. end Nov-Christmas Eve. Incl Grand Parade on the first Sunday of December.

EDINBURGH'S HOGMANAY: 557 3990. 4-6 days, end of Dec-1st Jan.

JAZZ

460 **HENRY'S JAZZ CELLAR:** 467 5200. Morrison St opp cinema nr corner with
C3 Lothian Rd. Sounds of every stripe fill the tiny floor of this crowded basement. W/ends and other nights. Gr vibe. Mellow crowd. Till 3am.

THE QUEEN'S HALL: 668 2019. See above.

BANNERMAN'S: 556 3254. 212 Cowgate.

FOLK MUSIC

461 **SANDY BELL'S:** 225 2751. Forrest Rd. Famous and forever. Sometimes you
D3 could look in and wonder why; other times you know you're in exactly the right place.

462 **WEST END HOTEL:** 225 3656. Palmerston Pl. A good place to stay or just to
B3 hang out with the Highlanders. Some trad folk live at w/ends and whenever. (63/INDIVIDUAL HOTELS)

463 **THE ROYAL OAK:** 557 2976. Infirmary St. A folk institution. Locals drink in the
D3 tiny bar upstairs during the day. Live sessions kick-off downstairs every night around 10pm with well-kent faces dropping in occasionally for the tunes and singaround. Till 2am 7 days.

464 **CASTLE ARMS:** 225 7432. 6 Johnston Terr. Fairly small, good atmos. Trad folk
C3 sessions almost every night.

CEILIDHS

465 **WEST END HOTEL:** 225 3656. 35 Palmerston Pl. Edin's Heilan' hame hotel has
B3 occasional sessions of music/singing and storytelling (more like a trad ceilidh) but no dancing. This is where to come (or phone) to find out where the others are (occasional ceilidhs held in the church hall nearby). (63/INDIVIDUAL HOTELS)

466 **CALEDONIAN BREWERY:** 623 8066. 42 Slateford Rd. Ceilidhs most Sats in the
xA4 Festival Hall in the brewery 7pm-1am. Bands vary but the couple of hundred heuchin' teuchin' punters have a good time regardless. (342/REAL-ALE PUBS)

LIVE ROCK & POP & BEST CLUBS

467
xA3
INGLISTON EXHIB CENTRE & MURRAYFIELD STADIUM: Rarely used, biggies only (U2, the Stones, the Pope).

468
D2
PLAYHOUSE THEATRE: 0870 6063424. Greenside Pl. Major theatre in Scotland, most regular programme, holds 3,000. More infrequent as concert venue while they get through the musicals (apparently endless supply).

469
C3
USHER HALL: 228 1155. Lothian Rd. Gr auditorium. Classier acts. Recently refurbed so looking good.

THE QUEEN'S HALL: 668 2019. See above (457/UNIQUE VENUES).

470
xA4
THE CORN EXCHANGE: 477 3500. Newmarket Rd. 8km SW of city centre. Used to be the Edin slaughterhouse – say no more. It's now a multi-purpose megabar and venue. Capacity of 2500 so you'd expect to see major touring bands. Rough (tho not so rough) equivalent of Glasgow Barrowlands.

471
D3
LA BELLE ANGÈLE: 225 7536. 11 Hastie's Close. Combines its role as a DJ club and live-music venue well. Rm has attitude and atmos. Some showcases, parties and special nights.

472
D2
BARONY BAR: 557 0546. 81 Broughton St. Late Sun afternoon/eve perfect pub gig. 'Bert's band' includes many Edin musos and kent faces incl members of The Proclaimers. A long-running Sun spot. (312/UNIQUE EDIN PUBS)

473
xE1
NOBLE'S: 554 2024. 44a Constitution St. Dependable bar food and real ales in a fine-sized rm. Real mix of bands on a Fri/Sat, comedy on Thurs, open-mic on Sun. Phone to confirm.

474
D3
THE LIQUID ROOM: 225 2564. Top of Victoria St. Probably the city's best turned-out venue for live music. Enter at st level and descend to watch bands before they go on to greater things (or not). Also a major club venue.

475
D3
THE ATTIC: 225 8382. Dyer's Close, Cowgate. Small upstairs club bar featuring new indie and undergroundy bands.

476
D3
THE VENUE: 557 3073. Calton Rd, behind Waverley Stn. Edin's major live venue at club level with well-established dance clubs among many. For live music, it's on the club circuit, so often notable bands and the best of the Scottish wannabes. Watch for posters & flyers.

477
D3
SUBWAY: 225 6766. Cowgate, under George IV Bridge. Cavernous grungey rock 'n' roll. Fairly studenty, live music some nights, DJs on others playing 1960s to cheesy dance and chart. 5pm-3am daily. Also **SUBWAY WEST END**, 23 Lothian Rd – 229 9197. Glitzier than its Cowgate cousin. Nothing live. DJs playing indie, 1970s, 1980s.

478
E1
CC BLOOM'S: 556 9331. Greenside Pl. Late-night gay venue with bar upstairs (catch the floor show and eye contact generally). Report: 2153/GAY.

479
E2
EGO: 478 7434. 14 Picardy Pl. One of the major Edin club venues hosting regular big names such as **JOY**, **DISCO INFERNO**. 2 floors in former casino. thu-Sun. And all tomorrow's parties.

480
E2
THE BONGO CLUB: 556 5204. 14 New St. A small door in a big wall above a huge underground parking lot. Big windows onto small rooms where a committed crowd have created a club which is truly underground. No isms here incl ageism. Thu-Sun. Bongo looking for new home 2002.

481
C4
CAVENDISH: 228 3252. W Tollcross. Upstairs it hosts the long-running **MAMBO CLUB** (Sat). 2 floors – African/reggae/generally good vibes music for v mixed crowd – good for oldies who like to dance.

482
D3
CLUB MERCADO: 226 4224. 36-39 Market St. Probably Edinburgh's longest-running club venue. Recent revamp and an infusion of good club organisers means it's worth checking out – try Trendy Wendy's **TACKNO** or **TUNNEL OF LOVE**.

483
C3
WHY NOT?: 624 8311. 14 George St. Basement part of **THE DOME** (321/UNIQUE EDIN PUBS) – disco-mating venue for over-25s.

NEGOCIANTS: 225 6313. 45 Lothian St. Report: 350/PUBS WITH GOOD FOOD.

IGUANA: 220 4288. 41 Lothian St. Report: 373/HIP & STYLE BARS.

PO NA NA: 226 2224. 43b Frederick St. Report: 367/HIP & STYLE BARS.

SECTION 3

Glasgow

The telephone code for Glasgow is 0141
Refer to MAP B, *unless otherwise stated*

THE BEST HOTELS

484
xB1 ✔ ✔ **ONE DEVONSHIRE GARDENS:** 339 2001. 1 Devonshire Gdns. Off Gr Western Rd (the A82 W to Dumbarton). Long est as the smartest hotel in town & refurbishment in progress. Though change in ownership at TGP, One Devonshire still engenders the design vision of its original owner Ken McCulloch (who went on to invent the Malmaison chain). Hotel now occupies 4 out of the 5 townhouses on this elegant block set back from the busy rd west. Every rm is different but all have the things that we modern travellers look out for: DVD players, big beds, deep baths, thick carpets/towels/curtains. Many suites incl some doubles & super sumptuous. **TR:** 2, 4, 7, 9, 14 if you're Pavarotti-rich or just celebrating. Gordon Ramsay's Amaryllis restau a foodie experience in itself (528/BEST RESTAUS).

41RMS JAN-DEC T/T PETS CC KIDS LOTS

485
D3 ✔ **THE ARTHOUSE HOTEL:** 221 6789. 129 Bath St (style bar street), nr Sauchiehall Centre and above Sarti (567/ITALIAN RESTAUS), so gr coffee downstairs. Smart contemp town-house hotel with wide, tiled stairwell and funky lift to 3 floors of individual rms (so size, views, etc. vary). Fab gold embossed wallpaper in the hallways, notable stained glass and nice pictures and prints. Grill downstairs has tepanyaki and other Mod Br dishes. Bar, a fashionable rendezvous for this, prob the sexiest hotel stopover in town. **TR:** 129 & 204/5/6 (the Velvet Suites). 65RMS JAN-DEC T/T XPETS CC KIDS MED.EXP

486
D3 ✔ **LANGS:** 333 1500. Port Dundas Pl nr bus station and Concert Hall. Good-looking moderne high-rise hotel with designs – from lofty atrium/bar to penthouse suites on 5th floor. Every surface, sink & self-conscious detail tones into Japanese. Some beds better to look at than sleep in (sunken in the suites not so good). Satellite TV/DVD & Playstations in all rms. Oshi restau on ground floor with oriental pretension (nice plates) & spa (no pool, but treatments). 'Californian cuisine' at Las Brisas on mezzanine. Langs tries v hard to please. Provided you get a rm you like, they will. **TR:** Duplexes on first floor.

100RMS JAN-DEC T/T XPETS CC KIDS LOTS

487
C3 ✔ **THE MALMAISON:** 572 1000. 278 W George St. Sister hotel of the one in Edin and originally from the same stable and same team as One Devonshire (*see above*) so no surprise that this is an outstanding hotel. This 'chain' of good design hotels has spread since last we looked & the Glasgow Mal has all the features – well-proportioned rms (some suites), with CDs, cable, etc. – tho the location just off West End affords no gr views. However this is stylish excellence in a Blair New World. Cafe Mal downstairs contrasts with the woody clubbiness of The Brasseries (589/FRENCH RESTAUS).

72RMS JAN-DEC T/T XPETS CC KIDS MED.EXP

488
D3 **CARLTON GEORGE:** 353 6373. 44 W George St. Adj Queen St Stn and George Sq, this is a smart central option and apart from parking (a hike to car park behind the stn) prob the best hotel in the city centre for the business traveller. Its more fun than that though with a huge Irish bar downstairs and airy rooftop restau up top (**WINDOWS**). Residents' lounge and drinks in rm all on the house. Excl service and the usual comforts.

64RMS JAN-DEC T/T XPETS CC KIDS EXP

489
C4 **GLASGOW HILTON:** 204 5555. 1 William St. App from the M8 slip rd or from city centre via Waterloo St. It has a forbidding Fritz Lang/*Metropolis* appearance and entrance via underground car park is grim. But hotel is one of the best in town with good service and appointments. Japanese people made esp welcome. Huge atrium. 20 floors with top 3 'executive'. Views from here to N are stunning so all **TR**. Cameron's, the hotel's main restau, is present and correct, and the most highly Michelin-rated restau in town (though we don't agree). Minsky's bistro and Raffles bar are not so special. Shimla Pinks Indian cuisine makes a change. 319RMS JAN-DEC T/T PETS CC KIDS LOTS

490
C4 **THE MARRIOTT:** 226 5577. 500 Argyle St, nr motorway. Modern and functional business hotel on 12 floors. Parking is a test for the nerves. Nevertheless, there's a calm, helpful attitude from the staff inside; for further de-stressing you can hypnotise yourself by watching the soundless traffic on the Kingston Br o/side; or there's a pool to lap and separate gym. Mediterraneo restau ain't bad. No-smk floors. 300RMS JAN-DEC T/T PETS CC KIDS LOTS

491 **HOLIDAY INN:** 0800 897121. 161 W Nile St. Another block off the old block. In
D3 the city centre nr Concert Hall. Gym, but no pool, restau but not gr shakes.
Holiday Inn Xpress adj is better value (25% less). Both rec here because of loca-
tion & good standard.   113/58RMS JAN-DEC T/T XPETS CC KIDS LOTS/MED.INX

492 **THE MILLENNIUM HOTEL:** 332 6711. 50 George Sq. Situated on the sq which
D3 is the municipal heart of the city and next to Queen St Stn (trains to Edin and
pts N), Glasgow will be going on all about you and there's a conservatory terr,
serving breakfast and afternoon tea, from which to watch. Bedrms vary great-
ly; some perhaps overdone and we think over dear. Busy brasserie.
117RMS JAN-DEC T/T PETS CC KIDS LOTS

493 **THE MOAT HOUSE:** 306 9988. Congress Rd. Beside the SECC, on the Clyde, this
B4 towering, glass monument to the 1980s feels like it's in a constant state of
'siege readiness'. Science Centre & Tower gleam & twinkle on the opp bank &
there's a footbridge across. Some good river views from the 16 floors. The
Marine Restau, in the lobby, has a good reputation and ring-side seating for
river-gazing. Somewhat removed from city centre (about 3km, you wouldn't
want to walk), it's esp handy for SECC and Armadillo goings-on.
293RMS JAN-DEC T/T PETS CC KIDS LOTS

494 **THE CENTRAL HOTEL:** 221 9680. Gordon St. Once the last word in gracious
D3 living, the elegance is now distinctly faded, although a certain atmos still
remains in the sweep of the staircase and in the grandiose public rms. Rms
(recently refurb) are individual, though may be small (and too hot). 60 singles
reflecting commercial traveller past. Corridors stretch forever but you're at the
hub of a gr city.   222RMS JAN-DEC T/T PETS CC KIDS EXP

INDIVIDUAL HOTELS

495 ✓ ✓ **ST JUDE'S:** 352 8800. 190 Bath St. Off-shoot of Soho's Groucho Club in
C3 collaboration with well-sussed Glasgow guys, but little similarity & no
membership reqd. Tho designery (by prop Bobby Patterson), both bar & esp
restau (543/RESTAUS) have stood the test of recent times & are pop haunts of the
Glasgow glitt & litt eratti. Rms more clever than comfy methinks, but excl service.   6RMS JAN-DEC T/T XPETS CC XKIDS MED.EXP

496 ✓ **CATHEDRAL HOUSE:** 552 3519. 28-32 Cathedral Sq/John Knox St. Next
E3 to the Cathedral (some rms o/look) and close to the Merchant City, this
detached old building has been tastefully & recently refurbed into a café-bar
(with occasional live music), a separate restau (check opening though) and
comfortable bedrms above. Discreet and informal hospitality for the traveller;
much as it always has been here, in the ancient heart of the city.
8RMS JAN-DEC T/T PETS CC KIDS MED.EXP

497 ✓ **PIPERS' TRYST:** 353 0220. McPhater St. Visible from dual carriageway nr
D2 STV HQ at Cowcaddens, but hard to get to the street in a car. Hotel
upstairs from café-bar of the adj piping centre & whole complex a beautiful
conversion of an old church & manse. Centre has course, conferences & a
museum, so staying here is to get close to Highland culture.
8RMS JAN-DEC T/T XPETS CC KIDS MED.EXP

498 ✓ **INN ON THE GREEN:** 554 0165. 25 Greenhead St which is hard to find
xE4 (follow or get a taxi), but is close to Glas E End & Merchant City. Hotel &
long-est restau on corner of Glas defining green place. Individually run & furnished with woody, tartan and even Gothic feel. Nice touches (picnic hampers
in rms) though some furnishings perhaps a slat too far. Subterranean restau is
both intimate & a group-night-out kind of place with piano player & occ
singers. Carefully & caringly run.   18RMS JAN-DEC T/T PETS CC KIDS MED.INX

499 ✓ **THE TOWN HOUSE:** 357 0862. 4 Hughenden Terr. Quiet st off Gr Western
xB1 Rd via Hyndland Rd, o/looking rugby & cricket grounds. Same area as
One Devonshire (484/HOTELS) for a fraction of the price. Spacious rms faithfully restored – even if you don't happen to live in a well-appointed town house
on a gracious terr yourself, you'll feel at home. Close to the W End. Don't confuse with the Townhouse Hotel, Royal Cres.
10RMS JAN-DEC T/T XPETS CC KIDS MED.INX

500 ✔ **NUMBER 52 CHARLOTTE STREET:** Serviced apartments in superb con-
E5 version of the one remaining Georgian town house in historic (now decimated) st betw the Barrows Market and Glas Green. Tobacco Merchant's
house by Robert Adam refurb by NTS. V good rates for
bedrm/lounge/kitchen; everything but breakfast. One-night lets poss, units
sleep 2-5. 7RMS JAN-DEC X/T XPETS CC KIDS MED.INX

501 **THE BRUNSWICK:** 552 0001. 104-108 Brunswick St. V contemporary, minimal-
E4 ist hotel in Merchant City. Bright and cheerful rms economically designed to
make use of tight space; low Japanese-style beds. Good base for nocturnal
forays into pub and club land. Restau has had mixed response, but breakfast
v pleasant. The penthouse suite is excl.

21RMS JAN-DEC T/T XPETS CC KIDS MED.EXP

502 **RAB HA'S:** 572 0400. 83 Hutcheson St. Rms above a pub in the urban heart of
E4 the Merchant City that have had a recent overhaul. Good food and friendly
folk make this a place to go if you're in the know. But noisy late night and if
you lie in. 4RMS JAN-DEC T/T PETS CC XKIDS MED.INX

503 **THE MERCHANT LODGE HOTEL:** 552 2424. 52 Virginia St. Conversion of the
D4 old Tobacco Merchant's house (in Merchant City) that has managed to retain
the original staircase (ask the porter to take your bags, there's no lift).
Surprisingly quiet area nr shops; in the gay zone (in case you didn't notice).
Rms vary, look first. 40RMS JAN-DEC T/T PETS CC KIDS CHP

504 **BABBITY BOWSTER:** 552 5055. 16-18 Blackfriars St. This late 18th-century
E4 town house was pivotal in the redevelopment of the Merchant City and
famous for its bar (698/REAL-ALE PUBS, 714/PUB FOOD) and beer gdn,
Schottische restau upstairs & rms above with basic facs. A v Glasgow hostelry.

6RMS JAN-DEC T/X XPETS CC XKIDS MED.INX

505 **KIRKLEE:** 334 5555. 11 Kensington Gate. In a city curiously short of appealing
xB1 & individual GHs here at least is one to rec – a tidy Edwardian house and most
notably a tidy gdn in a leafy suburb nr Botanics and Byres Rd. Lots of pics.

9RMS JAN-DEC T/T XPETS CC KIDS MED.INX

506 **THE WHITE HOUSE:** 339 9375. 12 Cleveden Cres. Not a hotel, but self-cater-
xA1 ing apartments nr Botanics. A friendly hame from hame in this civilised crescent & a sensible alternative, esp if there are a few of you or you are staying a
week. Refurb in progress at TGP. Some quiet mews out back.

32UNITS JAN-DEC T/T PETS CC KIDS MED.INX

507 **OLD SCHOOLHOUSE:** 333 7600. 194 Renfrew St. Poss best option in row of
D3 GH uphill from Sauchiehall St & nr Art College. This house stands alone & is
less labyrinthine than the others – **THE VICTORIAN HOUSE** (332 0129) at no
214 (the most expansive) & the **RENNIE MACKINTOSH** (333 9992) at no 218
in which are displayed the worst excesses of cheap retro Mockintosh. All 3 are
similarly priced. Check rms first if poss.

17/60/24RMS JAN-DEC T/T PETS CC KIDS MED.INX

TRAVEL LODGES

508 ✔ **CITY INN:** 240 1002. Finnieston Quay by the big crane on the riverside &
B4 nr the SECC. Recent block makes most of Clydeside location with deck &
views. Designed by Andy Doulin of The Point in Edin (55/HOTELS), rms here are
a cut above the usual tho not large. Uniformity is at least thought out. City
Café on ground floor takes itself seriously as a restu. Recent price hike &
improvements elevates from the economy travel lodge to the designer
almost boutique hotel. River's the thing. 164RMS JAN-DEC T/T
XPETS CC XKIDS MED.INX

509 ✔ **BEWLEY'S:** 353 0800. 110 Bath St. In the downtown section of Bath St but
D3 nr the style bars & designer restaus, a bed block with more taste & character than most. Thought, for example, has gone into the choice of prints in
rms & halls. Loop, a credible restau on ground floor (561/BISTROS). Good accom
& facs at this price. 103RMS JAN-DEC T/T PETS CC KIDS MED.INX

510 **PREMIER LODGE:** 221 1000. 10 Elmbank Gdns, above Charing Cross Stn. Once
C3 an office block, now a vast city-centre budget hotel, with no frills and no pretence, but a v adequate rm for the night. Not a pile of charm and you would-
n't want to spend your holidays here, but its functionalism, anonymity and
urban melancholy may suit the very modern traveller. M8 rms less quiet.
Restau & bar tho the excl Baby Grand is opp & open late (553/BISTROS). Rm rate
a good deal £46 at TGP.   278RMS JAN-DEC T/T XPETS CC KIDS MED.INX

511 **NOVOTEL:** 222 2775. 181 Pitt St. Branch of the French bed-box empire in quiet
C3 corner nr w end Sauchiehall St. Nothing much to distinguish, but brass/restau
is bright enough & Novotel beds are v good. Small bathrms. The 2- as opposed
to the 3-star **IBIS:** 225 6000 is adj. If it's merely a bed for the night you want,
it's much cheaper & hard to see what difference a star makes. They're both
pretty soulless.   139/141RMS JAN-DEC T/T PETS CC KIDS MED.INX/CHP

512 **HOLIDAY INN EXPRESS:** 0800 897121. Corner of Stockwell and Clyde St (tho
D4 only 5 rms on the river). Functional bed-box that's still a good deal. All you do
is sleep here. Nr Merchant City, so plenty of restaus, nightlife and other distractions and curiously midway betw 2 of Glasgow's oldest, funkiest bars The
Scotia and Victoria (681/680/PUBS). Another Express adj Holiday Inn but this
one best (491/HOTELS).   128RMS JAN-DEC T/T XPETS CC KIDS MED.INX

THE BEST HOSTELS

*The SYHA is the Scottish Youth Hostel Association, of which you have to be a
member (or a member of an affiliated organization from another country) to stay
in their many hostels round Scotland. Phone 01786 451181 for details, or contact
any YHA hostel.*

513 ✓ **SY HOSTEL:** 332 3004. 7 Park Terr. Close to where the old Glas hostel used
B2 ✓ to be in Woodlands Terr, in the same area of the W End nr the univ and
Kelvingrove Park. This building was converted in 1992 from the Beacons
Hotel, which was where rock 'n' roll bands used to stay in the 1980s. Now the
bedrms are converted into dorms for 4-6 (some larger) and the public rms are
common rms with TV, games, café, etc. Still feels more like a hotel than a hos-
tel and is a gr place to stay. Late opening. You must be a member of the YHA.
See above.   150BEDS

514 ✓ **GLASGOW BACKPACKERS:** 332 9099. 17 Park Terr. Along from the SYH
B2 ✓ (*see opposite*), the funkier alternative. Mostly dorms (4-8 people) but
some twins available. Only open summer months. Close to W End thrills and
spills.   102BEDS

515 ✓ **BAIRD HALL, STRATHCLYDE UNIV:** 553 4148. 460 Sauchiehall St. The
C3 ✓ landmark Grade A-listed Art Deco building near the Art School and the
W End. Originally the Beresford Hotel, built 1937 and once Glasgow's finest (v
Miami Beach). 200 beds in vacs and 11 AYR. Spartan, almost drab, though the
rms are fine, like an American Y. Reeks of nostalgia as well as disinfectant.
Dining-rm, TV and reading rm. Lots of groovy places nearby such as Bar Ce
Lona, Variety Bar, Baby Grand and the Griffin. All are listed further on.

200BEDS

516 **MURRAY HALL, STRATHCLYDE UNIV:** 553 4148. Cathedral St. Modern, but
E3 not sterile block of single rms on edge of main campus and facing towards
Cathedral. Part of large complex (also some student flats to rent by the week)
with bar/shop/laundrette. Quite central, close to Merchant City bars. Vacs only.

70BEDS

517 **EURO HOSTEL GLASGOW:** 222 2828. 318 Clyde St. A v central independent
D4 hostel block at the bottom of Union/Renfield St and almost o/looking the
river. Mix of single, twin or dorm accom, but all en-suite & clean. Breakfast
included in price but at TGP no café/kitchen facs. Games & TV room, laundry
& internet access. Open AYR.   364BEDS

*Note: Both Strathclyde and Glasgow univs have several other halls of residence
available for short-term accom in the summer months. Phone: Glasgow 330 5385
or Strathclyde 553 4148 (central booking).*

THE BEST HOTELS OUTSIDE TOWN

518
MAP 1
C2
✓ **CAMERON HOUSE, NR BALLOCH, LOCH LOMOND:** 01389 755565. A82 dual carriageway through W End or via Erskine Br and M8. 45km NW of centre. Highly regarded mansion-house hotel complex with excellent leisure facs in 100 acres open grounds on the bonny banks of the loch. Sports incl 9-hole golf (& 10km L Lomond course – 1959/GOLF), good pool, tennis and a busy marina for sailing/windsurfing, etc. Notable restau (The Georgian Rm with 3 AA rosettes) and all-day brasserie. Many famous names have holed up here; it's a short helicopter hop to Glasg.

96RMS JAN-DEC T/T XPETS CC KIDS TOS LOTS

519
MAP 6
B3
✓ **THE BLACK BULL HOTEL, KILLEARN:** 01360 550215. 2 The Sq. A81 towards Aberfoyle, take the rt fork after Glengoyne Distillery, and the hotel is at the top end of the village next to the church. Recent refurb & rethink of what was always a notable pub/restau by chef/owners Ian Macmaster. Clubby casual bar/grill & finer dining conservatory restau. Nice art on the walls. Garden. Rms tasteful, comfy & well priced.

14RMS JAN-DEC T/T PETS CC KIDS MED.INX

520
MAP 1
C2
✓ **GLEDDOCH HOUSE, LANGBANK, NR GREENOCK:** 01475 540711. Take M8/A8 to Greenock, then B789 signposted Langbank/Houston, then 2km – hotel is signed. 30km W of centre by fast rd. A château-like country-house hotel, formerly the home of the Lithgow shipping family. High above the Clyde estuary, there are spectacular views across to Dumbarton Rock and the Kilpatrick Hills. Rms not lavish but comfortable – only a few have the view. Reputable dining-rm strong on Scottish ingredients. 18-hole golf course (773/SPORTS FACS); health club, tiny pool. 38RMS JAN-DEC T/T PETS CC KIDS TOS LOTS

521
MAP 1
D3
✓ **NEW LANARK MILL HOTEL, LANARK:** 01555 667200. From Glasgow, take M74, then follow signs for Lanark and esp New Lanark, the conservation vill of Robert Owen (45 mins). Excl retreat from Glasgow, where you wake up on the banks of the Clyde and sleep to the sound of its running water. Serene spot tho' many visitors. Good walks by river (1562/WATERFALLS) and an excl restau in Lanark (10 mins), La Vigna (487/RESTAUS CLYDE VALLEY).

38RMS JAN-DEC T/T PETS CC KIDS MED.INX

522
MAP 1
C2
✓ **THE LODGE ON LOCH LOMOND:** 01436 860201. Edge of Luss on A82 N from Balloch. About 40 mins W End. Linear not lovely, but gr lochside setting. Rms above restau & wood-lined rms o/look the bonny banks with balconies & saunas, tho' Luss is not everybody's cup of tea (and sausage roll). Restau also has the view and terrace and is surprisingly good; booking may be necessary w/ends. 29RMS JAN-DEC T/T PETS CC KIDS MED.INX

523
MAP 6
B3
STRATHBLANE COUNTRY HOUSE HOTEL: 01360 770491. 20km N and only 20mins from Maryhill Rd on a good day (follow A81, the Milngavie rd, to Strathblane). A civilised lodging to N of city with decent informal brasserie. Rms individual, reasonably well appointed; carefully chosen pictures from Glasgow's Roger Bilcliffe Gallery. 10RMS JAN-DEC T/T PETS CC KIDS EXP

524
MAP 1
D3
BOTHWELL BRIDGE HOTEL, BOTHWELL: 01698 852246. Uddingston t/off from M74, 15km SE of centre. Main St. Nr castle (1720/O/SIDE GLAS). Comfortable, family-run hotel with an Italian ambience. V kid-friendly.

90RMS JAN-DEC T/T XPETS CC KIDS EXP

525
MAP 6
C3
CULCREUCH CASTLE HOTEL, FINTRY: 01360 860555. Off B818 in Campsie Fells, 32km N of centre via A81 Milngavie rd from Glas. Fintry is well kept and in a valley betw the Fells and the Fintry Hills. Some fine walking (749/WALKS O/SIDE THE CITY). Ancestral home of the Galbraiths with many old features, incl a half-tester bed. Dungeons converted into bar/bistro. Many weddings, so check w/ends. 8RMS JAN-DEC T/T PETS CC KIDS TOS MED.INX

526
MAP 1
C2
THE INVERKIP HOTEL, INVERKIP: 01475 521478. M8 from Glas then A8 and A78 from Pt Glas heading S for Largs. 50km W of centre. The most reasonable place to stay on this part of the Clyde coast. 6RMS JAN-DEC X/T PETS CC KIDS INX

527
MAP 1
A4
KIRKTON HOUSE, CARDROSS: 01389 841951. A814, past Helensburgh to Cardross village then N up Darleith Rd. Kirkton House is 1km on rt. 18th-century Scottish farmhouse that combines rustic charm with *every* mod con. Nr L Lomond. 6 RMS FEB-NOV T/T PETS CC KIDS MED.INX

528 ✓ ✓ **AMARYLLIS at ONE DEVONSHIRE GARDENS:** 337 3434. Glasgow's
xB1 most stylish hotel (484/BEST HOTELS) now boasts the Glas satellite of
one of the UK's most controversial & Michelin-regarded chefs: Gordon
Ramsay. Chef here is David Dempsey tho menu is studded with Ramsay staples. Food seductive & invariably perfectly turned out. Service from a flurry of
waiters a tad overbearing. Rm simply elegant – we are here to worship the
food & wonder. Inx for this level of cuisine & compared with other hedonistic
nights on the town though not much on the wine-list less than £30. **SD**: the
Ramsay repertoire. Lunch Wed-Fri, dinner Wed-Sun. Cl Mon, Tues and LO
10.30pm. EXP

529 ✓ ✓ **LE CHARDON D'OR:** 248 3801. 176 W Regent St. Brian Maule's (for-
D3 merly head chef at the Roux brothers' famed Le Gavroche) Golden
Thistle in French opened to less than effulgent reviews in summer 2001 with
speculation as to whether this was a serious challenge to Gordon Ramsay.
Well … it depends. Ambience is similar tho staff here less frenetic. Food most-
ly excellent with classic French approach and hits all the contemporary notes.
All in all hard to fault but not a fun night out even with the 'celebration selec-
tion'. Glasgow is fortunate to have acquired both the above. **SD**: ham hock
lentil salad with sherry vinaigrette. Sea bass & crushed potatoes. Lunch Mon-
Fri, LO 10.30pm. Cl Sun. EXP

530 ✓ ✓ **NAIRN'S:** 353 0707. 13 Woodside Cres, nr Charing Cross. Ubiquitous
B2 telly chef Nick Nairn's notable Glas townhouse restau in quiet W end
crescent. After initial foray into restau with rms territory & duplex dining, this is
the new stripped-down Nairns & a discreet treat. Intimate rm, excl service &
Nick's no-nonsense perfectly presented dishes – lunch: 3 starters/main & puds,
dinner 4 of each. **SD**: seared fish, confit of duck, parfait. cl Sun, Mon, LO 9.45 pm.
MED

531 ✓ ✓ **GAMBA:** 572 0899. 225a W George St. Mellow minimalist seafood
C3 restau in basement at corner of W Campbell St. Straight-talking
menu so expect prawn cocktail, sole meunière. Fashionable rendezvous. Glas
people love Gamba tho Michelin or AA have failed to recognise. **SD** from chef
Derek Marshall: fish soup, scallops with Thai dipping sauce & sticky rice. MED

532 ✓ ✓ **QUIGLEY'S:** 331 4060. 158 Bath St. TV chef John Quigley's dream has
C3 'come home'. V big, v Glasgow operation on stylee Bath St with long,
high-ceilinged restau upstairs & vast bar (Lowdown) below street (718/STYLE
BARS). Menu contemp Scottish with nice presentation & nae nonsense. Tapas
& lighter bar menu avail downstairs. Affordable wine-list. This place new at
TGP designed to do well. Chef: usually the man himself. 7 days lunch (not
Sat/Sun) & dinner. LO 11pm. MED

533 ✓ ✓ **THE UBIQUITOUS CHIP:** 334 5007. 12 Ashton Lane. Ronnie
A1 Clydesdale's cornerstone of culinary Glasgow. 2-storey, covered
courtyard draped with vines, off a bar-strewn cobbled lane in the heart of the
W End, heaped with accolades over 30 yrs in residence. The main bit is still one
of the most atmospheric of rms tho some say service can slip. The menu is
exemplary – the best of Scottish seafood, game and beef and fine, original
cooking. An outstanding wine list. Chip upstairs open w/ends but the simpler
menu here is also avail in the courtyard. **SD**: Dishes with long list of ingredients, ea Scottish provenance noted eg the black pudding is Rothesay black
pudding, raspberries from Blairgowrie. Daily lunch and 6.30-11pm. EXP

534 ✓ ✓ **CORINTHIAN:** 552 1107. 191 Ingram St. Beautiful restau in a fabu-
E4 lous Merchant City building nr George Sq (and GOMA). Bars on same
floor (677/GR GLAS PUBS) and 'members' club' above, but restau most impressive part. Vaulted rm in immaculate condition could be Vienna. 'Cosmopolitan,
modern European cuisine' from chef Pascal Eck. Good service – wines exp but
overall an affordable de-luxe dining experience. 7 days. Cl Sat lunch. LO 10pm.
SD: Bouillabaisse. MED

535 ✓ ✓ **STRAVAIGIN:** 334 2665. 28-30 Gibson St. Constantly changing, inno-
B2 vative and consciously eclectic menu from award-winning chef
Colin Clydesdale. Mixes cuisines, esp Asian and Pacific Rim. 'Think global, eat

local'. Pleasant café-bar upstairs is more continental. Excellent, affordable food without the foodie formalities and open later than most. **SD**: Ever-changing with precise long list of ingredients too long to mention here. Mon-Thu 5-11pm, Fri-Sat lunch & 5pm-12midnight, Sun 5pm-12midnight. Now also **STRAVAIGIN 2:** 334 7165 (see 550/BISTROS) INX/MED

536 ✓ **ROCOCO:** 221 5004. 202 W George St. corner of Wellington St and just
C3 along from Bouzy Rouge to which it is related (555/BISTROS). But this is the upmarket, fine dining and impeccable service version. Basement but light & one of the most beautiful rms in the city. Excl contemp menu has the lot in the mix. Nice private dining area and smokers courtyard o/side for post-prandial chat and coffee. Chef Mark Tamburrini **SD**: Daube of beef with horseradish pommes purée. Lunch and LO 10pm, cl Sun.

537 ✓ **THE BUTTERY:** 221 8188. 652 Argyle St. Central but curious location for
B3 Glas's long-est and consistently top-end restau, recently (at TGP) refurbished & reinvented. Cosy atmos retained. Tick also remains although early for us to assess. Chef Willy Deans and 3-rosette kitchen staff from Auchterarder House (1144/CO HOUSE HOTELS) should ensure that the Buttery's reputation remains intact & may go to greater things. Tues-Sat, lunch & LO 10pm (not Sat lunch). EXP

538 ✓ **ROGANO:** 248 4055. 11 Exchange Pl. Betw Buchanan St and Queen St. An
D3 institution in Glas since the 1930s. Décor replicating a Cunard ship, the *Queen Mary*, is the major attraction. *The* place to take visiting friends or clients, even if just for cocktails. Restau spacious, perennially fashionable, with fish and seafood the specialities. Downstairs has a lighter/cheaper menu, and though a bit sub-Rogano its informality is easier on the pocket. Restaurant: lunch and 6-10.30pm. Café Rogano: lunch and 6-11.30pm (Fri-Sat until 12midnight, Sun until 10pm). Chef Andy Cummings **SD**: lobster thermidor, oysters. EXP.MED

539 ✓ **LA PARMIGIANA:** 334 0686. 447 Gr Western Rd. Simply the best Italian
B1 for many discriminating Glaswegians (convenient location nr Kelvin Br – usually parking nearby), the favourite posh place to eat pasta & vitello but that's just for starters. Main courses elaborate with Italian take on local provision. Lunch (good deal 'pre-theatre' menu). LO 11pm. Cl Sun. **SD**: char-grilled scallops with olive oil. (568/ITALIAN RESTAUS) MED

540 ✓ **ST JUDE'S:** 352 8800. 190 Bath St. The restau of the hotel in fashionable
C3 Bath St that's related to London's Groucho Club (tho no membership reqd). Bar in basement with snackier menu till 8pm (not Suns), but restau serves modern British menu in lofty, light retro-chic surroundings & it's easy to eat here. Chef Martin Teplitzky is inspired by Larousse Gastronomique but you'd never notice (that's a compliment!). **SD**: grilled scallops in squid ink pasta. Lunch Mon-Fri, dinner 7 days. LO 10/10.30pm. MED

541 **GONG:** 576 1700. 17 Vinicombe St which is off Byres Rd at the Botanics end.
A1 Sophisticated, some might say OTT remodelling of old cinema by the same people who have The Corinthian (above) & Arta (622/WORLD RESTAUS). Bamboo-strutted dining area flanked by bars (one open non-diners) by United Designers (who did Met, London & Clarence, Dublin). Appearances however aren't everything & the food from the Easy Eating menu is surprisingly good. Grazy format to menu. Some inspired twists to salads, pastas, meat & fish mains. Tibetan cool & cocktails. The West End just got chic & East. 7 days, lunch thro dinner, LO 11pm.

542 **AIR ORGANIC:** 564 5200. 36 Kelvingrove St. Much-applauded, media-friendly
A3 bar/café and upstairs restau in W End. Proprietor Colin McDougal and designer Dene Happell have created an airy and stylish ambience for the purposefully organic bar and cuisine. This includes beer and wine list, bar snacks and a full menu upstairs. Perhaps dated now (opened 99 but this was style before content & this is Glasgow), but still a cool place to eat. Food innovative fusion esp Pacific Rim. **SD**: Bento Box (tuna best), tempura, sticky rice, miso soup – the works. Bar: food LO 9pm. Restau LO 11pm, 12midnight w/ends. (711/PUB FOOD). INX

543 **THAI FOUNTAIN:** 332 2599. 2 Woodside Cres, Charing Cross. Same ownership
B2 as Amber Regent (*see below*), this is probably Glasgow's best Asian restau. Genuinely Thai and not at all Chinese. Innovative dishes with gr diversity of

flavours and textures, so sharing several is best. Of course you will eat too much. Cl Sun. **SD**: weeping tiger beef. (602/FAR-EASTERN RESTAUS)   MED

544 **THE CABIN:** 569 1036. 996 Dumbarton Rd. Way down, follow Whiteinch.
xA2 Beautifully cooked fresh seafood and Scottish game, home-made Irish soda bread and delicious puds. Excl vegn choice. You'll probably have to linger after dinner, when Wilma, legendary waitress and *chanteuse*, does her diva thing. A Glas original. BYOB (wine only) if you like. Tue-Fri lunch, Tue-Sat dinner. LO 9pm. **SD**: Bisque or chowder, bread 'n' butter pud.   MED

AMBER REGENT: 50 W Regent St. Report: 604/FAR-EASTERN.

KILLERMONT POLO CLUB: 2002 Maryhill Rd. Report: 593/INDIAN.

THE BEST BISTROS AND CAFÉ-BARS

548
B3,
MAP 1
D3
✓ **MITCHELL'S:** 204 4312. 2 branches, W at 157 North St on the left bank of M8 at the Mitchell Library, next to the Bon Accord (696/REAL-ALE PUBS), and S at Waterside Rd, Carmunnock (644 2255). Both have diff menus from individual chefs. North St is flagship & esp good for meat eaters. *The* place for informal and v good food with a genuine bistro atmos. Lunch Tues-Fri & LO 10pm/10.30pm. Cl Sun/Mon. Southside cl Mon/Tues. INX

549
C3,A2
✓ **GORDON YUILL and COMPANY:** 572 4052. 257 W Campbell St and 2 Byres Rd (337 1145). First there was Gordon Yuill, Rogano's manager for 17 years (he had seated everybody), then there was W Campbell St, then with same menu, ambience & always miraculously the man himself, another one on the corner of Byres Rd & Dumbarton Rd. When you enter here, you leave Partick behind. This is the one we like esp for late supper. But both are open for b/fast & the stylish, contemp menu (incl bistro classics) with excl service continues all day. News at TGP that he was about to replicate again. 7 days 8am-10.30pm (Byres Rd from noon). Long hrs; this boy works hard. INX

550
A1
✓ **STRAVAIGIN 2:** 334 7165. 8 Ruthven Lane. Just off Byres Rd thro' vennel opp underground stn. Off-shoot of **STRAVAIGIN** (536/BEST RESTAUS), one of Glasgow's finest. Similar eclectic often inspirational but lighter menu somewhere betw the upstairs bar and downstairs finer dining of the mothership. Smallish rms (upper brighter) so book w/ends. 7 days all day from 11/12 to 11/midnight. INX

551
A2
✓ **NO. SIXTEEN:** 339 2544. 16 Byres Rd. Tiny restau on 2 postage stamp floors at the bottom end of Byres Rd now est as hugely pop W End haunt – so you prob have to book. Winning combo is good bistro food, no fuss and good value. Sublime puds. Lunch and LO 10pm. Cl Sun. Best book! INX

552
E4
✓ **FARFELU:** 552 5345. 89 Candleriggs. Upstairs from (and same proprietor as) fairly fashionable Bar 91 and opp Merchant Sq, where there are other not-so-good restaus. Contemporary British menu and modern look. This often not-busy restau serves some of the best food in the Merchant City, so it's a good bet even at w/ends. Esp reasonable early even menu. Lunch & LO 10pm. Cl Sun. INX

553
C3
✓ **BABY GRAND:** 248 4942. 3-7 Elmbank Gdns. Inviting haven among highrise office blocks opp hotel (510/LESS EXP HOTELS); a downtown-USA location. (Go behind the King's Theatre down Elmbank St, rt at gas stn and look for the hotel.) Narrow rm with bar stools and banquettes, often with background music from resident mad pianist. Char-grilled fish, steak & specials or you can graze. Decent bottle of wine for a fiver betw 5-7pm & best late meal in town. Daily 8am-midnight (2 on w/ends). (656/LATE RESTAUS) CHP

554
E3
✓ **FRANGO:** 552 4433. 15 John St by the Italian Centre. With tables o/side at front on st & back in courtyard. Alan Tomkins' (Gamba, Papingo) latest venture & once again the quality of food & wine-list is excl – prob better than it needs to be on a sunny day & discreetly so at night when the Merchant City can be quiet. Mod British menu full of gr ideas. This is probably the best casual food nr George Square. 7 days 9am-10.30pm (11pm w/ends). INX

555
C3
✓ **BOUZY ROUGE:** 221 8804. 111 W Regent St. Key restau in the Bouzy Rouge chain, made by the enterprising Brown family & one of the few chains we heartily endorse (also in Edin & Sheriffmuir, where they have a hotel (873/CENTRAL HOTELS). An excellent bistro for eclectic, affordable contemporary food and wine. Good vegn choice. 7 days, lunch & LO 9.30pm (10.30pm w/ends). INX

556
D3
✓ **PAPINGO:** 332 6678. 104 Bath St. A bistro in a basement among many (in the streets round here) but as many Glaswegians know, food, service & wine-list here are spot-on. Chef David Clunas' contemp Scottish menu in Michelin & AA. A perennial fave. Lunch & LO 10/10.30pm. Cl Sun lunch. MED

557
xB1
LUX/STAZIONE: 576 7576. 1057 Gr Western Rd. Nr Gartnavel Hospital, which for non-Glaswegians means a long way down Gr Western Rd from the Botanic corner. Informal Italian bar/bistro & the rather more formal **LUX** (upstairs) in former station. Both have relaxed ambience. O/side tables in summer. Lux

quite highly rated by some (Michelin 3 forks) & more relaxed than other city centre Mod-Brit eateries. 7 days, lunch and 5-11pm. Lux dinner only. Cl Sun/Mon.   MED/INX

558 **OTAGO:** 337 2282. 61 Otago St. Reworked neighbourhood caff, now most def-
B1 initely a restau/café with a lighter daytime menu, giving way to the full meat/fish/game after 6pm. Mediterraneo slant & excl wine-list. Open 7 days 11am–10pm. LO 9.30pm.   CHP

559 **COTTIER'S:** 357 5827. 93 Hyndland Rd. Off the top of Hyndland St nr
xA1 Highburgh Rd. Converted church that encompasses a theatre, a bar, etc; regu-lar live music (811/ESS. CULTURE/CLUBS) and benches o/side. Restau with South/Central American menu made up of light, spicy dishes. Theatre stages range of music throughout the yr. A v broad church. (667/SUN BREAKFAST and other references.) 7 days. LO 10.30 (later w/ends).   INX

560 **KOOKS:** 334 9682. 1355 Argyle St. View to Kelvingrove. Chilled music, eclectic
B3 décor and menu. Chef is vegn, but does do Stornoway black pudding. Much organic. Cool spot. 7 days, late AM - late PM (cl 6pm Mon/Tues).   INX

561 **LOOP:** 572 1472. 64 Ingram St, Merchant City (main rd for traffic nr
E4 Fruitmarket venue) and 110 Bath St in Bewley's Hotel (354 7705). Contemp
D3 cafe-restau, light and stylish design, seems to meet with general Glaswegian approval (Bath St often packed). Menu hits all the right buttons for suits thro' to clubbers; risottos to club sandwich & fries. Lunch & LO 10.30 (Bath St from 7am for Bewley's b/fast). 7 days, 11am – LO 10.30pm.   MED

562 **ARTHOUSE GRILL:** 572 6002. 129 Bath St. Basement restau of excellent
D3 Arthouse Hotel (485/BEST HOTELS); enter through fab foyer or off st. Brasserie-type menu, incl lots of seafood and simple meat dishes alongside genuine (sit-round) tepanyaki grill. Sometimes food is not most fab, but popular spot on style street & good atmos. 7 days lunch and dinner. LO 10/10.30pm.   INX

563 **CUL DE SAC:** 334 8899. 44 Ashton Lane, the main lane off Byres Rd with the
A1 Grosvenor Cinema and The Ubiquitous Chip (534/BEST RESTAUS). Perennially fashionable crêperie/diner dedicated to serving good, simple food with flair, even wit. The atmos is relaxed and conversational, the burgers are famously good. New ownership at TGP Bar & 'Attic' upstairs. (666/SUN BREAKFAST). Daily 12noon-11pm (Fri-Sat later).   CHP

564 **BAR BREL:** 342 4966. 39 Ashton Lane. Another Billy McAnnanie (Baby Grand,
A1 Cottier's) translation of an idea from elsewhere. This is a Gallic bar/bistro across the lane from the Cul de Sac (see above). Flagstone floor, metal tables and enormous folding doors. No mistaking the Belgian influence in the cook-ing; fat, crispy chips served with large bowls of steaming mussels, or with steak. Belgian beers and ok wine list. Daily 11am-10.30, bar midnight.   INX

565 **TRON CAFÉ-BAR:** 552 8587. 63 Trongate. Attached to the important Tron
E4 Theatre, this buzzing bar/bistro has New Glas written all over it. Bar on st & 'Victorian' rm in back (not open at all times). Decent house wines and an eclectic menu. Not always the best grub in the city, but definitely up there for atmos and generally good vibes. Food until 10.30/11pm.   CHP

✓ **FIREBIRD:** 334 0594. 321 Argyle St. Recently more bistrotastic than only pizza, for which it's renowned, but report: 583/BEST PIZZA.

✓ **CAFÉ GANDOLFI:** 552 6813. 64 Albion St. Last but right up there with the best. See Report: 634/BEST TEAROOMS.

THE BEST ITALIAN RESTAURANTS

567
D3 ✔ **FRATELLI SARTI:** 248 2228, 133 Wellington St, and 204 0440 (best number for bookings), 121 Bath St. Glasgow's famed *emporio d'Italia* combining a **deli/wine shop** in Wellington St, **wine shop** in Bath St and **bistro** in each. Gr bustling atmos. Cultivated and celebrated by anyone who has ever managed to get a table at lunchtime. Good pizza, specials change every day, *dolci* and *gelati* in super-calorific abundance. LO 10.30pm. Wellington St cl Sun. (586/PIZZA, 643/COFFEE). Sarti expanded 2000 so now a **restaurant** at 43 Renfield St (corner of W George St, 572 7000), for finer Italian dining in elegant rm with exceptional marble tiling & wine-list. Same menu as others, but more ristorante specials. 7 days. Lunch & LO 10pm. INX/MED (RESTAU)

568
B1 ✔ **LA PARMIGIANA:** 334 0686. 447 Gr Western Rd. Sophisticated ristorante that blends trad service and contemporary Italian cuisine into a seamless performance. Carefully chosen dishes and wine list; solicitous service. Milano rather than Napoli. Expect to find Italians (who consider this to be one of the city's gr restaus – 542/BEST RESTAUS). Mon-Sat lunch and 6-11pm. Cl Sun. MED

569
D3 ✔ **L'ARIOSTO:** 221 0971. 92 Mitchell St. Old-style ristorante but they'd not want to think of themselves as a tratt. Set in an indoor courtyard nr Buchanan St, this is full-blown Tuscan fare with flair & a long way from Est Est Est (below). Gr wine list with good house. Lunch & LO 11pm. Cl Sun. MED

570
B4 **LA FIORENTINA:** 420 1585. 2 Paisley Rd W. Not far from river and motorway over Kingston Br, but app from Eglinton St (A77 Kilmarnock Rd). It's at the Y-jnct with Govan Rd. Trad tratt Little Tuscany (and pizzeria next door) in a fine listed building. Always busy, usually seafood specials and off-hand waiters. As Italian as you want it to be, enormous menu and wine list. Mon-Sat lunch and 5.30-11pm (though LO 9.30pm). Cl Sun. MED

571
C3 **EST EST EST:** 248 6262. 21–25 Bothwell St. Glas version of Edin George St mega-restau, as this UK chain expands. Spacious, contemporary, stylish – pity, then, about the food. Service looks good, but may not deliver. Blair New Britain loves this kind of dining out. 7 days. LO 10pm (10.45 w/ends) and bar till midnight. INX

572
C3 **PAPERINO'S:** 332 3800. 283 Sauchiehall St. Ordinary-looking though smart restau is better than the rest; down to the Giovanazzi brothers who also own La Parmigiana (*see above*) and The Big Blue (713/PUB FOOD). Perfect pasta and good service. 7 days. LO 11pm/12midnight. INX

573
A1 **ANTIPASTI:** 337 2737. 337 Byres Rd. Popular restau on 2 levels that spills onto the st in warm weather. Good pasta. Breakfast time until late (12midnight w/ends). Also at 305 Sauchiehall St (332 9002). Same hours, same mezzanine, food and vibe. 7 days. LO 10.30pm/11.30pm. INX

574
xC5 **ARIGO:** 636 6616. 67 Kilmarnock Rd, Shawlands. Smart little Italian joint on busiest stretch of this main drag. Spare, colour-tint décor. Some surprises on the menu. Friendly, efficient service & nice touches. **ARIGO CENTRO:** 353 6616. 85 Renfield St is recent uptown addition. Mediterranean kind of menu, inexpensive with integrity. Both 7 days, lunch and LO 10.30pm. INX

LA VIGNA: Lanark. Report: 847/CLYDE VALLEY.

THE TRUSTY TRATTS

Old style family-run restaurants (real Italians) with familiar pasta/pizza staples & the rest. There are many of these in Glasgow & elsewhere but these are the best.

575
D3 ✔ **RISTORANTE CAPRESE:** 332 3070. 217 Buchanan St. Basement café nr the Concert Hall. Glaswegians (and footballers) love this place judging by the wall-to-wall gallery of happy smiling punters. Our fave too! Checked tablecloths and crooning in the background create the authentic 'mamma mia' atmos. Friendly service, constantly mobbed (well, not *mobbed*). LO 10/11pm. Cl Sun. Book at w/ends. INX

576 **TREVI:** 334 3262. 526 Gr Western Rd. Tiny family-run tratt with celebrity
B1 ✓ photos next to cool football memorabilia on the walls. The staff can get
a bit distracted on international fixture nights. Loyal clientele lap up the pasta
(along with pollo, veal & other carne). Mama Donata does the sauces & the
puds. Lunch: Mon-Fri. Dinner 7 days. LO 10.30/11.30pm. . INX

577 **LA SCARPETTA, BALLOCH:** 01389 758247 Balloch Rd nr the bridge. Not per-
xB1 haps many reasons to linger in Balloch – the busy lochside (Lomond) here is
not one of them, but this family–run restau is. Fave of writer A. L. Kennedy (she
ain't easy to please) and now us. 7 days LO 10.30pm INX

578 **SAL E PEPE:** 341 0999. 18 Gibson St. Although a recent invention, this popu-
B2 lar W End spot has all the atmos of an old-fashioned family tratt. Small, with
mezzanine floor, it's always busy. Home-made puds & specials to complement
the P and the P. Open for b/fast 9.30-11pm. (Suns from noon). INX

579 **MASSIMO'S:** 332 3227. 57 Elmbank St. Basement tratt opp King's Theatre,
C3 here for yonks but rel recent makeover has lightened it up a lot. Friendly staff
serve up the usuals & some unusual Italian variants; good pizza. INX

580 **ROMA MIA:** 423 6649. 164 Darnley Rd nr The Tramway on the S Side (& the
xC5 best option pre-/post-theatre). Expanded, v family-friendly tratt, members of
'Ciao Italia' (denoting a 'real' Italian restau). Lunch & LO 10pm. Cl Sun/Mon. INX

581 **LITTLE TUSCANY:** 420 1585. Next to and part of **LA FIORENTINA** (570/ITAL-
B4 IAN RESTAUS), the less full-on alternative. Many locals prefer. INX

THE BIG BLUE: 445 Gr Western Rd. Report: 584/PIZZA.

DI MAGGIO'S: Royal Exchange Sq & branches: 650/KIDS.

THE BEST PIZZA

582 **PIZZA EXPRESS:** 221 3333. 151 Queen St and 402 Sauchiehall St (332
D4, D3 ✓ 6965). The national chain who set the pizza standard, here in 2 well-situ-
ated and classy restaus. Always a reliable standby when pizza's the only thing
you can agree on; it's sometimes handy that you can't book. INX

583 **FIREBIRD:** 334 0594. 1321 Argyle St. Big-windowed, spacious bistro at
A3 ✓ the far W end of Argyle St. Mixed modern menu but notable for wood-
smoked dishes, of which their light, imaginative pizzas are excellent. Even
menu improved of late. Noon-10/10.30pm (bar midnight/1am). INX

584 **BIG BLUE:** 357 1038. 445 Gt Western Rd on corner of Kelvinbridge & with ter-
B1 race o/looking river. Bar & restau together so noise can obliterate meal & con-
versation later on. Lots of other dishes & morsels, but the big thin pizzas here
are special. 7 days lunch & LO 9.45pm (w/ends 10.30pm). INX

585 **LITTLE ITALY:** 339 6287. 205 Byres Rd. Ready-made slices (well, slabs of pizza)
A1 and 3 sizes of made-to-order takeaway pies. Not the best pizza in your W End,
but this is a Byres Rd fave esp the window seats, early & later. Mon-Thu 8am-
10pm, Fri-Sat 8am-1am, Sun 10am-10pm. (675/TAKEAWAY) INX

586 **SARTI:** 248 2228. 133 Wellington St and 121 Bath St. Excellent, thin-crust pie,
D3 buffalo mozzarella and freshly-made *pomodoro*. 6 days, 8am-10pm. Only Bath
St on Suns. Full report: 567/ITALIAN RESTAUS. INX

587 **SANNINO:** 332 8025, 61 Bath St, and 332 3565, 61 Elmbank St and larger also
D3, C3 subterranean version at 61 Bath St (332 8025). Famous for its enormous 16"
pizzas, made for sharing (there's also the 9"). You can half and half the toppings. 7 days, 12noon-10.30 (midnight w/ends). INX

THE BEST FRENCH RESTAURANTS

588
D3
✔ ✔ **LE CHARDON D'OR:** 248 3801. 176 W Regent St. Superlative French-style restau. Report: 529/BEST RESTAUS.

589
C3
✔ **MALMAISON:** 221 6401. 278 W George St. The brasserie in the basement of the hotel (487/BEST HOTELS) with the same setup as Edin & elsewhere and a v similar menu. Excellent brasserie ambience in meticulously designed woody salon. Seating layout and busy waiters mean lots of buzz; also private dining-rms and the adjacent **CAFÉ MAL** in bright contrast. Fixed-menu lunch Mediterranean style with daily specials. 7 days, lunch and LO 10.30pm.　　MED

590
C2
✔ **CAFÉ DU SUD:** 332 2054. 8 Clarendon St. Popular intimate restau tucked away behind St George's Cross. Mediterranean/French-style cooking from French husband and Glaswegian wife team who run it with an emphasis on the personal touch. Everything fresh and home-made incl the bread. Better book. Lunch: Fri/Sat only. Dinner LO 10pm. Cl Sun/Mon.　　INX

591
D3
78 ST VINCENT: 221 7710. 78 St Vincent St. Based on century-old Le Chartier restau in Paris (on railway carriages in fact), this restau is related to the Leonardo's chain of Italian joints. Impressive split-level rm with a high ceiling and a big mural by Glas artist Donald McLeod. Stylish cuisine balancing the tried and tested with some touches of originality. They say 'Scottish food with a continental twist'. Slightly formal with an atmos of discreet efficiency. Not bad wines. Lunch (not Sun) and LO 10.30pm (10.45pm Sat-Sun).　　MED

592 ✔ ✔ **MOTHER INDIA:** 221 1663. 28 Westminster Terr. Legendary Glas
B3 restau for Indian home-cooking in a laid-back but stylish setting & where the food rarely lets you down. Many faves & specialities by people who know how to work the flavours & textures. House wine & Kingfisher beer but for 85p corkage you can BYOB. At w/ends & many other nights you will have to book. Take-away too. Lots of vegn choice. V relaxed neighbourhood atmos. 7 days, lunch and LO 11pm, 11.30pm Fri/Sat. INX

593 ✔ **KILLERMONT POLO CLUB:** 946 5412. 2022 Maryhill Rd. Under new own-
xC1 ers but same chef and still one of the most refreshingly different Indian restaus in Scotland. Within a hill-top restau, at the Milngavie end of Maryhill Rd, you will find courteous manners, attentive service and a clubby atmos in the front rm, which is kept as a shrine to all things polo. The food is light, experimental and the spices are sprinkled with care. Indian cuisine is taken seriously. Their Dum Pukht menu (slow cooked) has been a huge success. 7 days noon-11.30pm. INX/MED

594 ✔ **THE WEE CURRY SHOP:** 353 0777. 7 Buccleuch St nr Concert Hall & STV.
D3 Tiny outpost of Mother India above, a neighbourhood home-style cook-ing curry shop, just as they say. Cheap, always cheerful. Stripped-down menu & a sweetie to go. House red & white & Kingfisher but can BYOB. No CC. Lunch & LO 10.30pm. Cl Sun. CHP

595 ✔ **SHISH MAHAL:** 339 8256. 68 Park Rd. First-generation Indian restau that
B1 still, after 30 yrs, remains one of Glasgow's faves. A major refurb brought it back into the light. Menu also completely recharged and the toilets almost posh. Many different influences in the cooking & still committed. 7 days. Till 11pm/12midnight. Can BYOB. INX

596 ✔ **ASHOKA ASHTON LANE:** 357 5904. 19 Ashton Lane and the **ASHOKA**
A1, B3 **WEST END:** 339 0936. 1284 Argyle St. Part of the burgeoning Harlequin Restaurants chain, they have always been good, simple and dependable places to go for curry but have kept up with the times. Nothing surprising about the menus, just sound Punjabi via Glasgow fare. Good takeaway service (0800 195 3 195). Lunch & LO 11.30pm (not lunch W End Mon/Tues). Both 7 days, lunch and open till 12midnight (W End even later). INX

597 **CRÈME DE LA CRÈME:** 221 3222. 1071 Argyle St. The biggest, the most flash
B3 (and God knows they love flash) restau in town – so *they* say. Still at the edge of all things curried and they even show movies (*sic*), incl cartoons (653/KID-FRIENDLY). Frequently busy with office parties and leaving-dos. Behind the flambé and the razzmatazz this is a restau that is run with some care and, dare we say, determination. 7 days, lunch (not Sun) and LO midnight. MED

598 **CAFÉ INDIA:** 248 4074. 171 N St. Enormous brasserie, big on a glamour that
B3 seems a bit time-warped now, but the food is pretty good. Similar Crème de la Crème (above, same owners). The extensive menu is busy with herbs and spices and is not merely hot. A night on the town kind of joint. Buffet and à la carte, Sun-Mon. 7 days, lunch and LO 11.30pm/12midnight. INX

599 **KAMA SUTRA:** 332 0055. 331 Sauchiehall St. Part of the Ashoka group
C3 (above), this restau is better than most in this lager-and-curry-laden belt of the W End. An extensive, almost fusion menu, each dish comes with a break-down of contents and region of origin. Extracts from the original Indian sex-guide dotted here and there are peered at, surreptitiously, tho this all seems a bit ragged now. 7 days, lunch and till 12midnight. (Not Sun). INX

600 **THE ASHOKA:** 221 1761. 108 Elderslie St. Confusingly, no relation to the
B3 Ashokas above. Designery interior but that old pink pakora sauce still runs through the veins. Once voted No. 1 in the 'Best curry houses in Scotland' – that's a matter of taste but the buffet is popular & these curries will run & run! Mon-Sat lunch, 7 days dinner. LO 11.30pm. INX

601 **BALBIR'S:** 334 0084. 11 Hyndland St in Partick. Many fans of this fairly nonde-
xA2 script but 'classic' Glas Punjabi restau. Gr detail in the dishes, some with nei-ther oils nor butter & lots for vegns. Real integrity here. Can BYOB. Dinner only LO 11pm/midnight. INX

THE BEST FAR-EASTERN RESTAURANTS

THAI

602 ✓ **THAI FOUNTAIN:** 332 2599. 2 Woodside Cres. Charing Cross, nr M8,
B2 Mitchell Library, etc. The best Thai in town (and probably in Scotland).
Owned by Chinese Mr Chung but the Thai chefs know a green curry from a
red. Tom yam excellent and weeping tiger beef v popular with those who really just want a steak. Lots of prawn and fish dishes and real vegn choice. Lunch
and LO 11pm. Cl Sun. MED

603 ✓ **THAI SIAM:** 229 1191. 1191 Argyle St (W End side). Trad homely (if dimly lit)
A3 atmos but fashionable clientele who swear it has the prawniest crackers
and greenest curry in town. Prop/chef Pawina Kennedy ensures authenticity and
a packed house at w/ends. Lunch Mon-Fri LO 11pm. Cl Sun. MED

CHINESE

604 ✓ **AMBER REGENT:** 331 1655. 50 W Regent St. Elegant Cantonese restau
D3 that prides itself on courteous service and the quality of its food. The
menu is trad, the atmos too. Has v interior feel. Creditable wine list, quite
romantic at night and a good business lunch spot. Only Glas Chinese restau
in AA & Michelin. Lunch, LO 10.30pm w/ends 11/11.30pm. Cl Sun. MED

605 ✓ **LOON FUNG:** 332 1240. 417 Sauchiehall St. Poss Glasgow's most 'respect-
C3 ed' Cantonese, the place where the local Chinese community meet for
lunch on a Sun/Mon/Tue. Pace is fast and friendly while the food, as you would
expect, is fresh and authentic. Everybody on chopsticks. Even a noticeboard of
Hong Kong/Beijing flights. 7 days, 12noon-10/11pm. MED

606 ✓ **PEKING INN:** 332 8971. 191 Hope St. Smart, urban kind of Chinese restau
D3 on busy corner (with W Regent St) but light, relaxing room. Famous for its
spicy, Szechuan specials; and nights on town. Lunch, LO 11pm (w/ends 12). MED

607 ✓ **CHINA TOWN:** 353 0037. 42 New City Rd. Just off centre but nr
C2 Cowcaddens, under the m/way. Here you're in Hong Kong (almost).
Endless food for lunch (esp Sun) or dinner. Divine dim sum. If you love Chinese
food, you must come here. 7 days, noon-11.30pm. INX

608 **HO WONG:** 221 3550. 82 York St, in city centre nr river, betw Clyde St and
D4 Argyle St. Discreet, urbane Pekinese/Cantonese restau which relies on its reputation and makes few compromises. Décor dated now, but still up-market
clientele; roomful of suits at lunch and champagne list. Notable for seafood
and duck. Good Szechuan. Lunch (not Sun) and LO 11/11.30pm. MED

609 **CHOW:** 334 9818. 98 Byres Rd. Away from the other downtown Chinese
D4 restaus, this is the contemp, smarter & recent W End version. Broad menu incl
speciality Singapore noodles & Szechuan dishes. Good vegn choice. T/away &
delivery. 7 days lunch & dinner (Sun from 4.30pm). INX

610 **THE NOODLE BAR:** 333 1883. 482 Sauchiehall St. Authentic, Chinese-style
C3 noodle bar, 100m from Charing Cross. Along with **CANTON EXPRESS** opp at
407 Sauchiehall St (332 0145), two gr fast food joints with genuine, made on
the spot – in the wok – food late into the AM. Quite groovy in a West End way.
7days, 12noon-5am. (657/655/LATE-NIGHT RESTAUS) CHP

JAPANESE

611 ✓ **OKO:** 572 1500. 68 Ingram St. On main st of Merchant City area, out east. The
D4 Japanese conveyor belt to the stars (local ex pop star Jim Kerr had a hand in
setting this up). Reasonably authentic Japanese nibbles come past and can add
up to quite a bill. Booths best. Tues-Sun, all day. LO 10/11pm. Bar later. MED

612 **ICHIBAN:** 204 4200. 50 Queen St & 184 Dumbarton Rd. Noodle bar based
D4 loosely on the Wagamama formula. Ramen, udon, soba noodle dishes; also
chow meins, tempuras and other Japanese snacks. Long tables, eat-as-it-
comes 'methodology'. Light, calm, hip. 7 days. Lunch and LO 10pm (w/ends
10.30pm). INX

FUSION

613 ✓ **FUSION:** 339 3666. 41 Byres Rd. Stylish, reasonably authentic and small
A2 (few tables up on mezzanine, few down) Japanese bistro at bottom end
of Byres Rd. Beef, chicken, salmon and vegn sushi/sashimi combos from open
galley kitchen. Good value. T/away sushi. Generally minimalist approach, incl
wines and puds. 7 days (not Sun lunch). LO 10/11pm.   CHP

613a ✓ **OPUS:** 204 1150. 150 St Vincent St. Top-end contemp restau. Sound
C3 Scottish ingredients given Asian outing. Crisp service. Good & 'grand'
desserts. Still settling in at TGP, but this could become a top spot again after
demise of former Eurasia. Open early & late, LO 10.30pm (Fri/Sat later) & bar till
2am.   CHP

614 **MAO:** 564 5161. Corner of Brunswick and Wilson St in Merchant City. Bright, hip
E4 east-Asian restau transplanted not, of course, from Beijing but from Dublin. Good
service, right-on wine-list. Asian beers & smoothies. Nice rice. Open all day. 7 days.
LO 10/11pm.   INX

615 **OSHI:** 333 5702. Pt Dundas Pl. The ground floor restau of Langs Hotel
D3 (486/HOTELS) with adj spa sees itself as an 'urban retreat'. It is a v nice space & food
has improved from a shaky start. More fusion than Japanese with sushi platters
alongside rib-eye & spicy fries. Tries hard. 7 days noon-10pm.   INX

616 **SPICE GARDEN:** 429 2222. 11 Clyde Pl. Designer Asian restau (Italian bar, open-
C4 plan kitchen). Sky TV to entertain you if your companion don't. Enormous menu
for 'all tastes' predom S Asian. Open v late so pop post-club spot. 7 days 6pm-1am
(but 4am license applied for at TGP).   INX

THE BEST MEXICAN RESTAURANTS

*Glas has innumerable restaus and café-bars with Mexican choices on a menu
that mixes food from all over (best to stick to the potato skins). The places below
are close to genuine Mex (UK style):*

617 ✓ **PANCHO VILLA'S:** 552 7737. 26 Bell St. Bright, colourful restau free of the
E4 cluttered cantina stereotype, run by real, live Mexican, Maira Nunez.
Menu in Spanish/ingredients in English. No burritos ('an American invention').
Plenty of veggie choices but you really have to try the *albondigas en salsa*
(that's spicy meatballs). Mon-Sat lunch and 6-11pm, Sun 6-10.30pm.   INX

618 **LA COCINA:** 572 0435. 53 West Regent St, Glas's newest Mexican, after recent
D4 reshuffle. Usual staples, but more adventurous possibilities. Good seafood
choice. Cool music. Lunch & LO 10pm (bar open later). Cl Sun.

THE BEST RESTAURANTS FROM AROUND THE WORLD

PACIFIC RIM

620
B2 ✓ **STRAVAIGIN:** 334 2665. 28-30 Gibson St. The best fusion restau in town with influences from all over, though mainly E of Suez. Report: 536/BEST RESTAUS. Also **STRAVAIGIN 2:** 334 7165. Report: 550/BEST BISTROS.　　MED

EASTERN EUROPEAN

621
B1 ✓ **OBLOMOV:** 339 9177. 372 Gr Western Rd, nr Kelvinbridge and 24 Candleriggs (552 4251). Bar/restau with E European 'bohemian' twist. W End branch best, here it's small (12 tables) in raised dining area with light and bar meals during day and heartier à la carte. Most dishes have Euro influence with some classics, e.g. blinis, goulash, strudel. Drink vodka. Often must book! Lunch and LO 8.30pm. Bar till 12midnight/1am. (710/PUB FOOD). New ownership at TGP so change possible.　　INX

SPANISH

622
E4 ✓ **ARTA:** 552 2101. Old Cheesemarket, Walls St. Not strictly speaking a restau but once you've negotiated the hugely OTT bar (usually packed), there's a cantina above (but not beyond) the mêlée. Catalan-style tapas-based menu with Italian pizzas thrown in. Good bread part of a grazing menu. You'd want to be up for it. See also 678/UNIQUE PUBS. Wed-Sun 5pm-11pm, Fri/Sat till midnight (bar 1 hr later).　　INX

623 **LA TASCA:** 204 5188. 39 Renfield St. Tapas bar chain thing, this their first in
D3 Scotland. What Est Est Est has done for mass Italian food, this does for Spanish. Tapas here bear little relation to Barcelona or Bilbao, but the ambience is OK mas o menos. Packed at w/ends. Paella for two and some puds. 7 days, all day LO 10.30pm (Sun 10pm). Bar later.　　CHP

CENTRAL AMERICAN

624 **CUBA NORTE:** 552 3505. 17 John St. Cavernous Cuban restau underneath
E3 'The Italian Centre', a rare example of appropriate pairing (ethnic food & place). This space, esp when there's a live band on or DJs, actually feels like Havana might. Follows success of Edin version (208/CENTRAL AM RESTAUS), but this much bigger. Good at w/ends – eat, dance, get lively. Menu Central American-ish & better than you'd think (or know after a few Cuba Libres). Salsa classes contribute to the weirdly authentic mix. 7 days lunch & LO 11pm (bar midnight/1am).　　INX

GREEK

625 **CAFÉ SERGHEI:** 429 1547. 67 Br St, just over the Jamaica St (or Glas) Br. Greek
D4 island evenings on a bleak rd heading S, a restau in an interesting conversion of a former bank with upstairs balcony beneath impressive cupola. In a tough world, this place has survived. Talkative waiters advise and dispense excellent Greek grub, incl vegn dishes. Fri is Greek dancing night. Lunch (not Sun) and 6-11pm, 7 days.　　INX

BELGIAN

626 **BAR BREL:** 342 4966. 39 Ashton Lane. Kind of Belgian? Report: 564/BEST
A1 BISTROS.

THE BEST SEAFOOD AND FISH

627
C3
✓ ✓ **GAMBA:** 572 0899. 225a W George St, in basement at corner of W Campbell St. Another seafood bistro which happens to be one of the best restaus in the city (532/BEST RESTAUS). Fashionable clientele enjoy stylish setting and snappy service, as well as excellent fresh fish unfussily presented à la mode. Exemplary wine list. Unlike many, open on Mon (cl Sun). Lunch and dinner. LO 10.30pm but may stay open later so check. (532/BEST RESTAUS) MED

628
A2
✓ **TWO FAT LADIES:** 339 1944. 88 Dumbarton Rd. A landmark Glas restau re-establishing itself after departure of proprietor/chef Calum Mathieson. Notable team at helm of v seaworthy boat should continue to keep the Fat Ladies at the forefront of seafood restaus in the city. Lunch & dinner. Cl Mon. MED

629
MAP 1
D2
✓ **GINGERHILL:** 956 6515. Hillhead St, Milngavie. Upstairs at the end of the main st in this northern suburb of Glas (you are at the start of the W Highland Way), a restau which used to be run entirely by women but now by chef/owner Alan Burns who is a man. One meat dish on offer otherwise unpretentious seafood in comfy upstairs bistro. Life is easier here (esp if you don't have to drive home). One dinner sitting only, Thu-Sat (other nights by arrangement); light lunches Mon-Sat. BYOB (& licence applied for 2002) no corkage. MED

630
D3
✓ **MUSSEL INN:** 572 1405. 157 Hope St. Downtown location for light, bright bistro (big windows) recently landed (2001) from Edinburgh. Mussels, scallops, oysters & vegn option, but mussels in variant concoctions & kilo pots are the thing. The 2 Mussel Inns are a chain in the making, but this formula is sound & the owners do know their oysters. Noon-10pm. Cl Suns. INX

ROGANO: 11 Exchange Pl. Report: 541/BEST RESTAUS.

THE BEST VEGETARIAN RESTAURANTS

631
B2, C2
✓ **GRASSROOTS CAFÉ:** 333 0534. 97 St George's Rd beneath St George's Studios nr Charing Cross. This is the caff offshoot of Grassroots (the deli) round the corner at 48 Woodlands Rd (1432/DELIS): serving proper vegn & vegan food. Nutritious, worthy – all this, but round the world dishes as vegn food should be and some simply splendid salads. Calming as well as healthy. 7 days. 10am-10pm. CHP

632
E4
THE 13TH NOTE: 553 1638. 50-60 King St. Old-style veggie hangout – a good attitude/good vibes café-bar with live music downstairs. Big range menu from excellent vegeburgers to Indian and Greek dishes. All suitable for vegans. Organic booze on offer, but also normal Glasgow bevvy. 7 days, 12noon-12midnight. Food LO 10pm. Also 13th Note Club at Clyde St. (810/CULTURE).

633
B1
BAY TREE: 334 5898. 403 Gr Western Rd. Long-established vegan restau nr Kelvinbridge. Wide range of dishes, esp Greek, Turkish and Arabic (owners are Iraqis). All strictly vegan, the sole concession being milk (on request) & cheddar cheese (this is Glasgow!). 7 days till 9pm (Sun till 8pm). (663/B/FAST). CHP

THE GRANARY: 82 Howard St, nr St Enoch Centre. A wholefood & trad tearm straight off a Scottish village street, but this just round the corner from the mall. Report: 638/BEST TEAROOMS.

Restaurants serving particularly good vegn food but not exclusively vegn:

THE UBIQUITOUS CHIP and **THAI FOUNTAIN**. Reports: 534/545/ BEST RESTAUS.

BABY GRAND, FRANGO, ST JUDE'S and **TRON CAFÉ-BAR**. Reports: 553/554/565/BEST BISTROS, 543/BEST RESTAUS.

MOTHER INDIA. 28 Westminster Terr. Report: 592/INDIAN RESTAUS.

CAFÉ GANDOLFI. 64 Albion St. Report: 634/BEST TEAROOMS.

THE BEST TEAROOMS AND COFFEE SHOPS

634 ✓ ✓ **CAFÉ GANDOLFI:** 552 6813. 64 Albion St, Merchant City. For over 20
E4 yrs a definitive & landmark meeting/eating place – bistro menu, but casual ambience of a tearm or coffee shop. Bohemian, Europe-somewhere atmos. Stained glass and heavy, over-sized wooden furniture create a unique ambience that has stood the fashionability test. The food is light and imaginative and served all day. You may have to queue. 7 days, 9am-11.30pm, Sun from 12noon. (660/SUN BREAKFAST). Another Gandolfi at Habitat in Buchanan St (331 1254) prob the best place to eat in the shopping quarter. Store hrs.

635 ✓ ✓ **TINDERBOX:** 339 3108. 189 Byres Rd, on busy corner with
A1 Highburgh Rd. Stylish, designery but unlikely to date, state-of-the-art neighbourhood coffee shop. Stuff for kids, stuff to buy. Snacks and Elektra, the good-looking coffee machine. Gr people-watching potential inside and out. 7 days, 7.45am-11pm (Suns from 8.45am).

636 ✓ **TCHAI-OVNA:** 357 4524. 42 Otago Lane off Otago St and round the back.
B1 A 'house of tea' hidden away on the banks of the Kelvin with verandah & gdn terrace. A boho tearm which could be E Europe, N Africa or Kathmandu but not Glasgow. 70 kinds of tea, soup, organic s/wiches & cakes. Jazz on Weds. A real find. 7 days 11am-10pm.

637 ✓ **WHERE THE MONKEY SLEEPS:** 226 3406. 182 W Regent St adj Compass
D3 Gallery & in basement below Chardon D'Or (529/BEST RESTAUS): its commercial & spiritual opposite. Exhib space ie hanging as well as hanging out. Coffee, soups & picmix s/wiches. T/way & nearby delivery. Cool people place. 7 days. 7am-7pm. (Sat from 9am, Sun 11am).

638 ✓ **THE GRANARY:** 226 3770. 82 Howard St, beside/behind the glass pyra-
D4 mid of the St Enoch Centre towards river. A calm style-free oasis away from shop till you drop Argyle St. Serves mainly vegn dishes but the emphasis is on home-baking. The apple pie is still the best in town. Hard to believe that this place exists in an area decimated by the mall-mongers. *Vive la resistance!* Mon-Sat 9am-5pm, Sun from 10am.

639 ✓ **NORTH STAR:** 946 5365. 108 Queen Margaret Drive. Portuguese deli-
xB1 cum-espresso bar. Minimalist approach to design and product range but you always find something you must have. All home-made except bread. Yum tortilla. Can BYOB. 7 days Mon-Sat. 8am-7/8pm. Sun 11am-6pm.

640 **THE WILLOW TEAROOMS:** 217 Sauchiehall St. On a balcony above a jewellery
C3, D4 & souvenir shop with a sister tearoom at 97 Buchanan St. Both celebrate the Rennie Mackintosh connection big time and under the discerning eye of proprietor Anne Mulhern, recreate the interiors of the original Miss Cranston's Tearooms he designed. 30 blends of loose-leaf tea, all manner of cakes, scones and sandwiches and now, hold on … a wee glass of wine. Mon-Sat 9.30am-4.30pm. Sun from noon. Buchanan St best by the way. (789/MACKINTOSH)

641 **ART LOVER'S CAFÉ:** 353 4779. 10 Dumbreck Rd, Bellahouston Park. On the
xA5 ground floor of House for an Art Lover, a building based on drawings left by Rennie Mackintosh (791/MACKINTOSH). Bright rm more ambient than Willow Tearooms (above) and a counterpoint to the usual wrought iron, purply, swirly Mockintosh caffs elsewhere. This is unfussy & elegant. Garden views. Soup 'n' sandwiches, but also set & à la carte menus so a serious lunch spot. 7 days 10am-5pm (Fri/Sat till 3pm).

642 **BRADFORDS:** 245 Sauchiehall St. Since 1924 the coffee shop/restau upstairs
C3 from the flagship shop of this local and estimable bakery chain. Familiar wifie waitresses, the macaroni cheese is close to mum's and the cakes and pies from downstairs represent Scottish bakery at its best. Mon-Sat 9am-5.30pm.

643 **FRATELLI SARTI:** 248 2228. 133 Wellington St and 121 Bath St. Full report:
D3 567/ITALIAN RESTAUS. Definitive Italian version. 8am-10pm. Cl Sun.

644
A2 ✓ ✓ **UNIVERSITY CAFÉ:** 87 Byres Rd. When your granny, in the lines of the well-known song, was 'shoved aff a bus', this is where she was taken afterwards and given a wee cup of tea to steady her nerves. People have been coming here for generations to sit at the 'kneesy' tables and share the salt and vinegar. Run by the Verecchia family who administer advice, sympathy and pie, beans and chips with equal aplomb. A gem. Daily till 10pm (w/ends till 10.30pm). Cl Tue. Takeaway open later.

645
xC5 ✓ ✓ **THE UNIQUE:** 223 Allison St. Not exactly central, but if you're on the S-side you'll find the best fish 'n' chips in town here. Through the curtain in the café they serve lunches, fish teas and spam fritters. Veg oil used. Old-fashioned hrs, viz 8.15am-1.15pm, 3-8pm. That's right, 8pm – closed!

646
A1 ✓ **GROSVENOR CAFÉ:** 31 Ashton Lane, behind Byres Rd nr Hillhead Stn. For over 30 yrs they've been cramming us in. Orig cheery caff and all-day breakfast has moved upstairs & gets even posher in eve with wider menu. This place was/is a Glas institution & should survive its 21st century makeover unscathed. 7 days, 9am-10.30pm (Mon till 6pm, Sun 10am-5pm).

647
xE4 ✓ **COIA'S CAFÉ:** 473 Duke St. Since 1928, supplying this E End high st with ice cream, gr deal breakfasts and the kind of comforting lunch (they might call it dinner) café-bar places just cannot do. There's a telly in the corner lots of Glas chat at the tables. Sit-in or takeaway. Sweeties of all sorts; and Havana cigars. 7 days, 7.30am-9pm (LO 7.30pm); Sun from 11am.

648
xC1 **CAFE D'JACONELLI:** 570 Maryhill Rd nr the Queen's Cross Church (784/MACK-INTOSH). Neighbourhood caff with toasties, macaroni cheese and award-winning ice-cream to go that's been here for ever. This is the disappearing Glasgow, but used often as a film location (Trainspotting, Carla's Song). Get yourself a banquette. 7 days, 9am-10pm.

649
xA5 **ALLAN'S SNACK BAR:** 6 Storie St, Paisley. Off the High St, a chip shop with classic greasy spoon adj and a chips-with-everything menu in a Paisley days-gone-by atmos. Happy waitresses. Mon-Thu 11am-7pm, Fri-Sat 11am-8pm. Cl Sun.

JACK MCPHEE'S: 285 Byres Rd.

KID-FRIENDLY PLACES

650 **DI MAGGIO'S:** 334 8560. 61 Ruthven Lane, off Byres Rd, W End; 632 4194, 1038
A1 Pollokshaws Rd, on a busy corner S of the river; and 248 2111, 21 Royal
xC5 Exchange Sq. 'Our family serving your family' they say & they do. Bustling,
D4 friendly pizza joints with good Italian attitude to bairns. There's a choice to
defy the most finicky kid. High chairs, special menu. In summer, o/side tables
in Exchange Sq so the kids can run around. 7 days.

651 **TGI FRIDAY'S:** 221 6996. 113 Buchanan St. The Glas branch of the national
D3 chain adored by kids because of the way they get fussed over and are given,
pretty much, a free run of the place. The food is from everywhere via America
and when added, free-hand, to the crayon drawings on the tablecloth, can
look quite spectacular. Huge range of cocktails available for parents who may
need them. Face-painter at w/ends. 7 days, 11.30am-11.30pm, Sun till 11pm.

652 **HARRY RAMSDEN'S:** Paisley Rd W, beside M8 flyover – not far from centre,
B4 but difficult without a car. Not a bad branch of the national chain that caters
well for kids. Greasy, cooked in lard and in cheerfully tacky surroundings, the
chips and peas, sausage and fishcakes come in kids' portions and there's a
playground to throw up into before you get back in the car.

653 **CRÈME DE LA CRÈME:** 221 3222. 1071 Argyle St. Big (huge), bustling Indian
B3 emporium which makes special allowances for kids (there are 40 high chairs
available!), incl cartoons on giant screens. Tempt them with a korma; there is
ice cream. 7 days, lunch and LO 11.30pm. (597/INDIAN RESTAUS)

THE BEST LATE-NIGHT RESTAURANTS

654 ✓**INSOMNIA:** 564 1700. 38 Woodlands Rd. 24hr café/deli that dispenses
B2 food, infusions, strong coffee and drinks to those who just *will not go to
their beds*. In a rm full of higgledy-piggledy bits of furniture, baths full of gold-
fish and a clock noticeable by its absence, Glasgow's demi-monde plot and
sip tea into the wee hrs of the afternoon. The clientele & the menu & the vibe
changes thro'out the long day. **7 days, 24hr. 2002 UPDATE: NOW CLOSED**

655 ✓**CANTON EXPRESS:** 332 0145. 407 Sauchiehall St. The first fast-food
C3 Chinese joint on this block; still the genuine Chinese article. Not as wok-
tastic as once was, but still feels like Hong Kong to us. **7 days, 12noon-4am.**

656 ✓**BABY GRAND:** 248 4942. Elmbank Gardens by Charing Cross Stn &
C3 Premier Lodge skyscraper hotel (behind King's Theatre). Not easy for
strangers to find, but persevere – this is an excl bar/diner at any time of day
(553/BISTROS), but comes into its own after 10pm when just about everywhere
that's decent is closing. Char-grilled food & grazing contemp menu. Piano
player & night-time people. **Daily till 1am, Fri/Sat till 2am.**

657 **THE NOODLE BAR:** 333 1883. 482 Sauchiehall St. Major competition to the
C3 above (even gets the edge in opening hrs). Authentic, Chinese fast food, no
frills (ticket service and eezee-kleen tables). The noodle is 'king' here; cooking
is taken seriously. (610/FAR-EASTERN RESTAUS) **7 days, 12noon-5am.**

658 **SLEEPLESS ON SAUCHIEHALL:** 332 9290. 415 Sauchiehall St. Opp Garage
C3 club & v post-pub/club clientele. Giant screen, American diner menu, all night
b/fasts, good shakes. **7 days 8.30pm-5.30am.**

659 **STRAVAIGIN & STRAVAIGIN 2:** 334 2665 & 334 7165. Gibson St & Ruthven
B2, A1 Lane off Byres Rd. Worth remembering that both these excl restaus
(536/RESTAUS & 550/BISTROS) serve food to **11pm & midnight w/ends.**

SPICE GARDEN: 492 2222. 11 Clyde Pl (616/FUSION RESTAUS). Late-night retreat
just over the river. **Till 4am (bar 1am).**

PIZZA EXPRESS: Sauchiehall St/Queen St. (582/PIZZAS) **11.30pm.**

CRÈME DE LA CRÈME: 1071 Argyle St. Report: 597/INDIAN RESTAUS. **11.30pm.**

ASHOKA ASHTON LANE: Ashton Lane. (596/INDIAN RESTAUS) **12.30pm.**

GOOD PLACES FOR SUNDAY BREAKFAST

660 ✓ **CAFÉ GANDOLFI:** 552 6813. 64 Albion St. Atmospheric rm, with soft day-
E4 light filtering through the stained glass and the comforting, oversized wooden furniture. This is a pleasant start to another Sun, that day of rest and more shopping made even better with some baked eggs, a pot of tea and the Sun papers (634/BEST TEAROOMS). **From 12noon.**

661 ✓ **TINDERBOX:** 339 3108. Corner Byres Rd & Highburgh St. Gr café/diner
A1 open early to late (635/COFFEE SHOPS). **From 8.45am.**

662 **GRASSROOTS CAFÉ:** 97 St George's Rd at Charing X. An especially calm &
C2 healthy Sun thing (631/VEGN RESTAUS) and it **opens at 10am.**

663 **BAY TREE:** 403 Gr Western Rd. This worthy, old-style vegn caff (633/VEGN
B1 RESTAUS) provides another antidote to the toxins of Sat night. Hearty vegan breakfast is served all day. **From 9am.**

664 **LOOP:** 354 7705. 110 Bath St the ground floor of Bewley's Hotel for whom it
D3 supplies daily b/fast hence early start. All the usual & some contemp twists in mod restau surroundings. B/fast menu till 11am. **From 8am.**

665 **BABBITY BOWSTER:** 552 5055. 16 Blackfriars St. The seminal Merchant City
E4 bar/hotel recommended for many things (714/PUB FOOD, 705/DRINKING OUT-DOORS), but worth remembering as one of the best and earliest spots for Sun breakfast. **From 10am.**

666 **CUL DE SAC:** 44 Ashton Lane, off Byres Rd. Kind of an institution now tho'
A1 b/fast starts earlier than before upstairs in **THE ATTIC (from 9am)** – tiny tables, best at bar. Downstairs a smart relaxed place to phase into Sun. Fry-up includes potato scones and comes in a vegn version, and there are the better-than-average burgers and exotic crêpes. Brunch **12.30pm-4pm.** New owner-ship at TGP so may change. (563/BEST BISTROS)

667 **COTTIER'S:** 93 Hyndland St, off Hyndland Rd. Off the top of Hyndland St nr
xA1 Highburgh Rd. Deep in the hefty-mortgage belt of Hyndland, this converted church probably gets more of a congregation now than it ever did. Eclectic menu from fruit plate to the full monty and eggs benedict to cajun kedgeree. Papers provided (559/BEST BISTROS). **12noon-4pm.**

668 **UPSTAIRS AT THE CHIP:** 334 5007. 12 Ashton Lane. 'Sair heid' or not, their
A1 Bloody Marys are the best in town and combined with a veggie breakfast (gr potato crowdie), famously restorative. Selection of papers. Unhurried (534/BEST RESTAUS). **From 12.30pm.**

THE BEST TAKEAWAY PLACES

669
A1 ✔ **HEART and BUCHANAN:** 334 7626. 308 Byres Rd. Deli & t/away but more what Fiona Buchanan describes as a 'traiteur', the French idea that excl food can be pre-prepared & you just take it home & reheat it. Certainly an extraordinary daily changing menu is produced in the kitchens downstairs according to a published menu of the week. Lots of other carefully selected goodies to go. Fiona puts her 'heart' into this place, it's a major plus to living around here. 7 days 8.30am-9.30pm. Suns 12-7pm.

670
xC5 **MISE EN PLACE:** 424 4600. 122 Nithsdale Rd. S-side specialist caterer, deli & t/away run by Suzanne Ritchie. Food to go incl soup/sandwiches, pastas & tarts. All home-made. Everything from dinner *à deux* to full-on alfresco bash with cool waiters and other trimmings. Delivered to your door or drop in for delish lunch. Small caff next door. Mon-Fri 9.15am-5.45pm, Sat 9.15am-4pm.

671
A1 **NAKED SOUP:** 334 6200. 106 Byres Rd. First of the new soup-to-go places that we might expect to take hold in Scotland. Perhaps not best location for office lunches, but otherwise absolutely the right idea. 8 fresh (organic where poss) soups daily, gr salads (esp cous cous) & (perhaps too) thick smoothies. Sit-in or go. 7 days, 9am-8pm, Sun 12-5pm.

672
D3 **PRET À MANGER:** 34 Sauchiehall St, St Vincent St, Bothwell St & presumably more on the way. Smart, formulaic but has wiped the floor with the more trad sandwich bars. Food comes with philosophy, but it didn't stop them selling out to McDonald's! 7 days 8am-5.30pm (Thur-Sat till 6pm, Sun 10-5pm).

673
D3 **YUM:** 229 0258. 130 W Regent St. Styly, basement to-go bar in office & gallery belt. 'Classic' & fancy s/wich selection, melts and 2 soups changing daily. Smoothies & sushi – all the 2002 stuff. Can deliver. 8am-4pm. Cl w/ends.

674
B2 **GRASSROOTS:** 353 3278. 20 Woodlands Rd, Charing X. Food to go, but mainly big organic deli. Vegn ready meals, bespoke s/wiches. 7 days 8am-8pm, Sat 9-6pm, Sun 11-5pm.

675
A1 **LITTLE ITALY:** 339 6287. 205 Byres Rd. Basic, but a Byres Rd old faithful. Pizza focaccia and pasta (585/PIZZA), freshly-baked breads, ice cream, loadsa Italian wines and a no' bad (meaning 'not at all bad') cup of coffee. Mon-Thu 8am-10pm, Fri-Sat 8am-1am, Sun 10am-10pm.

UNIQUE GLASGOW PUBS

Those pubs you won't find anywhere else.

676 ✓ ✓ **THE HORSESHOE:** 17 Drury St. A mighty pub since the 19th cent in
D3 the small st betw W Nile and Renfield Sts nr Central stn. Early example of this style of pub, dubbed 'gin palaces'. Island rather than horseshoe bar ('the longest in the UK') impressive selection of alcohols and an upstairs lounge where they serve high tea. The food is amazing value (707/PUB FOOD). All kinds of folk. Daily till 12midnight.

677 ✓ ✓ **CORINTHIAN:** 191 Ingram St. Mega makeover of impressive listed
D4 building to form cavernous bar/restau, 2 comfy lounge/cocktail bars and a restau (535/BEST RESTAUS) nr George Sq and Gallery of Modern Art. Awesome ceiling in main rm much much better than megabars elsewhere. Food in main rm ok, excl in restau. Older, richer, well-heeled clientele, some Armani. Totally Glas. 7 days, till 12midnight. (Piano bar Thur-Sun).

678 ✓ ✓ **ARTA:** Old Cheesemarket, Walls St, Merchant City. Nr & rel to
E4 Corinthian (above) & similar scale of vision completely realised. This massive OTT bar/restau/club somewhere betw old Madrid & new Barcelona could prob only happen in Glasgow. Tapas type menu upstairs (622/WORLD RESTAUS) & down the full-on Glas drinking, dressing up & chatting up experience. Go thro' that curtain into a dream or just possibly a nightmare. Wed-Sun from 5pm-1am (Thu/Fri/Sat till 3am).

679 ✓ **THE HALT BAR:** 160 Woodlands Rd. Edwardian pub largely unspoiled,
B2 unchanged but always kept up with the times. Original counter and snug intact. Always gr atmos – model of how a pub should look and feel. Live music and DJs Wed & w/ends. (801/ESS.CULTURE/LIVE MUSIC) Open till 11pm (12midnight w/ends).

680 ✓ **VICTORIA BAR:** 157 Bridgegate. 'The Vicky' is in the 'Briggait', one of Glas's
D4 oldest streets, nr the Victoria Br over the Clyde. Once a pub for the fishmarket and open odd hrs, now it's a howf for all those who like an atmos that's old, friendly and uncontrived. Real ales. Mon-Sat till 12midnight, Sun till 11pm. (800/CULTURE)

681 ✓ **SCOTIA BAR:** 112 Stockwell St. Nr the Victoria (*see above*), late-1920s
D4 Tudor-style pub with a low-beamed ceiling and intimate, woody 'snug'. Long the haunt of folk musicians, writers and raconteurs. Music and poetry sessions, folk and blues. Daily till 12midnight. (799/CULTURE)

682 ✓ **CLUTHA VAULTS:** 167 Stockwell St. This and the pubs above are part of
D4 the same family of trad Glas pubs. The Clutha (ancient name for the Clyde) has a Victorian-style interior and an even longer history. Known for live music. Mon-Sat till 12midnight, Sun till 11pm. (802/CULTURE)

683 **UISGE BEATHA:** 246 Woodlands Rd. 'Oo-i-skay Bay' (or something like that)
B2 means 'the water of life' and is a unique Highland outpost in the city. Shooting-lodge chic in 3 diff rms; all cosy. More than a mere draught of the Gael. Good grub at lunchtime. Related to one of the gr Highland bars, The Drover's Inn, Inverarnan. Sun-Thu till 11pm, Fri-Sat till 12midnight.

684 **BAR 10:** 10 Mitchell Lane, off Buchanan St. Opp new Lighthouse and nr the
D4 Tunnel, this was one of the orig 'cool' & pre-club bars before the Glas style-bar explosion. Dating now but remarkably resilient to fashionista trends, the Ben Kelly interior still looks good. Food till 4.30pm, then snax. Regular DJs at w/ends. (717/HIP)

685 **REPUBLIK BIER HALLE:** 9 Gordon St. Beer cellar extraordinaire, the creation of
D3 well-known Glasg entrepreneur & mover/shaker Colin Barr. Huge list of Belgians, Czechs & incl Mongolian, Moroccan, Scottish beers. Stews, dogs & goulash to go with. You can smell the meat & the teen spirit. 7 days 12-12pm.

686 **LISMORE:** 206 Dumbarton Rd, main rd w after Byres Rd. Lismore/Lios mor
xA2 named after the long island off Oban. Gr neighbourhood (Partick) bar that welcomes all sorts. Gives good atmos, succour and malts. Daily till 12pm.

687 **BEN NEVIS:** Argyle St nr Crème de la Crème (597/RESTAUS). Owned by same
B3 people as Lismore (above). An excl makeover in contemp but not faux-Scottish style. Small & pubby, the Deuchars is spot-on. Live music Weds.

688 **THE MITRE:** 12 Brunswick St, but more in the lane behind Trongate opp the
E4 backwards EMPIRE sign by Douglas Gordon. V new dressed-down Glasgow in trad old Glas pub. Cheap grub. Karaoke upstairs Sat. Till 11pm, 12midnight w/ends.

THE BEST OLD 'UNSPOILT' PUBS

The following places don't have to pretend to be old. Most close no later than 11pm/midnight.

HORSESHOE: 17 Drury St. Report: 676/UNIQUE PUBS.

HALT BAR: 160 Woodlands Rd. Report: 679/UNIQUE PUBS.

VICTORIA BAR: 157 Bridgegate. Report: 680/UNIQUE PUBS.

SCOTIA BAR: 112 Stockwell St. Report: 681/UNIQUE PUBS.

CLUTHA VAULTS: 167 Stockwell St. Report: 682/UNIQUE PUBS.

THE MITRE: Lane off Brunswick St/Argyle St. Report: 688/UNIQUE PUBS.

689 ✔ **THE GRIFFIN (AND THE GRIFFINY AND THE GRIFFINETTE):** 266 Bath
C3 St. Corner of Elmbank St nr King's Theatre. Built 1903 to anticipate the completion of the theatre and offer the patrons a pre-show pie and a pint. Stand at the Edwardian Bar like generations of Glaswegians. Main bar still retains 'snug' with a posh, etched-glass partition; booths have been added but the atmos is still 'Old Glasgow'. Sun-Thu till 11pm, Fri-Sat till 12midnight. Amazingly cheap lunches (706/PUB FOOD).

690 **THE SARACEN'S HEAD:** Gallowgate, nr Barrowlands. An establishment of this
xE4 name has existed in the neighbourhood since 1755, playing host to a multitude of characters; not least Boswell and Johnson, on the return leg of their grand Highland tour. This, the most recent incarnation, opened in 1905 and is famous for its lethal cider. The atmos is more 'wild west end' than E End, & Baird's across the st (see below) serves the stronger shot of culture, but the Sarrie Heid is still pure dead brilliant. 7 days, Cl 10.30pm weekdays.

691 **STEPS:** 66 Glassford St. Tiny pub & barely noticed but has the indelible marks
E4 of better by-gone days. In no way celebrated like Rogano (541/RESTAUS), but also refers to the *Queen Mary* with stained glass & gr panelling. V typical, friendly Glasgow. Often, there are free snacks on the house. A real find.

692 **M J HERAGHTY:** 708 Pollokshaws Rd. More than a touch of the Irish here and
xC5 easily more authentic than recent imports. A local with loyal regulars who'll make you welcome; old pub practices still hold in this howff in the sowff. Ladies' loos introduced in 1996! Sun-Thu till 11pm, Fri-Sat till 12midnight.

693 **BRECHIN'S:** 803 Govan Rd. Nr jnct with Paisley Rd W and motorway over-
A5 pass. Established in 1798 and, as they say, always in the same family. A former shipyard pub which is close in heart & soul to to Rangers FC. It's behind the statue of shipbuilder Sir William Pearce (which, covered in sooty grime, was known as the 'Black Man') and there's a feline 'rat-catcher' on the roof (making it a listed building). Unaffected neighbourhood atmos, some flute-playing. Mon-Sat till 11pm, Sun till 6.30pm.

694 **THE OLD TOLL BAR:** 1 Paisley Rd W. Opp the site of the original Parkhouse
B4 Toll, where monies were collected for use of the 'turnpikes' betw Glas and Greenock. Opened in 1874, the original interior is still intact; the *fin de siècle* painted glass and magnificent old gantry preserved under order. A 'palace pub' classic. Real ale and some single malts. 7 days till 11pm.

695 **BAIRD'S BAR** and **THE DISTRICT:** 2 bars from opp sides of the gr divide.
E4 **BAIRD'S** in the Gallowgate adj Barrowlands is a Catholic stronghold green to
xA5 the gills where, on days when Celtic play at home up the rd in Parkhead, you'd have to be in by 11am to get a drink. **THE DISTRICT,** 252 Paisley Rd W, Govan, nr Ibrox Park, is where Rangers supporters gather and rule in their own blue heaven. Both pubs give an extraordinary insight into what makes the Glas time-bomb tick. Provided you aren't wearing the wrong colours (or say something daft), you'll be very welcome in either.

Pubs on other pages may purvey real ale, but the following are the ones where they take it seriously and/or have a good choice.

696 ✓ **BON ACCORD:** 153 N St. On a slip rd of the motorway swathe nr the
B3 Mitchell Library. One of the first real-ale pubs in Glas. Good selection of malts and up to 12 beers; always Theakstons, Deuchars & IPA plus many guest ales on hand pump. Food at lunchtime and light bites till 8pm. Light, easy-going atmos here, but they do take their ale seriously; there's even a 'tour' of the cellars if you want it. Mon-Sat till 12midnight, Sun till 11.00pm.

697 **TENNENT'S:** 191 Byres Rd. Nr the always-red traffic lights at Univ Ave, a big,
A1 booming watering-hole of a place where you're never far away from the horseshoe bar and its several excellent hand-pumped ales, incl several Scottish & many guests. Revamped only a little but the old crowd will always be there with the new.

698 **BABBITY BOWSTER:** 16 Blackfriars St. In a pedestrianised part of the
E4 Merchant City and just off the High St, a highly successful pub/restau/hotel (504/INDIVIDUAL HOTELS); but the pub comes first. Caledonian, Deuchars, IPA & well-chosen guests. Many malts & cask cider. Food all day (714/PUB FOOD), occasional folk music (esp Sun), o/side patio (705/DRINK OUTDOORS) and exhibs.

699 **BLACKFRIARS:** 36 Bell St on corner of the Merchant City. Mixed crowd in this
E4 a' thing to a' body kind of pub (food till 7pm, then bites, also comedy & jazz programme). Ind Coope, Burton guest beers, bottled & draught Euro beers. Till 11/12pm.

700 **THE HORSESHOE:** 17 Drury St. Gr for lots of reasons (676/UNIQUE GLAS PUBS),
D3 not the least of which is its range of beers: Caledonian, Greenmantle, Maclays and Bass on hand pump.

701 **VICTORIA BAR:** 157 Bridgegate. Another pub mentioned before (680/UNIQUE
D4 GLAS PUBS) where IPA, Maclays and others can be drunk in a dark woody atmos enlivened by occasional trad music (767/FOLK MUSIC).

PLACES TO DRINK OUTDOORS

702 **LOCK 27:** 1100 Crow Rd. At the very N end of Crow Rd beyond Anniesland, an
xA1 unusual boozer for Glas: a canalside pub on a lock of the Forth and Clyde Canal (745/WALKS IN THE CITY), a touch English (a v wee touch), where of a summer's day you can sit o/side. Excellent bar food, always busy. 7 days.

703 **COTTIER'S:** 357 5825. 93 Hyndland St. First on the left after the swing park on
xA1 Highburgh Rd (going W) and the converted church is on your rt, around the corner. Gr place for many reasons (559/BEST BISTROS, 667/SUN BREAKFAST), but a cold beer on a hot day sitting in leafy shade is one of the best; or into the evening – life can be good! 7 days.

704 **ASHTON LANE:** As soon as the sun comes out, so do the punters. With the
A1 **CUL DE SAC** and **BAR BREL** at one end and **JINTY MCGUINTY'S** at the other, benches suddenly appear and the whole lane becomes a cobbled, alfresco pub. It's the nearest Glas gets to Euro, even Dublin, drinking. 7 days.

705 **BABBITY BOWSTER:** 552 5055. 16 Blackfriars St. Unique in the Merchant City
E4 for several reasons (698/REAL-ALE PUBS, 714/PUB FOOD), but in summer certainly for its napkin of gdn in an area bereft of greenery. Though enclosed by surrounding sts, it's an oasis many head for. Feels like Soho, Soho NYC? Naw, feels like Glas. Always good crack. 7 days.

PUBS WITH GOOD FOOD

706
C3
✓✓ **THE GRIFFIN:** 266 Bath St. On corner of Elmbank St across from King's Theatre. The Griffin, the Griffiny and the Griffinette: they're always there on that corner and your basic pie/chips/beans *and a pint* will not be bettered at this price (£2.80 lunchtime, the equivalent 80 yrs ago of 8 old pence). Other staples available and a more elaborate menu in the lounge or the Griffinette next door. Food: 12noon-2.30pm and evenings till 7pm. Pub till 12midnight. (689/'UNSPOILT' PUBS)

707
D3
✓✓ **THE HORSESHOE:** 17 Drury St. This classic pub to be recommended for all kinds of reasons. But lunch is a particularly good deal with 3 courses for £2.80 (pie and beans still 80p), and old favourites on the menu like mushy peas, macaroni cheese, jelly and fruit. Lunch 12noon-2.30pm and all afternoon upstairs, incl high tea till 7pm (not quite the same atmos, but pure Glas). Pub open daily till 12midnight. (676/UNIQUE GLAS PUBS)

708
B2
✓✓ **STRAVAIGIN:** 28-30 Gibson St. Excellent pub food upstairs from one of the best restaus in town. Doors open on to sunny Gibson St & mezzanine above. Crowded maybe, but inspirational grub & no fuss. Nice wines to go with. 7 days all day & LO 10pm. Report: 536/BEST RESTAUS.

709
C3
✓✓ **LOWDOWN:** 331 4061. 158 Bath St. Vast below street level bar underneath Quigley's (533/RESTAUS). Spacious & opening on to sunken terrace with loungy furniture. Stylish look & clientele & easy eating menu by the irrepressible & eponymous Mr Quigley. Food all day till 11pm.

710
B1
✓ **OBLOMOV:** 339 9177. 372 Gr Western Rd, Kelvinbridge. A creation of Ron McCulloch (designer and entrepreneur of this parish) changing hands at TGP. Sepia, softly-lit pre-war kinda atmos. Booths and chaises, big drapes. Crepuscular dining-rm. Contemporary menu. Their food is good and not too foreign. (621/RESTAUS). 7 days. Served 11.30am-8.30pm. Menu & times may change.

711
A3
✓ **AIR ORGANIC:** 564 5200. 36 Kelvingrove St nr the park. Restau upstairs was once flavour of the month (2000), but snackier food in bar, e.g. Thai curry sandwiches, sushi boxes; still a hip place to graze. Open fire among cool minimalism and music. 7 days, 11am–11pm. (544/BEST RESTAUS)

712
B3
✓ **McPHABB'S:** 221 0770. 23 Sandyford Pl. 2 blocks W of Charing Cross. Gr Scottish/Irish bar food; smoked haddies, salmon and steaks, beef and Guinness stew, etc. Given the 'parliamentary seal of approval' by local MP George Galloway who particularly rates the stew. 7 days, open till 12midnight at w/ends. Food till 9pm.

713
B1
THE BIG BLUE: 445 Gr Western Rd. A modern bar/bistro in a gr uptown location literally on the (river) Kelvinside. Drinking may drown the eating later on, but till mid/late-evening there's excellent Italian pasta/pizza pub grub. LO 10/10.30pm. Bar 12midnight.

714
E4
BABBITY BOWSTER: 16 Blackfriars St. Already listed as a pub for real ale and as a hotel (there are rms upstairs), the food is mentioned mainly for its Scottishness (haggis and stovies) and all-day availability. It's also pleasant to eat o/side on the patio/gdn in summer. There is a restau upstairs (lunch Mon–Fri, dinner Mon–Sat) but we prefer down. Also breakfast served from 8am (Sun 10am). (698/REAL-ALE PUBS, 504/INDIVIDUAL HOTELS)

715
E4
BLACKFRIARS: 36 Bell St. Candleriggs is one of the focal points in the Merchant City. Gr Glas pub for all-round ambience, provision of real ale and music, and food available all day (meals till 7pm, then 'bites') (but drinkers loud after 9pm). 699/REAL ALES.

716
MAP 1
C3
FOX AND HOUNDS, HOUSTON: On B790 village main st in Renfrewshire, 30km W of centre by M8 jnct 29 (A726), then cross back under motorway on B790. Village pub with real fire and dining-rm upstairs for family meals and suppers. Folk come from miles around. Sunday roasts. Lunch and 6-10pm (all day w/ends).

717 ✓ **BAR 10:** 221 8353. 10 Mitchell Lane, halfway up Buchanan St pedestrian
D4 precinct on the left in the narrow lane that also houses the Lighthouse design centre. There's an NYC look about this joint that is so loved by its habitués, they still pack it at w/ends almost 10 yrs after it arrived. Ben Kelly design has worn well. Food, DJs & pre-club preparations. 7 days till midnight. (684/UNIQUE PUBS)

718 ✓ **LOWDOWN:** 331 4061. 158 Bath St Opened mid 2001 this, the lower
C3 down bar of Quigley's (533/BEST RESTAUS) quickly became an immensely popular place to gather & graze (709/PUB FOOD) & for that matter gaze (dressed-to-go crowd). This place looks likely to last.

719 ✓ **ARCHES:** 0901 022 0300 (box office). 253 Argyle St. The fab bar/café of
B3 the fab Arches Theatre (on whose board I sit), the club & experimental theatre space recently refurbished with millennium money. Design by Timorous/Taller (see Strata below), this is an obvious pre-club pre-theatre space, but works at any time. Food & DJs & lots going on. Even if you're only in Glas for the w/end, you must come here. (Is that alright Andy?)

720 ✓ **GROUCHO:** 352 8800. 190 Bath St. Further along Bath St (from Lowdown
C3 above), another bar below stairs that seems likely to outlive the Bath St explosion. This, the bar of St Jude's (495/HOTELS, 543/BEST RESTAUS) is minimal-ist but still fuzzy & friendly. Good cocktails. Food till drinking takes over & open till midnight 7 days.

721 **STRATA:** 221 1888. 45 Queen St. Was 'Style Bar of the Year, 2000', but we won't
D4 hold that against them. Nothing hugely obvious to distinguish this from a clutch of others, but somehow it works. Done by Timorous Beasties & One Food Taller (ubiquitous Glas design team), the room is not intrusive & the food is better than most. Food till 10pm, bar midnight.

722 **BARGO:** 553 4771. 80 Albion St. In the Merchant City, this spacious, designer-
E4 theque is in demand for fashion shoots and, of course, high-glam posing on a Sat night. Can be attractively, if not spookily, quiet during the week when sur-prisingly OK food is served. Opens on to st in summertimes sometimes.

723 **CUL DE SAC:** 649 4717. 44 Ashton Lane. The upstairs bar and **ATTIC** is a peren-
A1 nial W End fave. Close to the underground for that last-minute dash into town to beat club curfews. (563/BEST BISTROS)

724 **CANDY BAR:** 353 7420. 185 Hope St .Still stylee after all these years (well 4), a
D3 good place to look, linger and even eat (food till 8pm) - eclectic new menu incl a decent fish 'n' chips. Minimalist chic with the odd flourish. 7 days noon till midnight.

725 **POLO LOUNGE:** 553 1221. 84 Wilson St. Urbane and stylish bar/disco by the
E4 irrepressible Stefan King. Unmistakably gay in the heart of the quarter (not him, it). Clubbable rather than clubby crowd (until later on) arranged around the comfortable furniture; at w/ends you go downstairs to disco. Mellow Sun afternoons; papers and jazz. (2063/GAY GLAS)

726 **BAR 91:** 552 5211. 91 Candleriggs. A better bar among many of this ilk here-
E4 abouts, food also (the restau Farfelu is upstairs – 552/BISTROS), tho it stops at 6pm to make way for pre-club ministrations.

AIR ORGANIC: 36 Kelvingrove St. Report: 711/PUB FOOD.

727 ✓✓ **KELVINGROVE ART GALLERY AND MUSEUM:** 287 2699. At westerly
A2 extension of Argyle St and Sauchiehall St by Kelvingrove Park. Huge
Victorian sandstone edifice with awesome atrium. On the ground floor is a nat-
ural history/Scottish history museum. The upper salons contain the city's superb
British and European art collection. There are strong contemporary exhibs as
well as the permanent collection. Tearoom. Museum of Transport (734/OTHER AT-
TRACTIONS) across the rd. Mon-Thurs, Sat 10am-5pm, Fri & Sun 11am-5pm. FREE

728 ✓✓ **THE BURRELL COLLECTION AND POLLOK PARK:** 287 2550. S of river
xC5 via A77 Kilmarnock Rd (over Jamaica St Br) about 5km, following signs
from Pollokshaws Rd. Set in rural parkland, this award-winning modern gallery
was built to house the eclectic acquisitions of Sir William Burrell. Showing a
preference for medieval works, among the 8,500 items the magpie magnate
donated to the city in 1944 are artefacts from the Roman empire to Rodin. The
building itself integrates old doorways and whole rms reconstructed from
Hutton Castle. Self-serve café and restau on the ground floor. Pollok House and
Gdns further into the park (with works by Goya, El Greco and William Blake) is
worth a detour and has, below stairs, the better tearoom. Both open Mon-Thurs,
Sat 10am-5pm, Fri & Sun 11am-5pm. (746/WALKS IN THE CITY)   FREE

729 ✓ **GLASGOW CATHEDRAL/PROVAND'S LORDSHIP:** 552 6891/553 2557.
xE3 Castle St. Across the rd from one another they represent what remains of
the oldest part of the city, which (as can be seen in the People's Palace, *see
below*) was, in the early 18th century, merely a ribbon of streets from here to
the river. The present Cathedral, though established by St Mungo in AD 543,
dates from the 12th century and is a fine example of the v real, if gloomy,
Gothic. The house, built in 1471, is a museum which strives to convey a sense
of medieval life. Watch you don't get run over when you re-emerge into the
21st century and try to cross the st. In the background, the Necropolis piled
on the hill invites inspection and offers a viewpoint and the full Gothic perspective (tho' best not to go alone). Call for opening times.

730 ✓ **THE PEOPLE'S PALACE:** 554 0223. App via the Tron and London Rd, then
xE5 turn rt into Glas Green. This has long been a folk museum *par excellence*
wherein, since 1898, the history, folklore and artefacts of a proud city have
been gathered, cherished and displayed. But this is much more than a mere
museum; it is the heart and soul of the city and together with the Winter Gdns
adj, shouldn't be missed, to know what Glasgow's about. Tearoom in the
Tropics, among the palms and ferns of the Winter Gdns. Opening times as
other museums (*see above*).   FREE

731 ✓ **GLASGOW SCIENCE CENTRE:** 420 5000/5010. On S Side of Clyde opp
A4 SECC, Glasgow's newest attraction built with Millennium dosh. App via
Kingston Br (from city) and Govan t/off, then rt fork at 'the angel', or walk from
SECC complex by 'Bell's Bridge'. Impressive titanium-clad mall, Imax cinema &
127m-high tower. 4 floors of interactive exhibs, planetarium & theatre. Rolling
story of the city with the science and the view. Separate tickets or combos
(only 20 people with 2 lifts at a time for the tower). 7 days 10am-6pm.   ADM

732 **ST MUNGO MUSEUM OF RELIGIOUS LIFE AND ART:** 553 2557. In the
xE3 Cathedral precinct or sq dubbed 'Ft Weetabix' by Glas cabbies. Opened with
some gnashing of teeth and wringing of hands in 1993, it houses art and artefacts representing the world's 6 major religions arranged tactfully in an attractive stone building with a Zen gdn in the courtyard. The dramatic Dalí
Crucifixion seems somehow lost, and the assemblage seems like a good and
worthwhile vision not quite realised. But if you like your spirituality shuffled
but not stirred, this is for you. The punters' comments board is always …
enlightening. Opening times as other museums (*see above*).   FREE

733 **HUNTERIAN MUSEUM AND GALLERY:** 330 4221/5431. Univ Ave. On one side
A1 of the st, Glasgow's oldest museum with geological, archaeological and social
history displayed in a venerable building. The cloisters outside and the **UNI-
VERSITY CHAPEL** should not be missed. Across the st, a modern block contains part of Glasgow's exceptional civic collection – Rembrandt to the
Colourists and the Glas Boys, as well as one of the most complete collections
of any artist's work and personal effects to be found anywhere, viz that of

Whistler. It's fascinating stuff, even if you're not a fan. There's also a print gallery and the superb **MACKINTOSH HOUSE** (785/MACKINTOSH). Mon-Sat 9.30am-5pm (M. House closed daily 12.30-1.30pm).   FREE

THE OTHER ATTRACTIONS

734
A2
✔ ✔ **MUSEUM OF TRANSPORT:** 287 2720. Off Argyle St behind the Kelvin Hall. May not seem your ticket to ride, but this is one of Scotland's most fascinating museums. Has something for everybody, esp kids. The reconstruction of a cobbled Glas st c1938 is an inspired evocation. There are trains, trams and unique collections of cars, motorbikes and bicycles. And model ships in the Clyde rm, in remembrance of a mighty river. Make a donation and the Mini splits in two. Mon-Thur, Sat 10am-5pm, Fri & Sun 11am-5pm.   FREE

735
xB1
✔ ✔ **BOTANIC GARDENS AND KIBBLE PALACE:** 334 2422. Gr Western Rd. Smallish park close to R Kelvin with riverside walks (744/WALKS IN THE CITY), and pretty much the 'dear green place'. Kibble Palace (built 1873) is the distinctive domed glasshouse with statues set among lush ferns and shrubbery from around the (mostly temperate) world. A wonderful place to muse and wander. Gdns open till dusk; palace 10am-4.45pm (4.15pm in wint).

736
D4
✔ ✔ **GALLERY OF MODERN ART:** 229 1996. Queen St. Central, controversial and housed in former Stirling's Library, Glasgow's big visual arts attraction opened in a hail of art world bickering in 1996. Then director Julian Spalding's choice of inclusion raised to record levels both the ire of critics and the interest of the public. This 'Modern Art' incl contemporary and populist from elsewhere, but little from the influential movements and bugger all from the Saatchi side in which many Glas artists have made notable contributions. Smart café up top. Same hrs as MOT (*see above*).   FREE

737
xE4
✔ ✔ **THE BARROWS:** (pronounced 'Barras') The sprawling st and indoor market area in the E End of the city around the Gallowgate. As with all gr markets, it's full of character and characters and it's still possible to find bargains and collectibles. Everything from clairvoyants to the latest scam. Purists, of course, point out that its glory days are well over & commercialisation has killed it, but it's still pure Glasgow. Sat and Sun only 10am-5pm.

738
C2
THE TENEMENT HOUSE: 333 0183. 145 Buccleuch St. Nr Charing Cross but can app from nr the end of Sauchiehall St and over the hill. The typical 'respectable' Glas tenement kept under a bell-jar since Our Agnes moved out in 1965. She had lived there with her mother since 1911 and wasn't one for new-fangled things. It's a touch claustrophobic when busy and is distinctly voyeuristic, but, well … your house would be interesting, too, in 50 yrs time if the clock were stopped. Daily, Mar-Oct 2-5pm.   ADMN

739
E4
SHARMANKA KINETIC GALLERY & THEATRE: 552 7080. 2nd floor, 14 King St, Trongate. A small and intimate experience cf most others on this page, but an extraordinary one. The gallery/theatre of Russian emigre Eduard Bersindsky shows his meticulous and amazing mechanical sculptures. Unlike others in this list, the gallery is open for specific performances only so call to check times (usually 4 pers week).   ADMN

740
xC5
GREENBANK GARDENS: 639 3281. 10km SW of centre via Kilmarnock Rd, Eastwood Toll, Clarkston Toll and Mearns Rd, then signposted (3km). A spacious oasis in the suburbs; formal gdns and 'working' walled gdn, parterre and woodland walks around elegant Georgian house. V Scottish. Gdns open AYR 9.30am-dusk, shop/tearoom Apr-Oct 11am-5pm.   NTS

741
D3
CITY CHAMBERS: 287 4018. George Sq. The hugely impressive building along the whole E end of Glasgow's municipal central sq. This is a wonderfully over-the-top monument to the days when Glas was the second city of the empire. Guided tours Mon-Fri, 10.30am and 2.30pm.   FREE

742
MAP 1
C2
FINLAYSTONE ESTATE: 01475 540505. 30km W of city centre via fast M8/A8, signed off dual carriageway just before Pt Glas. Delightful gdns and woods around mansion house with many pottering places and longer trails (and ranger service). Visitor centre and conservatory tearoom. AYR 7 days, 10am-5pm.

743 **THE PRIDE O' THE CLYDE:** 07711 250969. Amsterdam-style water-bus ferry-
C4 ing passengers between Glasgow (board at Broomielaw, Jamaica Bridge) and
Braehead Shopping & Leisure Centre (board at Maritime Heritage Centre). A
35-min journey incl commentary on the sights & history of the Clyde.
Refreshments avail. Plans to expand business & add pick-up/drop-off points
at Tall Ship and Science Centre. AYR. ADMN

PAISLEY ABBEY: 15km from Glas. Report: 1816/ABBEYS.

BOTHWELL CASTLE, UDDINGSTON: 15km E, via M74. Report: 1720/RUINS.

THE BEST WALKS IN THE CITY

See page 10 for walk codes.

744 **KELVIN WALKWAY:** A path along the banks of Glasgow's other river, the
B1 Kelvin, which enters the Clyde unobtrusively at Yorkhill but first meanders
through some of the most interesting parts and parks of the NW city. Walk
starts at Kelvingrove Park through the Univ and Hillhead district under Kelvin
Br and on to the celebrated Botanic Gdns (735/OTHER ATTRACTIONS). The trail
then goes N, under the Forth and Clyde Canal (*see below*) to the Arcadian
fields of Dawsholm Park (5km), Killermont (posh golf course) and Kirkintilloch
(13km from start). Since the river and the canal shadow each other for much
of their routes, it's possible, with a map, to go out by one waterway and return
by the other (e.g. start at Gr Western Rd, return Maryhill Rd).

START: Usual start at the Eildon St (off Woodlands Rd) gate of Kelvingrove
Park or Kelvin Br. St parking only. 2-13+KM XCIRC BIKE 1-A-1

745 **FORTH AND CLYDE CANAL TOWPATH:** The canal, opened in 1790 and once
D2 a major short cut for fishing boats and trade betw Europe and America, pro-
xC1 vides a fascinating look round the back of the city from a pathway that
stretches on a spur from Pt Dundas just N of the M8 to the main canal at the
end of Lochburn Rd off Maryhill Rd and then E all the way to Kirkintilloch and
Falkirk, and W through Maryhill and Drumchapel to Bowling and the Clyde
(60km). Much of the route is through the forsaken or redeveloped industrial
heart of the city, past waste ground, warehouses and high flats, but there are
open stretches and curious corners and, by Bishopbriggs, it's a rural waterway.
More info from British Waterways (01324 671217). At TGP, the Edin-Glas canal
link is now navigable with just the Falkirk section to finish – due for completion Mar 2002.

START: (1) Top of Firhill Rd (gr view of city from Ruchill Park, 100m further on
– 757/BEST VIEWS). (2) Lochburn Rd (*see above*) at the confluence from which to
go E or W to the Clyde. (3) Top of Crow Rd, Anniesland where there is a canalside pub, Lock 27 (702/DRINK OUTDOORS), with tables o/side, real ale and food
(12noon-7/8pm). (4) Bishopbriggs Sports Centre, Balmuildy Rd. From here it is
6km to Maryhill and 1km in other direction to the 'country churchyard' of
Cadder or 3km to Kirkintilloch. All starts have some parking.
ANY KM XCIRC BIKE 1-A-1

746 **POLLOK COUNTRY PARK:** The park that (apart from the area around the
xC5 gallery and the house – 728/MAIN ATTRACTIONS) most feels like a real country
park. Numerous trails through woods and meadows. The leisurely guided
walks with the park rangers can be educative and more fun than you would
think (632 9299 for details). Burrell Collection and Pollok House and Gdns are
obvious highlights. There's an 'old-fashioned' tearoom in the basement of the
latter serving excellent range of hot, home-made dishes, soups, salads, s/wich-
es as well as usual cakes & tasties. Open 7 days 10am-4.30pm (616 6410). Enter
by Haggs Rd or by Haggs Castle Golf Course. By car you are directed to the
entry rd off Pollokshaws Rd and then to the car park in front of the Burrell.
Train to Shawlands or Pollokshaws W from Glas Central Stn.

747 **MUGDOCK COUNTRY PARK:** 956 6100. Not perhaps within the city, but one
MAP 1 of the nearest and easiest escapes. Park which incl Mugdock Woods (SSSI) and
D2 2 castles is NW of Milngavie. Regular train from Queen St Stn takes 20 min,
then follow route of W Highland Way for 4km across Drumclog Moor to S
edge of park. In summer, shuttlebus will meet the trains at Milngavie Stn and

take you right into park. By car to Milngavie by A81 park is 5km N. Well signed. 5 car parks, main one incl Craigend Visitor Centre. Many trails marked out and further afield rambles. This is a godsend betw Glas and the Highland hills.

5-20KM CAN BE CIRC BIKE 1-A-2

748   **CATHKIN BRAES:** S edge of city with views. Report: 755/BEST VIEWS.
xA5

EASY WALKS OUTSIDE THE CITY

See page 11 for walk codes.

749   **CAMPSIE FELLS:** Range of hills 25km N of city best reached via Kirkintilloch
xC1   or Cumbernauld/Kilsyth. Encompasses area that includes the Kilsyth Hills, Fintry Hills and Carron Valley betw. (1) Good app from A803, Kilsyth main st up the Tak-me-Doon (*sic*) rd. Park by the golf club and follow path by the burn. It's poss to take in the two hills to left as well as Tomtain (453m), the most easterly of the tops, in a good afternoon; views to the E. (2) Drive on to the jnct (9km) of the B818 rd to Fintry and go left, following Carron Valley reservoir to the far corner where there is a forestry rd to the left. Park here and follow track to ascend Meikle Bin (570m) to the rt, the highest peak in the central Campsies. (3) The bonny village of Fintry (525/HOTELS O/SIDE TOWN) is a good start/base for the Fintry Hills and Earl's Seat (578m). (4) Campsie Glen – a sliver of glen in the hills. App via Clachan of Campsie on A81 (decent tearoom) or from viewpoint high on the hill on B822 from Lennoxtown-Fintry. This is the easy Campsie intro.   10KM+ CAN BE CIRC XBIKE 2-B-2

750   **GLENIFFER BRAES, PAISLEY:** Ridge to the S of Paisley (15km from Glas) has
MAP 1   been a favourite walking-place for centuries. M8 or Paisley Rd W to town cen-
C3   tre then: (1) S via B775/A736 towards Irvine or (2) B774 (Causeyside St then Neilston Rd) and sharp rt after 3km to Glenfield Rd. For (1) go 2km after last houses, winding up ridge and park/start at Robertson Park (signed). Here there are superb views and walks marked to E and W. (2) 500m along Glenfield Rd is a car park/ranger centre (0141 884 3794). Walk up through gdns and formal parkland and then W along marked paths and trails. Eventually, after 5km, this route joins (1).   2-10KM CAN BE CIRC MTBIKE 1-A-2

751   **GREENOCK CUT:** 45km W of Glas. Can app via Pt Glas but simplest route is
MAP 1   from A78 rd to Largs. Travelling S from Pt Glas take first left after IBM, signed
C2   L Thom. Lochside 5km up winding rd. Park at Cornalees Br Centre (01475 521458). Walk left along lochside rd to Overton (5km) then path is signed. The Cut, an aqueduct built in 1827 to supply water to Greenock and its 31 mills, is now an ancient monument. Gr views from the mast over the Clyde. Another route to the rt from Cornalees leads through a glen of birch, rowan and oak to the Kelly Cut. Both trails described on board at the car park.

15/16KM CIRC MTBIKE 1-B-2

752   **MUIRSHIEL:** General name for vast area of 'Inverclyde' W of city, incl Greenock
MAP 1   Cut (*see above*), Castle Semple Country Park and Lunderston Bay, a stretch of
C2   coastline nr the Cloch Lighthouse on the A770 S of Gourock for littoral amblings. Best wildish bit is Muirshiel Country Park itself (01505 842803), with trails, a waterfall and Windy Hill (350m). Nothing arduous, but a breath of air. From Pt Glas head S on A761 for Kilmacolm then S for Lochwinnoch on B786.

753   **THE WHANGIE:** On A809 N from Bearsden about 8km after last r/bout and
MAP 1   2km after the Carbeth Inn, is the car park for the Queen's View (756/BEST
D2   VIEWS). Once you get to the summit of Auchineden Hill, take the path that drops down to the W (a half-rt-angle) and look for crags on your rt. This is the 'back door' of The Whangie. Carry on and you'll suddenly find yourself in a deep cleft in the rock face with sheer walls rising over 10m on either side. The Whangie is more than 100m long and at one pt the walls narrow to less than 1m. Local mythology has it that The Whangie was made by the Devil, who lashed his tail in anticipation of a witchy rendezvous somewhere in the N, and carved a slice through the rock, where the path now goes.

5KM CIRC XBIKE XDOGS 1-A-1

754   **CHATELHÉRAULT, nr HAMILTON:** Jnct 6 off M74, well signposted into
MAP 1   Hamilton, follow rd into centre, then bear left away from main rd where it's
D3   signed for A723. The gates to the 'château' are about 3km o/side town. A drive

leads to the William Adam-designed hunting lodge of the Dukes of Hamilton, set amid ornamental gdns with a notable parterre and extensive grounds. Tracks along the deep, wooded glen of the Avon (ruins of Cadzow Castle) lead to distant glades. Good walks and ranger service (01698 426213). House open 10.30am-4.30pm, walks at all times. 2-7KM CIRC BIKE 1-A-2

THE BEST VIEWS OF THE CITY AND BEYOND

Refer to Map 1 on pages 328–329.

755 **CATHKIN BRAES, QUEEN MARY'S SEAT:** The southern ridge of the city on
C5 the B759 from Carmunnock to Cambuslang, about 12km from centre. Go S of river by Albert Br to Aikenhead Rd which continues S as Carmunnock Rd. Follow to Carmunnock, a delightfully rural village, and pick up the Cathkin Rd. 2km along on the rt is the Cathkin Braes Golf Club and 100m further on the left is the park. Marvellous views to N of the Campsies, Kilpatrick Hills, Ben Lomond and as far as Ben Ledi. Walks on the Braes on both sides of the rd.

756 **QUEEN'S VIEW, AUCHINEDEN:** Not so much a view of the city, more a per-
MAP 1 spective on Glasgow's Highland hinterland, this short walk and sweeping
D2 vista to the N has been a Glaswegian pilgrimage for generations. On A809 N from Bearsden about 8km after last r/bout and 2km after the Carbeth Inn which is a v decent pub to repair to. Busy car park attests to its popularity. The walk, along path cut into ridgeside, takes 40-50 min to cairn, from which you can see The Cobbler (1864/HILLS), that other Glas favourite, Ben Ledi and sometimes as far as Ben Chonzie 50km away. The fine views of L Lomond are what Queen Victoria came for. Further on is The Whangie (*see opp*). 1-A-1

757 **RUCHILL PARK:** An unlikely but splendid panorama from this overlooked, but
xC1 well-kept park to the N of the city nr the infamous Possilpark housing estate. Go to top of Firhill Rd (past Partick Thistle football ground) over Forth and Clyde Canal (745/WALKS IN THE CITY) off Garscube Rd where it becomes Maryhill Rd. Best view is from around the flagpole; the whole city among its surrounding hills, from the Campsies to Gleniffer and Cathkin Braes (*see above*), becomes clear.

758 **BAR HILL AT TWECHAR, nr KIRKINTILLOCH:** 22km N of city, taking A803
xE2 Kirkintilloch t/off from M8, then the 'low' rd to Kilsyth, the B8023, bearing left at the 'black-and-white br'. Next to Twechar Quarry Inn, a path is signed for Bar Hill and the Antonine Wall. Steepish climb for 2km, ignore strange dome of grass. Over to left in copse of trees are the remains of one of the forts on the wall which was built across Scotland in the 2nd century AD. Ground plan explained on a board. This is a special place with strong history vibes and airy views over the plain to the city which came a long time after. 1-A-2

759 **BLACKHILL, nr LESMAHAGOW:** 28km S of city. Another marvellous outlook,
xE2 but in the opp direction from above. Take jnct 10/11 on M74, then off the B7078 signed Lanark, take the B7018. 4km along past Clarkston Farm, head uphill for 1km and park by Water Board mound. Walk uphill through fields to rt for about 1km. Unprepossessing hill which unexpectedly reveals a vast vista of most of E central Scotland. 1-A-2

760 **PAISLEY ABBEY:** Every so often on Abbey 'open days', the tower of this amaz-
MAP 1 ing edifice can be climbed. The tower (restored 1926) is 50m high and from
D2 the top there's a grand view of the Clyde. This is a rare experience, but phone TIC (889 0711) or Abbey itself (889 7654, am) for details; could be your lucky day. M8 to Paisley; frequent trains from Central Stn. (1816/GREAT ABBEYS)

761 **LYLE HILL, GOUROCK:** Via M8 W to Greenock, then round the coast to rela-
MAP 1 tively genteel old resort of Gourock where the 'Free French' worked in the
C2 yards during the war. A monument has been erected to their memory on the top of Lyle Hill above the town, from where you get one of the most dramat-ic views of the gr crossroads of the Clyde (Holy L, Gare L and L Long). Best vantage-point is further along the rd on other side by trig pt. Follow British Rail stn signs, then Lyle Hill. There's another gr view of the Clyde further down the water at **HAYLIE, LARGS**, the hill 3km from town reached via the A760 rd to Kilbirnie and Paisley. The island of Cumbrae lies in the sound and the sunset.

CAMPSIE FELLS and **GLENIFFER BRAES**: 749/750/WALKS O/SIDE THE CITY.

THE BEST OF THE SPORTS FACILITIES

SWIMMING AND INDOOR SPORTS CENTRES

The best 2 pools, Arlington Baths (332 6021) and the Western Baths (339 1127), are private. Temporary memberships may be negotiable. Others are:

762 **WHITEHILL POOL:** 551 9969. Onslow Dr parallel to Duke St at Meadowpark St
xE4 in the E End nr Alexandra Park (not open all day, every day so phone for times). 25m pool with sauna/multigym (Universal).

763 **NORTH WOODSIDE LEISURE CENTRE:** 332 8102. Braid Sq. Not far from St
B2 George's Cross nr Charing Cross at the bottom of Gr Western Rd. In a rebuilt area; follow AA signs. Modern pool (25m) and sauna/steam/sun centre plus the usual fitness suite & classes. Mon 10am, Tue & Thur 9.30am, Wed & Fri 7.30am all till 9pm; Sat/Sun 10am-4pm.

764 **POLLOK LEISURE CENTRE:** 881 3313. Cowglen Rd. Not a do-your-lengths
xA5 kind of a pool – more a family water outing. Mon-Fri 9.30am (Tue 10am)-9pm, Sat/Sun 10am-4pm.

765 **GOUROCK BATHING POOL:** 01475 631561. On rd S, an open-air heated pool
xA5 on the Clyde. Gr prospect for summers like they used to be. May-Sept. (1997/SWIMMING POOLS)

766 **KELVIN HALL INTERNATIONAL SPORTS ARENA:** 357 2525. Argyle St by
A2 Kelvingrove Museum and Art Gallery (727/MAIN ATTRACTIONS). Major venue for international indoor sports competitions, but open otherwise for weights/ badminton/tennis/athletics/climbing. Book hr-long sessions. No squash.

767 **SCOTSTOUN LEISURE CENTRE:** 959 4000. Danes Dr. Huge state-of-the-art
xA2 sports multiplex. 10 lane pool, indoor halls and outdoor pitches. Mon, Wed, Fri 7.30am-10pm, Tue/Thur 9am-10pm, Sat/Sun 9am-6pm. (1992/LEISURE CENTRES)

768 **TOLLCROSS PARK LEISURE CENTRE:** 763 2345. Wellshot Rd, Tollcross.
xE4 Another biggie. 10 lane pool, indoor halls, split-level fitness suite. Mon-Fri 7am (Thu 10am)-9pm, Sat 9am-5pm, Sun 9am-4pm.

769 **ALLANDER SPORTS COMPLEX:** 942 2233. Milngavie Rd, Bearsden, 16km N of
xC1 centre via Maryhill Rd. Best by car. Squash (2 courts), sports halls, snooker, badminton, swimming pool, fitness suite (open late, but times vary). All refurbished & upgraded late 2001. Waiting list for gym.

GOLF COURSES

Glas has a vast number of parks and golf courses. The following clubs are the best open to non-members. Refer to Around Glasgow map on pages 326–327.

770 **CATHKIN BRAES:** 634 0650. Cathkin Rd, SE via Aikenhead Rd/Carmunnock Rd
xC5 to Carmunnock village, then 3km. Best by car. Civilised hilltop course on the S edge of the city. Non-members Mon-Fri (though probably not Fri am).

771 **HAGGS CASTLE:** 427 3355. Dumbreck Rd nr jnct 22 of the M8; go straight on
xC5 to clubhouse at first r/bout. Part of the grounds of Pollok Park; a convenient course, perhaps overplayed. Non-members Mon-Fri.

772 **POLLOK GOLF CLUB:** 632 1080. On the other side of the White Cart Water and
xC5 Pollok House and rather more up-market. Well-wooded parkland course, flat and well kept, but not cheap. Women not permitted to play.

773 **GLEDDOCH, LANGBANK:** 01475 540704. Excellent 18-hole course adj and
xA5 part of Gleddoch House Hotel (520/HOTELS O/SIDE TOWN). Restricted play.

TENNIS

774 Public courts (Apr-Sep), membership not required: **KELVINGROVE PARK** 6
B2, courts, **QUEEN'S PARK** 6 courts, **VICTORIA PARK** 6 courts. Courts open
xC5, 12noon-8pm.
xA3

THE BEST GALLERIES

Apart from those listed previously (MAIN ATTRACTIONS, OTHER ATTRACTIONS) *the following galleries are always worth looking into. The* Glasgow Gallery Guide, *free from any of them, lists all the current exhibs.*

775 ✓✓ **GLASGOW PRINT STUDIOS:** 552 0704. 22 & 25 King St. Influential
E4 and accessible upstairs gallery with print work on view and for sale from many of Scotland's leading and rising artists. Cl Sun & Mon. Print Shop over rd.

776 ✓✓ **TRANSMISSION GALLERY:** 552 4813. 28 King St. Cutting edge and
E4 often off-the-wall work from contemporary Scottish and international artists. Reflects Glasgow's increasing importance as a hot spot of conceptual art. Stuff you might disagree with. Cl Sun & Mon.

777 ✓✓ **THE MODERN INSTITUTE:** 248 3711. 73 Robertson St. Not really a
C4 gallery – more a concept. Cutting-edge art ideas and occasional events. Sometimes exhibs, incl Glasgow Art Fair.

778 ✓✓ **THE GLASGOW ART FAIR:** George Sq in tented pavilions. Held
D3 every yr in mid-Apr. Most of the galleries on this page and many more are represented; highly selective and good fun. (2150/WHERE TO BUY ART)

779 ✓ **COMPASS GALLERY:** 221 6370. 178 W Regent St. Glasgow's oldest estab-
C3 lished commercial contemporary art gallery. Their 'New Generation' exhib in Jul-Aug shows work from new graduates of the art colleges and has heralded many a career. Combine with the other Gerber gallery (*see below*). Cl Sun.

780 ✓ **CYRIL GERBER FINE ART:** 221 3095. 148 W Regent St. British paintings
C3 and esp the Scottish Colourists and 'name' contemporaries. Gerber, the Compass (*see above*), and Art Exposure (*see below*) have Christmas exhibs where small, accessible paintings can be bought for reasonable prices. Cl Sun.

781 **ART EXPOSURE GALLERY:** 552 7779. 19 Parnie St. Behind the Tron Theatre.
E4 Showcase gallery with a friendly, down-to-earth attitude exhibiting the work of contemporary/graduate Scottish artists. Sort of 'affordable'. Cl Sun.

782 **SHARMANKA KINETIC GALLERY:** 552 7080. Report: 739/OTHER ATTRACTIONS.
E4

THE MACKINTOSH TRAIL

The gr Scottish architect and designer Charles Rennie Mackintosh (1868–1928) had an extraordinary influence on contemporary design.

783 ✓✓✓ **GLASGOW SCHOOL OF ART:** 353 4500. 167 Renfrew St.
C2 Mackintosh's supreme architectural triumph. It's enough almost to admire it from the st (and maybe best, since this is v much a working college) but there are guided tours at 11am and 2pm (Sat 10.30am & 11.30am) of the sombre yet light interior, the halls and library. You might wonder if the building itself could be partly responsible for its remarkable output of acclaimed painters. Temp exhibitions in the Mackintosh Gallery. The Tenement House (738/OTHER ATTRACTIONS) is nearby.

784 ✓✓ **QUEEN'S CROSS CHURCH:** 870 Garscube Rd, where it becomes
xC1 Maryhill Rd (corner of Springbank St). Built 1896-99. Calm and simple, the antithesis of Victorian Gothic. If all churches had been built like this, we'd go more often. The HQ of the Charles Rennie Mackintosh Society (946 6600), which was founded in 1973. Mon-Fri 10am-5pm, Sat 10am-2pm, Sun 2-5pm.   DONATION

785 ✓✓ **MACKINTOSH HOUSE:** 330 5431. Univ Ave. Opp and part of the
A1 Hunterian Museum (733/MAIN ATTRACTIONS) within the univ campus. The Master's house has been transplanted and methodically reconstructed from the next st (they say even the light is the same). If you've ever wondered what the fuss is about, go and see how innovative and complete an artist, designer and architect he was, in this inspiring yet habitable set of rms. Mon-Sat 10am-5pm, Sun 11am-5pm.   FREE

786 ✓ ✓ **SCOTLAND STREET SCHOOL MUSEUM:** 287 0500. 225 Scotland St.
B5 Opp Shields Rd underground and best app by car from Eglinton St (A77 Kilmarnock Rd over Jamaica St Br). Entire school (from 1906) preserved (and recently renovated) as museum of education through Victorian/ Edwardian and wartimes. Original, exquisite Mackintosh features, esp tiling, and powerfully redolent of happy school days. This is a uniquely evocative time capsule. Café and temporary exhibs. Mon-Sat 10am-5pm, Sun 2-5pm.   FREE

787 ✓ **THE LIGHTHOUSE:** 221 6362. Mitchell Lane, off Buchanan St by USC
D4 Clothing store. Glasgow's legacy from its yr as UK City of Architecture and Design. Changing exhibs in Mackintosh's 1893–5 building for *The Glasgow Herald* newspaper. Also houses an interpretation centre on the gr architect with fantastic rooftop views from the corner tower. Mon, Wed, Fri, Sat 10.30am-5.30pm, Tue 11am-5.30pm, Thu 10am-7pm, Sun 12-5pm.   ADM

788 ✓ **THE HILL HOUSE, HELENSBURGH:** 01436 673900. Upper Colquhoun St.
MAP 1 Take Sinclair St off Princes St (at Romanesque tower and TIC) and go 2km
C2 uphill, taking left into Kennedy Dr and follow signs. A complete house incorporating Mackintosh's typical total unity of design, built for Walter Blackie in 1902-4. Much to marvel over and wish that everybody else would go away and you could stay there for the night. There's even a library full of books to keep you occupied. Tearoom; gdns. Apr-Oct 1.30-5.30pm. Helensburgh is 45km NW of city centre via Dumbarton (A82) and A814 up N Clyde coast.   ADMN

789 **THE WILLOW TEAROOMS:** Sauchiehall St and Buchanan St. The café he de-
D3, D4 signed (or what's left of it); where to go for a break on the trail (640/TEAROOMS).

790 **MARTYR'S PUBLIC SCHOOL:** 287 8955. Parson St. Latest renovation and pub-
xE3 lic access to another spectacular Mackintosh building. Check those roof trusses.   FREE

791 **HOUSE FOR AN ART LOVER:** 353 4770. Bellahouston Park. 10 Dumbreck Rd.
xA5 Take the M8 W, then the M77, turn rt onto Dumbreck Rd and it's on your left. These rms were designed, nearly a century ago, specifically, it would seem, for willowy women to come and go, talking of Michelangelo. Detail is the essence of Mackintosh, and there's plenty here, but the overall effect is of space and light and a complete absence of clutter. Design shop and Café (641/BEST TEA-ROOMS) on the ground floor. Phone for opening times.   ADMN

ESSENTIAL CULTURE

UNIQUE VENUES

792 ✓ ✓ **THE CITIZENS' THEATRE:** 429 0022. Gorbals St, just over the river.
D5 Fabulous main auditorium and 2 small studios. Drama at its v best. One of Britain's most influential theatres, esp for design. Refurbished with lottery funds. Love the theatre, love this theatre.

793 ✓ ✓ **THE TRAMWAY:** 422 2023. 25 Albert Dr on S side. Studio, theatre
xC5 and vast performance space. Dynamic and widely influential with an innovative and varied programme from all over the world. Seasonal programme. New gdn project imminent 2002.

794 ✓ **CCA:** 332 7521. Centre for Contemporary Arts, 350 Sauchiehall St. Major
C3 refurb of central arts-lab complex for all kinds of performance & visual arts presentation. Impressive atrium/courtyard houses cool café/restau called Tempus. Watch press for CCA programme.

795 ✓ **THE ARCHES:** 221 4001. 253 Argyle St. Experimental and vital theatre on
D4 a tight budget in the railway arches under the tracks of Central Stn. Andy Arnold will not lie down. Opening times vary. W/end clubs among the best (813/ESS. CULTURE/CLUBBING IT). Major renovations unveiled in 2001 contributed to this venue becoming one of the most exciting in UK.

796 **THE TRON THEATRE:** 552 4267. 63 Trongate. Contemporary Scottish theatre
E4 and other interesting performance, esp music. Gr café-bar with food before and *après* (565/BEST BISTROS).

797 **GLASGOW FILM THEATRE:** 332 6535. Rose St at downtown end of
C3 Sauchiehall St. Known affectionately as GFT, has café/bar and 2 screens for essential art house flicks.

798
xE4 ✓ ✓ ✓ **BARROWLAND BALLROOM:** 552 4601. Gallowgate. When its lights are on, you can't miss it. The Barrowland is world-famous and for many bands one of their favourite gigs. It's tacky and a bit run-down, but distinctly venerable; and with its high stage and sprung dance floor, perfect for rock 'n' roll. The Glas audience is one of 'the best in the world'. True!

FESTIVALS

THE WEST END FESTIVAL: 341 0844. 2 weeks in June. Neighbourhood and arts fest that incl parade in Byres Rd and a lot of drinking.

GLASGOW INTERNATIONAL JAZZ FESTIVAL: 552 3552. 1 week in July. Scotland's most credible jazz (in its widest sense) prog over diff venues.

GLASGOW ART FAIR: 552 6027. 4 days in Apr. (2150/WHERE TO BUY ART)

CELTIC CONNECTIONS: 353 8000. 3 weeks in Jan.

HOGMANAY: 552 6027. 31 December. Not on the same scale as Edin. Usually a stage in George Sq (ticketed) and smaller ones in Merchant City (free).

JAZZ MUSIC

BABY GRAND: 248 4942. 3-7 Elmbank Gardens.

BLACKFRIARS: 552 5924. 36 Bell St.

CORINTHIAN: 552 1101. 191 Ingram St.

FOLK MUSIC

799
D4 ✓ **SCOTIA BAR:** 552 8681. 112 Stockwell St. The folk club and writers' retreat and all things non-high cultural. Always the 'right folk' here. (681/UNIQUE GLAS PUBS)

800
D4 ✓ **VICTORIA BAR:** Briggait. Nr the Scotia (*see above*) and a similar set-up. Fri and Sat night sessions of Irish/Scottish trad music. (680/UNIQUE GLAS PUBS)

801
B2 ✓ **THE HALT BAR:** 564 1527. Woodlands Rd. Among a mixed music programme, always some folk for the kind of folk who inhabit the bar. (679/UNIQUE GLAS PUBS)

802
D4 ✓ **CLUTHA VAULTS:** 552 7520. 167 Stockwell St. E end nr Clyde. Gr atmos for the drink and the music. Mixed programme: readings, bluegrass, open mic slot. (682/UNIQUE GLAS PUBS)

ISLAY INN: 334 1055. Argyle St.

CEILIDHS

803
C4 ✓ **THE RENFREW FERRY:** Enter by Clyde Pl via Jamaica St Br from N of river or Br St. A real ferry moored on the Clyde – brilliant ambience for ceilidhs and gigs of all kinds. Usually once a month but check *The List* or *Evening Times*. Tickets at quay or in advance from Ticket Centre, Candleriggs (227 5511), they sell out fast. Visitors and locals. Gr bands.

804
D4 **THE RIVERSIDE:** 248 3144. Fox St, off Clyde St. The place that started the ceilidh revival in Glas. Upstairs in quiet st, the joint is jumping. Fri-Sat from 8pm, fills up quickly. Good bands. Good, mixed crowd.

LIVE ROCK & POP AND BEST CLUBS

805
A3 **SECC:** 248 3000. 0870 040 4000. Finnieston Quay beyond the city centre and, for many, beyond the pale as far as concerts are concerned (big shed, not big on atmos), but there are 3 different-sized halls for mainly arena-sized acts and everyone from pop to Pav and U2 have played here (but not Madge).

806
A3 **CLYDE AUDITORIUM, aka THE ARMADILLO:** Adj to the SECC. A smaller theatre space, a belter for concerts, but not big enough for the megas.

BARROWLANDS BALLROOM: The dancehall! See Unique Venues, above.

807 **KING TUT'S WAH WAH HUT:** 221 5279. 272 St Vincent St. Every bit as good as
C3 its namesake in Alphabet City used to be; the room for interesting new bands,
make-or-break atmos and cramped. Bands on the club circuit play to a damp
and appreciative crowd. See flyers. Doors open 8.30pm. Tickets at bar or Tower
Records, Argyle St.

808 **NICE 'N' SLEAZY:** 333 9637. 421 Sauchiehall St at the W End. Not esp sleazy
C3 and fairly rock 'n' roll. Popular art school hang-out. Every flavour of alco-pop
and voddie to drink. Good indie jukebox and PlayStation for hire. Bands
downstairs (esp Thu-Sun) with a nominal entrance charge. Usually from 9pm.
All over before midnight.

809 **THE CATHOUSE:** 248 6606. 15 Union St, and **THE GARAGE:** 332 1120.
D4, C3 Sauchiehall St, W End (same owners). Live rock clubs with mixed programme
on various nights depending on availability of touring bands (other 'clubs' on
other nights). Recent broadening of musical taste so no longer necessary to
turn up with leather strides and pointy boots. Tickets in advance from Tower
Records, Argyle St.

810 **THE 13TH NOTE:** 553 1638. CAFE 60 King St and CLUB, Clyde St (243 2177).
E4 The vegn restau in King St (632/VEGN RESTAUS) and the gig thing down nr the
river. Various combos of the indie or merely hip in both. These are the ones to
watch. Most nights 8pm-midnight. Clubs on 4 times a week till 3am. Tue-Sun
8pm-3.30am.

811 **COTTIER'S:** 357 5825. 93 Hyndland St. In the densely populated quadrant
xA1 betw Dumbarton Rd and Byres Rd. A neighbourhood atmos to this converted
church (not in, but off the top of Hyndland St nr Highburgh Rd); it has the
same management as the Baby Grand (553/BEST BISTROS) and Cathedral
House (496/INDIVIDUAL HOTELS). Restau upstairs (559/BEST BISTROS). Bar and theatre, on the ground level, serve as a platform for local talent and cult-ish acts
from abroad. Regularly features special gigs with 3 or more bands on the bill
and, occasionally, entire, musically-themed, w/ends. Expect good program-
ming.

BLACKFRIARS, THE HALT, SCOTIA BAR, THE CLUTHA VAULTS: See above in
Folk. All have varied programme of live music incl 'open mic' spots. Free.

812 **GLASGOW ROYAL CONCERT HALL:** 287 5511 2 Sauchiehall St. Full prog of
D3 mainly classical music but also a civilised theatre for more thoughtful pop.

CLUBBING IT

813 **CLUBS AT THE ARCHES:** 0907 022 0300. At the Arches Theatre, Argyle St (see
D4 above), w/ends only. Glasgow's finest. 2/3 vaulted archways, serious sound
system and v up-for-it crowd. Best clubs: Colours, Inside Out, Slam one-offs.
Monthly Sunday Social, all-day chill out.

814 **THE TUNNEL:** 204 1000. 84 Mitchell St. Once defined club culture in Glas. Still
D4 high-glam quotient and designer ambience with vogue-ish crowd. W/ends
(Ark and Triumph) and student nights. On same circuit as Liverpool's Cream so
big-name DJs every month.

815 **TRASH:** 572 3372. 197 Pitt St. Mega disco thing in city centre. Student-ish
C3 crowd so not teensy. Clubs vary, till 3am.

816 **ARCHAOS:** 204 3189. 25 Queen St. Dance emporium on 3 floors, incl Betty's
D4 Mayonnaise. Central dance floor has state-of-the-art lighting. Balconies upstairs
for action-checking and chilling. Atmos more rarified the higher you go.

817 **YANG:** 248 8484. 33 Queen St. Same crowd as Archaos *above*, but newer and
D4 fresher. Different clubs/DJs each night but open all week from 6pm.

818 **ALASKA:** 248 1777. 142 Bath Lane. Lane behind Bath St (behind the Spy Bar –
C3 same management). Laid-back bar area, hard-hitting dance floor. Cool as in …
1999.

819 **MAS:** 221 7080. 23 Royal Exchange Sq. Colin Barr's drinking and dancin' club
D4 upstairs opp Gallery of Modern Art. Hot local & often interesting imported
DJs. Check this. Best clubs: Subculture & Optimo. Wed-Mon 11pm-3am.

SECTION 4

Regional Hotels and Restaurants

THE BEST HOTELS AND RESTAURANTS IN ARGYLL

See also 2250/BEST OF OBAN. *Refer to Map 1.*

820
B1
✓ ✓ **AIRDS HOTEL, PORT APPIN:** 01631 730236. 32km N of Oban 4km off A828. A gourmet experience and all round welcome from the Allens awaits you here in this refined hotel in a charming corner of Scotland. Member of cosmopolitan *Relais et Châteaux* group (and in all the other guide-books that count). Many ingredients come from v nearby incl a lovingly tend-ed kitchen gdn; Graeme Allen is a consummate chef. Nice short walk behind the house. The family guesthouse up the rd is a cheaper stopover. Lismore passenger ferry 2km away (2202/MAGIC ISLANDS).

12RMS (+4) FEB-DEC T/T XPETS CC KIDS LOTS/MED.EX

EAT One of the best meals you will find in the N (and S, E and W). EXP

821
B1
✓ **TAYCHREGGAN, KILCHRENAN:** 01866 833211. Signed off A85 just before Taynuilt, 30km from Oban and nestling on a bluff by L Awe in imposing countryside. Quay for the old ferry to Portsonachan is nearby with boats available. Loch side inn which just gets better with a restau where even locals come the long and winding (and enchanting) rd to eat. Pleasant rms and bar. That awesome loch is always there outside for pre- and post-prandi-al strolls (midges may come too). Some new rooms 2002. Gr pub 1 km walk away (1271/PUBS). 19RMS JAN-DEC T/T PETS CC KIDS TOS LOTS

EAT Jerome Prodanu's nicely judged menu is French and interesting. EXP

822
C2
✓ **ROYAL HOTEL, TIGHNABRUAICH:** 01700 811239. Roger and Bea McKie took this over in 1997 and have transformed it totally. Nice food (Roger), professional front of house (Bea), art on the walls that you'll like, rms looking over to Bute, good whisky list … and they sponsor the local shinty team! Good people with good taste. 11RMS JAN-DEC T/T PETS CC XKIDS TOS MED.EX

823
C2
✓ **GEORGE HOTEL, INVERARAY:** 01499 302111. Main st of interesting town on L Fyne with credible attractions (2256/HOLIDAY CENTRES). Ancient inn (1770) with real atmosphere in bar. Rms recently refurb & tastefully so in a Highland chic kind of way. Open fire, gr grub & locals in the bar. This hotel is exceptionally good value. 12RMS JAN-DEC X/T PETS CC KIDS MED.INX

824
B2
KILFINAN HOTEL, KILFINAN: 01700 821201. 13km from Tighnabruaich on B8000. A much-loved hotel with some changes since last we visited. Classic quiet getaway inn (quiet as the graveyard adj) with long-standing rep for food in bar and dining rm. We haven't eaten recently (reports please) but for a MED.EX retreat on a quiet peninsula, still a good bet.

11RMS JAN-DEC T/T PETS CC KIDS MED.EX

825
C2
LOCH FYNE HOTEL, INVERARAY: 01499 302148. Another surprisingly fine hotel in this charming town. On main A83 towards Lochgilphead o/looking loch. Part of British Trust Hotels; this one of their best. Pleasing & simple design makeover with mere touch of tartan. Pool & facs.

68RMS JAN-DEC T/T PETS CC KIDS MED.INX

826
B2
STONEFIELD CASTLE HOTEL, TARBERT (ARGYLL): 01880 820836. Just o/side town on the A83, a castle which evokes the 1970s more than preced-ing centuries. Splendid gdns leading down to L Fyne. The surrounding luxuri-ant gdns are fabulous. Dining-rm with baronial splendour and staggering views. Friendly, flexible staff; overall, it seems quintessentially Scottish and ok, esp for families (1158/KIDS) though style people may moan. They prefer that you have dinner too. (MED). 33RMS JAN-DEC T/T PETS CC KIDS TOS MED.EX

827
C2
ARDENTINNY HOTEL, ARDENTINNY, nr DUNOON: 01369 810209. 20km N via A880/A885. Trad, Clydeside inn by Glen Finart forest adj L Long. Beer gdn on cove with moorings. Long est good rep but new ownership 2001. Refurb still in progress. We'd still stop for a beer, and are keen to hear what the hotel's like – reports please. You can still get there on the yellow water taxi though (L Goil Cruisers 01301 703349).

9RMS JAN-DEC X/T PETS XCC KIDS INX

828 **WEST LOCH HOTEL, TARBERT (ARGYLL):** 01880 820283. Picturesque 1710
C2 former coaching inn on the cusp of Kintyre, just o/side of Tarbert on A83.
Within easy reach of ferries to Islay, Gigha and Arran. Lovely views of loch over
rd, nice staff, relaxed atmos, coaching inn character remains. Good food, relaxing though roadside rms may be noisy. Feel at home here (1189/INNS).

9RMS JAN-DEC X/T PETS CC KIDS MED.INX

829 **COLUMBA HOTEL, TARBERT:** 01880 820808. Ideal budget hotel on water
B2 front in this perfect Argyll town. 'Net Store' bar v popular with yachties and
locals. They closed the 'gym' but now one of the rooms has an en suite sauna!

10RMS JAN-DEC T/T PETS CC KIDS TOS MED.INX

830 **BARRIEMORE, OBAN:** 01631 566356. Corran Esplanade. This hotel, the v last
B1 one in a st full of them along the coast to Ganavan, is a good bet if you're in
Oban. Front rms have excellent views of Kerrera and Lorne. B&B only.

13RMS MAR-OCT X/T PETS CC KIDS INX

ARDANAISEIG, LOCH AWE: 01866 833333 (1147/COUNTRY-HOUSE HOTELS).
ISLE OF ERISKA: 01631 720371. 20km N of Oban (1139/COUNTRY-HOUSE HOTELS).
LOCH MELFORT: 01852 200233. 22km S of Oban (1146/COUNTRY-HOUSE
HOTELS).
ARDSHEAL HOUSE: 01631 740227. 45km N of Oban (1143/COUNTRY-HOUSE
HOTELS).

RESTAURANTS

831 ✓ **CHATTERS, DUNOON:** 01369 706402. 58 John St next to Safeway. Rosie
C2 Macinnes' excellent restau in town rather than on esplanade is, by itself,
a good reason for getting the ferry. The Cowal peninsula awaits your explorations (and Benmore Gdns 1376/GARDENS). Bar menu and à la carte, and a
small gdn for drinks or lunch on a good day. All delightful. Wed-Sat only, lunch
and dinner.

MED

832 **CREGGANS INN, STRACHUR:** 01369 860279. 2km N Strachur on A815 to
C2 Cairndow, a busy rd in summer along L Fyne. Road house bar/restau and more
formal dining-rm in a place once notable as the fiefdom of Sir Fitzroy & Lady
Maclean, but now under new ownership. 14 rms upstairs with some fine views
of loch. Reports please on food.

CHP/MED/EXP

THE BEST HOTELS AND RESTAURANTS IN AYRSHIRE & CLYDE VALLEY

See also 2244/AYR. Refer to Map 1.

833 ✓✓ **TURNBERRY HOTEL, TURNBERRY:** 01655 331000. Not just a hotel
C4 on the Ayrshire coast, more a way of life centred on golf. Looks over
the 2 courses which are difficult to get on unless you're a guest (1941/GREAT
GOLF). All that should be expected of a world-class hotel except, perhaps, the
buzz; but plenty of golf chat and time moving slowly. The spa complex adj has
state-of-the-art 'treatments', even exercise. Get purified and detoxed at the
spa for a mere £115 – but it buys you two-and-a-half hours! Brasserie here has
excl 'light' all day menus; main dining-rm looks over the courses to Ailsa Craig
beyond – dinner only, and epic Sun lunch.

221RMS JAN-DEC T/T PETS CC KIDS TOS LOTS

EAT The Terrace Brasserie is the light place to eat; pastas, risottos, etc. Main
restau has 2 AA rosettes.

MED/EXP

834 ✓✓ **GLENAPP CASTLE, by BALLANTRAE:** 01465 831212. New upmar-
C4 ket jewel in the crown for S Ayrshire (full report: 1142/SUPERLATIVE
COUNTRY HOUSE HOTELS).

835 ✓ **CULZEAN CASTLE, nr MAYBOLE:** 01655 760615. 18km S of Ayr (coast rd
C4 most pleasant), this is accom in the suites of Culzean, the house itself
(1695/CASTLES) so a bed for the night rarely comes as posh as this (includes
the famous Eisenhower suite). Rates are exp, but incl afternoon tea. Dinner
(incl wine) is avail at additional £45pp. The cliff-top setting, the gdns & the vast

grounds are superb. 10.30am check-out seems a bit peremptory.

6 SUITES APR-OCT T/T XPETS CC KIDS TOS LOTS

836 ✓ **GLEDDOCH HOUSE, LANGBANK, nr GREENOCK:** 01475 540711. 35km
C2 from Glas by fast rd – M8/A8 t/off marked Langbank/Houston after jnct
31, follow signs. Set in extensive grounds (including 18-hole golf course), with
commanding view of Clyde by Dumbarton Rock (but only from a few rms).
Small leisure club adj. Excellent conservatory and dining-rms. Most civilised
place to stay close to Glas.   38RMS JAN-DEC T/T PETS CC KIDS TOS MED.EX

EAT Excellent restau with 2 AA rosettes. Scottish accents.   EXP

837 ✓ **THE IVY HOUSE, AYR:** 01292 442336. North Park on the Alloway Rd,
C3 almost feels like the country. Cosy, well-appointed rms with bathrms bor-
dering on the lavish. Seriously good restau.

5RMS JAN-DEC T/T PETS CC KIDS MED.EX

EAT One of the best meals in Ayrshire, tho at a price.   EXP

838 **ENTERKINE HOUSE, nr ANNBANK, by AYR:** 01292 521608. Opened in
C3 autumn 2000 with v self-consciously upmarket style (initially they wouldn't
let our man in because no shirt & tie). Chef Douglas Smith v good indeed
Whether you like the ambience or not, go eat. But don't wear combat trousers.

6RMS JAN-DEC T/T XPETS CC XKIDS LOTS

839 **MONTGREENAN, nr KILWINNING:** 01294 557733. Take A736 (5km) from the
C3 A78 around Irvine and several r/bouts later you arrive in a surprisingly woody
enclave and a civilised country-house hotel (phone for directions). Woody
and friendly inside too, and run by the estimable Leckies. Interior was looking
fresher on last visit. Restau open non res.

21RMS JAN-DEC T/T PETS CC KIDS TOS LOTS

840 **PIERSLAND HOTEL, TROON:** 01292 314747. Craig End Rd opp Portland Golf
C3 Course which is next to Royal Troon (1942/GREAT GOLF). Mansion house of
some character and ambience much favoured for weddings. Wood-panelling,
open fires, lovely gdns only a 'drive' away from the courses (no preferential
booking on Royal, but Portland usually poss) and lots of gr golf nearby. 2 AA
rosettes for the food.   28RMS JAN-DEC T/T PETS CC KIDS TOS EXP

841 **LOCHGREEN HOUSE, TROON:** 01292 313343. Part of the Costley and Costley
C3 empire in this neck of the woods, Lochgreen (adj to Royal Troon Golf Course)
the most full-on upmarket. The **BRIG O' DOON** at Alloway is the romance-
and-Rabbie Burns hotel (01292 442466), lots of weddings and only 5 rms,
while **HIGHGROVE** (01292 312511) is that bit more intimate, just outside
Troon. All operate at a very acceptable standard – Highgrove has 2 AA
rosettes, Lochgreen has 3. These Costleys also have a good roadside inn – the
COCHRANE at Gatehead, nearby.

842 **SHIELDHILL CASTLE, QUOTHQUAN, nr BIGGAR:** 01899 220035. Well S of the
D3 Clyde, Glasgow & anywhere, a countryside retreat just off the B7016 Biggar-
Carnwath. Mostly dates from late 16thC but older bits go back to 1199.
Famous guests include a certain Mr Mandela. Pick yr rm carefully and you get
a 4-poster and a jacuzzi. 2 AA rosettes for the food.

16RMS JAN-DEC T/T PETS CC KIDS TOS EXP/LOTS

843 **WILDING'S HOTEL & RESTAURANT, MAIDENS:** 01655 331401. Maidens is
C4 coastal vill in S Ayrshire, S of Maybole & lovely Culzean (1695/CASTLES), so a
good base. Run by Brian Sage restaurateur, whose Wilding's used to be in
Girvan, this is perhaps more a restau with rms. Many o/look serene harbour.
Overall a wee gem.   10RMS JAN-DEC T/T PETS CC KIDS MED.INX

EAT May be a drive for dinner, but a beautiful spot & excl menu. Food LO 9pm.

MED

RESTAURANTS

844 ✓ **FOUTERS, AYR:** 01292 261391. 2a Academy St. Off Sandgate. The best
C3 meal in town. Laurie and Fran Black, amazingly how many years on? Still
caring about food and wine and Scotland's efforts to do better. Creative cooking and here the phrase 'best local ingredients' means what it says. Tues-Sat:
lunch and LO 10.30pm. Sun: dinner only.   MED

845 ✔ **BRAIDWOODS, nr DALRY:** 01294 833544. First find Dalry; near the Esso
C3 garage take the small rd to Saltcoats and the restau is discreetly signed
around a mile out that rd. Once you find Keith and Nicola's place, you'll be glad
you made the effort. Michelin star, TOS awards, nice people, great food. Best
meal in the shire. Wed/Sun lunch and Tues-Sat dinner.   MED

846 ✔ **RISTORANTE LA VIGNA, LANARK:** 01555 664320. 40 Wellgate. Famously
D3 good Italian restau in a back st in Lanark. Unexpected, and quite a find if
you're lost in the badlands. Lunch Mon-Sat, dinner 7 days.   MED

847 **THE WHEATSHEAF, SYMINGTON, nr AYR & PRESTWICK:** 01563 830307. Off
C3 main A77 (2km), just N of main Prestwick r/about. Roadside & village inn
tucked away off main rd with big local rep for wholesome pub grub. No fuss,
gr service. Report 1291/PUB FOOD.

848 **PAPILLONS, GOUROCK:** 01475 633998. Main st above the trad Victoria pub;
C2 still not in the foodie guides but big local reputation. German owner. Lunch
Tues-Sun, dinner Tues-Sat.   INX

849 **FINS, FAIRLIE, nr LARGS:** 01475 568989. 8 km S of Largs on A78. Excellent
C3 seafood bistro. Report: 1338/SEAFOOD RESTAUS.   MED

850 **MACCALLUMS, THE HARBOUR, TROON:** 01292 319339. Harbourside
C3 seafood bistro. Report: 1330/SEAFOOD. If MacCallums is full, closer to town
you'll find **CELLARS** at 147 Templehill (01292 317448) next to the Anchorage
Hotel. Not eaten but friends tell us it's worth stopping.   MED/INX

851 **MALIN COURT, TURNBERRY:** 01655 331457. Just up the rd from that other
C4 Turnberry hotel, and a good eats alternative. TOS and a brace of AA rosettes
thanks to Andrea Beach's Franco–Scot menu. Looks a bit 'suburban bungalow'
from outside but don't let it put you off.   MED

852 **THE GATHERING, KILMARNOCK:** 01563 529022. 43 John Finnie St. Right by
C3 the station, handy and all things to all people: restau, bar, and DJs Thurs-Sat
late.   INX

THE BEST HOTELS AND RESTAURANTS IN THE SOUTH-WEST

See also 2245/BEST OF DUMFRIES. *Refer to Map 9.*

853
A3 ✓✓ **KNOCKINAAM LODGE, PORTPATRICK:** 01776 810471. Tucked away on dream cove, historic country house full of fresh flowers, gr food, sea air and informal, but v good service. Run by Canadians who know and love what they're doing. Their enjoyment is yours (1141/COUNTRY-HOUSE HOTELS). Up for sale in 2001 but we expect and hope they'll be around for a year or two yet.
10RMS JAN-DEC T/T PETS CC KIDS TOS LOTS

EAT Best meal in the S. from outstanding chef, Tony Pierce. Fixed menu – lots of unexpected treats. *Michelin* Star.
EXP

854
A3 ✓ **CORSEWALL LIGHTHOUSE HOTEL, STRANRAER:** 01776 853220. A718 to Kirkcolm 3km, B738 to Corsewall 6km (follow signs). Wild location on cliff top. Cosily furnished clever but cramped (or snug) conversion. Best with a suite and a close personal friend. The adj fully functioning lighthouse (since 1817) makes for surreal evenings. Better since new owner took over in 2000.
6RMS (+ SUITES) JAN-DEC T/T PETS CC KIDS EXP

855 **KIRROUGHTREE HOTEL, NEWTON STEWART:** 01671 402141. On A712. Built
B3 1719, Rabbie Burns was once here. Extensive country house newly refurb with heavy drapes and plush atmos. Original panelled hall and stairs, spacious rms. Food here gets 3 AA rosettes and is probably the main reason for coming. New man in kitchen – Ralph Mueller, formerly at the Kilfinan on Cowal consolidating rep for food.
17RMS FEB-DEC T/T PETS CC KIDS TOS LOTS

856 **BALCARY BAY, AUCHENCAIRN, nr CASTLE DOUGLAS:** 01556 640311. 20km
C3 S of Castle Douglas and Dalbeattie. Off A711 at end of shore rd. Watch fishermen casting their nets in the hazy bay. Ideal base for walking and birdwatching. Refurbed over winter 2000/1, good man in the kitchen (Charles Kelly) and a pebble beach from which you watch the stars appear after dinner.
20RMS MAR-NOV T/T PETS CC KIDS TOS EXP

857 **CLONYARD HOUSE, COLVEND, nr ROCKCLIFFE, nr DALBEATTIE:** 01556
C3 630372. On Solway Coast rd nr Rockcliffe and Kippford (1514/COASTAL VILLAGES; 1935/ COASTAL WALKS) but not on sea. Later extension to house provides bedrms adj to patio gdn with own private access and ... aviary! Friendly family, decent pub grub, but sad to report that the parrot flew away (not a euphemism – it actually did escape!) 15RMS JAN-DEC T/T PETS CC KIDS MED.INX

858 **CORSEMALZIE HOUSE, nr WIGTOWN:** 01988 860254. Find Wigtown (S of
B3 Newton Stewart) then take the B7005 towards Luce Bay, heading W. The hotel is around halfway along. Trad granite pile with comfortable rms and beautiful bluebell woods. Fishin' and shootin' for those who want it.
14RMS MAR-JAN T/T XPETS CC KIDS MED.EXP

859 **COMLONGON CASTLE, CLARENCEFIELD, nr DUMFRIES:** 013878 70283.
D3 14km SE of Dumfries. Early 20th-century house with 15th-century castle that has been in the Ptolomey family since 1984. More investment since younger gen took over. Aims for the full-on McCastle experience so attracts loads of wedding business from N of England. Fab 4-posters and philosophical bedspreads ('Cogito ergo sum'). Nice gdns. Heraldic/film set atmos. Good for B&B if you catch it between weddings!
12RMS FEB-DEC T/T XPETS CC KIDS MED.EX

860 **GOOD SPOTS IN KIRKCUDBRIGHT:** pronounced 'cur-coo-bree'; a gem of a
C3 town. On a street filled with posh B&Bs the **GLADSTONE HOUSE** stands out (High St 01557 331734) while the cheaper option is **GORDON HOUSE** (also High St, round corner, 01557 330670) which boasts an Italian restau. **SELKIRK ARMS** (yup, High St, 01557 330402) is much more your 'proper hotel' and with 2 AA rosettes, the best food in town.

861 **ANCHOR, KIPPFORD:** 01556 620205. Seaside hotel in cute vill 3km off main
C3 A710. Good pub food and atmos (*see below*).
7RMS (+ COTT) JAN-DEC X/T PETS CC KIDS INX

862 **ABBEY ARMS & CRIFFEL INN, NEW ABBEY, nr DUMFRIES:** 01387
C3 850489/850244. Opp each other on village sq, comfy rms above village inns with loads of atmos nr Sweetheart Abbey and Criffel (1869/HILLS) 12km S of Dumfries. CHP

RESTAURANTS

863 ✓ **THE PLUMED HORSE, CROSSMICHAEL, nr CASTLE DOUGLAS:** 01556
C3 670333. Just N of Castle Douglas on A713. Amazing find in unexpected surroundings – serious food by chef Tony Borthwick. After only 3 yrs firmly est on foodie map of Scotland. Michelin star & other food guides routinely praise it to the skies. Expect first-class ingredients and real flair. Lunch Tues-Fri and Sun, dinner Tues-Sat. MED.EXP

864 **THE CROWN, PORTPATRICK:** 01776 810216. Harbourside hotel/pub restau
A3 with better than your av pub-grub. Goes like a fair in summer. Lounge and conservatory. Most excl chips. 7 days. LO 10pm. Now has competition next door from the **WATERFRONT**. Crown is the better pub, newcomer has more mod rms. INX

865 **CAMPBELLS, PORTPATRICK:** 01776 810314. Further round harbour from
A3 Crown, above. More upmarket but medium range seafood bistro. Unpretentious fishy fare (some pork/lamb/beef/duck/chicken dishes ie something for everyone). 7 days lunch and LO 10pm. Cl Mon and Jan – Mar. INX

866 **ANCHOR, KIPPFORD:** 01556 620205. Waterfront hotel/bar on the 'Scottish
C3 Riviera'. Gr atmos in snug lounges and gr for family meals. 7rms above (so also rec as an inx hotel, above). 7 days, lunch and dinner. CHP

867 **THE SELKIRK ARMS, KIRKCUDBRIGHT:** 01557 330402. At east end of High st.
C3 Small country hotel with surprisingly good cuisine. Conservatory dining rm and less formal bistro. Lunch and dinner 7-9.30pm (bistro from 6pm). 7 days. INX/MED

868 **THE AULD ALLIANCE, KIRKCUDBRIGHT:** 01557 330569. Solway scallops and
C3 salmon, etc. 7 nights. Franco-Scottish flavour. Open Easter-Oct for dinner only (and Sun lunch) but the quieter it gets, the less they open so call and book. MED

869 **CARLO'S, CASTLE DOUGLAS:** 211 King Street, 01556 503977. Bustling atmos
C3 in small rm with odd green phone box. Best Italian food in S. Open Tues-Sun from 6.30pm – until 9.30 in winter, until you stop eating in summer. INX

870 **HULLABALOO, DUMFRIES:** 01387 259679. At the Robert Burns Centre, W side
00 of the river. Wraps, steaks, burgers etc done in the mod style; contemporary look and well run. Macy Gray on the speakers as you gaze on the Nith. Summer daily 11am-9/10pm (sometimes later), winter Tues-Sat only. INX

THE BEST HOTELS AND RESTAURANTS IN CENTRAL SCOTLAND

See also 2252/BEST OF STIRLING. *Refer to Map 6.*

871
C2
✔ ✔ **CROMLIX HOUSE, DUNBLANE:** 01786 822125. 3km from A9 and 4km from town on B8033; first follow signs for Perth, and then Kinbuck. A long drive through an old estate with splendid mature trees to this spacious country mansion both sumptuous and comfortable (fabulous bathrooms). Ailsa and David Assenti have a firm but not formal touch with gr attention to detail & service. No leisure facs – this is a place for rest & respite. Walk the 3000 sylvan acres & fishing lochs (the House Loch nearby comes complete with swans and solitude), Paul Devonshire's 2 AA rosette menu.

14RMS (8 SUITES) FEB-DEC T/T PETS CC KIDS TOS LOTS

EAT Non-residents: drive that drive for dinner (or Sun lunch)! Gr conservatory.

EXP

872
C2
✔ ✔ **THE ROMAN CAMP, CALLANDER:** 01877 330003. Behind the main st (at E or Stirling end), away from the tourist throng and with extensive gdns on the R Teith; another, more elegant world. Roman ruins nearby, but the house was built for the Dukes of Perth and has been a hotel since the war. Rms low-ceilinged and snug; period furnishings; some rms small, many magnificent. 10 new rms to be added 2002. In the old building corridors do creak. Delightful drawing rm and conservatory. Oval dining-rm v sympatico. Private chapel should a prayer come on and, of course, many weddings. Rods for fishing – the river swishes past the lawn.

14RMS (+10) JAN-DEC T/T PETS CC KIDS TOS LOTS

EAT Dining-rm effortlessly the best food in town (with chef Ian McNaught).

EXP

873
00
✔ **BOUZY ROUGE at the SHERIFFMUIR INN, SHERIFFMUIR nr DUNBLANE:** 01786 823285. On old rd across the moor (app from A9 or via Dunblane or Bridge of Allan). Old coaching inn at crossroads transformed by Bouzy Rouge of Edin/Glas fame (555/GLAS BISTROS) into contemp restau with rms. Now the smartest stopover in the area & v much worth the short detour into the back of beyond. Gr swimming spot nearby (1629/SWIMMING HOLES).

4RMS JAN-DEC T/T PETS CC KIDS MED.INX

874
C3
STIRLING HIGHLAND, STIRLING: 01786 475444. Reasonably sympathetic conversion of former school (with modern accom block) in the historic section of town on rd up to castle. Serviceable businessy hotel in prime location; light 17m pool. 'Sophisticated' Scholars restau up top (2 AA rosettes); the Italian bistro, Rizzios at st level, is not so *al dente*, but pleasant enough.

78RMS JAN-DEC T/T PETS CC KIDS MED.EX/EXP

875
B3
LAKE HOTEL, PORT OF MENTEITH: 01877 385258. A v lake side hotel on the Lake of Menteith in the purple heart of the Trossachs. Good centre for touring and walking. The Inchmahome ferry leaves from nearby (1831/MARY, CHARLIE AND BOB). 5 rms o/look lake (and are more exp, but worth the extra). Splendid conservatory for sunset supper. Clean air and/or dirty w/end.

16RMS JAN-DEC T/T PETS CC KIDS TOS MED.EX

876
C2
HILTON DUNBLANE HYDRO, DUNBLANE: 01786 822551. One of the huge hydro hotels left over from the last health boom, many bought & now tarted up by Hilton. Nice views for some and a long walk down corridors for most. Exercise in Living Well gym and the pool. It's a dinner-dance and wedded world.

210RMS JAN-DEC T/T PETS KIDS CC TOS EXP

877
A2
INVERARNAN HOTEL/THE DROVER'S INN, INVERARNAN: 01301 704234. N of Ardlui on L Lomond and 12km S of Crianlarich on the A82. Much the same as it was when it began in 1705; bare floors, open fires, shared facs and heavy drinking (1265/BLOODY GOOD PUBS). Highland hoolies here much recommended. Bar staff wearing kilts look like they mean it. Rms are not Gleneagles. A wild place in the wilderness. They also now own the Stagger Inn across the road (704274). 16 en suite rooms & restau. 10RMS JAN-DEC X/X PETS CC KIDS CHP

878 **HOTELS IN KILLIN:** Killin is a v Highland sort of a place, famous for the Falls of
B1   Dochart, the rocky course of the river that runs through the town. Mighty Ben
Lawers is nearby and it is a good gateway for pts N and W. There are 2 good
inexp hotels. **THE KILLIN HOTEL:** 01567 820296. V Scottish, tartan everywhere, old-fashioned feel; conservatory on front. **DALL LODGE:** 01567
820217. Smaller, more personal, many *objets* and 4 Tourist Board whatsits
(Killin only 2). Both hotels on main st.

32/10RMS JAN-DEC T/T PETS CC KIDS MED.INX

879 **GEAN HOUSE, ALLOA:** 01259 720101. Former hotel now part of Inglewood
D3   Conference Centre but the Edwardian mansion designed by Lutyens is stunning and rms may be available depending on their calendar. Stylish comfort,
terraced gdns. Phone for details.

RESTAURANTS

880 ✓ **BLACK BULL, KILLEARN:** 01360 550215. Good-looking village, 30mins N
B3   of Glasgow betw L Lomond (Drymen) and the Campsies. Excellent pub
food and conservatory restau. New owners & contemp makeover 2001 bodes
well for this always highly regarded inn close to heart & hinterland of Glas. Not
visited at TGP but we know this team & they know what we want. See
519/HOTELS OUTSIDE TOWN. In Killearn for a run, check also **THE OLD MILL**
(1302/PUB FOOD).

MED

881 ✓ **CREAGAN HOUSE, STRATHYRE:** 01877 384638. End of the village on
B2   main A84 for Crianlarich. Creagan House is the place to eat in Rob Roy
country and there are some wonderful walks pre and *après* (1866/HILLS). They
have 5 inexp rms and the Gunns (incl the v large red setter) are an extremely
congenial bunch. Gordon Gunn is also an innovative and individualist chef (2
AA rosettes) and ingredients do come local, incl the gdn. You eat in a pleasant
baronial dining-rm & can pat the dog after dinner. Cl Feb.

MED

882 ✓ **CROSS KEYS HOTEL AND BAR, KIPPEN:** 01786 870293. Main st of
C3   couthie town 15km W of Stirling by A811. Award-winning pubfood in
bars and restau setting (same menu). Gr for families and generally for informal
unpretentious approach and atmos. A wee treasure. (1293/PUB FOOD). LO
9.00pm.

INX

883 ✓ **THE ALLAN WATER CAFÉ, BRIDGE OF ALLAN:** Caff that's been here for
C3   ever at the end of the main st in Bridge of Allan. Original features, gr feel,
gr fish 'n' chips and, of course, the ice cream (1366/CAFÉS). 7 days, 9am-9pm.

CHP

885 ✓ **BOUZY ROUGE at the SHERIFFMUIR INN, SHERIFFMUIR nr DUN-**
C3   **BLANE:** 01786 823285. Old Sheriffmuir rd behind Dunblane (& Br of
Allan). Trad coaching inn given Bouzy Rouge treatment (see above). 'Casual
gourmet dining' in bar & surprisingly large restau. LO 9/10 pm. Book w/ends.

4RMS JAN-DEC T/T PETS CC KIDS MED.INX

886 **GLENSKIRLIE HOUSE, BANKNOCK:** 01324 840207. On A803 Kilsyth-
D2   Bonnybridge road, not far (15 mins) Stirling or Falkirk. Mansion house serving
bar lunches and serious dining. We haven't eaten but big local rep. Reports
please. 7 days lunch & dinner (not Mon lunch). CHP/EXP

THE BEST HOTELS AND RESTAURANTS IN THE BORDERS

See also 2248/BEST OF THE BORDER TOWNS, p. 313. Refer to Map 8.

887 ✓✓ **ROXBURGHE HOTEL, nr KELSO:** 01573 450331. The best country-
C2 house hotel in the Borders. Owned by the Duke and Duchess of
Roxburghe, who have a personal input. Rms distinctive, all light with green
views. Reliable wine list (by the Duke) and menu (safe and satisfying). The 18-
hole golf course has broadened appeal – it's challenging and championship
standard and in a beautiful riverside setting. Non-res can play (1960/GOLF).
Compared with other country-house hotels, the Roxburghe is good value.
Personal, not overbearing service. And last summer a black crow flew down
the chimney and into my room (twice!) – how natural, or supernatural, is that?
22RMS JAN-DEC T/T PETS CC KIDS TOS EXP

EAT Where to go for fine dining and wining in the E Borders. Chef Keith Short.
Also Fairways Brasserie o/looking golf course open w/ends. EXP

888 ✓✓ **CRINGLETIE HOUSE, PEEBLES:** 01721 730233. Country house 5km
B2 from town just off A703 Edin rd (35km). Late 19th-century Scottish
baronial house in 28 acres owned by Wren Group who have Auchterarder
House (1144/CO HOUSE HOTS). Comfortable & civilised. Conservatory does light
lunches and nice aft tea. Walled gdn provides all fruit and veg. Tennis and
putting green. 14RMS JAN-DEC T/T PETS CC KIDS TOS LOTS

EAT Gracious dining (o/looking) conservatory & gdn. Friendly escape. EXP

889 ✓ **BURTS, MELROSE:** 01896 822285. In Market Sq/main st, some (double-
C2 glazed) rms o/look. Busy bars, esp for food, The dining-rm is where to eat
in this part of the Borders. Trad, but comfortably modernised small town
hotel, though some rms also feel small. Convenient location. Good service
(1821/ABBEYS; 1880/HILL WALKS; 1481/GARDENS). Where to stay for the Sevens,
but try getting in! 20RMS JAN-DEC T/T PETS CC KIDS TOS MED.EX

EAT Jolly and busy bar; more refined dining-rm has 2 AA rosettes. EXP

890 ✓ **EDENWATER HOUSE, EDNAM, nr KELSO:** 01573 224070. Find Ednam on
C2 Kelso–Swinton rd B6461, 4 km. Discreet manse-type house beside old
kirk and o/look graveyard and tranquil green countryside. You have the run of
the home of Jeff & Jacqui Kelly & Jacqui's superb cooking. Good wines, good
life. Even a smoking rm. 4RMS JAN-DEC X/T XPETS CC KIDS MED.INX

891 ✓ **CHURCHES, EYEMOUTH:** 01890 750401. Albert Rd on corner of rd down
D1 to harbour surrounded by churches. Surprising boutique hotel in fishing
town that's seen some hard times. Modern Habitat decor with some flourish-
es. Stylish dining rm & conservatory & tables o/side in summer. Only a short
detour (5km) from A1. 6RMS JAN-DEC T/T PETS CC KIDS MED.INX–EXP

892 ✓ **LODGE at CARFRAEMILL, nr LAUDER:** 01578 750750. On A68 and can't
C2 miss it, 8km N of Lauder. Old coaching type lodging with recent refurb.
This sure beats a motel! Old-style Aga-type cooking, a good stop on the rd for
grub & a gateway to the Borders. Nice for kids.
10RMS JAN-DEC T/T PETS CC KIDS MED.INX–EXP

893 **DRYBURGH ABBEY HOTEL, nr ST BOSWELLS:** 01835 822261. Secluded, ele-
C3 gant 19th-century house in Abbey grounds banking R Tweed. Peaceful atmos;
good tho small swimming pool. Lovely riverside walks. Abbey pure romance
by moonlight. 38RMS JAN-DEC T/T PETS CC KIDS TOS EXP

894 **PHILIPBURN, SELKIRK:** 01750 720747. 1km from town centre on A707
B3 Peebles Rd. Excl hotel for families, walkers, weekend away from it all. Selkirk is
a good Borders base. Restaurant and bar-bistro and rare outdoor pool (with 2
gdn rms o/looking). Comfy rms & then, luxury rms.
17RMS JAN-DEC T/T PETS CC KIDS TOS EXP

895 **JEDFOREST COUNTRY HOTEL, nr JEDBURGH:** 01835 840222. On A68 about
C3 12km from the border at Carter Bar (the first hotel in Scotland!) and 5km from
Jedburgh, my home town. Refurb rms and notable restau (French chef, 2 AA
rosettes). You must walk down to that river Jed.
8RMS JAN-DEC T/T XPETS CC KIDS MED.INX

896   **EDNAM HOUSE, KELSO:** 01573 224168. Just off town sq, o/look R Tweed; a
C2   majestic Georgian mansion with v old original features incl some of the
guests! Dated in a comfy way, fishing regalia dotted around; the restau's river
view is , however, the main attraction.

32RMS JAN-DEC T/T PETS CC KIDS TOS MED.INX

897   **CLINT LODGE, ST BOSWELLS:** 01835 822027. Phone for directions. On B6356
C3   (1588/SCENIC ROUTES). Small country GH in gr border country with tranquil
views from rms. Good home cooking.   5RMS JAN-DEC X/T PETS XCC KIDS INX

898   **CADDON VIEW, INNERLEITHEN:** 01896 830208. Pirn Rd. Hotel in the doctor's
B2   house, comfy & tasteful rms. Excl restau dinner & b/fast from French chef/prop.
Many glowing recs from readers.   6RMS JAN-DEC X/T PETS CC KIDS MED.INX

899   **FAUHOPE, MELROSE:** 01896 823184. Borders house in sylvan setting o/look-
C2   ing Tweed. Only 3 rms but run by Sheila Robson who also has Marmions (see
below), so worth a stopover.   3RMS JAN-DEC T/X PETS CC KIDS INX

AND 6 SUPERB COUNTRY INNS

WHEATSHEAF, SWINTON: 01890 860257. (1291/PUBFOOD)

AULD CROSSKEYS INN, DENHOLM: 01450 870305. (1313/PUBFOOD)

HORSESHOE INN, EDDLESTON: 01721 730225. (1312/PUBFOOD)

TRAQUAIR ARMS, TRAQUAIR: 01896 830229. (1195/ROADSIDE INNS)

THE CRAW INN, AUCHENCROW: 01890 761253. (1194/ROADSIDE INNS)

CROSSKEYS INN, ETTRICKBRIDGE: 01750 52224. (1186/ROADSIDE INNS)

RESTAURANTS

EATING IN MELROSE (the Borders' best bet):

900   ✓   **MARMION'S:** 01896 822245. Buccleuch St nr the abbey. Local fave bistro,
C2   now going a long time, but on our last visit it was better food-wise than
ever. Lunch and dinner. Cl Sun.   INX

901   ✓   **KING'S ARMS:** 01896 822143. High St. Excl bar food in 17th cent coach-
C2   ing inn. The locals' choice. LO 9pm (9.30pm Sat).

902   ✓ **CHAPTERS, GATTONSIDE, nr MELROSE:** 01896 823217. Over the R
C2   Tweed (you could walk by footbridge as quick as going round by car).
Kevin & Nicki Winsland's surprising bistro – a bit of a find. Huge choice from à
la carte and specials. Tues–Sat dinner only.   MED

903   **THE HOEBRIDGE INN, GATTONSIDE, nr MELROSE:** 01896 823082. More old-
C2   style, but superior & imaginative pub fd with flair.   INX

   BURTS and **CRINGLETIE** (*see above*): Burts for best dining hereabouts,
Cringletie for country treat (Cringletie is nr Peebles).

   All the inns listed above for accomm also serve great food (some esp noted).

904   **SUNFLOWER RESTAURANT, PEEBLES:** 01721 722420. Bridgegate off Main
B2   St at Veitches corner. Long-standing spot for restau, but good again. Cafe
menu during day & nice for kids. Thu/Fri/Sat for dinner 7–9 pm. Cl Suns.   INX

905   **LAZEL'S, PEEBLES:** 01721 730233. Restaurant in the bowels of the Hydro
B2   (1157/FAMILY HOTELS), but real chef so good for lunch if passing thro' or Fri/Sat
dinner. Modern makeover & menu, but well below stairs.   INX/MED

906   **CASTLEGATE TEAROOMS and RESTAURANT, JEDBURGH:** 01835 862592.
C3   26 Castlegate nr Abbey. Home-made food incl puds in homely parlour. Not
licensed BYOB. Lunch and dinner 7 days.   INX

907   **CULTER MILL, nr BIGGAR:** 01899 220950. A respite from the frustration of
A2   crawling along in a convoy on the A702 (the main Edin – S route). Neatly converted mill – fuel for the rd. Bistro daily 12-8pm, restau 6.30-10pm. In Coulter,
just S of Biggar.   INX

THE BEST HOTELS AND RESTAURANTS IN THE LOTHIANS

See Section 2 for Edin. Refer to Map 7.

908
B1
✔✔ **GREYWALLS, GULLANE:** 01620 842144. On the coast, 36km E of Edin off A198 just beyond Gullane towards N Berwick. O/looks Muirfield, the championship course (no right of access) and nr Gullane's 3 courses and N Berwick's 2 (1945/1946/GREAT GOLF). No grey walls here but warm sandstone and light, summery public rms in this Lutyens-designed manor with gdns attributed to Gertrude Jekyll. It's the look that makes it special and the roses are legendary. Occasional literary lunches and sculpture gdns. Library like a London club, and service. Golf ain't everything but it helps. 22RMS APR-OCT T/T PETS CC XKIDS TOS LOTS

EAT Fine and subtle dining in elegant rm adj course; experienced chef Simon Burn is a confident player. Wine list has depth and character. EXP

909
A1
✔✔ **CHAMPANY INN nr LINLITHGOW:** 01506 834532. Excl restau with rms nr M9 jnct 3 (Edinburgh-Stirling), 30rms Edin city centre, 15 mins airport. Convenient high standard hotel adj nationally famous restau (94/EDIN RESTAUS) esp if you love your meat. Separate b/fast rm. Superlative wine-list, esp S. African vintages. 16RMS JAN-DEC T/T XPETS CC XKIDS LOTS

EAT As mentioned, the best meal in West Lothian. INX/EXP

910
B1
MARINE HOTEL, NORTH BERWICK: 01620 892406. The rather shabby old seaside hotel of N Berwick reeks of holidays gone by – you almost expect to see Margaret Rutherford on the putting green. Due for £8M refit by new owners so it should look nice after that. Snooker, open-air swimming pool. O/looks Links and Fidra. Good for kids and golf. 83RMS JAN-DEC T/T PETS CC KIDS EXP

911
B1
OPEN ARMS, DIRLETON: 01620 850241. Dirleton is 4km from Gullane towards N Berwick. Comfortable, pricey and rather precious hotel in centre of village, opp ruins of castle. Location means it's a golfers' haven and special packages are available. Restau has two AA whatsits.
10RMS JAN-DEC T/T PETS CC KIDS TOS LOTS

912
B1
THE OLD ABERLADY INN: 01875 870503. Main St. Straightforward drop inn with simple, well-kept rms, a good farmhouse-style bistro with interesting menu and a trad howf for drinks and bar food 6–9.30 pm. Popular with golfers – OK for anyone. 8RMS JAN-DEC T/T PETS CC KIDS MED.INX

913
B1
TWEEDDALE ARMS, GIFFORD: 01620 810240. One of two inns in this heart of E Lothian village 9km from the A1 at Haddington, within easy reach of Edin. Set among rich farming country, Gifford is conservative and couthy. Some bedrms small, but public rms pleasant if chintzy. Has been here forever so smells like a country inn should. 16RMS JAN-DEC T/T PETS CC KIDS MED.INX

RESTAURANTS

914
B1
✔ **THE WATERSIDE, HADDINGTON:** 01620 825674. 115 Waterside. On the river, opp side of the pedestrianised old br from St Mary's (1799/CHURCHES). Upstairs restau is more of a pink napkin affair, bistro/bar down has various rms. Separate vegn menu. This was the pioneer bistro in these parts, now owned by major brewery. Daily lunch/supper, LO 10pm. INX

915
B1
✔ **DROVER'S INN, EAST LINTON:** 01620 860298. Bridge St, middle of neat vill just off A1. Pub with good atmos; bistro downstairs and more elaborate dining up. Beer gdn out back. Lunch and dinner all areas, LO 9.30pm Pub till 11pm. Courtesy buses so … Don't drink and drove now! INX/MED

916
A2
THE OLD BAKEHOUSE, WEST LINTON: 01968 660830. Jens and Anita Steffen – no strangers to this book – opened this place early in 2000. Just a place that feels really cared for. Everything made on the premises, and a nice line in smorrebrod too. Lunch and dinner, Wed-Sun. MED

917
B1
MUSEUM OF FLIGHT CAFE, nr HADDINGTON: 01620 880838. Café in Nissan Hut run by home-cooking locals. Scones, sandwiches and soup and excl bacon sarnies to keep you going on your sortie. AYR 10.30–5.00. ☕ INX

918 **POLDRATE'S, HADDINGTON:** 01620 826882. On B6369 out of Haddington to
B1 Lennoxlove and Gifford. Converted mill; bistro atmos, under recent change of
ownership so service and menu upgraded. Tues-Sun lunch and dinner (not
Sun/Mon) LO 9.00pm.   INX-MED

919 **CREEL, DUNBAR:** 01368 863279. Nr harbour of this seaside town, cosy pan-
B1 elled captain's cabin serving original unstuffy menu in old smuggler's howff.
Emphasis on locally caught fish. Charming service. Thurs–Sun lunch and din-
ner (6.30 (Sun 5) –9pm).   INX-MED

920 **THE OLD CLUBHOUSE, GULLANE:** 01620 842008. E Links Rd behind main st,
B1 on corner of Green. Large woody clubhouse; a bar/bistro serving food all day
till 9.45pm. Gr busy atmos. Surprising wine selection; but puds are bought in.
                                                                                  INX

921 **LIVINGSTON'S, LINLITHGOW:** 01506 846565. Thro arch at E end of High St
A1 opp PO. Cottage conversion with conservatory and gdn – a quiet bistro with
imaginative modern Scottish cuisine. 2AA rosettes. Tues-Sat, lunch and dinner.
Cl Jan.   INX

922 **MARYNKA, LINLITHGOW:** 01506 840123. Next door to 4 Marys. Stylish,
A1 bright, modern town restaurant with bistro-cool lunches and serious dinners.
Small New World wine list & Iain Mellis cheese to end. Din Tues–Sat 6–10.30
Lunch Mon–Sat 12–2.   INX–MED

923 **TIGH BALLA, TORPHICHEN, nr BATHGATE:** 01506 652133. Oasis of Scottish
A1 trad cuisine in rural setting. Modern bungalow among old Scots pines serving
excellent range of dishes. Unfashionable decor but owners enthuse. Lunch &
dinner 7 days.   MED

THE BEST HOTELS AND RESTAURANTS IN FIFE

See also 2246/BEST OF DUNFERMLINE AND KIRKCALDY, *p. 304*; 2257/HOLIDAY CENTRES: ST ANDREWS, *p.318. Refer to Map 5.*

924 ✓ ✓ **OLD COURSE, ST ANDREWS:** 01334 474371. This world-famous
C2 hotel is the one you come to first on the A91 from N or W. Unlike many de luxe hotels in the UK, this has lightness to it and accessibility – it is after all surrounded by greens and full of golfers coming and going. Most rms o/look the famous course and sea (immaculate and tastefully done with no fac or expense spared), as do the Sands Brasserie and less informal Road Hole Grill up top. Bar here also for lingering views and whisky in the glass. Truly gr for golf, but anyone could unwind here, towelled in luxury. Spa well appointed. Small but beautiful pool.   146RMS JAN-DEC T/T PETS CC KIDS TOS LOTS

EAT Rd Hole Grill for spectacular dinner esp in late light summer. Sands on ground floor for lighter and later food. Both excl.   EXP/MED

925 ✓ **BALBIRNIE HOUSE, MARKINCH:** 01592 610066. Signed from the rd sys-
B3 tem around Glenrothes (3km) in surprisingly sylvan setting of Balbirnie Country Park. One of the most sociable and comfortable country-house hotels in the land, with high standards in service and décor that's easy to be at home with. Library Bar leads on to tranquil gdn. Orangery restau has 2 AA rosettes and good wine list. Their 'pamper breaks' – aft tea on arrival, Bucks Fizz with b/fast are a gr deal *à deux*. No leisure facs, but good golf in the park. Wake to the thwack of balls!   30RMS JAN-DEC T/T PETS CC KIDS TOS LOTS

EAT Elegant hotel dining and bistro for lunch. 2 AA rosettes.   EXP

926 ✓ **RUFFLETS, ST ANDREWS:** 01334 472594. 4km from centre via Argyle St
C2 opp W Pt along Strathkinness Low Rd past univ playing fields. Serene feel to this country-house hotel on edge of town. The celebrated gdns are a joy. Garden restau fine dining with 2 AA rosettes and more informal bar/brasserie. Cosy rms.   22RMS JAN-DEC T/T PETS CC KIDS TOS EXP

927 **KILCONQUHAR CASTLE ESTATE, nr ELIE:** 01333 340501. On B942 nr
C3 Colinburgh, 3km from Elie (that famously nice town). Mainly time-share villas (newer ones seem fairly naff), but 'club rms' available in castle itself with access to all facs incl pool, tennis, golf and esp riding. Daily rates poss. Bistro and posher dining rm in baronial setting.
9RMS JAN-DEC T/T PETS CC KIDS MED.INX

928 **CAMBO ESTATE, nr CRAIL:** 01333 450313. 2km E of Crail on A917. Huge coun-
D2 try pile in glorious gdns on the coastal rd betw St Andrews and Crail. Only few flats (and 2 cotts), but this is self/c in the grand manner. Rattle around, pretend you're house guests and be grateful you don't have to pay the bills.
4&2COTTS JAN-DEC X/X PETS CC KIDS MED.INX

929 **THE GOLF HOTEL, ELIE:** 01333 330209. Earlsferry end of favourite village
C3 (1515/COASTAL VILLAGES) o/look not bad golf (1955/GOLF). Mixed reports here, listed mainly for the location.   22RMS MAR-OCT T/T PETS KIDS MED.INX

930 **THE SHIP INN, ELIE:** 01333 330246. 6 basic rms in rock View adj pub notable
C3 for food and good life (1298/PUB FOOD) close to beach in an excellent neuk of Fife. Summer only.   6RMS JAN-DEC X/X PETS CC KIDS CHP

931 **THE HERMITAGE, ANSTRUTHER:** 01333 310909. Small B&B-type family
D3 house in the essential East Neuk town. Tasteful (unlike most round here) and friendly. The Cellar (*see Restaurants below*) for the eating-out treat of your stay.
4RMS JAN-DEC X/X XPETS CC KIDS INX

932 **WOODSIDE HOTEL, ABERDOUR:** 01383 860328. Refurb inn in main st of
B4 pleasant village with prize-winning rail stn, castle and church (1791/CHURCH-ES), coastal walk and nearby beach. This is where to come from Edin (by train, of course) with your bit on the side. 20RMS JAN-DEC T/T PETS CC KIDS MED.INX

933 **FORTH VIEW, ABERDOUR:** 01383 860402. Brilliant setting by a jagged jetty
B4 on the Forth beneath a cliff for airy walks (and famed for rock-climbing). On foot by path from harbour; or car from corner of Silver Sands beach car park,

by extreme track. Accom is basic in family house, but you wake up with Edin over the sea. **HAWCRAIG HOUSE** opp 01383 860335 a bit fancier and rec by *Which* but has only 2 rms. 5RMS APR-OCT X/X PETS CC KIDS CHP

INN ON NORTH STREET, ST ANDREWS: 01334 474664. Cool place. Report: 2257/ST ANDREWS.

SANDFORD HILL: 01382 541802. 7km S of Tay Br. Underrated country-house hotel in N Fife nr Dundee. Report: 1149/COUNTRY-HOUSE HOTELS.

PEAT INN nr CUPAR: 01334 840206. The definitive 'restaurant with rooms' (*see below*).

RESTAURANTS

934
C2
✓✓ **THE PEAT INN, nr CUPAR and ST ANDREWS:** 01334 840206. At a crossroads of the county, the hamlet of Peat Inn (signed from all over), for 30 years one of the gr Scottish restaus and David Wilson our first and still outstanding chef. Standards have improved immeasurably and now you don't need to go 50 miles to be sure of superb food. But on occasion come here – it is still an epicurean experience with classic cuisine on a no-nonsense menu and superb wine-list. 8 cottage rms for staying the night. 3 AA rosettes. Tues-Sat 1-3pm and 7-9.30pm. EXP

935
D3
✓✓ **THE CELLAR, ANSTRUTHER:** 01333 310378. This classic bistro the one place in Fife I wish I could go more often. Off courtyard behind Fisheries Museum in this busy E Neuk town (1515/COASTAL VILLAGES) – you'd call this entrance unassuming. As is the whole app, though seafood here is among the v best you'll find in Scotland. Peter Jukes sources only the best produce. One meat dish, excl complementary wine-list. Pure atmos. Fri–Sun lunch and 6.30–9.30 7 days. Times may change. (1328/SEAFOOD RESTAUS) MED

936
C2
✓✓ **OSTLER'S CLOSE, CUPAR:** 01334 655574. Down a close of the main st, Amanda and Jimmy Graham run a bistro/restau that has Cupar on the gastronomic map (for almost 20 yrs). Intimate, cottagy rms. Amanda out front also does puds, Jimmy a star in the kitchen. Often organic, big on wild mushrooms. Fri/Sat lunch & Tues–Sat 7-9.30pm. MED

937
C3
✓ **THE SEAFOOD RESTAURANT, ST MONANS:** 01333 730327. Excl atmos & food in old St Monans up hill from harbour. Report:1341/SEAFOOD RESTAUS. INX

938
B3
THE GREENHOUSE, FALKLAND: 01337 858400. St on corner of main st of delightful mid-Fife vill (1696/CASTLES, 1879/HILL WALKS, 1907/GLEN WALKS). Light and friendly cafe-bistro serving supper & brunch (Fri/Sat/Sun). All home-made, mostly organic (incl wine-list). Cl Mon/Tues. LO 9.00pm. INX

939
B3
OLD RECTORY, DYSART: 01592 651211. 2km E of Kirkcaldy (5km centre); still worth the drive from town or anywhere W Fife. Loyal regulars wouldn't go anywhere else. Tues-Sat lunch; Tues-Sun dinner. MED

940
B3, D3
VALENTE'S, KIRKCALDY & THE ANSTRUTHER FISH BAR: 2 gr fish 'n' chip shops with queues every day. Famously good, that's why! (1347/1358/FISH AND CHIPS). CHP

941
C3
WOK & SPICE, ST MONANS: 01333 730888. On main A917 rd turning past St Monans. Not a caff but a takeaway. Sizzling woks, proper rice, a taste of real Malaysian food (forget the chips). This would work in Edin or Glas. When in Fife, order here (they deliver betw N. Largo & Crail). 7 days 4.30 til whenever. CHP

THE SHIP INN, ELIE: 01333 330246. Report: 1298/PUB FOOD.

BEST RESTAURANTS IN ST ANDREWS: See p. 318–319.

THE BEST HOTELS AND RESTAURANTS IN PERTHSHIRE AND TAYSIDE

See also DUNDEE HOTELS AND RESTAURANTS, p. 145–147; 2251/CENTRES: PERTH, p. 312; and 2255/HOLIDAY CENTRES: PITLOCHRY, p. 317. Refer to Map 4.

942 ✔ ✔ **BALLATHIE HOUSE, nr PERTH:** 01250 883268. 20km N of Perth and
C3 more fully reported in the town section (2251/PERTH), but a true country-house hotel on the Tay that you fall in love with. Good dining, good fishing; good for the w/end away. New riverside rms are pretty nice.

43RMS JAN-DEC T/T PETS CC KIDS TOS LOTS

EAT Award-winning chef Kevin MacGillivray. Gr local produce esp beef/lamb.

EXP

943 ✔ ✔ **KINLOCH HOUSE, nr BLAIRGOWRIE:** 01250 884237. 5km W on
C3 A923 to Dunkeld. A country house with open views to the Sidlaw Hills. Panelled and galleried, and rather formally attired and run. Nice pool and health suite discreetly tucked away. Food is spectacular and PC (some organic). J/T preferred. Gr malt whisky selection. 3 AA rosettes.

20RMS JAN-DEC T/T PETS CC KIDS TOS EXP

944 ✔ **KINFAUNS CASTLE, PERTH:** 01738 620777. A90 Dundee rd (Perth 7km).
C3 Sumptuous country-house hotel in convenient v central location nr Perth and motorway. Glorious staircase, ceilings and wood panelling and 16 spacious suites. Slightly corporate feel (and many biz gatherings). Many oriental artefacts (UK owner lives Hong Kong). Restau open to non res consistently gets 2 AA rosettes.

16RMS FEB-DEC T/T PETS CC KIDS LOTS

945 ✔ **HILTON DUNKELD HOUSE, DUNKELD:** 01350 727771. Former home of
B3 Duke of Atholl, a v large impressive country house on the banks of the R Tay in beautiful grounds (some time-share) just outside Dunkeld. Leisure complex with good pool etc and many other activities laid on. V decent menu. Fine for kids. Pleasant walks. Not cheap but often good deals available. Huge but does fill up, so book early! 96RMS JAN-DEC T/T PETS CC KIDS LOTS

946 ✔ **ROYAL HOTEL, COMRIE:** 01764 679200. Central sq of cosy town, a sym-
B3 pathetic and stylish upgrading of trad small-town hotel. Excellent restau with good light and superb pub out back with real ale and atmos (1280/REAL ALES). Exquisite rugs and pictures. A pleasing bit of style in the county bit of the country. Delightful restau and bar meals. New owners 2001 also own Tufton Arms in Cumbria. 11RMS JAN-DEC T/T XPETS CC KIDS MED.EX

947 **HUNTINGTOWER HOTEL, nr PERTH:** 01738 583771. 3km from town, 1km
C3 ring rd (direction Crieff). Serviceable, good looking hotel in gdns close to Perth and the rds north and west. Report: (2251/PERTH).

34RMS JAN-DEC T/T PETS CC KIDS TOS EXP

948 **CASTLETON HOUSE, EASSIE, nr GLAMIS:** 01307 840340. 13km W of Forfar,
C3 25km N of Dundee. App from Glamis, 5km SW on A94. Family-run country-house hotel with good restau. Not over-pricey or stuffy; bar meals as well as dining-rms/conservatory. Popular Sun lunch.

6RMS JAN-DEC T/T PETS CC KIDS TOS EXP

949 **PINE TREES HOTEL, PITLOCHRY:** 01796 472121. A safe haven in visitor-ville –
B2 it's above the town and above all that (there are many mansions here). Take Larchwood Rd off W end of main st. Woody gdns, woody interior. Piano-player at Sat dinner. Scots owners. With taste (nice rugs).

19RMS JAN-DEC T/T XPETS CC KIDS MED.EX

950 **KILLIECRANKIE HOTEL, KILLIECRANKIE:** 01796 473220. 5km N of Pitlochry.
B2 Village inn ambience; cosy rms of individual character. Carefully run. Gr food. Plenty walks round about. 10RMS MAR-DEC T/T PETS CC KIDS TOS EXP

EAT V fine home-cooking in restau and bar (LO 9.30pm no booking in bar). In every guide book that counts. Pop over from Pitlochry. INX

951 **KENMORE HOTEL, KENMORE:** 01887 830205. Ancient coaching inn (tho now
B3 Best Western) in quaint conservation village. Excellent prospect for golfing (at Taymouth Castle adj, 1971/GOLF IN GREAT PLACES) and fishing. On river (Tay)

itself with terrace and restau o/looking. Comfy rms. Front area of hotel best with real fires. 39RMS JAN-DEC T/T PETS CC KIDS MED.INX

952 **GLEN CLOVA HOTEL:** 01575 550350. Nr end of Glen Clova, one of the gr
C2 Angus Glens (1546/GLENS), on B955 25km N of Kirriemuir. A walk/climb/country retreat hotel recently refurb & now v comfy. Superb walking nearby. Often full. 10RMS JAN-DEC T/T XPETS CC KIDS INX

953 **COLLEARN HOUSE, AUCHTERARDER:** 01764 663553. Off main st.
B4 Extravagant Victorian mansion with exceptional stained glass. Comfy rms, huge beds. Pleasant gdn. 8RMS JAN-DEC T/T XPETS CC KIDS EXP

954 **GUINACH HOUSE, ABERFELDY:** 01887 820251. On A826 Crieff rd and among
B3 the famous 'Birks' (1921/WOODLAND WALKS). Small mansion in pleasant gdn. Chef prop Bert MacKay always has 2 AA rosettes. Best place to eat for miles. 7RMS JAN-DEC X/T PETS CC KIDS TOS MED.EX

955 **ATHOLL ARMS, BLAIR ATHOLL:** 01796 481205. Main st opp castle, the major
B2 attraction hereabouts (1698/CASTLES), close to estate and Glen Tilt. New ownership refurb continues. Magnificent lofty dining-rm, the old ballrm for the castle. Eat by candlelight. A v Highland experience. Cosy bar with real fire and ales (and food, LO 9.30 pm). 31RMS JAN-DEC T/T PETS CC KIDS INX

956 **DALMUNZIE HOUSE, SPITTAL O' GLENSHEE, nr BLAIRGOWRIE:** 01250
C2 885224. 3 km from Perth–Braemar rd close to Glenshee ski slopes & good base for Royal Deeside without Deeside prices. 9 hole golf-course for fun. Food adequate (1 AA rosette). Hills all around. Fire to come home to. 17RMS JAN-DEC T/T PETS CC KIDS TOS MED.INX

957 **BIRNAM WOOD HOUSE by DUNKELD:** 01350 727782. Perth rd in Birnam vill
B2 off rd to Dunkeld 2 mins A9. Edwardian house restored & furnished in keeping. We haven't stayed but excl reports. Lavish b/fast, even meals poss – good rep for food. Reports please. 5RMS JAN-DEC X/X PETS CC KIDS INX

GLENEAGLES: 01764 662231 (1140/COUNTRY-HOUSE HOTELS).

KINNAIRD HOUSE: 01796 482440 (1136/COUNTRY-HOUSE HOTELS).

AUCHTERARDER HOUSE: 01764 663646 (1144/COUNTRY-HOUSE HOTELS).

OLD MANSION HOUSE, AUCHTERHOUSE: 01382 320366 (1109/DUNDEE HOTELS).

CRIEFF HYDRO, CRIEFF: 01764 655555. Superb for many reasons, esp kids. Quintessentially Scottish (1152/KIDS).

ARDEONAIG, LOCH TAY nr KILLIN: 01567 820400 (1218/GET AWAY FROM IT ALL).

RESTAURANTS

958 ✓ ✓ **ANDREW FAIRLIE at GLENEAGLES:** 01764 694267. The 'other'
B4 restau apart from main dining rm in this de-luxe resort hotel (1140/CO HOUSE HOTELS) & comfortably the best meal to be had in this & many other counties. Mr Fairlie comes with big rep, a Michelin star & good PR. Understated opulence in interior rm and confident French food of a v superior nature. Joanna Blythman gave it 10/10 but many lady critics like a good-looking chef who can cook. Mon-Sat dinner only. LO 10 pm. EXP

959 ✓ ✓ **LET'S EAT, PERTH:** 01738 643377. Corner of Kinnoull St. Tony Heath
C3 and Shona Drysdale's perfect county town eaterie. Cuisine without the trappings, but all the rt trimmings. Extremely good value and many awards. MED

960 ✓ ✓ **63 TAY STREET, PERTH:** 01738 441451. 63 Tay St on newly devel-
C3 oped riverside rd and walk. Award winning young chef Jeremy Wares in kitchen, Shona out front running a small tight ship. Contemp light rm and Modern Brit cuisine with hand-picked ingredients (incl wild garlic when we were there). The boy will do well! Tues–Sat lunch, LO 9 pm. Book w/ends. MED

961 ✓ **THE BUT 'N' BEN, AUCHMITHIE, nr ARBROATH:** 01241 877223. 2km off
D3 A92 N from Arbroath, 8km to town or 4km by cliff-top walk. Village perched on cliff top where ravine leads to small cove and quay. Adj cottages converted into cosy restau open noon-2.30pm for lunch, 4-5.30pm for high-

tea (2 sittings Sun, no dinner), 7pm-9.30pm for dinner. Cl Tue. Menus vary but all v Scottish and informal with emphasis on fresh fish/seafood. Brilliant value – Margaret Horn continues to provide a Scottish experience for her ain folk and all others.　　　　　　　　　　　　　　　　　　　　　　　　INX

962 **GORDON'S, INVERKEILOR, nr ARBROATH:** 01241 830364. Halfway betw
D3 Arbroath and Montrose on the main st. A restau with rms (3) which has won loadsa accolades incl 2 AA rosettes. They say 'modern Scottish cooking'. We say yeah. Closed Mon (residents only). Lunch except Mon, Tues & Sat (booking essential). Dinner except Mon.　　　　　　　　　　　　　　　　　　MED

963 **LOCHSIDE LODGE, BRIDGEND OF LINTRATHEN:** 01575 560340. 9km from
C3 Alyth towards Glenisla on B954 past Reekie Linn (1563/WATERFALLS), or via Kirriemuir. Deep in watery countryside. Converted stone steading nr loch; gr setting, good food. Accom (3rms). Lunch/dinner LO 9pm. Cl Sun even.　　MED

964 **CARGILLS, BLAIRGOWRIE:** 01250 876735. Cosy wine bar ambience, busy à la
C3 carte menu and blackboard. Serviceable, reliable and a bit of a hidden gem. Unprepossessing frontage, but on river side. Adj coffee shop/gallery. The place to eat in this corner of the country. LO 9/10pm. Cl Tues.　　　　　INX

965 **OLD ARMOURY, PITLOCHRY:** 01796 474281. On rd from main st that winds
B2 down to Salmon Ladder attraction. Old Black Watch armoury gives spacious, light bistro ambience and nice terrace/tea gdn. We haven't tried at TGP, but looks like there's a gr place to eat in Pitlochry at last. Easter–Sept 7 days noon–LO 9.30pm. Good pre-theatre supper.　　　　　　　　　　　INX/MED

966 **THE LOFT, BLAIR ATHOLL:** 01796 481377. Off the A9, in vill turn left at Bridge
B2 of Tilt Hotel. Odd kind of location (corner of a caravan park) for this solidly rep-utable restau. Chef Paul Collins was 'Rural Chef of the Year' 2002. Hearty food with a good combo of new and traditional touches in lofty setting. Bistro & finer dining menus. Lunch and LO 9.30pm. Cl Sun/Mon.　　　　　　　　INX

967 **THE BANK, CRIEFF:** 01764 656575. 32 High St opp TIC and town clock. Prob
B3 best food in cosy Crieff (you may want a meal out from the Hydro) in former bank. Chef/prop Bill McGuigan's modern Scottish cooking. Feb–Dec. Tues–Sun lunch & dinner (Cl Sun even).　　　　　　　　　　　　　　　　　　MED

968 **CROFTBANK HOUSE, KINROSS:** 01577 863819. Stn Rd; on the M9: 1km on
C4 main rd from motorway jnct. Discreet hotel with notable dining-rm (2 AA rosettes). Also bar meals (5rms). Cl Sun dinner and Mon.　　　　　　MED

969 **GROUSE AND CLARET, KINROSS:** 01577 864212. Heatheryford on other (W)
00 side of jnct, about 1km. On fishing lochans, converted farm buildings with popular pleasant restau and 3 rms. Cl Sun Mon.　　　　　　　　　　INX

970 **DEIL'S CAULDRON, COMRIE:** 01764 670352. 27 Dundas St on bend of A85
B3 main rd thro' town and rd to Glen Lednock. Cottage restau with simple, effec-tive menu like haggis and neeps, moules et frites. Lunch Sat/Sun. Dinner Tues–Sun LO 8.30pm.　　　　　　　　　　　　　　　　　　　　INX

　　　KERACHER'S, PERTH: 01738 449777 (2251/PERTH)　　　　　　　MED

　　　ROYAL HOTEL, COMRIE: 01764 679200 (see above)　　　　　　MED

THE BEST HOTELS AND RESTAURANTS IN THE NORTH-EAST

Excludes city of Aberdeen (see pp. 140–44). See 2258/ROYAL DEESIDE. *Refer to Map 3.*

971
B3
✓✓ **DARROCH LEARG, BALLATER:** 01339 755443. On main A93 at edge of town. The Franks continue to enhance the reputation of this Deeside mansion esp for food (long in the family). With superior standards, but a relaxed ambience and an excellent dining-rm, it is the best in this hotel-studded town. Three AA rosettes; other Deeside hoteliers aspire to its good standards. Comfortable, informal with attentive and considerate staff. No bar, but civilised drinks before and *après*. Good base for touring.

18RMS FEB-DEC T/T PETS CC KIDS TOS LOTS

EAT Conservatory dining-rm and one of best restaus in NE; Chef David Mutter continues to hit the heights. Nice gdn view, fab food. EXP

972
C3
✓✓ **RAEMOIR HOUSE, BANCHORY:** 01330 824884. 5km N from town via A980 off main st. Mansion in the country just off the Deeside conveyor belt which gets everything right Old-fashioned comfy rms given contemporary details. Flowers everywhere. 9-hole golf and tennis. Stable annex and self-cat apts. The Bishop-Milnes have made tremendous improvements to what has always been a fave co-house retreat. Chef John Barber has 2 AA rosettes. 21RMS & SELF-CAT JAN-DEC T/T PETS CC KIDS TOS LOTS

973
B2
✓ **CRAIGELLACHIE HOTEL, CRAIGELLACHIE:** 01340 881204. The quintessential Speyside hotel, off A941 Elgin to Perth and Aber rd by the br over Spey. Esp good for fishing, but well placed for walking (Speyside Way runs along bottom of gdn, see 1895/LONG WALKS) and distillery visits (1466/WHISKY). Informal; some fab rms. Nice snug and, of course, this is where to drink the drink. 25RMS JAN-DEC T/T XPETS CC KIDS TOS MED.EX

974
C2
✓ **PITTODRIE HOUSE, PITCAPLE:** 01467 681444. Large 'family' mansion house on estate in one of the best bits of Aberdeenshire with Bennachie above. 40km Aber but 'only 30mins from airport' via A96. Follow signs off B9002. Lots of activities available on the estate, croquet lawn, billiards and lots of comfortable rms. Exquisite walled gdn 500m from house. Not struck on the food, but friendly service. Nice snug bar with gr whisky selection.

27RMS JAN-DEC T/T PETS CC KIDS TOS LOTS

975
D2
✓ **UDNY ARMS, NEWBURGH:** 01358 789444. A975 off A92. Village pub with gr food and character run by the Craig family for many yrs. Rms tasteful and individually furnished. Folk come from Aber (22km) to eat here. Golf course Cruden Bay (1950/GREAT GOLF) 16km N and walks beside Ythan estuary (1683/WILDLIFE). 26RMS JAN-DEC T/T XPETS CC KIDS TOS MED.INX

EAT Excellent grub in bar or dining-rm. Good ambience and the dessert assiette is a gobsmacker. Lunch; LO 9.30pm. They say that this was where Sticky Toffee Pudding was invented & the lady is still around. MED

976
B3
✓ **HILTON CRAIGENDARROCH, BALLATER:** 013397 55858. On the Braemar rd (A93). Part of a country-club/time-share operation with elegant dining, good leisure facs and discreet resort-in-the-woods feel. Part of the new expanded Hilton empire in the UK, so expect consistent & improving standards. 2 restaus, one by pool and the conscientiously up-market Oaks. Lodges can be available on short lets, a good idea for a group holiday or w/end. Barbacoa, an outside bar-b-que, is v pleasant when the weather permits.

45RMS JAN-DEC T/T XPETS CC KIDS TOS LOTS

977
C2
MELDRUM HOUSE, OLDMELDRUM: 01651 872294. 1km from village, 30km N of Aber via A947 Banff rd. Immediately impressive and solid establishment – Scottish baronial style. Set amid new 18-hole golf course (private membership, but guests can use) landscaped & managed to high standard (gr practice range). Rms have atmos & nice furnishing – many orig antiques & chosen pictures. Reports on dining please. 9RMS JAN-DEC T/T PETS CC KIDS TOS LOTS

978 **SEAFIELD HOTEL, CULLEN:** 01542 840791. On the main Brae; an activity-ori-
B1 ented hotel with lots to do on nearby Seafield estate (hunt, shoot, fish). Single
rms can be a bit pokey but there's a comfortable lounge with a fair range of
malts. Restau good for fresh fish. Mr and Mrs Cox run an exemplary family
hotel.   22RMS JAN-DEC T/T PETS KIDS CC MED.INX

979 **THE MANSION HOUSE, ELGIN:** 01343 548811. In town centre (beneath the
B1 left hand of the statue on the hill). Comfortable and elegant town house in a
comfortable and gentle town with 'leisure facs', incl small pool/gym and drop-
in (v small) bistro. Nice dining-rm. 23RMS JAN-DEC T/T XPETS CC KIDS TOS LOTS

980 **BANCHORY LODGE HOTEL, BANCHORY:** 01330 822625. A sporting-lodge
C3 hotel nr town centre, but superbly situated on the banks of the Dee. No longer
hold fishing rts, but can arrange. Public rms and many bedrms o/look the river.
Sporty rather than staid atmos. Fight for the tables by the window for dinner.
People come back, like the fish.   22RMS FEB-DEC T/T PETS CC KIDS EXP

981 **DELNASHAUGH INN, BALLINDALLOCH, nr GRANTOWN ON SPEY:** 01807
B2 500255. Road-side and Speyside (actually the Avon, pron 'Arn') inn, comfy,
unpretentious. On bend of A95 betw Craigellachie and Grantown nr confluence of main rds and rivers. Laura Ashley/Sarah Churchill décor, not minimalist, but simple. Food also. Much ado about fishing.
                                                         9RMS JAN-DEC T/T PETS CC KIDS MED.EX

982 **CASTLE HOTEL, HUNTLY:** 01466 792696. Behind Huntly Castle ruin; app from
C2 town through castle entrance and then over R Deveron up impressive drive.
Large but family-scale lodge-house; former seat of the Dukes of Gordon. Rms
have character and views tho' fairly basic. Fishing fixed.
                                                         19RMS JAN-DEC T/T PETS CC KIDS MED.INX

983 **ARCHIESTOWN HOTEL, ARCHIESTOWN:** 01340 810218. Main st of small vil-
B2 lage in heart of Speyside nr Cardhu Distillery (1468/WHISKY). A village inn with
comfortable rms and celebrated food in bistro setting (LO 8.30pm). Fishers
and locals.   8RMS FEB-SEPT T/T PETS CC KIDS MED.EX

984 **WATERSIDE INN, PETERHEAD:** 01779 471121. Edge of town on A952 to
D2 Fraserburgh on tidal R Ugie. Standard, well-run modern hotel, recommended
for its service and convenience and because it's the best option around. Good
for kids (1161/KIDS).   109RMS JAN-DEC T/T PETS CC KIDS MED.EX

985 **GRANT ARMS, MONYMUSK:** 01467 651226. The village inn on a remarkable
C3 small square, a good centre for walking (1876/HILLS), close to the 'Castle Trail'
(1708/CASTLES; 1764/COUNTRY HOUSES) and with fishing rts on the Don. Rms in
hotel & (9) round courtyard are v basic, but the food esp in the bar, is why we
come.   17RMS JAN-DEC T/T PETS CC KIDS MED.INX

EAT Best pub food for miles, and dining. Daily lunch, 6.30-9pm.   INX

986 **BRAEMAR LODGE, BRAEMAR:** 013397 41627. Down-home granite country
A3 house where the owners won't look down their nose at muddy walkers. Few
frills but a haven after a long day in the Cairngorms. Have a whisky. Log cabins for hire out back.   7RMS JAN-DEC X/T PETS CC KIDS MED.INX

RESTAURANTS

987 ✓ **LAIRHILLOCK, nr STONEHAVEN:** 01569 730001. 15km S of Aber off A92.
C3 Excellent country pub and restau, good for kids. Full report 1067/ABER
RESTAUS; 1289/PUB FOOD.

988 ✓ **TOLBOOTH, STONEHAVEN:** 01569 762287. Excl location on Stonehaven
C4 Harbour & brill brill (well, more likely sea bass). Report: 1337/SEAFOOD
RESTAUS.

989 ✓ **THE OLD MONASTERY, nr BUCKIE:** 01542 832660. Leave A89 at Buckie
B1 jnct for Drybridge, 4 km, restau at top of hill & consequently has brilliant
views. Also v good food, still with 2 AA rosettes in long-established setting.
Good atmos. Tues-Sun Lunch and LO 8.30/9pm (not Sun dinner).   EXP

990 ✓ **MILTON RESTAURANT:** 01330 844566. On main A93 Royal Deeside rd
C3 4km E of Banchory opp the entrance to Crathes (1473/GARDENS;
1765/COUNTRY HOUSES). Roadside and surprisingly contemporary café/restau
in old steading adj craft vill of varying quality. Light and exceedingly pleasant

space. Menu from brunch-lunch-aft tea (till 5pm)-supper, then dinner so they cater for everything (& rather well). 7 days, LO 9.45pm.   INX

991 **STATION RESTAURANT, BALLATER:** 01339 755050. Centre town nr TIC.
B3 Restoration of Victorian tearm in v capable hands of the Franks who have Darroch Learg (see above) so you know the food will be good. Open for b/fast (bacon sarnie to pain au chocolat) through to supper with gr cream teas in betw (all home-baking). 7 days but cl Mon/Tues dinner. Wint hrs may differ.
                                                                                     INX

992 **HORSEMILL RESTAURANT, CRATHES, nr BANCHORY:** 01330 844525. Adj
C3 magnificent Crathes (1765/COUNTRY HOUSES; 1473/GARDENS) so lots of reasons to go off the Deeside rd (A93) & up the drive. More tearm than restau but some hot dishes eg haggis & neeps with the excl home-baking mm ... meringues. Open AYR lunch/aft tea till 5pm.   INX

993 **ST TROPEZ, BANCHORY:** 01330 822216. Bridge St behind and parallel to
C3 main st opp TIC. A bit off the beaten track, this discreet & authentically French restau is the best place to eat hereabouts. Moroccan chef-prop has got the measure of the Deeside dearth in good places to eat out. Pleasantly bour-geoise, nice people. 7 days in summer, but phone to check.   MED

994 **FAGINS, WHITEHILLS nr BANFF:** 01261 861321. Loch St on rt as you app this
C1 coastal village 3km W of Banff off B9139. Long-standing local reputation for surf 'n' turf suppers cooked in galley kitchen in corner of dining-rm above an unpromising pub. Honest to goodness food with some flair but don't expect a Terence Conran eating-out experience. Wed-Sat dinner, LO 9pm. Lunch Sun only.   INX

THE BLACK-FACED SHEEP, ABOYNE: 01339 887311 (1379/TEARMS). Note, plans to open for supper in newly expanded set-up in 2002.

THE BEST HOTELS AND RESTAURANTS IN THE HIGHLANDS

See also Ft William, p. 306; Ullapool, p. 315; Skye, p. 292; Western Isles, p. 294. Refer to Map 2.

995
C3
✓ ✓ **INVERLOCHY CASTLE, FORT WILLIAM:** 01397 702177. 5km from town on A82 Inverness rd, Scotland's flagship Highland (*Relais et Châteaux*) hotel. Now less stuffy than it used to be, but still stuffed with sumptuous furnishings, objects and occasional film stars, luminaries and royalty. Everything you expect of a 'castle'; the epitome of grandeur and service. Huge colourful, comfortable rms, set in acres of rhododendrons with rainbow trout in the lake and the big Ben over there. Eat in tho this is not a drop-in kind of a dining rm (3 AA rosettes). 17RMS JAN-DEC T/T PETS CC KIDS LOTS

996
D2
✓ ✓ **THE BOATH HOUSE, AULDEARN, nr NAIRN:** 01667 454896. Signed from the main A96 3km E of Nairn. A small country-house hotel in a classic & immaculately restored mansion - Don & Wendy Matheson's family home. Add chef Charlie Lockley & you're in for a memorable stay. Spa/gym in basement, massage on hand & delightful grounds (& beautiful Brodie nearby – 1694/CASTLES) with a lake. Eat well, sleep well, chill out. 7RMS JAN-DEC T/T PETS CC KIDS TOS LOTS

EAT Consummate chef, ambience & ingredients just right. MED

997
D2
✓ ✓ **CLIFTON HOUSE, NAIRN:** 01667 453119. Seafield St off A96 to Inverness. A suburban mansion o/look park and seafront of genteel town nr Inverness. For over 50yrs one of the most distinctly individual hotels in the Highlands run by the inimitable J Gordon MacIntyre and full of his good taste and flowers from the gdn. Sometimes he chefs though his son does most. Excellent wine list. Sept-June there are musical and theatrical evenings; (send for prog). Every rm is a different experience; dinner is not merely a meal. It's a house party and demonstrates that all the management training, spas, trouser-presses and unctuous waiters in the world will never make up for style – and this is truer than ever. 12RMS JAN-DEC X/X PETS CC KIDS EXP

EAT Dining never dull, often dramatic. Hand-picked excellent value wine list. EXP

998
C2
✓ ✓ **CULLODEN HOUSE, INVERNESS:** 01463 790461. 5km E of town nr A9, follow signs for Culloden village, not the battlefield. Hugely impressive, Georgian mansion and lawn a big green duvet on edge of suburbia and, of course, history. The most conscientiously de luxe hotel hereabouts. Some fab gdn suites, and great food when last ate there. 28RMS JAN-DEC T/T PETS CC KIDS TOS LOTS

999
D3
✓ **THE CROSS, KINGUSSIE:** 01540 661166. Off main st at traffic lights, 200m uphill then left into glen. Tasteful hotel in converted tweed mill by river which gurgles o/side most windows. Some rms recent refurb so better than ever. Restau superb. 9RMS MAR-NOV T/X XPETS CC XKIDS TOS EXP

EAT To stay, you're expected to eat; you'd be mad not to. Open non-res for the best restau in the ski-zone. Ruth Hadley mastercook in kitchen (with Becca), Tony outfront with excl wine-list, cheeseboard & chat. Fixed menu. Cl Tues.

1000
C2
✓ **DOWER HOUSE, nr MUIR OF ORD:** 01463 870090. On A862 between Beauly and Dingwall, 18km NW of Inverness and 2km N of village. Charming, personal place; you are a house guest so you have to fit in. Cottagey-style small country house, with comfy public rms. Also self-cat lodge house. 5RMS JAN-DEC T/T PETS CC XKIDS EXP

EAT Consummate chef Robyn Aitchison, simple, sophisticated. Fixed menu. MED

1001
C2
✓ **DUNAIN PARK, INVERNESS:** 01463 230512. 6km SW town on A82 Ft William rd. Mansion-house just off the rd, a quiet and more civilised alternative to hotels in town, esp for those on business. Some good deals out of season. Nice gdns, small pool and sauna; real countryside beyond. Notable restau/dining-rm with sound Scottish menu; lots of creamy puds. Excellent wine and malt list. Nice people who care, and enviro-friendly gdn. 13RMS JAN-DEC T/T PETS CC KIDS TOS EXP

EAT Ann Nicholl's no-nonsense menu and sideboard of delicious puds. MED

1002
C2 ✓ **GLENMORISTON TOWN HOUSE HOTEL, INVERNESS:** 01463 223777. One of the many mansions/hotels on the riverside below the castle, but this unquestionably the best; indeed the best in town. Italian owners so Mediterranean style menus in dining-rm and bar/bistro (2 AA rosettes). Hotel opp Eden Court Theatre so handy for most Invernusion things, but also Ness Island walks for peace & quiet. 15RMS JAN-DEC T/T PETS CC KIDS MED.EXP

EAT Restau (open non-res) **LA RIVIERA** for best Italian dining in town (MED). Same owners have the RIVA bistro.

1003
C2 ✓ **THE SUMMER ISLES HOTEL, ACHILTIBUIE:** 01854 622282. 40km from Ullapool with views over the isles; Stac Polly and Suilven are close by to climb. V popular restau, comfortable rms above; with *Swiss Family Robinson* log cabins in gdns. Adj pub offers similar quality food at half the price.
13RMS APR-OCT T/X PETS CC XKIDS TOS EXP

EAT Fairly formal dining, but awfully good. All would-be restaurateurs should be shown this cheeseboard. Seafood lunches and bar meals a must if nearby.
MED.EX

1004
MAP 1
B2 ✓ **CRINAN HOTEL:** 01546 830261. At the w end of the Crinan Canal, Nick Ryan and Frances Macdonald's place has splendid situation o/looking the canal lock, art (by Frances), two excellent restaus (1327/SEAFOOD RESTAUS) & gr pub with food. Legendary sunsets & the endless fascination of boats coming thro' the lock. Bliss! 22RMS JAN-DEC T/T PETS CC KIDS TOS LOTS

1005
B2 ✓ **POOL HOUSE HOTEL, POOLEWE:** 01445 781272. Often we've driven by here and been unmoved, but what a change. Recent refurb by the Harrisons has put Pool House right up there with the Torridon tops. Formerly owned by Osgood MacKenzie who founded the gdns up the road (1472/ GARDENS), it now has 4 themed suites and one single room. Chef John Moir does a fine job with the scallops that come from 'just out there'. Simultaneously special and personable. 5RMS MAR-DEC T/T XPETS CC XKIDS TOS LOTS

1006
C2 ✓ **LOCH TORRIDON HOTEL, L TORRIDON, nr KINLOCHEWE:** 01445 791242. At the end of Glen Torridon in immense scenery. Highland Lodge atmos, big hills to climb. Report: 1204/GET-AWAY-FROM-IT-ALL
20RMS JAN-DEC T/T XPETS CC XKIDS TOS LOTS

1007
C2 **BUNCHREW HOUSE, nr INVERNESS:** 01463 234917. On A862 Beauly rd only 5km from Inverness yet completely removed from town; on the wooded shore of the Beauly Firth. Dining-rm and some bedrms o/look water; you might see Ben Wyvis. Gr club bar, esp for late dram. Graham and Janet Cross have really built their wedding business – afternoon tea on the lawn when sunny unmissable. 14RMS JAN-DEC T/T PETS CC KIDS TOS EXP

1008
C2 **COUL HOUSE, CONTIN, nr STRATHPEFFER:** 01997 421487. Comfortable country-house hotel on the edge of the wilds with some elegant public rms, partic the octagonal lounge. Family-run (Martyn and Ann Hill) with nice dogs. Well-kept lawns where a piper plays in summer (Fri evenings). V Taste of Scotland menu, Martyn keeps an excellent wine list and they have a small bistro now too. 20RMS JAN-DEC T/T PETS CC KIDS TOS MED.EX

1009
C3 **POLMAILY HOUSE, DRUMNADROCHIT, LOCH NESS:** 01456 450343. 5km from Drumnadrochit on A831 to Cannich in Glen Urquhart and nr awesome Glen Affric (1541/GLENS). Unpretentious country-house retreat in lived-in unmanicured grounds. Many walks; tennis, riding and covered-in pool. Small, comfy public rms, individual bedrms. Sensible dinner and wine list. Everything on hand for kids (1155/KIDS), but ok for those without. The house and the glen are yours. 10RMS JAN-DEC T/T PETS CC KIDS EXP

1010
C3 **LODGE ON THE LOCH, ONICH:** 01855 821237. In my view the best hotel in this strip S of Ft William (16km). Notable relaxed ambience, colour scheme, furnishings etc. Hydrotherapy massage, showers, double jacuzzis, mature hippy colour scheme in parts, posh toiletries, and CD players. The inimitable Jackie Burns in charge. 17RMS MAR-OCT T/T PETS CC XKIDS TOS MED.EX-EXP

1011
C3 **ONICH HOTEL, ONICH, by FORT WILLIAM:** 01855 821214. As above 16km S on main A82, one of many roadside and in this case, loch side hotels which are more attractive than many in Ft William. Onich is the best value and some of its rms o/look L Linnhe. Busy bars and grassy terrace.
27RMS JAN-DEC T/T PETS CC KIDS TOS MED.EX

1012 **HOLLY TREE, KENTALLEN, ARGYLL:** 01631 740292. On A828 Ft William
C4 (Ballachulish) – Oban rd, 8km S of Ballachulish Bridge. On road and sea and
once the railway; formerly a station. Now a slightly idiosyncratic hotel with
decor of mixed taste (incl Mockintosh), but fab views from bdrms and dining
rm. Nice for kids. 10RMS JAN-DEC T/T PETS CC TOS EXP

1013 **KINLOCHBERVIE HOTEL, KINLOCHBERVIE:** 01971 521275. The only show in
C1 town o/looking important fishing pt (go see evening fish market). 1970s kind
of rms and restau, bar and bistro. 14RMS JAN-DEC T/T PETS CC KIDS EXP

ACKERGILL TOWER, nr WICK: 01955 603556 (1259/HOUSE PARTIES).

RESTAURANTS

1014 ✓ ✓ **OLD PINES, nr SPEAN BRIDGE:** 01397 712324. Medium-priced din-
C3 ing in inexp hotel, still one of the best meals in the Highlands (with
big table and crocks). How Sukie Barber does it with all those kids, God knows,
but the food can be brilliant. Essentially an award-winning restau with rms.
Kids may eat with theirs. Carefully selected & amazingly reasonable wine list
with topical gags. Cl Sun eve and Mon, but phone to check. No smk. See also
1021/LESS EXP HIGHLAND HOTELS. MED

1015 **MANSFIELD HOUSE HOTEL, TAIN:** 01862 892052. Smart baronial-style hotel
D2 on Scotsburn Rd (rms are LOTS). Owners, the Lauritsen family, know their business – a serious kitchen with a Scottish slant and 2 AA rosettes. MED

1016 **2 QUAIL RESTAURANT, DORNOCH:** 01862 811811. Castle St. Looks like a
D2 townhouse on the outside, a cosy library on the inside. New arrival in this
book, already has 2 AA rosettes. Altogether splendid and good call the Carrs
who run it. Mod Franco-Scot flavour. Dinner only Tues-Sat. MED

1017 **DUNDONNELL HOTEL, DUNDONNELL:** 01854 633204. At E end of Little Loch
C2 Broom, nr Ullapool. Bar and restaurant choices; your chef is one Isabel. Food
MED (28 rms if you want to stay). 2 AA rosettes. MED

GOOD LESS EXPENSIVE HOTELS IN THE HIGHLANDS

Refer to Map 2.

1018 ✓ ✓ **THE CEILIDH PLACE, ULLAPOOL:** 01854 612103. Jean Urquhart's
C2 unconventional app and individual hotel still out in front; an oasis
up-N. What started out in the 1970s as a coffee/exhibition shop in a boat shed,
has spread along this row of cottages now comprising a restau, bookshop,
self-serve wholefood/coffee area, and bedrms upstairs. In winter food is
served in front of the roaring fire in the Parlour Bar. Bunkhouse across the rd
offers cheaper accom but is not a substitute for the hotel. Live music and
events throughout the yr, or you can simply sit on the lounge/terrace upstairs
and wonder about Ullapool. 23RMS JAN-DEC T/X PETS CC KIDS EXP

EAT Coffee shop/bistro 8am-11pm. Restau service sometimes slips when
busy, but we'll come back here forever. MED

1019 ✓ ✓ **THE ALBANNACH, LOCHINVER:** 01571 844407. 2km up rd to
C1 Baddidarach as you come into Lochinver on the A837, at the br.
Lesley and Colin have created a unique and comfortable haven in their 18th-
century house. The suite in the grounds used to be a byre; the croft walk
behind has gr views over the water to Suilven. After one of their artfully crafted dinners you get the sun on the terrace o/looking the gdn (you have to go
there to smoke) and drink in the tranquillity; and their whisky.
5RMS MAR-DEC T/X XPETS CC XKIDS MED.INX

EAT When in Assynt, eat at The Albannach. When not, plan to go. MED

1020 ✓ **AUCHENDEAN LODGE, DULNAIN BRIDGE, nr GRANTOWN ON SPEY:**
D3 01479 851347. An urbane enclave in an area of stunning scenery nr
Aviemore skiing and Whisky Trail. Tastefully and cosily furnished Edwardian
lodge with log fires, good malts and cellar, and books. Food with flair and
imagination with many ingredients from the kitchen gdn (like 47 – yes 47 –

varieties of potatoes) TOS award for using local produce. Esp good with mushrooms. Intimate. Dinner can turn into a house party as Ian patiently serves: Eric takes care of the kitchen.

5RMS (& FLAT) JAN-DEC X/T PETS CC KIDS TOS GF MED.EX

EAT Most imaginative menu in wide area of S Speyside, incl Aviemore.   MED

1021 ✓ **OLD PINES, nr SPEAN BRIDGE:** 01397 712324. 3km Spean Br via B8004
C3   for Garlochy at Commando Monument. This award-winning 'restau with rms' is a home from home. Open-plan pine cabin with log fires, games, enough books for a public library, neat bedrooms and a huge new polytunnel (where bits of yr dinner come from). Enjoy Sukie Barber's exceptional cooking and the ducks on the stream (1153/KIDS; 1014/HIGHLAND HOTELS).

8RMS JAN-DEC X/X XPETS CC KIDS TOS MED.INX

EAT It's a restau first; worth drive from Fort William.   MED

1022 ✓ **BOAT HOTEL, BOAT OF GARTEN:** 01479 831258. Centre of vill o/looking
D3   the steam train line & golf course (1965/GOLF). Gr old style (Victorian/ 1920s) hotel recently refurb with good restau which has 2 AA rosettes, bar the locals use (good bar meals) & an all-round feeling of a good place to be in the 1920s (best rms those).   32RMS JAN-DEC T/T PETS CC KIDS MED.INX

1023 **GLENFINNAN HOUSE HOTEL, GLENFINNAN:** 01397 722235. Victorian man-
B3   sion with lawns down to L Shiel and the Glenfinnan Monument over the water. No shortbread-tin twee or tartan carpet here; instead a warm welcome from the MacFarlanes. You are piped into dinner and the refurbed bar has gr atmos. A cruise on this stunning loch in the ex-admiralty launch prob a must! (1242/SCOTTISH HOTELS).   17RMS APR-OCT X/X PETS CC KIDS MED.INX-EXP

1024 **GLENGARRY CASTLE, INVERGARRY:** 01809 501254. A family-run hotel in the
C3   Highlands for over 40 yrs, now in the charge of young Donald MacCallum. Lichen on the balustrades, honeysuckle as you walk to the loch and a ruined castle in the grounds. Perhaps better for romance and atmos than fine dining.

26RMS MAR-NOV T/T PETS CC KIDS MED.EX

1025 **KINKELL HOUSE nr DINGWALL:** 01349 861270. 15 km n of Inverness, 2km
C2   from main A9 taking B9169 E signed Easter Kinkell. Mansion house in farming country (the Black Isle) with rms o/look the Firth & Ben Wyvis. Gr local rep for food.   10RMS JAN-DEC T/T PETS CC KIDS TOS MED.INX

EAT Best in the Black Isle. Local produce. Book w/ends.   MED

1026 **THE PLOCKTON INN, PLOCKTON:** 01599 544222. Neat village inn and
B3   seafood restau in neat little seaside vill (1508/COASTAL VILLAGES). Some good cask ale (Burton's, London Pride etc). Simple, quiet tasteful rms. Bar and bistro, mainly seafood. Tables on terrace in summer, back gdn for kids.

9RMS JAN-DEC T/T PETS CC KIDS MED.INX

1027 **LOCH MAREE HOTEL, TALLADALE:** 01445 760288. On A832 15km from
B2   Kinlochewe and rt by the loch side (1568/LOCHS). A Highland fishing hotel catering for discriminating tourists (incl Queen Victoria) since 1872. But the aristos have gone and so have many of the fish. Not all though. Somehow, in the care of the remarkable Ann Henderson, that makes it all the better. Good for Torridon walking and near Inverewe (1472/GARDENS).

20RMS MAR-NOV T/T PETS CC KIDS MED.INX

1028 **TONGUE HOTEL, TONGUE:** 01847 611206. One village, more than one hotel
C1   – which is best? At the moment we reckon this one has the edge. Former Duke of Sutherland hunting lodge – and he'd probably still like it.

16RMS MAR-OCT X/T PETS CC KIDS TOS MED.EX

1029 **TIGH-AN-EILEAN, SHIELDAIG:** 01520 755251. Lovely freshly-furnished hotel
B2   on waterfront o/look Scots Pine island on loch. The Fields run a pleasant house – the locale has that serene otherness. Chris is a folk-buff so look out for music in the adj pub. Dinner (MED) is well worth having. The view remains fab, just like the Colin Baxter postcard.   11RMS APR-OCT X/X PETS CC KIDS EXP

1030 **EDDRACHILLES HOTEL, nr SCOURIE:** 01971 502080. Excellent location for a
C1   quiet and polite hotel at Badcall Bay. Handy for Handa (1663/BIRDS) or go for a walk on a beach.   12RMS MAR-OCT T/T XPETS CC XKIDS MED.EX

1031 **SUTHERLAND ARMS HOTEL, GOLSPIE:** 01408 633234. Roadside inn at N end
D2 of town nr Dunrobin Castle and Big Burn Walk (1908/GLEN WALKS). First coaching inn in Scotland changed hands yet again in 2001: a stopover on the way north.
14RMS JAN-DEC T/T PETS CC KIDS INX

1032 **DORNOCH CASTLE HOTEL, DORNOCH:** 01862 810216. Atmos 16th-century
D2 castle in main st. Dinner in the dungeons (huge stone fireplace) and drinks upstairs in the turreted bar o/look cathedral. Bedrms in old part and new wing. Beach and golf nearby (1952/GREAT GOLF). Recent new owners & much needed rolling refurb in progress. Now on the Madonna wedding trail, so lively w/ends.
18RMS JAN-DEC T/T PETS CC KIDS MED.EX

1033 **LOVAT ARMS, BEAULY:** 01463 782313. Best hotel of many in main st of mar-
C2 ket town 20km from Inverness. Relaxed, welcoming family-run hotel with gr bar meals and comfy public rms. Much tartan upstairs.
28RMS JAN-DEC T/T PETS CC KIDS TOS MED.EX

1034 **TOMICH HOTEL, TOMICH, nr DRUMNADROCHIT:** 01456 415399. The inn of
C3 a quiet conservation village, part of an old estate on the edge of Guisachan Forest. Nr fantastic Plodda Falls (1553/WATERFALLS) and Glen Affric (1541/GLENS). Basic facs, but use of pool nearby in farm steading (9am-9pm); esp good for fishing holidays. 25km drive from Drum by A831.
8RMS JAN-DEC T/T PETS CC KIDS MED.INX

1035 **PORT-NA-CON, nr DURNESS:** 01971 511367. Ken and Lesley Black's guest-
C1 house on this idyllic shore is gr value. New conservatory since last time, brilliant for browsing the extensive library or just gazing at the Bens (Loyal and Hope). Seafood from the loch often on the dinner menu (INX). Non-residents should book. If they're full, Lesley might be able to find you a rm at her mum's house in Durness.
4RMS JAN-DEC X/X PETS CC KIDS CHP

1036 **THE OLD SMIDDY, LAIDE:** 01445 731425. This book doesn't feature many
B2 B&Bs, but after those readers' letters … Kate MacDonald's place in jolie Laide (Gruinard Bay, Wester Ross on the A832) is one of the superior examples. She's a fine cook and does serious dinners (book then BYOB) but if you want to stay these are only 3rms (and self-cat cottages out the back).
3RMS APR-NOV X/T PETS XCC XKIDS MED.EX

1037 **NAVIDALE HOUSE, by HELMSDALE:** 01431 821258. Just off main rd N of
D1 Helmsdale, signed. We haven't stayed, but reports are good.
16RMS FEB-OCT X/T PETS CC KIDS TOS INX

1038 **CORRIECHOILLE LODGE, by SPEAN BRIDGE:** 01397 712002. Around 3km
C3 out of Spean Bridge on the small rd by the station. Justin & Lucy Swabey getting 4-star acclaim from all over. When we visited they were out but we like the look of this place and reports reach us of spectacularly good value B&B & dinner with views towards the Grey Corries & Aonach Mor.
5RMS MAR-OCT X/T XPETS CC XKIDS INX

1039 **GARIMORE, S MORAR:** 01687 450268. On main A830 (rd to the Isles) betw
B3 Arisaig & Mallaig & opp Cambusdarak (the 'Local Hero') beach. We haven't stayed, but this antique-filled GH comes heartily rec. B&B (dinner) & P&Q (peace & quiet).
7RMS JAN-DEC X/X PETS CC KIDS INX

GLENELG INN, GLENELG: 01599 522273 (1184/INNS).

TOMDOUN HOTEL, nr INVERGARRY: 01809 511218 (1192/INNS).

OLD LIBRARY LODGE, ARISAIG: 01687 450651 – report 1048/INX HIGHLAND RESTAURANTS.

Refer to Map 2.

1040 ✓ **CAFÉ NUMBER ONE, INVERNESS:** 01463 226200. Castle St. A favourite
C2 spot to eat in the Highland capital. See 2249/INVERNESS for full report. INX

1041 ✓ **OLD STATION, SPEAN BRIDGE:** 01397 712535. Richard and Helen
C3 Bunney's excl railway stn-restau conversion. Gr Scottish contemp cooking. We still say their single AA rosette should be 2. W coast seafood, and good
vegn selection. Apr-Oct Tues-Sun 11-5.30pm, dinner Fri-Sat only 6.30-9pm.
MED

1042 ✓ **SEAGREEN, KYLE OF LOCHALSH:** 01599 534388. Café by day and dinner
B3 at night. Eclectic and cosy atmos with wholefood products to buy, art
exhibitions and books. Seafood restau at night in adj funky dining rm. Fiona
Begg's amazingly good-value menu from locally caught/produced ingredients. Some vegn dishes, nice puds. Local cheeses and handmade chocolates
with your decaff. Restau May-Sept; LO 9pm; café AYR 10am-6pm (1314/VEGN
RESTAUS). MED

1043 ✓ **THE SEAFOOD RESTAURANT, KYLE OF LOCHALSH:** 01599 534813. Gt
B3 atmos bistro nr (and still an actual station platform) the busy port, off the
rd to Skye and with that bridge in the distance. Seafood (with unusual dress-
ings; 'raspberry and poppy seed') and vegn selection. Apr-Oct: lunch Mon-Sat
10am-3pm; dinner 7 days 6.30-9pm. V popular. Phone to book & check opening hrs (may vary edge of season). MED

1044 ✓ **OFF THE RAILS, PLOCKTON:** 01599 544423. On the platform of this
B3 working railway stn; but no droopy sandwiches here, just good home-
baking and snacks in the day then blackboard specials and evening menu
later. 10am-9.30pm in summer. Weekends only in winter. White choc bread
and butter pud! (Also 1508/COASTAL VILLAGES). INX

1045 ✓ **LA MIRAGE, HELMSDALE:** 01431 821615. Dunrobin St nr the Br Hotel. A
D1 little piece of Las Vegas in Caithness; this glitterati parlour is a novelty in
this wee village by the sea. Snacks of every kind all day; with life-size photos
of the inimitable proprietor Nancy Sinclair and various celebs gracing the
walls. Up for sale at TGP, sad to say. Great fish and chips while it survives and
we hope it does cause we love Nancy to bits. INX

1046 **HAMBLETTS, AVIEMORE:** 01479 810300. Main st (s end). At last a decent
D3 café/restau in benighted Aviemore. All day menu, supper at night (may cl late
afternoon for turnaround). Nice rm, light food; perfectly acceptable here. LO
10pm (maybe earlier in wint).

1047 **THE BOATHOUSE, KINCRAIG:** 01540 651394. 2km from village towards
D3 Feshiebridge along L Insh. Part of L Insh Water sports (2012/WATER SPORTS), a
balcony restau o/look beach and loch. Fine setting and ambience, friendly
young staff (but they come and go). Some vegn. Salmon from the loch. You're
in competition with the ospreys. Bar menu and home-baking till 6pm; supper
till 8.30pm, bar 11pm. Apr-Oct. CHP

1048 **OLD LIBRARY LODGE, ARISAIG:** 01687 450651. Nr the end of the infamous
B3 'Road to the Isles' just as they start to hove into view. Converted stables with
6 bedrms (MED.INX) above and behind. Hot and cold lunch snacks (INX)
11.30am-2.30pm. Good selection of not only seafood but also meat and veg
for the evening table d'hôte (MED) 6.30-9.30pm, booking advisable. Quay and
beach nearby (with boats to Rum, Eigg and Muck), bask in the sunset behind
them. INX

1049 **OLD SCHOOL, INSHEGRA, nr KINLOCHBERVIE:** 01971 521383. B801 Betw
C1 Rhiconich and Kinlochbervie. Not exactly converted but *adapted*, which is
what makes it atmos (the huge ruler on the wall helps). Snacks and kids' menu
during day; 3 courses at night with nursery puds. The world map from 1945 is
not the only nostalgia. Gourmet it is not, but you're usually glad you stopped.
Dinner daily 6-8pm, perhaps only Easter-Sept as from 2002. Phone to check.
INX

1050 **RIVERSIDE BISTRO, LOCHINVER:** 01571 844356. On way into tov
C1   Self-serve during day; vast array of Ian Stewart's home-made pies
     ic cakes. You can eat in, sit out at the picnic tables, or take away. C
     bistro beside river serves v popular meals at night; using local s
     son, vegn – something for everyone incl, apparently, Michael Winner (though
     don't let that put you off). Food 10am-8pm although bistro menu kicks in at
     6.30pm   MED

1051 **THE OYSTERCATCHER, PORTMAHOMACK, nr TAIN:** 01862 871560. On
D2   promontory of the Dornoch Firth (Tain 15km) this hidden seaside village
     could bring back childhood memories (even somebody else's). New owners in
     2001 (the Robertsons) and even more murals than before. The fishtank is still
     there and the menu more shellfishy. Still has a good name locally. Open Tues-
     Sun in July and Aug, Wed-Sun rest of season. Winter hours tbc. Meanwhile
     11.45am-4.30pm, then from 6.30pm on those open days.   CHP

1052 **MORANGIE HOUSE, TAIN:** 01862 892281. On way into/out of Tain from A9.
D2   Popular locally for its food; nicely kept hotel with 26 rms (EXP). A very TOS
     menu, but you're in very TOS environment. Wynne family run a good house.
     Lunch and 6-9.30pm.   MED/INX

1055 **FALLS OF SHIN COFFEE SHOP, nr LAIRG:** Self-serve café/restau in the visitor
C2   centre and shop across the rd from the Falls of Shin on the Achany Glen rd
     8km S of Lairg (1567/WATERFALLS). Excellent basic food, among best I've seen
     in similar situations. Somebody there cooks and cares. Mar-Oct daily 9.30am-
     6pm. Cl mid-Dec to end Feb. Other times, weekends only.   CHP

1054 **THE DUNNET HEAD TEA-ROOM, DUNNET HEAD, nr THURSO:** 01847
D1   851774. 15km N of Thurso on the coast rd via Castletown. New owners as from
     2000, the Sparks. Still an excellent stop en route to Dunnet Head, going or
     coming. Three B&B rooms for those who have travelled quite far enough,
     Easter-Oct. Food Easter-Sep 12-3pm then 6-9pm. Cl Wed.   INX

1055 **KYLESKU HOTEL, nr KYLESTROME:** 01971 502231. On A894; tucked down
C1   beside L Glencoul where the boat leaves to see Britain's 'highest waterfall'
     (1558/WATERFALLS). New ownership since last edition (Patrick Gilmore) 8 rms
     for those enchanted by the view, Mar-Oct. Fab setting with Quinag looming &
     longing to be climbed.   INX

THE BEST PLACES TO STAY IN AND AROUND ABERDEEN

It's been said before, but in oil city, hotels are expensive. But remember, though full during the week, many places offer surprisingly good w/end deals. Refer to Map 3.

1056 ✓✓ **MARCLIFFE OF PITFODELS:** 01224 861000. N Deeside Rd (en route to Royal Deeside 5km from Union St). Aberdeen's premiere hotel. On the edge of town, a successful mix of the intimate and the spacious, the old (mansion house) and the new (1993 refurb). Personally run by the Spence family, the sort of hoteliers whom no detail or guest's face escapes. 2 excellent restaus, breakfast in light conservatory. Often dinners and dos attended by the gr and the good Aberdonians; always efficient and friendly service.

42RMS JAN-DEC T/T PETS CC KIDS TOS LOTS

1057 ✓ **MARYCULTER HOUSE HOTEL, MARYCULTER:** 01224 732124. Another out-of-town hotel, in the same direction as Ardoe below but 7km further on. Excellent situation on banks of Dee with river side walks and an old grave-yard and ruined chapel. Newer annex; 8/9 rms o/look river. Poacher's Bar (best) and dining-rm. Many weddings here, so be prepared if over w/end. Hotel on site of 13th C preceptory. Cocktail bar v Knights Templar.

23RMS JAN-DEC T/T XPETS CC KIDS LOTS

1058 **ARDOE HOUSE, BLAIRS:** 01224 867355. 12km SW of centre on the S Deeside (it's poss to turn off the A92 from Stonehaven and the S at the first br and get to the hotel avoiding the city). The Dee is on other side of rd from hotel, but nearby. A granite chunk of Scottish Baronial with few, but more individual rms and an annex where most rms have pleasant countryside views. TOS menu gets 2 AA rosettes. Leisure facs & all-round fairly reliable biz hotel.

112RMS JAN-DEC T/T PETS CC KIDS TOS LOTS

1059 **THE PATIO HOTEL:** 01224 633339. Beach Boulevard. Accom in the Beach pleasure zone, slightly apart from both the dire mall-type development & the beautiful long seafront that it dominates. Serviceable biz hotel wins no archi-tectural plaudits from the o/side, but is comfortable and contemporary in its inner courtyard. Lightsome though bedrms have curiously wee windows. Own pool etc. Not far to Silver Darling for dinner (1010/ABER RESTAUS).

124RMS JAN-DEC T/T PETS CC KIDS EXP./ LOTS

1060 **CALEDONIAN THISTLE HOTEL:** 01224 640233. Victorian edifice on Union Terr. Of several city centre hotels just off Union St, this always seems the most easy to deal with, the most calm and efficient. Dining rm & refurb bar/brasserie. Some nice suites o/looking the Gardens. 80RMS JAN-DEC T/T PETS CC KIDS TOS LOTS

1061 **SIMPSON'S HOTEL:** 01224 327777. 59 Queen's Rd. V late 90s hotel (peach & turquoise thro' out) which tries hard to please. Huge bar & brasserie/restau adj is hugely pop (local star Paul Whitecross, the chef) – they say it 'evokes a Roman bath house'. 'Classic', 'Executive' rms & suites have some decor but diff sizes. Modern people will prob like all this; take your sunglasses.

50RMS JAN-DEC T/T XPETS CC KIDS TOS MED.EXP/LOTS

1062 **ATHOLL HOTEL:** 01224 323505. 54 King's Gate, a busy rd in w towards Hazelhead. An Aber stalwart, the sort of place you put your rellies and join them for dinner or a bar meal. I've never stayed, but people say this is the best among many mansions. Hotel says it's 'in a class of its own'.

35RMS JAN-DEC T/T XPETS CC KIDS MED.EX

1063 **THE BRENTWOOD HOTEL:** 01224 595440. 101 Crown St. In an area of many hotels and guesthouses to the S of Union St, this one's garish appearance belies a surprisingly commodious hostelry that is a better prospect than most. An adequate business hotel on a budget. Close to Union St and bars/restaus. Bar meals recommended and the ale is real.

65RMS JAN-DEC T/T PETS CC KIDS MED.INX

1064 **TRAVELODGE:** 01224 584555. 9 Bridge St tho' actually o/looking Union St bang in the middle which is why it's incl here. Usual conversion of office block into serviceable bedbox, but given Abd prices, this is a v reasonable billet.

97RMS JAN-DEC T/T XPETS CC KIDS CHP

1065 **THE CULTS HOTEL, CULTS:** 01224 867632. 9km from centre on A93 Deeside rd so well-placed for touring/Castle Trail. Fine roadside pub/hotel with local following and quite comfortable esp the 4 rms adj above the Post Office (sic). Bar is friendly & full of golf.　　　10RMS JAN-DEC T/T PETS CC KIDS MED.INX

1066 **HOSTELS: SYHA:** 8 Queen's Rd, an arterial rd to W. Grade 1 hostel 2km from centre (plenty buses). No café. Rms mainly for 4 to 6 people. You can stay out till 2am. Other hostels and self-catering flats c/o Univ, of which the best is probably the **ROBERT GORDON'S**, 01224 2621344. Campus in Old Aberdeen which is good place to be though 6km city centre has univ halls accom 01224 272664. Vacs only.

THE BEST RESTAURANTS IN ABERDEEN

THE TOPS

1067 ✓ ✓ **THE LAIRHILLOCK INN:** 01569 730001. Not in the city at all, but a roadside inn at a country crossroads to the S, reached off either the rd to Stonehaven or the S Deeside Rd W. Easiest is: head S on main A92, turn off at 'Durris' then 5km. Long-famous for its pub food (1289/PUB FOOD), informal atmos and posher restau, new owners determined to keep the rep. Restau now called 'Crynoch'. Likely to remain notable for good atmos, cheeseboard & malt selection & still worth the drive from town. Restau: dinner and Sun lunch. Cl Tues. LO 9.30pm. Inn: 7days lunch and LO 10pm.　　　MED/INX

1068 ✓ ✓ **SILVER DARLING:** 01224 576229. Didier Dejean's breakthrough bistro still going strong in this perfect spot poss the best location of any seafood (or other) restau in the land. Not so easy to find – head for Beach Esplanade, the lighthouse and harbour mouth (Pocra Quay). The light winks and boats glide past. Upstairs dining-rm not large (best to book) & you want to be by the window. Mostly chargrilled; the smell pleasantly pervades. Different menu for lunch and dinner, changes seasonally and depends on the catch. Apposite wines, wicked desserts. Mon-Fri lunch, Mon-Sat dinner 7-9.30pm.　EXP

1069 ✓ **THE FOYER:** 01224 582277. 82a Crown St. Remarkable in that this busy, contemporary restau with good mod-British cuisine & gr service is part of a local charity org who help homeless & disadvantaged people. No hint of charity here, but you can satisfy your conscience as well as your appetite for food & tasteful surroundings. Can't help thinking there should be more places like this. Lunch onwards LO 9.30pm. Cl Sun/Mon.　　　INX

1070 ✓ **DAG:** 01224 581177. 25 Crown St opp Foyer (above) Bar with downstairs dining-rm. Excl light menu mainly down to chef who was leaving at TGP, but this rep too good to lose, so hopefully standards will continue, tho' menu may change. Reports please. Lunch & LO 10pm. Cl Sun/Mon.　　　INX

1071 ✓ **OLIVE TREE:** 01224 208877. 32 Queen's Rd. A late 90s addition to smart dining in the Granite City and Mike Reilly certainly made sure it had the look & the good management. Bargain lunches and suppers (5.30-7pm) preferred (INX). Service and presentation tip top. The Olive Branch adj is curiously more Spar than special. Mon-Sat L and LO 10pm.　　　EXP

SEAFOOD

✓ ✓ **SILVER DARLING:** 01224 576229. The Tops (*see above*).

1072 ✓ **THE ASHVALE:** 01224 596981. 46 Gt Western Rd nr Union St and branches (incl Elgin, Br of Don, Inverurie and Brechin). The famous Ashvale fish 'n' chip shop, the NE equivalent of Harry Ramsden's, but we'd all say better, esp here at original branch. Sit in (room for 300) or take away. Long, varied menu; you'd be daft not to have fresh fried fish (1349/FISH AND CHIPS).　　　INX

1073 ✓ **ATLANTIS at the MARINER HOTEL:** 01224 591403. 349 Gr Western Rd. Those that know where to go in Aber for excellent fish and seafood may not necessarily go to Silver Darling or the Ashvale, but come here. Hotel dining-rm atmos is not too evident (tables in conservatory) and the fish v good. Moderately priced wines. Lunch (not Sat) and dinner LO 9.30pm.　　　MED

1074 **BISTRO VERDE:** 01224 586180. The Green (down steps from Union St at Virgin megastore). Unpretentious fish restau (one steak, one chicken dish) with blackboard daily catch. Nice place. Lunch & LO 10pm. cl Sun/Mon.   INX

ITALIAN

1075 ✓ **LITTLE ITALY:** 01224 572240. 79 Holburn St nr W end of Union St. The authentic good-fun and esp late-night Italian eaterie. Usual pasta/pizza mix. Can be raucous. Small & gets crowded. 7 days LO 11.15pm.   MED

1076 **BORSALINO:** 01224 732902. Peterculter on main A93 (after Rob Roy Br), 15km W of city centre but famously worth the drive. For over 20yrs Franco's unlikely cantina in a roadside cottage. Looking a little tired now, but a corner of Tuscany on a sunny day. Dinner only. Cl Mon.   MED

1077 **POLDINO'S:** 01224 647777. 7 Little Belmont St. Enduring haunt of Aberdonians in search of pasta etc. Good Italian home-cooking, incl puddings. City centre, always buzzy. Mon-Sat lunch and 6-10.45pm.   INX

1078 **CARMINE'S PIZZA:** 01224 624145. 32 Union Terr. This tiny slice of a rm for *the* best pizza in town and on the wall, a few famous faces who've eaten them. Take away (to the Gardens opp). real authentic pasta. Noon-5.30pm. Cl Sun.
CHP

EASTERN

1079 ✓ **THE ROYAL THAI:** 01224 212922. Crown Terr (off Crown St which is off Union St). The first and still one of the best of the welcome Asian invasion. 'Banquets' with sample dishes are a good idea. Good service, moody lighting. Daily lunch and 7-11pm. Same owners have the more recent CHINATOWN, see below.   MED

1080 **CHINATOWN:** 01224 211111. 11 Dee St Close to Union St, the smart new Chinese restau with designed decor & menu. Prob the closest to the old cuisine with a contemp twist. 7 days lunch and LO 11pm.   MED

1081 **YU:** 01224 580318. 347 Union St. Central, stylish, airy and relaxed and now longstanding Peking Chinese. Good fish; light sauces. Daily lunch and 7-11pm.   MED

1082 **NARGILE:** 01224 636093. 77 Skene St. Turkish survivor that made its regulars happy for 18yrs. Turkish owner, who also has t/away Meze Cafe at 3 Rose St (same name) open v late, and another **NARGILE** in Edin (173/BEST MED FOOD). Doric staff, reliable meze, kebabs, swordfish etc. 7 days, Cl lunch. 11pm Sun 10pm.   MED

BISTROS

1083 ✓ **THE VICTORIA:** 01224 621381. Upstairs at 140 Union St. Not a bistro as such, more a luncheon & tearm, but too good not to mention. Same staircase & foyer as adj jewellery & gift emporium so an odd alliance. Gr light menu, everything home-made & terribly well incl the bread & the biscuits. 9am-5pm (6.30pm Thur). Cl Sun.   INX

1084 ✓ **HOWIE'S:** 01224 639500. 50 Chapel St. Opened summer 2001. We haven't tried at TGP, but we know Howie's from Edin where there are several branches (119/EDIN BISTROS), so it's reasonable to suppose that this will be every bit as good & will give other Aber diners a run for their money.   INX

1085 **OWLIES:** 01224 649267. Littlejohn St. All-day brasserie in warehouse setting, a long-time Aber fave. Tapas bar d/stairs but also available up. Imaginative menu with good vegn choice. Gr value early even specials 5.30-7.30pm. Tues-Sat LO 10pm (11 w/ends). Good atmos, good attitude.   INX

1086 **THE WILD BOAR:** 01224 625357. 19 Belmont St. Narrow, intimate and usually buzzing bar-bistro that's stood the time test. From big cake selection to steaks/noodles to Thai additions. Caff turns into bar (open midnight). Food 12-7.30pm.   INX

1087 **THE LEMON TREE:** 01224 642230. 5 W North St. From E end of Union St heading for beach, W North St is off King St. Excellent arts centre with café-bar/restau. Food ok rather than fantastic, but gr ambience. Lunch only Tues-Sun. INX

1088 **LA BONNE BAGUETTE:** 01224 644445. Off Union St down steps at side of graveyard. Très popular and quite French café. Pâtisserie, snacks (baguettes, etc.) and specials. Daytime only 8.30am-5pm. Cl Sun. CHP

1089 **LA BAMBA:** 01224 590088. Crown Terr. Tex-Mex with attitude hits town. Good buzz. A party place but passable grub too. People do salsa after the salsa. May have seatings at w/ends (7pm & 9pm). Otherwise 7 days 5.30pm-LO 10pm.
INX

THE BEST PUBS AND CLUBS IN ABERDEEN

PUBS WITH ATMOSPHERE

1090 ✓ **THE PRINCE OF WALES:** 7 St Nicholas Lane, just off Union St at George St. An all-round gr pub always mentioned in guides and one of the best places in the city for real ale: Old Peculier, Caledonian 80/-, Younger's No 3 and guest beers. V cheap self-service food at lunchtime. Lots of wood, flagstones, booths. Large area but gets v crowded. 7 days, 11am-midnight (11pm Sun).

1091 ✓ **UNDER THE HAMMER:** 11 N Silver St. Basement bar along the st from above, v intimately Aberdonian and a good place to meet them. Slightly older and mixed crowd. Only open evenings (till midnight) and best late on. My kind of place. Last time I visited (Fri night, late) a single girl sat in the corner with a pint & a book. How cool is that?

1092 **THE BLUE LAMP:** Gallowgate. Snug pub with nice ambience and long-established clientele and up the st large stone-floored lounge (The Blue Lampie) with gr atmos and live music w/ends (so open 1am). Pub has pics of that '83 team and a jukebox unchanged forever.

1093 **MA CAMERON'S INN:** Little Belmont St. The 'oldest pub in the city' (though the old bit is actually a small portion of the sprawling whole – but there's a good snug). No nonsense oasis in buzzy street. Food: lunch and early evening. Cl Sun.

1094 **THE GLOBE:** 13 N Silver St. Urban and urbane bar in single rm – a place to drink coffee as well as lager, but without self-conscious, pretentious 'café-bar' atmos. Known for its food at lunch and 5-7.45pm (not w/ends) and for live music – jazz and blues in the corner.

1095 **THE LEMON TREE:** 5 W North St. A theatre (upstairs) and a spacious bar/restau on st level where there's lunchtime food (1087/ABER RESTAUS) and a mixed programme of entertainment. Phone (01224 642230) or watch for fliers, but prog will include comedy, jazz, folk, pop and cabaret. No membership required though only open when there's something on.

CONTEMPORARY PUBS

1096 **COLLEGE:** Alfred Pl at W end of Union St. Hugely popular 'sports' and MTV kind of bar by Q Brasserie with stylish interior. Screens hanging everywhere for the footie, boxing, and other bodies disporting and competing as they do around the bar.

1097 **THE OLD TOWN SCHOOL:** Little Belmont St as Ma Cameron's above, but the v up-to-date equivalent with everything from themed interior, balcony and patio to many ales, gr wine selection (by glass), malts and grub (till 9pm, w/ends 8pm). All works pretty well so does heave.

1098 **PARAMOUNT:** Bon Accord St. Designer café-bar looking a little worn now, but v popular and gr place to check out the club scene (flyers etc). You wouldn't want to eat here. Till midnight.

1099 **ESKOBAR:** 18 Bridge St. Basic dance/grungy bar with food during the day, DJs at night and aspirins available from the toilet vending machine. Becomes a club at night on lower level (see below).

1100 **BLUE:** Bon Accord St adj Via Milano & actually in the mini-shopping mall (bouncers at the entrance on the st). Difficult to see the appeal here, but summer 2001, this was cool. 7 days till midnight.

1101 **ILLICIT STILL:** Betw Broad St and Netherkirkgate. Studenty, wooden real ale labyrinth with brews from Tomintoul among others. Also bar food. Not a bad mix. 7 days till midnight.

1102 **JUSTICE MILL LANE and WINDMILL BRAE:** Many pubs to choose from. JM Lane has bigger selection and slightly older age gp. All loud and lively. For the up-for-it crowd (& the oil workers).

CLUBS

With more ready cash than most, the Aberdonian has many clubs to choose from. Once again we tried loads, those below are the ones we recommend. Open Fri-Sun mostly, but check flyers for details.

1103 ✓ **MINISTRY:** 01224 211661. 16 Dee St off Union St. Converted church and, after all these yrs still a good bet mainly because proprietor Mike Wilson put it together properly in the first place. Studenty but a pleasant mix – in Aber they generally don't mind oldies on the dancefloor. You have to be 'smart' on Sats; students and guest DJs on Suns.

1104 **PO NA NA:** 5 Union St. Northern outpost of the late-night raver pub/club chain. 7 nights 10pm-2am.

1105 **ESKO:** 18 Bridge St. The club labyrinth of the pub on the corner (above). If you're in the pub at 10pm you're in the club, otherwise pay am from door on the street below (Windmill Brae) this allows the pub to open late. It is pretty much a lager-laden & alcopop experience.

1106 **CHE VIVA at the METRO HOTEL:** Market St. Indie subterranean beatbox in the basement of this plastic hotel. No bad attitude, moustaches, or white slingbacks thank you! Yet more dancing underground.

1107 **LAVA:** 01224 648000. 9 Belmont St. Probably the most versatile of the Aber clubs. 2 floors offering resident DJs (everything from soul, & retro to hip hop & house) plus live bands & some guest DJs. Six nights a week. Open till 2am.

1108 **THE PALACE:** 01224 581135. 5 Bridge Pl. V popular with student crowd, partic on the alternative/indie Mon & Fri. More varied & mainstream on Thurs and hardcore rock on Sat. Open till 2am.

THE BEST HOTELS IN AND AROUND DUNDEE

Refer to Map 4.

1109 ✓ **THE OLD MANSION HOUSE, AUCHTERHOUSE:** 01382 320366. 15km NW of centre on B954 to Alyth (take Coupar Angus rd from ring route). Every important Scot in history is reputed to have stayed in this 16th-century castellated hse. Quirky and quaint but beautifully done, this is the real McCoy. Tranquil co house 20 mins from town. Fine dining, bistro & surprising outdoor (v small) pool. 6 RMS JAN-DEC T/T PETS CC KIDS TOS EXP

EAT Elegant dining in the green world beyond Dundee. EXP

1110 **HILTON:** 01382 229271. On riverside adj Olympic Centre nr Discovery Point. Serviceable, mainly business hotel with little charm but reasonable facs. Living Well leisure centre with ok pool. Brasserie & some rms o/look the Tay. 3 nights here and you might want to jump in. Casino of all things! 129RMS JAN-DEC T/T PETS CC KIDS EXP

1111 **THE QUEEN'S HOTEL:** 01382 322515. Nethergate/Perth Rd. Recent Best Western makeover has obliterated charm ('Nosey Parker's brasserie' – I ask you), but convenient location bang in the middle nr Arts Centre. Some back rms o/looking distant R Tay are best.

47RMS JAN-DEC T/T PETS CC KIDS MED.EX

1112 **THE SHAFTESBURY:** 01382 669216. 1 Hyndford St just off Perth Rd (about 3km from city centre). A suburban (jute baron's) mansion converted into a comfortable hotel with neat back gdn. All rms different; loungeable lounge. Decent value. 12RMS JAN-DEC T/T PETS CC KIDS INX

1113 **FISHERMAN'S TAVERN:** 01382 775941. Broughty Ferry, Fort St nr the river/sea. Rms above and beside but noise not bad esp new rms adj which are en-suite – others more basic but chp. Excl pub (*see below*) and grub. Gr location nr riverside and nr ship for gr grub (1131/DUNDEE RESTAU).

14RMS (5 EN-SUITE) JAN-DEC T/T PETS CC KIDS CHP.INX

1114 **HOTEL BROUGHTY FERRY, BROUGHTY FERRY:** 01382 480027. 16 W Queen St. On main rd into the 'Ferry' (*see below*). Cleanly refurb inside, with conservatory. Pool and sauna rm lurking surprisingly in the basement. On busy corner, but calm inside. Bar and Bombay Brasserie serving Indian & à la carte that was good enough for Michelin 2001. 16RMS JAN-DEC T/T XPETS CC KIDS MED.INX

1115 **WOODLANDS, BROUGHTY FERRY:** 01382 480033. From Broughty Ferry main st, take left after 1.5km into Abercromby St, second left into Panmure Terr. High falutin' house in substantial acreage. Recent refurb & good disabled access. Popular out-of-town wedding venue quite complete with small swimming pool and gym. 38RMS JAN-DEC T/T PETS CC KIDS MED.INX

SANDFORD HILL: 01382 541802. Excellent rural retreat over the water 7km S of Tay Br via A92/914 (1149/COUNTRY-HOUSE HOTELS).

SWALLOW HOTEL: 01382 641122. Modern, all-purpose chain hotel on town ring rd, but good for families (1162/KIDS).

HOSTELS: There is no S.Y.H. in the area, although in summer months univ hall accom is available – info from TO. 01382 527527. **THE WHITE HOUSE** 208 Broughty Ferry Rd. Caters for backpackers.

1116 ✓ **THE SHIP INN:** 01382 779176. On front at Broughty Ferry. Weathered by the R Tay since the 1800s, this cosy pub has sustained smugglers, fishermen and foody folk alike. Bar and upstairs restau; no-nonsense Scottish menu and picture windows o/look the Tay. Lunch and 5-10.30pm, w/ends noon-10.30pm. CHP

1117 ✓ **JUTE at DUNDEE CONTEMPORARY ARTS:** 01382 432000. Perth Rd. The bar/cafe/restau of the arts centre which is Dundee's most contemporary space and menu. Also gallery, cinema, classy craft shop. A good rendezvous. Snacks during day. Good coffee. 7 days 10.30am-midnight. Lunch and dinner LO 9/9.30pm. CHP

1118 ✓ **SOUTH KINGENNIE HOUSE:** 01382 350562 Out of town. From A92 nr Arbroath rd take B978 to Kellas (2km). At app to village, restau signed to rt (1km along). Major Sun lunch destination for Dundonians needing a lungful of air, an eyeful of green fields and a stomach full of roast beef with all the trimmings. Modern Scottish menu at other times. Cl Sun evening and Mon. MED

1119 ✓ **THE AGACAN:** 01382 644227. 113 Perth Rd. Fabled bistro for Turkish eats and wine. OTT frontage and much art on the walls. Bohemian ambience & you smell the meat (veggies go meze). Cl Mon. INX

1120 ✓ **PIZZA EXPRESS:** 01382 226677. 31a Albert Sq behind McManus Galleries. Dundee branch of the dependable pizza chain. Easily the classiest looking restau in town. Less crowded than PEs elsewhere – Dundonians unimpressed by the slightly more exp pizza, may actually prefer Pizza Hut. Oh, well! 7 days LO 10pm (11pm w/ends). INX

1121 **HOWIE'S:** 01382 322999. 25 Tay St. The estimable Howie's with 3 notable easy-eating establishments in Edin has come N to Aber (1084/ABER RESTAUS) & here in Dundee's emerging 'cultural quarter'. Here there's a bar/café, 2 floor restau & 4 rms. Too new at TGP to assess, but we know it will work. 7 days. Times TBA. INX

1122 **CAFE MONTMARTRE:** 01382 739313. 289 Brook St, Broughty Ferry. Charming and genuine bistro with extensive menu. French/Algerian cuisine incl N African wines. Gr value. 7 days (cl Mon lunch), LO 9.45pm CHP

1123 **CAFÉ BUONGIORNO:** 01382 221179. 11 Bank St. Fairly authentic Italian job behind shopping centre. Prob best Italian in town. Excl pasta. 9-9.30pm. Cl Suns. MED

1124 **VISOCCHI'S:** 01382 779297. 40 Gray St, Broughty Ferry. More of a café than the original Kirriemuir branch caff. After almost 70yrs they're still making mouthwatering Italian flavoured ice creams (*amaretto, cassata* etc.) alongside home-made pasta and snacks. CHP

1125 **ROYAL OAK:** 01382 229440. 167 Brook St nr W Pt. Excellent pub food with an Indian emphasis that's quietly quirky. Dundee's funky find. Bar and dining-rm. Lunch and LO 9pm. INX

1126 **GULISTAN HOUSE:** 01382 738844. Queen St in Broughty Ferry (on main rd in/out) in converted church. Perennially popular curry in a church. In many curry guides & with many hygiene certificates on display, a clean curry & prob a good one can be expected here. INX

1127 **JAHANGIR:** 01382 202022. 1 Session St at West Port. Another Dundee fave with taste only in the curry. Many pubs nearby so 10 pints then a tikka masala for some – not pleasant! INX

1128 **BYZANTIUM:** 01382 228866. Corner of Session St on busy Hawkhill. A pebbledash box opp Jahangir (above). Med but mostly E of Med cuisine. Joanna Blythman not impressed, nor me but makes a change from curry or pizza & definitely among the best in town. INX

1129 **MANDARIN GARDEN:** 01382 227733. 40 Tay St. V acceptable Chinese. Low key décor, peaceful atmos; food is the thing. Excellent seafood and different meats covered sauce-u-like but also MSG. Dinner only 5-11pm. INX

1130 FISHER & DONALDSON: Whitehall St off High St. Trad bakers among v best in Scotland (1401/BAKERS) with elevated tearm. Snacks & all their fine fare. Mon-Sat LO 4.45pm. CHP

... AND DRINK

1131 THE FISHERMAN'S TAVERN: 12 Fort St, Broughty Ferry. Good pub lunches here, but notable for real ales. Listed 17th-century fisherman's cottage, snug portside atmos. Also accom (1113/HOTELS). 11am-midnight (1am Thur-Sat).

1132 LAING'S: Roseangle, off Perth Rd. V popular with 20s-30s crowd. Beer gdn gets crowded in summer, typical pub food to fill you up and the *de rigeur* Banoffee pie. 11am-11.30pm.

1133 MERCANTILE BAR: Commercial St. Huge newly fashioned trad style pub with circular gallery brimming with regulars. Food till 7pm. V mixed crowd.

1134 TAYBRIDGE BAR: 129 Perth Rd. Legendary drinking place. Est 1867: the smoke-filled gloom of a Dundee afternoon. When Peter Howson runs out of Glaswegian gnarled heads, he might come here. Women are present, but usually accompanied by their 'man'.

1135 PUBS IN THE WEST PORT: THE GLOBE, TALLY'S, THE PARAMOUNT, THE DOGHOUSE etc: Popular student and 20-something hang-outs in W Port (end of S Tay St & off Marketgait; behind univ). The Irish one more authentic than usual.

SECTION 5

Particular Places to Eat and Stay throughout Scotland

SUPERLATIVE COUNTRY-HOUSE HOTELS

1136
MAP 4
B3
✓ ✓ **KINNAIRD, DUNKELD:** 01796 482440. 12km N of Dunkeld (Perth 35km) via A9 and B898 for Dalguise. In Kinnaird estate, a bucolic setting beneath woody ridge of Tay Valley, this country house envelops you with good taste and comfort. Good, unobtrusive service from friendly arrival to sad departure. You get a teddy on your bed and there's a stylish 'K' on everything. Gr snooker rm and drawing rm warmed by open fires. J/T preferred. Elegant dining; chef Trevor Brooks gets 3 AA rosettes. Silently beyond the grounds and river, endless traffic ploughs N and S on the A9. One day you'll have to join it again. Until then, live Kinnaird. Also 9 superb individual cottages (esp 'Castle Peroch') for more privacy.

9RMS (9 COTT) JAN-DEC T/T PETS CC KIDS LOTS

1137
MAP 6
C2
✓ ✓ **CROMLIX HOUSE, DUNBLANE:** 01786 822125. Full report (871/CENTRAL HOTELS), but one of the best country-house hotels in the UK. Vast and fabulously sylvan grounds, fastidious service, excellent food. Go rest!

1138
MAP 3
C3
✓ ✓ **RAEMOIR HOUSE, BANCHORY:** 01330 824884. 5 km N from town via A980. Scotland's most recently improved co house hotel. Historical with contemp comforts & excl dining. Report 972/NE HOTELS.

1139
MAP 1
B1
✓ ✓ **ISLE OF ERISKA, LEDAIG:** 01631 720371. 20km N of Oban (signed from A85 nr Benderloch Castle). As you drive over the Victorian iron br onto the isle (a real island), you enter a more tranquil and gracious world. Its 300 acres are a sanctuary for wildlife; you are not the only guests. The famous badgers, for example, come almost every night to the door of the bar for their milk. Comfortable baronial house with fastidious service and facs. Highly picturesque 9 hole golf, gr 17m pool (and gym) (excl in summer when it opens on to the gdn). Also putting, tennis and clay shooting; it's all there if you feel like action, but it's v pleasant just to stay still (and aromatherapy is avail). Dining, with a Scottish flavour and impeccable local ingredients from a rich backyard and bay, has 3 AA rosettes under chef, Robert MacPherson - unquestionably one of the top Scots.

17RMS FEB-DEC T/T PETS CC KIDS TOS LOTS

1140
MAP 4
B4
✓ ✓ **GLENEAGLES, AUCHTERARDER:** 01764 662231. Off A9 Perth-Stirling rd and signposted. Scotland's truly luxurious resort hotel. For facs on the grand scale others pale into insignificance; it is an international destination. Only the sun may be missing, but the famous golf (3 courses), the Equestrian Centre, Shooting School, Falconry Centre and Country Club make up for the climate. The Club has 2 pools and outdoor tubs. The newly refurb bedrms are esp contemporary elegant. Strathearn Restau is a foodie heaven but fabulously expensive. Also Club bistro lighter and brighter. Andrew Fairlie's intimate dining rm, considered by some to offer the best dining in Scotland, was new 2001. Report 958/PERTHSHIRE RESTAUS. When you are in love and rich go here; there are no cheap w/ends.

236RMS JAN-DEC T/T PETS CC KIDS TOS LOTS

1141
MAP 9
A3
✓ ✓ **KNOCKINAAM LODGE, PORTPATRICK:** 01776 810471. An ideal place to lie low; an historic Victorian house nestled on a cove. The Irish coastline is the only thing on the horizon, apart from your considerate N American hosts proffering discreet service, excellent food (chef Tony Pierce excels with a fixed menu which is full of surprises). Up for sale at TGP but we hope to see them there a while yet. 15km S of Stranraer, off A77 nr Lochans.

10RMS MAR-DEC T/T PETS CC KIDS TOS LOTS

1142
MAP 9
A2
✓ ✓ **GLENAPP CASTLE, nr BALLANTRAE:** 01465 831212. Victorian pile just S of Ballantrae on minor rd. V discreet. Home of Inchcape family for most of 20thC, opened as a hotel in first year of 21st. Run by Graham and Fay Cowan (Fay's family has other hotels in the SW). Amazing restoration on a house that fell into disuse in the 1990s. Excellent and studied service, good food, impeccable environment. Quality costs but the price is inclusive of just about everything, so relax and join this effortless house party.

17RMS EASTER-OCT T/T PETS CC KIDS LOTS AND LOTS

1143
MAP 2
C4
✓ ✓ **ARDSHEAL HOUSE, KENTALLAN:** 01631 740227. On A828 Oban-Ballachulish rd (7km S of bridge), signposted then 2km rough track. Neal & Philippa Sutherland's small, elegant co house in lovely grounds o/looking L Linnhe. Good brekkie, excl dinner. Enveloping & not exp.

6RMS MAR-NOV T/T XPETS CC KIDS TOS MED.EX

1144
MAP 4
B4

✓ **AUCHTERARDER HOUSE, AUCHTERARDER:** 01764 663646. Off B8062 Crieff rd 3km from this village more commonly associated with Gleneagles. It is more intimate and personal and there are few activities to - impinge on your slobbing out. Famous people have always come here and are discreetly and sumptuously accommodated. Public rms formal verging on gloomy; conservatory bar exquisite. Dining by candlelight in silk-lined rms. Chef Willy Deans is gr on detail (2AA rosettes).

15RMS JAN-DEC T/T PETS CC KIDS TOS LOTS

1145
MAP 4
C3

✓ **BALLATHIE HOUSE, KINCLAVEN, nr BLAIRGOWRIE and PERTH:** 01250 883268. Superb situation on R Tay; culinary delights, comfortable, relaxing: a chance to enjoy the finer things in (Perthshire) life. Merits longer mention than this, but because it is handy for Perth and probably the best place to stay nr the town; full report and codes: 2251/PERTH.

1146
MAP 1
B2

✓ **LOCH MELFORT, ARDUAINE, nr OBAN:** 01852 200233. 22km S of Oban on the A816 and on one of the most commanding sites on this picturesque coast. The fabulous view is not everything, but the rms and the restau make the most of it. 20 rms in an annex have either patios or (better) balconies. Large light dining-rm with notable seafood (EXP); Skerry Bistro (MED) more informal fare. The wonderful Arduaine Gardens (1479/GARDENS) run by the NTS are adj.

26RMS MAR-DEC T/T PETS CC KIDS TOS EXP

1147
MAP 1
C1

✓ **ARDANAISEIG, LOCH AWE:** 01866 833333. 16km from Taynuilt signed from main A85 to Oban down beautiful winding rd and 7km from Kilchrenan. In sheltered landscaped gdns dotted with funny faux Roman statuary and sculptures that burst from the rhododendrons. Nice to wander in even if you're not a guest – go for afternoon tea or lunch. On a promontory of the loch. Rooms have partic antiques, and decor. O/side by the loch, deer wander and bats flap at dusk. Pure romance. Chef Gary Goldie deserves some plaudits too.

16RMS MAR-DEC T/T PETS CC KIDS TOS LOTS

1148
MAP 2
B3

✓ **ARISAIG HOUSE, ARISAIG:** 01687 450622. On A830, rd to the Isles from Ft William to Mallaig. 2km before Arisaig and 18km from Mallaig in stunning countryside on one of Scotland's most romantic coasts. The Smither family smothers you with their good taste. 3AA. The gdns are a joy. Civilised and relaxed. Fuller report: 1240/SCOTTISH HOTELS. Note: Arisaig closing at end of 2002 season.

12RMS MAR-NOV T/T XPETS CC XKIDS LOTS

1149
MAP 5
C2

✓ **SANDFORD HILL, nr WORMIT (nr DUNDEE & ST ANDREWS):** 01382 541802. 7km S of Tay Bridge via A92 and A914, 100m along B946 to Wormit. In an unpromising landscape of quarries and pigfarms, a civilised withdrawal from the jams of Dundee and bunkers of St Andrews. An austere mansion with unusual layout and mullioned windows looking out to gorgeous gdns. Wild but romantic tennis court (someday they must get it back in use), pub lunches (pity about Jack Vettriano in the bar). 750 acres adj farmland of 'activities' – clay-pigeon shooting, fishing in Farm Loch, off-road driving.

16RMS JAN-DEC T/T PETS CC KIDS TOS EXP

1150
MAP 2
B2

✓ **FLODIGARRY COUNTRY HOUSE, SKYE:** 01470 552203. Nr Staffin, 32km N of Portree. Set on the face of a hill with amazing views across Staffin bay and the mighty Quirang behind. Gr crack in the bar (sessions at the drop of a fiddle) and lounge; the piano is often played. Flora MacDonald's cottage in the grounds with its tastefully refurbished bedrooms offers a rare opportunity actually to stay in a romantic place redolent of this island's history. The Butlers have created a relaxed atmos. Great sky and great Skye all around you.

19RMS (7 IN COTT) JAN-DEC T/X PETS CC KIDS TOS EXP

1151
MAP 2
D3

✓ **CORROUR HOUSE, AVIEMORE:** 01479 810220. Small country house 3km from the concrete moor of Aviemore, handy for the ski slopes. Without airs but not without graces, this family-run hotel is good value. Young deer in the gdn at daybreak, fine-size rms, the best deal for miles.

8RMS JAN-DEC T/T PETS CC KIDS TOS MED.INX

2 COUNTRY HOUSE HOTELS IN THE BORDERS

THE ROXBURGHE HOTEL nr KELSO: 01573 450331 Report: 887/BORDERS

CRINGLETIE HOUSE nr PEEBLES: 01721 730233. Report: 888/BORDERS

HOTELS THAT WELCOME KIDS

1152
MAP 4
B3
✓ ✓ **CRIEFF HYDRO, CRIEFF:** 01764 655555. A national institution and still a family business; your family is part of theirs. App via High St, turning off at Drummond Arms Hotel uphill then follow signs. Vast Victorian pile with activities for everybody from bowlers to babies. Still run by the Leckies from hydropathic beginnings but with continuous refurbs, incl the fabulous winter gdns moving graciously with the times. The Brasserie (best for food) is open all day. Gr tennis courts, riding school, Lagoon Pool. Tiny cinema shows family movies; nature talks, donkey rides. Kids endlessly entertained (even while you eat). The new chalets in grounds are certainly among the best in Scotland. Gr for family get-togethers.

225RMS JAN-DEC T/T PETS CC KIDS TOS MED.INX

1153
MAP 2
C3
✓ ✓ **OLD PINES, nr SPEAN BRIDGE:** 01397 712324. 3km Spean Br via B8004 for Gairlochy at Commando Monument. Bill and Sukie Barber have 8 kids so will be unfazed by the demands of yours. Amazing value. One level pine log cabin – all bedrms individually furnished; bunk beds with wee teddies to cuddle and take home. Playrm with books, videos and games for kids of all ages, and the Barber brood are also on hand to play with. Menagerie of animals around the stream (many ducks) and Sukie's legendary cooking. Kids can eat separately (not pizza and chips). (1014/BEST HIGHLANDS RESTAUS).

8RMS JAN-DEC X/X XPETS CC KID TOS MED.INX

1154
MAP 2
B3
✓ **GLENFINNAN HOUSE, GLENFINNAN:** 01397 722235. Just off the 'Road to the Isles' (the A830 from Ft William to Mallaig). V large Highland 'hoose' with so many rms and such large gdns you can be as noisy as you like. Great intro to the Highland heartland; music, scenery and local characters. Cruise of the loch leaves from the foot of the lawn. (1023/INEXP HIGHLAND HOTELS). Note: this is not poshed-up accom.   17RMS APR-OCT X/X PETS CC KIDS MED.INX-EXP

1155
MAP 2
C3
POLMAILY HOUSE, nr DRUMNADROCHIT: 01456 450343. 5km from main L Ness rd at Drumnadrochit via A831 to Cannich (and glorious Glen Affric), a good country-house hotel for adults that is excellent for kids. The Whittington-Davis's have 4 themselves. Their lucky kids and yours have lots to do in the gdns – trout pond where older kids can fish, pet rabbit run, bikes, indoor swimming pool, pool room. Tree house and swing up the back esp popular. Separate kids' meal time; special rates.

12RMS + 2SUITES JAN-DEC T/T PETS CC KIDS MED.EX

1156
MAP 2
A1
BAILE-NA-CILLE, TIMSGARRY, UIG, HARRIS: 01851 672242. 58km W of Stornoway, a long way to go, perhaps, and although this isolation might be more usually sought by adults, the beach here is one that kids will remember all their lives – wide, safe, untouched. Kids eat earlier and they will be tired. 3 sitting rms (one with TV, one smk – otherwise not). Boat trips to deserted islands in nice weather. 2 lower price rms in annex.

6+2RMS MAR-OCT X/X PETS CC KIDS MED.INX

1157
MAP 8
B2
PEEBLES HYDRO, PEEBLES: 01721 720602. Innerleithen Rd. One of the first Victorian hydros, now more Butlins than Bath. Huge grounds, corridors (you get lost) and floors of rms where kids can run around. New pool & leisure facs. Entertainment and baby-sitting services. V traditional and refreshingly untrendy. Rms vary. Dining rm is vast and hotel-like. Lazels bistro downstairs is light, contemp and refreshingly good (905/BORDER EATS).

137RMS JAN-DEC T/T PETS CC KIDS TOS MED.INX/EXP

1158
MAP 1
B2
STONEFIELD CASTLE HOTEL, TARBERT: 01880 820836. O/side Tarbert on A83 on slopes of L Fyne with wonderful views. A real castle with 60 acres of woody grounds to explore. Full report and codes: 826/ARGYLL HOTELS.

1159
MAP 2
C4
ISLES OF GLENCOE HOTEL, BALLACHULISH: 01855 811602. Beside the A82 Crianlarich to Ft William: a modern hotel and leisure centre jutting out onto L. Leven. Adventure playground o/side and nature trails. Conservatory restau o/looking the water, adj. to refurb lounge. Mysteryworld next door shut because of the 2001 foot and mouth – it may not reopen. We won't miss it! Snacks in the restau all day, new age Celtic-themed gift shop (*sic*). Glencoe and 2 ski areas nearby.   39RMS JAN-DEC T/T PETS CC KIDS MED.INX/EXP

1160 **HILTON COYLUMBRIDGE, nr AVIEMORE:** 01479 810661. 8km from Aviemore
MAP 2 Centre on B970 rd to ski slopes and nearest hotel to them. 2 pools of decent
D3 size, sauna, flume, etc. Plenty to do in summer and winter (1652/KIDS) and certainly where to go when it rains. Best of the often-criticised Aviemore corporate hotels, the most facs, huge new shed with kids' play area, staff wandering
around in animal costumes and kids' diner.
175 (INCL FAMILY)RMS JAN-DEC T/T PETS CC KIDS LOTS

1161 **WATERSIDE INN, PETERHEAD:** 01779 471121. Edge of town on A952 to
MAP 3 Fraserburgh. Modern hotel with pool etc and some activities for kids. Aden
D2 Country Park nearby (1649/KIDS). Kids' menu and meal times and family rms.
Ugie and Deedee (the bears) are a gr success, but you wouldn't want to take
them to bed. Adventure playground. Go-karts. Sometimes special family
w/ends. 109(16 FAMILY)RMS JAN-DEC T/T PETS CC KIDS TOS MED.EX

1162 **SWALLOW HOTEL, DUNDEE:** 01382 631200. Conveniently placed on the
MAP 4 edge of town, just off ring rd system and the rd in from Perth. A link in the
C3 commercial chain; but pleasantly sprawling with surprisingly lush gdns,
nature trails and leisure facs. Deals available. 107RMS JAN -
DEC T/T PETS CC KIDS EXP

THE BEST HOSTELS

For hostels in EDINBURGH, *see p. 29; for* GLASGOW, *see p. 77. SYHA Info: 01786
891400. Central reservations (SYHA) 01541 553255.*

1163 ✓ ✓ ✓ **CARBISDALE CASTLE, CULRAIN, nr BONAR BRIDGE:** 01549
MAP 2 421232. The flagship hostel of the SYHA, an Edwardian castle in
C2 terraced gdns o/looking the flood plain of a river on the edge of the
Highlands. Once the home of the exiled King of Norway, it still contains original works of art (nothing of gr value though the sculptures are elegant). The
library, ballrm, lounges are all in use and it's only a few quid a night. Shared
dorms as usual but no chores. Kitchens and café. Bike hire in summer; lots
scenic walks. Stn (from Inverness) 1km up steep hill. Buses:
Inverness/Thurso/Lairg. 80km Inverness, 330km Edin. 226 beds.

1164 ✓ **STIRLING:** 01786 473442 Fax 445715. Modern conversion in gr part of town,
MAP 6 close to castle, adj ancient graveyard and with fine views from some rms.
C3 One of the new hotel-like hostels with student-hall standard and facs. Many
oldies & internat tourists. B'fast incl or self-catering. Access till 2am. 130 beds.

1165 ✓ **LOCH LOMOND S.Y.H.:** 01389 850226 Fax 850623. Alexandria,
MAP 1 Dumbarton. Built in 1866 by George Martin, the tobacco baron (as
C2 opposed to the other one who produced the Beatles), this is hostelling on the
grand scale. Towers and turrets, galleried upper-hall, space for banqueting
and a splendid view across the loch, of where you're going tomorrow. 30km
Glas. Stn (Balloch) 4km. Buses 200m. Access till 2am. 184 beds.

1166 **THE BORDERS** *There are some ideal wee hostels in this hill-walking tract of*
MAP 8 *Scotland (where it all began). These 2 are esp good, one grand, one very small.*
C2, B3

MELROSE: 01896 822521. Grade 1, 90 beds, v popular. Well-appointed mansion looking across to the Abbey; student-hall standard.

BROADMEADOWS: 8km from Selkirk off A708, the first hostel in Scotland
(1931) is a cosy howff with a stove and a view.

1167 **INVERNESS STUDENT HOSTEL:** 01463 236556. Independent hostel at 8
MAP 2 Culduthel Rd opp the SYH, uphill from town centre (some dorms have views).
C2 Run by same folk who have the great Edin one (85/HOSTELS), with similar laid-
back atmos and camaraderie. Hostels seem to be springing up all over. If this
is full ask at the TIC.

1168 **ROWARDENNAN, LOCH LOMOND:** 01360 870259. The hostel at the end of
MAP 6 the rd up the E (less touristy) side of L Lomond from Balmaha and Drymen.
B3 Large, well managed and modernised and on a water-side site. On W
Highland Way and obvious base for climbing Ben Lomond (1884/MUNROS).
Good all-round activity centre and lawns to the loch of your dreams.
Rowardennan Hotel boozer nearby.

1169 **HOSTELLING IN THE HEBRIDES:** Simple hostelling in the crofting communities of Lewis, Harris and the Uists. Run by a trust to maintain standards in the spirit of Highland hospitality with local crofters acting as wardens. Lewis, Harris and one each in N and S Uist. No advance bookings necessary or accepted (suggests they will always fit you in). No smk and no Sun arrival or departure. Check local TICs for details (2240/WESTERN ISLES). Also:

1170 **AM BOTHAN, HARRIS:** 01859 520251. At Leverburgh in the S of S Harris a
MAP 7 bunkhouse handbuilt & personally run – a bright, cool building with contemp
A2 feel. Good disabled facs. Caff, shop nearby. 18 spaces. Check also 2101/MUSEUMS for the new hostel in a Blackhouse a little further N (N Lewis).

1171 **TOBERMORY, MULL:** 01688 302481. Looks out to Tobermory Bay. Central rel
MAP 1 high standard hostel v busy in summer. 39 places 7 rms (4 on front). Kitchen.
B1 Internet. Nr ferry to Ardnamurchan main Oban ferry 35km away (1512/VILLS).

1172 **GLENCOE:** 01855 811219. Deep in the glen itself, 3km off A82/4km by back rd
MAP 2 from Glencoe village and 33km from Ft William. Modern timber house o/look-
C4 ing river; especially handy for climbers and walkers. Clachaig pub, 2km for
good food and crack. (Also 1581/SCENIC ROUTES; 1852/SPOOKY PLACES;
1826/BATTLEGROUNDS; 1270/PUBS; 1981/SKIING; 1899/SERIOUS WALKS.)

1173 **RATAGAN:** 01599 511243. 29km from Kyle of Lochalsh, 3km Shiel Br (on A87).
MAP 2 A much-loved Highland hostel on the shore of L Duich and well situated for
B3 walking and exploring some of Scotland's most celebrated scenery e.g. 5
Sisters of Kintail/Cluanie Ridge (1901/SERIOUS WALKS), Glenelg (1582/SCENIC
ROUTES), 1751/PREHISTORIC SITES), Falls of Glomach (1552/WATERFALLS). From
Glenelg there's the short and dramatic crossing to Skye through the Kylerhea
narrows (continuous, summer only), quite the best way to go.

1174 **INDEPENDENT HOSTELS IN SKYE: DUN FLODIGARRY, nr STAFFIN:** 01470
MAP 2 552212. In far N 32km from Portree beside Flodigarry Country-House Hotel,
B2 whose pub is one of the best on the island and has great ceilidhs (2239/SKYE),
and amidst big scenery. O/looks sea. Bunkrms for 2-6 (holds up to 54) and
great refectory. Open AYR.

1175 **SKYE BACKPACKERS GUEST HOUSE, KYLEAKIN:** 01599 534510. Convenient
MAP 2 guest house with mainly 4-bunk rms and smallish gantry/lounge nr br for last/
B3 first stop on what used to be the island. Open AYR. There are many other in-
dependent hostels on Skye incl 2 in Portree. This has laundry service & internet.

1176 **GLEN FESHIE, nr AVIEMORE:** 01540 651323. Privately-run hostel in farm-
MAP 2 house by the rd-side in Glen Feshie, signed Achlean from Feshiebridge on the
D3 B970. A walkers' refuge which has a genuine, friendly atmos. Store sells basics;
free porridge, but also meals provided. Good base for Cairngorm walking
(1902/SERIOUS WALKS). 4 places incl 3 rms for 4. Open AYR.

1177 **FALKLAND BACKPACKERS:** 01337 857710. Back Wynd behind main st of
MAP 5 Fife's most charming inland village (1696/PALACE, 1907/WALKS). Refurb, friend-
B3 ly, linen provided, log fire. Gr organic restau round corner (938/RESTAU). Prob
best cheap stay in the county.

1178 **POTTERY BUNKHOUSE, LAGGAN BRIDGE nr A9:** 01528 544231. On rd E-W
MAP 2 nr L Laggan, homely bunkhouse & pottery/caff. Lounge o/look hills, wood
C3 stove, hot tub on deck. AYR.

1179 **MOUNT COLDINGHAM SANDS YOUTH HOSTEL, COLDINGHAM off A1:**
MAP 8 01890 771298. Impressive position & views over N Sea, N of Berwick. Usual
D1 ascetics of hostel life (SYH) but vill has some facs. Gr surfing & kayaking spot.
Cl Oct-Mar.

THE BEST ROADSIDE, SEASIDE AND COUNTRYSIDE INNS

1180
MAP 2
A2
✓ ✓ **THE THREE CHIMNEYS, COLBOST, SKYE:** 01470 511258. 7km W of Dunvegan on B884 to Glendale. Rms in a new build across the yard from the excl and long-established Three Chimneys restau (2223/ISLAND RESTAU) called **THE HOUSE OVER-BY.** Roadside tho few cars and within sight and smell of the sea. Exceptionally high standard split-level rms with own doors to the sward. Breakfast lounge, s/serv v healthy buffet. A model of its kind in the Highlands, hence often full. 8RMS JAN-DEC T/T PETS CC KIDS LOTS

1181
MAP 1
C1
✓ **BRIDGE OF ORCHY HOTEL, BRIDGE OF ORCHY:** 01838 400208. Unmissable on the A82 (the rd to Glencoe, Ft William and Skye) 11km N of Tyndrum. Old inn extensively refurbished and run as an excl stopover hotel. Simple, quite stylish rms. Hearty pub grub and dining. Good spot for the malt on the W Highland Way (1893/LONG WALKS). Also 54-bed bunkhouse (v chp). Under new management at TGP, but expect good things from the dynamic McKnights. 10RMS JAN-DEC T/T PETS CC KIDS MED.INX

1182
MAP 1
D2
✓ **BOUZY ROUGE at the SHERIFFMUIR INN:** 01786 823285. Narrow Sheriffmuir rd off A9 but also app via Dunblane or more scenically from Bridge of Allan. Historic coaching inn with stylish makeover by the people with the hugely popular restau chain (555/GLASGOW). Boutique hotel standard rms and contemp dining. Excl value and restful location (873/CENTRAL HOTELS). 4RMS JAN-DEC T/T PETS CC KIDS MED.INX

1183
MAP 2
C3
✓ **CLUANIE INN, GLENMORISTON:** 01320 340238. On main rd to Skye 15km before Shiel Br, a trad inn surrounded by the mt summits that attract the walkers and travellers who frequent the place. Club house adj has some group accom while inn rms can be high-spec – one with sauna, one with jacuzzi! Ideal place to crash after a long haul in the hills. Good bar food LO 9pm. The Cluanie Ridge and the 5 Sisters await you in the morning (1901/SERIOUS WALKS). 14RMS+1 JAN-DEC T/X PETS CC KIDS INX-MED.EX

1184
MAP 2
B3
✓ **GLENELG INN, GLENELG:** 01599 522273. At the end of that gr rd over the hill from Shiel Br on the A87 (1582/SCENIC ROUTES)…well, not quite the end because you can drive further round to ethereal L Hourn, but this halt is a v civilised hostelry of fame and infamy. Decent food, good drinking, snug lounge. Gdn with tables and views. Charming rms. From Glenelg, take the best route to Skye (7/FAVOURITE JOURNEYS). 6RMS APR-OCT X/X PETS XCC KIDS MED.EXP

1185
MAP 1
A1
✓ **ARGYLL HOTEL, IONA:** 01681 700334. On beautiful, turquoise bay betw Iona & Mull on rd betw ferry & abbey. Daytrippers come & go but here you can really chill and roam this remarkable island. Cosy rms (1 suite), good food (esp vegn) The real peace & quiet and that's just sitting on the bench outside – this is Colourist country & this is where they would have stayed. 16RMS EASTER-OCT X/X PETS CC KIDS MED.INX

1186
MAP 8
B3
CROSS KEYS INN and COURTYARD COTTAGES, ETTRICKBRIDGE, nr SELKIRK: 01750 52224. Well not that nr Selkirk, but 12 km down beautiful B7009 & the historic valley of the Ettrick. James Hogg country excl for walking, fishing, getting away. 2/3 bedrm houses adj pub are light & spacious. Pub cosy & cluttered but choose food carefully. 5RMS JAN-DEC X/T PETS CC KIDS INX

1187
MAP 4
A3
FORTINGALL HOTEL, FORTINGALL, nr ABERFELDY: 01887 830367. 15km from Aberfeldy but close to fabulous Glen Lyon (1542/GLENS). Trad inn, log fire bar, some refurb ongoing. Often booked. The 'oldest tree' in Europe is next door in the churchyard. Good for fishing and walking and kids are welcomed. 10RMS MAR-NOV T/T PETS CC KIDS MED.INX

1188
MAP 2
B2
THE STEIN INN, WATERNISH, SKYE: 01470 592362. Off B886 the Dunvegan-Portree rd, about 10km Dunvegan. In row of cottages on waterside. The 'oldest inn on Skye' with gr pub (open fire, good grub) & comfortable small rms above. Gr value in a special spot. Excl seafood restau adj (1332/SEAFOOD RESTAUS). 5RMS JAN-DEC X/X PETS CC KIDS CHP

1189 **WEST LOCH HOTEL, TARBERT:** 01880 820283. Beside A83 just W of Tarbert;
MAP 1 ideal stopover en route to the islands. Comfortably furnished; with original
B2 features sympathetically retained. Board games and books dotted around,
children welcome in relaxed, friendly atmos. Good value, but roadside rms
may be noisy. And doesn't that staff member suit her leather trousers … ?
8RMS JAN-DEC X/T PETS CC KIDS MED.INX

1190 **PIER HOUSE, PORT APPIN:** 01631 730302. An inn at the end of the rd (the
MAP 1 minor rd that leads off the A828 Oban to Ft William) and at the end of the
B1 'pier', where the tiny passenger ferry leaves for Lismore (2202/MAGIC ISLANDS).
Bistro restau with decent seafood (1345/SEAFOOD RESTAUS) in gr setting. Comfy
motel-type rms o/look the sea and island and jazzy lounge.
11RMS JAN-DEC T/T XPETS CC KIDS MED.EX

1191 **GLENISLA HOTEL, KIRKTON OF GLENISLA:** 01575 582223. 20km NW of
MAP 4 Kirriemuir via B951 at head of this secluded story-book glen. A home from
C2 home: hearty food, real ale and local colour. Fishers, stalkers, trekkers and
walkers all come by. Miles from the town literally and laterally. Newish owners
making improvements. A non-TV kind of a place (portable avail on demand,
pay-phone in foyer).
6RMS JAN-DEC X/X PETS CC KIDS INX

1192 **TOMDOUN HOTEL, nr INVERGARRY:** 01809 511218. 20km from Invergarry,
MAP 2 12km off the A87 to Kyle of Lochalsh. A 19th-century coaching inn that
C3 replaced a much older one; off the beaten track but perfect (we do mean perfect) for fishing, walking (L Quoich and Knoydart have been waiting a long
time for you) and naturalising. Superb views over Glengarry and Bonnie
Prince Charlie's country. New owners making improvements.
10RMS JAN-DEC X/X PETS CC KIDS INX

1193 **ST MICHAELS INN, nr ST ANDREWS:** 01334 839220. On A919 towards
MAP 5 Dundee, 12km from St Andrews. At crossrds, a 200-year-old inn, seems
C2 Englishy, often busy, with pub food and restau. Plenty of golf and other attractions within reach. Good bet given cost of board in St Andrews.
8RMS JAN-DEC X/T PETS CC XKIDS INX

1194 **CRAW INN, AUCHENCROW, nr RESTON:** 01890 761253. 5 km A1 and well
MAP 8 worth short detour into Berwickshire countryside. Quintessential inn with
D1 cosy pub & dining rm. Funky furniture, simple rms. Food so-so, wines a surprise.
3RMS JAN-DEC X/X PETS CC XKIDS CHP

1195 **TRAQUAIR ARMS, INNERLEITHEN:** 01896 830229. 100m from the A72
MAP 8 Gala–Peebles rd towards Traquair, a popular village and country inn that
B2 caters for all kinds of folk (and, at w/ends, large numbers of them). Notable for
bar meals, real ale and family facs. Rms recently refurb. Nice gdn out back. All
food v home-made.
10RMS JAN-DEC T/T PETS CC KIDS MED.INX

1196 **THE KAMES HOTEL, TIGHNABRUAICH:** 01700 811489. Frequented by pass-
MAP 1 ing yachtsmen who moor alongside and pop in for lunch. Good base for all
C2 things offshore; marine cruises or a nostalgic journey on a 'puffer', with a gr
selection of malts to warm you up before or after. New owners since last time,
the Andrews. Hotel on a rolling refurb, keen to be seen as an inn with rms.
Great bar.
10RMS JAN-DEC X/T PETS CC KIDS MED.INX

1197 **BRIDGE OF CALLY HOTEL, BRIDGE OF CALLY:** 01250 886231. Wayside pub
MAP 4 on a bend of the road betw Blairgowrie and Glenshee/Braemar (the ski zone
C3 and Royal Deeside). Cosy and inexpensive betw gentle Perthshire and the
wilder Grampians. Newish owners.
9RMS JAN-DEC T/T PETS CC KIDS INX

1198 **CLACHAIG INN, GLENCOE:** 01855 811252. Basic accom but you will sleep
MAP 2 well, esp after walking/climbing/drinking, which is what most people are
C4 doing here. Gr atmos both inside and out. Food avail bar/lounge and dining
rm.
20RMS JAN-DEC X/T XPETS CC KIDS INX

1199 **MOULIN HOTEL, PITLOCHRY:** 01796 472196. Kirkmichael Rd; at the landmark
MAP 4 crossrds on the A924. Rms above and beside notable pub for food and esp
B2 ales – they brew their own out the back. (1279/REAL ALES).
16RMS JAN-DEC T/T MED.INX

1200
MAP 1
B2
CULFAIL HOTEL by KILMELFORD: 01852 200274. On A816 20 km S of Oban and nr a gr bit of W Highland coast that includes Seil Island, Luing etc. A trad roadside hostelry incl the 'Tartan Puffer' Bar B Q restau. A gantry full of choice single malt whiskies and bar food provided as and when. A friendly hotel with a lounge that speaks of time and travellers gone by.

12RMS JAN-DEC X/T PETS CC KIDS MED.INX

1201
MAP 1
B2
GALLEY OF LORNE, ARDFERN: 01852 500284. Roadside/seaside inn in yachty haven of Ardfern. Salts, locals and other worthies mingle at the bar and the restau/bistro is good for families early in the evening and for drinking much wine later on. Rms basic, but new owners may improve. Ardfern itself is a good berth.

JAN-DEC X/T PETS CC KIDS INX

1202
MAP 2
C3
GLENMORISTON ARMS HOTEL, INVERMORISTON, LOCH NESS: 01320 351206. On main A82 betw Inverness (45km) and Ft Augustus (10km) at the Glen Moriston corner, and quite the best corner of this famous loch side to explore. Busy local bar, fishermen's tales. Bistro over-by (LO 8.30pm) table o/side in summer. Bar meals look ok and extensive malt list – certainly a good place to drink them.

8RMS JAN-DEC T/T PETS CC KIDS MED.INX

ANCHOR HOTEL, KIPPFORD: 01556 620205. Report: 866/SW HOTELS/RESTAUS

THE OLD ABERLADY INN: 01875 870503 Report: 912/LOTHIANS HOTELS

THE GREAT GET-AWAY-FROM-IT-ALL HOTELS

1203 ✓✓✓ **SKIBO CASTLE, DORNOCH:** 01862 894600. A vast estate once
MAP 2 home to the formidable Carnegies (those halls in NYC,
D2 Dunfermline, etc.). They declared it to be 'heaven on earth' which may be your
sentiment too. Now like an Edwardian 'gentleman's' club you can sample the
atmos once, but to return you join the club. Some club! The sumptuous castle
retains its original furnishings (silk wallpaper, panelling, etc.) and the service
from your discreet 'hosts' is exemplary. Lodges in the grounds offer more privacy, with the obligatory golf course, spa, gym and beach, all oases of relaxing
indulgence – vintage Rolls Royces take you around. You get the feeling they
weren't that bothered about the publicity boost when Maddy got married
here. Phone for details. LOTS AND LOTS

1204 ✓ **LOCH TORRIDON, GLEN TORRIDON, nr KINLOCHEWE:** 01445 791242.
MAP 2 Impressive former hunting lodge on lochside, surrounded by majestic
B2 mts. A comfortable but cosy baronial house with very upmarket atmos. For all
that, it's been focusing on outdoor activities lately like clay-pigeon shoots,
mountain bikes or fishing. Lots of walking possibilities and Diabeg nearby
(1518/COASTAL VILLAGES). 20RMS JAN-DEC T/T XPETS CC XKIDS TOS LOTS

1205 ✓ **MONACHYLE MHOR, nr BALQUHIDDER:** 01877 384622. Not so very
MAP 6 remote, but seems so once you've negotiated the thread of rd alongside
B2 Loch Voil from Balquhidder (only 11km from the A84 Callander-Crianlarich rd)
and Rob Roy's now famous grave (1810/GRAVEYARDS). Farmhouse o/looking L
Voil from the magnificent Balquhidder Braes. Friendly, cosy and inexp; a place
to relax in summer or winter. Rms in courtyard annex are best (5), but all have
character. Fishing. Food fairly fab, well-sourced ingredients, 2 AA rosettes.
Tastefully done, gr informal atmos.
5+5RMS+2 COTT JAN-DEC T/T PETS CC KIDS TOS MED.INX

1206 ✓ **TIRORAN HOUSE, ISLE OF MULL:** 01681 705232. SW corner on rd to Iona
MAP 1 from Craignure then B8035 round Loch na Keal. 1 hr Tobermory but you
B1 don't ever have to go there. Family-friendly small co house in gr gdns by the
sea. Excl food from sea & kitchen gdn in vine-hung conservatory. Lovely rms
(esp the gdn one). Wolsey Lodge but you don't eat together. Find this place!
6RMS+2COTT MAR-NOV X/X XPETS CC KIDS MED.EXP

1207 ✓ **ARGYLL HOTEL, IONA:** 01681 700334. Quintessential island hotel on the
MAP 1 best of small islands just large enough to get away for walks & explore
A1 (2194/ISLANDS) & you can hire bikes (or bring). Abbey is nearby (1814/ABBEYS).
3 lounges (1 with TV, 1 with sun) & 1 lovely suite (with wood-burning stove)
new in 2002. Good home-grown/made food.
15RMS(1SUITE) APR-OCT X/X PETS CC KIDS MED.INX

1208 ✓ **BOUZY ROUGE at the SHERIFFMUIR INN:** 01786 823285. The old rd
MAP 6 across the moor app via A9, from Dunblane or Bridge of Allan (see The
C2 Ochils: 1881/HILLS). Excl food in pub or restau by the BR people (555/GLAS
BISTROS) & 4 stylish rms, a real surprise in this isolated spot (though only 20
mins from Stirling). Not many walks adj but a real sense of being at the cross-
roads to nowhere. 4RMS JAN-DEC T/T PETS CC KIDS MED.INX

1209 ✓ **CORSEWALL LIGHTHOUSE HOTEL nr STRANRAER:** 01776 853220. Only
MAP 9 15mins from Stranraer (via A718 to Kirkcolm) and follow signs, but way
A3 up on the peninsula and as it suggests a hotel made out of a working lighthouse. Gordon Ward took over in 2000 and doing well. Romantic and offbeat,
decent food too, and there are attractions nearby (Portpatrick 30 mins).
6RMS (+ SUITES IN GROUNDS) JAN-DEC T/T PETS CC KIDS EXP

1210 **GLENMORANGIE HOUSE:** 01862 871671. Cadboll, by Fearn, nr Tain. On the lit-
MAP 2 tle peninsula E of Tain – phone to ask for directions. Owned by the whisky
D2 people since '89, they decided to open it up in '98. Still used for corporate
entertainment by Glenmorangie and other companies – Sting stayed here
when Madonna got hitched at Skibo. But the public can come too. Chef has
good rep. Class not just in the glass. 9RMS JAN-DEC T/X XPETS CC XKIDS EXP

1211   **THE PIER HOUSE, INVERIE, KNOYDART:** 01687 462347. Currently the only rest
MAP 2   on this far-away peninsula, though good grub at the pub nearby (1268/BLOO
B3   GOOD PUBS). Accessible on foot (sic) from Kinlochourn (25km) or Bruce Watt's bo
from Mallaig (Mon, Wed, Fri). Friendly couple offer warm hospitality in their hom
and surprisingly good cooking for somewhere so remote; rovers often retur
Some say the better and certainly remoter option is the **DOUNE STONE LODG**
01687 462667; 5km up the single rd. We couldn't stay, but it comes much recom
mended.   4RMS MAR-OCT X/X XPETS XCC KIDS TOS C

1212   **CLOVA, GLEN CLOVA HOTEL, nr KIRRIEMUIR:** 01575 550350. Well, not that
MAP 4   Kirriemuir; 25km N to head of glen on B955 and once you're there there's nowhe
C2   else to go except up. Recent upgrading & makeover. Rms all en-suite. Walkers' b
Superb walking hereabouts (e.g. L Brandy and the classic path to L Muick). A
inexp get-away-from-it all.   10RMS JAN-DEC T/T XPETS CC KIDS II

1213   **APPLECROSS INN, APPLECROSS:** 01520 744262. At the end of the rd (the Pass
MAP 2   the Cattle which is often snowed up in winter, so you can really disappear) N
B2   Kyle of Lochalsh and W of Strathcarron. Now Judith Fish is sole owner she's drafte
in a proper chef (who has worked with Michelin starred peers) and upgraded th
rms. Homely with the odd kitsch flourish but a half pint of prawns and some R
Cuillin? You're laughing!   7RMS JAN-DEC X/X PETS CC KIDS II

1214   **TOMICH HOTEL nr CANNICH:** 01456 415399. 8km from Cannich which is 20k
MAP 2   from Drumnadrochit. Fabulous Plodda Falls are nearby (1553/WATERFALLS). Co
D3   country inn in conservation village with added bonus of use of swimming pool
nearby steading. Good base for outdoorsy w/end. Glen Affric across the way.
       8RMS FEB-NOV T/T PETS CC KIDS MED.I

1215   **INVERVAR LODGE, GLEN LYON:** 01887 877206. A brilliant retreat in Glen Lyo
MAP 4   Run by a Swiss/German couple they seem to be doing everything right. Delicio
A3   food free-range/organic wherever poss, open fire, good vibes. BYOB. Glen Lyon,
course, is amazing (1542/GREAT GLENS). Changes afoot – phone first.
       4RMS DEC-OCT X/X PETS CC KIDS I

1216   **MULLARDOCH HOUSE, nr CANNICH, nr DRUMNADROCHIT:** 01456 41546
MAP 2   Leaving L Ness at Drumnadrochit up Glen Urquhart to Cannich (20km), then foll
C3   R Cannich to head of glen (12km) where it's blocked by the mighty Mullardo
Dam. Almost tangible pressure as this cosy Edwardian shooting lodge lies below
but only herds of red deer wander here and with 11 Munros within 20mins, it'
good place to wander, too. Good for hunters/shooters/fishers. Their tick is repo
edly long overdue, but we didn't make it up the glen again, so can't award o
Reports please! Fixed dinner at 8pm.   6RMS JAN-DEC T/T PETS CC KIDS MED

1217   **DALILEA HOUSE, nr ACHARACLE:** 01967 431253. East end of Ardnamurch
MAP 2   Young Ms Macaulay has been surely building her reputation here in the old fa
B3   ly farmhouse since '96. The cooking gets plaudits from TOS & the overall ambier
gets thumbs up from us. Non residents can dine (MED) but do book. The Macau
ancestors keep a watchful eye on Mairi in the dining rm … (Phone for directio
       5RMS MAR-OCT X/X PETS CC KIDS TOS I

1218   **ARDEONAIG, LOCH TAY:** 01567 820400. On narrow and scenic S Loch Tay rd m
MAP 4   way betw Kenmore and Killin. An airy roadside inn by the water opp Ben Lawe
A3   Friendly staff. Cosy public rms and bar. Upstairs library with cool books and drea
view of the Ben. Good food. Love that loch!   14RMS JAN-DEC T/X PETS CC KIDS MED

1219   **CAPE WRATH HOTEL, nr DURNESS:** 01971 511212. 3km S Durness just off A838; on
MAP 2   to Cape Wrath Ferry (1933/COASTAL WALKS) which takes you to Britain's farthest-flu
C1   corner and the Cliffs of Clo Mor. O/looking the loch, the sparsely furnished hotel is p
ular with fisherman; passing tourists also shoal up for lunch. Fishing on 2 rivers incl
ing the celebrated Dionard and lochs. Durness Golf nearby (1975/GOLF) and the
some of Britain's most spectacular and undisturbed coastline to wander. Excl vie
from some rms down Kyle of Durness; like a setting for something morose by Ibser
       18RMS APR-OCT X/X PETS CC KIDS MED.I

1220   **LADYBURN, MIDDLE OF NOWHERE, AYRSHIRE:** 01655 740585. On the B7
MAP 9   Girvan to Crosshill, find the turnoff 2 miles from Crosshill marked for campsite/c
B2   avan park. Ladyburn's around a mile up there. Small and discreet country ho
with AA rosette and sense of decorum. 5RMS EASTER-OCT T/T XPETS CC XKIDS LO

1221 **SPRINGBANK COTTAGE, ST ABBS:** 018907 71477. Centre of the village next
MAP 8 to St Abbs harbour, 5km from the A1. Not a hotel, certainly a B&B but defi-
D1 nitely a gr place to get away. Small and friendly cottage (no smk) with an outdoors tea gdn open all year, popular with divers – bring a wetsuit when raining. Walk in St Abb's Head nature reserve (1682/WILDLIFE RESERVES). Few rms so
often full in summer. 3RMS FEB-DEC X/T PETS CC KIDS CHP

1222 **TUSHIELAW INN, ETTRICK VALLEY:** 01750 62205. Further down the valley
MAP 8 (15 miles Selkirk) a cosy retreat. Only 3 rms, but good value. Both this country
B3 inn and the Cross Keys, below, are in wildly beautiful James Hogg country
(1849/LITERARY PLACES) about 1 hr from Edinburgh.
3RMS JAN-DEC X/T PETS CC KIDS CHP

1222a **MOOR OF RANNOCH HOTEL, RANNOCH STATION:** 01882 633238. Beyond
MAP 4 Pitlochry and the Trossachs and far W via L Tummel and L Rannoch (B8019
A2 and B8846) so a wonderful journey to the edge of Rannoch Moor. Literally the
end of the road but an exceptional find in the middle of nowhere. Quirky
rooms, great restau (open to non-residents). Many readers rave about this
place. 5RMS JAN-DEC X/X PETS CC KIDS MED INX

ALSO …

KNOCKINAAM LODGE, nr PORTPATRICK: 01776 810471. Report: 853/SW
BEST HOTELS

THREE CHIMNEYS, SKYE: 01470 511258. Report: 1180/ROADSIDE INNS,
2223/ISLAND RESTAU.

CROSS KEYS, ETTRICKSHAWS, THE BORDERS: 01750 52224. Report:
1186/ROADSIDE INNS.

ACKERGILL TOWER, nr WICK: 01955 603556. Report: 1259/HOUSE PARTIES.

SOME HIGHLAND AND ISLAND PLACES TO CAMP

In Scotland the Best we don't do caravan life style. In fact, because we spend a lot of time behind them on Highland roads, WE HATE CARAVANS, but wild camping is a different matter. Although probably irresponsible to encourage wild camping, it's a good and inexp way to experience Scotland, provided you are sensitive to the environment and respect the rights of farmers and other landowners.

1223 **KINTRA, ISLAY:** Bowmore-Port Ellen rd, take Oa turn-off then follow signs
MAP 1 7km. Restau and bar at end of rd with long beach one way, wild coastal walk
A3 the other. Camping (room also for a few caravans) on grassy strand looking out to sea; not a formal site but facs available. Also bunkhouse.

1224 **LOCHAILORT:** A 12km stretch S from Lochailort on the A861, along the
MAP 2 southern shore of the sea loch itself. A flat, rocky and grassy foreshore with a
B3 splendid seascape and backed by brooding mtns. Nearby is L nan Uamh where Bonnie Prince Charlie landed (1838/MARY, CHARLIE AND BOB). Once past the salmon farm laboratories, you're in calendar scenery; the Glenuig Inn at the southern end is a fine pub to repair to. No facs except the sea.

1225 **MULL:** Calgary Beach 10km from Dervaig, where there are toilets; also S of
MAP 1 Kilchronan on the gentle shore of L Na Keal where there is nothing but the sky
B1 and the sea. Ben More is in the background (1887/MUNROS).

1226 **GLEN ETIVE, nr BALLACHULISH and GLENCOE:** One of Scotland's gr unoffi-
MAP 2 cial camping grounds. Along the rd/river side in a classic glen (1544/GLENS)
C4 guarded where it joins the pass into Glencoe by the awesome Buachaille Etive Mor. Innumerable grassy terraces and small meadows on which climbers and walkers have camped for generations, and pools to bathe in (1616/SWIMMING HOLES). The famous Kingshouse Pub is 2km from the foot of the glen for sustenance, malt whisky and comparing midge bites.

1227 **OLDSHOREMORE, nr KINLOCHBERVIE and ACHMELVICH, nr LOCHINVER:**
MAP 2 2 superb beaches with grassy links and nr villages for supplies, the pub etc.
C1 Achmelvich has official campsite, Oldshoremore (and neighbouring coves) has only you.

CAMPING WITH THE KIDS

Caravan sites and camp grounds that are especially kid-friendly, with good facilities and a range of things to do (incl a good pub).

Key: HIRE *Caravans for rent* XHIRE *No rental caravans available*
X CVAN *Number of caravan pitches* X TENT *Number of tent pitches*

1228 **GLEN MORE CAMP SITE, nr AVIEMORE:** 01479 861271. 9km from Aviemore
MAP 2 on the road to the ski slopes, the B970. Across the road from the Glen More
D3 Visitor Centre and adj to L Morlich Watersports Centre (2013/WATER SPORTS). Extensive grassy site on loch side with trees and views of the mountains. Loads of activities include watery ones esp the reindeer (1652/KIDS) and at the Coylumbridge Hotel (1160/HOTELS THAT WELCOME KIDS) where there's a pool and The Fun House – a separate building full of stuff to amuse kids of all ages (soft play, mini golf, etc). Well stocked shop at site entrance.

DEC-OCT XHIRE 240TENT

1229 **TAYMOUTH HOLIDAY CENTRE, KENMORE:** 01887 830226. On the A827 road
MAP 1 leading out of picturesque vill at the end of L Tay. The campsite is part of a
D1 centre which also includes cottages to rent and a bistro as well as numerous facs. Close to Croft-Na-Caber Water Sports (2014/WATER SPORTS) which has everything that you can do on a boat, board, etc and the Crannog Centre (1737/PREHISTORIC SITES). Kenmore Hotel (951/HOTELS TAYSIDE) good for pub food – the kids can run about on the terraces. MAR-OCT XHIRE MANY TENT

1230 **CARFRAEMILL CAMPING & CARAVANNING SITE:** 01578 750697. Just off
MAP 8   A697 where it joins the A68 near Oxton. Small, sheltered and friendly camp-
C2   site in the green countryside with trickling burn. 4 chalets for hire on site.
Good gateway to the Borders (Melrose 20km). The Lodge (or Jo's Kitchen as it
is also known) adj has gr family restau where kids made v welcome (play area
and the food they like, etc).   MAR-OCT XHIRE 60TENT

1231 **SANDS HOLIDAY CENTRE, GAIRLOCH:** 01445 712152. On L Gairloch with
MAP 2   views to the islands, a large park with its own sandy beach. Kids' play area but
B2   plenty to do and see in Gairloch itself plus walking, fishing, etc.
APR-OCT HIRE 100CVAN 200TENT

1232 **BOAT OF GARTEN CARAVAN PARK:** 01479 831652. In vill itself, a medium-
MAP 2   sized, slightly regimented site tailored to families with play area for the kids
D3   and even cots available to rent for the very wee. Cabins on site if the Scottish
weather gets too much. Lots on doorstep to keep the kids happy, incl brilliant
Landmark Centre (1657/KIDS) and Loch Garten ospreys (1670/BIRDS).
AYR HIRE 37TENT

1233 **OBAN DIVERS CARAVAN PARK, OBAN:** 01631 562755. 1.5 miles out of Oban.
MAP 1   Quiet, clean and friendly ground with stream running through. All sorts of
B1   'extras' such as undercover cooking area, BBQ, adventure playground. In case
of severe downpours, you can always escape to the 6-berth bunk room. No
dogs. A good base for day trips incl Rare Breeds Farm and Sealife Centre
(1659/KIDS).   MAR-OCT XHIRE 30CVAN 32TENT

1234 **SHIELING HOLIDAYS, CRAIGNURE, MULL:** 01680 812496. 35km from
MAP 1   Tobermory but right where the ferry comes in. Gr views and a no-nonsense,
B1   thought-of-everything camp park. Self-catering shielings or hostel beds if you
prefer. Loads to do and see, incl nearby Torosay and Duart Castles (1701/
1702/CASTLES) and fun and novel Mull Light Railway.
APR-OCT XHIRE 30CVAN 30TENT

1235 **CASHEL CARAVAN AND CAMPSITE, ROWARDENNAN:** 01360 870234.
MAP 1   Forestry Commission site on the quieter shores of L Lomond in Queen
C2   Elizabeth Forest Park. Excellent facilities and tons to do in the surrounding
area which incl Ben Lomond and plootering by the loch.
MAR-OCT XHIRE 100CVAN 135TENT

1236 **SCOUTSCROFT HOLIDAY CENTRE, COLDINGHAM:** 01890 771338. Massive
MAP 8   coastal park with every fac under the sun, include restau, burger bar, cabaret
D1   bar, sports bar. Not everyone's cup of tea but the kids will love it and adults
will love the kids' activity prog (summer only) and play area.
MAR-NOV HIRE 30CVAN 60TENT

THE BEST VERY SCOTTISH HOTELS

1237
MAP 2
C2

✓ ✓ **THE CEILIDH PLACE, ULLAPOOL:** 01854 612103. Off main st near pt for the Hebrides, this place more than any other in the Highlands encapsulates Scottish trad culture and hospitality and interprets it in a contemporary manner. Caters for all sorts: there's an excellent hotel above (with a truly comfortable lounge – you help yourself to drinks) and a stylish if not punctilious restau below. A bar with occasional live music and gr bar meals. A bunkhouse across the way with cheap and cheerful (though thin-walled) accom and a bookshop where you can browse through the best new Scottish literature. Scottishness is all here and nothing embarrassing in sight.

23RMS JAN-DEC T/X PETS CC KIDS EXP/CHP

1238
MAP 2
C1

✓ ✓ **THE ALBANNACH, LOCHINVER:** 01571 844407. 2km up rd to Baddidarach as you come from S into Lochinver on A837, at the br. Lovely 18th-century house in one of Scotland's most scenic areas, Assynt, where the mtns can take your breath away even without going up them (1861/1862/FAVOURITE HILLS). Colin & Lesley have created a quite exceptional Highland retreat. You unwind in tasteful, informal surroundings. The food is the best for miles. No smk. *5RMS MAR-DEC X/X XPETS CC XKIDS MED.INX*

1239
MAP 3
B3

✓ **KILDRUMMY CASTLE HOTEL, nr ALFORD, ABERDEENSHIRE:** 01975 571288. 60km W of Aberdeen via A944, through some fine bucolic scenery and the green Don valley to this spectacular location with the real aura of the Highlands. Well placed if you're on the 'Castle Trail', this comfortable chunk of Scottish Baronial has the redolent ruins of Kildrummy Castle on the opposite bluff and a gorgeful of gdns betw. Some rms small, but all v Scottish. Romantic in autumn when the gdns are good. J/tie for dinner.

16RMS FEB-DEC T/T PETS CC KIDS TOS EXP

1240
MAP 2
B3

✓ **ARISAIG HOUSE, ARISAIG:** 01687 450622. Another hotel in Bonnie Prince Charlie country on the 'Road to the Isles'; here there's a cave at the foot of their fields (and wonderful gdns) where he once hid – it's very near where he landed (1837/MARY, CHARLIE AND BOB). Of course it's not just any other hotel, but an elegant country house which succeeds in the apparently rare combination of refinement and r&r. Good manners, but very Scots. *Relais and Châteaux.* Chef, Duncan Gibson gets 3 AA rosettes for cooking, the Smither family and excl staff do the rest. Note: hotel closed for 2003 season - the Smithers get their home back.

12RMS MAR-NOV T/T XPETS CC XKIDS TOS LOTS

1241
MAP 2
B3

✓ **EILEAN IARMAIN, SKYE:** 01471 833332. Situated in Sleat area on S of island, this snug Gaelic inn nestles in the bay and is the classic island hostelry. A dram in your rm awaits you; from the adj whisky company. Bedrms in hotel best but cottage annex quieter. New suites in adj steading more exp. Food real good in d. rm or pub. Mystic shore walks. Gallery with selected exhibs and shop nearby. *12RMS+4SUITES JAN-DEC T/T PETS CC KIDS EXP/LOTS*

1242
MAP 2
B3

✓ **GLENFINNAN HOUSE, GLENFINNAN:** 01397 722235. Off the Road to the Isles (A830 Ft William to Mallaig). The MacFarlanes recently celebrated a quarter century of running their hotel in this historic house (1839/MARY, CHARLIE AND BOB). Some refurb without losing its charm, the huge rms remain intimate and cosy with open fires. Legendary sessions and ceilidhs wherever there's a gathering in the house and you get piped into dinner. Solitude still achievable in the huge grounds, or fishing or dreaming on L Shiel (boat available). Day trips to Skye and small islands, nearby.

17RMS APR-OCT X/X PETS CC KIDS MED.INX-EXP

1243
MAP 2
C4

✓ **BALLACHULISH HOUSE, BALLACHULISH:** 01855 811266. On A828 nr south side of the bridge, not to be confused with the nearby hotel. Major investment here since last we visited, new owners and new prop – Marie McLaughlin. House v Scottish and makes much more of its historical background (Appin murder, Glencoe etc) – tasteful update of 17thC laird's place. We only had breakfast but the word is the chef here is pretty good. Range of rms so not just for special occasions.

8RMS JAN-DEC T/X XPETS CC KIDS MED.EX/EXP/LOTS

1244
MAP 1
C3

✓ **SAVOY PARK, AYR:** 01292 266112. 16 Racecourse Rd. In a street and area of many indifferent hotels this one, owned and run by the Henderson family for over 40 yrs, is a real Scottish gem. Many weddings here but that's the only drawback. Period features, gdn, not too much tartan, but a warm cosy lived-in atmos. Round one of the fireplaces, 'blessed be God for his giftis', the Hendersons (and I) would agree.   15RMS JAN-DEC T/T PETS KIDS MED.INX

CRIEFF HYDRO, CRIEFF: 01764 655555. The quintessential Scottish family hotel. (1152/HOTELS FOR KIDS).

STONEFIELD CASTLE, TARBERT: 01880 820836 (826/ARGYLL HOTELS).

REAL RETREATS

1245
MAP 9
D2

✓ ✓ ✓ **SAMYE LING, ESKDALEMUIR, nr LOCKERBIE/DUMFRIES:** 01387 373232. Bus or train to Lockerbie/Carlisle then bus (Mon-Sat) to Boreland (0345 090510) or taxi (01576 470480). 2km from village, community consists of an extraordinary and inspiring temple incongruous in these border parts. The complex comprises main house (with some accom), dorm and guesthouse blocks many single rms, a café (open 7 days 9am-5pm) and shop. Further up the hill, real retreats – months and years – in some annexes. Much of Samye Ling, a world centre for Tibetan Buddhism, is still under construction under the supervision of Tibetan masters, but they offer daily and longer stays (£15-25) and courses in all aspects of Buddhism, meditation, tai chi, Alexander Technique, etc. Daily timetable, from prayers at 6am and work period. Breakfast/lunch and soup, etc. for supper at 6pm; all vegn. Busy, thriving community atmos; some space cases and holier-than-thous, but rewarding and unique and thriving. This is Buddhism with no celebrity, pure & simple. Their recent acquisition, **HOLY ISLAND**, off Arran, will be an architectural and environmental landmark when completed. Meanwhile a small centre is reached by a boat from the pier at Lamlash, accom limited. Phone Samye Ling for details.

1246
MAP 3
A2

✓ ✓ **PLUSCARDEN, between FORRES and ELGIN:** 01343 890257. Signed from main A96 (11km from Elgin) in a sheltered glen S-facing with a background of wooded hillside, this is the only medieval monastery in the UK still inhabited by monks. It's a deeply calming place. The (Benedictine) community keep walled gdns and bees. 7 services a day in the glorious chapel (1815/ABBEYS) which visitors can attend. Retreat for men (15 places) and women (separate, self-catering) with no time limit and no obligatory charge. Write to the Guest Master Brother Gabriel, Pluscarden Abbey, by Elgin IV30 8VA; no telephone bookings. Men eat with monks (mainly vegn). Restoration/building work always in progress (of the abbey and of the spirit).

1247
MAP 3
A1

✓ ✓ **FINDHORN COMMUNITY, FINDHORN, nr FORRES:** 01309 690311. The world-famous spiritual community (now a foundation) begun by Peter Caddy and Dorothy Maclean in 1962, a village of mainly caravans and cabins on the way into Findhorn on the B9011. Open as an ordinary caravan park and visitors can join the community as 'short-term guests' eating and working on-site but probably staying at recommended B&Bs. Full programme of courses and residential workshops in spiritual growth/dance/ healing, etc. Accom mainly at Cluny Hill College in Forres. Many other aspects and facs available in this cosmopolitan and well-organised new-age township. Excl shop (1437/DELIS) and cafe – the Green Room (1317/VEGN).

1248
MAP 1
C3

COLLEGE OF THE HOLY SPIRIT, MILLPORT, ISLAND OF CUMBRAE: 01475 530353. Continuous ferry service from Largs (hourly in winter), then 6km bus journey to Millport. Off main st through gate in the wall, into grounds of the Cathedral of the Isles (1685/CHURCHES) and another more peaceful world. A retreat for the Episcopal Church since 1884, there are 19 simple but comfortable rms in the college next to the church with B&B or full board (around £20). No set schedule but morning and evening prayer each day, Eucharist on Sun and occasional concerts in summer. Warden available for direction and spiritual counselling. Fine library. Bike hire available on island. Phone 'the Provost'. Try the island's gr café (1367/CAFÉS).

1249 CARBERRY TOWERS, MUSSELBURGH, nr EDINBURGH: 0131 665 3135.
MAP 7   Sitting in extensive, well-kept grounds 3km S of Musselburgh, parts of this
B1   fine old house date back to the 15th century. Now a Christian residential and
conference centre, most accom is in new block 50m away; student-hall standard. Courses for church workers/group weekends which visitors may sometimes join. Not a quiet retreat but inexp for a break; high on 'renewal', low on
rock 'n' roll.

1250 NUNRAW ABBEY, GARVALD, nr HADDINGTON: 01620 830228. Cistercian
MAP 7   community earning its daily bread with a working farm in the land surround-
B1   ing the abbey – but visitors can come and stay for a while and get their heads
together in the Sancta Maria Guesthouse (a house for visitors is part of their
doctrine). Payment by donation. V Catholic monastic ambience throughout.
Guesthouse is 1km from the monastery, a modern complex built to a trad
Cistercian pattern. Services open to visitors.

1251 SALISBURY CENTRE, EDINBURGH: 0131 667 5438. 2 Salisbury Rd.
MAP A   'Community and creative resource' in Georgian house on capital's Southside,
xE4   est 1973 by Dr Winifred Rushforth, psychotherapist and dream specialist. Not
a retreat in the isolated sense, although 'w/end retreats' are possible. Classes
during week and w/end workshops in meditation, healing, aromatherapy,
massage, yoga, shiatsu, tai chi and pottery. Organic gdn, therapy rm, some
basic accom.

1252 CAMAS ADVENTURE CENTRE, MULL: 01681 700367. Part of Iona
MAP 1   Community (2 others on Iona; this one is aimed at yoof and youth) near to
A1   Fionnphort in S of island (good bus service). No electricity, cars, TV or noise
except the waves and the gulls. Outdoor activities (e.g. canoeing, hillwalking).
2 dorms; share chores. Week-long stays. You'll probably have to relate.

FOR THE BEST HOUSE PARTIES

Place you can hire for families or friends & have to yourself.

1253 **MYRES CASTLE:** 01337 828350. 2 km Auchtermuchty on Falkland rd. Well-
MAP 5 preserved castle/family home in stunningly beautiful gdns. High country life
B2 though at a price. 9 rms individually & recently refurb to exceptional standard.
Formal dining rm, funky kitchen and impressive billiard rm. The perfect set-
ting for a murder mystery shindig. Central to all Fife attractions esp Falkland &
St Andrews. £3000 per night but can take 16.

1254 **CARBISDALE CASTLE, CULRAIN, NR BONAR BRIDGE:** 01549 421232.
MAP 2 Another castle and hugely impressive but on a per head basis, v inexpensive.
C2 Carbisdale is the flagship hostel of the SYHA (1163/BEST HOSTELS gives directions). From Nov-Feb you can hire the whole place so big Highland hoolies
over Xmas/Hogmanay are an option. More than 150 people can be accom in
the 32 rms (varying from singles to 12-bed dorms). Per night price £1200-
1500. Bring your own chef or muck in. You get the whole place to yourself.
Other SYHA hostels can be hired Oct-May. Check 0870 1553255.

1255 **GLEN FESHIE HOSTEL, nr AVIEMORE:** 01540 651323. At other end of scale
MAP 2 from above, a friendly, independent hostel in the superb walking countryside
D3 nr Cairngorm and Aviemore. A max of 15 people in dorms of 4, twins and a
single. Meals provided or self-cater. Main report 1176/BEST HOSTELS.

1256 **KINLOCH CASTLE, RUM:** 01687 462037. An extraordinary house party venue.
MAP 2 Report 2219/ISLAND HOTELS but poss to hire all 5 opulent rms and fantastical
B3 bathrooms as well as the more basic hostel accom (a max of 58 bed spaces).
Price will vary depending on your needs so call to discuss. Common rooms,
restau (staffed summer only) and self-catering facs. Rum not that easy to get
to but a wild landscape awaits. Run by Scottish Natural Heritage.

1257 **AMHUINNSUIDHE CASTLE, HARRIS:** 01876 500329. On far W at S end of N
MAP 2 Harris, 20 km from Tarbert. Like Myres above, this castle (pron 'Aven-suey') is
A2 really only available for groups (conferences, courses) so is esp good for your
own party. Luxury accom in 8 v individ bedrms – up to 15 people. Excl food –
there are regular cookery courses by Rosemary Shrager. Hunting, shooting
and fishing facs on hand and golf (1968/GOLF; superb walking, eg the Lost
Glen, 2230/ISLAND WALKS). Castle for sale at TGP. Check by phone.

1258 **PARTIES ON SKYE:** Of several options on this most popular of island destina-
MAP 2 tions, try: **GRESHORNISH HOUSE:** 01470 582266. Fairly remote and on its
B2 own peninsula, o/look L Greshornish, a small co house hotel that you could
have for yourself. Billiard rm and open fires. Food to order. Report 2239/SKYE.
STEIN INN, WATERNISH: 01470 592362. In N W off Dunvegan-Portree rd in
ribbon of houses by the sea. 5 rms above atmos pub adj gr seafood cottage
(2239/SKYE RESTAUS). Easy to feel at home here and very Skye.

1259 **ACKERGILL TOWER, nr WICK:** 01955 603556. Deluxe retreat in distant north.
MAP 2 Totally geared for parties and groups (mostly corporates). 6 times a year, eg
D1 Valentines/Hogmanay, you can join their 'House Parties'. Fixed price (£625 for
3 nights in 2002) all inclusive. You'll prob have to mingle.

1260 **MELDRUM HOUSE, OLDMELDRUM:** 01651 872294. Of several small/med co
MAP 3 house hotels that might be taken over, this is a good one and highly individ.
C2 Lovely open fires everywhere. Stuffed with antiques, selected pics and atmos.
Can accom up to 18 (all twins and doubles). Esp good for golfers with 18-hole
course/prof/practice range in grounds. Doubtless a deal can be struck. Report
977/BEST HOTELS NE.

1260a **GLENN HOUSE, TRAQUAIR:** 01896 830210. On A709 4km from vill in stun-
MAP 8 ning Border scenery, the notable family home of the Tennants (Colin Tennant
B2 the man who made Mustique and host to royalty). House reeks of atmosphere
and echoes of swinging parties gone by. Hire complete (incl Princess
Margaret's bedroom), ballroom, snooker room, etc. for up to 40 people. £4K
per 48 hrs, meals extra but you can BYOB. Live like they did! 22 rms.

National Trust for Scotland *have many interesting properties they rent out for
w/ends or longer.* 0131-243 9331 *for details.*

GET-AWAY WEEKENDS

1261 LOCHAWESIDE
MAP 1
WHERE TO STAY
TAYCHREGGAN (821/ARGYLL HOTELS); **ARDANAISEIG** (1147/COUNTRY-HOUSE HOTELS).

WHERE TO EAT AND DRINK
LOCK 16, CRINAN HOTEL (1327/SEAFOOD); **KILCHREGGAN INN** (1271/PUBS), **KILMARTIN HOUSE** (1315/VEGN).

WHERE TO VISIT
THE WOODS (1916/WOODLAND WALKS); **TEMPLE WOOD** (1738/PREHISTORIC SITES). **KILMARTIN MUSEUM** (2110/MUSEUMS, 1315/VEGN)

1262 TARBERT, ARGYLL
MAP 1
WHERE TO STAY
STONEFIELD (826/ARGYLL HOTELS; 1158/KIDS); **THE COLUMBA** (829/ARGYLL HOTELS); **WEST LOCH** (828/ARGYLL HOTELS).

WHERE TO EAT AND DRINK
THE ANCHORAGE (1336/SEAFOOD RESTAUS); **WEST LOCH** (*as above*); **AN TAIRBERT CENTRE** W on A83 (*see below*).

WHERE TO VISIT
The **VILLAGE** itself; **ISLAY/JURA** (by ferry from Kennacraig, 7km S, *see p. 297*); **GIGHA** (by ferry from Tayinloan 14km SW); **ARRAN** (by ferry from Claonaig 9km SE) **TARBERT CASTLE** (1723/RUINS) **& SKIPNESS CASTLE; AN TAIRBERT CENTRE** for kids.

1263 SPEYSIDE
MAP 3
WHERE TO STAY
CRAIGELLACHIE, DELNASHAUGH, MANSION HOUSE (*pp. 130–31*).

WHERE TO EAT AND DRINK
ARCHIESTOWN HOTEL BISTRO: 01340 810218. Well-known spot locally for good (2 AA rosettes) informal dining. LO 8.30pm.

AUCHENDEAN LODGE: a bit further S (nr Grantown) but imaginative cuisine (1020/INEXP HIGHLAND HOTELS).

WHERE TO VISIT
DISTILLERIES: *p. 189*; **SPEYSIDE WAY:** 1895/LONG WALKS; **BALLENDALLOCH CASTLE:** on A95 midway betw Grantown and Craigellachie. Family big house with pleasant Speyside gdns. Apr-Sept 10am-5pm.; **ELGIN CATHEDRAL:** 1716/RUINS; **JOHNSONS:** 2068/WOOLLIES; **CHRISTIES OF FOCHABERS:** 2082/GARDEN CENTRES; **JUST ART:** 2143/ART

1264 EAST NEUK OF FIFE
MAP 5
WHERE TO STAY
See p. 125-26 FIFE HOTELS/RESTAUS. Note also; **THE BELVEDERE:** way back at **WEST WEMYSS** (*see* KIRKCALDY, *p. 310*); **ANSTRUTHER, THE HERMITAGE:** 01333 310909; **ELIE, THE SHIP INN:** 01333 330246; **ELIE, GOLF HOTEL:** 01333 330209 (929/FIFE HOTELS).

WHERE TO EAT AND DRINK
THE CELLAR, ANSTRUTHER (1328/SEAFOOD RESTAUS); **THE ANSTRUTHER FISH BAR or RESTAU** (1358/FISH AND CHIPS); **THE PEAT INN** (934/FIFE BEST RESTAUS); **OSTLER'S CLOSE, CUPAR** (936/FIFE BEST RESTAUS); **THE SHIP, ELIE** (1298/PUB FOOD); **OLD RECTORY, DYSART** (939/FIFE BEST RESTAUS); **SEAFOOD CABIN, ST MONANS** (1341/SEAFOOD).

WHERE TO VISIT
THE SECRET BUNKER (2099/MUSEUMS); **CHAIN WALK, ELIE** (1940/COASTAL WALKS); **CRAIL POTTERY** (2034/CRAFTS); **ST ANDREWS ATTRACTIONS** (*p. 324*); **GOLF, ST ANDREWS** (*see p.259*); **FISHERIES MUSEUM, ANSTRUTHER** (2119/MUSEUMS); **ISLE OF MAY** (1666/BIRDS); **THE VILLAGE OF FALKLAND**.

SECTION 6

Good Food and Drink

Pubs in EDIN, GLAS, ABER *and* DUNDEE *are listed in their own sections.*

1265
MAP 6
A2
✔ ✔ **DROVER'S INN, INVERARNAN:** A famously Scottish drinking den/hotel on the edge of the Highlands just N of Ardlui at the head of L Lomond and 12km S of Crianlarich on the A82. Smoky, low-ceilinged rooms, open ranges, whisky in the jar, stuffed animals in the hall and kilted barmen; this is nevertheless the antithesis of the contrived Scottish tourist pub.

1266
MAP 1
B1
✔ ✔ **THE MISHNISH, TOBERMORY:** The Mish has had its refit, but it's still the real Tobermory. 7 days till late. Usually live music from Scot trad to DJs and indie. Gr pub grub, open fire.

1267
MAP 2
C3
✔ ✔ **CLUANIE INN:** 01320 340257. On A87 at head of L Cluanie 15km before Shiel Br on the long rd to Kyle of Lochalsh. A wayside inn with good pub food, a restau and the accom walkers want. Perfect base for climbing/ walking (esp the Five Sisters of Kintail, 1901/SERIOUS WALKS), a cosy refuge, especially the jacuzzi. LO 9pm for food.

1268
MAP 2
B3
✔ **OLD FORGE, INVERIE, KNOYDART:** 01687 462267. A warm haven for visitors to this remote peninsula. Suddenly you're part of the community, real ales and real characters, real pub grub. Stay along the rd. (1211/GET-AWAY-FROM-IT-ALL)

1269
MAP 1
B2
✔ **TIGH-AN-TRUISH, CLACHAN, ISLE OF SEIL:** 01852 300242. Beside the much-photographed 'Bridge over the Atlantic' which links the 'Isle' of Seil with the 'mainland'. On B884, 8km from B816 and 22km S of Oban. Country pub with 2 apartments above (with views of br). A place where no one cares how daft your hair looks after a hard day's messing about on boats. Food LO 8.30pm. (Mar-Oct)

1270
MAP 2
C4
✔ **CLACHAIG INN, GLENCOE:** 01855 811252. Deep in the glen itself down the rd signed off the A82, 5km from Glencoe village. Both the pub with its wood-burning stove and the lounge are woody and welcoming. Real ale and real climbers and walkers. Handy for hostel 2km down rd. Decent food (in bar/lounge or dining rm) and good, inexp accom. They have beerfests – Oct one is quite a biggie.

1271
MAP 1
C1
KILCHRENAN INN, KILCHRENAN, LOCH AWE: On the corner where the wonderful, woody rd that winds along the N bank of the long loch from Ford turns N to Taynuilt. Nr Taychreggan Hotel (821/ARGYLL HOTELS) & Ardanaiseig (1147/CO HOUSE HOTS), but much cheaper grub & a friendly alternative to country house ways. Self-cat accom avail. Food LO 8.45pm.

1272
MAP 2
A3
CASTLEBAY BAR, BARRA: Adj Castlebay Hotel. Brilliant bar. All human life is here. More Irish than all the Irish makeovers on the mainland. Occasional live music, conversations with strangers.

1273
MAP 2
C2
PHOENIX, INVERNESS: 108 Academy St. Trad horseshoe bar. Always lively. The lounge is the place to relax with robust food (macaroni cheese & chips) and a pint of Deuchars IPA. However, **BLACKFRIARS** on Academy St also has its fans – inc researchers for this book! Good cask ale and regular live music.

1274
MAP 9
D1
TIBBIE SHIELS INN: Off A708 Moffat-Selkirk rd. Occupies its own particular place in Scottish culture, esp literature (1849/LITERARY PLACES) and in the Border hills SW of Selkirk where it nestles between 2 romantic lochs. On Southern Upland Way (1561/WATERFALLS) a good place to stop and refuel.

1275
MAP 9
B3
THE MURRAY ARMS and THE MASONIC, GATEHOUSE OF FLEET: 2 adj, unrelated pubs that just fit perfectly into the life of this gr wee town. Murray has accom and restau-style food but it's the Masonic that has the best atmos and pub grub.

1276
MAP 2
C3
LOCK INN, FORT AUGUSTUS: Busy canalside (Caledonian Canal which joins L Ness in the distance) pub for locals and visitors. Good grub (you should book for the upstairs restau) The Gilliegorm, reasonable malts. Food LO 9.45pm. Some live music.

GREAT PUBS FOR REAL ALE

*For pubs in **EDINBURGH**, see pp. 55–60, **GLASGOW** p. 97–101.*

1277 ✓ **FISHERMAN'S TAVERN, DUNDEE:** In Broughty Ferry, but not too far to
MAP 4   go for gr atmos and the best collection of ales in the area. In Fort St near
C3   the seafront. Regular ales and many guests. Low-ceilinged and friendly
(1131/DUNDEE PUBS). Inx accom adj (1113/DUNDEE HOTS).

1278 ✓ **THE PHEASANT, HADDINGTON:** On corner where main st divides. Old-
MAP 7   style, real-ale howff claiming to have the best selection in E Lothian. No
B2   arguments from us. Rare guests on tap, and local Belhaven brewed along the
road in Dunbar. Busy market-town atmos; pool and frequent live music. Mind
the parrot and 'spirited' locals at weekend.

1279 ✓ **MOULIN INN/HOTEL, PITLOCHRY:** 2km uphill from main st on rd to Br
MAP 4   of Cally, an inn at a picturesque crossrds since 1695. Some rms and restau,
B2   but notable mainly for cosy (partly smoky) bar and brewery out back from
which comes 'Moulin Light' and the 'Ale of Atholl'. Live music some Sun. Food
LO 9.30pm.

1280 ✓ **ROYAL HOTEL, COMRIE:** Main sq; public bar is behind hotel. By same
MAP 4   people who have the Bow Bar and Cloisters in Edin, a rare combination
B3   of stylish and right-on ambience, sort of city meets the country. Guests and
regulars, which incl Earthquake Ale (made by Caledonian), exclusive to pub.
Live music. Beer gdn. V pleasant in summer.

1281 ✓ **THE FOUR MARYS, LINLITHGOW:** Main st nr rd up to palace so handy for
MAP 7   a pint after schlepping around the historical attractions. Mentioned in
A1   most beer guides. Half a dozen ales on tap incl various guests. Beer festivals
May and Oct. Notable malt whisky collection and popular locally for lunches
(daily) and evening meals (Thurs-Sat, LO 8.45pm). Open 7 days.

1282 **THE TAPPIT HEN, DUNBLANE:** By the cathedral. Good ales (incl the Wallace),
MAP 6   atmos and live music. A real find in these parts.
C2

1283 **MARINE HOTEL, STONEHAVEN:** Popular local on great harbour front with
MAP 3   seats o/side; juke box and bar meals inside. Youngish crowd. Has won awards
C4   for its cask ales – various on tap. Lounge/restau upstairs. Open all day.

1284 **THE WOOLPACK, TILLICOULTRY:** Via Upper Mill St (signed 'Mill Glen') from
MAP 6   main st on your way to the Ochils. They come far and wide to this ancient pub.
D3   Bar food and a changing selection of ales which they know how to keep. Sup
after stroll.

1285 **CLACHNAHARRY INN, INVERNESS:** On A862 Inverness-Beauly rd just out-
MAP 2   side Inverness o/looking firth with beer gdn. Long list of regulars posted, 5/6
C2   on tap when we visited, also Clachnaharry Village Ale, and three Tomintouls
'from the wood'. Heaven!

1286 **THE SHORE INN, PORTSOY:** Down at the harbour so good atmos (& ales).
MAP 3   Food all day in summer, weekends only in winter. The place to drink when you
C1   come for the Trad Boats fest (25/EVENTS)

1287 **THE OLD INN, GAIRLOCH:** Southern app on A832 nr golf course, an 'old inn'
MAP 2   across an old br; a goodly selection of malts. Some real ales in the cellar.
B2   Tourists and locals mix in season, live music some nights, and now with the
tasteful Origin Studio Gallery adj, things are looking up in Gairloch.

1288 **BETTY NICOL'S, KIRKCALDY:** 297 High St at the E end. Innkeepers who know
MAP 5   and love their ales. Gr selection with usually 8 posted. Check also the FEAURS
B3   ARMS in this town (2246/BEST KIRKCALDY). Open 7 days.

PUBS THAT SERVE THE BEST FOOD

Pubs in EDIN, GLAS, ABER and DUNDEE are listed in their own sections.

1289 ✔ ✔ **LAIRHILLOCK, nr NETHERLEY, STONEHAVEN:** 01569 730001.
MAP 3 Known forever for gr pubfood and more gourmet restau: open
C3 evenings – LO 9.30pm – and Sun lunch (1067/ABER RESTAUS). Inn (7 days lunch
& dinner) more informal and downright friendly. Fine for kids. Superb cheese
selection, notable malts and ales. Can app from S Deeside Rd, but simplest
direction for strangers is: 15km S of Aber by main A92 towards Stonehaven,
then signed Durris, go 5km to country crossrds. New owners 2001.

1290 ✔ ✔ **BOUZY ROUGE at the SHERIFFMUIR INN:** 01786 823285.
MAP 6 Sheriffmuir rd 'behind' Dunblane and Bridge of Allan or from A9.
C2 Contemp food unexpectedly stylish at this far flung crossrds and tasteful rms
upstairs. Report: 873/CENTRAL HOTELS.

1291 ✔ ✔ **THE WHEATSHEAF, SWINTON, betw KELSO and BERWICK:** 01890
MAP 8 860257. A hotel pub in an undistinguished village about halfway
D2 betw the 2 towns (18km) on the B6461. In deepest, flattest Berwickshire, Alan
and Julie Reid serve up the best pub grub you've had since England. AA pub
fd of the yr. 7 rms adj. An all-round excl hostelry. Lunch, 6-9.30pm. Cl Mon.

1292 ✔ **LION & UNICORN, THORNHILL, TROSSACHS:** 01786 850204. On A873
MAP 1 off A84 rd betw the M9 and Callander & nr Lake of Menteith. On main rd
D2 thro' nondescript vill. They come from mls around. Cosy dining areas & gdn.
Changing menu, not fancy. 7 days. LO 9pm.

1293 ✔ **THE CROSS KEYS, KIPPEN:** 01786 870293. Here forever in this quiet
MAP 6 backwater town off the A811 15km W of Stirling. Bar meals by coal fire, à
C3 la carte and family restaus. A real pub food haven, for a'body. LO 9.30pm.

1294 ✔ **THE BYRE, BRIG O'TURK:** 01877 376292. Off A821 at Callander end of the
MAP 6 village adj Dundarroch Hotel and L Achray. Country inn in deepest
B2 Trossachs. Blackboard table d'hôte in bar or (no smk) restau. Best pub food for
a long way in any direction. Lunch and 6-9pm.

1295 ✔ **WHEATSHEAF INN, SYMINGTON, nr AYR:** 01563 830307. 2km A77.
MAP 1 Pleasant village off the unpleasant A77 with this busy coaching inn
C3 opposite church. Folk come from miles around to eat (book at w/ends)
honest-to-goodness pub fare in various rms (roast beef every Sunday). Menu
on boards. Beer gdn. LO 10pm.

1296 ✔ **ARCHIESTOWN HOTEL, ARCHIESTOWN:** 01340 810218. On square of
MAP 3 small Speyside vill, more a bistro perhaps than a mere pub, but men-
B2 tioned here because it is top quality, unpretentious pub grub & so you don't
miss it. See also 983/NE HOTELS. Cl Oct-Feb.

1297 ✔ **KYLESKU HOTEL, KYLESKU:** 01971 502231. Off A894 betw Scourie and
MAP 2 Lochinver in Sutherland. A hotel and pub with a gr quayside location on
C1 L Glencoul where boats leave for trips to see the 'highest waterfall in Europe'
(1558/WATERFALLS, 1055/INEXP HIGHLAND RESTAUS). A friendly atmos with local
fish, seafood (esp with legs) and yummy desserts. Noon-9.30pm. New owners.

1298 ✔ **SHIP INN, ELIE:** Pub on the bay at Elie, the perfect toon in the pic-
MAP 5 turesque East Neuk of Fife (1515/COASTAL VILLAGES). Bar and rm through
C3 back, but food mainly in refurbished boathouse next door and bistro above
(good view, book w/ends). Same menu throughout and blackboard specials.
Real popular place esp in summer when terrace o/looking the beach goes like
Bondi. LO 9.00pm. Also has 6 chp rms adj in summer (01333 330246).

1299 **COCHRANE INN, GATEHEAD:** 01563 570122. Part of the Costley and Costley
MAP 1 hotel empire (840/HOTELS IN AYRSHIRE). A very trim and ivy-covered inn – most
C3 agreeable. On the A759 Troon to Kilmarnock. Phone if you get lost – for non-
natives, everything in this shire seems hard to find.

1300 **UNICORN INN, KINCARDINE:** 01259 739129. More a restau in a former pub
MAP 5 than a pub with food, and a surprisingly good place to eat hereabouts.
A3 Chef/prop Tony Budde former chef at Scottish Parliament making a go of it in
a place that once had a big reputation then closed for a bit. Tony building it
up again. Lunch & dinner Tues-Sat. LO 9.30.

1301
MAP 6
D3
STRATHALLAN HOTEL, DOLLAR: Chapel Pl. All round good pub (with 4 inexp rms above) in back st of couthie and tidy town. Ales, malts, a games selection and beer gdn. Looking a shade shabby now but more reports please. Gr walks nearby (1905/GLEN AND RIVER WALKS).

1302
MAP 6
B3
OLD MILL, KILLEARN: 01360 550068. Main St. The 'other' gr pub in Killearn (Black Bull more upscale 519/HOTELS OUTSIDE TOWN) but this is cosy, friendly, all an old pub should be (old here is from 1774). Pub & restau. Log fires, nice for kids. Garden. 7 days 12-9.30pm, Sun from 12.30.

1303
MAP 5
B3
HUNTING LODGE HOTEL, FALKLAND : 01337 857226. Main st of much visited town in central Fife, opp the fabulous Palace (1696/CASTLES). All day menu of mainly stalwarts like 80/- ale steak pie and macaroni cheese. Beer gdn a bit removed. Open 7 days. LO 8pm.

1304
MAP 7
B1
GOBLIN HA' HOTEL, GIFFORD: 01620 810244. Twee village in the boondocks; one of 2 hotels (913/LOTHIANS HOTELS). This, the one with the gr name, serves a decent pub lunch and supper (6-9pm; 9.30pm on Fri and Sat) in lounge and more basic version in the pub. Conservatory and gdn; kids' play area.

1305
MAP 7
B1
DROVER'S INN, E LINTON: 01620 860298. A village off A1, 35km from Edin. A notable & hospitable E Lothian hostelry within reach of city. Restau upstairs, bistro with blackboard specials down. Can eat alfresco in summer with trains whooshing by (354/EDIN PUBS WITH GOOD FOOD). Big portions, not so vegn. LO 9.30pm.

1306
MAP 4
B4
TORMAUKIN INN, GLENDEVON: 01259 781252. On A823 through wooded Glen to Auchterarder, 36km E of Stirling, 16km W of M90 at jnct 6/7. Rdside inn with very pleasant accom (12 rms/MED.INX), à la carte restau and fine pub meals. Vegn dishes. W/ends busy. Lunch and 5.30-9.30pm. All day Sun.

1307
MAP 2
D3
OLD BRIDGE INN, AVIEMORE: Off Coylumbridge rd at S end of Aviemore as you come in from A9 or Kincraig. 100m main st but sits in hollow. An old inn like it says with basic à la carte and more interesting blackboard specials. Three cask ales on tap. Kids' menu, ski-bums welcome. Lunch and 6-9pm. In summer, tables over rd go down to river.

1308
MAP 9
A3
THE CROWN, PORTPATRICK: 01776 810261. Hugely popular pub on harbour with tables o/side in summer. Light, airy conservatory at back serving freshly caught fish. 12rms above. Locals and Irish who sail over for lunch (sic). Excl chips LO 10pm.

1309
MAP 9
C3
OLD SMUGGLERS, AUCHENCAIRN: 01556 640331. An alternative place to stay to the Balcary Bay in this old smuggling stretch of the Solway coast (though only 3 rms). Good pub grub and robust village crack. LO 10pm.

1310
MAP 9
C3
THE ANCHOR, KIPPFORD: The place to eat on the 'Scottish Riviera', esp if you've walked over from Rockcliffe (2km). In summer, tables o/side look (over the rd) to the silted Solway. Elbow to elbow inside with all ages enjoying grub, good family pub with games rm and kids menu.

1311
MAP 4
C3
THE SHIP INN, BROUGHTY FERRY: Excellent seafront (Tay estuary) snug pub with food upstairs and down (best tables at window upstairs). Famous for clootie dumpling (but not in summer). 7 days, lunch and 5-10pm (1116/DUNDEE EAT AND DRINK).

1312
MAP 8
A2
HORSESHOE INN, EDDLESTON, nr PEEBLES: 01721 730225. 5km N on A703 to Edin, this rdside inn is more a restau than just a pub. Lunch & dinner LO 11pm bar, 9pm food (Sun all day till 8pm). A hostelry worth a stop-over, there are 8 bedrms out-back by the church. Good value top on the way to the Borders.

1313
MAP 8
C3
THE AULD CROSS KEYS INN, DENHOLM, nr HAWICK: 01450 870305. Not a lot to recommend in Hawick, so Peter and Heather Ferguson's village pub with rms is worth the 8km journey on the A698 Jedburgh rd. On the Green, with pub and dining lounges through the back. Blackboard menu, heaps of choice. Real fire & candles. Excl Sun high tea (4-6.30pm). Open late Thur-Sat (Sun 11pm).

FOX AND HOUNDS, HOUSTON: 01505 612448. (716/GLAS PUBS WITH GOOD FOOD)

OLD CLUBHOUSE, GULLANE: 01620 842008. Report: 920/LOTHIANS HOTELS

THE BEST VEGETARIAN RESTAURANTS

Not surprisingly, perhaps, there are precious few completely vegetarian restaus in Scotland. But there are lots in EDIN *(see p. 41) and some in* GLAS *(see p. 91).*

1314 ✔ **SEAGREEN, KYLE OF LOCHALSH:** 01599 534388. On edge of town, rd to
MAP 2 Plockton. Café/bookshop/wholefood during the day (open AYR); in
B3 another rm is a seafood restau at night (May-Sept). Fiona Begg's varied and
artistic menu demonstrates just how innovative vegn cookery can be. Vegan
selection. No whiff of bacon sarnies here among the books. No smk. Organic
ales and wine. 7 days but phone for opening o/side season. MED

1315 ✔ **KILMARTIN HOUSE CAFE, KILMARTIN:** 01546 510278. Attached to early
MAP 1 peoples museum (2110/MUSEUMS) in Kilmartin Glen & on main rd N of
B2 Lochgilphead. Light food in gr space. Creative cookery using gdn herbs, etc.
Soups, quiches, cakes. 7 days, hot food till 3pm, cakes till 5pm. CHP

1316 ✔ **AN TUIREANN, PORTREE, SKYE:** Off Uig (then Struan) rd (at the Co-op).
MAP 2 Excl gallery cafe and restau with contemp menu; salads, hot meals,
B2 snacks. Prob best coffee on Skye and soups. 10am-4.30pm. Cl Sun. Changing
exhibs. CHP

1317 ✔ **GREEN ROOM at FINDHORN COMMUNITY, FINDHORN:** You will go a
MAP 3 long way in the N to find real vegn food, so it may be worth the detour
A1 from the main A96 Inverness–Elgin rd, to Findhorn and the famous commune
(1247/RETREATS) where there is a gr deli (1437/DELIS) and a pleasant caff by the
'Hall'. 7 days till 5pm and evens if event in the hall. CHP

1318 ✔ **CAFE NA LUSAN, OBAN:** 01631 567268. 9 Craigard Rd nr main st (uphill
MAP 1 & nr the Studio restau). Simple, non-pretentious caff serving vegn/vegan
B1 & organic food where poss, incl wines/beers. Internet & facs downstairs. Gr sal-
ads. 7 days. 11.30-9.30pm (till 3.30pm Sun/Mon). INX

1319 **THE MOUNTAIN RESTAURANT, GAIRLOCH:** 01445 712316. Vegn-friendly
MAP 2 restau with conservatory and tables outside with mt view. Bookshop and adj
B2 Nature Shop with every kind of spiritual whatsits you may want. We've had
complaints about the price of tea and scones – and the candlelit dinners in
the eve (July-Aug only) are 'ample'. Just the job after a day on the hill, but far
from dainty. V American, and surprisingly seems to spark debate about all
kinds of things. What do you think? Reports please. Easter-Oct. INX

THE BEST VEGETARIAN-FRIENDLY PLACES

EDINBURGH *and* GLASGOW *cafés and restaus are mentioned in their own sections, see p. 41 and p. 91.*

1320 ## ORKNEY

WOODWICK HOUSE, EVIE, ORKNEY: 01856 751330. B&B, seals, music and woodland. (2242/ORKNEY)

1321 ## HIGHLANDS
MAP 2

THE CEILIDH PLACE, ULLAPOOL: 01854 612103 (1018/INEXP HIGHLAND HOTELS).

CAFÉ NUMBER ONE, INVERNESS: 01463 226200 (2249/INVERNESS).

BOOKSHOP CAFE, INVERNESS: 01463 239947 (2249/INVERNESS).

DUNNET HEAD TEAROOM, nr THURSO: 01847 851774 (1054/INEXP HIGH-LAND RESTAUS).

THREE CHIMNEYS, SKYE: 01470 511258 (2223/ISLAND RESTAUS).

OLD SCHOOL, DUNVEGAN, SKYE: 01470 521421 (2239/SKYE)

THE SEAFOOD RESTAURANT, KYLE OF LOCHALSH: (1043/INEXP HIGHLAND RESTAUS).

RIVERSIDE BISTRO, LOCHINVER: 01571 844356 (1050/INEXP HIGHLAND RESTAUS).

CAFÉ BEAG, FORT WILLIAM: 01397 703601 (2247/FT WILLIAM).

OLD STATION, SPEAN BRIDGE: 01397 712535 (1041/INEXP HIGHLAND RESTAUS)

1322 NORTH EAST
MAP 3

LEMON TREE, ABERDEEN: 01224 642230 (1087/ABER RESTAUS).

OWLIES, ABERDEEN: 01224 649267 (1085/ABER RESTAUS).

MILTON RESTAURANT, BANCHORY: 01330 844566 (990/NE HOTELS)

1323 ARGYLL
MAP 1

THE CLIFTON COFFEE SHOP, TYNDRUM: 01838 400271 (1378/TEAROOMS).

ARISAIG HOUSE HOTEL, ARISAIG: 01687 450622 (1148/COUNTRY-HOUSE HOTELS).

AN TAIRBEART HERITAGE CENTRE, TARBERT: 01880 820190. On A83 S. Family fare.

JULIE'S COFFEE HOUSE, OBAN: 01631 565952. (2250/OBAN).

1324 FIFE AND LOTHIANS
MAPS 5, 7

THE GREEN HOUSE, FALKLAND: 01337 858400.

OSTLER'S CLOSE, CUPAR: 01334 655574 (936/FIFE RESTAUS).

THE VINE LEAF, ST ANDREWS: 01334 477497 (2257/ST ANDREWS).

BRAMBLES, ST ANDREWS (1398/TEAROOMS).

WATERSIDE BISTRO, HADDINGTON: 01620 825674 (914/LOTHIANS RESTAUS).

DROVER'S INN, EAST LINTON: 01620 860298 (354/EDIN PUB FOOD).

1325 CENTRAL:
MAP 6

LET'S EAT, PERTH: 01738 643377 (959/PERTHSHIRE RESTAUS).

BOUZY ROUGE at the SHERIFFMUIR INN: 01786 823285 (873/PUB FOOD).

MONACHYLE MHOR nr BALQUHIDDER: 01877 384622 (1205/GET-AWAY-FROM-IT-ALL).

KILLIECRANKIE HOTEL BAR, KILLIECRANKIE: 01796 473220 (950/PERTHSHIRE HOTELS).

1326 SOUTH AND SOUTH WEST:
MAP 8

MARMIONS, MELROSE: 01896 822245 (900/BORDERS EATS).

CHAPTERS, GATTONSIDE: 01896 823217 (902/BORDERS EATS).

THE BEST SEAFOOD RESTAURANTS

For seafood restaus in EDINBURGH, *see p. 40; for* GLASGOW, *see p. 91.*

1327
MAP 1
B2
✓✓ **CRINAN HOTEL, CRINAN:** 01546 830261. 8km off A816. On coast, 60km S of Oban (Lochgilphead 12km) at head of the Crinan Canal which joins L Fyne with the sea. O/side on the quay is the boat which has landed those massive prawns, sweet clams and other creatures with legs or valves, which are cooked v simply and brought on heaped tureens to your table. Inside a choice of the 'Westward' dining rm on the ground floor or Lock 16 the top floor bistro with a stunning view of the Sound of Jura (latter not always open) or pub grub in the cosier bar. This hotel has long been one of the gr seafood restaus in the UK. Nick Ryan presides; the wife's pictures are everywhere (and not just here).   EXP

1328
MAP 5
D3
✓✓ **THE CELLAR, ANSTRUTHER:** 01333 310378. The best in SE Scotland. Behind Fisheries Museum in busy East Neuk of Fife town. Fish and shellfish from only the best waters, some meat options. Cosy French bistro atmos. Full Report: 935/FIFE RESTAUS.   MED

1329
MAP 3
D3
✓✓ **SILVER DARLING, ABERDEEN:** 01224 576229. Down by harbour. For many yrs one of the best restaus in the city and the NE. Exquisite chargrilled seafood. Report: 1068/ABER RESTAUS.   MED

1330
MAP 1
C3
✓✓ **MACCALLUM'S OF TROON OYSTER BAR:** 01292 319339. Right down at the quayside, so follow the long rd all the way by car. Too far to walk! Red brick building with discreet sign, so eyes peeled. Lovely fish, great atmos, unpretentious and worth the trip even from Glasgow. Tues-Thurs lunch and dinner, Fri-Sat dinner only, Sun 12-6.   MED

1331
MAP 4
C3
✓ **KERACHER'S, PERTH:** 01738 449777. Corner of South St and Scott St. Seafood bar at street level, airy restau upstairs. Keracher's are major fish wholesalers & supply most of the best hotel dining rms in Perthshire, so they know their mullet. Vegn & meat options. Lunch and dinner LO 10pm. Cl Sun/Mon.   INX/MED

1332
MAP 2
B2
✓ **LOCHBAY SEAFOOD, SKYE:** 01470 592235. 12km N Dunvegan; A850 to Portree, B886 Waternish peninsula coastal route. A scenic Skye drive leads you to the door of this small cottage at end of the village row. O/looks water where your scallops, prawns & oysters have surfaced. Main dishes served unfussily with home-made chips or baked potatoes. Puds from clootie dumpling to crème brûlée. Simply v good – you'll need to book. Apr-Oct; lunch & LO 8.30ish. Cl Sat/Sun.   MED

1333
MAP 1
C2
✓ **LOCH FYNE SEAFOOD AND SMOKERY:** 01499 600264. On A83 the L Lomond to Inveraray rd, 20km Inveraray/11km Rest and Be Thankful. Landmark roadside restau and all-round seafood experience on the way out or the way home west. In summer you may have to book or wait; people come from afar for the oysters and the smokery fare, esp the kippers. Spacious, though the booths can seem cramped. House white (other whites and whisky) well chosen. Birlinn tapas bar for snacks & restau. Same menu all day; LO 8.30pm. Shop sells every conceivable packaging of salmon, etc.; shop 8pm.   INX

1334
MAP 1
B1
✓ **THE WATERFRONT, OBAN:** 01631 563110. On the waterfront at the station. Upstairs from unimposing entrance a light, airy rm which is poss serving the best food in town. Blackboard specials change daily. At last somewhere in Oban to linger on the way to the ferry. Mar–Dec. L and LO 9pm.   MED

1335
MAP 2
B2
✓ **KISHORN SEAFOOD BAR:** 01520 733240. On A896 at Kishorn on rd betw Lochcarron (Inverness) and Sheildaig nr the rd over the hill to Applecross (1583/ROUTES). Fresh local seafood in a roadside diner. Light, bright and a real find in the middle of beautiful nowhere. Courtesy of the enthusiastic Viv Rollo. Apr-Oct daily 10-6pm (July-Aug until 9pm).   MED

1336
MAP 1
B2
✓ **THE ANCHORAGE, TARBERT:** 01880 820881. Former staffer Clare Johnson took over 2000 and she's getting it so right. Good quayside location, menu changes daily, bistro-like and a sunny place to eat – reflecting the sunny Clare. Easter-Oct daily, LO 9pm, winter Tues-Sat. Cl Jan. Dinner only – maybe occ lunches. Call her!   MED

1337
MAP 3
C4
✔ **THE TOLBOOTH, STONEHAVEN:** 01569 762287. On corner of harbour, one of the best restaus in the area in a great setting – oldest building in town. Upstairs bistro with interesting seafood menu served with flair and integrity; good wine list, some real bargains. Tues-Sat 6-9.30pm. Cl lunch. MED

1338
MAP 1
C3
✔ **FINS, FAIRLIE, nr LARGS:** 01475 568989. On main A78 S of Fairlie a seafood bistro, smokery (Fencebay Fisheries), shop and craft/cookshop. Roadside fish farm bistro, best place to eat for miles in any direction. Chef Gillian Dick uses exemplary restraint and the wine list is similarly to the point. Lunch and dinner. Cl Mon. New conservatory. INX

1339
MAP 1
C3
✔ **CREELERS, BRODICK, ARRAN:** 01770 302810. Just outside Brodick on rd N to castle in a modern tourist plaza-plex. Definitely back on the upswing last we passed. Good staff, good kitchen, fab seafood. When in Arran … Easter-Oct. Cl Mon. MED

1340
MAP 2
C2
✔ **MOREFIELD MOTEL, ULLAPOOL:** 01854 612161. Mariner's Restaurant – Neptune's seafood platter, great fish and vegn all on offer in this quirky popular venue on a kind of housing estate. Bar meals are great and selection of seafood amazing; close your eyes and enjoy. People drive 100 miles for this meal – nuff said. INX.MED

1341
MAP 5
C3
THE SEAFOOD RESTAURANT, ST MONANS, FIFE: 01333 730327. West end of East Neuk Village. Simple title and no fuss in the menu either. Conservatory & terrace o/looks sea, waves lap, gulls mew etc. Bar menu lunch and dinner LO 10pm Cl Sun even & Mon. MED

1342
MAP 9
A3
CAMPBELL'S, PORTPATRICK: 01776 810314. Friendly, harbourside restau of recent origin ('99). Some meat dishes, but mainly seafood. Sardines were nice. 7 days lunch and LO 10pm. Cl Jan-Mar and Mons. MED

1343
MAP 2
C3
CRANNOG, FORT WILLIAM: 01397 705589. Opinion is divided about this converted boathouse but it was high-season pandemonium when last in FW so couldn't even get a table! Given location, fish should be good – no excuses now! Daily AYR, lunch and dinner. MED

1344
MAP 2
C1
SEAFOOD CAFÉ, TARBET, nr SCOURIE: 01971 502251. Charming conservatory restau on cove where boats leave for Handa Island bird reserve (1663/BIRDS). Julian catches your seafood from his boat (he'll also take you on a cruise) and Jackie cooks it; they have the Rick Stein seal of approval. Cheesecake for dessert. It's so peaceful here you'll want to stay and can do so in adj self-catering barn. Located at end of unclassified rd off the A894 between Laxford Br and Scourie; best phone to check openings. Apr-Sept: Mon-Sat 12-8pm. Some Sun in summer. INX

1345
MAP 1
B1
THE PIERHOUSE, PORT APPIN: 01631 730302. At the end of the minor rd and 3km from the A828 Oban–Ft William rd in Pt Appin village rt by the tiny 'pier' where the passenger ferry leaves for Lismore. Locally caught seafood (Lismore oysters, Mallaig flatfish, hand-dived shellfish) is handed over fresh to the door by boat. Lively atmos, wine and wonderful view but it's best if they like you and they don't like us. (1190/INNS) INX

1346
MAP 2
B3
IN MALLAIG: The legendary Derek Cooper is said to rate **THE CABIN** (01687 462207) which also has a fish & chip takeaway, while the town's TOS contender is **THE FISH MARKET** (01687 462299). Just in case you're passing …

THE BEST FISH AND CHIP SHOPS

1347
MAP 5
B3
✔✔ **VALENTE'S, KIRKCALDY:** 01592 651991. 73 Overton Rd (not downtown version). Ask directions to this superb chippy in E of town; worth the detour and worth the queue when you get there. Phone if you're lost. Lard used. Till 11pm. Cl Wed.

1348
MAP B
xD5
✔✔ **THE UNIQUE, GLASGOW:** 223 Allison St. Not exactly central, but if you're on the S-side you'll find the best fish 'n' chips in town here. Through the curtain in the café, they serve lunches, fish teas and spam fritters. Veg oil used. Old-fashioned hours, viz 8.15am-1.15pm, 3.45-9pm. That's right, 9pm – closed.

1349
MAP 3
D3
✓ ✓ **THE ASHVALE, ABERDEEN, ELGIN, INVERURIE and BRECHIN:** Original restau (1985) at 46 Gt Western Rd nr Union St, and 2 other city branches. Restau and takeaway complex à la Harry Ramsden (they stick to dripping but veg oil supplied on request). Various sizes of haddock, sole, plaice. Home-made stovies, etc., all served fresh and fast though you may wait. Open 7 days, noon-1am; restau noon-11pm Sun-Thu; till midnight Fri/Sat.

1350
MAP 3
D3
✓ ✓ **THE NEW DOLPHIN, ABERDEEN:** Chapel St. Despite the pre-eminence of the Ashvale in Aberdeen, many would rather swear by this small, always busy place just off Union St. Few tables, superb takeaway. Till 1am and 3am w/ends.

1351
MAP A
C1
✓ ✓ **L'ALBA D'ORO, EDINBURGH:** Henderson Row, nr corner with Dundas St. Large selection of deep-fried goodies, incl many vegn-savouries. Inexpensive proper pasta, real pizzas and even the wine's ok. A lot more than your usual fry-up. Open until midnight. (167/EDIN PIZZA)

1352
MAP A
D2
✓ **THE RAPIDO, EDINBURGH:** 77 Broughton St. Legendary chippie. Popular with late-nighters stumbling back down the hill to the New Town, and the flotsam of the 'Pink Triangle.' 1.30am (3.30am Fri/Sat).

1353
MAP A
E1
✓ **THE DEEP SEA, EDINBURGH:** Leith Walk, opp Playhouse. Open late and often has queues but these are quickly dispatched. The haddock has to be 'of a certain size'. Trad menu. Still one of the best fish suppers you'll ever feed a hangover with. 2am-ish (3am Fri/Sat).

1354
MAP 4
C3
✓ **DEEP SEA, DUNDEE:** 81 Nethergate at bottom end of Perth Rd; v central. The Sterpaio family have been serving the Dundonians excellent fish 'n' chips since 1939; gr range of fish in veg oil. Café with aproned waitress service is a classic. so v trad, so very tasty. Mon-Sat, 11.30am-6.40pm.

1355
MAP 4
C3
✓ **HOLDGATE'S, PERTH:** 146 South St. For all of this century (est 1901), this brilliant caff shop has been frying up the F&C the way we like it. Sitting-room thro' the back is a model of minimalism and functionalism. This place will be here long after the chromey makeovers have come and gone. Go sample the simple. 7 days 12-8.30pm, Sun 4pm-8.30pm.

1356
MAP 4
D3
✓ **PEPPO'S, ARBROATH:** 51 Ladybridge St next to the harbour where those fish come in. Fresh as that and chips in dripping. Peppo has been here since 1951; John and Frank Orsi are carrying on the gr family trad and feeding the hordes. Tues-Fri 4-10pm, Sat-Mon till 8pm. Smell the smokies outside.

1357
MAP 3
C4
✓ **THE BERVIE CHIPPER, INVERBERVIE and STONEHAVEN:** Main st Inverbervie. Sit-in area up and downstairs and take-away. Gets through enormous amounts of haddock and cod. Lard used. Newer opening in Stoney on David St the rd to Aberdeen has queues out the door on Sat nights. Both open daily, noon-10.30pm (Inverbervie from 3pm in winter) 7 days.

1358
MAP 5
D3
✓ **THE ANSTRUTHER FISH BAR:** On the front in Fife seaside town (1515/COASTAL VILLAGES). They say best F&C UK 2000; the continuous queue suggests they may be right. Lard used. Eating in is cramped (cardboard trays etc) so takeaway best (walk round the harbour). 7 days 11.30-10.30pm.

1359
MAP 1
C3
✓ **WEST END, ROTHESAY:** 1 Gallowgate. Winner of awards (so many, we lose track) and unmissable if you're on Bute despite the ticket system. Only haddock, but wide range of other fries and fresh pizza. Uses expensive groundnut oil. Summer: 12-12am (Sun 4-11pm); winter 12-12am, Cl 2-4pm. Café in summer till 8pm. Cl Mon.

1360
MAP 8
D1
✓ **GIACOPAZZI'S, EYEMOUTH:** Harbour by the fishmarket (or what's left of it). A caff & takeaway with the catch on its doorstep. Dispensing excl F&C & their award-winning ice-cream quietly here in the far-flung SE corner of Scotland since 1900. 7 days 11am-9pm.

1361
MAP 9
C3
BALMORAL, DUMFRIES: Balmoral Rd. Seems as old and essential as the Bard himself. Now using groundnut oil, hence the best chip in the south. Out the Annan rd heading E, 1km from centre. Daily.

1362
MAP 1
B1
ONORIO'S, OBAN: George St. Legendary but this is where the wifie told me, 'Anyone who says you can fry good chips in vegetable oil is having you on, son.' This is bollocks, missus (*see above*). But their lardy chips are good and you're near the seafront to walk off the grease. Lunch 4-11.30pm. (Cl Sun winter.)

1363 **SANDY'S, STONEHAVEN:** Market Sq. The established Stoney Chipper, dealing
MAP 3 well with the recent competition (*see above*). Daily, LO 9pm. Big haddock.
C4

1364 **CORVI'S, BO'NESS:** Just squeezing in, included for its fine fish supper, and gr
MAP 6 home-made ice cream (1427/ICE CREAM).
D3

GREAT CAFÉS

For cafés in EDINBURGH, *see p. 51*, GLASGOW, *p. 93*.

1365 ✓✓✓ **NARDINI'S, LARGS:** 01475 674555. The Esplanade, Glas side. An
MAP 1 institution. The epitome of the seaside cafeteria and all the nos-
C3 talgia of Doon the Watter days. This airy brasserie with cake, ice cream and
chocolate counters and in the back a trad tratt with full Italian à la carte and
OK wines has a timeless formula which works as well today as it ever did. The
light fittings like almost everything else are true originals. But nothing lasts
forever and in summer 2001 Nardini's finally passed out of the hands of the
Nardini family. We shall watch future developments with interest – meantime,
pop down for high tea. Summer till late, winter till 8pm.

1366 ✓ **ALLAN WATER CAFÉ, BRIDGE OF ALLAN:** Henderson St (main st) beside
MAP 6 the eponymous br. Real whiff of nostalgia along with the fish'n'chips and
C3 the ice cream, which are the best around. Worth coming over from Stirling
(8km) for a takeaway or a seat in the comforting woody caff – and a reminisce
of the life before the mall and the burgering of your high st. 7 days, 8am-9pm.

1367 ✓ **THE RITZ CAFÉ, MILLPORT:** See Millport, see the Ritz. Since 1906 and
MAP 1 now in its fourth generation, the classic café on the Clyde. Somewhat
C3 overshadowed by Nardini's (*see above*) and a short ferry journey away (from
Largs, continuous; then 6km), but it should be an essential part of any visit to
this part of the coast, and Millport is not entirely without charm. Food 'n' chips,
frothy cappuccino, famous home-made ice cream (esp with melted marsh-
mallow). Something of 'things past'. 7 days, 10am-10pm forever.

1368 ✓ **TOGS, TROON:** Templehill nr main crossrds. There are 2 seaside caffs in
MAP 1 downtown Troon (the other, the pleasingly named Venice Café, is also
C3 good), but this is the one that did it for me – it even smells like a café should.
Fairy drops and vanilla fudge. 7 days 9am-6 or 8pm (from 10am on Sun).

1369 **THE MARKET BAR AND RESTAURANT, LANARK MARKET:** Hyndford Rd.
MAP 1 Betw the auction rings and only on auction days of which there are many esp
D3 Mon/Tues/Thurs, a café from a bygone era. Closed temp in 2001 (foot and
mouth) but we'll try again in 2002 – farmers and their sons usually cram the
tables for canteen cooking and to banter with the waitresses. Jump straight in
to a different culture.

1370 **THE CASTLE RESTAURANT, INVERNESS:** On rd that winds up to the castle
MAP 2 from the main st, nr the TO and the hostels. No pandering to tourists here, but
C2 this great caff has been serving chips with everything for 40 years. Pork chops,
prawn cocktail, perfect fried eggs. They work damned hard. 8am-8.30pm. Cl
Sun.

1371 **THE CAFÉ IN BRIG O'TURK IN THE TROSSACHS:** 01877 376267. Hanging
MAP 6 baskets of flowers o/side this shack are what you notice from the rd (the A821
B2 12km W of Callander) in the heart of the afternoon tea belt of the Trossachs.
But more substantial high teas are served: Highland stew, Cullen skink, whisky
spice cake. Not always open in even, so book.

1372 **BEN LEDI CAFE, CALLANDER:** Main st nr sq. Fish teas, and a sq meal.
MAP 6 Unprepossessing frontage, but here is the genuine, ungentrified article – who
C2 needs an internet cafe? Take away or sit in. The best ice cream for miles
around tho' we're told many locals now favour 'the other chip shop'. Cl Thu.

1373 **THE MELBOURNE, SALTCOATS:** 72 Hamilton St. A tatty 1950s leftover with
MAP 1 good coffee, good panini, breakfasts, filled rolls etc. Juke box nearly as cool as
C3 the lassies behind the counter! Used as a film location (*Late Night Shopping*).
Damned fine! Daily until 5pm.

THE BEST TEAROOMS AND COFFEE SHOPS

For EDINBURGH, *see p. 49; for* GLASGOW, *p. 92.*

1374
MAP A
E2

✓ ✓ **PLAISIR DU CHOCOLAT, EDINBURGH:** All other Edin places on p. 49, but this must feature here. A celebration of tea, France & the good life. Report 251/TEARMS.

1375
MAP B
E4

✓ ✓ **CAFE GANDOLFI, GLASGOW:** Glas's definitive tearm, long-standing & a formula that has not been bettered (not even at their Habitat venue). Report 634/TEARMS. Also in Glasgow the more recent and decidedly new wave **TCHAI-OVNA**. No chintz nor cream teas here, just good tchai and chat. Report 636/TEARMS.

1376
MAP 1
C3

✓ ✓ **TUDOR RESTAURANT, AYR:** 8 Beresford Terr, nr Odeon and Burns Monument Sq. High tea from 3.15pm, breakfast 9-11am. Roomy, well-used, full of life. Bakery counter at front (fab cream donuts and 'fly cemeteries' as they're supposed to be) and disdainful nippy waitresses in the body of the kirk. 9am-8pm Mon-Sat, 9pm July and Aug. Open Sun in season. Trad without being tacky.

1377
MAP 4
B7

✓ ✓ **THE POWMILL MILKBAR, nr KINROSS:** On the A977 Kinross (on the M90, jnct 6) to Kincardine Br rd, a real milkbar and a real slice of Scottish cack and cake. Apple pie and moist fly cemeteries – an essential stop on any Sunday run (but open every day). The paper plates do little justice to the confections they bear, but they are part of the deal, so don't complain! Hot meals and salads. Good place to take kids. 7 days, 9am-6pm (8pm summer, earlier in winter). (1905/GLEN AND RIVER WALKS)

1378
MAP 6
A1

✓ ✓ **THE CLIFTON COFFEE SHOP, TYNDRUM:** On A82, a strategically placed pit-stop on the drive to Oban or Ft William (just before the rd divides), with a Scottish produce shop and the 'Green Welly Shop' selling outdoor gear. Cakes and things v home-made, ditto the soup and some decent bottled ales. This is Scotland, ken? 7 days, 8.30am-5.30pm.

1379
MAP 3
C3

✓ ✓ **THE BLACK-FACED SHEEP, ABOYNE:** 01339 887311. Nr main Royal Deeside rd through Aboyne (A93) and TO, this excellent coffee shop/gift shop is well-loved by locals (and regulars from all over) but is thankfully missed by the bus parties hurtling towards Balmoral. Home-made breads and cakes, snacks; good coffee (real capp & espresso from Elektra machine). Expansion imminent at TGP, possibly with longer hrs. Look forward to supper! 10am-5pm, Sun from 11am.

1380
MAP 3
C4

✓ **THE (ART DECO) CARRON RESTAURANT, STONEHAVEN:** 01569 760460. 20 Carron St off main st nr the sq. They use 'art deco' in the title, but you couldn't miss the reference in this fantastic period piece faithfully restored & embellished. Open for b/fast thro lunch, aft tea & high teas until 6.30pm. We haven't tried the food at TGP but the building is fab.

1381
MAP 6
A3

✓ **THE COACH HOUSE, LUSS, LOCH LOMOND:** In the heart of Take The High Road country & this vill throngs with visitors. Gary & Rowena Grove's much (self) publicised success story also goes like the proverbial fair. Not all home-made but they'd need v big ovens. Nice loos, some o/side seating. 7 days 10am-5pm.

1382
MAP 1
B3

✓ **NORTH BEACHMORE FARM RESTAURANT, nr MUASDALE:** on A83 Tarbert–Campbeltown rd. Signposted up a steep track, 2km off the rd and into the hills. Matt and Eileen McInnes' home-cooking is v popular locally; you see why. Stunning views of the Sound of Gigha, (and on a clear day Ireland). Food excl too. Open AYR 10am-11pm. Cl weekdays in Nov.

1383
MAP 1
B1

✓ **THE GLASS BARN, TOBERMORY, MULL:** Up the hill at the edge of town 500m off Dervaig rd, 2km centre. Run by (and part of) the Reades' dairy farm the people who make the excellent Mull cheddar, but that's not the reason I'm recommending it. Rather, it's just gr what they've done with it – go see! A glass barn full of plants, hearty soup, farm bakes. Walk from the village – it will do you good. May-Sep; Mon-Fri (Cl Sun) 10am-4pm. Closed at TGP but re-opening expected 2002.

1384 ✓ **PUDDLEDUCKS, BLAIRLOGIE, nr STIRLING:** On main A91 in tiny village.
MAP 6 Hot dishes at lunch & snacks and a cabinet of delicious cakes, and I do
C3 mean delicious. Stock up on the way to the Ochils. There's a pavilion in the
extensive gdn (in fine weather). Garden always good for a stroll while you wait
to be called to your tiny table. 7 days 10.30-4.30pm.

1385 ✓ **KITTY'S TEAROOM, NEW GALLOWAY:** Main St of town in the forest.
MAP 9 Absolutely splendid. Sylvia Brown's steady hand in the kitchen, great
B3 cakes, good tea, and conversations between local ladies that are totally Alan
Bennett. 11am-7pm, Easter-Oct. Tues-Sun.

1386 **TULLY BANNOCHER FARM RESTAURANT:** 2km W on A85 to Lochearnhead.
MAP 4 Recommended roadside coffee shop/self-service diner with fairly trad hot
B3 dishes, salads, some baking. Handy for the delights of Comrie. Tables o/side.
Open till 7.30pm. Apr-Oct.

1387 **FLAT CAT GALLERY COFFEE-SHOP, LAUDER:** 2 Market St opp Eagle Hotel.
MAP 8 Speeding thro' Lauder (note speed camera at Edinburgh end) you might miss
C2 this cool coffee spot & serious gallery. Always interesting work & ethnic things.
Home-baking natch. 7 days till 5pm.

1388 **SILVER SPOON, PEEBLES:** Innerleithen Rd at end of main st adj Green Tree
MAP 8 hotel. Mumsy, definitely not funky tearoom, but with good attitude to baking
B2 (& mums). Perfectly Peebles! 7 days. 9-4.30pm (Sun 11-4pm).

1389 **ABBEY TEAROOM, MELROSE:** Nr TIC and abbey. Melrose must have a tea-
MAP 8 room & this is it! Some hot dishes (like macaroni cheese) & baked cakes (like
C2 Victoria cream sponge). Days, if not centuries could pass here while you tak
yer tea. 7 days, til 4.30pm.

1390 **THE RIVERSIDE and ABBEY ARTEFACTS, ABBEY ST BATHANS:** 01361
MAP 8 840312. By the trout farm, nr R Whiteadder in the middle of this rustic hamlet
C1 on the Southern Upland Way. A welcome place for a restau & gallery. Seasonal
menu. Light or 3-course lunches incl savoury flans, steaks, local seafood.
Cream teas. Tues-Sun 11am-5pm (4pm Oct-Easter). Cl Mons.

1391 **THE OLD BANK, DUMFRIES:** 95 Irish St, off High St. Coffee shop in converted
MAP 9 bank (revolving doors and cornices remain) on st where Burns lived. Delicate
C3 snacks, good puds and cakes. Looking a little dated now Sandbar has opened
opp (see 2245/BEST OF DUMFRIES). Mon-Sat 10am-4.30pm.

1392 **THE TEAROOM at CLATT, nr ALFORD and INVERURIE:** In the village hall in
MAP 3 the hamlet of Clatt where local ladies display gr home-made Scottish baking
C2 – like a weekly sale of work. Take A96 N of Inverurie, then B9002 follow sign for
Auchleven, then Clatt. Gr countryside. W/ends in summer 1pm-5pm.

1393 **THE HARBOUR CAFE, ROTHESAY:** 01700 505166, East Princes St. Internet
MAP 1 and espresso come to Bute. Surf the web, have a sandwich, or dinner. Urban
C3 outpost. Mon-Sat 11am-5pm, Sun 12-4pm. Sometimes closes on Tues, like the
rest of Bute.

1394 **GARDEN ROOM TEASHOP, ROCKCLIFFE:** On main rd in/out of this seaside
MAP 9 cul de sac. Best on sunny days when you can sit in the gdn. Snacks and cakes
C3 (though not all home-made). 10.30-5pm. Cl Mon & Tues.

1395 **COFFEE HOUSE, GRANTOWN-ON-SPEY:** 35 High St. Surprisingly authentic
MAP 2 Italian café with genuine Italian cakes, ice cream and espresso. They serve
D3 stew, pasta and gr ice-cream. Nice people run this place. Till 5pm.

1396 **COUNTRY KITCHEN, CROMARTY:** In great wee town in Black Isle 45km NE of
MAP 2 Inverness (1510/COASTAL VILLAGES) on corner of Church St. Award-winning
D2 home-baked cakes particularly good scones 10.30am-430pm. Cl Fri.

1397 **KIND KYTTOCK'S KITCHEN, FALKLAND:** Folk come to Falkland (1696/CAS-
MAP 5 TLES; 1879/HILL WALKS) for many reasons, not least for afternoon tea. Several
B3 choices, this the longest established and highly regarded. Omelettes, toasties,
baked potatoes, baking. Good service. 10.30am-5.30pm. Cl Mon.

1398 **BRAMBLES, ST ANDREWS:** 5 College St off Middle St. Small (incl entrance-
MAP 5 way) & always busy. Home-bakes & good vegn from cramped self-serv. 7 days
C2 till 5.30pm.

1399
MAP 6
C2
DUN WHINNY'S, CALLANDER: Off main st at Glas rd, a welcoming wee (but not twee) tearoom; not run by wifies. Banoffee pie kind of thing and clootie dumpling. There's a few naff caffs in Callander. This one still OK in my book.

1400
MAP 9
C3
ABBEY COTTAGE, NEW ABBEY: Literally over the lane from Sweetheart Abbey, this place serves a decent double espresso and fruit pie for a sunny afternoon when all you want to do is sit out and gawp at Devorguilla's pile opp (1820/ABBEYS). Easter-Oct daily, Oct-Dec weekends only. Cl Jan-Mar.

DUNNET HEAD TEAROOM nr THURSO: 15km N (1054/INEXP HIGHLAND RESTAUS).

THE BEST SCOTCH BAKERS

1401
MAP 5
C2
MAP 4
C3
✓ ✓ **FISHER & DONALDSON, DUNDEE/ST ANDREWS/CUPAR:** Main or original branch in Cupar and 3 in Dundee. Superior contemporary bakers along trad lines (born 1919) – surprising (and a pity) that they haven't gone further, although they do supply a few selected outlets (e.g. Jenners in Edin with pastries and the most excellent Dr Floyd's bread which is as good as anything you could make yourself). Main sq, Cupar; Church St, St Andrews; Whitehall St, 300 Perth Rd and Lochee, Dundee, which is v well served with decent bakers (*see below*). Dundee Whitehall has good tearm (1130/DUNDEE).

1402
MAP 4
C3
✓ **GOODFELLOW AND STEVEN and WALLACE'S, DUNDEE:** G&S have several branches in Dundee, Perth and Fife. Wallace's are famous for their pies and massive bridies, and have branches in Crichton St and Faraday St.

1403
MAP B
C3
✓ **BRADFORD'S:** 245 Sauchiehall St, Glas, and suburban branches in selected areas, i.e. they have not over-expanded; for a bakery chain, some lines seem almost home-made. Certainly better than all the industrial 'home'-bakers around. Individual fruit pies, for example, are uniquely yummy, and the all-important Scotch pie pastry is exemplary. (642/TEAROOMS.)

1404
MAP 1
D3
✓ **ALEXANDER TAYLOR'S, STRATHAVEN, nr LANARK:** 01357 521260. Specialising in huge array of savoury breads: sunflower, Bavarian, sourdough, black bun and, at Christmas, stollen. Also make all their shortbreads and oatcakes. Good & wholesome! Mon-Sat 8am-5.30pm (Sat from 7am!).

1405
MAP 6
C2
✓ **SCOTCH OVEN, CALLANDER:** Opp Royal Hotel in busy touristy main st and one of the best things about it. Good bread, rolls, cakes, the biggest, possibly the best, tattie scones and sublime doughnuts. Also featuring what may be the perfect Scotch pie pastry. Adj caff at side less convincing. Better to picnic on the Braes or by the river. Open 7 days.

1406
MAP 1
C2
✓ **BLACK'S OF DUNOON:** aka Cowal Cottage Bakery at 144 Argyll St, the main st of Dunoon. Popular for aeons, easily found opp the masonic lodge; loads of doughnuts and muffins. The old favourites shortbread, potato scones and the like still draw the queues.

1407
MAP 2
D2
CROMARTY BAKERY, CROMARTY: Bank St. One of the many reasons to visit this picturesque seaside town. Abundance of speciality cakes, organic bread, rolls & pies, baked daily on premises. Also tea, coffee, hot savouries & takeaway. Mon, Tue, Thu, Fri 8.30am-5.30pm; Wed 8.30am-1pm; Sat 8.30am-4 pm.

1408
MAP 4
B3
BREADALBANE BAKERY, ABERFELDY: 37 Dunkeld St. On rd out of town to Grandtully opp petrol stn. Home of Aberfeldy Whisky Cake (a rich fruit job with single malt flavour) and Holyrood Tarts (no, not Hollywood). Nice biscuits.

1409
MAP 2
D2
THE DORNOCH BAKERY, DORNOCH: Behind cathedral, a busy town bakery with a couple of tables in front of the ovens. Great selection of pies (esp fruit pies) and bread (esp milk bread). Often has queues.

1410
MAP 5
B3
PILLANS AND SONS, KIRKCALDY: Nr Harbour and end of High St. Poss one of the oldest family-run businesses in Scotland. Here for 120 yrs turning out their Scottish rolls and cakes and famous unconventional Scotch pies. Nostalgia and good Scots baking. Long may they remain Pillans, the Pie Shop.

1411
MAP 5
C3
D2
D3
ADAMSON'S IN FIFE: PITTENWEEM, ELIE, CRAIL, ANSTRUTHER and CUPAR: Baking in the kingdom since 1887, Adamson's is one of the few places that keeps trad bakery going, not succumbing to the creaming, or industrial yeasting of everything. Where else can you find puggy buns, Hedderwick buns or raggy biscuits? Mainly small neighbourhood shops – the one in Elie is out of Dr Finlay's Casebook. Original bake-house in Pittenweem. Go see!

1412
MAP 3
D3
AITKEN'S, ABERDEEN: Glenbervie Rd and Menzies Rd, Torry (a district of Aber over the br) and 202 Holburn St in city centre. Fancy cakes, pies and all the usual, but mainly notable as the place to get your rowies, the buttery rolls which are the Aberdonian contribution to breakfast (should give the croissant a run for its money). Aitken's rowies send Aberdonians into raptures all over the world.

1413
MAP 4
D3
McLAREN'S, FORFAR: Town centre next to Queens Hotel and in Kirriemuir. The best in town to sample the famous Forfar bridie, a meaty shortcrust pastie that'll keep you going all the way to Aber. **SADDLER'S** make an excl meringue.

THE BEST ICE CREAM

1414
MAP 7
B1
✓ ✓ **LUCA'S, MUSSELBURGH, nr EDINBURGH (and EDINBURGH):** 32 High St. Queues out the door in the middle of a Sun afternoon in February are testament to the enduring popularity of this almost-legendary ice cream boutique. 3 classic flavours (vanilla, choc and strawberry) and pure ingredients attract folk from Edin (14km) though there is now a branch in Edin at 16 Morningside Rd, a more designery Italian version (269/CAFÉS). In cafe thro the back, basic snacks, and you might have to wait, in Edin cafe upstairs more pizza/pasta and smart sandwiches. Mon-Sat 9am-10pm, Sun 10.30am-10pm. Edin hrs: 7 days 9am (10.30 Sun)-10pm. Luca's (wholesale) now spreading everywhere so look out for the sign.

1415
MAP 1
C3
✓ ✓ **MANCINI'S, THE ROYAL CAFÉ, AYR:** 11 New Rd, the rd to Prestwick. Ice cream that's taken seriously, entered for competitions and usually wins. Family biz for aeons. Massive no. of flavours at their disposal, always new ones. The plum was rather splendid on our last visit. Their sorbets taste better than the fruit they're made from. They were first with the ice-cream toastie. These Mancinis are champions of ice cream. 9.30am-11.00pm; cl Thu in winter.

1416
MAP 8
A2
✓ **THE CHOCOLATE BOX, BIGGAR:** Christine White's little sweetie and ice-cream shop, under her charge since '92. (Mr White makes the ice-cream in a factory by Lanark). Daily until 5pm. Sweet sustenance on the rd from/to Edinburgh.

1417
MAP 5
C2
✓ **JANETTA'S, ST ANDREWS:** 31 South St. Family firm since 1908. There are two Janetta's, but the one to adore is opp the Byre Theatre. Once only vanilla, Americans at the Open asked for other flavours. Now there are 52, & numerous awards. Also frozen yogs. Janetta's is another good reason for being a student at St Andrews. Sit-in café adj LO 5/5.30pm. 7 days 9am-6pm.

1418
MAP 8
B2
✓ **CALDWELL'S, INNERLEITHEN:** On the High St in this ribbon of a town between Peebles and Gala they've been making ice cream since 1911. Purists may bemoan the fact that they've succumbed to fancy flavours in the 21st cent, but their vanilla is still best. The shop still sells everything from Blue Nun to bicycles. Mon-Fri till 8.30pm, Sat/Sun 7.30pm.

1419
MAP 4
C2, C3
VISOCCHI'S, BROUGHTY FERRY/KIRRIEMUIR: Orig from St Andrews; ice-cream makers for 50 years and still with the café they opened in Kirriemuir in 1953. On the main drag of the Angus town (1546/GLENS), it's the local caff (v basic menu, no chips). Broughty Ferry (Dundee's seaside suburb) more middle-class, with a contemporary menu; home-made pasta as well as the peach melba. But whatever comes and goes, the ice cream will go on forever. 7 days (1124/DUNDEE EAT AND DRINK).

1420
MAP 3
D3
CASA MARCHINI, ABERDEEN: Gt Western Rd. New premises since last edition, past the Amatola hotel, then beside the shops. Superior ice cream in multi flavours and ice-cream cakes to trad Italian recipes. We haven't tried recently, more feedback on the Aberdeen ice-cream scene please. 7 days till 5.30pm.

1421
MAP 6
C3
THE ALLAN WATER CAFÉ, BRIDGE OF ALLAN: An old-fashioned café in an old-fashioned town, near the eponymous br in the main st since 1902. Fabulously good fish 'n' chips and ice cream. The former now dispensed from a modernised shop next door. Ice cream in the old woody atmos. One of the few that's not succumbed to flavours (only vanilla). 7 days, 8am-9pm.

1422
MAP 1
D2
COLPI'S, MILNGAVIE, GLASGOW: Opp Marks & Spencer in Milngavie centre (pron Mullguy) and there since 1928. Many consider this to be Glas's finest. Only vanilla at the cone counter but strawb/choc flake/amaretto/honeycomb to take home. There's another branch in Clydebank. Till 9pm, 7 days.

1423
MAP 1
D3
TORTOLANO'S, UDDINGSTON: 29 Main St. 15km E of city via M74, Uddingston t/off, at the lights where you turn for Bothwell Castle (1720/RUINS). Tiny confectioners/ice-cream shop with proper biscuit cones as an option and fab flavours (try the 'caramel shortcake') all home made and rather fantastic. Their loss, definitely our weight gain.

1424
MAP 1
C3
NARDINI'S, LARGS: On the Esplanade. No longer owned by the Nardini family, we doubt the ice cream will be any different. Some summers back I had an epiphany over a pistachio and vanilla on the esplanade. All became right with the world. In 2001, Keith said the comfort & the nostalgia was still there. Long may it linger. (1365/GREAT CAFÉS). Nardini's now rolling out the brand (several in Glasgow), but none will touch this, the original.

1425
MAP 9
C3
DRUMMUIR FARM, COLLIN, nr DUMFRIES: 5km off A75 (Carlisle/Annan) rd E of Dumfries on B724 (nr Clarencefield). A real farm producing real ice cream – still does supersmooth original and honeycomb, seasonal specials; on a fine day, sit out and chill. Easter-Sept daily to 5.30pm; Oct-Dec Sat-Sun until 5pm; Jan-Mar closed.

1426
MAP 9
B3
CREAM O' GALLOWAY, RAINTON, nr GATEHOUSE OF FLEET: 01557 814040. A75 take Sandgreen exit 2km, then left at sign for Carrick. Originally a dairy farm producing cheese, now you can watch them making the creamy concoctions which you find all over in 'good shops'. Nature trail, absolutely fab kids adventure play area, and decent organic café. Apr-Oct 11am-6pm.

1427
MAP 6
D3
CORVI'S, BO'NESS 'THE SEAVIEW CAFÉ': Seaview Pl, opp car park with tourist info. Downhome fish 'n' chip shop that serves home-made vanilla or strawberry ice cream in premises that look like an extended version of someone's parlour. Eat in or take away – the fish supper is the local choice. Mon-Tues 11am-6.30pm, Thurs-Sat 11am-7.30pm (seated area cl 4.30pm).

1428
MAP 2
D2
CAPALDI'S, BRORA: Never seems to change – all kinds of inventive flavours, the crème caramel was pretty good last time we passed. Daily until 8pm.

BEN LEDI CAFÉ, CALLANDER: Main St (1372/CAFÉS).

THE REALLY GOOD DELIS

1429
MAP A
E1
✔✔✔ **VALVONA AND CROLLA, EDINBURGH:** 19 Elm Row, nr top of Leith Walk. Since 1934, an Edin institution, the shop you show visitors. Full of smells, genial, knowledgeable staff and a floor-to-ceiling range of cheese (Ital/Scot, etc.), meats, oils, wines and more. Fresh veg trucked in from Milan markets, on-premises bakery, great café/bar (154/ITALIAN RESTAUS). Also demos, tastings, Fringe venue. Second to none and we can't say better than that! Cl Suns.

1430
MAP A
D3,xC4
B1
MAP B
B1
✔✔ **I.J. MELLIS, EDINBURGH & GLASGOW:** 3 branches Edin – Victoria St, Bruntsfield & Stockbridge & Kelvinbridge in Glas. Started out as the cheese guy, now more of a v select deli for food that's good & 'slow'. Coffees, hams, sausages, olives & seasonal stuff like apples & mushrooms (branches vary), so smells mingle. Irresistible! 7 days tho' times vary. See also 1452/CHEESES.

1431
MAP A
C2
✔ **GLASS & THOMPSON, EDINBURGH:** 2 Dundas St. Exemplary and contemporary New Town provisioner. Selective choice of Mediterranean – style goodies to eat or take away and bread/pâtisserie; also those all-important New Town dinner party essentials. Report: 262/TEAROOMS.

1432
MAP B
B2
✓ **GRASSROOTS ORGANIC, GLASGOW:** 48 Woodlands Rd, nr Charing Cross. First-class vegn food and provisions store, everything chemically unaltered and environmentally-friendly. Gr breads and sandwiches for lunch and the best organic fruit/veg range in town. Now with vegn restau round the corner (631/GLAS VEGN). 7 days 8am-8pm (Sat 9am-6pm, Sun 11am-5pm).

1433
MAP 8
B2
✓ **COOK'S FINE FOODS, PEEBLES:** 25 High St in midst of Peebles where people like a good bit of cheese. Here the selection is exemplary & they make bread, savouries & continental-type bakes. Sit-in for snacks; they also do outside catering. A place you'd expect to find in Edinburgh New Town. Tues-Sat 10am-6pm.

1434
MAP B
D3
✓ **SARTI'S, GLASGOW:** 113 Wellington St. Definitive corner of little Italy – a deli/tratt here and another eating place/wine shop in Bath St (567/ITALIAN RESTAUS). Feels like Italy.

1435
✓ **HEART and BUCHANAN, GLASGOW:** 380 Byres Rd. Gr deli & first-rate t/away. Report 669/T/AWAY.

1436
MAP B
xA1
✓ **DELIZIQUE, GLASGOW:** 66 Hyndland St nr Cottier's bar & theatre. Excl neighbourhood deli for the affluent Hyndlanders & others who roam & graze round here. Gr prepared meals & hand-picked goodies incl oils, hams, flowers & Mellis cheeses. 7 days 8am-8pm (earlier on Suns).

1437
MAP 3
A1
✓ **PHOENIX FINDHORN COMMUNITY, FINDHORN:** Serving the new age township of the Findhorn Community and therefore pursuing a conscientious app, this has become an exemplary and v high quality deli, worth the detour from the A96 Inverness-Elgin rd even if you have apprehensions about their 'thing'. Packed and carefully selected shelves; as much for pleasurable eating as for healthy. Till 6pm. (W/ends 5pm.) Cl Tue am.

1438
MAP A
C4
LUPE PINTOS, EDINBURGH: 24 Leven St nr King's Theatre. Unusual Latin deli (ie Mexican, Central American, Spanish). Where to go for chorizo, manchego and 20 kinds of tequila. T/away incl home-made burritos and the usual Tex-Mex. Every kind of chili & gr Riojas. 10am-6pm. Cl Suns.

1439
MAP B
D4
PECKHAM'S, CENTRAL STATION, GLASGOW: Best of several branches, most remarkable for its location in Glas's main station. From early train times to 11pm (midnight Fri/Sat, 10pm Sun), they've got everything you need from staples to fine wines and cheeses and a good range of up-market nibbles and quick meals. Their branch at Edinburgh Waverley is somehow not on the same … track. The better Edin branch is at 155 Bruntsfield Pl which is packed with goodies, tables o/side in summer. Open till midnight (incl wine).

1440
MAP 5
C2
BUTLER & CO, ST ANDREWS: 10 Church St. Excl deli by the people who have the seafood restau in St Monans (1341/SEAFOOD RESTAUS). Good range of Scottish and other cheeses. Cl Suns.

1441
MAP 3
B1
GORDON AND MACPHAIL, ELGIN: South St. Purveyors of fine wines, cheeses, meats, Mediterranean goodies, unusual breads and other epicurean delights to the good burghers of Elgin for nigh on a century. Traditional shopkeeping, in the style of the 'family grocer'. G & M are widely known as bottlers of lesser-known high-quality malts ('Connoisseurs' range) – on sale here. Some rare real ales by the bottle too. Mon-Sat 9am-5.15pm.

1442
MAP 7
B1
JACQUES & LAWRENCE, HADDINGTON: 37 Court St. Ex-Masterchef & École Culinaire caterers have teamed up to bring latest (local & far-flung) fine deli foods to E Lothian punters. Fast food of the home-made pasta & Thai green curry variety.

1443
MAP 8
B2
THE OLIVE TREE, PEEBLES: 7 High St. Small emporium packed with wide selection of European groceries plus local delicacies: beer, honey, cheese ad infinitum – specialises in farmhouse and unpasteurised cheeses.

1444
MAP A
xC4
GOURMET PASTA, EDINBURGH: 52 Morningside Rd (& small branch in arcade betw Cockburn St & N Bridge). Freshly-made pasta, sauces, tortes etc. Good for the instant dinner party. Cl Sun.

1444a
MAP A
C1
DIONIKA, EDINBURGH: Henderson Pl off Henderson Row at Dundas St. Recent Spanish emporium esp good for seafood and sausage. A surprising find. 7 days.

1445 **MULL or TOBERMORY CHEDDAR:** From Sgriob-Ruadh Farm (pron 'Skibrua'). Comes in big 50lb cheeses and 1lb truckles. Good, strong cheddar, one of the v best in the UK.

1446 **DUNSYRE BLUE/LANARK BLUE:** Made by Humphrey Errington at Carnwath. Next to Stilton, **DUNSYRE** (made from the unpasteurised milk of Ayrshire cows) is the best blue in the UK. It is soft, rather like Dolcelatte. **LANARK,** the original, is Scotland's Roquefort and made from ewes' milk. Both can vary but are excellent. Go on, live dangerously – unpasteurise your life.

1447 **LOCHARTHUR CHEESE:** Anything from this SW creamery is worth a nibble: the cheddar, CRIFFEL (mild), KEBBUCK (shaped like a dinosaur's tooth, semi-soft).

1448 **BONNET:** Hard goat's milk cheese from Anne Dorwood's farm at Stewarton in Ayrshire.

1449 **WESTER LAURENCETON CHEESES, FORRES:** Pam Rodway's excl organic cheeses: CAROLA, CALIFER (goat's milk) & the hard-to-get SWEETMILK CHEDDAR.

1450 **CABOC/CROWDIE/GRUTH DHU:** Widely available and established soft cheeses from Highland Fine Cheeses in Tain. **CROWDIE** is traditional cottage or crofters cheese, v basic; others made from double cream rolled in oatmeal/pepper. Rich and delicious; usually avail in wee 'logs'.

1451 **CAIRNSMORE:** A hard, tangy, cheddary cheese from Sorbie in Wigtownshire surprisingly made from ewes' milk, smoked or unsmoked.

AND WHERE TO FIND THEM

All the delis mentioned previously will have good selections (esp Valvona's and Delizique). Also:

1452
MAP A
D3,xC4
MAP B
xB1
✓ ✓ **I.J. MELLIS, EDINBURGH & GLASGOW:** 30a Victoria St, 205 Bruntsfield Pl and Baker's Pl, Stockbridge (Edin) and 492 Gr Western Rd (Glas). A real cheesemonger. Smell and taste before you buy. Cheeses from all over the UK in prime condition. Daily and seasonal specials. (1430/DELIS)

1453
MAP 3
D3
✓ **THE BIG CHEESE, ABERDEEN:** 22 Belmont St. The deli and cheese shop started by Linda Davidson under new ownership but still with v big cheeses from Scotland and the UK piled up around you. Snack bar opened '98 thro' back for cheese, snacks & nice cakes. 10am-5pm. Cl Sun/Mon.

1454
MAP A
B1
✓ **HERBIE, EDINBURGH:** 66 Raeburn Pl. Excellent selection. Clarissa Dickson Wright is a big fan. As usual she's right. As with Scottish cheeses, it's practically impossible here to find a Brie or a blue in less than perfect condition. All too moreish.

✓ **COOK'S FINE FOODS, PEEBLES:** Report: 1433/DELIS

1455
MAP 4
C3
✓ **MACDONALD'S CHEESE SHOP, RATTRAY nr BLAIRGOWRIE:** 2km Blairgowrie on rd to Glenshee and Braemar. Discreet 'shack' you could easily miss, but don't! Extraordinary selection of cheese esp Scottish and Swiss – only shop selling complete wheels of gruyère in Scotland. 7 days till 6pm (early closing Thur).

1456
MAP 1
C3
ISLAND CHEESES, ARRAN: 5km Brodick, rd to castle and Corrie. Excellent selection of their own (the well-known cheddars but many others esp crowdie with garlic and hand-rolled cream cheeses) and others. See them being made. 7 days.

1457
MAP 2
B3
WEST HIGHLAND DAIRY, ACHMORE, nr PLOCKTON: 01599 577203. Mr and Mrs Biss still running their great farm dairy shop selling their own cheeses (ewe and cow milk), yoghurt, ice cream and cheesecake. Mar-Dec dawn to dusk! Signed from village. If you're making the trip specially, phone first to check they're open.

HOUSE OF BRUAR, nr BLAIR ATHOLL: Roadside emporium (2032/SHOPPING).

PETER MACLENNAN, FORT WILLIAM: 28 High St.

SCOTTISH SPECIALITY FOOD, NORTH BALLACHULISH: By Leven Hotel.

JENNERS DEPARTMENT STORE, EDINBURGH: Princes St, top-floor.

AND CHEESEBOARDS IN THESE RESTAURANTS

MARTINS, EDINBURGH: 101/EDIN RESTAUS

UBIQUITOUS CHIP, GLASGOW: 534/GLAS RESTAUS

THE CROSS, KINGUSSIE: 999/HIGHLAND RESTAUS

SUMMER ISLES HOTEL, ACHILTIBUIE: 1003/HIGHLAND RESTAUS

WHISKY

THE BEST DISTILLERY TOURS

The process is basically the same in every distillery, but some are more atmospheric and some have more interesting tours, like these:

1458
MAP 1
A3
THE ISLAY MALTS: The big and cheering news is that **BRUICHLADDICH** is back in production after a hiatus of several yrs – tip of the hat to the new owners. Three tours daily Mon-Fri, twice daily on Sat (01496 850221). Elsewhere on Islay you can visit several of Scotland's most impressive distilleries and sample their gr malts. The distilleries here look like distilleries ought to. **LAGAVULIN** (01496 302400) and **LAPHROAIG** (01496 302418) are both nr Pt Ellen. They offer fascinating tours where your guide will lay on the anecdotes as well as the process and you get a feel for the life and history as well as the product of these world-famous places. At Laphroaig you can join their 'Friend' scheme (free) and own a piece of their hallowed ground. Lagavulin tours Mon-Fri by appointment, Laphroaig same. For the two up nr Port Askaig, call **BUNNAHABHAIN** on 840646 and **CAOL ILA** on 840207. **BOWMORE** (810441) has professional, more commercial, 1hr tours regularly (incl video show and the usual dram). **ARDBEG** (nr Port Ellen) is perhaps the most visitor-oriented and has a really good café where if you blunder in at mid morning and ask for toast, they make you some toast (302244). All these distilleries are in settings that entirely justify the romantic hyperbole of their advertising. Worth seeing from the o/side as well as the floor.

1459
MAP 3
B2
STRATHISLA, KEITH: 01542 783044. The oldest working distillery in the Highlands, literally on the strath of the Isla river and methinks the most evocative atmos of all the Speyside distilleries. The refurb made this an even classier halt for the malt. Used as the 'heart' of Chivas Regal, the malt not commonly available is still a fine dram. Apr-Oct, Mon-Sat 10am- 4pm; Sunday 12.30-4pm.

1460
MAP 2
B3
TALISKER, CARBOST, ISLE OF SKYE: From Sligachan-Dunvegan rd (A863) take B8009 for Carbost and Glen Brittle along the S side of L Harport for 5km. Skye's only distillery; since 1830 they've been making this classic after-dinner malt from barley and the burn that runs off the Hawkhill behind. A dram before the informative 40min tour. Good visitor centre. Apr-Oct 9am-4.30pm (winter 2-4.30pm). Cl w/ends except Sats July-Sept. Gr gifts nearby (2042/CRAFT SHOPS).

1461
MAP 7
B1
GLENKINCHIE, PENCAITLAND, nr EDINBURGH: 01875 342004. Only 25km from city centre (via A68 and A6093 before Pathhead), so popular. Founded in 1837 in a peaceful, pastoral place (it's 3km from the village) with its own bowling green; a country trip as well as a whisky tour. They have a 'silent season', so check (tho they still do a tour). State-of-the-art visitor centre. May-Sep tours daily until 4pm, Oct-Mar Mon-Fri until 4pm.

1462
MAP 4
B2
EDRADOUR, nr PITLOCHRY: Claims to be the smallest distillery in Scotland, producing single malts for blends since 1825 and limited quantities of the Edradour (since 1986) as well as the House of Lords' own brand. Guided tour of charming cottage complex every 20min. 4km from Pitlochry off Kirkmichael rd, A924; signed after Moulin village. Mar-Oct daily until 5pm. Nov-Dec Mon-Sat until 4pm cl Jan-Feb.

1463 **GLENTURRET, nr CRIEFF:** 2km from town off A85 to Comrie. A village has
MAP 4 almost been built around this quaint distillery, the oldest in Scotland (1775)
B3 with award-winning visitor centre. Continuous tours, restau and shop with
extensive range of branded products and exemplary marketing. Self-service
and waitress restau The Pagoda. The whisky itself has a smoky, roasted aroma;
you won't find it anywhere but here (and Harrods). Open AYR Mon-Sat
9.30am-4.30pm (last tour), and Sun from noon. Jan, Mon-Fri 11.30am-2.30pm.

1464 **HIGHLAND PARK, KIRKWALL, ORKNEY:** 01856 874619. 2km from town on
main A961 rd S to S Ronaldsay. The whisky is great and the award-winning
tour one of the best. The most northerly whisky in a class and a bottle of its
own. You walk through the floor maltings and you can touch the warm barley
and fair smell the peat. Good combination of the industrial and trad. Tours
every half hour Apr-Oct 10am-5pm (w/ends in summer only 12-5pm). Nov-
Mar 2pm tour only w/days.

THE BEST OF THE SPEYSIDE WHISKY TRAIL: *Well signposted but bewildering
number of tours, though by no means at every distillery. Many are in rather fea-
tureless industrial complexes and settings. These are the best along with
Strathisla (see above):*

1465 **THE GLENLIVET, MINMORE:** 01542 783220. Starting as an illicit dram cele-
MAP 3 brated as far S as Edin, George Smith licensed the brand in 1824 and founded
B2 this distillery in 1858, registering the already mighty name so that anyone else
had to use a prefix. After various successions and mergers, independence was
lost in 1978 when Seagrams took over. The famous Josie's Well, from which the
water springs, is underground and not shown, but small parties and a walk-
through which is not on a gantry make the tour as satisfying and as popular,
esp with Americans, as the product. Excellent reception centre with
bar/restau and shop. Apr-Oct, 10am-4pm. Sundays 12.30-4pm.

1466 **GLENFIDDICH, DUFFTOWN:** O/side town on the A941 to Craigellachie by the
MAP 3 ruins of Balvenie Castle. Well-oiled tourist operation and the only distillery
B2 where you can see the whisky bottled on the premises; indeed, the whole
process from barley to bar. Also the only major distillery that's free (incl dram).
AYR 9.30am-4.30pm not w/ends in winter. On the same rd there's a chance to
see a whisky-related industry/craft that hasn't changed in decades. The **SPEY-
SIDE COOPERAGE** is 1km from Craigellachie. You watch those poor guys from
the gantry (no chance to slack). AYR Mon-Fri 9.30am-4.30pm.

1467 **GLEN GRANT, ROTHES:** In Rothes on the A941 Elgin to Perth rd. A distillery
MAP 3 tour with an added attraction viz the gdns and orchard reconstructed around
B2 the shallow bowl of the glen of the burn that runs through the distillery. Tour
vouchers can be used there to take a dram in the delightful Dram Pavilion.
Apr-Oct 10-4pm, from 12.30pm on Sun.

1468 **CARDHU, CARRON:** Off B9102 from Craigellachie to Grantown through
MAP 3 deepest Speyside, a small if charming distillery with its own community, a
B2 millpond, picnic tables, etc. Owned by United Distillers, Cardhu is the 'heart of
Johnnie Walker' (which, amazingly, has another 30 malts in it). 10am-4.30pm
(6pm summer), Nov-Feb restricted hrs, check local TO. Mar-Nov, Mon-Fri.

1469 **DALLAS DHU, nr FORRES:** Not really nr the Spey (3km S of Forres on B9010)
MAP 3 and no longer a working distillery (ceased 1983), but instant history provided
A2 by HS and you don't have to go round on a tour. The wax workers are a bit
spooky; the product itself is more life-like. Apr-Sept 9.30-6.30, restricted hrs in
wint (01309 676548). HS

1470 **SCOTCH WHISKY HERITAGE CENTRE, EDINBURGH:** On Castlehill on last
MAP 3 stretch to Castle (you cannot miss it). Not a distillery of course, but a visitor
A2 attraction to celebrate all things that a tourist can take in about Scotland's
main export. Shop has huge range. 7 days 10-5.30pm.

WHERE TO FIND THE BEST SELECTION OF MALTS
GLASGOW

THE CASK AND STILL: 154 Hope St.

THE BON ACCORD: 153 North St.

EDINBURGH

✓ ✓ **SCOTCH MALT WHISKY SOCIETY:** The Vaults, 87 Giles St, Leith. Your search will end here. More a club (with membership) but visitors must be signed in.

✓ ✓ **BAR at THE SCOTSMAN HOTEL:** Almost 400 malts adorn the fine dining restau and can be tippled. (52/HOTELS)

BENNET'S: 8 Leven St by King's Theatre.

KAY'S BAR: 39 Jamaica St.

THE BOW BAR: 80 West Bow.

CADENHEAD'S: 172 Canongate. The shop with the lot.

CANNY MAN'S: 237 Morningside Rd.

BLUE BLAZER: Corner Spittal & Bread St (327/UNSPOILT PUBS).

REST OF SCOTLAND

LOCHSIDE HOTEL, BOWMORE, ISLAY: More Islay malts than you ever imagined in friendly local near the distillery. Malt whisky w/ends.

ARISAIG HOTEL, ARISAIG, nr MALLAIG: Small, civilised lounge and busy local. 100 malts move betw the bars.

KNOCKINAAM LODGE, PORTPATRICK: Comfortable country-house hotel; esp good lowland selection incl the (extinct) local Bladnoch (853/SW HOTELS).

CROMLIX HOUSE HOTEL, DUNBLANE: Excl and not overly expensive whisky list after dinner in civilised setting (871/CENTRAL HOTELS).

KINLOCH HOUSE HOTEL nr BLAIRGOWRIE (943/PERTHSHIRE BEST HOTELS).

THE BORESTONE BAR, STIRLING: St Ninians, Bannockburn rd 2km from centre. Staggering range of malts in truly authentic bar on a r/bout o/side Stirling. New owners since when we spied them here so now for show rather than sampling.

OBAN INN, OBAN: Good mix of customers, whisky and ale.

FISHERMAN'S TAVERN, BROUGHTY FERRY: (1113/DUNDEE EAT AND DRINK).

LOCK INN, FORT AUGUSTUS: Canalside setting, good food and plenty whisky.

CLACHAIG INN, GLENCOE: Over 100 malts to go with the range of ales and the range of folk that come here to drink after the hills (1270/BLOODY GOOD PUBS).

THE DROVER'S INN, INVERARNAN: Same as above, with around 75 to choose from and the rt atmos to drink them in (1265/BLOODY GOOD PUBS).

DUNAIN PARK HOTEL, INVERNESS: After dinner in one of the best places to eat hereabouts, there's a serious malts list to mull over (1001/HIGHLAND HOTELS).

THE BAR AT THE CRAIGELLACHIE HOTEL: Whiskies arranged around the cosy bar of this essential Speyside hotel and the river below (973/NE HOTELS).

PETER MACLENNAN, FORT WILLIAM: Main st, long-established emporium with big whisky section.

HOTEL EILEAN IARMAIN, SKYE: Also known as the Isleornsay Hotel (2207/ISLAND HOTELS); not the biggest range but one of the best places to drink (it).

LOCH FYNE WHISKIES, INVERARAY: Beyond the church on the A83 a shop with 400 malts to choose from in various sizes and disguises; and whisky ware.

SLIGACHAN HOTEL, SKYE: 01478 650204. On A87 (A850) 11km S of Portree. 71 malts in Seamus' huge cabin bar. Good real-ale selection; mid-Apr, Sept festivals. Adj bunkhouse and cottages, shop, laundry.

PITTODRIE HOUSE HOTEL, PITCAPLE: In the snug (974/NE HOTELS).

THE LAIRHILLOCK nr STONEHAVEN: Public bar (1289/PUB FOOD).

GORDON & MACPHAIL, ELGIN: The whisky provisioner and bottlers of the Connoisseurs brand you see in other shops and bars all over. From these humble beginnings over 100yrs ago, they now supply their exclusive and rarity range to the world. 9am-5.15pm. Cl Sun.

THE WHISKY SHOP, DUFFTOWN: The whisky shop in the main st (by the clock-tower) at the heart of whisky country. Within a few miles of numerous distilleries and their sales operations, this place stocks all the product (incl many halfs). 10am-5pm, Sun afternoons.

THE BEST MALTS AND WHEN TO DRINK THEM

Obviously, opinions vary. The following list is compiled from the consensus of several whisky buffs and 'authorities', but mainly Charlie Maclean who has several books under his belt. Vintages make a discernible difference to the connoisseur; the whiskies here are fine in any of their readily available forms.

BEFORE DINNER

Glenkinchie	LOWLAND
Glenmorangie	SPEYSIDE
Old Pulteney	HIGHLAND
Rosebank	LOWLAND

AFTER DINNER

Ardbeg	ISLAY	
Glenfarclas	SPEYSIDE	
Highland Park	ORKNEY	
Lagavulin	ISLAY	(pron 'Laga voolin')
Macallan	HIGHLAND	
Mortlach	SPEYSIDE	
Springbank	CAMPBELTOWN	
Strathisla	SPEYSIDE	
Talisker	SKYE	

ANYTIME

Aberlour	SPEYSIDE	
Bunnahabhain	ISLAY	(pron 'Boona-have-en')
Clynelish	HIGHLAND	
Cragganmore	SPEYSIDE	
Dalwhinnie	HIGHLAND	
Glenlivet	SPEYSIDE	
Glen Ord	HIGHLAND	
Oban	HIGHLAND	
Tamdhu	SPEYSIDE	(pron 'Tam do')

SECTION 7

Outdoor Places

THE BEST GARDENS

1471
MAP 1
B1
✓ ✓ **THE YOUNGER BOTANIC GARDEN, BENMORE:** 12km Dunoon on the A815 to Strachur. An 'outstation' of the Royal Botanic in Edin, gifted to the nation by Harry Younger in 1928, but the first plantations dating from 1820. Walks clearly marked through formal gdns, woody grounds and the 'pinetum' where the air is often so sweet and spicy it can seem like the v elixir of life. Redwood avenue, terraced hill sides, views; a gdn of different moods and fine proportions. Good walk nearby (1917/WOODLAND WALKS). Café. Mar-Oct 10-6pm. 🍵 ADMN

1472
MAP 2
B2
✓ ✓ **INVEREWE, POOLEWE:** on A832, 80km S of Ullapool. The world-famous gdns on a promontory of L Ewe. Begun in 1862, Osgood Mackenzie made it his life's work in 1883 and it continues with large crowds coming to admire his efforts. Helped by the ameliorating effect of the Gulf Stream, the 'wild' gdn became the model for many others. The guided tours (1.30pm Mon-Fri Apr-Sept) are probably the best way to get the most out of this extensive gdn. Gardens AYR; shop, visitor centre Mar-Oct. 🍵 ADMN

1473
MAP 3
C3
✓ ✓ **CRATHES, nr BANCHORY, ROYAL DEESIDE:** 25km W of Aber and just off A93. One of the most interesting tower houses (1765/COUNTRY HOUSES) surrounded by exceptional topiary and walled gdns of inspired design and tranquil atmos. Keen gardeners will be in their scented heaven. The Golden Garden (after Gertrude Jekyll) works particularly well and there's a wild gdn beyond the old wall that many people miss. All in all, a v *House and Garden* experience. Grounds open AYR 9.30am-sunset. 🍵 NTS ADMN

1474
MAP 4
B4
✓ ✓ **DRUMMOND CASTLE GARDENS, MUTHILL, nr CRIEFF:** Signed from A822, 2km from Muthill and then up a long avenue, the most exquisite formal gdns viewed first from the terrace by the house. A boxwood parterre of a vast St Andrew's Cross in yellow and red (esp antirrhinums and roses), the Drummond colours, with extraordinary sundial centrepiece; 5 gardeners keep every leaf in place. 7 days May-Oct 2-5pm (last adm). House not open to the public. ADMN

1475
MAP 9
A3
✓ ✓ **LOGAN BOTANICAL GARDENS, nr SANDHEAD, S of STRANRAER:** 16km S of Stranraer by A77/A716 and 2km on from Sandhead. Remarkable outstation of the Edin Botanics amongst sheltering woodland in the mild SW. Compact and full of pleasant surprises. Less crowded than other 'exotic' gdns. Their 'soundwands' giving commentary on demand make it all v interesting. Salad bar not bad. The Gunnera Bog is quite extraterrestrial. Mar-Oct; 7 days, 9.30am-6pm. 🍵 ADMN

1476
MAP 1
C2
✓ ✓ **CRARAE, INVERARAY:** 16km SE on A83 to Lochgilphead. Famed & fabulous. Recntly taken over by NTS so difficulties in staying open resolved. The wooded banks of L Fyne with gushing burn are as lush as the jungles of Borneo. Dawn till dusk. Vis centre till 5pm . NTS

1477
MAP 8
A2
✓ **DAWYCK, STOBO, nr PEEBLES:** On B712 Moffat rd off the A72 Biggar rd from Peebles, 2km from Stobo. Another outstation of the Edin Botanics; a 'recent' acquisition, though tree planting here goes back 300 yrs. Sloping grounds around the gurgling Scrape burn which trickles into the Tweed. Landscaped woody pathways for meditative walks. Famous for shrubs and blue Himalayan poppies. The chapel is closed. Gr walk on Drovers rd, 2km on Stobo Rd before entrance. Tiny basic tearoom. Mar-Oct 9.30am-6pm. ADMN

1478
MAP 1
C1
✓ **ANGUS' GARDEN, TAYNUILT:** 7km from village (which is 12km from Oban on the A85) along the Glen Lonan rd. Take first rt after Barguillen Gdn Centre. A gdn laid out by the family who own the centre in memory of their son Angus, a soldier, who was killed in Cyprus. On the slopes around a small loch brimful of lilies and ducks. Informal mix of tended and uncultivated (though wild prevails), a more poignant remembrance is hard to imagine as you while an hr away in this peaceful place. Open AYR. HONESTY BOX

1479
MAP 1
B2
✓ **ARDUAINE GARDEN, nr KILMELFORD:** 28km S of Oban on A816, one of Argyll's undiscovered arcadias gifted to the NTS and brought to wider attention. Creation of the microclimate in which the rich, diverse vegetation has flourished, influenced by Osgood Mackenzie of Inverewe and its restoration a testimony to 20yrs hard labour by the Wright brothers. Enter/park by L Melfort hotel, gate 100m. Until dusk. NTS

1480
MAP 1
B3
✓ **ACHAMORE GARDENS, ISLE OF GIGHA:** 1km from ferry. Walk or cycle from ferry (bike hire at post office at top of ferry rd); an easy day trip. The 'big house' on the island set in 65 acres. Lush tropical plants mingle with rhodies that flourish early (Feb-March): all due to the mild climate and head gardener's devotion. 2 marked walks (40mins/2hrs) start from the walled gdn (green route takes in the sea view of Islay and Jura). Density and variety of shrubs, pond plants and trees revealed as you meander around this enchanting spot. Leaflet guides at entrance. Open AYR. (2197/MAGICAL ISLANDS) ADMN

1481
MAP 8
C2
PRIORWOOD, MELROSE: Next to Melrose Abbey, a tranquil secret gdn behind high walls which specialises in growing flowers and plants for drying. Picking, drying and arranging is continuously in progress. Samples for sale. Run by enthusiasts on behalf of the NTS, they're always willing to talk stamens with you. Also includes an historical apple orchard with trees through the ages. Heavenly jelly on sale. Mon-Sat 10am-5.30pm; Sun 1.30-5.30pm. Cl 4pm wint. Dried flower shop. NTS ADMN

1482
MAP 8
B2
KAILZIE GARDENS, PEEBLES: On B7062 Traquair rd. Informal woodland gdns just out of town; not extensive but eminently strollable. Old-fashioned roses and wilder bits. Some poor birds in cages and the odd peacock. Courtyard teashop. Kids' corner. Fishing pond popular. Apr-Oct. ADMN

1483
MAP 3
C2
PITMEDDEN GARDEN, nr ELLON: 35km N of Aber and 10km W of the main A92. Formal French gdns recreated in 1950s on site of Sir Alex Seaton's 17th-century ones. The 4 gr parterres, 3 based on designs for gdns at Holyrood Palace, are best viewed from the terrace. Charming farmhouse 'museum' seems transplanted. For lovers of symmetry and an orderly universe only (but there is a woodland walk). May-Sept 10am-5.30pm. ☕ ⌕ NTS ADMN

1484
MAP 3
B3
CANDACRAIG GARDENS, STRATHDON: On A944 from Kildrummy to Alford which follows the Don through deep Aberdeenshire. A private walled cottage gdn and secret world in the wild country. Gallery has changing exhibits on a horticultural theme. A nice place to while away an afternoon. May-Sept 10am-5pm. For sale at TGP (01975 651226 for details).

1485
MAP 3
C2
PITTODRIE HOUSE nr INVERURIE: An exceptional walled gdn in the grounds of Pittodrie House Hotel at Chapel of Garioch in Aberdeenshire (974/NE HOTELS). 500m from house and largely unvisited by most of the guests, this secret and sheltered haven is both a kitchen gdn and a place for meditations and reflections (and possibly wedding photos).

1486
MAP 1
C2
ARDKINGLAS WOODLAND, CAIRNDOW: Off the A83 L Lomond to Inveraray rd. Through village to signed car park and these mature woodlands in the grounds of Ardkinglas House on the southern bank nr the head of L Fyne. Fine pines include the 'tallest tree in Britain'. Magical at dawn or dusk. 2km Loch Fyne Seafood (1333/SEAFOOD RESTAUS) where there is also a tree-shop gdn centre esp for trees & shrubs (2079/GARDEN CENTRES). HONESTY BOX

1487
MAP 1
B3
JURA HOUSE WALLED GARDEN: Ardfin, Jura. Around 5 miles from the ferry on the only rd. Keith went in 2001 on a wet night with the silver sky opening up over the water. A rare moment. Have one too! Open AYR. ADMN

1488
MAP 2
C2
THE HYDROPONICUM, ACHILTIBUIE: The 'Garden of the Future'; a weird indoor waterworld. Geraniums cluster round the pond by the café and other plants thrive in the microclimates. Apr-Sep. Tours: hourly. Limited hrs in Oct. Growing kits to buy (strawberries at Christmas?) 01854 622202. ADMN

1489
MAP 2
B4
ARD-DARAICH HILL GARDEN, ARDGOUR: 3 km S Ardgour at Corran Ferry (8/JOURNEYS) on A861 to Strontian. Private, labour of love 'hill' and wild gdn which you are at liberty to wander in. Specialising in rhodies, shrubs, trees. Nursery/small gdn centre. 01855 841248.

ROYAL BOTANIC GARDEN, EDINBURGH: 388/OTHER ATTRACTIONS.

BOTANIC GARDEN and KIBBLE PALACE, GLASGOW: 735/ATTRACTIONS.

THE BEST COUNTRY PARKS

1490
MAP 9
C2
✔ **DRUMLANRIG CASTLE, THORNHILL, nr DUMFRIES:** 01848 330248. On A76, 7km N of Thornhill in the W Borders in whose romance and history it's steeped, much more than merely a country park; spend a good day, both inside the castle and in the grounds. Apart from the art collection (Rembrandts, Leonardos, Holbeins) and the Craft Courtyard (2059/CRAFT SHOPS), the delights include: a stunning tearoom, woodland and riverside walks, an adventure playground, the 'Working Forge' and bike hire for further afield explorations along the Nith etc. Open May-Aug, Mon-Sun 11am-4pm.

1491
MAP 1
C3
✔ **MUIRSHEIL, nr LOCHWINNOCH:** Via Largs (A760) or Glas (M8, jnct 29 A737 then A760 5km S of Johnstone). N from village on Kilmacolm rd for 3km then signed. Muirshiel is name given to wider area, but park proper begins 6km on rd along the Calder valley. Despite proximity of conurbation (Pt Glas is over the hill), this is a wild and enchanting place for walking/picnics etc. Trails marked to waterfall and summit views. Extensive 'events' programme: www.clydemuirsheil.co.uk Escape!

1492
MAP 7
B1
JOHN MUIR COUNTRY PARK, nr DUNBAR, EAST LOTHIAN: Named after the 19th-century conservationist who founded America's National Parks (and the Sierra Club) and who was born in Dunbar. This swathe of coastline to the W of the town (known locally as Tyninghame) is an important estuarine nature reserve but is good for family walks and beachcombing. Can enter via B6370 off A198 to N Berwick or by 'cliff-top' trail from Dunbar (1685/WILDLIFE).

1493
MAP 1
D3
STRATHCLYDE PARK, between HAMILTON and MOTHERWELL: 15km SE of Glas. Take M8/A725 interchange or M74/jnct 5 or 6. Scotland's most popular country park, esp for water sports. From canoeing to parascending; you can hire the gear (2011/WATER SPORTS). Also; excavated Roman bath house, playgrounds, sports pitches and now that the trees are maturing, some pleasant walks. Nearby Baron's Haugh (1674/BIRDS) and Dalzell Country Park are more notable for their nature trails and gdns. (1770/MONUMENTS.)

1494
MAP 1
C2
FINLAYSTONE ESTATE, LANGBANK nr GREENOCK: A8 to Greenock, past Langbank, then signed. Grand mansion home to Chief of Clan Macmillan set in formal gdns in wooded estate. Lots of facs (tearm, craft shop etc), leafy walks, walled gdn. Rare magic. Oct-Mar w/ends only, Apr-Sep daily until 5pm.

1495
MAP 7
A1
ALMONDELL, nr EAST CALDER: 12km from Edin city bypass. Well-managed park in R Almond valley set amidst area of redundant industry. If you've just spent light yrs trying to exit from Livingston's notorious rd system, you'll need this green oasis with its walks in woods, meadows and along cinder tracks. Picnic sites, visitor centre with refreshments, kids' areas. A71 from bypass (Kilmarnock), then B7015 (Camp) for 7km. Park on rt just into E Calder. Walk ahead to woods.

1496
MAP 1
C2
HIRSEL COUNTRY PARK, COLDSTREAM: On A697, N edge town. 3000 acres grounds of Hirsel House (not open public). 2-4km walks thro' farmland & woods incl lovely lake. Museum, crafts, tearm. Quieter park than most.

1497
MAP 7
A1
MUIRAVONSIDE COUNTRY PARK: 5km W of Linlithgow on B825. Also signposted from J4 of the M9 Edin/Stirling. Former farm estate now run by the local authority providing 170 acres of woodland walks, parkland, picnic sites and a visitor centre for school parties or anyone else with an interest in birds, bees and badgers. Ranger service does guided walks Apr-Sep. Gr place to walk off that lunch at the not-too-distant Champany Inn (240/BURGERS).

1498
MAP 1
C3
EGLINTON nr IRVINE: Beside main A78 Largs to Ayr rd signed from Irvine/Kilwinning intersection. Spacious lungful of Ayrshire nr new town nexus and traffic tribulations. Visitor centre with interpretation of absolutely everything. Much made of the Eglintons' place in Scottish history. Park open all the time, visitor centre Easter-Oct. Network of walks.

MUGDOCK COUNTRY PARK, nr MILNGAVIE: Marvellous park close to Glas (5 car parks around the vast site). Report 747/CITY WALKS.

CULZEAN CASTLE PARK: Superb & hugely pop (1695/CASTLES).

TENTSMUIR, nr TAYPORT: Estuarine; John Muir, on Tay (1688/WILDLIFE).

ADEN, MINTLAW, nr PETERHEAD: 1649/KIDS.

HADDO HOUSE, ABERDEENSHIRE: Beautiful grounds (1754/CO HOUSES).

KELBURNE COUNTRY CENTRE, LARGS: 1638/KIDS.

THE BEST TOWN PARKS

1499
MAP A
C3

✓ ✓ **PRINCES ST GARDENS, EDINBURGH:** S side of Princes St. The greenery that launched a thousand postcards – millions probably – it's Edin. This former loch – drained around the time the New Town was built – is divided by the Mound. The eastern half has pitch and putt, Winter Wonderland and the Scott Monument (419/BEST VIEWS), the western has its much-photographed fountain, open-air café and space for locals and tourists to sprawl on the grass when sunny. You'll also find the the Ross Bandstand here – heart of Edinburgh's Hogmanay (36/BEST EVENTS) and the International Festival's gobsmacking fireworks concert (459/ANNUAL EVENTS). Louts with lager, senior citz on benches, Italian teens with daft wee rucksacks – all our lives are here. Till dusk.

1500
MAP 3
D3

✓ ✓ **HAZELHEAD PARK, ABERDEEN:** Via Queens Rd, 3km centre. Extraordinary park where the mysterious gardening skills of the Aberdonians are magnificently in evidence. Many facs incl a maze, mini-zoo, wonderful tacky tearoom and there are lawns, memorials and botanical splendours aplenty esp azalea gdn in spring and roses in summer. Gr sculpture.

1501
MAP 3
D3

✓ **DUTHIE PARK, ABERDEEN:** Riverside Dr along R Dee from the br carrying main A92 rd from/to Stonehaven. The other large well-kept park with duck pond, bandstand, hugely impressive rose gdns in summer, carved sculptures and the famous, though now somewhat shabby Winter Gdn of subtropical palms/ferns etc (10am-7.30pm summer, wint at dusk).

1502
MAP 5
A3

✓ **PITTENCRIEFF PARK, DUNFERMLINE:** The extensive park alongside the Abbey and Palace ruins gifted to the town in 1903 by Carnegie. Open areas, glasshouses, pavilion (more a function rm) but most notably a deep verdant glen criss-crossed with pathways. Lush, full of birds, good after rain.

1503
MAP 5
B3

BEVERIDGE PARK, KIRKCALDY: Also in Fife, another big municipal park with a duck and boat pond, wide-open spaces and many amusements (e.g. bowling, tennis, putting, paddling). Ravenscraig a coastal park on the main rd E to Dysart is an excellent place to walk. Gr prospect of town and Firth, coves and skerries.

1504
MAP 8
C3

WILTON LODGE PARK, HAWICK: Hawick not overfull of visitor attractions, but it does have a nice park with facs and diversions enough for everyone e.g. the civic gallery, rugby pitches (they quite like rugby in Hawick), a large kids' playground, a café and lots of riverside walks by the Teviot. Lots of my school friends lost their virginity in the shed here. All-round open-air recreation centre. S end of town by A7.

1505
MAP B
xC5

ROUKEN GLEN AND LINN PARK, GLASGOW: Both on S side of river. Rouken Glen via Pollokshaws/Kilmarnock rd to Eastwood Toll then rt. Good place to park is second left, Davieland Rd beside pond. Across park from here (or beside main Rouken Glen rd) is main visitor area with gdn centre, a Chinese restau, kids' play area and woodland walks (0141 577 3913 for info). Linn Park via Aikenhead and Carmunnock rd. After King's Park on left, take rt to Simshill Rd and park at golf course beyond houses. A long route there, but worth it; this is one of the undiscovered Elysiums of a city which boasts 60 parks. Ranger Centre (0141 637 1147) – activities, wildlife walks, kids' nature trails, horse-riding.

1506
MAP 4
C3

CAMPERDOWN PARK, DUNDEE: Calling itself a country park, Camperdown is the main recreational breathing space for the city and hosts a plethora of distractions (a golf course, a wildlife complex, mansion house etc). Situated beyond Kingsway, the ring-route; go via Coupar Angus rd t/off. Best walks across the A923 in the Templeton Woods.

1507
MAP 3
A2

GRANT PARK, FORRES: Forres is a frequent winner of the Bonny Bloom competitions. Grant Park, with its balance of ornamental gdns, open parkland and woody hill side, is the carefully tended rose in its crown. Good municipal facs like pitch and putt, playground. Cricket in summer and topping topiary. Through woods at top of Cluny Hill, a tower affords gr views of the Moray and Cromarty Firths and surrounding forest from which the town takes its name.

THE MOST INTERESTING COASTAL VILLAGES

1508 ✓ **PLOCKTON, nr KYLE OF LOCHALSH:** A Highland gem of a place 8km
MAP 2 over the hill from Kyle, clustered around inlets of a wooded bay on L
B3 Carron. Cottage gdns down to the bay and palm trees! Some gr walks over
headlands. Plockton Inn prob best bet for reasonable stay and eats (1026/LESS
EXP HIGHLAND HOTELS). Haven Hotel (01599 544223) also good place to eat.
Plockton Hotel (CHP, pub grub). It's not hard to feel connected with the village.

1509 ✓ **STROMNESS, ORKNEY MAINLAND:** 24km from Kirkwall and a different
kettle of fish. Hugging the shore and with narrow streets and wynds, it
has a unique atmos, both maritime and European. Some of the most singular
shops you'll see anywhere and the Orkney folk going about their business.
Park nr harbour and walk down the cobbled main st if you don't want to
scrape your paintwork (2242/ORKNEY; 2134/GALLERIES).

1510 ✓ **CROMARTY, nr INVERNESS:** At end of rd across Black Isle from Inverness
MAP 2 (45km NE), but worth the trip. Village with dreamy times-gone-by atmos,
D2 without being twee. Lots of kids running about and a pink strand of beach.
Delights to discover include: the east kirk, plain and aesthetic with countryside through the windows behind the altar; Hugh (the geologist) Miller's cot-
tage/Courthouse museum (2112/BEST HISTORY AND HERITAGE); Country Kitchen
(1396/TEAROOMS); Cromarty Bakery (1407/BEST SCOTCH BAKERS); the shore and
cliff walk (1939/COASTAL WALKS) and of course the dolphins (1681/DOLPHINS).

1511 **CULROSS, nr DUNFERMLINE:** By A994 from Dunfermline or jnct 1 of M90
MAP 5 just over Forth Rd Br (15km). Old centre conserved and being restored by NTS.
A3 Mainly residential and not awash with craft and coffee shops. More historical
than merely quaint; a community of careful custodians lives in the white, red-
pantiled houses. Footsteps echo in the cobbled wynds. Palace and Town
House open Apr/May/Sept 7 day 1pm-5pm. June-Aug 10am-5pm. Oct 1pm-
5pm. Interesting back gdns and lovely church at top of hill (1792/CHURCHES).
Pamphlet by Rights of Way Society available locally, is useful.

1512 **TOBERMORY, MULL:** Not so much a village, rather the main town of Mull, set
MAP 1 around a hill on superb Tobermory Bay. Ferry pt for Ardnamurchan, but main
B2 Oban ferry is 35km away at Craignure. Usually a bustling harbour front with
quieter streets behind; a quintessential island atmos. Some good inexp hotels
(and quayside hostel) well situated to explore the whole island. (2241/MULL;
2213/ISLAND HOTELS; 1171/BEST HOSTELS.)

1513 **PORT CHARLOTTE, ISLAY:** A township on the 'Rhinns of Islay', the western
MAP 1 peninsula. By A846 from the pts, Askaig and Ellen via Bridgend. Rows of white-
A3 washed, well-kept cottages along and back from shoreline. On rd in, there's an
island museum and a coffee/bookshop. Also a 'town' beach and one between
PC and Bruichladdich (and esp the one with the war memorial nearby). Quiet
and charming, not quaint. On Sat night, join the locals for a drink at the Loch
Indaal Hotel and see if the 'moonie' comes out. (2238/ISLAY; 2206/ISLAND HOTELS)

1514 **ROCKCLIFFE, nr DUMFRIES:** 25km S on Solway Coast rd, A710. On the
MAP 9 'Scottish Riviera', the rocky part of the coast around to Kippford (1935/COASTAL
C3 WALKS). A good rock-scrambling foreshore and a village with few houses and
Baron's Craig hotel; set back with gr views. Excl pub at Kippford (1310/BEST
FOOD) and tearoom at Rockcliffe (1394/TEAROOMS).

1515 **EAST NEUK VILLAGES:** The quintessential quaint wee fishing villages along
MAP 5 the bit of Fife that forms the mouth of the Firth of Forth, **CRAIL, ANSTRUTHER,**
C3, D3 **PITTENWEEM, ST MONANS** and **ELIE** all have different characters and attractions esp Crail and Pittenweem harbours, Anstruther as main centre and home
of Fisheries Museum (see also 1358/FISH AND CHIPS; FIFE HOTELS; 1666/BIRDS)
and perfect Elie (2026/WINDSURFING; 929/930/FIFE HOTELS; 1298/BEST FOOD;
1955/GREAT GOLF). Or see ST ANDREWS. Cycling good, traffic in summer not.

1516 **ABERDOUR:** Betw Dunfermline and Kirkcaldy and nr Forth Rd Br (10km E
MAP 5 from jnct 1 of M90) or, better still, go by train from Edin (frequent service:
B4 Dundee or Kirkcaldy); delightful station. Walks round harbour and to headland, Silver Sands beach 1km (416/EDIN BEACHES), castle ruins. (1791/CHURCHES;
932/933/FIFE HOTELS.)

1517 MORAY COAST FISHING VILLAGES: From Speybay (where the Spe,
MAP 3   into the sea) along to Fraserburgh, some of Scotland's best coastal scene
B1, C1 and many interesting villages in cliff/cove and beach settings. Esp notable
are **PORTSOY** with 17th-century harbour (1998/SWIMMING POOLS) – and see
25/EVENTS; **SANDEND** with its own popular beach and a fabulous one nearby (1524/BEACHES); **PENNAN** made famous by the film *Local Hero* (the
hotel/pub is cosy and cheap: 01346 561201); **GARDENSTOWN** with a walk
along the water's edge to **CROVIE** (pron 'Crivee') the epitome of a coast-
clinging community; and **CULLEN**, which is more of a town and has a gr
beach. (978/NE HOTELS.)

1518 DIABEG, WESTER ROSS: On N shore of L Torridon at the end of the unclassi-
MAP 2   fied rd from Torridon on one of Scotland's most inaccessible peninsulas.
B2   Diabeg (pron 'Jee-a-beg') is simply beautiful. Fantastic rd there and then
walk!

1519 DUNURE, AYR: 15km S of Ayr on A719, the coast rd past the Heads of Ayr
MAP 1   (cliff walks) 10km from Culzean (1695/CASTLES). Only a few cottages, a pub, an
C3   old harbour and the dramatic ruins of Dunure Castle, once the scene of hor-
rific tortures, now a kids' playground.

1520 ISLE OF WHITHORN: Strange faraway village at end of the rd, 35km S
MAP 9   Newton Stewart, 6km Whithorn (1748/PREHISTORIC SITES). Mystical harbour
B4   where low tide does mean low, saintly shoreline, a sea angler's pub (Steam
Packet) v good pub grub. Ninian's chapel round the headland not so uplifting but en route you'll see the *Solway Harvester* memorial by the ruins of the
19thC lifeboat house. The tragedy was in early 2000; by summer 2001 there
were still fresh flowers.

1521 CORRIE, ARRAN: Last but not least, the bonniest bit of Arran, best reached
MAP 1   by bike from Brodick (2237/ARRAN). I'd like a memorial bench on that shore-
C3   line.

KILORAN BEACH, COLONSAY: 9km from quay and hotel, past Colonsay House: parking and access on hill side. Described as the finest beach in the Hebrides, it does not disappoint, even in the rain. Craggy cliffs on one side, negotiable rocks on the other and, in betw, tiers of grassy dunes. The island of Colonsay was once bought as a picnic spot. This beach was probably the reason why.

A2

1523
MAP 1
B3
MACHRIHANISH: At the bottom of the Kintyre peninsula 10km from Campbeltown. Walk N from Machrihanish village, or from the car park on the main A83 to Tayinloan and Tarbert at pt where it hits/leaves the coast. A joyously long strand (8km) of unspoiled orange-pink sand backed by dunes and facing the 'steepe Atlantic Stream' all the way to Newfoundland (1962/GOLF IN GREAT PLACES).

1524
MAP 2
C1
SANDWOOD BAY, KINLOCHBERVIE: This mile-long sandy strand with its old 'Stack', is legendary, but therein lies the problem since now too many people know about it and you may have to share in its glorious isolation. Inaccessibility is its saving grace, a 7km walk from the sign off the rd at Balchrick (nr the cattle grid), 6km from Kinlochbervie; allow 3hrs return plus time there. More venturesome is the walk from the N and Cape Wrath (1933/COASTAL WALKS).

1525
MAP 2
C1
OLDSHOREMORE: The beach you pass on the rd to Balchrick, only 3km from Kinlochbervie. It's easy to reach and a beautiful spot: the water is clear and perfect for swimming, and there are rocky walks and quiet places. **POLIN**, 500m N, is a cove you might have to yourself.

1526
MAP 1
A3
ISLAY: SALIGO, MACHIR BAY and THE BIG STRAND: The first two are bays on NW of island via A847 rd to Pt Charlotte, then B8018 past L Gorm. Wide beaches; remains of war fortifications in deep dunes, Saligo perhaps the nicer. They say 'no swimming' so paddle with extreme prejudice. The Big Strand on Laggan Bay: along Bowmore-Pt Ellen rd take Oa t/off, follow Kintra signs. There's a restau/bar, accom, camping and gr walks in either direction, 8km of glorious sand and dunes (contains the Machrie Golf Course). An airy amble under a wide sky. (1961/GOLF IN GREAT PLACES; 1931/COASTAL WALKS.)

1527
MAP 1
C2
OSTAL BEACH/KILBRIDE BAY, MILLHOUSE, nr TIGHNABRUAICH: $^3/_4$km from Millhouse on B8000 signed Ardlamont, a track to rt at a white house (there's a church on the left) marked 'No Cars' (often with a chain across to restrict access). Park and walk $1^1/_2$km, turning rt after lochan. You arrive on a perfect white sandy crescent known locally as Ostal and, apart from the odd swatch of sewage, in certain conditions, a mystical secret place to swim and picnic. The N coast of Arran is like a Greek island in the bay.

1528
MAP 2
A2
SOUTH UIST: Deserted but for birds, an almost unbroken strand of beach running for miles down the W coast; the machair at its best early summer. Take any rd off the spinal A865; usually less than 2km. Good spot to try is t/off at Tobha Mor; real black houses and a chapel on the way to the sea.

1529
MAP 2
A2
SCARISTA BEACH, SOUTH HARRIS: On main rd S of Tarbert (15km) to Rodel. The beach is so beautiful that people have been married there. Hotel over the rd is worth staying just for this, but is also a gr retreat (2209/ISLAND HOTELS). Golf course on links (1968/GOLF IN GREAT PLACES). Fab in early evening. The sun also rises.

1530
MAP 4
D3
LUNAN BAY, nr MONTROSE: 5km from main A92 rd to Aber and 5km of deep red crescent beach under a wide northern sky. But'n'Ben, Auchmithie, is an excellent place to start or finish (961/PERTHSHIRE EATS) and good app (from S), although Gordon's restau at Inverkeilor is closer (962/PERTHSHIRE EATS). Best viewpoint from Boddin Farm 3km S Montrose and 3km from A92 signed 'Usan'. Often deserted.

1531
MAP 1
B2
JURA, LOWLANDMAN'S BAY: Not strictly a beach (there is a sandy strand before the headland) but a rocky foreshore with ethereal atmos; gr light and space. Only seals break the spell. Go rt at 3-arch br to first group of houses (Knockdrome), through yard on left and rt around cottages to track to Ardmenish. After deer fences, bay is visible on your rt, 1km walk away.

1532 **VATERSAY, OUTER HEBRIDES:** The tiny island joined by a causeway to Barra.
MAP 2 Twin crescent beaches on either side of the isthmus, one shallow and shel-
A3 tered visible from Castlebay, the other an ocean beach with rollers.
Dunes/machair; safe swimming. There's a helluva hill betw Barra and Vatersay
if you're cycling.

1533 **BARRA, SEAL BAY:** 5km Castlebay on W coast, 2km after Isle of Barra Hotel
MAP 2 through gate across machair where rd rt is signed Taobh a Deas Allathasdal.
A3 A flat, rocky Hebridean shore and skerries where seals flop into the water and
eye you with intense curiosity. The better-beach beach is next to the hotel.

1534 **WEST SANDS, ST ANDREWS:** As a town beach, this is hard to beat; it domi-
MAP 5 nates the view to W. Wide swathe not too unclean and sea swimmable. Golf
C2 courses behind. Consistently gets 'the blue flag', but beach buffs may prefer
Kinshaldy (1688/WILDLIFE), Kingsbarns (10km S), or Elie (28km S).

1535 **MORAY COAST:** Many gr beaches along coast from Spey Bay to Fraserburgh,
MAP 3 notably **CULLEN** and **LOSSIEMOUTH** (town beaches) and **NEW ABERDOUR**
B1, (1km from New Aberdour village on B9031, 15km W of Fraserburgh) and
C1, **ROSEHEARTY** (8km W of Fraserburgh) both quieter places for walks and pic-
D1 nics. One of the best-kept secrets is the beach at **SUNNYSIDE** where you walk
past the incredible ruins of Findlater Castle on the cliff top (how did they build
it? And what a place, on its grassed-over roof, for a picnic) and down to a cove
which on my sunny day was quite simply perfect. Take a left going into
Sandend 16km W of Banff and follow rd for 2km, turning rt and park in the
farmyard. Walk from here past dovecote, 1km to cliff. Also signed from A98. *See
also* 1938/COASTAL WALKS.

1536 **NORTH COAST:** To the W of Thurso, along the N coast, are some of Britain's
MAP 2 most unspoiled and unsung beaches. No beach bums, no Beach Boys. There
B1, C1 are so many gr little coves, you can have one to yourself even on a hot day, but
those to mention are: **STRATHY** and **ARMADALE** (35km W Thurso), **FARR** and
TORRISDALE (48km) and **COLDBACKIE** (65km). My favourite (which may be
called Ceannabeinne after the hill above it, but **PETE'S BEACH** is easier to
remember) is further along where L Eriboll comes out to the sea and the rd
hits the coast again 7km E of Durness. It's a small 100m cove flanked by walls
of oyster-pink rock and shallow turquoise sea; perfect. Excl inx GH nearby –
Port Na Con (1035/INX HIGHLAND HOTELS).

1537 **SANDS OF MORAR, nr MALLAIG:** 70km W of Ft William and 6km from
MAP 2 Mallaig, these easily accessible beaches may seem overpopulated on summer
B3 days and the S stretch nearest to Arisaig may have one too many caravan
parks, but they go on for miles and there's enough space for everybody. The
sand's supposed to be silver but in fact it's a v pleasing pink. Lots of rocky bits
for exploration. One of the best beachy bits is (coming from Mallaig) the next
bay after the estuary; park on the rd. And the bit nr the youth hostel,
Camusdarroch (where *Local Hero* was filmed), further from rd, is quieter and a
v good swathe of sand. Traigh, the golf course makes good use of the dunes
(1977/GOOD GOLF). Gr inx place to stay nearby – Garimore (1039/INX HIGHLAND
HOTELS).

1538 **THE BAY AT THE BACK OF THE OCEAN, IONA:** Easy 2km walk from frequent
MAP 1 ferry from Fionnphort, S of Mull (2194/MAGICAL ISLANDS) or hire a bike from the
A1 store on your left as you walk into the village (01681 700357). Paved rd most
of way. John Smith, who is buried beside the abbey, once told me that this was
one of his favourite places. Me too. And there's a gr inx hotel on Iona, The
Argyll (1207/GET AWAY FROM IT ALL).

1539 **DORNOCH and EMBO BEACHES:** The wide and extensive sandy beach of
MAP 2 this pleasant town at the mouth of the Dornoch Firth famous also for its golf
D2 links. 4km N, Embo Sands starts with caravan city, but walk N towards Golspie.
Embo is twinned with Kaunakakai, Hawaii!

1540 **PORT OF NESS, ISLE OF LEWIS:** Also signed Port Nis, this is the beach at the
MAP 2 end of the Hebrides in the far N of Lewis. Just keep driving – there are some
B1 interesting stops on the way (2146/ART, 2101/2/MUSEUMS) – until you get to
this tiny bay & harbour down the hill at the end of the rd. Anthony Barbour's
Harbour View Gallery full of his own work (which you find in many other gal-
leries & even postcards) is worth a visit (10am-5pm, cl Sun).

THE GREAT GLENS

1541
MAP 2
C3
✓ ✓ ✓ **GLEN AFFRIC:** Beyond Cannich at end of Glen Urquhart A831, 20km from Drumnadrochit on L Ness. A dramatic gorge that strikes westwards into the wild heart of Scotland. Superb for rambles (1904/GLEN AND RIVER WALKS), expeditions, Munro-bagging (further in, beyond L Affric) and even just tootling through in the car. Shaped by the Hydro Board, L Benevean nevertheless adds to the drama. Cycling good (bike hire in Cannich 01456 415251) as is the detour to Tomich and Plodda Falls (1553/WATERFALLS). Stop at Dog Falls (1623/PICNICS).

1542
MAP 4
A3
✓ ✓ ✓ **GLEN LYON, nr ABERFELDY:** One of Scotland's crucial places both historically and geographically, much favoured by fishers/walkers/Munro-baggers. Wordsworth and Tennyson, Gladstone and Baden Powell all sang its praises. Site of ground-breaking theatre 'The Path' in 2000. The Lyon is a classic Highland river tumbling through corries, gorges and riverine meadows. Several Munros are within its watershed and rise gloriously on either side. Rd all the way to the loch side (30km). Eagles soar over the remoter tops at the head of the glen. Stay at Invervar Lodge (12156/GET-AWAY-FROM-IT-ALL). Fishing permits from Fortingall Hotel on the way there (1187/INNS, 01887 830367).

1543
MAP 2
C3
✓ ✓ **GLEN NEVIS, FORT WILLIAM:** Used by many a film director; easy to see why. Ben Nevis is only part of magnificent scenery. Many walks and convenient facs (1559/WATERFALLS; 1900/SERIOUS WALKS). Not sure about the Braveheart car park or the 'legend' of Samuel's Stone; otherwise, it's a national treasure. Check Ft William p. 312 for eats, but nice pub.

1544
MAP 2
C4
✓ ✓ **GLEN ETIVE:** Off from more exalted Glencoe (and the A82) at Kingshouse, as anyone you meet in those parts will tell you, this truly is a glen of glens. And, as my friends who camp and climb here implore, it needs no more advertisement.

1545
MAP 2
C2
STRATHCARRON, nr BONAR BRIDGE: You drive up the N bank of this Highland river from the br o/side Ardgay (pron 'Ordguy') which is 3km over the br from Bonar Br. Rd goes 15km to Croick and its remarkable church (1797/CHURCHES). The river gurgles and gushes along its rocky course to the Dornoch Firth and there are innumerable places to picnic, swim and stroll further up. Quite heavenly on a warm day.

1546
MAP 4
C2
THE ANGUS GLENS: Glen Clova/Glen Prosen/Glen Isla. All via Kirriemuir. Isla to W is a woody, approachable glen with a deep gorge, on B954 nr Alyth (1563/WATERFALLS) and the lovely Glenisla Hotel (1191/INNS). Others via B955, to Dykehead then rd bifurcates. Both glens stab into the heart of the Grampians. 'Minister's Walk' goes betw them from behind the kirk at Prosen village over the hill to B955 before Clova village (7km). Glen Clova is a walkers' paradise esp from Glendoll 24km from Dykehead; limit of rd. Viewpoint. 'Jock's Rd' to Braemar and the Capel Mounth to Ballater (both 24km). Campsite and SYH. Also good hotel at Clova (952/PERTHSHIRE HOTELS) and famous 'Loops of Brandy' walk (2hrs, 2-B-2); stark and beautiful.

1547
MAP 1
C2
GLENDARUEL: The Cowal Peninsula on the A886 betw Colintraive and Strachur. Humble but perfectly formed glen of R Ruel, from Clachan in S (a kirk and an inn) through deciduous meadowland to more rugged grandeur 10km N. Easy walking and cycling. W rd best. Views L Fyne and Argyll from W ridge.
2-B-2

1548
MAP 1
B1
GLEN LONAN, nr TAYNUILT: Betw Taynuilt on A85 and A816 S of Oban. Another quiet wee glen, but all the rt elements for walking, picnics, cycling and fishing or just a run in the car. Varying scenery, a bubbling burn (the R Lonan), some standing stones and not many folk. Angus' Garden at the Taynuilt end should not be missed (1478/GARDENS). No marked walks; now get lost!
2-B-2

1549
MAP 9
B3
GLEN TROOL, nr NEWTON STEWART: 26km N by A714 via Bargrennan which is on the S Upland Way (1894/LONG WALKS). A gentle wooded glen of a place around L Trool. One of the most charming, accessible parts of the Galloway Forest Park. (1840/MARY, CHARLIE, BOB.) Start of the Merrick climb (1870/HILLS).

1550 **THE SMA' GLEN, nr CRIEFF:** Off the A85 to Perth, the A822 to Amulree and
MAP 4 Aberfeldy. Sma' meaning small, this is the valley of the R Almond where the
B3 Mealls (lumpish, shapeless hills) fall steeply down to the rd. Where the rd turns
away from the river, the long distance path to L Tay begins (28km). Sma' Glen,
8km, has good picnic spots, but they get busy and midgy in summer.

1551 **STRATHFARRAR, nr BEAULY or DRUMNADROCHIT:** Rare unspoiled glen
MAP 2 accessed from A831 leaving Drumnadrochit on L Ness via Cannich (30km) or
C2 S from Beauly (15km). Signed at Struy. Arrive at gatekeeper's house. Access
restricted to 25 cars per day (Cl Tue and Sun till 1.30pm). For access Oct-Mar
01463 761260; you must be out by 6pm. 22km to head of glen past lochs.
Good climbing, walking, fishing. Peace be with you.

THE MOST SPECTACULAR WATERFALLS

*One aspect of Scotland that really is improved by rain. All the walks to these falls
are graded 1-A-1 unless otherwise stated (see p. 11 for walk codes).*

1552 ✓✓ **FALLS OF GLOMACH:** 25km Kyle of Lochalsh off A87 nr Shiel Br, past
MAP 2   Kintail Centre at Morvich then 2km further up Glen Croe to br. Walk
C3 starts other side; there are other ways, (e.g. from the SY Hostel in Glen Affric),
but this is most straightforward. Allow 5/7 hrs for the pilgrimage to one of
Britain's highest falls. Path is steep but well trod. Glomach means gloomy and
you might feel so, peering into the ravine; from precipice to pool, it's 200m.
But to pay tribute, go down carefully to ledge. Vertigo factor and sense of
achievement both fairly high. (1173/HOSTELS.)   2-C-3

1553 ✓✓ **PLODDA FALLS, nr TOMICH, nr DRUMNADROCHIT:** A831 from L
MAP 2   Ness to Cannich (20km), then 7km to Tomich, a further 5km up
C3 mainly woodland track to car park. 200m walk down through woods of Scots
Pine and ancient Douglas Fir to one of the most enchanting woodland sites
in Britain and the Victorian iron br over the brink of the 150m fall into the
churning river below. The dawn chorus here must be amazing (though I'll
never hear it). Freezes into winter wonderland (ice climbers from Inverness
take advantage). Good hotel in village (1034/HIGHLANDS HOTELS).

1554 ✓ **FALLS OF BRUAR, nr BLAIR ATHOLL:** Close to the main A9 Perth-
MAP 4   Inverness rd, 12km N of B Atholl nr House of Bruar shopping experience.
B2 (2032/CRAFT SHOPS). Consequently, the short walk to lower falls is v consumer-
led but less crowded than you might expect. The lichen-covered walls of the
gorge below the upper falls (1km) are less ogled and more dramatic. Circular
path is well marked but steep and rocky in places. Tempting to swim on hot
days (1526/SWIMMING HOLES). ☕

1555 ✓ **GLENASHDALE FALLS, ARRAN:** 5km walk from br on main rd at Whiting
MAP 1   Bay. Signed up the burn side, but uphill and further on than you think, so
C3 allow 2hrs (return). Series of falls in a rocky gorge in the woods with paths so
you get rt down to the brim and the pools. Swim here, swim in heaven!   1-B-1

1556 **EAS FORS, MULL:** On the Dervaig to Fionnphort rd 3km from Ulva Ferry; a
MAP 1 series of cataracts tumbling down on either side of the rd. Easily accessible.
B1 There's a path down the side to the brink where the river plunges into the sea.
On a warm day swimming in the sea below the fall is a rare exhilaration.

1557 **EAS MOR, SKYE:** Glen Brittle nr end of rd. 24km from Sligachan. A mt water-
MAP 2 fall with the wild Cuillins behind and views to the sea. App as part of a serious
B3 scramble or merely a 30-min Cuillin sampler. Start at the Memorial Hut, cross
the rd, bear rt, cross burn and then follow path uphill.   2-C-2
Another impressive torrent of wild mt water is the **LEALT FALLS** about 20km
N of Portree on the A855 (before Kilt Rock). Beside rd; park walk and peer (you
can also get down to the beach).

1558 **EAS A' CHUAL ALUINN, KYLESKU:** 'Britain's highest waterfall' nr the head of
MAP 2 Glencoul, is not easy to reach. Kylesku is betw Scourie and Lochinver off the
C1 main A894, 20km S of Scourie. There are 2hr cruises at 11am/2pm May-Sept
(and 4pm July/Aug) outside hotel (1055/INEXP HIGHLAND RESTAUS). Falls are a
rather distant prospect, but you may be able to alight and get next boat. The
captain's rap will keep you going. There's also a track to the top of the falls

from 5km N of the Skiag Br on the main rd (4hrs return), but you will need to take directions locally. The water freefalls for 200m, which is 4 times further than Niagara (take pinch of salt here). There is a spectacular pulpit view down the cliff, 100m to rt.   2-C-3

1559 **STEALL FALLS, GLEN NEVIS, FORT WILLIAM:** Take Glen Nevis rd at r/bout
MAP 2 o/side town centre and drive 'to end' (16km) through glen. Start from the sec-
C3   ond car park you come to, following path marked Corrour, uphill through the
woody gorge with R Ness thrashing below. Glen eventually and dramatically
opens out and there are gr views of the long veils of the Falls. Precarious 3-
wire br for which you will also need nerves of steel. Always fun to see the
macho types bottle it.   3-A-3

1560 **CORRIESHALLOCH GORGE/FALLS OF MEASACH:** Jnct of A832 and A835,
MAP 2 20km S of Ullapool; possible to walk down into the gorge from both rds. Most
C2   dramatic app is from the car park on the A832 Gairloch rd. Staircase to swing
br from whence to consider how such a wee burn could make such a deep
gash. V impressive.

1561 **THE GREY MARE'S TAIL:** On the wildly scenic rd betw Moffat and Selkirk, the
MAP 9 A708. About halfway, a car park and signs for waterfall. 8km from Tibby Shiels
D2   Inn. The lower track takes 10/15mins to a viewing place still 500m from falls;
the higher, on the other side of the Tail burn, threads betw the austere hills
and up to L Skene from which the falls overflow (45/60mins). Mountain goats.

1562 **THE FALLS OF CLYDE, NEW LANARK, nr LANARK:** Dramatic falls in a long
MAP 1 gorge of the Clyde. New Lanark, the conservation village of Robert Owen the
D3   social reformer, is signed from Lanark. It's hard to avoid the 'award-winning'
tourist bazaar, but the riverbank has … a more natural appeal. The path to the
Power Station is about 3km, but the route doesn't get interesting till after it, a
1km climb to the first fall (Cora Linn) and another 1km to the next
(Bonnington Linn). Swimming above or below them is not advised (but it's gr).
Certainly don't swim on an 'open day', when they close the station and divert
all the water back down the river in a mighty surge (twice a year when we
asked; details from TIC: 01555 661661). There is a gr Italian restau in Lanark
and one of the mills is now a hotel (521/HOTELS O/SIDE GLASGOW). The strange
uniformity of New Lanark is better when the other tourists have gone home.

1563 **REEKIE LINN, ALYTH:** 8km N of town on back rds to Kirriemuir on B951 betw
MAP 4 Br of Craigisla and Br of Lintrathen. A picnic site and car park on bend of rd
C3   leads by 200m to the wooded gorge of Glen Isla with precipitous viewpoints
of defile where Isla is squeezed and falls in tiers for 100ft. Can walk further
along the glen. Loch side restau nearby (963/PERTHSHIRE EATS) and tearoom.

1564 **FALLS OF ACHARN nr KENMORE, LOCH TAY:** 5km along S side of loch on
MAP 4 unclass rd. Walk from nr bridge in township of Acharn; falls are signed.
B3   Steepish start then 1km up side of gorge; waterfalls on other side.

1565 **FALLS OF ROGIE, nr STRATHPEFFER:** Car park on A835 Inverness-Ullapool
MAP 2 rd, 5km Contin/10km Strathpeffer. Accessibility makes short walk (250m)
C2   quite popular to these hurtling falls on the Blackwater R. Br (built by T Army)
and salmon ladder (they leap in summer). Woodland trails marked, include a
circular route to Contin (1928/WOODLAND WALKS).

1566 **FOYERS, LOCH NESS:** On southern route from Ft Augustus to Inverness, the
MAP 2 B862 (1591/SCENIC ROUTES) at the village of Foyers (35km from Inverness). Park
C3   next to shops and cross rd, go through fence and down steep track to viewing places (slither-proof shoes advised). R Foyers falls 150m into foaming
gorge below and then into L Ness throwing clouds of spray into the trees (you
may get drenched). Occasionally the Hydro 'turn the water off' and it just
stops.

1567 **FALLS OF SHIN, nr LAIRG, SUTHERLAND:** 6km E of town on signed rd, car
MAP 2 park and falls nearby are easily accessible. Not quite up to the splendours of
C2   others on this page, but an excellent place to see salmon battling upstream
(best June-Aug). Visitor centre with extensive shop; the café/restau is v good
(1055/INX RESTAUS). ☕

THE LOCHS WE LOVE

1568
MAP 2
B2
✓ ✓ **LOCH MAREE:** A832 betw Kinlochewe and Gairloch. Dotted with islands covered in Scots pine hiding some of the best examples of Viking graves and apparently a money tree in their midst. Easily viewed from the rd which follows its length for 15km. Beinn Eighe rises behind you and the omniscient presence of Slioch is opposite. Aultroy Vistor Centre (5km Kinlochewe), fine walks from car park further on, good accom at L Maree Hotel (1027/INEXP HIGHLAND HOTELS).

1569
MAP 2
D3
✓ ✓ **LOCH AN EILEAN:** An enchanted loch in the heart of the Rothiemurchus Forest (1918/WOODLAND WALKS *for directions*). There's a good visitor centre. You can walk rt round the loch (5km, allow 1.5hrs). This is classic Highland scenery, a landscape of magnificent Scots pine.

1570
MAP 2
C3
✓ **LOCH ARKAIG:** 25km Ft William. An enigmatic loch long renowned for its fishing. From the A82 beyond Spean Br (at the Commando Monument) cross the Caledonian Canal, then on by single track rd through the Clune Forest and the 'Dark Mile' past the 'Witches' Pool' (a cauldron of dark water below cataracts), to the loch. Bonnie Prince Charlie came this way before and after Culloden; one of his refuge caves is marked on a trail.

1571
MAP 6
B2
LOCH LUBHAIR, nr CRIANLARICH: The loch you pass (on the rt) on the A85 to Crianlarich (4km), in Glen Dochart, the upper reaches of the Tay water system. Small, perfect, with bare hills surrounding and fringed with pines and woody islets. Beautiful scenery that most people just go past in the car heading for Oban or Ft William. Enquire locally for kayak hire.

1572
MAP 6
B2
LOCH ACHRAY, nr BRIG O' TURK: The small loch at the centre of the Trossachs betw **LOCH KATRINE** (on which the *SS Sir Walter Scott* makes thrice-daily cruises, 2 on Wed: 01877 376316) and **LOCH VENACHAR**. The A821 from Callander skirts both Venachar and Achray (picnic sites). Ben Venue and Ben An rise above: gr walks (1865/HILLS) and views. A one-way forest rd goes round the other side of L Achray thro Achray Forest (enter and leave from the Duke's Pass rd betw Aberfoyle and Brig O'Turk). Details of trails from forest vistor centre 3km N Aberfoyle. Bike hire at L Katrine/Callander/Aberfoyle – it's the best way to see these lochs.

1573
MAP 6
B2
GLEN FINGLAS RESERVOIR, BRIG O' TURK: And while we're on the subject of lochs in the Trossachs (see above) here's a hidden gem. Although it's man-made it's a real beauty surrounded by soft green hills & the odd burn bubbling in. App 'thro' Brig O'Turk houses (past the caff; 1371/CAFFS) and park 2km up road. Walk to right (not 'the Dam' rd although this an interesting 1km diversion on the way back). 5 km walk to head of loch or poss make the loop round it & back to dam (no path, lots of scrambling, boots only). Fabulous here in late summer light.

1574
MAP 3
B4
LOCH MUICK, nr BALLATER: At head of rd off B976, the S Dee rd at Ballater. 14km up Glen Muick (pron 'Mick') to car park, visitor centre and 100m to loch side. Lochnagar rises above (1889/MUNROS) and walk also begins here for Capel Mounth and Glen Clova (1546/GLENS). 3hr walk around loch and any number of ambles. The lodge where Vic met John is at the furthest pt (well it would be). Open aspect with grazing deer and not too much forestry.

1575
MAP 2
C1
LOCH ERIBOLL, NORTH COAST: 90km W of Thurso. The long sea loch that indents into the N coast for 15km and which you drive rt round on the main A838. Deepest natural anchorage in the UK, exhibiting every aspect of loch side scenery including, alas, fish cages. Ben Hope stands nr the head of the loch and there is a perfect beach (my beach) on the coast (1536/BEACHES). Walks from Hope.

1576
MAP 9
B3
LOCH TROOL, nr NEWTON STEWART: The small, celebrated loch in a bowl of the Galloway Hills reached via Bargrennan 14km N via A714 and 8km to end of rd. Woodland visitor centre/café on way. Good walks but best viewed from Bruce's Stone (1840/MARY, CHARLIE AND BOB) and the slopes of Merrick (1870/HILLS). An idyllic place.

1577 **LOCH MORAR, nr MALLAIG:** 70km W of Ft William by the A850 (a wildly
MAP 2 scenic route). Morar village is 6km from Mallaig and a single track rd leads
B3 away from the coast to the loch (only 500m but out of sight) then along it for
5km to Bracora. It's the prettiest part with wooded islets, small beaches, loch
side meadows and bobbing boats. The rd stops at a turning place but a track
continues from Bracorina to Tarbet and it's poss to connect with a post boat
and sail back to Mallaig on L Nevis around 3.30pm (check TIC). L Morar, joined
to the coast by the shortest river in Britain, also has the deepest water. There
is a spookiness about it and just possibly a monster called Morag. Nice GH
(Garimore) nearby (1039/INX HIGHLAND HOTELS).

1578 **LOCH TUMMEL, nr PITLOCHRY:** W from Pitlochry on B8019 to Rannoch (and
MAP 4 the end of the rd), L Tummel comes into view, as it did for Queen Victoria, scin-
B2 tillating beneath you, and on a clear day with Schiehallion beyond
(1608/VIEWS). This N side has good walks (1925/WOODLAND WALKS), but the S rd
from Faskally just o/side Pitlochry is the one to take to get down to the
lochside to picnic etc.

1579 **LOCH LUNDAVRA, nr FORT WILLIAM:** Here's a secret loch in the hills, but not
MAP 2 far from the well-trodden tracks through the glens and the sunny streets of Ft
C3 William. Go up Lundavra Rd from r/bout at W end of main st, out of town, over
cattle grid and on (to end of rd) 8km. You should have it to yourself; good picnic spots and gr view of Ben Nevis.

LOCH LOMOND: The biggest, maybe not the bonniest (1/BIG ATTRACTIONS)
with new vis centre opening 2002.

LOCH NESS: The longest; you haven't heard the last of it (4/BIG ATTRACTIONS).

1580 ✓ ✓ ✓ **ROTHESAY–TIGHNABRUAICH:** A886/A8003. The most cele-
MAP 1 brated part of this route is the latter, the A8003 down the side
C3 of L Riddon to Tighnabruaich along the hill sides which give the breathtaking
views of Bute and the Kyles, but the whole way, with its diverse aspects of loch
side, riverine and rocky scenery, is supernatural. Includes short crossing betw
Rhubodach and Colintraive.

1581 ✓ ✓ ✓ **GLENCOE:** The A82 from Crianlarich to Ballachulish is a fine
MAP 2 drive, but from the extraterrestrial L Ba onwards, there can be
C4 few rds anywhere that have direct contact with such imposing scenery. After
Kingshouse and Buachaille Etive Mor on the left, the mts and ridges rising on
either side of Glencoe proper are truly awesome. The new visitor centre, more
discreet than the former nr Glencoe village, sets the topographical and his-
torical scene. (1270/BLOODY GOOD PUBS; 1899/SERIOUS WALKS; 1826/BATTLE-
GROUNDS; 1852/SPOOKY PLACES; 1172/HOSTELS.)

1582 ✓ ✓ **SHIEL BRIDGE–GLENELG:** The switchback rd that climbs from the
MAP 2 A87 (Ft William 96km) at Shiel Br over the 'hill' and down to the coast
B3 opp the Sleat Peninsula in Skye (short ferry to Kylerhea). As you climb you're
almost as high as the surrounding summits and there's the classic view across
L Duich to the 5 Sisters of Kintail. Coming back you think you're going straight
into the loch! It's really worth driving to Glenelg (1184/INNS) and beyond to
Arnisdale and ethereal L Hourn (16km).

1583 ✓ **APPLECROSS:** 120km Inverness. From Tornapress nr Lochcarron for 18km.
MAP 2 Leaving the A896 seems like leaving civilisation; the winding ribbon
B2 heads into monstrous mts and the high plateau at the top is another planet.
It's not for the faint-hearted and Applecross is a relief to see with its camp-
site/coffee shop and a faraway inn. The Applecross Inn (confidently on the up).
1213/GET-AWAY-FROM-IT-ALL.

1584 ✓ **THE GOLDEN ROAD, SOUTH HARRIS:** The main rd in Harris follows the
MAP 2 W coast, notable for bays and sandy beaches (1529/BEACHES). This is the
A2 other one, winding round a series of coves and inlets with offshore skerries
and a treeless rocky hinterland – the classic Hebridean landscape, esp
Finsbay. Tweed is woven in this area; you can visit the crofts but it seems
impolite to leave without buying some tweedy token (2071/TWEED).

1585 **SLEAT PENINSULA, SKYE:** The unclassified rd off the A851 (main Sleat rd) esp
MAP 2 coming from S, i.e. take rd at Ostaig nr Gaelic College; it meets coast after 9km.
B3 Affords rare views of the Cuillins from a craggy coast. Returning to 'main' rd S
of Isleornsay, pop into the gr hotel pub there (2207/ISLAND HOTELS).

1586 **LOCHINVER–ACHILTIBUIE:** Achiltibuie is 40km from Ullapool; this is the
MAP 2 route from the N; 28km of winding rd/unwinding Highland scenery; through
C1 glens, mts and silver sea. Known locally as the 'wee mad rd' (it is maddening if
you're in a hurry). Passes Achin's Bookshop (2047/CRAFT SHOPS), the path to
Kirkaig Falls and the mighty Suilven.

1587 **LOCHINVER–DRUMBEG:** The coast rd N from Lochinver (20km) is also mar-
MAP 2 vellous; essential Assynt. Actually best travelled N-S so that you leave the
C1 splendid vista of Eddrachilles Bay and pass through lochan, moor and even
woodland, touching the coast again by sandy beaches (at Stoer a rd leads
7km to the lighthouse and the walk to the Old Man of Stoer, 1934/COASTAL
WALKS) and app Lochinver with one of the classic long views of Suilven.

1588 **LEADERFOOT–CLINTMAINS, nr ST BOSWELLS:** The B6356 betw the A68
MAP 8 and the B6404 Kelso–St Boswells rd. This small rd, busy in summer, links Scott's
C2 View and Dryburgh Abbey (1818/ABBEYS; best found by following Abbey
signs) and Smailholm Tower, and passes through classic Border/Tweedside
scenery. Don't miss Irvine's View if you want to see the Borders (1606/VIEWS).
Nice GH (897/BORDER HOTELS).

1589 **BRAEMAR–LINN OF DEE:** 12km of renowned Highland river scenery along
MAP 3 the upper valley of the (Royal) Dee. The Linn (rapids) is at the end of the rd, but
B3 there are river walks and the start of the gr Glen Tilt walk to Blair Atholl
(1902/SERIOUS WALKS). Deer abound.

1590 **BALLATER-TOMINTOUL:** This is the ski road to the Lecht (1982/SKIING), the
MAP 3 A939 which leaves the Royal Deeside rd (A93) W of Ballater before it gets real-
B3 ly royal. A ribbon of road in the bare Grampians, past the sentinel ruin Corgarff
(open to view, 250m walk) and the valley of the trickling Don. Rd proceeds
seriously uphill and main viewpoints are S of the Lecht. There is just nobody
for miles. Walks in Glenlivet estates S of Tomintoul.

1591 **FORT AUGUSTUS–DORES, nr INVERNESS:** The B862 often single-track rd
MAP 2 that follows and, for much of its latter length, skirts L Ness. Much quieter and
C3 more interesting than the main W bank A82. Starts off in rugged country and
follows the extraordinary straight rd built by Wade to tame the Highlands.
Reaches the loch side at Foyers (1566/WATERFALLS) and goes all the way to
Dores (15km from Inverness). There are paths to the shore of the loch.
Fabulous untrodden woodlands nr Errogie (marked) and the spooky grave-
yard adj Boleskin House where Aleister Crowley did his dark magic and Jimmy
Page of Led Zeppelin may have done his. 35km total; worth taking slowly.

1592 **THE DUKE'S PASS, ABERFOYLE–BRIG O'TURK:** Of the many rds through the
MAP 6 Trossachs, this one is spectacular though gets busy; numerous possibilities for
B2 stopping, exploration and gr views. Good viewpoint 4km from L Achray Hotel,
above rd and lay-by. One-way forest rd goes round L Achray. Good hill walking starts (1865/1866/1867/FAVOURITE HILLS) and L Katrine Ferry (2km) 3 times
a day Apr-Oct (01877 376316). Bike hire at L Katrine, Aberfoyle and Callander.

1593 **GLENFINNAN–MALLAIG:** The A830, Road to the Isles. Through some of the
MAP 2 most impressive and romantic landscapes in the Highlands, splendid in any
B3 weather (it does rain rather a lot) to the coast at the Sands of Morar
(1537/BEACHES). This is deepest Bonnie Prince Charlie country (1839/MARY,
CHARLIE AND BOB) and demonstrates what a misty eye he had for magnificent
settings. The rd is shadowed for much of the way by the West Highland
Railway, which is an even better way to enjoy the scenery (10/FAVOURITE JOUR-
NEYS).

1594 **LOCHAILORT–ACHARACLE:** Off from the A830 above at Lochailort and turn-
MAP 2 ing S on the A861, the coastal section of this gr scenery is superb esp in the
B3 setting sun. This is the rd to Castle Tioram, which should not be missed
(1715/RUINS); Michael McGregor's new wildlife centre nearby shouldn't be
either (1622/KIDS).

1595 **AMULREE–KENMORE:** The unclassified single track and often v narrow rd
MAP 4 that leads from the hill-country hamlet of Amulree to cosy Kenmore signed
B3 Glen Quaich. Past L Freuchie, a steep climb takes you to a plateau ringed by
magnificent (distant) mts to L Tay. Steep descent to L. Tay and Kenmore. Don't
forget to close the gates.

1596 **PURE PERTHSHIRE, MUTHILL–COMRIE:** A route which takes you through
MAP 4 some of the best scenery in central Scotland and ends up (best this way
B4 round) in Comrie with its teashops and other pleasures (1386/TEAROOMS;
1624/PICNICS). Leave Muthill by Crieff rd turning left (2km) into Drummond
Castle grounds up a glorious avenue of beech trees (gate open 2-5pm). Visit
gdn (1474/GARDENS) then continue through estate. At gate, go rt, following
signs for Strowan. V quiet rd; we have it to ourselves. First jnct, go left following signs (4km). At T-jnct, go left to Comrie (7km).

THE CLASSIC VIEWS

For views of and around EDINBURGH *and* GLASGOW *see p. 67 and p. 106... ...views from hill or mt tops are included here.*

1597
MAP 2
B2
✓ ✓ ✓ **THE QUIRANG, SKYE:** Best app is from Uig direction taking the rt-hand unclassified rd off the hairpin of the A855 above and 2km from town (more usual app from Staffin side is less of a revelation). View (and walk) from car park, the massive rock formations of a towering, contorted ridge. Solidified lava heaved and eroded into fantastic pinnacles. Fine views also across Staffin Bay to Wester Ross. (2234/ISLAND WALKS.)

1598
MAP 2
C2
✓ ✓ ✓ The views of **AN TEALLACH** and **LIATHACH:** An Teallach, that gr favourite of Scottish hill walkers (40km S of Ullapool by the A835/A832), is best viewed from the side of Little L Broom or the A832 just before you get to Dundonald.

The classic view of the other great Torridon mts (Beinn Eighe and Liathach together, 100km S by rd from Ullapool), for those who can't imagine how (or why) you would attempt to go up them, is from the track around L Clair which is reached from the entrance to the Coulin estate off the A896, Glen Torridon rd (be aware of stalking). These mts have to be seen to be believed.

1599
MAP 2
B2
✓ ✓ From **RAASAY:** There are a number of fabulous views looking over to Skye from Raasay, the small island reached by ferry from Sconser (2192/MAGICAL ISLANDS). The panorama from Dun Caan, the hill in the centre of the island (444m) is of Munro proportions, producing an elation quite incommensurate with the small effort required to get there. Start from the rd to the 'N End'.
2-B-2

1600
MAP 1
C2
✓ ✓ **THE REST AND BE THANKFUL:** On A83 L Lomond-Inveraray rd where it's met by the B828 from Lochgoilhead. In summer the rest may be from driving stress and you may not be thankful for the camera-toting masses, but this was always one of the most accessible, rewarding viewpoints in the land. Surprisingly, none of the encompassing hills are Munros but they are nonetheless dramatic. There are mercifully few carpets of conifer to smother the grandeur of the crags as you look down the valley.

1601
MAP 2
B3
✓ **ELGOL, SKYE:** End of the rd, the B8083, 22km from Broadford. The classic view of the Cuillins from across L Scavaig and of Soay and Rum. Cruises (Apr-Oct) in the *Bella Jane* (0800 731 3089) or the *Kaylea Jayne* (01687 462447) to the famous corrie of L Coruisk, painted by Turner, romanticised by Walter Scott; with 90mins ashore. A journey you'll remember.

1602
MAP 2
C2
✓ **THE SUMMER ISLES, ACHILTIBUIE:** The Summer Isles are a scattering of islands seen from the coast of Achiltibuie (and the lounge of the Summer Isles Hotel 1003/HIGHLANDS HOTELS) and visited by boat from Ullapool. But the best place to see them, and the stunning perspective of this western shore is on the road to Altandhu, possibly to the pub there. On way to Achiltibuie, turn rt thro Polbain, on about 2.5km. There's a bench. Sit on it, drink in the sunset.

1603
MAP 2
B3
CAMAS NAN GEALL, ARDNAMURCHAN: 12km Salen on B8007. 4km from Ardnamurchan's Natural History Centre (1561/KIDS) 65km Ft William. Coming esp from the Kilchoan direction, a magnificent bay appears below you, where the rd first meets the sea. Almost symmetrical with high cliffs and a perfect field (still cultivated) in the bowl fringed by a shingle beach. Car park viewpoint and there is a path down. Deer graze around here.

1604
MAP 2
C3
GLENGARRY: 3km after Tomdoun t/off on A87, Invergarry-Kyle of Lochalsh rd. Lay-by with viewfinder. An uncluttered vista up and down loch and glen with not a house in sight (pity about the salmon cages). Distant peaks of Knoydart are identified, but not L Quoich nestling spookily and full of fish in the wilderness at the head of the glen. Bonnie Prince Charlie passed this way.

1605
MAP 8
C2
SCOTT'S VIEW, ST BOSWELLS: Off A68 at Leaderfoot Br nr St Boswells, signed Gattonside. 'The View', old Walter's favourite (the horses still stopped there long after he'd gone), is 4km along the rd (Dryburgh Abbey 3km further; 1818/ABBEYS). Magnificent sweep of his beloved Border country, but only in one direction. If you cross the rd and the stile and head up the hill towards the jagged standing stone that comes into view, you reach …

_06 **IRVINE'S VIEW:** The full panorama from the Cheviots to the Lammermuirs.
MAP 8 This, the finest view in southern Scotland, is only a furlong further. This is
C3 where I'd like my bench – unfortunately some bastard has erected a horrible
phone mast up there (not that I don't use a moby myself – about all the time).

1607 **THE LAW, DUNDEE:** Few cities have such a single good viewpoint. To N of the
MAP 4 centre, it reveals the panoramic perspective of the city on the estuary of the
C3 silvery Tay. Best to walk from town; the one-way system is a nightmare, tho
there are signposts.

1608 **QUEEN'S VIEW, LOCH TUMMEL, nr PITLOCHRY:** 8km on B8019 to Kinloch
MAP 4 Rannoch. Car park and 100m walk to rocky knoll where pioneers of tourism,
B2 Queen Victoria and Prince Albert, were 'transported into ecstasies' by the view
of L Tummel and Schiehallion (1578/LOCHS; 1925/WOODLAND WALKS). Their
view was flooded by a hydro scheme after WW2, but you get the idea.

1609 **CALIFER, nr FORRES:** 7km from Forres on A96 to Elgin, turn rt for 'Pluscarden',
MAP 3 follow narrow rd for 5km. Viewpoint is on rd and looks down across Findhorn
A2 Bay and the wide vista of the Moray Firth to the Black Isle and Ben Wyvis.
Fantastic light.

1610 **THE MALCOLM MEMORIAL, LANGHOLM:** 3km from Langholm and signed
MAP 9 from main A7, a single-track rd leads to a path to this obelisk raised to cele-
D2 brate the military and masonic achievements of one John Malcolm. The eulo-
gy is fulsome esp compared with that for Hugh MacDiarmid on the cairn by
the stunning sculpture at the start of the path (1778/MEMORIALS). Views
from the obelisk, however, are among the finest in the S, encompassing a vista from
the Lakeland Fells and the Solway Firth to the wild Border hills. Path 1km.

1611 **DUNCRYNE HILL, GARTOCHARN, nr BALLOCH:** Gartocharn is betw Balloch
MAP 1 and Drymen on the A811, and this view, was recommended by writer and out-
C2 doorsman Tom Weir as 'the finest viewpoint of any small hill in Scotland'. Turn
up Duncryne rd at the E end of village and park 1km on left by a small wood
(a sign reads 'Woods reserved for Teddy bears'). The hill is only 470ft high and
'easy', but the view of L Lomond and the Kilpatrick Hills is superb.

1612 **BLACKHILL, LESMAHAGOW, nr GLASGOW:** 28km S of city. Another marvel-
MAP 1 lous outlook, but in the opp direction from above. Take jnct 10/11 on M74,
D3 then off the B7078 signed Lanark, take the B7018. 4km along past Clarkston
Farm, head uphill for 1km and park by Water Board mound. Walk uphill
through fields to rt for about 1km. Unprepossessing hill which unexpectedly
reveals a vast vista of most of E central Scotland.   1-A-2

1613 **TONGUE:** From the causeway across the kyle, or following the minor rd to
MAP 2 Talmine on the W side, look S to the ben, or north to the small islands off the
C1 coast.

1614 **GOING TO DUNURE:** (1519/COASTAL VILLAGES). Heading N on the A719 from
MAP 1 Turnberry to Ayr, you can detour down the minor rd to Dunure. But at the
C3 viewpoint you also get Ailsa Craig, Arran, the Ayrshire Coast and Culzean
Castle sitting grandly a few miles south. Behold the Ayrshire coast!

SUMMER PICNICS AND GREAT SWIMMING HOLES

Care should be taken when swimming in rivers; don't take them for granted. Kids should be watched. Most of these places are trad local swimming and picnic spots where people have swum for yrs, but rivers continuously change their course and their nature. Wearing sandals or old sports shoes is a good idea.

1615
MAP 2
B3

✓ ✓ **THE FAIRY POOLS, GLEN BRITTLE, SKYE:** On a hot day, this is one of the best places on Skye to head for; swimming in deep pools with the massif of the Cuillins around you. One pool has a stone br you can swim under. Head off A863 Dunvegan rd from Sligachan Hotel (*see p. 190*) then B8009 and Glenbrittle rd. 7km down just as rd begins to parallel the glen itself, you'll see a river coming off the hills. Park in lay-by on rt. 1km walk, follow this up. Lady Clair Macdonald recs also, the pools at Torrin nr Elgol.

1616
MAP 2
C4

✓ ✓ **THE POOLS IN GLEN ETIVE:** Glen Etive is a wild, enchanted place where people have been camping for yrs to walk and climb in the Glencoe area. There are many grassy landings at the river side as well as these perfect pools for bathing. The first is about 6km from the main Glencoe rd, the A82 at Kingshouse, but just follow the river and find your own. Take midge cream for evening wear. Lots.

1617
MAP 2
D3

✓ ✓ **FESHIEBRIDGE:** At the br itself on the B970 betw Kingussie and Inverdruie nr Aviemore. 4km from Kincraig. Gr walks here into Glen Feshie and in nearby woodland, but under br a perfect spot for Highland swimming. Go down to left from S. Rocky ledges, clear water. One of the best but cold even in high summer.

1618
MAP 6
A2

✓ ✓ **ROB ROY FALLS, nr INVERARNAN:** A82 N of Ardlui and 3 km past The Drover's Inn (1265/BLOODY GOOD PUBS). Sign on the rt (Picnic Area), height restriction so watch your Landcruiser. Park, then follow the path to the main waterfall where you'll be able to glimpse a secluded upper pool, through the trees. There's an overhanging rock face on one side and smooth slabs at the edge of the falls. Natural suntrap in summer, but the water is 'Baltic' at all times.

1619
MAP 8
B2

✓ **NEIDPATH, PEEBLES:** 2km from town on A72, Biggar rd; sign for castle. Park by Hay Lodge Park or poss the lay-by past the castle track (sometimes by the castle itself). Idyllic setting of a broad meander of the Tweed, with medieval Neidpath Castle, a sentinel above. Two 'pools' (3m deep in av summer) linked by shallow rapids which the adventurous chute down on their backs. Usually a rope-swing at upper pool. TAKE CARE. Also see (1910/GLEN AND RIVER WALKS).

1620
MAP 8
C1

✓ **THE WHITEADDER, nr ABBEY ST BATHANS:** Can walk in from village or from Toot corner (1882/HILL WALKS); past Edenshall brochs then follow river 2km further. Easier via A6112 to Duns (6km from A1 at Granthouse), rd to rt marked Abbey St Bathans, go 500m to first corner, then rough track signed for brochs for 1km to river side at swing br. 3 superb rocky pools with the br above. Midges can be menacing, so take the lotion; river shoes useful. River pron 'Whit-adir'.

1621
MAP 3
A2

✓ **RANDOLPH'S LEAP nr FORRES:** Spectacular gorge on the mythical Findhorn which carves out some craggy scenery on its way to a gentle coast. This secret glade and fabulous swimming hole are behind a wall and it's difficult to describe how to find them succinctly (*see* 1915/WOODLAND WALKS *for directions*), but it's S of Forres and Nairn and nr Logie Steading, a courtyard of good things. One Randolph of course once leapt here; we just bathe and lie under the trees dreaming of gods (and maybe satyrs).

1622
MAP 2
C3

STRATHMASHIE, nr NEWTONMORE: On A86 Newtonmore/Dalwhinnie (on A9) to Ft William rd 7km from Laggan, watch for Forest sign, small off rd car park and lay-by. River follows rd. Last visit: another coachload of backpack tourists. Ah well … and I used to have it to myself.

1623 **DOG FALLS, GLEN AFFRIC:** Half-way along Glen Affric rd from Cannich
MAP 2 before you come to the loch, a well-marked picnic spot and gr place to swim
C3 in the peaty waters surrounded by the Caledonian Forest (with trails). Birds well
sussed to picnic potential – your car covered in tits – Hitchcock or what?
(1904/GLEN AND RIVER WALKS).

1624 **Nr COMRIE:** 2 great pools of different character nr the neat little town in
MAP 4 deepest Perthshire. **THE LINN,** the town pool: go over humpback br from
B3 main A85 W to Lochearnhead, signed The Ross. After 2km there's a parking
place on left. River's relatively wide, v pleasant spot. For more adventurous,
GLENARTNEY is past Cultybraggan training camp (follow signs), (5km) and
then MoD range on left until a ruined cottage on rt. Park and walk down to
river in glen. What with the twin perils of the Army and the Comrie Angling
Club, you might feel you have no right to be here, but you do and this stretch
of river is marvellous. Respect the farmland. Follow rd further for more gr picnic spots. Comrie has gr pub/hotel bistro (946/PERTHSHIRE HOTELS) & tearm
(1386/TEAROOMS).

1625 **NORTH SANNOX BURN, ARRAN:** Park at the North Sannox Bridge on the
MAP 1 A841 (rd from Lochranza to Sannox Bay) and follow the track W to the deer
C3 fence and treeline (1km). Just past there you will find a gt pool with small
waterfall, dragonflies and perhaps even an eagle or two above.

1626 **FALLS OF BRUAR, nr BLAIR ATHOLL:** Just off A9, 12km N of Blair Atholl. 250m
MAP 4 walk from **HOUSE OF BRUAR** car park and shopping experience
B2 (2032/CRAFTS) to lower fall (1554/WATERFALLS) where there is an accessible
large deep pool by the br. Cold, fresh mt water in a woody gorge. The proximity of the 'retail experience' can make it all the more daring.

1627 **THE OTTER'S POOL, NEW GALLOWAY FOREST:** A clearing in the forest
MAP 9 reached by a track, 'The Raider's Rd', running from 8km N of Laurieston on the
B3 A762, for 16km to Clatteringshaws Loch. The track, which is only open Apr-
Oct, has a toll of £2 and gets busy. It follows the Water of Dee and halfway
down the rd – the Otter's Pool. A bronze otter used to mark the spot (it got
nicked) and it's a place mainly for kids and paddling; but when the dam runs
off it can be deep enough to swim. Rd closes dusk. (1926/WOODLAND WALKS.)

1628 **ANCRUM:** A secret place on the quiet Ale Water (out of village towards
MAP 8 Lilliesleaf, 3km out 500m from farm sign to Hopton – a recessed gate on the
C3 rt before a bend and a rough track). A meadow, a Border burn, a surprisingly
deep pool to swim. Arcadia!

1629 **PARADISE, SHERIFFMUIR, nr DUNBLANE:** A pool at the foot of an unex-
MAP 6 pected leafy gorge on the moor betw the Ochils and Strathallan. Here the
C3 Wharry Burn is known locally as 'Paradise', and for good reason. Take rd from
'behind' Dunblane or Br of Allan to the Sheriffmuir Inn (873/PUB FOOD); head
downhill (back) towards Br of Allan and park 1km after the hump back br.
Head for the pylon & you'll find the river. Swim/picnic then back to the pub. It
can be midgy and it can be perfect.

1630 **POTARCH BRIDGE & CAMBUS O'MAY on the DEE:** 2 places on the 'Royal'
MAP 3 Dee, the first by the reconstructed Victorian br (and nr the hotel) 3km E of
B3 Kincardine O'Neill. Cambus another stretch of river E of Ballater (6km). Locals
swim, picnic on rocks, etc, and there are forest walks on the other side of rd.
The brave jump off the bridge at Cambus – best just to watch. Gr tearm near-
by – The Black Faced Sheep in Aboyne (1379/TEAROOMS).

1631 **INVERMORISTON:** On main L Ness rd A82 betw Inverness and Ft Augustus,
MAP 2 this is the best bit. R Moriston tumbles under an ancient br. Perfectly
C3 Highland. Ledges for picnics, invigorating pools, ozone-friendly. Nice beech
woods. Tavern/bistro nearby (1202/INNS).

1632 **DULSIE BRIDGE, nr NAIRN:** 16km S of Nairn on the A939 to Grantown, this
MAP 2 locally revered beauty spot is fabulous for summer swimming. The ancient
D2 arched br spans the rocky gorge of the Findhorn (again) and there are ledges
and even sandy beaches for picnics and from which to launch yourself or paddle into the peaty waters.

STRATHCARRON, nr BONAR BRIDGE: Pick your spot (1545/GLENS).

GOOD PLACES TO TAKE KIDS

CENTRAL:

1633
MAP A
xA3
✓ ✓ **EDINBURGH ZOO:** 0131 334 9171. Corstorphine Rd. 4km W of Princes St. A large and long-established zoo, where the natural world from the poles to the plains of Africa is ranged around Corstorphine Hill. Enough huge/exotic/ghastly creatures and friendly, amusing ones to fill an overstimulated day. The penguins and the seals do their stuff at set times. More familiar creatures hang out at the 'farm'. Café and shop stocked with PC toys and souvenirs. Open 7 days, 9am-4.30pm (till 5pm, Mar). 9am-6pm Easter onwards, but times set to change 2002 so check first.

✓ ✓ **OUR DYNAMIC EARTH, EDINBURGH:** 0131 550 7800. Holyrood Rd. Edinburgh's major kids' attraction. Report 383/ATTRACTIONS.

✓ ✓ **MUSEUM OF CHILDHOOD, EDINBURGH:** 0131 529 4142. 42 High St. An Aladdin's cave of toys for all ages. 392/ATTRACTIONS.

1634
MAP 7
B1
✓ **EDINBURGH BUTTERFLY FARM & INSECT WORLD, nr DALKEITH and EDINBURGH:** 0131 663 4932. On A7, signed Eskbank/Galashiels from ring rd (1km). Part of a gdn centre complex and the swish **BIRDS OF PREY CENTRE** (flying displays; kids can handle some of the birds, phone for details 0131 654 1720). As for the bugs, the butterflies are delightful but kids will be far more impressed with the scorpions, locusts and other assorted uglies on show. Red-kneed tarantula not for the faint-hearted. 7 days, 9.30am-5pm (10am-5pm in winter).

1635
MAP A
GLASGOW SCIENCE CENTRE: 0141 420 5000. Glasgow's newest and most flash attraction. State-of-the-art interactive, landmark tower & Imax. Report 731/MAIN ATTRACTIONS.

1636
MAP A
D3
EDINBURGH DUNGEONS: 556 6700. Market St. Multimillion très contrived experience takes you thro a ghoulish history of Scottish nasties. Hammy of course, but kids will love the monorail. 7 days 10am-6pm.

1637
MAP 4
B3
AUCHINGARRICH WILDLIFE CENTRE, nr COMRIE: 4km from main st turning off at br then signed. Sympathetic corralling in picturesque Perthshire Hills. Excl for kids. Huge playbarn. Daily hatchings & lots of baby fluffy things, some of which you can hold. Don't ask what happens to them when they grow up! Good place to start sex education. Emus and meerkats especially weird. Apr-Oct(ish) 10am-dusk. Coffee shop till 5pm.

1638
MAP 1
C3
KELBURN COUNTRY CENTRE, LARGS: 2km S of Largs on A78. Riding school, gdns, woodland walks up the Kel Burn and a central visitor/consumer section with shops/exhibits/cafés. Wooden stockade for clambering kids; commando assault course for exhibitionist adults and less doddering dads. Falconry displays (and long-suffering owl). Secret Forest in the woods. Combine with Vikingar (1989/LEISURE CENTRES) for an exhausting day. Stock up with Nardini's ice cream (1424/ICE CREAM). 7 days 10am-6pm. Apr-Oct. Grounds only in wint 11-5pm.

FIFE AND DUNDEE:

1639
MAP 5
B4
✓ **DEEP SEA WORLD, N QUEENSFERRY:** 01383 411411. The aquarium in a quarry which may be reaching its swim-by date. Park'n'ride system and buses from Edin, or better still by *Maid of the Forth* from S Queensferry (9/FAVOURITE JOURNEYS). Habitats are viewed from a conveyor belt where you can stare at the fish and diverse divers teeming around and above you. Maximum hard sell to this all-weather attraction, but kids like it even when they've been queueing for aeons (ask about the 'fast track' route). Cafe is fairly awful, but nice views. Open AYR 7 days: summer 10am-6pm; winter 11am-5pm.

1640
MAP 4
C3
✓ **SENSATION, DUNDEE:** 01382 228800. Greenmarket across r/bout from Discovery Pt and adj DCA (2128/GALLERIES). Purpose-built indoor kids infotainment attraction. With basis in Dundee's 'Discover Yourself' & 'Scientific Centre of Excellence' claims, this is an innovative and v interactive games room with a message. We all learn something. 7 days 10am-5pm.

1641
MAP 4
C3
✓ **VERDANT WORKS, DUNDEE:** 01382 225282. West Henderson's Wynd nr Westport. Heritage museum that recreates workings of a jute mill. Sounds dull, but brilliant for kids and grown-ups. Report: 2100/MUSEUMS. ☕

1642
MAP 5
C2

✓ **CRAIGTON PARK, ST ANDREWS:** 01334 473666. 6km SW of St Andrews on the Pitscottie rd. An oasis of fun: bouncy castles, trampolines, putting, crazy golf, boating lake, a train thro the grounds, adventure playgrounds and glasshouses. A perfect day's amusement esp for nippers. Easter-Sept; 10.30am-6.30pm, 7 days.

1643
MAP 4
C3

CAMPERDOWN PARK, DUNDEE: The large park just off the ring-road system (the Kingsway and via A923 to Coupar Angus) with a wildlife centre and a nearby play complex. Animal-handling at w/ends. 'Over 80 species'. Open AYR, but centre 10am-4.30pm, earlier in winter (1506/TOWN PARKS).

SOUTH AND SOUTH WEST:

1644
MAP 1
C3

✓ **THE BIG IDEA, IRVINE:** 08708 404030. Opened in 2000 in blaze of publicity, TBI bills itself as the world's first inventor centre. Lots of hands-on contraptions for the kids to try, and an area where they assemble various models then get to use them. Not cheap and the sponsorship is a little intrusive but all the stuff about Nobel (of Prize fame) and the local history should sustain the grown-ups – TBI is where Nobel started the British Dynamite Co. Interesting exterior, lots of space, café etc. Open AYR, call for times.

1645
MAP 1
C3

✓ **KIDZ PLAY, PRESTWICK:** 01292 475215. Off main st at Station rd, past stn to beach and to rt. Big shed soft play area for kids. Everything that the little blighters will like in the throwing-themselves-around department. Shriek city. Sun-Thur 9.30am-7pm. Fri-Sat 9.30am-7.30pm.

1646
MAP 1
D3

LOUDOUN CASTLE, nr GALSTON: Theme park for the S of Glas hinterland. Just off A71 Kilmarnock-Edin rd (go from Glas via A77 Kilmarnock rd). Behind the ruins of the said Loudon Castle (burned out in 1941), a fairground which includes the 'largest carousel in Europe' and massive 'chairy plane', has been transplanted in the old walled gdn. Nice setting; well kids may not notice the setting, but they won't forget the chairy plane. Open Easter-Sep.

1647
MAP 1
D2

PALACERIGG COUNTRY PARK, CUMBERNAULD: 01236 720047. 6km E of Cumbernauld. 740 acres of parkland; ranger service, nature trails, picnic area and kids farm. 18-hole golf course and putting green. Exhib area with changing exhibits about forestry, conservation etc. Open AYR: 7 days; daylight hrs. Visitor centre and tearoom till 6pm in summer, 4.30pm winter.

DRUMLANRIG CASTLE, nr DUMFRIES: 1490/COUNTRY PARKS.

CREAM O' GALLOWAY, RAINTON: Ice cream & gr play area. 1426/ICE CREAM.

NORTH-EAST

1648
MAP 3
C1

✓ **MACDUFF MARINE AQUARIUM:** On seafront E of the harbour, a family attraction for this under-rated Moray Firth port. Under-rated perhaps because neighbouring Banff gets more attention from tourists, but Duff House (2132/GALLERIES) gets fewer visitors than this user- and child-friendly sea-life centre. All the fish seem curiously happy with their lot and content to educate and entertain. Open AYR 10-5pm.

1649
MAP 3
D2

✓ **ADEN, MINTLAW, nr PETERHEAD:** (pron 'Ah-den'). Country park just beyond Mintlaw on A950 16km from Peterhead. Former grounds of mansion with walks and organised activities and events. Farm buildings converted into Heritage Centre (kids free), café etc. Adventure playground. AYR.

1650
MAP 3
C3

✓ **STORYBOOK GLEN, nr ABERDEEN:** Fibreglass fantasy land in verdant glen 16km S of Aber via B9077, the S Deeside rd, a nice drive. Characters from every fairy tale and nursery story dotted around 20-acre park. Their fixed manic stares give them a spooky resemblance to people you may know. Older kids may find it tame – no guns, no big technology but nice for little 'uns. Indoor play area. Mar-Oct 10-6pm. Nov-Feb w/ends only 11-4pm.

1651
MAP 3
D3

✓ **SARTROSPHERE, ABERDEEN:** Nr beach (off Beach Boulevard, nr Patio Hotel), Scotland's 'original interactive science centre'. Hands on, it is! Granny will learn as much as she can take in. AYR. 7 days 10am-5pm.

HIGHLANDS

1652 ✓ **THE CAIRNGORM REINDEER HERD nr AVIEMORE:** 01479 810363. Stop
MAP 2 at Centre (shop, exhibition) to buy tickets and follow the guide in your
D3 vehicle up the mountain. From here, 20 min walk. At Glenmore Forest Park on
rd from Coylumbridge 12km from Aviemore. Real reindeer aplenty in reasonably authentic free-ranging habitat (when they come down off the cloudy
hillside in winter with snow all around). They've come a long way from
Sweden (in 1952). 1hr 30min trip. They are so ...small. 11am AYR plus 2.30pm
in summer. Wear appropriate footwear and phone if weather looks threatening.

1653 ✓ **LEAULT FARM nr KINCRAIG:** Actually on fast bit of the main A9, but eas-
MAP 2 ier to find by looking for sign 1km S of Kincraig on the B9152. Working
D3 farm with daily sheepdog trials where Neil Ross demonstrates his extraordinary facility with dogs and sheep (and ducks). By all accounts this is gr spec-
tacle and is totally authentic in this setting. Usually noon and 4pm (May-Oct,
also 10 and 2pm July/Aug). Cl Sat.

1654 **AN TAIRBEART ARTS CENTRE, TARBERT:** 01880 821116. Just on the edge of
MAP 1 town as you approach from the S. Multifaceted arts centre with gallery, gigs,
B2 craft workshops and more – particularly all the summer programme stuff
they run for kids. If basket-making in a yurt don't float your boat, making kite-
things or coracles might. Tues-Sat 10am-6pm, AYR.

1655 **THE HIGHLAND WILDLIFE PARK, KINCRAIG:** On B9152 betw Aviemore and
MAP 2 Kingussie. Large drive-through 'reserve' run by Royal Zoological Society with
D3 wandering herds of deer, bison etc and pens of other animals. 'Habitats', but
mostly cages. Must be time to bring back bears and wolves – sort out the deer
and liven up the caravan parks. Open 10-6pm (July/Aug 7pm, wint 4pm).

1656 **HIGHLAND AND RARE BREEDS FARM, ELPHIN, nr ULLAPOOL:** 01854
MAP 2 666204. Charming croft with over 30 'breeds' from the Soay sheep of St Kilda
C1 to Tamworth pigs; many feathered friends. A genuine working farm set on
either side of the rd (A835 26km N of Ullapool) that's v hooves and hands-on.
There's always a baby something to pet. Farmwork demos and tours. The sun
seems to shine here all day. July and Aug only, 10am-5pm; 7 days.

1657 **LANDMARK CENTRE, CARRBRIDGE:** 01479 841614. A purpose-built tourist
MAP 2 centre with audiovisual displays and a gr deal of shopping. Gr for kids mess-
D3 ing about in the woods on slides, in a 'maze' etc, in a large adventure playground, Microworld or (esp squealy) the Wildwater Coaster. The Tower may be
too much for Granny but there are fine forest views. Open AYR 7 days till 5pm.

1658 **ISLAY WILDLIFE INFO & FIELD CENTRE, PORT CHARLOTTE:** 01496 850288.
MAP 1 Fascinating wildlife centre for all ages. Activity rm and organised day trips.
A3 (1690/WILDLIFE; 2238/ISLAY).

1659 **SEALIFE CENTRE, OBAN:** 16km N on the A828. On the shore of L Creran this
MAP 1 one of the oldest of a number of UK waterworlds still the best (another in **ST**
B1 **ANDREWS**). Environmentally conscientious they 'rescue' seals and house
numerous aquatic life. The 'World of the Jellyfish' is the ultimate lava lamp
(Aug/Sept). Café/shop/adventure playground. Open summer, 10am-6pm. (call
for winter hrs 01631 720386)

1660 **RARE BREEDS FARM, OBAN:** 4km from town via Argyll Sq, then S (A816)
MAP 1 bearing left at church, past golf course. Weird and wonderful collection of ani-
B1 mals in hill side pens and runs and a touchy-feely barn, who seem all the more
peculiar because they're versions of familiar ones. Leaving the caging ques-
tions aside, it's a funny farm for kids and the creatures seem keen enough for
the attention and crumbs from the tearoom table. New owners. 7 days in season.

1661 **ARGYLL WILDLIFE PARK, INVERARAY:** 4km W of town on A83. Another zoo-
MAP 1 type place, but with many native animals in more or less their natural habitat.
C2 Lots of them just wander and waddle about. Set amongst pinewoods on the
braes of L Fyne, there are probably even a few animals (e.g. mink and foxes),
trying to get in. A snowy wallaby has recently joined the many badgers, wild-
cats, deer and multifarious wildfowl. Apr-Oct, 10-5pm, 7 days.

1662 **NATURAL HISTORY CENTRE, ARDNAMURCHAN:** 01972 500209. A861
MAP 2 Strontian, B8007 Glenmore 14km. Photographer Michael McGregor's award
B3 winning interactive exhib; a bit of a surprise out here. Kids will enjoy, adults
may be impressed. Tearoom. Mon-Sat; 10.30am-5.30pm. Sun; 12-5.30pm.

THE BEST PLACES TO SEE BIRDS

See p. 215 for WILDLIFE RESERVES, *many of which are good for bird-watching.*

1663
MAP 2
C1
✓ ✓ **HANDA ISLAND, nr SCOURIE, SUTHERLAND:** Take the boat from Tarbet Pier 6km off A894 5km N of Scourie and land on a beautiful island run by the Scottish Wildlife Trust as a sea bird reserve. Boats (Apr-mid Sept though fewer birds after Aug) are continuous depending on demand (01971 502347). Crossing 30mins. Small reception hut and 2.5km walk over island to cliffs which rise 350m and are layered in colonies from fulmars to shags. Allow 3 to 4hrs. Perhaps you can persuade the boatman to go to see the cliffs and the formidable stack from below. Though you must take care not to disturb the birds, you'll be eye to eye with seals and bill to bill with razorbills. Eat at the seafood café on the cove when you return (1344/SEAFOOD RESTAUS). Mon-Sat only.

1664
MAP 9
C3
✓ ✓ **CAERLAVEROCK, nr DUMFRIES:** 17km S on B725 nr Bankend, signed from rd. The WWT Caerlaverock Wetlands Centre (01387 770200) has undergone quite a few changes of late. Still an excellent place to see whooper swans, barnacle geese and more (countless hides, observatories, viewing towers) but also now has a right-on café, as well as farmhouse-style accom for up to 14 (INX). More than just birds too: natterjack toads, badgers. Not just for twitchers – tyros in slingbacks also welcome. Eastpark Farm, Caerlaverock. Centre open daily AYR 10am-5pm.   ADMN

1665
MAP 1
A1
✓ ✓ **LUNGA and THE TRESHNISH ISLANDS:** Off Mull. Sail from Iona or Fionnphort or Ulva ferry on Mull to these uninhabited islands on a 5/6hr excursion which probably takes in Staffa and Fingal's Cave. Best months are May-July when birds are breeding. Some trips allow 3hrs on Lunga. Razorbills, guillemots and a carpet of puffins oblivious to your presence. This will be a memorable day. Boat trips (01688 400242) or check Tobermory TIC (01688 302182) who will advise of other boatmen. All trips dependent on sea conditions.

1666
MAP 5
D3
✓ ✓ **ISLE OF MAY, FIRTH OF FORTH:** Island at mouth of Forth off Crail/ Anstruther reached by daily boat trip from Anstruther Harbour (01333 310103), May-Oct 9am-2.30pm depending on tides. Boats hold 40-50; trip 45mins; allows 3hrs ashore. Island (including isthmus to Rona) 1.5km x 0.5km. Info centre and resident wardens. See guillemots, razorbills and kittiwakes on cliffs and shags, terns and thousands of puffins. Most populations increasing. This place is strange as well as beautiful. The puffins in early summer are, as always, engaging.

1667
MAP 7
B1
✓ **THE LAGOON, MUSSELBURGH:** On E edge of town behind the racecourse (follow rd round, take turn-off signed Levenhall Links), at the estuarine mouth of the R Esk. Waders, sea birds, ducks aplenty and often interesting migrants on the mudflats and wide littoral. The 'lagoon' itself is a manmade pond behind with hide and attracts big populations (both birds and binocs). This is the nearest diverse-species area to Edin (15km) and in recent yrs has become one of the most significant migrant stopovers in the UK.

1668
MAP 3
C4
✓ **FOWLSHEUGH, nr STONEHAVEN:** 8km S of Stonehaven and signed from A92 with path from Crawton. Sea bird city on spectacular cliffs where you can lie on your front and look over. The cliffs are 75m high; take gr care. 80,000 pairs of 6 species esp guillemots, kittiwakes, razorbills and also fulmar, shag, puffins. Poss to view the birds without disturbing them and see the 'layers' they occupy on the cliff face. Or go by boat thrice weekly in summer from Stonehaven Harbour (check TIC for details 01224 624824). Best seen May-July.

1669
MAP 4
B3
✓ **LOCH OF THE LOWES, DUNKELD:** 4km NE Dunkeld on A923 to Blairgowrie. Properly managed (Scottish Wildlife Trust) site with doublefloored hide and permanent binocs. Main attractions are the captivating ospreys (from early Apr-Aug/Sept). Nest 100m over loch and clearly visible. Their revival is well documented, including diary of movements, breeding history etc. Also otters and pine martens. Hide 10am-5/6pm.

1670
MAP 2
D3

✓ **LOCH GARTEN, BOAT OF GARTEN:** 3km village off B970 into Abernethy Forest. Famous for the ospreys and so popular that access may be restricted until after the eggs have hatched. 2 car parks: the first has nature trails through Scots pine woods and around loch; other has the main hide 300m away. Extraordinary palaver considering there's only one pair and there are no fish in the loch so they don't feed there (anyhow fish farms are easier). Och, but they are magnificent.

1671
MAP 1
A2

✓ **ISLAY, LOCH GRUINART, LOCH INDAAL:** RSPB reserve. Take A847 at Bridgend then B8017 turning N and rt for Gruinart. The mudflats and fields at the head of the loch provide winter grazing for huge flocks of Barnacle and Greenland geese. They arrive, as do flocks of fellow bird-watchers, in late Oct. Hides and good vantage points near rd. The Rhinns and the Oa in the S sustain a huge variety of bird life.

1672

✓ **MARWICK HEAD, ORKNEY MAINLAND:** 40km NW of Kirkwall, via Finstown and Dounby; take left at Birsay after L of Isbister cross the B9056 and park at Cumlaquoy. Spectacular sea bird breeding colony on 100m cliffs and nearby at the Loons Reserve, wet meadowland, 8 species of duck and many waders. Orkney sites include the Noup cliffs on Westray, North Hill on Papa Westray and Copinsay, 3km E of the mainland. The remoter, the merrier.

1673 **ORKNEY PUFFINS:** 'Wildabout' tour's dusk puffin patrol (01856 851011). Or go solo at Costa Head, Brough of Birsay and Westray; check Kirkwall TIC for latest.

1674
MAP 1
D3

BARON'S HAUGH, MOTHERWELL: nr Strathclyde Park. From Motherwell Civic Centre, take rd for Hamilton then left (1km) up Leven St, bearing rt to end (there are signs). RSPB reserve of woodland, marsh and scrub by R Clyde; a sanctuary in a heavily built-up area. Furthest of 4 hides is 1.5km walk. The wide variety of habitats offers a surprising range of species esp in winter. Dalzell Country Park adj, has trails.

1675
MAP 7
B1

THE BASS ROCK, off NORTH BERWICK: 01620 892838. 'Temple of gannets'. A gr-guano encrusted spaceship take-off ramp sticking out of the Forth and where Davie Balfour was imprisoned in RLS's *Catriona* (aka *Kidnapped II*). Weather-dependent boat trips available May-Sep courtesy of Mr Marr, from N Berwick harbour (also to nearby Fidra). Phone for details.

1676
MAP 7
B1

SCOTTISH SEABIRDS CENTRE, N BERWICK: 01620 890202. Recently opened visitor attraction nr Harbour o/looking Bass Rock and Fidra. Video and other state-of-the-art technology makes you feel as if the birds are next to you. Viewing deck for dramatic perspective of gannets diving (140kmph!) 10am-4 winter. Later opening summer.

1677
MAP 4
D2

MONTROSE BASIN WILDLIFE CENTRE: 1.5km south of Montrose on the A92 to Arbroath. V accessible Scottish Wildlife Trust centre, opened in '95, overlooks the estuarine basin that hosts various residents and migrants. Good for twitchers and kids. And autumn geese. Apr-Oct daily 10.30am-5pm. Nov-Mar daily 10.30pm-4pm.

1678
MAP 2
D1

FORSINARD NATURE RESERVE: By road, 44km from Helmsdale on the A897, or the train stops on route to Wick/Thurso. RSPB reserve, acquired in '95 following public appeal. 17, 500 acres of flow country and the birds that go with it: divers, plovers, merlins and hen harriers. Reserve open AYR; visitor centre Apr-Oct daily 9am-6pm.

1679
MAP 4
C2

LOCH OF KINNORDY, KIRRIEMUIR: 4km W of town on B951, an easily accessible site with 2 hides o/look loch and wetland area managed by RSPB. Geese in winter, gulls aplenty; always tickworthy.

1680
MAP 3
D2

STRATHBEG, nr FRASERBURGH: 12km S off main Fraserburgh-Peterhead rd, the A952 and signed 'Nature Reserve' at Crimond. Wide, shallow loch v close to coastline, a 'magnet for migrating wildfowl' and from the (unmanned) reception centre at loch side it's poss to get a v good view of them. Marsh/fen, dune and meadow habitats. In winter 30,000 geese/widgeon/mallard/swans and occasional rarities like cranes and egrets. Binocs in centre and 2 other hides; marked route around.

WHERE TO SEE DOLPHINS, WHALES PORPOISES AND SEALS

1681
MAP 2
MAP 3

✓✓ *The coast around the N of Scotland offers some of the best places in Europe from which to see whales and dolphins and, more ubiquitously, seals. You don't have to go on boat trips, though of course you get closer, the boatman will know where to find them and the trip itself can be exhilarating. A list of operators is given below. Dolphins are most active on a rising tide esp May-Sept.*

MORAY and CROMARTY FIRTHS, nr INVERNESS and CROMARTY:

The best area in Scotland. The population of bottlenose dolphins in this area well exceeds 100 and they can be seen AYR.

THE DOLPHINS AND SEALS OF THE MORAY FIRTH CENTRE: Just N of the Kessock Br on the A9 and adj the Tourist Information Centre (01463 731505). Underwater microphones pick up the chatterings of dolphins and porpoises and there's always somebody there to explain. Apr-Nov, 7 days 10am-5pm.

CROMARTY: Any vantage around the town is good esp S Sutor for coastal walk and an old lighthouse cottage has been converted into a research station run by Aberdeen Uni. **CHANONRY POINT, FORTROSE**, E end of pt beyond lighthouse is the *best* place to see dolphins from land in Britain. Occasional sightings can also be seen at **BALINTORE**, opp Seaboard Memorial Hall; **TARBERT NESS** beyond **PORTMAHOMACK**, end of path through reserve further out along the Moray Firth poss at **BURGHEAD**, **LOSSIEMOUTH** and **BUCKIE, SPEY BAY** and **PORTKNOCKIE.**

NORTH WEST

On the W coast, esp nr Gairloch the following places may offer sightings of orcas, dolphins and minke whales mainly in summer.

RUBHA REIDH nr GAIRLOCH: 20km N by unclassified rd beyond Melvaig. Nr the Carn Dearg Youth Hostel W of Lonemore where rd turns inland is good spot.

GREENSTONE POINT N of LAIDE on the A832 nr Inverewe Gardens and Gruinard Bay. Harbour porpoises here Apr-Dec and minke whales May-Oct.

RED POINT of GAIRLOCH: by unclassified rd via Badachro. High ground looking over N Minch and S to L Torridon. Harbour porpoises often along this coast.

OTHER PLACES

MOUSA SOUND, SHETLAND: 20km S of Lerwick (1736/PREHISTORIC SITES).

ARDNAMURCHAN, THE POINT: The most westerly point (and lighthouse) on this wildly beautiful peninsula. Go to end of rd or park nr Sanna Beach and walk round. Sanna Beach is worth going to just to walk the strand. Visitor centre with tearoom and toilets.

STORNOWAY, ISLE OF LEWIS: Heading out of town for Eye Peninsula, at Holm nr Sandwick S of A866 or from Bayble Bay (all within walking distance).

BEST SEALIFE CRUISES

DOLPHIN ECOSSE, CROMARTY: 01381 600323. Intimate and informative tours. 2 trips per day. Booking essential.

MORAY FIRTH DOLPHIN CRUISES, INVERNESS: 01463 731866. 5 trips per day.

SUMMER ISLES CRUISES: 01854 622200. Seals & seabirds abound round these beautiful islands. 2 trips per day plus all day special.

WILDLIFE CRUISES, JOHN O' GROATS: 01955 611353. Puffins, seabirds, seals. June-Aug. 2.30pm daily.

SEA.FARI ADVENTURES: Based in **EDINBURGH** (0131 331 5000), **OBAN** (01852 300003) and **SKYE** (01471 833316). Sealife adventure boating specialists. Range of eco-tours & trips in fast, inflatable boats. Same product at 3 locations.

ON THE ISLANDS

SEA-LIFE SURVEYS, MULL: 01688 400223. Various packages from relaxed four hour trip to the more intense eight hour. Small groups on comfortable boat. Good percentage of dolphin & whale sightings.

TURUS MARA, MULL: 08000 858786. Daytrips from Ulva Ferry. Various itineraries taking in bird colonies of Treshnish Isles, Staffa & Iona. Dolphins, whales, puffins & seals. Booking essential.

SHETLAND WILDLIFE & BRESSABOATS, SHETLAND: 01950 422483. Award-winning tours – from day trips to seven-day wildlife holidays. Sealife, birds, whales and otters.

ISLAND CRUISING, LEWIS: 01851 672381. Wildlife, birdwatching and diving cruises around the Western Isles and St Kilda.

STROND WILDLIFE CHARTERS, HARRIS: 01859 520204. From one hour to full day boat trips to see seals & birdlife of the Sound of Harris. Pay per boat, not per person.

There are two glass-bottom boat companies offering trips in **SKYE. FAMILY PRIDE II** (01471 822037) operate from Broadford Bay and concentrate on the reefs round the local islands. **SEAPROBE ATLANTIS** (0800 9804846) are based on the mainland at Kyle (just over the bridge) and stay around Kyle of Lochalsh area. Sit underwater in the 'gallery' so better viewing advantage.

WILDLIFE WALKS

WILDLIFE SAFARIS, MULL: 01680 300441. All day (10am-5pm; not Sat) tour with local expert. Possible sightings of otters, eagles, seals and falcons. Numerous pick-up points. Book in advance.

WILDABOUT, ORKNEY: 01856 851011. Various trips with experienced guides. Wildlife plus history & folklore.

OUT & ABOUT TOURS, LEWIS: 01851 612288. Ex-countryside ranger leads groups of all sizes on guided walks and day trips of Lewis and Harris. Experience the landscape, culture and wildlife of the islands.

Otters can be seen all over the NW Highlands in sheltered inlets, esp early morning and late evening and on an ebb tide. Skye is one of best places in Europe to see them. Go with:

OTTER SURVIVAL FUND, BROADFORD: 01471 822487 organise guided walks for all wildlife and might pt you in the rt direction.

OTTER HAVEN, KYLERHEA: Basically a viewing hide with CCTV, binoculars and a knowledgeable warden (not always there). Seabirds & seals too and a forest walk. 500m walk along a track from car park signposted on road out of Kylerhea.

GREAT WILDLIFE RESERVES

These wildlife reserves are not merely bird-watching places. Most of them are easy to get to from major centres; none requires permits.

1682
MAP 8
D1

✓✓ **ST ABB'S HEAD, nr BERWICK:** 22km N Berwick, 9km N Eyemouth and only 10km E of main A1. Spectacular cliff scenery (1936/COASTAL WALKS), a huge sea bird colony, rich marine life and a varied flora make this a place of fascination and diverse interest. Good view from top of stacks, geos and cliff face full of serried ranks of guillemot, kittiwake, razorbill etc. Hanging gdns of grasses and campion. Behind cliffs, grassland rolls down to the Mire L and its varied habitat of bird, insect and butterfly life and vegetation. Superb.

1683 **SANDS OF FORVIE and THE YTHAN ESTUARY, NEWBURGH:** 25km
MAP 3 ✔ ✔ N of Aber. Cross br o/side Newburgh on A975 to Cruden Bay and
D2 park. Path follows Ythan estuary and, bearing N, enters the largest dune system in the UK undisturbed by man. Dunes in every aspect of formation.
Collieston, a 17/18th-century fishing village arranged in terraces on the cliffs,
is 5km away. The various coastal habitats support the largest population of
eiders in UK (esp June) and huge numbers of terns. Plenty to see even from
main rd lay-bys; also hides.

1684 **BEINN EIGHE:** Bounded by the A832 and A896 W of Kinlochewe, this first
MAP 2 ✔ National Nature Reserve in Britain includes one of the remaining frag-
C2 ments of old Caledonian pinewood on the S shore of Loch Maree and rises to
the rugged mountain tops with their spectacular views & varied geology.
Excellent woodland and mountain trails. Start from roadside car park (on
A832 4km from Kinlochewe). 3km nearer the village on this road is a visitor
centre.

1685 **JOHN MUIR COUNTRY PARK, DUNBAR:** The vast park betw Dunbar and N
MAP 7 Berwick named after the naturalist/explorer who was born in Dunbar and
B1 who, in founding Yellowstone National Park in the US, is regarded as the father
of the Conservation movement. Includes estuary of the Tyne (park also known
as Tyninghame), cliffs, sand spits and woodland, it covers a wide range of habitats. Many bird species (e.g. 30 waders), crabs, lichens, sea and marsh plants.
Enter at E extremity of Dunbar at Belhaven, off the B6370 from A1; or off A198
to N Berwick 3km from A1. Or better, walk from Dunbar by 'cliff top trail' (2km).

1686 **LOCHWINNOCH:** 30km SW of Glas via M8 jnct 29 then A737 and A760 past
MAP 1 Johnstone. Also from Largs 20km via A760. Reserve is just o/side village on
C3 loch side and comprises wetland and woodland habitats. A serious 'nature
centre' incorporating an observation tower. Hides and marked trails; and a
birds-spotted board. Shop and coffee shop. Good for kids. Centre 10am-5pm
(cl Thurs). RSPB

1687 **INSH MARSHES, KINGUSSIE:** 4km from town along B970 (after Ruthven
MAP 2 Barracks, 1728/RUINS), a reserve run by RSPB but with much more than just
D3 birds to see. Trail (3km) marked out through meadow and wetland and a note
of species to look out for (including 6 types of orchid). Also 2 hides (250m and
450m) high above marshes, vantage points to see waterfowl, birds of prey,
otters and deer.

1688 **TENTSMUIR, betw NEWPORT and LEUCHARS:** The northern tip of Fife at the
MAP 5 mouth of the Firth of Tay, reached from Tayport or Leuchars via the B945.
C2 Follow signs for Kinshaldy Beach taking rd that winds for 4km over flat and
then forested land. Park amongst Corsican pine plantation (car park closes
9pm in summer) and cross dunes to broad strand which many consider to be
a better beach than the W Sands, St Andrews. Walks in both direction: W back
to Tayport, E towards Eden Bird Sanctuary. Also 4km circular walk of beach
and forest. Hide 2km away at Ice House Pond. Seals often watch from waves
and bask in summer. Lots of butterflies. Waders aplenty and, to E, one of UK's
most significant populations of eider. Most wildfowl offshore on Abertay Sands.

1689 **VANE FARM:** RSPB reserve on S shore of L Leven, beside and bisected by
MAP 5 B9097 off jnct 5 of M90. Easily reached and v busy visitor centre with obser-
B3 vation lounge and education/orientation facs. Hide nearer loch side reached
by tunnel under rd. Nature Trail on hill behind through heath and birchwood
(2km circ). Good place to introduce kids to nature watching.

1690 **ISLAY WILDLIFE INFO & FIELD CENTRE, PORT CHARLOTTE:** Jam-packed
MAP 1 info centre that's v 'hands-on' and interactive. Up-to-date displays of geology,
A3 natural history (rocks, skeletons, sealife tanks). Recent sightings of wildlife,
flora and fauna lists, video rm, reference library. Kids' area and activity days
when staff take you on a tour around the surrounding area. Expansion plans
so more facs perhaps in 2002-03. Quietly attractive staff, odd opening hours.
10am-3pm Apr-Oct. Cl Wed and Sat, open to 5pm July-Aug.

1691 **BALRANALD, NORTH UIST, WESTERN ISLES:** W coast of N Uist reached by
MAP 2 the rd from Lochmaddy, then the Bayhead t/off at Clachan Stores (10km N).
A2 We have listened for the corncrake, this being one of its last strongholds but
so far not a cheep. However here and there are… Many species; many different habitats.

SECTION 8

Historical Places

THE BEST CASTLES

NTS: Under the care of the National Trust for Scotland. Hrs vary. HS: Under the care of Historic Scotland. Standard hrs are: Apr-end Sept Mon-Sat 9.30am-6.30pm; Sun 2-6.30pm. Oct-Mar Mon-Sat 9.30am-4.30pm; Sun 2-4.30pm.

1692
MAP 6
C3

✓ ✓ ✓ **STIRLING CASTLE:** Dominating the town and the plain, this like Edin Castle is worth the hype and the history. And like Edin, it's a timeless attraction that can withstand waves of tourism as it survived the centuries of warfare for which it was built. Despite this primary function, it does seem a v civilised billet, with peaceful gdns and rampart walks from which the views are excellent (esp the aerial view of the Royal Gdns, 'the cup and saucer' as they're known locally). Incls the Renaissance Palace of James V and the Great Hall of James IV recently restored to full magnificence. Some rock legends also play here in summer (Bob Dylan in 2001). The Costa caff is a bit of a letdown in these historical circumstances.   HS

1693
MAP A
C3

✓ ✓ ✓ **EDINBURGH CASTLE:** Edin city centre. Impressive from any angle and all the more so from inside. Despite the tides of tourists and time, it still enthralls. Superb perspectives of the city and of Scottish history. Stone of Destiny now up there with the Crown Jewels as Big Attraction. Café and restau (superb views) with efficient, but uninspiring catering operation; open only castle hrs and to castle visitors (377/MAIN ATTRACTIONS).   HS

1694
MAP 3
A2

✓ ✓ **BRODIE CASTLE, nr NAIRN:** 6-7km W of Forres off main A96. More a (Z plan) tower house than a castle, dating from 1567 and still lived in by the Brodie of Brodie. With a minimum of historical hocum, this 16/17th-century, but mainly Victorian, country house is furnished from rugs to moulded ceilings in the most excellent taste. Every picture (v few gloomies) bears examination. The nursery and nanny's rm, the guest rms, indeed all the rms, are eminently habitable. I could live in the library. There are regular musical evenings and other events (01309 641371 for event programme). Tearoom and informal walks in grounds. An avenue leads to a lake; in spring the daffodils are famous. Apr-Sept 11am-5.30pm; Sun 1.30-5.30pm. W/ends in Oct. Grounds open AYR till sunset.   NTS

1695
MAP 1
C4

✓ ✓ **CULZEAN CASTLE, MAYBOLE:** 24km S of Ayr on A719. Impossible to convey here the scale and the scope of the house and the country park. Allow some hrs esp for the grounds. Castle is more like a country house and you examine from the other side of a rope. From the 12th century, but rebuilt by Robert Adam in 1775, a time of soaring ambition, its grandeur is almost out of place in this exposed cliff-top position. It was designed for entertaining, and the oval staircase is magnificent. Wartime associations (esp with President Eisenhower) plus the enduring fascination of the aristocracy. 560 acres of grounds including cliff-top walk, formal gdns, walled gdn, Swan Pond (a must) and Happy Valley. Harmonious home farm is visitor centre with café, exhibits and shop etc. Open Apr-Oct 11am-5.30pm. Many special 'events'. Culzean is pron 'Cullane'. And you can stay (835/AYRSHIRE HOTELS).   NTS

1696
MAP 5
C3

✓ ✓ **FALKLAND PALACE, FALKLAND:** Middle of farming Fife, 15km from M90 jnct 8. Not a castle at all, but the hunting palace of the Stewart dynasty. Despite its recreational rather than political role, it's one of the landmark buildings in Scottish history and in the 16th century was the finest Renaissance building in Britain. They all came here for archery, falcony and hunting boar and deer on the Lomonds; and for Royal Tennis which is displayed and explained. Still occupied by the Crichton-Stewarts, the house is dark and rich and redolent of those days of 'dancin and deray at Falkland on the Grene'. Apr-Oct 11-5.30pm, from 10am in summer. Sun 1.30-5.30pm. 938/FIFE RESTAUS. Gr walks from village (1879/HILL WALKS). (1907/GLEN WALKS).   NTS

1697
MAP 2
D2

✓ **CAWDOR CASTLE, CAWDOR, nr NAIRN and INVERNESS:** The mighty Cawdor of Macbeth fame. The family clear off for the summer and leave their romantic yet habitable castle, sylvan grounds and gurgling Cawdor Burn to you. Pictures from Claude to John Piper and Conroy, a modern kitchen as fascinating as the enormous one of yore. Even the 'tartan passage' is nicely done. The burn is the colour of tea. An easy drive (25km) to Brodie (1694/CASTLES) means you can see two of Scotland's most appealing castles in one day. Gdns are gorgeous. May-early Oct, 7 days, 10am-5.30pm, 9-hole golf.

1698
MAP 4
B2
✓ **BLAIR CASTLE, BLAIR ATHOLL:** Impressive from the A9, the castle and the landscape of the Dukes of Atholl (present duke not present); 10km N of Pitlochry. Hugely popular; almost a holiday camp atmos. Numbered rms chock-full of 'collections': costumes, toys, plates, weapons, stag skulls, walking sticks – so many things! Upstairs, the more usual stuffed apartments including the Jacobite bits. Walk in the policies (incl 'Hercules Gdn' with tranquil ponds). Apr-Oct 10am-6pm.

1699
MAP 4
C3
✓ **GLAMIS, FORFAR:** 8km from Forfar via A94 or off main A929, Dundee-Aber rd (t/off 10km N of Dundee, a picturesque app). Fairy-tale castle in majestic setting. Seat of the Strathmore family (Queen Mum spent her childhood here) for 300 yrs; every rm an example of the interior of a certain period. Guided tours (continuous/50mins duration). Restau/gallery shop haven for tourists. Mid Apr-mid Oct, 10am. Last admn 4.45pm. Italian Gdns & nature trail well worth 500m walk.

1700
MAP 1
C3
✓ **BRODICK CASTLE, ARRAN:** 4km from town (bike hire 01770 302868/302009). Impressive, well-maintained castle, exotic formal gdns and extensive grounds. Goat Fell in the background and the sea through the trees. Dating from 13th century and until recently home of the Dukes of Hamilton. An over-antlered hall leads to liveable rms with portraits and heirlooms, an atmos of long-ago afternoons. Tangible sense of relief in the kitchens now all the entertaining is over. Robert the Bruce's cell is not so convincing. Easter-Oct daily until 4pm (last adm). Marvellous grounds open AYR.   NTS

1701
MAP 1
B1
✓ **DUART CASTLE, MULL:** 13th-century ancestral seat of the Clan Maclean who take up residence for the summer and clan gatherings. Quite a few modifications over the centuries as methods of defence grew in sophistication but with walls as thick as a truck and the sheer isolation of the place it must have made any prospect of attack seem doomed from the outset. Of course the only attacking that gets done these days is on scones in the tearoom but some scent of the old bloodthirst still remains. May-Oct 10.30am-6pm. ☕

1702
MAP 1
B1
TOROSAY CASTLE, MULL: 3km from Craignure and the ferry. A Victorian *arriviste* in this strategic corner where Duart Castle has ruled for centuries. Not many apartments open but who could blame them – this is a family home, endearing and eccentric esp their more recent history (like Dad's Loch Ness Monster fixation). The heirlooms are valuable because they have been cherished and there's a human proportion to the house and its contents which is rare in such places. The gdns, attributed to Lorimer, are fabulous, esp the Italianate Statue Walk, and are open AYR. The Mull Light Railway from Craignure is one way to go. Tearoom. Mar-Oct 10am-6pm. Gardens AYR.

1703
MAP 2
B2
DUNVEGAN CASTLE, SKYE: 3km Dunvegan village. Romantic history and setting, though more baronial than castellate, the result of mid-19th-century restoration that incorporated the disparate parts. Necessary crowd management leads you through a series of rms where the Fairy Flag, displayed above a table of exquisite marquetry, has pride of place. Gdns down to the loch, where boats leave the jetty 'to see the seals'. Busy café and gift shop at gate side car park.

1704
MAP 2
B3
EILEAN DONAN, DORNIE: On A87, 13km before Kyle of Lochalsh. A calendar favourite, often depicted illuminated; and with the balloon hovering above, an abiding image from the BBC promo still running at TGP. Inside it's a v decent slice of history for the price. The Banqueting Hall with its Pipers' Gallery must make for splendid dinner parties for the Macraes. Much military regalia amongst the bric-a-brac, but also the impressive Raasay Punchbowl partaken of by Johnson and Boswell. Mystical views from ramparts. Apr-Oct, 10-5.30pm.

1705
MAP 4
B3
CASTLE MENZIES, WEEM, nr ABERFELDY: In Tay valley with spectacular ridge behind (there are walks here in the Weem Forest, part of the Tummel Valley Forest Park; separate car park). On B846, 7km W of Aberfeldy, through Weem. The 16th-century stronghold of the Menzies (pron 'Ming-iss'), one of Scotland's oldest clans. Sparsely furnished with odd clan memorabilia, the house nevertheless conveys more of a sense of Jacobite times than many more brimful of bric-a-brac. Bonnie Prince Charlie stopped here on the way to Culloden. Open farmland situation, so manured rather than manicured grounds. Apr-Oct 10.30am-5pm, Sun 2-5pm. Tearoom.

1706 **SCONE PALACE, nr PERTH:** On A93 rd to Blairgowrie and Braemar. A 'great
MAP 4   house', the home to the Earl of Mansfield and gorgeous grounds. Famous for
C3   the 'Stone of Scone' on which the Kings of Scotland were crowned, and the
Queen Vic bedroom. Maze and pinetum. Many contented animals greet you
and a plethora of peacocks. Easter–Oct 7days 9.30am-4.45pm (last adm.) Fri
only in wint 10am-4pm.

1707 **KELLIE CASTLE, nr PITTENWEEM, FIFE:** Major castle in Fife. Dating from 14th
MAP 5   century restored by Robert Lorimer, his influence evidenced by magnificent
C3   plaster ceilings and furniture. The gdns, nursery and kitchen recall all the old
Victorian virtues. The old-fashioned roses still bloom for us. Easter and May-
Sept 1.30-5.30pm, w/ends only Oct. Grounds open AYR.   ADMN

1708 **CRAIGIEVAR, nr BANCHORY:** 15km N of main A93 Aber-Braemar rd betw
MAP 3   Banchory and Aboyne. A classic tower house, perfect like a porcelain minia-
C3   ture. Random windows, turrets, balustrades. Set amongst sloping lawns and
tall trees. Limited access to halt deterioration (only 8 people at a time) means
you are spared the shuffling hordes, but don't go unless you are respecter of
the NTS conservation policy. Check local TICs for latest opening hrs, but probably Easter-Sept 1.30pm. Last entry 4.45pm.   NTS

1709 **DRUM CASTLE (the IRVINE ANCESTRAL HOME), nr BANCHORY:** 1km off
MAP 3   main A93 Aberdeen-Braemar rd betw Banchory and Peterculter and 20km
C3   from Aberdeen centre. For 24 generations this has been the seat of the
Irvines. Our lot! Gifted to one William De Irwin by Robert the Bruce, it
combines the original keep, a Jacobean mansion and Victorian expansionism.
I have twice signed the book in the Irvine Rm and wandered through the
accumulated history hopeful of identifying with something. Hugh Irvine, the
family 'artist' whose extravagant self-portrait as the Angel Gabriel raised eye-
brows in 1810, seems more interesting than most of my soldiering forebears.
Give me a window seat in the library! Grounds have a peaceful walled rose
gdn (Apr-Oct 10-6pm). House: Easter-Sept 1.30-5.30, Oct w/ends only. Tower
can be climbed for gr views.   NTS

1710 **BALMORAL, nr BALLATER:** On main A93 betw Ballater and Braemar. Limited
MAP 3   access to the house (i.e. only the ballrm – public functions are held here when
B3   they're in residence) so grounds (open Apr-July) with Albert's wonderful trees
are more rewarding. For royalty rooters only, and if you like
Landseers …Crathie Church along the main rd has a good rose window, an
altar of Iona marble. John Brown is somewhere in the old graveyard down
track from visitor centre, the memorial on the hill is worth a climb for a
poignant moment and the view of the policies. The Crathie services have
never been quite the same Sunday attraction since Di and Fergie on a prince's
arm.

1711 **DUNROBIN CASTLE, GOLSPIE:** The largest house in the Highlands, the home
MAP 2   of the Dukes of Sutherland who once owned more land than anyone else in
D2   the British Empire. It's the first Duke who occupies an accursed place in Scots
history for his inhumane replacement, in these vast tracts, of people with
sheep. His statue stands on Ben Bhraggie above the town (1774/MONUMENTS).
Living the life of English grandees, the Sutherlands transformed the castle
into a *château* and filled it with their obscene wealth. Once there were 100
servants for a house party of 20 and it had 30 gardeners. Now it's all just history. The gdns are still fabulous. The castle and separate museum are open
May-mid Oct. Check 01408 633177 for times. One of the few castles you might
want to raze on first sight; the motto above the windows says 'sans peur'. Gets
the pulse racing.   ADMN

CRATHES, nr BANCHORY: 1473/GARDENS; 1765/COUNTRY HOUSES.

FYVIE, ABERDEENSHIRE: 1764/COUNTRY HOUSES.

FASQUE, nr STONEHAVEN: 1756/COUNTRY HOUSES.

FLOORS CASTLE, KELSO: 1760/COUNTRY HOUSES.

TRAQUAIR, INNERLEITHEN: 1758/COUNTRY HOUSES.

THIRLESTANE, LAUDER: 1763/COUNTRY HOUSES.

THE MOST INTERESTING RUINS

HS: *Under the care of Historic Scotland. Standard hrs are: Apr-end Sept Mon-Sat 9.30am-6.30pm; Sun 2-6.30pm. Oct-Mar Mon-Sat 9.30am-4.30pm, Sun 2-4.30pm. 'Friends of Historic Scotland' membership: 0131 668 8600 or any of the manned sites (annual charge but then free admn).*

1712
MAP 7
A1

✓ ✓ ✓ **LINLITHGOW PALACE:** Impressive from the M9 and the S app to this the most agreeable of W Lothian towns, but don't confuse the magnificent Renaissance edifice with St Michael's Church next door, topped with its controversial crown and spear spire. From the richly carved fountain in the courtyard, to the Gr Hall with its adj huge kitchens, you get a real impression of the lavish lifestyle of the court. Apparently 'underperforms' as an attraction for Historic Scotland, so King's Fountain under wraps for glam restoration. HS

1713
MAP 9
C3

✓ ✓ **CAERLAVEROCK, nr DUMFRIES:** 17km S by B725. Follow signs for Wetlands Reserve (1664/BIRDS), but go past rd end. Fairy-tale fortress within double moat and manicured lawns, the daunting frontage being the apex of an uncommon triangular shape. Since 1270, the bastion of the Maxwells, the Wardens of the W Marches. Destroyed by Bruce, besieged in 1640; now with siege engine and AV voiced by Time Team's Tony Robinson. The whole castle experience. HS

1714
MAP 3
C4

✓ **DUNNOTTAR CASTLE, nr STONEHAVEN:** 3km S of Stonehaven on the coast rd just off the A92. Like Slains further N, the ruins are impressively and precariously perched on a cliff top. Historical links with Wallace, Mary Queen of Scots (the odd night) and even Oliver Cromwell, whose Roundheads besieged it in 1650. Mel Gibson's *Hamlet* was filmed here (bet you don't remember that) and the Crown Jewels of Scotland were once held here. 400m walk from car park. Can walk along cliff top from Stonehaven (2km). Mar-Oct 9am-6pm, Sun 2-5pm. Nov-Mar weekdays only 9-dusk.

1715
MAP 2
B3

✓ **CASTLE TIORAM, nr ACHARACLE:** Romantic ruin where you don't need the saga to sense the place, and maybe the mystery is better than the history. 5km from A861 just N of Acharacle. A sign on the foreshore says 'Don't get stranded'; the walk across a short causeway adds to the experience. Future of this ruin under review at TGP. Pron 'Cheerum'. Musical beach at nearby Kentra Bay (1937/COASTAL WALKS).

1716
MAP 3
B1

✓ **ELGIN CATHEDRAL, ELGIN:** Follow signs in town centre. Set in a meadow by the river, a tranquil corner of this busy market town, the scattered ruins and surrounding graveyard of what was once Scotland's finest cathedral. The nasty Wolf of Badenoch burned it down in 1390, but there are some 13th-century and medieval renewals. The octagonal chapterhouse is especially revered, but this is an impressive and evocative slice of history. Guided tours are v good. Around the corner, there's now a biblical gdn planted with species mentioned in the Bible. (May-Sept, daily). HS ADMN

1717
MAP 3
B3

✓ **KILDRUMMY CASTLE, nr ALFORD:** 15km SW of Alford on A97 nr the hotel (1239/SCOTTISH HOTELS) and across the gorge from its famous gdns. Most complete 13th-century castle in Scotland, an HQ for the Jacobite uprising of 1715 and an evocative and v Highland site. Here the invitation in HS advertising to 'bring your imagination' is truly valid. Apr-Sep 9.30am-6.30pm. HS

1718
MAP 2
A3

✓ **KISIMULL CASTLE, ISLE OF BARRA:** The medieval fortress, home of the MacNeils that sits on a rocky outcrop in the bay 200m offshore. Originally built in the 11th century, it was burnt in the 18th and restored by the 45th chief, an American architect, but was unfinished when he died in 1970. An essential pilgrimage for all MacNeils, it is fascinating and atmospheric for the rest of us, a grim exterior belying an unusual internal layout – a courtyard that seems unchanged and rms betwixt renovation and decay. Now run by HS, it's open every day in season & has a gift shop. You phone or flip board when you want to visit & they come in the boat (01871 810313). Phone for wint hrs or enq TIC. HS

1719 **EDZELL CASTLE, EDZELL:** 2km village off main st, signed. Pleasing red sand-
MAP 4   stone ruin in bucolic setting – birds twitter, rabbits run. Notable walled
D2   parterre gdn created by Sir David Lindsay way back in 1604. The wall niches
         are nice. Lotsa lobelias! Mary Queen of Scots was here (of course).   HS

1720 **BOTHWELL CASTLE, UDDINGSTON, GLASGOW:** 15km E of city via M74,
MAP 1   Uddingston t/off into main st and follow signs. Hugely impressive 13th-century
D3   ruin, the home of the Black Douglas, o/look Clyde (with fine walks). Remark-
         able considering proximity to city that there is hardly any 20th-century intru-
         sion except yourself. Pay to go inside or just sit and watch the Clyde go by.HS

1721 **FORT GEORGE, nr INVERNESS:** On promontory of Moray Firth 18km NE via
MAP 2   A96 by village of Ardersier. A vast site and 'one of the most outstanding
D2   artillery fortifications in Europe'. Planned after Culloden as a base for George
         II's army and completed 1769, it has remained unaltered ever since and allows
         a v complete picture. May provoke palpitations in the Nationalist heart, but
         it's heaven for militarists and altogether impressive. It's hardly a ruin of course,
         and is still occupied by the army.   HS

1722 **DUNOLLIE CASTLE, OBAN:** Just o/side town via Corran Esplanade towards
MAP 1   Ganavan. Best to walk to or park on Esplanade and then walk 1km. (No park-
B1   ing on main rd below castle.) Bit of a scramble up and a slither down (& the
         run itself is note 'safe), but the views are superb. More atmospheric than
         Dunstaffnage and not commercialised. You can climb one flight up, but the
         ruin is only a remnant of the gr stronghold of the Lorn Kings that it was. The
         Macdougals, who took it over in the 12th century, still live in the house below.

1723 **TARBERT CASTLE:** Tarbert, Argyll. Strategically and dramatically o/look the
MAP 1   sheltered harbour of this epitome of a West Highland pt. Unsafe to clamber
B2   over, it's for the timeless view rather than an evocation of tangible history that
         it's worth finding the way up. Steps on Harbour Rd next to dental surgery.

1724 **KILCHURN CASTLE, LOCH AWE:** The romantic ruin at the head of L Awe, vis-
MAP 1   ited either by a short walk (1km) from car park off the main A85 5km E of
C1   Lochawe village (betw the Stronmilchan t/off and the Inveraray rd) or by a
         fetching wee steamboat from Loch Awe Pierhead (by the station) – call 01838
         200440 for details. Pleasant spot for loch reflections. If you go by boat, take tea
         in the railway carriage cafe while you're waiting.

1725 **ST ANDREWS CATHEDRAL:** The ruins of the largest church in Scotland
MAP 5   before the Reformation, a place of gr influence and pilgrimage. St Rule's Tower
C2   and the jagged fragment of the huge W Front in their striking position at the
         convergence of the main streets and o/look the sea, are remnants of its gr
         glory. 7 days 9.30-6.30pm (wint 4.30). Suns 2-4.30pm.

1726 **CRICHTON CASTLE, nr PATHHEAD:** 6km W of A68 at Pathhead (28km S Edin)
MAP 7   or via A7 turning E, 3km S of Gorebridge. Massive Border keep dominating the
B1   Tyne valley on knoll with church ruin nearby. Spectacular 'range' built late
         16th century. 500m walk from Crichton village. Good picnic spots below by
         the river. Open Apr-Sept. See 405/EASY WALKS.   ADMN HS

1727 **TANTALLON CASTLE, NORTH BERWICK:** 5km E of town by coast rd; 500m to
MAP 7   dramatic cliff top setting with views to Bass Rock. Dates from 1350 with mas-
B1   sive 'curtain wall' to see it through stormy weather and stormy history. The
         Red Douglases and their friends kept the world at bay. Wonderful beach
         nearby (413/BEACHES).   ADMN HS

1728 **RUTHVEN BARRACKS, KINGUSSIE:** 2km along B970 and visible from A9 esp
MAP 2   at night when it's illuminated, these former barracks built by the English
D3   Redcoats as part of the campaign to tame the Highlands after the first
         Jacobite rising in 1715, were actually destroyed by the Jacobites in 1746 after
         Culloden. It was here that Bonnie Prince Charlie sent his final order, 'Let every
         man seek his own safety', signalling the absolute end of the doomed cause.
         Life for the soldiers is well described and visualised. Open AYR.   HS

1729 **URQUHART CASTLE, DRUMNADROCHIT, LOCH NESS:** 28km S of Inverness
MAP 2   on A82. The classic Highland fortress on a promontory o/look L Ness visited
C3   every yr by bus loads and boat loads of tourists. Photo opportunities galore
         amongst the well-kept lawns and extensive ruins of the once formidable
         stronghold of the Picts and their scions, finally abandoned in the 18th
         century. New visitor facs to cope with demand.   ADMN HS

1730 **DOUNE CASTLE, DOUNE:** Follow signs from centre of village which is just off
MAP 6 A84 Callander-Dunblane rd. O/look the R Teith, the well-preserved ruin of a
C3 late 14th-century courtyard castle with a Gr Hall and another draughty rm
where Mary Queen of Scots once slept. Nice walk to the meadow begins on
track to left of castle.
ADMN HS

1731 **SLAINS CASTLE, betw NEWBURGH and CRUDEN BAY:** 32km N of Aber off
MAP 3 the A975 perched on the cliffs. Obviously because of its location, but also
D2 because there's no reception centre/postcard shop or guided tour, this is a
ruin that talks. Your imagination, like Bram Stoker's (who was inspired after
staying here, to write Dracula), can be cast to the winds. The seat of the Earls
of Errol, it has been gradually disintegrating since the roof was removed in
1925. Once, it had the finest dining-rm in Scotland. The waves crash below, as
always. Be careful!

THE BEST PREHISTORIC SITES

1732 ✓ ✓ ✓ **SKARA BRAE, ORKNEY MAINLAND:** 32km Kirkwall by
A965/B9655 via Finstown and Dounby. Can be a windy walk to
this remarkable shoreline site, the subterranean remains of a compact village
5,000 yrs old. It was engulfed by a sandstorm 600yrs later and lay perfectly
preserved until uncovered by another storm in 1850. Now it permits one of
the most evocative glimpses of truly ancient times in the UK.
ADMN HS

1733 ✓ ✓ **THE STANDING STONES OF STENNESS, ORKNEY MAINLAND:**
Together with the Ring of Brodgar and the great chambered tomb
of Maes Howe, all within walking distance of the A965, 18km from Kirkwall, this
is as impressive a ceremonial site as you'll find anywhere. From same period as
Skara Brae. The individual stones and the scale of the Ring are v imposing and
deeply mysterious. The burial cairn is the finest megalithic tomb in the UK.
Seen together, they will stimulate even the most jaded sense of wonder.
HS

1734 ✓ ✓ **THE CALLANISH STONES, ISLE OF LEWIS:** 24km from Stornoway.
Take Tarbert rd and go rt at Leurbost. The best preserved and most
unusual combination of standing stones in a ring around a tomb, with radiat-
ing arms in cross shape. Predating Stonehenge, they were unearthed from the
peat in the mid-19th century and have become the major historical attraction
of the Hebrides. Other configurations nearby. At dawn there's nobody else
there (except camping New-Agers). Visitor centre out of sight is a good one
with a nice caff. Cl Sun. Free. ☕
HS

1735 ✓ **THE CLAVA CAIRNS nr CULLODEN nr INVERNESS:** Here long before the
MAP 2 most infamous battle in Scottish and other histories; well worth finding.
D2 Not so well marked but continue along the B9006 towards Cawdor Castle,
that other gr historical landmark (1697/CASTLES), taking a rt at the Culloden
Moor Inn and follow signs for Clava Lodge (holiday homes), picking up HS
sign to rt. Chambered cairns in grove of trees. Really just piles of stones, but
the death rattle echo from 5,000 yrs ago is perceptible to all esp when no one
else is there. Remoteness inhibits new age attentions and allows more private
meditations in this extraterrestrial spot.
HS

1736 ✓ **THE MOUSA BROCH, SHETLAND:** On small island of Mousa, off Shetland
mainland 20km S of Lerwick, visible from main A970; but to see it properly, take boat (01950 431367). Isolated in its island fastness, this is the best
preserved broch in Scotland. Walls are 13m high (originally 15m) and galleries
run up the middle, in one case to the top. Solid as a rock, this example of a
uniquely Scottish phenomenon would once have been a v des res. Also
JARLSHOF in the far S next to Sumburgh airport has remnants and ruins from
Neolithic to Viking times – 18th century, with esp impressive 'wheelhouses'.
ADMN

1737 ✓ **CRANNOG CENTRE, ABERFELDY:** Adj Croft-Na-Caber Water Sports
MAP 4 Centre on L Tay (2014/WATER SPORTS). Superb reconstruction of iron-age
B3 dwelling (there are several under the loch). Credible and worthwhile archeo-
logical project now gr for kids & conveys history well. Displays in progress and
human story told by pleasant humans. Open Apr-Oct 10am-5.30pm.

1738
MAP 1
B2

✔ **KILMARTIN GLEN, nr LOCHGILPHEAD, TEMPLEWOOD:** 2km S of Kilmartin and 1km (signed) from A816 and across rd from car park, 2 distinct stone circles from a long period of history betw 3000-1200 BC. Story and speculations described on boards. Pastoral countryside and wide skies. There are other sites in the vicinity, and an excl museum/café (MUSEUMS/2110).   HS

1739

TOMB OF THE EAGLES, ORKNEY MAINLAND: 33km S of Kirkwall at the foot of S Ronaldsay; signed from Burwick. A 'recent' discovery, the excavation of this cliff cave is on private land. You call in at the house first and they'll tell you the whole story. Then there's a 2km walk. Allow time; ethereal stuff.   ADMN

1740
MAP 7
A1

CAIRNPAPPLE HILL, nr LINLITHGOW, WEST LOTHIAN: App from the 'Beecraigs' rd off W end of Linlithgow main st. Go past the Beecraigs t/off and continue for 3km. Cairnpapple is signed. Cairn and remnants of various rings of stones evince the long sequence of ceremonial activities that took place on this high, windy hill betw 2800 and 500 BC. Atmos even more strange by the very 20th-century communications mast next door.   ADMN HS

1741
MAP 9
B3

CAIRNHOLY, between NEWTON STEWART/GATEHOUSE: 1km off main A75. Signed from rd, a pleasant walk up the glen side. A mini Callanish of standing stones around a burial cairn on v human scale and in a serene setting with another site (with chambered tomb) 150m up the farm track. Excellent view – sit and contemplate what went on 4000–6000 years ago. Farmhouse has B&B – not stayed.

1742
MAP 4
D2

THE BROWN AND WHITE CATERTHUNS, KIRKTON OF MENMUIR, nr BRECHIN: 5km uphill from war memorial at Menmuir, then signed 1km. Lay-by with obvious path to both on either side of the rd. White easiest (500m uphill). These iron-age hill top settlements give tremendous sense of scale and space and afford an impressive panorama of the Highland line. Colours refer to the heather-covered turf and stone of one and the massive collapsed ramparts of the White. The Picts, on the other hand, were blue (according to Mel Gibson).

ABERDEENSHIRE PREHISTORIC TRAIL

1743
MAP 3
C3

EAST AQUHORTHIES STONE CIRCLE, nr INVERURIE, ABERDEENSHIRE: Signed from B993 from Inverurie to Monymusk. A circle of pinkish stones with 2 grey sentinels flanking a huge recumbent stone set in the rolling country-side of the Don Valley. Look at Bennachie then wonder what they got up to … (1876/HILLS)

1744
MAP 3
C2

LOANHEAD OF DAVIOT STONE CIRCLE, nr INVERURIE, ABERDEENSHIRE: Head for the village of Daviot on B9001 from Inverurie; or Loanhead, signed off A920 rd betw Oldmeldrum and Insch. The site is 500m from top of village. Impressive and spooky circle of 11 stones and one recumbent from 4000/5000 BC. Unusual second circle adj encloses a cremation cemetery from 1500 BC. Remains of 32 people were found here. Obviously, an important place for God-knows-what rituals.

1745
MAP 3
C2

ARCHAEOLINK nr INSCH, ABERDEENSHIRE: Geographically betw the 2 sites above and within an area of many prehistoric remnants, a more recent inter-pretative centre. Impressively modern app to history both from exterior and within, where interactive and audiovisual displays bring the food hunter-gatherer past into the culture hunter-gatherer present. Up the hill, 3 adaptable staff members alternate as Iron/Bronze/Stone Age natives or visiting Romans. Apr-Oct 11am-5pm.   ADMN

1746
MAP 2
D1

THE GREY CAIRNS OF CANSTER, nr WICK: 20km S of Wick, a v straight rd (signed for Cairns) heads W from the A9 for 8km. The cairns are instantly iden-tifiable nr the rd and impressively complete. The 'horned cairn' is the best in the UK. In 2500 BC these stone-piled structures were used for the disposal of the dead. You can crawl inside them if you're agile (or at night, brave). Nearby, also signed from A9 is:

1747 **HILL O' MANY STANES, nr WICK:** Aptly named place with extraordinary
MAP 2 number of small standing stones; 200 in 22 rows. If fan shape was complete,
D1 there would be 600. Their v purposeful layout is enigmatic and strangely
stirring.

1748 **THE WHITHORN DIG, WHITHORN:** Excavation site, medieval priory, shrine of
MAP 9 St Ninian and Whithorn Dig visitor centre and café (opened 1999). More than
B3 enough to keep the whole family occupied – enthusiastic staff. Christianity in
Scotland? This was ground zero (also 1520/COASTAL VILLAGES). Easter-Oct
10.30-5pm daily.

1749 **THE MOTTE OF UR, nr DALBEATTIE:** Off B794 N of Dalbeattie and 6km from
MAP 9 main A75 Castle Douglas to Dumfries rd. Most extensive bailey earthwork cas-
C3 tle in Scotland dating from 12th century. No walls or excavation visible but a
gr sense of scale and place. Go through village of Haugh and on for 2km S.
Looking down to rt at farm buildings the minor rd crosses a ford; park here,
cross footbridge and head to rt – the hillock is above the ford.

1750 **BAR HILL, nr KIRKINTILLOCH:** A fine example of the low ruins of a Roman
MAP 1 fort on the Antonine Wall which ran across Scotland for 200 yrs early ad. Gr
D2 place for an out-of-town walk (758/VIEWS).

1751 **THE BROCHS, GLENELG:** 110km from Ft William. Glenelg is 14km from the
MAP 2 A87 at Shiel Br (1582/SCENIC ROUTES). 5km from Glenelg village in beautiful
B3 Glen Beag. The 2 brochs, Dun Trodden and Dun Telve, are the best preserved
examples on the mainland of these mysterious 1st-century homesteads. Easy
here to distinguish the twin stone walls that kept out the cold and the more
disagreeable neighbours. Free.   HS

1752 **BARPA LANYASS, NORTH UIST:** 8km S Lochmaddy, visible from main A867
MAP 2 rd, like a hat on the hill (200m away). A 'squashed' beehive burial cairn dating
A2 from 1000 BC, the tomb of a chieftain. It's largely intact and you can explore
inside, crawling through the short entrance tunnel and down through the yrs.

1753 **SUENO'S STONE, FORRES:** Signposted from Grant Pk (1507/TOWN PARKS).
MAP 3 More late Dark Age than prehistoric, a 9th or 10th C carved stone, 6m high in
A2 its own glass case. Pictish, magnificent; arguments still over what it shows.

GREAT COUNTRY HOUSES

1754 ✓ ✓ **HADDO HOUSE:** Tarves, by Ellon. 01651 851440. Designed by
MAP 3 William Adam for the Earl of Aberdeen, the Palladian-style mansion
C2 well known for its musical evenings. Not so much a house, more a leisure land
in the best poss taste, with country park to wander, a pleasant café, estate
shop and gentle education. Austere inside perhaps, but the basements are
the place to ponder. The window by Burne-Jones in the chapel is glorious. Excl
programme of events, both NTS and Haddo House Trust. ☕   NTS

1755 ✓ ✓ **MOUNT STUART, BUTE:** 01700 503877. Unique Victorian Gothic
MAP 1 house; echoes 3rd Marquis of Bute's passion for mythology, astron-
C3 omy, astrology and religion. Amazing splendour and scale, but atmos intimate
and romantic. Beautiful Italian antiques, notable paintings and fascinating
attention to detail with surprising humourous touches. Equally grand gdns,
with walks and sea views. Stylish visitor centre opened 2001 – straight out of
the pages of *Wallpaper* magazine. May-Oct 11am-4.30pm. Also open Easter
w/end and every other w/end in April. Cl Tue/Thu. ☕

1756 ✓ ✓ **FASQUE, betw STONEHAVEN and MONTROSE**: W of A92 at
MAP 3 Laurencekirk and through Victorian Fettercairn to Fasque, one of
C4 the most fascinating old houses you'll ever be permitted to wander through
on your own (or accompanied by the enthusiastic custodian). Home of
Gladstone (4 times Prime Minister) whose descendants still live in the W wing.
Shut down in 1939 till the 1970s, the world before and betw the wars was preserved and is still there for faded-grandeur connoisseurs to savour and all of
us to sense. Best is below stairs. May-Sept 7 days 11am-5.30pm. Take no
souvenirs. One of *the* best tearooms.

1757
MAP 8
D2
✓ **MANDERSTON, DUNS:** Off A6105, 2km down Duns-Berwick rd. Described as the swan-song of the Gr Classical House, one of the finest examples of Edwardian opulence in UK. All the more fascinating because the family still live there. Below stairs as fascinating as up; sublime gdns (don't miss the woodland gdn on other side of the lake, or the marble dairy). Open May-end Sept, Thu/Sun 2-5.30pm.

1758
MAP 8
B2
✓ ✓ **TRAQUAIR, INNERLEITHEN:** 01896 830323. 2km from A72 Peebles-Gala rd. Archetypal romantic Border retreat steeped in Jacobite history (ask about the Bear gates). Human proportions, liveability and lots of atmos. An enchanting house, a maze (20th cent) and tranquil duck pond in the gdn. Traquair ale still brewed. 1745 cottage tearoom, pottery and candle-making. Apr-Oct 12.30-5.30pm (opens 10.30am June-Aug). Crafty, folky fair in Aug. Woodland walks.

1758a
MAP 8
B1
✓ **NEWHAILES, MUSSELBURGH nr EDINBURGH:** 0131 653 5599. Newhailes Rd, well signed from Portobello end of Musselburgh. NTS flag-ship project 'stabilising' the microcosm of 18th cent history encapsulated here & uniquely intact. Gr rococo interiors, v liveable, esp library. A rural sanctuary nr the city. Guided tours (of 10) must be booked in advance. AYR.

1759
MAP 7
B1
GOSFORD HOUSE nr ABERLADY, EAST LOTHIAN: On A198 betw Longniddry and Aberlady, the Gosford estate is behind a high wall and strangely stunted vegetation. Imposing house with centre block by Robert Adam and the wing you visit by William Young who did Glas City Chambers. The Marble Hall houses the remarkable collections of the unbroken line of the Earls of Wemyss. Priceless art, informally displayed. Superb grounds. July only. Check local TICs.

1760
MAP 8
C2
FLOORS CASTLE, KELSO: 01573 223333. More vast mansion than old castle, the ancestral home of the Duke of Roxburghe, o/look with imposing grandeur the town and the Tweed. 18th-century with later additions. You're led round lofty public rms past family collections of fine furniture, tapestries and porce-lain. Priceless; spectacularly impractical. Good gdn centre (2080/GARDEN CEN-TRES). Annual event prog (phone for details) or floorscastle.com. ☕

1761
MAP 8
C2
MELLERSTAIN, nr GORDON/KELSO: 01573 410225. Home of the Earl of Haddington, signed from A6089 (Kelso-Gordon) or A6105 (Earlston-Greenlaw). One of Scotland's gr Georgian houses, begun by Wm Adam in 1725, completed by Robert. Outstanding decorative interiors esp the library & spectacular exterior. May-Sept 12.30-5pm (not Sat).

1762
MAP 8
D2
PAXTON, nr BERWICK: 01289 386291. Off B6461 rd to Swinton and Kelso about 6km from A1. Country park & Adam mansion with Chippendales, Trotters and a picture gallery which is an outstation of the National Gallery. They've made a very good job of the wallpapering. 80 acres woodland to walk. Restored Victorian boathouse and salmon fishing museum on the R Tweed. Tours (1hr) every 45mins, Apr-Oct 11am-5pm. Garden 10am-sunset.

1763
MAP 8
C2
THIRLESTANE, LAUDER: 01578 722430. 2km off A68. A castellate/baronial seat of the Earls and Duke of Lauderdale and family home of the Maitlands; it must take some upkeeping. Extraordinary staterooms, esp plaster work; the ceilings must be seen to be believed. In contrast, the nurseries (with toy col-lection), kitchens and laundry are more approachable. Apr-Oct 10.30am-5pm (last adm 4.15pm).

1764
MAP 3
C2
FYVIE, ABERDEENSHIRE: 40km NW Aber, an important stop on the 'Castle Trail' which links the gr houses of Aberdeenshire. Before opulence fatigue sets in, see this pleasant baronial pile first. It was lived-in until the 1980s so feels less remote than most. Fantastic roofscape and ceilings. The *best* tearoom. Tree-lined acres; loch side walks. June, July, Aug 11am-4.45pm; Sept, Oct, Apr, May 1.30-4.45 pm; cl wint.   NTS

1765
MAP 3
C3
CRATHES, nr BANCHORY: 25km W of Aber on A93. Amidst superb gdns (1473/GARDENS) a 'fairy-tale castle', a tower house which is actually interesting to visit. Up and down spiral staircases and into small but liveable rms. The notable painted ceilings and the Long Gallery at the top are all worth linger-ing over. 350yrs of the Burnett family are ingrained in this oak. Apr-Oct 11am-5.30pm. Grounds open AYR 9.30am-dusk. Excl tearm (990/NE RESTAUS). ☕

ABBOTSFORD, nr MELROSE: Home of Walter Scott (1850/LITERARY PLACES).

GREAT MONUMENTS, MEMORIALS AND FOLLIES

These sites are open at all times and free unless otherwise stated.

1766
MAP 1
A3
✓ ✓ **THE AMERICAN MONUMENT, ISLAY:** On the SW peninsula of the island, known as the Oa (pron 'Oh'), 13km from Pt Ellen. A monument to commemorate the shipwrecks in nearby waters, of 2 American ships, the *Tuscania* and the *Ontranto*, both of which sank in 1918 at the end of the war. The obelisk o/look this sea – which is often beset by storms – from a spectacular headland, the sort of disquieting place where you could imagine looking round and finding the person you're with has disappeared. Take rd from Pt Ellen past Maltings marked Mull of Oa 9km, through gate and left at broken sign. Park and walk 1.5km steadily uphill to monument. Bird life good in Oa area.   1-A-2

1767
MAP 6
C3
✓ **WALLACE MONUMENT, STIRLING:** Visible for miles and with gr views, though not as dramatic as Stirling Castle. App from A91 or Br of Allan rd. 150m walk from car park (or minibus) and 246 steps up. Victorian gothic spire marking the place where Scotland's gr patriot swooped down upon the English at the Battle of Stirling Br. Mel Gibson's *Braveheart* increased visitors though his face on the Wallace statue is thanks too far. In the 'Hall of Heroes' the new heroines section requires a feminist leap of the imagination. The famous sword is v big. Cliff top walk through Abbey Craig woods is worth detour. Monument open daily 10am-5pm (or later in summer 01786 472140), w/ends in winter till 4pm.   ADM

1768
MAP 2
B2
THE GRAVE OF FLORA MACDONALD, SKYE: Kilmuir on A855, Uig-Staffin rd, 40km N of Portree. A 10ft-high Celtic cross supported against the wind, high on the ridge o/look the Uists from whence she came. Long after the legendary journey, her funeral in 1790 attracted the biggest crowd since Culloden. The present memorial replaced the original, which was chipped away by souvenir hunters. Dubious though the whole business may have been, she still helped to shape the folklore of the Highlands.

1769
MAP 1
D3
CARFIN GROTTO, MOTHERWELL: Between Motherwell and the M8, take the B road into Carfin and it's by the Citroen dealership. Gardens and pathways with shrines, pavilion, chapel and memorials. Latest (June 2001) unveiled by Irish An Taoiseach Bertie Ahern – to those who died, suffered or emigrated during the Great Famine 1845–51. A major Catholic centre and never less than thought-provoking as the rest of us go station to station. Carfin Pilgrimage Centre adj open daily (10am-7pm May-Oct, 10am-5pm Nov-Apr). Grotto open at all times.

1770
MAP 1
D3
HAMILTON MAUSOLEUM, STRATHCLYDE PARK: Off (and visible from) M74 at jnct 5/6, 15km from Glas (1493/COUNTRY PARKS). Huge, over-the-top/over-the-tomb (though removed 1921) stone memorial to the 10th Duke of Hamilton. Guided tours daily (Easter-Sept at Wed/Sat/Sun 3pm and, even better, evenings on request; winter Wed/Sat/Sun at 2pm). Eerie and chilling and with remarkable acoustics – the 'longest echo in Europe'. Give it a shout or take your violin. Info and tickets from Hamilton Museum: 01698 328232.

1771
MAP 8
C3
PENIEL HEUGH, nr ANCRUM/JEDBURGH: (pron 'Pinal-hue'.) An obelisk visible for miles and on a rise which offers some of the most exhilarating views of the Borders. Also known as the Waterloo Monument, it was built on the Marquis of Lothian's estate to commemorate the battle. It's said that the woodland on the surrounding slopes represents the positions of Wellington's troops. From A68 opposite Ancrum t/off, on B6400, go 1km past 'Woodland Centre' up steep, unmarked rd to left for 150m. Park, walk up through woods.

1772
MAP 7
B1
THE HOPETOUN MONUMENT, ATHELSTANEFORD nr HADDINGTON: The needle atop a rare rise in E Lothian and a gr vantage point from which to view the county from the Forth to the Lammermuirs and Edinburgh over there. Off A6737 Haddington to Aberlady rd on B1343 to Athelstaneford. Car park and short climb. Tower usually open and viewfinder boards at top. Good gentle 'ridge' walk E from here.

1773 **THE PINEAPPLE, AIRTH:** From Airth N of Grangemouth, take A905 to Stirling
MAP 6 and after 1km the B9124 for Cowie. It sits on the edge of a walled gdn at the
C3 end of the drive. 45ft high, it was built in 1761 as a gdn retreat by an unknown
architect and remained 'undiscovered' until 1963. How exotic the fruit must
have seemed in the 18th century, never mind this extraordinary folly. Open
AYR; oddly enough, you can stay here (2 bedrms, 01628 825925).

1774 **THE MONUMENT ON BEN BHRAGGIE, GOLSPIE:** Atop the hill (pron
MAP 2 'Brachee') that dominates the town, the domineering statue and plinth (over
D2 35m) of the dreaded first Duke of Sutherland; there's a campaign group that
would like to see it demolished, but it survives yet. Climb from town fountain
on marked path. The hill race go up in 10mins but allow 2hrs return. His private view along the NE coast is superb (1711/CASTLES; 2105/MUSEUMS).

1775 **McCAIG'S TOWER or FOLLY, OBAN:** Oban's gr landmark built in 1897 by
MAP 1 McCaig, a local banker, to give 'work to the unemployed' and as a memorial to
B1 his family. It's like a temple or coliseum and time has mellowed whatever
incongruous effect it may have had originally. The views of the town and the
bay are magnificent and it's easy to get up from several points in town centre.
(*See* OBAN, p. 316.)

1776 **THE VICTORIA MEMORIAL TO ALBERT, BALMORAL:** Atop the fir-covered
MAP 3 hill behind the house, she raised a monument whose distinctive pyramid
B3 shape can be seen peeping over the crest from all over the estate. Desolated
by his death, the 'broken-hearted' widow had this memorial built in 1862 and
spent so much time here, she became a recluse and the Empire trembled.
Path begins at shop on way to Lochnagar distillery, 45mins up. Forget
Balmoral (1710/CASTLES), all the longing and love for Scotland can be felt here,
the gr estate laid out below.

1777 **THE PROP OF YTHSIE, nr ABERDEEN:** 35km NW city nr Ellon to W of A92, or
MAP 3 pass on the 'Castle Trail' since this monument commemorates one George
C2 Gordon of Haddo House nearby, who was prime minister 1852-55 (the good-
looking guy in the first portrait you come to in the house). Tower visible from
all of rolling Aberdeenshire around and there are reciprocal views should you
take the easy but unclear route up. On B999 Aber-Tarves rd and 2km from
entrance to house. Take rd for the Ythsie (pron 'icy') farms, 100m. Stone circle
nearby.

1778 **THE MONUMENT TO HUGH MacDIARMID, LANGHOLM:** Brilliant piece of
MAP 9 modern sculpture by Jake Harvey on the hill above Langholm 3km from A7 at
D2 beginning of path to the Malcolm obelisk from where there are gr views
(1610/VIEWS). MacDiarmid, our national poet, was born in Langholm in 1872
and, though they never liked him much after he left, the monument was commissioned and a cairn beside it raised in 1992. The bare hills surround you. The
motifs of the sculpture were used by Scotland's favourite Celtic rock band,
Runrig, on the cover of their 1993 album, *Amazing Things*.

1779 **MURRAY MONUMENT, nr NEW GALLOWAY:** Above A712 rd to Newton
MAP 9 Stewart about halfway betw. A fairly austere needle of granite to commemo-
B3 rate a 'shepherd boy', one Alexander Murray, who rose to become a professor
of Oriental Languages at Edinburgh Univ in early 19th century. 10min walk up
for fine views of Galloway Hills; pleasant waterfall nearby. Just as he,
barefoot ...

1780 **SMAILHOLM TOWER, nr KELSO and ST BOSWELLS:** The classic Border
MAP 8 tower; plenty of history and romance and a v nice place to stop, picnic what-
C2 ever. Good views. Nr main rd B6404 or off smaller B6937 – well signposted.
Open Apr-Sept 9.30am-6.30pm (Sun from 2pm). But fine to visit at any time
(1588/SCENIC ROUTES).

1781 **AIKWOOD TOWER nr SELKIRK:** 8km SE via B7009 to Ettrickbridge. Not a
MAP 8 memorial or folly but the restored 16th cent tower which is now the home of
B3 Lord David and Judy Steel. Exhib of life and times of James Hogg (1849/LITER-
ARY PLACES) and 'medieval gdn'. May-Sept Tues/Thur/Sun 2pm-5pm.

SCOTT MONUMENT, EDINBURGH: 419/VIEWS.

THE MOST INTERESTING CHURCHES

All 'generally open' unless otherwise stated; those marked (*) have public services.

1782
MAP 1
C1

✓ ✓ ***ST CONAN'S KIRK, LOCH AWE:** A85 33km E of Oban. Perched amongst trees on the side of L Awe, this small but spacious church seems to incorporate every ecclesiastical architectural style. Its building was a labour of love for one Walter Campbell who was perhaps striving for beauty rather than consistency. Though modern (begun by him in 1881 and finished by his sister and a board of trustees in 1930), the result is a place of ethereal light and atmos, enhanced by and befitting the inherent spirituality of the setting. There's a spooky carved effigy of Robert the Bruce, a cosy cloister and the most amazing flying buttresses. A place to wander and reflect.

1783
MAP 7
A1

✓ ✓ ***ROSSLYN CHAPEL, ROSLIN:** 12km S of Edin city centre. Take A702, then A703 from ring-route rd, marked Penicuik. Roslin village 1km from main rd and chapel 500m from village crossroads above Roslin Glen (402/WALKS OUTSIDE THE CITY). Freemason central and New Age fuel station: stories abound of the Holy Grail hidden in the walls and for the next few yrs there's a metal hood to protect the roof. For such a wee chapel, visitors can spend hrs wandering around working the place out with help from copious guidance notes. Founded by a 15th-century Sinclair, Prince of Orkney, who reinterred his illustrious 13th-century ancestor here (the latter just happened to be a Grand Prior of the Knights Templar). All holy meaningful stuff in a *Foucault's Pendulum* sense. But a special place. Episcopalian. Mon-Sat 10-5pm, 12-4.45pm Sun. Coffee shop.

1784

✓ ✓ **THE ITALIAN CHAPEL, ORKNEY MAINLAND:** 8km S of Kirkwall at Lamb Holm and the first causeway on the way to St Margaret's Hope. In 1943, Italian PoWs brought to work on the Churchill Barriers transformed a Nissen hut, using the most meagre materials, into this remarkable ornate chapel. The meticulous *trompe l'œil* and wrought-iron work are a touching affirmation of faith. At the other end of the architectural scale, **ST MAGNUS CATHEDRAL** in Kirkwall is a gr edifice, but also filled with spirituality.

1785
MAP B
xC1

✓ ✓ **QUEEN'S CROSS CHURCH, GLASGOW:** 870 Garscube Rd where it becomes Maryhill Rd at Springbank St. C R Mackintosh's only church. Fascinating and unpredictable in every part of its design. Some elements reminiscent of The Art School (built in the same year 1897) and others, like the tower, evoke medieval architecture. Bold and innovative, now restored and functioning as the headquarters of The Mackintosh Society. Mon-Fri 10.00am-5pm, Sat 10am-2pm, Sun 2pm-5pm. No services. (784/MACKINTOSH.)

1786
MAP 9
C2

✓ ***DURISDEER PARISH CHURCH, nr ABINGTON AND THORNHILL:** Off A702 Abington-Thornhill rd and nr Drumlanrig (1490/COUNTRY PARKS). If I lived in this village in the hills, I'd go to church more often. It's exquisite and the history of Scotland is writ on the stones. The Queensberry marbles (1709) are displayed in the N transept and there's a cradle roll and a list of ministers from the 14th century. The plaque to the two brothers who died at Gallipoli is especially touching, while Covenanter tales are writ on the gravestones.

1787
MAP 1
C3

*CATHEDRAL OF THE ISLES, MILLPORT ON THE ISLAND OF CUMBRAE: Frequent ferry service from Largs is met by bus for 6km journey to Millport. Lane from main st by Newton pub, 250m then through gate. The smallest 'cathedral' in Europe, one of Butterfield's gr works (other is Keble Coll, Oxford). Here, small is outstandingly beautiful. (1248/RETREATS; 1367/CAFÉS.)

1788
MAP 2
A2

ST CLEMENTS, RODEL, SOUTH HARRIS: Tarbert 40km. Classic island kirk in Hebridean landscape. Go by the Golden Road (1584/ROUTES). Simple cruciform structure with tower, which the adventurous can climb. Probably influenced by Iona. Now an empty but atmospheric shell, with blackened effigies and important monumental sculpture. Goats in the churchyard graze amongst the headstones of all the young Harris lads lost at sea in the Gr War. There are other fallen angels on the outside of the tower.

1789
MAP 2
A3

*ST MICHAEL'S CHAPEL, ERISKAY, nr SOUTH UIST/BARRA: That rare example of an ordinary modern church without history or grand architecture, which has charm and serenity and imbues the sense of well-being that a religious centre should. The focal pt of a relatively devout Catholic community who obviously care about it. Alabaster angels abound. O/look Sound of Barra. A real delight whatever your religion.

1790 ***ST ATHERNASE, LEUCHARS:** The parish church on a corner of what is essen-
MAP 5 tially an Air Force base spans centuries of warfare and architecture. The
C2 Norman bell tower is remarkable. If locked, key at church opp.

1791 ***ST FILLAN'S CHURCH, ABERDOUR:** Behind ruined castle in this pleasant
MAP 5 seaside village (1516/COASTAL VILLAGES), a more agreeable old kirk would be
B4 hard to find. Restored from a 12th-century ruin in 1926, the warm stonework
and stained glass create a v soothing atmos (church open at most times, but
if closed the graveyard is v fine).

1792 ***CULROSS ABBEY CHURCH:** Top of Forth-side village full of interesting
MAP 5 buildings and windy streets (1511/COASTAL VILLS). Worth hike up hill (signed
A3 'Abbey', ruins are adj) for views and this well-loved and looked-after church. Gr
stained glass (see Sandy's window), often full of flowers.

1793 ***DUNBLANE CATHEDRAL:** A huge nave of a church built around a Norman
MAP 6 tower (from David I) on the Allan Water and restored 1892. The wondrously
C2 bright stained glass is mostly 20th-century. The poisoned sisters buried under
the altar helped change the course of Scottish history.   HS

1794 ***ST MACHAR'S CATHEDRAL, ABERDEEN:** The Chanonry in 'Old Aberdeen'
MAP 3 off St Machar's Dr about 2km from centre. Best seen as part of a walk round
D3 the old 'village within the city' occupied mainly by the university's old and
modern buildings. Cathedral's fine granite nave and twin-spired W Front date
from 15th century, on site of 6th-century Celtic church. Noted for heraldic ceiling and 19/20th-century stained glass. Seaton Park adj has pleasant Don-side
walks and there's the old Brig o' Balgownie. Church open daily 9am-5pm.

1795 ***THE EAST LOTHIAN CHURCHES at ABERLADY, WHITEKIRK, ATHELSTANE-**
MAP 7 **FORD:** 3 charming churches in bucolic settings; quiet corners to explore and
B1 reflect. Easy to find. All have interesting local histories and in the case of
Athelstaneford, a national resonance – a 'vision' in the sky nr here became the
flag of Scotland, the saltire. An innovative audiovisual display explains.
Aberlady my favourite.

1796 **ABERCORN CHURCH, nr S QUEENSFERRY:** Off A904. 4 km W 11th cent kirk
MAP 7 nestling among ancient yews in a sleepy hamlet, untouched since Covenanter
A1 days. St Ninian said to have preached to the Picts here and Abercorn once on
a par with York and Lindisfarne in religious importance. Church always open.

1797 **CROICK CHURCH, nr BONAR BRIDGE:** 16km W of Ardgay, which is just over
MAP 2 the river from Bonar Br and through the splendid glen of Strathcarron
C2 (1545/GLENS). This humble and charming church is chiefly remembered for its
place in the history of the Highland clearances. In May 1845, 90 folk took shelter in the graveyard around the church after they had been cleared from their
homes in nearby Glencalvie. Not allowed even in the kirk, their plight did not
go unnoticed and was reported in *The Times*. The harrowing account is there
to read, and the messages they scratched on the windows. Sheep graze all
around.

1798 ***THOMAS COATES MEMORIAL CHURCH, PAISLEY:** Built by Coates (of
MAP 1 thread fame), an imposing edifice, one of the grandest Baptist churches in
C3 Europe. A monument to God, prosperity and the Industrial Revolution. Open
Apr-Sept Mon/Wed/Fri 2-4pm, service on Sun at 11am.

1799 ***THE LAMP OF THE LOTHIANS, ST MARY'S COLLEGIATE, HADDINGTON:**
MAP 7 Follow signs from E main st. At the risk of sounding profane or at least trite,
B1 this is a church that's really got its act together, both now and throughout
ecclesiastical history. It's beautiful and in a fine setting on the R Tyne, with
good stained glass and interesting crypts and corners. But it's obviously v
much at the centre of the community, a lamp as it were, in the Lothians.
Guided tours, brass rubbings (Sat), summer recitals (Sun afternoon). Coffee
shop and gift shop. Don't miss Lady Kitty's gdn nearby, including the secret
medicinal gdn, a quiet spot to contemplate (if not sort out) your condition.
Mon-Sat 10am-4pm. Sun 1pm-4pm.

1800
MAP 4
B3
*DUNKELD CATHEDRAL: In town centre by lane to the banks of the Tay at its most silvery. Medieval splendour amongst lofty trees. Notable for 13th-century choir and 15th-century nave and tower. Parish church open for edifying services and purposes.

1801
MAP 9
D3
RUTHWELL CHURCH, RUTHWELL: 10 miles SE Dumfries, B724 nr Clarencefield. Collect keys from Mrs Coulthard, Kirkyett House (bungalow where you turn off the main rd); she's the fount of all knowledge concerning this important building. Unique 18ft Runic Cross within Church, dating from 7th century. Carvings depict Biblical scenes with monk's inscription of 'The Holy Rood' poem. Fascinating history of its creation, preservation during the religious troubles of 1640, and subsequent restoration in 1823 by the community. Buy the guidebook from Mrs C. And some postcards!

1802
MAP 1
B2
KEILLS CHAPEL, S of CRINAN: The chapel at the end of nowhere. From Lochgilphead, drive towards Crinan, but before you get there, turn S down the B8025 and follow it for nearly 20km to the end. Park at the farm then walk the last 200m. You are 7km across the Sound from Jura, at the edge of Knapdale. Early 13thC chapel (simple) but houses some remarkable cross slabs and a 7thC cross. Wave to the ghosts.   HS

ST GILES CATHEDRAL, EDINBURGH: 393/OTHER ATTRACTIONS.

GLASGOW CATHEDRAL/UNIVERSITY CHAPEL: 729/733/MAIN ATTRACTIONS.

THE MOST INTERESTING GRAVEYARDS

1803
MAP B
xE3
✓✓ **GLASGOW NECROPOLIS:** The vast burial ground at the crest of the ridge, running down to the river, that was the focus of the original settlement of Glas. Everything began at the foot of this hill and, ultimately, ended at the top where many of the city's most famous (and infamous) sons and daughters are interred within the reach of the long shadow of John Knox's obelisk. Generally open (official times), but best if you can get the full spooky experience to yourself. Check with the TIC 0141 204 4400. (729/MAIN ATTRACTIONS.)

1804
MAP A
E2,
E3,
D3,
C1,
B2
EDINBURGH: CANONGATE: On left of Royal Mile going down to Palace. Adam Smith and the tragic poet Robert Fergusson revered by Rabbie Burns (who raised the memorial stone in 1787 over his pauper's grave) are buried here in the heart of Auld Reekie. Tourists can easily miss this one. **GREYFRIARS:** A place of ancient mystery, famous for the wee dog who guarded his master's grave for 14yrs, for the plundering of graves in the early 18th century for the Anatomy School and for the graves of Allan Ramsay (prominent poet and burgher), James Hutton (the father of geology), William McGonagall (the 'world's worst poet') and sundry serious Highlanders. Annals of a gr city are written on these stones. **WARRISTON:** Warriston Rd by B&Q or end of cul-de-sac at Warriston Cres (Canonmills), up bank and along railway line. Overgrown, peaceful, steeped in atmos. Gothic horrorland (some of those cruising guys may like that sort of thing). **DEAN** is an Edinburgh secret.

1805
MAP 1
B2
ISLE OF JURA: Killchianaig graveyard in the N. Follow rd as far as it goes to Inverlussa, graveyard is on rt, just before hamlet. Mairi Ribeach apparently lived until she was 128. In the south at Keils (2km from rd N out of Craighouse, bearing left past Keils houses and through the deer fence), her father is buried and he was 180! Both sites are beautiful, isolated and redolent of island history, with much to reflect on, not least the mysterious longevity of the inhabitants.

1806
MAP 1
B3
CAMPBELTOWN CEMETERY: Campbeltown. Odd, but one of the nicest things about this end-of-the-line town is the cemetery. It's at the end of a row of fascinating posh houses, the original merchant and mariner owners of which will be interred in the leafy plots next door. Still v much in use after centuries of commerce and seafaring disasters, it has crept up the terraces of a steep and lush overhanging bank. The white cross and row of WW2 headstones are partic affecting.

1807
MAP 1
C4
KIRKOSWALD KIRKYARD nr MAYBOLE and GIRVAN: On main rd through village betw Ayr and Girvan. The graveyard around the ruined Kirk famous as the burial place of the characters in Burns' most famous poem and a must for Burns fans and thrill seekers. Tam O'Shanter, Souter Johnnie and Kirkton Jean all lie here.

1808
MAP 7
B1
HUMBIE CHURCHYARD: Humbie, E Lothian 25km SE of Edin via A68 (t/off at Fala). This is as reassuring a place to be buried as you could wish for; if you're set on cremation, come here and think of earth. Deep in the woods with the burn besides; after-hrs the sprites and the spirits must have a hell of a time.

1809
MAP 8
C3
ANCRUM GRAVEYARD, nr JEDBURGH: The quintessential country church-yard; away from the village (2km along B6400), by a lazy river (the Ale Water) crossed to a farm by a humpback br and a chapel in ruins. Elegiac and deeply peaceful (1628/PICNICS).

1810
MAP 6
B2
BALQUHIDDER CHURCHYARD: Chiefly notable as the last resting place of one Rob Roy Macgregor who was buried in 1734 after causing a heap of trou-ble hereabouts and raised to immortality by Sir Walter Scott and Michael Caton-Jones. Despite well-trodden path, setting is poignant. For best reflec-tions head along L Voil to Inverlochlarig. Beautiful Sunday evening concerts in kirk July/Aug. (check with local TICs). Nice walk from back corner signed 'Waterfall' & gr long walk to Brig O' Turk. Tearoom in **OLD LIBRARY** in vill is cosy & couthie, with v good cakes.

1811
MAP 6
C3
LOGIE OLD KIRK, nr STIRLING: A crumbling chapel and an ancient graveyard at the foot of the Ochils. The wall is round to keep out the demons, a burn gur-gles beside and there are some fine and v old stones going back to the 16th century. Take rd for Wallace Monument off A91, 2km from Stirling, then first rt. The old kirk is beyond the new.

1812
MAP 2
C2
CHISHOLM GRAVEYARD, nr BEAULY: Last resting place of the Chisholms and 3 of the largest Celtic crosses you'll see anywhere, in a secret and atmos-pheric woodland setting. 10km S Beauly on A831 to Struy, 1km before Cnoc Hotel opp Erchless Estate and through a white iron gate on rt. Walk 250m.

1813
MAP 2
D1
TUTNAGUAIL, DUNBEATH: An enchanting cemetery 5km from Dunbeath, Neil Gunn's birthplace, and found by walking up the 'Strath' he describes in his book *Highland River* (1848/LITERARY PLACES). With a white wall around it, this graveyard, which before the clearances once served a valley community of 400 souls, can be seen for miles. Despite isolation, it's still used.

THE GREAT ABBEYS

1814
MAP 1
A1
✔ ✔ **IONA ABBEY:** This hugely significant place of pilgrimage for new age and old age pilgrims and tourists alike is reached from Fionnphort, SW Mull, by frequent Calmac Ferry (5min crossing). Walk 1km. Here in 563 BC St Columba began his mission for a Celtic Church that changed the face of Europe. Cloisters, graveyard of Scottish kings and, marked by a modest stone, the inscription already faded by the weather, the grave of John Smith, father of our Blair New World. Regular services. Good shop (2049/CRAFT SHOPS). Residential courses and retreats (MacLeod Centre adj, 01681 700404) include a 'Christmas house party' (2194/MAGICAL ISLANDS). HS

1815
MAP 3
A2
✔ ✔ **PLUSCARDEN ABBEY, betw FORRES and ELGIN:** A fully working monastic community (1246/RETREATS) in one of the most spiritual of places. Founded by Alexander II in 1250 and being restored since 1948. Benedictine services (starting with Matins at 5am through Prime-Terce-Sext-None-Vespers at 6pm and Compline at 8.05pm) open to public. The ancient honey-coloured walls, the brilliant stained glass, the monks' Gregorian chant: the whole effect is a truly uplifting experience. The bell rings down the valley. Open at all times.

1816
MAP 1
C3
✔ ✔ **PAISLEY ABBEY:** Town centre. An abbey founded in 1163, razed (by the English) in 1307 and with successive deteriorations and renova-tions ever since. Major restoration in the 1920s brought it to present-day cathedral-like magnificence. Exceptional stained glass (the recent window complementing the formidable Strachan E Window), an impressive choir and

an edifying sense of space. Sunday Services (11am, 12.15pm, 6.30pm) are superb, esp full-dress communion and there are open days (1st Sat July, 2nd Sat Sept) with coffee in the cloisters, organ music and the tower open for climbing. Otherwise Abbey open AYR Mon-Sat 10am-3.30pm. Café/shop.

1817 ✓ ✓ **JEDBURGH ABBEY:** The classic abbey ruin; conveys the most com-
MAP 8   plete impression of the Border abbeys built under the patronage of
C3   David I in the 12th century. Its tower and remarkable Catherine window are still intact. Excavations have unearthed example of a 12th-century comb. It's now displayed in the excellent visitor centre which brilliantly illustrates the full story of the abbey's amazing history. Best view from across the Jed in the 'Glebe'. Apr-Sep 9.30am-6.30pm, Oct-Mar until 4.30pm. Sun 2-4.30pm.   HS

1818 ✓ **DRYBURGH ABBEY, nr ST BOSWELLS:** One of the most evocative of
MAP 8   ruins, an aesthetic attraction since the late 18th century. Sustained innu-
C2   merable attacks from the English since its inauguration by Premonstratensian Canons in 1150. Celebrated by Sir Walter Scott, buried here in 1832 (with his biographer Lockhart at his feet), its setting, amongst huge cedar trees on the banks of the Tweed is one of pure historical romance. 4km A68. (1605/VIEWS.)
   HS

1819 **CROSSRAGUEL ABBEY, MAYBOLE:** 24km S of Ayr on A77. Built 1244, one of
MAP 1   first Cluniac settlements in Scotland, an influential and rich order, stripped in
C4   the Reformation. Now an extensive ruin of architectural distinction, the ground plan v well preserved and obvious. Open daily.   HS

1820 **SWEETHEART, NEW ABBEY nr DUMFRIES:** 12km S by A710. The endearing
MAP 9   and enduring warm red sandstone abbey in the shadow of Criffel, so named
C3   because Devorguilla de Balliol, devoted to her husband (he of the Oxford College), founded the abbey for Cistercian monks and kept his heart in a cas- ket which is buried with her here. No roof, but the tower is intact. (862/SW HOTELS.) Nice tearoom adj if you can sit out and gaze at the ruins while eating yr fruit pie.   HS

1821 **MELROSE ABBEY:** Another romantic setting, the abbey seems to give an
MAP 8   atmos to the whole town. Built by David I (what a guy!) for Cistercian monks
C2   from Rievaulx from 1136, there wasn't much left, spiritually or architecturally, by the Reformation. Once, however, it sustained a huge community, as evinced by the widespread excavations. There's a museum of abbey, church and Roman relics; soon to include Robert the Bruce's heart, recently excavat- ed in the gdns. Nice Tweed walks can start here. Same hrs as Jed.   HS

1822 **ARBROATH ABBEY:** 25km N of Dundee. Founded in 1178 and endowed on an
MAP 4   unparalleled scale, this is an important place in Scots history. It's where the
D3   Declaration was signed in 1320 to appeal to the Pope to release the Scots from the yoke of the English (you can buy facsimiles of the yellow parchment; the original is in the Scottish Records Office in Edin). It was to Arbroath that the Stone of Destiny (on which Scottish kings were traditionally crowned) was returned after being 'stolen' from Westminster Abbey in the 1950s and is now at Edinburgh Castle.   HS

1823 **FORT AUGUSTUS ABBEY:** On the site of the old 18thC fort, an abbey
MAP 2   appeared in 1876 (Benedictine) thanks to the 15th Lord Lovat. The monks
c3   were there until 1998 and in 2001 FAA opened as a visitor attraction. Wild mix of styles (v mod church) and it may have developed by the time you're read- ing this. Great history – 'Ecce lex'. And take a walk to the loch. Daily, AYR 10am-6pm.   ADMN

THE GREAT BATTLEGROUNDS

Chosen for accessibility and sense of history as well as historical significance.

1824 **CULLODEN, INVERNESS:** Signed from A9 and A96 into Inverness and about
MAP 2 8km from town. Extensive battlefield on either side of the rd before you even
D2 get to the (v full-on) visitor centre. Positions of the clans and the troops
marked out across the moor; flags enable you to get a real sense of scale. If
you go in spring you see how wet and miserable the Moor can be (the battle
took place on 16 April 1746). No matter how many other folk are there wandering down the lines, a visit to this most infamous of battlefields can still
leave a pain in the heart. Centre 9am-5.30pm (winter 10am-4pm) Cl 2 weeks
in Jan. Ground open at all times for more personal Cullodens.   NTS

1825 **BATTLE OF THE BRAES, SKYE:** 10km Portree. Take main A850 rd S for 3km
MAP 2 then left, marked 'Braes' for 7km. Monument is on a rise on rt. The last battle
B2 fought on British soil and a significant place in Scots history. When the clearances, uninterrupted by any organised opposition, were virtually complete
and vast tracts of Scotland had been depopulated for sheep, the Skye crofters
finally stood up in 1882 to the Government troops and said enough is
enough. A cairn has been erected nr the spot where they fought on behalf of
'all the crofters of Gaeldom', a battle which led eventually to the Crofters Act
which has guaranteed their rights ever since. At the end of this rd at
Peinchorran, there are fine views of Raasay (which was devastated by clearances) and Glamaig, the conical Cuillin, across L Sligachan.

1826 **GLENCOE:** Not much of a battle, of course, but one of the most infamous mas-
MAP 2 sacres in British history. Much has been written (John Prebble's *Glencoe* and
C4 others) and the new visitor centre provides audiovisual scenario. There's the
Macdonald monument nr Glencoe village and the walk to the more evocative
Signal Rock where the bonfire was lit, now a happy wood-land trail in this
doom-laden landscape. Many gr walks. (1852/SPOOKY PLACES.)

1827 **SCAPA FLOW, ORKNEY MAINLAND and HOY:** Scapa Flow, surrounded by
various of the southern Orkney islands, is one of the most sheltered anchor-
ages in Europe. Hence the huge presence in Orkney of ships and personnel
during both wars. The Germans scuttled 54 of their warships here in 1919 and
many still lie in the bay. The *Royal Oak* was torpedoed in 1939 with the loss of
833 men. Much still remains of the war yrs (especially if you're a diver,
2024/DIVING): the rusting hulks, the shore fortifications, the Churchill Barriers
and the ghosts of a long-gone army at Scapa and Lyness on Hoy. Excl 'tour' on
MV Guide with remote controlled camera exploring 3 wrecks. 01856 811360.

1828 **LILLIARD'S EDGE, nr ST BOSWELLS:** On main A68, look for Lilliard's Edge
MAP 8 Caravan Park 5km S of St Boswells; park and walk back towards St Boswells to
C3 the brim of the hill (about 500m), then cross rough ground on rt along ridge,
following tree-line hedge. Marvellous view attests to strategic location. 200m
along, a cairn marks the grave of Lilliard who, in 1545, joined the Battle of
Ancrum Moor against the English 'loons' under the Earl of Angus. 'And when
her legs were cuttit off, she fought upon her stumps'. An ancient poem etched
on the stone records her legendary … feet.

1829 **KILLIECRANKIE, nr PITLOCHRY:** The first battle of the Jacobite Risings where,
MAP 4 in July 1689, the Highlanders lost their leader Viscount (aka Bonnie) Dundee,
B2 but won the battle, using the narrow Pass of Killiecrankie. One escaping soldier
made a famous leap. Well-depicted scenario in visitor centre; short walk to 'The
Leap'. Battle viewpoint and cairn is further along rd to Blair Atholl, turning rt
and doubling back nr the Garry GH and on, almost to A9 underpass (3km from
visitor centre). You get the lie of the land from here. Many good walks.

1830 **BANNOCKBURN, nr STIRLING:** 4km town centre via Glas rd (it's well sign-
MAP 6 posted) or jnct 9 of M9 (3km), behind a rather sad hotel. Some visitors might
C3 be perplexed as to why 24 June 1314 was such a big deal for the Scots and,
apart from the 50m walk to the flag-pole and the huge statue, there's not a lot
doing. But the visitor centre does bring the scale of it to life, the horror and the
glory. The battlefield itself is thought to lie around the orange building of the
High School some distance away, and the best place to see the famous wee
burn is from below the magnificent Telford Br. Ask at centre (5km by road).

MARY, CHARLIE AND BOB

MARY QUEEN OF SCOTS 1542–87

LINLITHGOW PALACE: Where she was born (1712/RUINS).

HOLYROOD PALACE, EDINBURGH: And lived (379/MAIN ATTRACTIONS).

1831
MAP 6
B3
INCHMAHOME PRIORY, PORT OF MENTEITH: The ruins of the Priory on the island in Scotland's only lake, where the infant Queen spent her early years in the safe keeping of the Augustinian monks. Short journey by boat from quay nr lake hotel. Signal the ferryman by turning the board to the island, much as she did. Apr-Oct. 7 days. Last trip 5.15pm (3.15 Oct). Delights of the Trossachs surround you. Gr tearm nearby (1375/TEARMS) & good pub fd on way home (1292/PUB FD). HS

1832
MAP 8
C3
MARY QUEEN OF SCOTS' HOUSE, JEDBURGH: In gdns via Smiths Wynd off main st. Historians quibble but this long-standing museum claims to be 'the' house where she became ill in 1566, but somehow made it over to visit the injured Bothwell at Hermitage Castle 50km away. Tower house in good condition; displays and well-told saga. Easter-Nov 10am-3.30pm (4.30 June-Aug), Sun 1-4pm. Wint hrs vary slightly.

1833
MAP 4
C4
LOCH LEVEN CASTLE, nr KINROSS: The ultimate in romantic penitentiaries; on the island in the middle of the loch and clearly visible from the M90. Not much left of the ruin to fill out the fantasy, but this is where Mary spent 10 months in 1568 before her famous escape and her final attempt to get back the throne. Sailings Apr-Sept, 9am-6pm in small launch from Kirkgate Park. 7min trip, return as you like.

1834
MAP 9
C3
DUNDRENNAN ABBEY, nr AUCHENCAIRN and KIRKCUDBRIGHT: Mary Queen of Scots got around and there are innumerable places, castles and abbeys where she spent the night. This, however, was where she spent her last one on Scottish soil. She left next day from Pt Mary (nothing much to see there except a beach – it's 2km along the rd that skirts the sinister MoD range – the pier's long gone and … well, there's no plaque). The Cistercian abbey of Whitemonks (established 1142), which harboured her on her last night, is now a tranquil ruin. HS

'In my end is my beginning,' she said, facing her execution which came 19 yrs later.

1836
MAP 7
B1
Her 'death mask' is displayed at **LENNOXLOVE HOUSE**, nr **HADDINGTON**; it does seem on the small side for someone who was supposedly 6 feet tall!

1835
MAP 3
C3
BLAIR MUSEUM nr PETERCULTER, ABERDEEN: Recently opened museum in the old Catholic College at Blairs on the S Deeside Rd. Massive & austere former college cl 1986, empty at TGP but adj chapel a repository for religious artefacts, history of the seminary & the 'official' memorial portrait of the recently dead queen – the start of the legend. May-Oct 12-4pm cl Mon. A lock of Bonnie Prince Charlie's hair is also here (but no T-shirts).

BONNIE PRINCE CHARLIE 1720–88

1837
MAP 2
A3
PRINCE CHARLIE'S BAY, ERISKAY: The uncelebrated, unmarked and beautiful beach where Charlie first landed in Scotland to begin the Jacobite Rebellion. Nothing much has changed and this crescent of sand with soft machair and a turquoise sea is still a secret place. 1km from township heading S. (2199/MAGICAL ISLANDS.)

1838
MAP 2
B3
LOCH NAN UAMH, nr ARISAIG, THE PRINCE'S CAIRN: 7km from Lochailort on A830, 48km Ft William. Signed from the rd, a path leads down to the left. This is the 'traditional' spot (pron 'Loch Na Nuan') where Charlie embarked for France in Sept 1746, having lost the battle and the cause. The rocky headland also o/look the bay and skerries where he'd landed in July the year before to begin the campaign. This place was the beginning and the end and it has all the romance necessary to be utterly convincing. Is that a French ship out there in the mist?

1839 **GLENFINNAN:** The place where he 'raised his standard' to rally the clans to
MAP 2 the Jacobite cause. For a while on that August day in 1745 it had looked as if
B3 only a handful were coming. Then they heard the pipes and 600 Camerons
came marching from the valley (where the viaduct now spans). That must
have been one helluva moment. Though it's thought that he actually stood on
the higher ground, there is a powerful sense of place and history here. The visitor centre has an excellent map of Charlie's path/flight through Scotland –
somehow he touched all the most alluring places! Tower can be climbed. NTS

CULLODEN, nr INVERNESS: 1824/BATTLEGROUNDS.

ROBERT THE BRUCE 1274–1329

1840 **BRUCE'S STONE, GLEN TROOL, nr NEWTON STEWART:** 26km N by A714 via
MAP 9 Bargrennan (8km to head of glen) which is on the S Upland Way (1894/LONG
B3 WALKS). The fair Glen Trool is a celebrated spot in the Galloway Forest Park
(1549/GLENS). The stone is signed and marks the area where Bruce's guerrilla
band rained boulders down on the pursuing English in 1307 after they had
routed the main army at Solway Moss. Good walking, incl Merrick
(1870/HILLS).

1841 **BANNOCKBURN, nr STIRLING:** The climactic battle in June 1314, when Bruce
MAP 6 decisively whipped the English and got himself the kingdom (though
C3 Scotland was not recognised as independent until 1328, just before his
death). The scale of the skirmish can be visualised at the visitor centre, but not
so readily 'in the field' (1830/BATTLEGROUNDS).

1842 **ARBROATH ABBEY:** Not much of the Bruce trail here, but this is where the
MAP 4 famous Declaration was signed that was the attempt of the Scots nobility
D3 united behind him to gain international recognition of the independence
they had won on the battlefield. What it says is stirring stuff; the original is in
Edin (1822/ABBEYS). HS

1843 **DUNFERMLINE ABBEY CHURCH:** Here, at last, some tangible evidence, his
MAP 5 tomb. Buried in 1329, his remains were discovered wrapped in gold cloth,
A3 when the site was being cleared for the new church in 1818. Many of the
other gr kings, the Alexanders I and III, were not so readily identifiable (Bruce's
ribcage had been cut to remove his heart). With gr national emotion he was
reinterred underneath the pulpit. The church (as opposed to the ruins and
Norman nave adj) is open Apr-Sept 10am-4.30pm. Gr café in Abbot House
thro graveyard (2103/MUSEUMS). Look up & see Robert carved on the skyline.

1844 **MELROSE ABBEY:** On his deathbed Bruce asked that his heart be buried here
MAP 8 after it was taken to the Crusades to aid the Army in their battles. A likely lead
C2 casket thought to contain it was excavated from the chapter house and it did
date from the period. It was reburied here and is marked with a stone. I think
we can believe in this! HS

THE IMPORTANT LITERARY PLACES

1845 **ROBERT BURNS (1759–96), ALLOWAY, AYR AND DUMFRIES:** A well-marked
MAP 9 heritage trail through his life and haunts in Ayrshire and Dumfriesshire. His
C3 howff at Dumfries is v atmospheric. Best is at **ALLOWAY:** The Auld Brig o'
Doon and the Auld Kirk where Tam o' Shanter saw the witches dance are more
evocative than the Monument and surrounding gdns or, 1km up the rd, the
cottage (his birthplace; little atmos) and the state-of-the-art Tam o' Shanter
Experience where you are 'transported back to 18th-century Ayrshire by 20th-
century technology' (I don't think he'd have been overimpressed – the shop
here is a temple of tat).**BURNS & A' THAT** festival underway at TGP. Details TIC.

1846 **AYR:** The Auld Kirk off main st by river; graveyard with diagram of where his
MAP 1 friends are buried; open at all times. **DUMFRIES:** House where he spent his
C3 last yrs and mausoleum 250m away at back of a kirkyard stuffed with extrav-
MAP 9 agant masonry. 10km N of Dumfries on A76 at **ELLISLAND FARM** is the most
C3 interesting of all the sites. The farmhouse with genuine memorabilia e.g. his
mirror, fishing-rod, a poem scratched on glass, original manuscripts. There's his
favourite walk by the river where he composed 'Tam o' Shanter' and a strong
atmos about the place. Farmer/curator Les Byers will let you in to see when
he's at home. **BROW WELL, nr RUTHWELL** on the B725 20km S Dumfries and
nr Caerlaverock (1664/BIRDS), is a quiet place, a well with curative properties
where he went in the latter stages of his illness. Not many folk go to this one.

1847 **LEWIS GRASSIC GIBBON (1901–35), ARBUTHNOT, nr STONEHAVEN:**
MAP 3 Although James Leslie Mitchell left the area in 1917, this is where he was born
C3 and spent his formative years. Visitor centre (01561 361668; Feb-Oct 7 days
10am-4.30pm) at the end of the village (via B967, 16km S of Stonehaven off
main A92) has details of his life and can point you in the direction of the
places he writes about in his trilogy, *A Scots Quair*. The first part, *Sunset Song*,
is generally considered to be one of the gr Scots novels and this area, the
HOWE OF THE MEARNS, is the place he so effectively evokes. Arbuthnot is
reminiscent of 'Kinraddie' and the churchyard 1km away on the other side of
rd still has the atmos of that time of innocence before the war which pervades
the book. His ashes are here in a grave in a corner. From 1928 to when he died
7yrs later at the age of only 34, he wrote an incredible 17 books.

1848 **NEIL GUNN (1891–1973), DUNBEATH, nr WICK:** Scotland's foremost writer
MAP 2 on Highland life, only recently receiving the recognition he deserves, was
D1 brought up in this NE fishing village and based 3 of his greatest yarns here,
particularly *Highland River*, which must stand in any literature as a brilliant
evocation of place. The **STRATH** in which it is set is below the house (a nondescript terraced house next to the Stores) and makes for a gr walk
(1909/GLEN AND RIVER WALKS). There's a commemorative statue by the harbour,
not quite the harbour you imagine from the books. Gunn also lived for many
yrs nr **DINGWALL** and there is a memorial on the back rd to Strathpeffer and
a wonderful view in a place he often walked (on A834, 4km from Dingwall).

1849 **JAMES HOGG (1770–1835), ST MARY'S LOCH, ETTRICK:** 'The Ettrick
MAP 8 Shepherd' who wrote one of the great works of Scottish literature,
B3 *Confessions of a Justified Sinner*, was born, lived and died in the valleys of the
YARROW and the **ETTRICK**, some of the most starkly beautiful landscapes in
Scotland. **ST MARY'S LOCH** on the A708, 28km W of Selkirk: there's a com-
memorative statue looking over the loch and the adj and supernatural seem-
ing L of the Lowes. On the strip of land betw is **TIBBIE SHIELS** pub (and hotel),
once a gathering place for the writer and his friends (e.g. Sir Walter Scott) and
still a notable hostelry. Across the valley divide (11km on foot, part of the S
Upland Way 1894/LONG WALKS), or 25km by rd past the Gordon Arms Hotel is
the remote village of **ETTRICK**, another monument and his grave (and Tibbie
Shiels') in the churchyard. His countryside is stark and beautiful. The James
Hogg exhib is at Aikwood (1781/MONUMENTS).

1850 **SIR WALTER SCOTT (1771–1832), ABBOTSFORD, MELROSE:** No other place
MAP 8 in Scotland (and few anywhere) contains so much of a writer's life and work.
C2 This was the house he rebuilt from the farmhouse he moved to in 1812 in the
countryside which he did so much to popularise. The house is still lived in by
his descendants and the library and study are pretty much as he left them,

including 9,000 rare books, antiquarian even in his day. There are pleasant grounds and topiary and a walk by the Tweed which the house o/look. His grave is at **DRYBURGH ABBEY** (1818/ABBEYS). House open Apr-Oct 10am-5pm; Sun 2-5pm (in summer 10am).

1851 **ROBERT LOUIS STEVENSON (1850–94), EDINBURGH:** Though Stevenson
MAP 7 travelled widely – lived in France, emigrated to America and died and was
MAP A buried in Samoa – he spent the first 30 yrs of his short life in Edin. He was born and brought up in the New Town, living at **17 HERIOT ROW** from 1857-80 in a fashionable town house which is still lived in (not open to the public). Most of his youth was spent in this newly built and expanding part of the city in an area bounded then by parkland and farms. Both the **BOTANICS** (388/OTHER ATTRACTIONS) and **WARRISTON CEMETERY** (1804/GRAVEYARDS) are part of the landscape of his childhood. However, his fondest recollections were of the **PENTLAND HILLS** and, virtually unchanged as they are, it's here that one is following most poignantly in his footsteps. The 'cottage' at **SWANSTON** (a delightful village with some remarkable thatched cottages reached via the city bypass/Colinton t/off or from Oxgangs Rd and a br over the bypass; the village nestles in a grove of trees below the hills and is a good place to walk from), the ruins of **GLENCORSE CHURCH** (ruins even then and where he later asked that a prayer be said for him) and **COLINTON MANSE** can all be seen, but not visited. The fact is, Edinburgh has no Stevenson Museum (though his lifetime was relatively recent and his acclaim international). Pity that the **HAWES INN** in South Queensferry where he wrote *Kidnapped* has recently had its history obliterated by a brewery makeover.

IRVINE WELSH (c1958–): Literary immortality awaits confirmation. Tours (*that* toilet etc) likely any day. **ROBBIE'S BAR:** might suffice (328/'UNSPOILT' PUBS); you will hear the voices.

THE REALLY SPOOKY PLACES

1852 **HIDDEN VALLEY, GLENCOE:** The secret glen where the ill-fated Macdonalds
MAP 2 hid the cattle they'd stolen from the Lowlands and which became (with poli-
C4 tics and power struggles) their undoing. A narrow wooded cleft takes you betw the imposing and gnarled '3 Sisters' Hills and over the threshold (God knows how the cattle got there) and into the huge bowl of Coire Gabhail. The place envelops you in its tragic history, more redolent perhaps than any of the massacre sites. Park on the A82 5km from the visitor centre 300m W of 2 white buildings (one as steading) on either side of the rd (Alt-na-reigh). Cross rd and follow clear path down to and across the R Coe. Ascend keeping burn to left; 1.5km further up, it's best to ford it. Allow 3hrs. (1826/BATTLEGROUNDS.)   2-B-2

1853 **UNDER EDINBURGH OLD TOWN:** Two mentions here – Mary King's Close, a
MAP A medieval st under the Royal Mile closed in 1753; and the Vaults under North
D3 Br – built in the 18th century and sealed up around the time of the Napoleonic Wars. History underfoot for unsuspecting tourists and locals alike. Mercat Tours (0131 557 6464) will take you both places. Glimpses of a rather smelly subterranean life way back then. It's dark during the day, and you wouldn't want to get locked in. Plans afoot to develop this site at TGP.

1854 **THE YESNABY STACKS, ORKNEY MAINLAND:** A cliff top viewpoint that's so
MAP ? wild, so dramatic and, if you walk near the edge, so precarious that its super-naturalism verges on the uneasy. Shells of lookout posts from the war echo the melancholy spirit of the place. ('The bloody town's a bloody cuss/No bloody trains, no bloody bus/And no one cares for bloody us/In bloody Orkney' – first lines of a poem written then, a soldier's lament.) Nr Skara Brae, it's about 30km from Kirkwall and way out west.

1855 **THE FAIRY GLEN, SKYE:** A place so strange, it's hard to believe that it's mere-
MAP 2 ly a geological phenomenon. Entering Uig on the A855 (becomes A87) from
B2 Portree, there's a turret on the left (Macrae's Folly). Take rd on rt marked Balnaknock for 2km and you enter an area of extraordinary conical hills which, in certain conditions of light and weather, seems to entirely justify its legendary provenance. Your mood may determine whether you believe they were good or bad fairies, but there's supposed to be an incredible 365 of these grassy hillocks, some 35m high – how else could they be there?

1856 **CLAVA CAIRNS, nr CULLODEN, INVERNESS:** Nr Culloden (1824/BATTLE-
MAP 2 GROUNDS) these curious chambered cairns in a grove of trees nr a river in the
D2 middle of 21st-century nowhere can be seriously Blair Witch (1735/PREHIS-
TORIC SITES for details).

1857 **THE CLOOTIE WELL on the road betw TORE on the A9 and AVOCH:** Spooky
MAP 2 spooky place on the rd towards Avoch and Cromarty 4km from the r/bout at
C2 Tore N of Inverness. Easily missed, but it's on the rt side of the rd going E. What
you see is hundreds of rags (actually pieces of clothing) hanging on the
branches of trees around the spout of an ancient well. They go way back up
the hill behind and have probably been here for decades. Don't wish you were
here. This has what you'd call strong (but strange) vibrations.

1858 **BURN O' VAT, nr BALLATER:** This impressive and rather spooky glacial curios-
MAP 3 ity on Royal Deeside is a popular spot and well worth the short walk. 8km
B3 from Ballater towards Aberd on main A93, take A97 for Huntly for 2km to the
car park at the Muir of Dinnet nature reserve. Some scrambling to reach the
huge cavern from which the burn flows to L Kinord. Forest walks, busy on fine
weekends, but v odd when you catch it quiet.

1859 **CRICHOPE LINN, nr THORNHILL:** A supernatural sliver of glen inhabited by
MAP 9 water spirits of various temperaments (and Spanish schoolkids on the wrong
C2 day – go figure). Take rd for Cample on A76 Dumfries to Kilmarnock rd just S
of Thornhill; at village (2km) take left for 2km. Discreet sign and gate in bank
on rt is easy to miss, but quarry for parking 100m further on, on left, is more
obvious. Take care – can be very wet and very slippy. Gorge is a 10-min schlep
from the gate. More than dignity has been lost.

1860 **SALLOCHY WOOD, LOCH LOMOND:** B837, N of Balmaha, look for Sallochy
MAP 6 Wood car park on the left. Cross back over the rd, away from L Lomond, and
B3 follow the trail signs, up the hill. After the large cedar tree, the path takes you
into the woods. Slippery going (on the exposed tree roots) then an unexpected clearing in middle of dense undergrowth. This is the ruined hamlet of
Wester Sallochy. Surrounded by gloomy conifers, the roofless buildings still
stand, awaiting the return of their long-dead tenants. Not a place to visit at
night, but some do, and they leave their mark …

THE NECROPOLIS, GLASGOW: 1803/GRAVEYARDS.

HAMILTON MAUSOLEUM, STRATHCLYDE PARK: 1770/MONUMENTS.

LOANHEAD OF DAVIOT, nr OLDMELDRUM, ABERDEENSHIRE: 1744/PREHIS-
TORIC SITES.

SECTION 9

Strolls, Walks and Hikes

Popular and notable hills in the various regions of Scotland but not including Munros or difficult climbs. Always best to remember that the weather can change v quickly. Take an OS map on higher tops. See p. 11 for walk codes.

1861
MAP 2
C1

✓ ✓ **SUILVEN, LOCHINVER:** From close or far away, this is one of Scotland's most awe-inspiring mountains. The 'sugar loaf' can seem almost insurmountable, but in good weather it's not so difficult. Route from Inverkirkaig 5km S of Lochinver on rd to Achiltibuie, turns up track by Achin's Bookshop (2047/CRAFT SHOPS) on the path for the Kirkaig Falls; once at the loch, you head for the Bealach, the central waistline through an unexpected dyke and follow track to the top. The slightly quicker route from the N (Glencanisp) following a stalkers' track that eventually leads to Elphin, also heads for the central breach in the mt's defences. Either way it's a long walk in; 8km before the climb. Allow 8hrs return. At the top, the most enjoyable 100m in the land and below – amazing Assynt. 731m. Take OS map.   2-C-3

1862
MAP 2
C1

✓ ✓ **STAC POLLAIDH/POLLY, nr ULLAPOOL:** This hill described variously as 'perfect', 'preposterous' and 'gr fun', certainly has character and, rising out of the Sutherland moors on the rd to Achiltibuie off the A835 N from Ullapool, demands to be climbed. Route everyone takes is from the car park by L Lurgainn 8km from main rd. Head for the central ridge which for many folk is enough; the path to the pinnacles is exposed and can be off-putting. Best half day hill climb in the N. 613m. Allow 3-4hrs return.   2-B-3

1863
MAP 1
C3

✓ **GOAT FELL, ARRAN:** Starting from the car park at Cladach before Brodick Castle grounds 3km from town, or from Corrie further up the coast (12km). Worn path, a steady climb, rarely much of a scramble but a rewarding afternoon's exertion. Some scree and some view! 874m. Allow 5hrs.   2-B-2

1864
MAP 1
C2

✓ **THE COBBLER (BEN ARTHUR), ARROCHAR:** Perennial favourite of the Glas hill walker and, for sheer exhilaration, the most popular of 'the Arrochar Alps'. A motorway path ascends from the A83 on the other side of L Long from Arrochar (park in lay-bys nr Succoth rd end; there are always loads of cars) and takes 2.5-3hrs to traverse the up'n'down route to the top. Just short of a Munro at 881m, it has 3 tops of which the N peak is the simplest scramble (central and S peaks for climbers). Way not marked; consult.   2-B-3

FIVE MAGNIFICENT HILLS IN THE TROSSACHS

1865
MAP 6
B3

✓ **BEN VENUE and BEN AN:** 2 celebrated tops in the Highland microcosm of the Trossachs around L Achray, 15km W of Callander; strenuous but not difficult and with superb views. Ben Venue (727m) is the more serious; allow 4-5 hrs return. Start from Kinlochard side at Ledard or more usually from behind L Achray Hotel: 100m along 'Forest Path' go left and then it's waymarked. Ben An (415m) starts with a steep climb from the main A821 along from the time-share mansions. Scramble at top. Allow 2 to 3hrs.   2-B-3

1866
MAP 6
B2

BENN SHIAN, STRATHYRE: Another Trossachs favourite and not taxing. From village main rd (the A74 to Lochearnhead), cross bridge opp Monro Hotel, turn left after 200m then path to rt at 50m a steep start through woods. O/look vil-lage and views to Crianlarich and Ben Vorlich (*see below*). 600m. 1.5hrs.   2-B-3

1867
MAP 6
B3

DOON HILL, THE FAERIE KNOWE, ABERFOYLE: Legendary hillock in Aberfoyle, only 1hr up and back, so a gentle elevation into faerie land. The tree at the top is the home of the 'People of Quietness' and there was once a local minister who had the temerity to tell their secrets (in 1692). Go round it 7 times and your wish will be granted, go round it backwards at your peril (well, you wouldn't would you?). Go from end of main st and opp jnct of Trossachs/Callander rd take small rd turning left at the Covenanter.   1-B-1

1868
MAP 6
B3

BEN VORLICH: The big hill itself is also approached from the S Lochearn rd; from Ardvorlich House 5km from A84. Enter 'East Gate' and follow signs for open hillside of Glen Vorlich. Track splits after 1.5km, take right then SE side of come to N ridge of mountain. Allow 5hrs ret.   2-B-3

1869 **CRIFFEL, NEW ABBEY, nr DUMFRIES:** 12km S by A710 to New Abbey, which
MAP 9   Criffel dominates. It's only 569m, but seems higher. Exceptional views from
  C3   top as far as English lakes and across to Borders. Granite lump with brilliant
        outcrops of quartzite. The annual race gets up and back to the Abbey Arms in
        under an hr; you can take it easier. Start 3km S of village, t/off A710 by one of
        the curious painted bus shelters signed for Ardwell Mains Farm. Park before
        the farm buildings and get on up.   2-A-2

1870 **MERRICK, nr NEWTON STEWART:** Go from bonnie Glen Trool via Bargrennan
MAP 9   14km N on the A714. Bruce's Stone is there at the start (1840/MARY, CHARLIE
  B2   AND BOB). The highest peak in S Scotland (843m), it's a strenuous though
        straightforward climb in glorious scenery. 4hrs.   2-B-3

1871 **NORTH BERWICK LAW:** The conical volcanic hill, a beacon in the E Lothian
MAP 7   landscape. **TRAPRAIN LAW** nearby, is higher, tends to be frequented by rock
  B1   climbers, but has major prehistorical significance as a hillfort citadel of the
        Goddodin and a definite aura. NBL is easy and rewarding – leave town by Law
        Rd, path marked beyond houses. Car park and picnic site. Views 'to the
        Cairngorms' (!) and along the Forth.   BOTH 1-A-1

1872 **RUBERSLAW, DENHOLM, nr HAWICK:** The smooth hummock that sits above
MAP 8   the Teviot valley and affords views of 7 counties, incl Northumberland. At
  C3   424m, it's a gentle climb taking about 1hr from the usual start at Denholm Hill
        Farm (private land, be aware of livestock). Leave Denholm at corner of Green
        by shop and go past post office. Take left after 3km to farm.   2-A-2

1873 **TINTO HILL, nr BIGGAR and LANARK:** A favourite climb in S/Central
MAP 1   Scotland with easy access to start from A73 nr Symington, 10km S of Lanark.
  D3   Park 100m behind Tinto Hills farm shop, after stocking up with rolls and juice.
        Good track, though it has its ups and downs before you get there. Braw views.
        707m. Allow 3hrs.   2-A-2

1874 **CONIC HILL, BALMAHA, LOCH LOMOND:** An easier climb than the Ben up
MAP 6   the rd and a good place to view it from, Conic, on the Highland fault line, is
  B3   one of the first Highland hills you reach from Glas. Stunning views also of L
        Lomond from its 358m peak. Ascend thro woodland from the corner of
        Balmaha car park. Watch for buzzards and your footing on the final crumbly
        bits. May be closed for lambing season Apr-May. 1.5hrs up.   2-A-2

1875 **KINNOULL HILL, PERTH:** Various starts from town (the path from beyond
MAP 4   Branklyn Gdn on the Dundee Rd is less frequented) to the wooded ridge
  C3   above the Tay with its tower and incredible views to S from the precipitous
        cliffs. Surprisingly extensive area of hill side common and it's not difficult to
        get lost. The leaflet/map from Perth TIC helps. Local lurv spot after dark. 1-A-1

1876 **BENNACHIE, nr ABERDEEN:** The pilgrimage hill, an easy 528m often busy at
MAP 3   w/ends but never a let-down. Various trails take in 'the Taps'. Trad route from
  C3   Rowan Tree nr Chapel of Garioch (pron 'Geery') signed Pittodrie off A96 nr
        Pitcaple. Also from Essons car park on rd from Chapel-Monymusk, which is
        steeper. Or from other side the Lord's Throat rd, a longer, more forested app
        from banks of the Don. All car parks have trail-finders. From the fortified top
        you see what Aberdeenshire is about. 2hrs. Bennachie's soulmate, **TAP O'**
        NOTH, is 20km W. Easy app via Rhynie on A97 (then 3km).   2-B-2

1877 **DUNADD, KILMARTIN, N of LOCHGILPHEAD:** 8km N on A816. Less of a hill,
MAP 1   more of a lump, but it's where they crowned the kings of Dalriada for half a
  B2   millennium. Stand on top when the Atlantic rain is sheeting in and … you get
        wet like the kings did. Kilmartin House Museum nearby for info & gr food
        (2110/MUSEUMS).   2-B-2

The following ranges of hills offer walks in various directions and more than one summit. They are all accessible and fairly easy. See p. 12 for walk codes.

1878
MAP 2

WALKS ON SKYE: Obviously many serious walks in and around the Cuillins (1890/MUNROS, 1898/SERIOUS WALKS), but almost infinite variety of others. Can do no better than read a gr book, *50 Best Routes on Skye and Raasay* by Ralph Storer (avail locally), which describes and grades many of the must-dos.

1879
MAP 5
B3

LOMOND HILLS, FIFE, nr FALKLAND: The conservation village lies below a prominent ridge easily reached from the main st esp via Back Wynd (off which there's a car park). More usual app to both E and W Lomond, the main tops, is from Craigmead car park 3km from village towards Leslie trail-finder board. The celebrated Lomonds (aka the Paps of Fife), aren't that high (West is 522m), but they can see and be seen for miles. Also start from radio masts up rd from A912 E of Falkland.   3-10KM CIRC XBIKES 2-A-2

An easy rewarding single climb is **BISHOP'S HILL**. Start opp the church in Scotlandwell. A steep path veers left and then there are several ways up. Allow 2hrs. Gr view of L Leven, Fife and a good swathe of Central Scotland. Gliders glide over from the old airstrip below.

1880
MAP 8
C2

THE EILDONS, MELROSE: The 3 much-loved hills or paps visible from most of the Central Borders and easily climbed from the town of Melrose which nestles at their foot. Leave main sq by rd to stn (the Dingleton rd), after 100m a path begins betw 2 pebble-dash houses on the left. You climb the smaller first, then the highest central one (422m). You can make a circular route of it by returning to the golf course. Allow 1.5hrs.   3KM CIRC XBIKES I-A-2

1881
MAP 6
D3

THE OCHILS: Usual app from the 'hillfoot towns' at the foot of the glens that cut into their S-facing slopes, along the A91 Stirling-St Andrews rd. Alva, Tillicoultry and Dollar all have impressive glen walks easily found from the main streets where tracks are marked (1905/GLEN AND RIVER WALKS). Good start nr Stirling from the Sheriffmuir rd uphill from Br of Allan or steep rd from the old graveyard (1811/GRAVEYARDS), both about 3km, look for pylons and a lay-by on the rt (a reservoir just visible on the left). There are usually other cars here. A stile leads to the hills which stretch away to the E for 40km and afford gr views for little effort. Highest point is Ben Cleugh, 721m. Swimming place nearby is Paradise (1629/PICNICS).   2-40KM SOME CIRC XBIKES 1/2-B-2

1882
MAP 7
B2

THE LAMMERMUIRS: The hills SE of Edin that divide the rich farmlands of E Lothian and the valley of the Tweed in the Borders. Mostly a high wide moor land but there's wooded gentle hill country in the watersheds of the southern rivers and spectacular coastal scenery betw Cockburnspath and St Abbs Head. (1682/WILDLIFE; 1936/COASTAL WALKS.) The eastern part of the S Upland Way follows the Lammermuirs to the coast (1894/LONG WALKS). Many moorland walks begin at the car park at the head of Whiteadder Reservoir (A1 to Haddington, B6369 towards Humbie, then E on B6355 through Gifford), a mysterious loch in the bowl of the hills. Excellent walks also centre on Abbey St Bathans to the S – head off A1 at Cockburnspath. Through village (1620/TEAROOMS) to Toot Corner (signed 1km) and off to left, follow path above valley of Whiteadder to Edinshall Broch (2km). Further on, along river (1km), is a swing bridge and a fine place to swim (1520/PICNICS). Circular walks possible; ask in village.   5-15KM SOME CIRC MTBIKES 1/2-B-2

1883
MAP 8
D3

THE CHEVIOTS: Not strictly in Scotland, but they straddle the border and Border history. There are many fine walks starting from Kirk Yetholm (incl the Pennine Way which stretches 400km S to the Peak district and St Cuthbert's Way; 1897/LONG WALKS) incl an 8km circular route of typical Cheviot foothill terrain. See 'Walking in the Scottish Borders' avail from all Border TICs (an excl guide). Most forays start at Wooler 20km from Coldstream and the border. Cheviot itself (2,676ft) a boggy plateau, Hedgehope via the Harthope Burn more fun.

THE CAMPSIE FELLS, nr GLASGOW: 749/WALKS OUTSIDE THE CITY.

THE PENTLAND HILLS, nr EDINBURGH: 400/WALKS OUTSIDE THE CITY.

SOME GREAT MUNROS

There are almost 300 hills in Scotland over 3,000ft as tabled by Sir Hugh Munro in 1891. Munro-bagging is popular and numerous books give route details. The Munros selected here have been chosen for their relative ease of access both to the bottom and thence to the top. They all offer rewarding climbs. None should be attempted without proper clothing (esp boots) and sustenance. You may also need an OS map. The weather can change quickly in the Scottish mts.

1884
MAP 6
B3
BEN LOMOND, ROWARDENNAN, LOCH LOMOND: Many folk's first Munro, given proximity to Glas (soul and city). It's not too taxing a climb and has rewarding views (in good weather). 2 main ascents: 'tourist route' is easier, from toilet block at Rowardennan car park (end of rd from Drymen), well-trodden all the way; or 500m up past Youth Hostel, a path follows burn – the 'Ptarmigan Route'. Circular walk poss. 974m. 3hrs up.

1885
MAP 2
C2
AN TEALLACH, TORRIDON: Sea-level start from Dundonnell on the A832 S of Ullapool, so easy to find. This, one of the most awesome peaks in Scotland is not the ordeal it looks. Path well trod and once up there are gr scrambling opportunities for the nimble. Peering over the pinnacle of Lord Berkeley's Seat down to L na Sheaallag is a jaw-drop. Take a day (a good day). 1,062m.

1886
MAP 2
B2
BEINN ALLIGIN, TORRIDON: The other gr Torridon trek – you may as well go for it! Car park by br on rd to Inveralligin and Diabeg, walk thro woods over moor by tumbling river. Left at fork then a steepish pull up onto the Horns of Alligin. You can cover 2 Munros in a circular route that takes you across the top of the world, up there with mighty Liathach and Beinn Eighe. 985m.

1887
MAP 1
B1
BEN MORE, MULL: The 'cool, high ben' sits in isolated splendour, the only Munro, bar the Cuillins, not on the mainland. Sea-level start from lay-by on the coast rd B8073 that skirts the southern coast of L Na Keal at Dhiseig House, then a fairly clear path through the bleak landscape. Can be slightly tricky nr the top (don't think about it without good boots), but there are fabulous views across the islands. 966m.

1888
MAP 2
C2
BEN WYVIS, nr GARVE: Standing apart from its northern neighbours, you can feel the presence of this mt from a long way off. Just to N of main A835 rd from Inverness-Ullapool and v accessible from it, park 6km N of Garve (48km from Inverness) and follow marked path by stream and through the forest. Vast plantations all around but you leave them behind and the app to the summit is by a soft and mossy ridge. Magnificent 1,046m.

1889
MAP 3
B4
LOCHNAGAR, nr BALLATER: Described as a fine, complex mt, its nobility and mystique apparent from afar, not least Balmoral Castle. App via Glen Muick (pron 'Mick') rd from Ballater to car park at L Muick (1574/LOCHS). Path to mt well signed and well trodden. 18km return, allow 6-8hrs. Steep at top. Apparently on a clear day you can see the Forth Br. 1,155m.

1890
MAP 2
B3
BLA BHEINN, SKYE: The magnificent massif, isolated from the other Cuillins, has a sea-level start and seems higher than it is. The *Munro Guide* describes it as 'exceptionally accessible'. It has an eerie jagged beauty and – though some scrambling is involved and it helps to have a head for exposed situations – there are no serious dangers. Take B8083 from Broadford to Elgol thro Torrin, park 1km S of the head of L Slapin, walking W at Allt na Dunaiche along N bank of stream. Bla Bheinn (pron 'Blahven') is an enormously rewarding climb. Rapid descent for scree runners, but allow 8hrs. 928m.

1891
MAP 4
A3
BEN LAWERS, between KILLIN and ABERFELDY, PERTHSHIRE: The massif of 7 summits includes 6 Munros that dominate the N side of L Tay. They are linked by a twisting ridge 12km long that only once falls below 800m and, if you're v fit, it's poss to do the lot in a single day starting from the N or Glen Lyon side. The Munro beginner or non-bagger should start and plan route at the visitor centre 5km off the A827 nr Lawers.

1892
MAP 4
A3
MEALL NAN TARMACHAN: The part of the ridge to the W of Lawers (above), which takes in a Munro and several tops, is not arduous and is immensely impressive. In 3hrs you can get up, along some of it and back, and feel gr for the rest of the week. Start 1km further on from NTS visitor centre down 100m track and through gate. Head up into saddle, paths indistinct, but just climb. At the top the path becomes clear, as does your reason for being here.

LONG WALKS

Once again, these walks require preparation, route maps, v good boots etc. But don't carry too much. Sections are always poss. See p. 12 for walk codes.

1893 **THE WEST HIGHLAND WAY:** The 150km walk which starts at Milngavie 12km
MAPS o/side Glas and goes via some of Scotland's most celebrated scenery to
1, 2 emerge in Glen Nevis before the Ben. The route goes: Mugdock
Moor-Drymen-L Lomond-Rowardennan-Inversnaid-Inverarnan-Crianlarich-
Tyndrum-Br of Orchy-Rannoch Moor-Kingshouse Hotel-Glencoe-The Devil's
Staircase-Kinlochleven. The latter part from Br of Orchy is the most dramatic.
The Br of Orchy Hotel (01838 400208) (1181/ROADSIDE INNS) and Kingshouse
(01855 851259), both historic staging posts, are recommended, as is the
Drover's Inn, Inverarnan (877/CENTRAL HOTELS). It's a good idea to book accom
(allowing time for muscle fatigue) and don't take too much stuff. Info
leaflet/pack from shops or Ranger Service (01389 722600).

MAP 1 **START:** Officially at Milngavie (pron 'Mull-guy') Railway Stn (reg service from
D2 Glas Central, also buses from Buchanan St Bus Stn), but actually from
Milngavie shopping precinct (Douglas St) 500m away; an inauspicious ramp
down to Allander River by the side of Victoria Wine and then behind Mackay's
clothes shop. However, the countryside is close. Start from other end 1km
down Glen Nevis rd from r/bout on A82 N from Ft William. Way is well marked,
but you must have a route map.   2-B-3

1894 **THE SOUTHERN UPLAND WAY:** 350km walk from Portpatrick S of Stranraer
MAP 9 across the Rhinns of Galloway, much moorland, the Galloway Forest Park, the
A3 wild heartland of Southern Scotland, then through James Hogg country
(1849/LITERARY PLACES) to the gentler E Borders and the sea at Pease Bay (offi-
cial end, Cockburnspath). As long as there's no foot and mouth of course.
Route is Stranraer-New Luce-Dalry-Sanquhar-Wanlockhead-Beattock-St
Mary's L-Melrose-Lauder-Abbey St Bathans. The first and latter sections are
the most obviously picturesque but highlights include L Trool, the Lowther
Hills, St Mary's L, R Tweed. Usually walked W to E, the SU Way is a formidable
undertaking … (Info from Ranger Service: 01835 830281).

START: Portpatrick by the harbour and up along the cliffs past the lighthouse.
or Cockburnspath. Map is on side of shop at Cross.   2-B-3

1895 **THE SPEYSIDE WAY:** A long distance route which generally follows the valley
MAP 3 of the R Spey from Buckie on the Moray Firth coast to Aviemore in the
foothills of the Cairngorms (there are plans to complete the route to
Newtonmore in the next couple of years), with side spurs to Dufftown up Glen
Fiddich (7km) and to Tomintoul over the hill between the R Avon (pron 'A'rn')
and the R Livet (24km). The main stem of the route largely follows they valley
bottom, criss-crossing the Spey several times – a distance of around 100km,
and is less strenuous than SU or WH Ways. The Tomintoul spur has more hillwalking character and rises to a gr viewpoint at 600m. Throughout walk you
are in whisky country with opportunities to visit Cardhu, Glenlivet and other
distilleries nearby (1468/WHISKY). Info from Ranger Service: 01340 881266.

START: Usual start is from coast end. Spey Bay is 8km N of Fochabers; the first
marker is by the banks of shingle at the river mouth.   1-A-3

1896 **GLEN AFFRIC:** In enchanting Glen Affric and L Affric beyond (1904/GLEN AND
MAP 2 RIVER WALKS; 1541/GLENS; 1623/PICNICS), some serious walking begins on the
C3 32km Kintail trail. Done either W-E starting at the Morvich Outdoor Centre
2km from A87 nr Shiel Br, or E-W starting at the Affric Lodge 15km W of
Cannich. Route can include one of the approaches to the Falls of Glomach
(1552/WATERFALLS).   2-C-3

1897 **ST CUTHBERT'S WAY:** From Melrose in Scottish Borders (where St Cuthbert
MAP 8 started his ministry) to Lindisfarne on Holy Island off Northumberland (where
C2 he died). 100km but many sections easy. Bowden–Maxton a stroll by the
Tweed esp fine. Check local TICs.   2-A-3

None of these should be attempted without OS maps, proper equipment and preparation. Hill or ridge walking experience may be essential.

1898
MAP 2
B3
THE CUILLINS, SKYE: Much scrambling and, if you want it, serious climbing over these famously unforgiving peaks. The Red ones are easier and many walks start at the Sligachan Hotel on the main Portree-Broadford rd. Every July there's a hill race up Glamaig; the conical one which o/look the hotel. Most of the Black Cuillins incl the highest, Sgurr Alasdair (993m), and Sgurr Dearg, 'the Inaccessible Pinnacle' (978m), can be attacked from the campsite or the youth hostel in Glen Brittle. Good guides are *Introductory Scrambles from Glen Brittle* by Charles Rhodes, or *50 Best Routes in Skye and Raasay* by Ralph Storer both available locally, but you will need something. Take extreme care! (2/BIG ATTRACTIONS; 1174/1175/HOSTELS; 1555/WATERFALLS; 1890/MUNROS; 1615/PICNICS.)   3-C-3

1899
MAP 2
C4
AONACH EAGACH, GLENCOE: One of several poss major expeditions in the Glencoe area and one of the world's classic ridge walks. Not for the faint-hearted or the ill-prepared. It's the ridge on your rt for almost the whole length of the glen from Altnafeadh to the visitor centre (where you might consult over the route). Start from the main rd and once you're up and have hopped across, do resist the descent from the last summit (Sgorr nam Fiannaidh) to the welcoming bar of the Clachaig Hotel. On your way, you'll have come close to heaven, seen Lochaber in its immense glory and recon-noitred some fairly exposed edges and pinnacles. As I've said before, go with somebody good. (1581/SCENIC ROUTES; 1270/BLOODY GOOD PUBS; 1172/ HOS-TELS; 1826/BATTLEGROUNDS.)   3-C-3

1900
MAP 2
C3
BEN NEVIS: Start on Glen Nevis rd, 5km Ft William town centre by br opp youth hostel or from visitor centre (4km town) over br and past Achintee Farm (gentler start). These paths lead to the same main route which continues to the top (many consider the tourist route to be v dull, but it is the safest). Allow the best part of a day (and I do mean the best – the weather can turn quickly here). Many people are killed every yr, even experienced climbers. It is the biggest, though not the best; you can see 100 Munros on a clear day (i.e. about once a yr.) You climb it because … well, because you have to. Go pre-pared (but you can hire boots etc on Glen rd).   2-B-3

1901
MAP 2
C3
THE FIVE SISTERS OF KINTAIL and THE CLUANIE RIDGE: Both generally started from A87 along from Cluanie Inn (1267/BLOODY GOOD PUBS) and they will keep you rt; usually walked E to W. Sisters is an uncomplicated but inspir-ing ridge walk, taking in 2 Munros and 2 tops. It's a hard pull up and you descend to a point 8km further up the rd (so arrange transport). Many side spurs to vantage-points and wild views. The Cluanie or S ridge is a classic which covers 7 Munros. Starts at inn; 2 ways off back onto A876. Both can be walked in a single day (Cluanie allow 9hrs). (1173/HOSTELS.)   3-C-3

From the Kintail Centre at Morvich off A87 nr Shiel Br another long distance walk starts to Glen Affric (1896/LONG WALKS).

1902
MAP 2
D3
GLEN MORE FOREST PARK: from Coylumbridge and L Morlich; 32km. (2) joins (3) beyond L Morlich and both go through the Rothiemurchus Forest (1923/WOODLAND WALKS) and the famous **LAIRIG GHRU**, the ancient Rt of Way through the Cairngorms which passes betw Ben Macdui and Braeriach. Ascent is over 700m and going can be rough. This is one of the gr Scottish trails. At end of June, the Lairig Ghru Race completes this course E-W in 3.5hrs, but generally this is a full-day trip. The famous shelter, Corrour Bothy betw 'Devil's Point' and Carn A Mhaim, can be a halfway house. Nr Linn of Dee, routes (1) and (2/3) converge and pass through the ancient Caledonian Forest of Mar. Going E-W is less gruelling and there's Aviemore to look forward to!

GLEN AFFRIC: Or rather beyond Glen Affric and L Affric (1904/GLEN WALKS; 1541/GLENS), the serious walking begins (1896/LONG WALKS).

GLEN AND RIVER WALKS

See also GREAT GLENS, *p. 198. Walk codes are on p. 11.*

1903 **GLEN TILT, BLAIR ATHOLL:** A walk of variable length in this classic Highland
MAP 4 glen, easily accessible from the old Blair Rd off main Blair Atholl rd nr Bridge
B2 of Tilt Hotel, car park by the (v) old bridge. Trail leaflet from park office and
local TICs. Fine walking and unspoiled scenery begins only a short distance
into the deeply wooded gorge of the R Tilt, but to cover the circular route it's
necessary to walk to 'Gilbert's Br' (9km return) or the longer trail to Gow's Br
(17km return). Begin here also the gr route into the Cairngorms leading to the
Linn of Dee and Braemar, joining the track from Speyside which starts at
Feshiebridge or Glenmore Forest (1902/SERIOUS WALKS).

UP TO 17KM CIRC XBIKE 1-B-2

1904 **GLEN AFFRIC, CANNICH, nr DRUMNADROCHIT:** Easy short walks are
MAP 2 marked and hugely rewarding in this magnificent glen well known as the first
C3 stretch in the gr E-W route to Kintail (1901/SERIOUS WALKS) and the Falls of
Glomach (1552/WATERFALLS). Starting pt of this track into the wilds is at the
end of the rd at L Affric; there are many short and circular trails indicated here.
Car park is beyond metal rd 2km along forest track towards Affric Lodge (cars
not allowed to lodge itself). Track cl in stalking season. Easier walks in famous
Affric forest from car park at Dog Falls. 7km from Cannich (1623/PICNICS).
Waterfalls and spooky tame birds. Good idea to hire bikes at Drumnadrochit
or Cannich (01456 415251). Don't miss Glen Affric (1541/GLENS).

5/8KM CIRC BIKE 1-B-2

1905 **DOLLAR GLEN, DOLLAR, nr STIRLING:** The classic fairy glen in Central
MAP 6 Scotland, positively hoaching with water spirits, reeking of ozone and euphor-
D3 ic after rain. 20km from Stirling by A91, or 18km from M90 at Kinross jnct 6.
Start from top of tree-lined ave on either side of burn or from further up rd
signed Castle Campbell where there's a car park and a path down into glen.
The Castle at head of glen is open 7 days till 6pm (Oct-Mar till 4pm), and has
boggling views. There's a circular walk back or take off for the Ochil Tops, the
hills that surround the glen. There are also first-class walks (the hill trail is more
rewarding than the 'Mill Trail') up the glens of the other hillfoot towns, Alva
and Tillicoultry; they also lead to the hills (1881/HILL WALKS).

3KM + TOPS CIRC XBIKE 1-A-2

1906 **RUMBLING BRIDGE, nr DOLLAR:** Formed by another burn running off the
MAP 6 same hills, an easier short walk in an Ochil Glen with something of the chas-
D3 mic experience and the added delight of the unique double br (built 1713).
There's a pt here at the end of one of the walkways under the br where you
are looking into a Scottish jungle landscape as the Romantics imagined. Nr
Powmill on A977 from Kinross (jnct 6, M90) then 2km. Nearby is **BRIDGE
BYGONES**, an antique/coffee shop (w/ends till 5pm) and esp **THE POWMILL
MILKBAR** serving excellent home-made food for 40 yrs. It's 5km W on the
A977. Open 7 days till 5pm (6pm weekends) (1377/TEAROOMS). Go after your
walk! 3KM CIRC XBIKE 1-A-1

1907 **FALKLAND, FIFE:** If you're in Falkland for the Palace (1696/CASTLES) or the tea-
MAP 5 room (1397/TEAROOMS), this short amble up an enchanting glen should be
B3 added to your afternoon. Head thro vill for Falkland Estate and School (an
activity centre for visiting groups) – you can take a car into the estate signed
'Cricket Club' – and gdns are behind it. Glen and path are obvious. Gushing
burn, waterfalls – you can even walk behind one of them! Good café/restau in
vill (938/FIFE RESTAUS). 3KM CIRC XBIKE 1-A-2

1908 **THE BIG BURN WALK, GOLSPIE:** A non-taxing, perfect little glen walk
MAP 2 through lush diverse woodland. Variations poss, but start just beyond
D2 Sutherland Arms (1031/HIGHLAND INEXP HOTELS) in the garage yard which is
just off the A9 before Dunrobin Castle. Go past derelict mill and under aqueduct following river. A real supernature trail unfolds with ancient tangled
trees, meadows, waterfalls, cliffs and much wildlife. 3km to falls, return via
route to castle woods for best all-round intoxication. 6KM CIRC XBIKE 1-B-1

1909 **THE STRATH at DUNBEATH:** The glen or strath so eloquently evoked in Neil
MAP 2 Gunn's *Highland River* (1848/LITERARY PLACES), a book which is as much about
D1 the geography as the history of his childhood. A path follows the river for
many miles. A leaflet from the Dunbeath Heritage Centre points out places on
the way. It's a spate river and in summer becomes a trickle; hard to imagine
Gunn's salmon odyssey. It's only 500m to the broch, but it's worth going into
the hinterland where it becomes quite mystical (1813/GRAVEYARDS).   1-A-1

1910 **TWEEDSIDE, PEEBLES:** The river side trail that follows the R Tweed from town
MAP 8 (Hay Lodge Park) past Neidpath Castle (1619/PICNICS) and on through classic
B2 Border wooded countryside crossing river either 2.5km out (5km round trip),
at Manor Br 6km out (Lyne Footbr, 12km). Pick up 'Walking in the Scottish
Borders' at local TIC.   5/12KM CIRC XBIKE 1-A-1

Other good Tweedside walk between Dryburgh Abbey and Bemersyde
House grounds and at Newton St Boswells by golf course.

1911 **GLEN LEDNOCK, nr COMRIE:** Can walk from Comrie or take car further up to
MAP 4 monument or drive further into glen to reservoir (9km) for more open walks.
B3 From town take rt off main A85 (to Lochearnhead) at Deil's Cauldron restau.
Walk and Deil's Cauldron (waterfall and gorge) are signed after 250m. Walk
takes less than 1hr and emerges on rd nr Lord Melville's monument (climb for
gr views back towards Crieff, about 25 mins). Other walks up slopes to left
after you emerge from the tree-lined gorge rd.   3/5KM CIRC XBIKE 1-A-1

1912 **BRIDGE OF ALVAH, BANFF:** Details: 1927/WOODLAND WALKS, mentioned here
MAP 3 because the best bit is by the river and the br itself. The single span crossing
C1 was built in 1772 and stands high above the river in a sheer-sided gorge. The
river below is deep and slow. In the rt light it's almost Amazonian.

1913 **THE GANNOCHY BRIDGE AND THE ROCKS OF SOLITUDE, nr EDZELL:** 2km
MAP 4 N of village on B966 to Fettercairn. There's a lay-by after br and a wooden door
D2 in wall. Through it is another green world and a path above the rocky gorge
of the R North Esk (1km). Huge sandstone ledges over dark peaty pools. You
don't have to be alone (well maybe you do).   2KM XCIRC XBIKE 1-A-1

1914 **Nr TAYNUILT:** A walk (recommended by readers) which takes in education
MAP 1 with recreation. It goes via Bonawe Ironworks (2118/MUSEUMS) and L Etive
C1 along the river side to a swing br and thence to Inverawe Smokehouse (open
to the public; café). Walk back less interesting but all v nice. Ask in Taynuilt for
start.   10 KM CIRC BIKE 1-A-1

WOODLAND WALKS

1915 **RANDOLPH'S LEAP nr FORRES:** Tricky to explain how to find this spectacu-
MAP 3 lar gorge of the plucky little Findhorn lined with beautiful beechwoods and a
A2 gr place to swim or picnic (1621/PICNICS), so listen up. Go either: 10km S of
Forres on the A940 for Grantown, then the B9007 for Ferness and Carrbridge.
1km from the sign for Logie Steading (2149/BUY ART) and 500m from the narrow stone br, there's a pull-over place on the bend. The woods are on the
other side of the rd. Or: take the A939 S from Nairn or N from Grantown and
at Ferness take the B9007 for Forres. Approaching from this direction, it's
about 6km along the rd; the pull-over is on your rt. If you come to Logie
Steading you've missed it; don't – you will miss one of the sylvan secrets of
the N.

1916 **LOCHAWESIDE:** Unclassified rd on N side of loch betw Kilchrenan and Ford
MAP 1 centred on Dalavich. Illustrated brochure available from local hotels around
B2, C2 Kilchrenan and Dalavich post office, describes 6 walks in the mixed, mature
forest all starting from car parking places on the rd. 3 starting from the
Barnaline car park are trail-marked and could be followed without brochure.
Avich Falls route crosses R Avich after 2km with falls on return route. Inverinan
Glen is always nice. The track from the car park N of Kilchrenan on the B845
back to Taynuilt isn't on the brochure, may be less travelled and also fine. The
pub at Kilchrenan is a cracker (1271/PUBS).   2-8KM CIRC XBIKE 2-A-2

1917 **PUCK'S GLEN nr DUNOON:** Close to the gates of the Younger Botanic
MAP 1 Garden at Benmore (1471/GARDENS) on the other side of the A815 to Stracher
C2 12km N of Dunoon. A short, exhilarating woodland walk from a convenient

car park. Ascend thro' trees then down into a faery glen, foll the burn back to the rd. Some swimming pools.   3KM CIRC XBIKE 1-A-1

1918 **ROTHIEMURCHUS FOREST, nr AVIEMORE:** The place to experience the
MAP 2 magic and the majesty of the gr Caledonian Forest and the beauty of Scots
D3 pine. App from B970, the rd that parallels the A9 from Coylumbridge to
Kincraig/Kingussie. 2km from Inverdruie nr Coylumbridge follow sign for L an
Eilean; one of the most perfect lochans in these or any woods. Loch circuit
5km (1569/LOCHS). Good free brochure for all forest activities from TICs.

1919 **ARIUNDLE OAKWOODS:** Strontian. 35km Ft William via Corran Ferry. Walk
MAP 2 guide brochure at Strontian TO. Many walks around L Sunart and Ariundle:
B3 rare oak and other native species. You see how v different Scotland's landscape was before the Industrial Revolution used up the wood. Start over town
br, turning rt for Polloch. Go on past Cosy Knits, with good home-baking café
and park. 2 walks; well marked.   5KM CIRC MTBIKE 1-A-2

1920 **BALMACARRA, LOCHALSH WOODLAND GARDEN:** 5km S Kyle of Lochalsh
MAP 2 on A87. A woodland walk around the shore of L Alsh, centred on Lochalsh
B3 House. Mixed woodland in fairly formal gdn setting where you are confined
to paths. Views over to Skye. A fragrant and verdant amble.
                                                                   KM CIRC XBIKE 1-A-1

1921 **THE BIRKS O' ABERFELDY:** Circular walk through oak, beech and the birch (or
MAP 4 birk) woods of the title, easily reached and signed from town main st (1km).
B3 Steep-sided wooded glen of the Moness Burn with attractive falls esp the
higher one spanned by br where the 2 marked walks converge. This is where
Burns 'spread the lightsome days' in his eponymous poem.
                                                                   3KM CIRC XBIKE 1-A-2

1922 **THE HERMITAGE, DUNKELD:** On A9 2km N of Dunkeld. Popular, easy, accessi-
MAP 4 ble walks along the glen and gorge of R Braan with pavilion o/look the Falls
B3 and, further on, 'Ossian's Cave'. Also uphill Craig Vean walks starts here to good
view pt (2km). Several woody walks around Dunkeld/Birnam – good leaflet
from TIC.   2KM CIRC XBIKE 1-A-1

1923 **GLENMORE FOREST PARK, nr AVIEMORE:** Along from Coylumbridge (and
MAP 2 adj Rothiemurchus) on rd to ski resort, the forest trail area centred on L
D3 Morlich (sandy beaches, good swimming, water sports). Visitor centre has
maps of walk and bike trails and an activity programme.

1924 **ABOVE THE PASS OF LENY, CALLANDER:** A walk through mixed forest
MAP 6 (beech, oak, birch, pine) with gr Trossachs views. Start from main car park on
C2 A84 4km N of Callander (the Falls of Leny are on opp side of rd, 100m away)
on path at back, to the left – path parallels rd at first (don't head straight up).
Way-marked and boarded where marshy, the path divides after 1km to head
further up to crest (4km return) or back down (2km).
                                                           2 OR 4KM CIRC XBIKE 1-A-2

1925 **LOCH TUMMEL WALKS, nr PITLOCHRY:** The mixed woodland N of L Tummel
MAP 4 reached by the B8019 from Pitlochry to Rannoch. Visitor centre at Queen's
B2 View (1608/VIEWS) and walks in the Allean Forest which take in some historical sites (a restored farmstead, standing stones) start nearby (2-4km). There
are many other walks in area and the Forest Enterprise brochure is worth following (available from visitor centre and local TICs). (1578/LOCHS.)

1926 **THE NEW GALLOWAY FOREST:** Huge area of forest and hill country with
MAP 9 every type and length of trail incl section of S Upland Way from Bargrennan
B3 to Dalry (1894/LONG WALKS). Visitor centres at Kirroughtree (5km Newton
Stewart) and Clatteringshaws L on the 'Queen's Way' (9km New Galloway)
with easy routes around them. Glen and L Trool are v fine (1549/GLENS); the
'Retreat Oakwood' nr Laurieston has 5km trails. Kitty's in New Galloway has
great cakes and tea (1385/TEAROOMS). There's a river pool on the Raiders' Rd
(1627/PICNICS). One could ramble on …

1927 **DUFF HOUSE, BANFF:** Duff House itself is the major attraction around here
MAP 3 (2132/PUBLIC GALLERIES), but if you've time it would be a pity to miss the wood-
C1 ed policies and the meadows and riverscape of the Deveron. An illustrated
map on the back of the free brochure for the house (available from local TICs)
shows the route. To the Br of Alva where you should be bound is about 7km
return. See also 1912/GLEN AND RIVER WALKS.

1928 **TORRACHILTY FOREST and ROGIE FALLS nr CONTIN and STRATHPEFFER:**
MAP 2 Enter by old br just o/side Contin on main A835 W to Ullapool or further along
C2   (4km) at Rogie Falls car park. Shame to miss the falls (11565/WATERFALLS), but
the woods and gorge are pleasant enough if it's merely a stroll you need. Ben
Wyvis further up the rd is the big challenge (1888/MUNROS).

1929 **ABERNETHY FOREST nr BOAT OF GARTEN:** 3km from village off B970, but
MAP 2 hard to miss because the famous ospreys are signposted from all over
D3   (1670/BIRDS). Nevertheless this woodland reserve is a tranquil place among
native pinewoods around the loch with dells and trails. Many other birdies
twittering around your picnic. They don't dispose of the midges.

1930 **FOCHABERS** on main A98 about 3km E of town are some excellent woody
MAP 3 and winding walks around the glen and Whiteash Hill (2-5km). Further W on
B2   the **MORAY COAST: CULBIN FOREST** – head for Cloddymoss or Kentessack
off A96 at Brodie Castle 12km E of Nairn. Acres of Sitka in sandy coastal forest.

WHERE TO FIND SCOTS PINE

*Scots pine, along with oak and birch etc, formed the gr Caledonian Forest which
once covered most of Scotland. Native Scots pine is v different from the regimented rows of pine trees that we associate with forestry plantations and which now
drape much of the countryside. It is more like a deciduous tree with reddish bark
and irregular foliage; no two ever look the same. The remnants of the gr stands of
pine that are left are beautiful to see, mystical and majestic, a joy to walk among
and no less worthy of conservation perhaps than a castle or a bird of prey. Here
are some places you will find them:*

ROTHIEMURCHUS FOREST: 1918/WOODLAND WALKS.

GLENTANAR, ROYAL DEESIDE: Nr Ballater, 10-15km SW of Aboyne.

Around Braemar and **GRANTOWN-ON-SPEY**.

STRATHYRE, nr CALLANDER: S of village on rt of main rd after L Lubnaig.

ACHRAY FOREST, nr ABERFOYLE: Some pine nr the Duke's Pass rd, the A821
to L Katrine, and amongst the mixed woodland in the 'forest drive' to L Achray.

BLACKWOOD OF RANNOCH: S of L Rannoch, 30km W of Pitlochry via
Kinloch Rannoch. Start from Carie, fair walk in. 250-year-old pines; an important site.

ROWARDENNAN, L LOMOND: End of the rd along E side of loch nr Ben
Lomond. Easily accessible pines nr the loch side, picnic sites etc.

Shores of **LOCH MAREE** and around **LOCH CLAIR, GLEN TORRIDON:** Both nr
the **BEINN EIGHE NATIONAL NATURE RESERVE** (1684/GREAT WILDLIFE
RESERVES). Visitor Centre on A832 N of Kinlochewe.

GLEN AFFRIC, nr DRUMNADROCHIT: 1541/GLENS. Biggest remnant of the
Caledonian Forest in classic glen. Many strolls and hikes poss. Try Dog Falls (on
main rd) for Affric introduction.

*Native pinewoods aren't found S of Perthshire, but there are fine plantation
examples in southern Scotland at:*

GLENTRESS, nr PEEBLES: 7km on A72 to Innerleithen. Mature forest up the
burn side, though surrounded by commercial forest.

SHAMBELLIE ESTATE, nr DUMFRIES: 1km from New Abbey beside A710 at
the Shambellie House, 100yds sign. Ancient stands of pine over the wall
amongst other glorious trees; this is like virgin woodland. Planted 1775–1780.
Magnificent.

1931
MAP 1
A3
✔ ✔ **KINTRA, ISLAY:** On Bowmore-Pt Ellen rd take Oa t/off: then Kintra signed 7km. Good restau/bar with B&B in season, a place to camp (1223/HIGHLAND CAMPING), a fabulous beach (1526/BEACHES) which runs in opp direction and a notable golf course behind it (1961/GOLF IN GREAT PLACES). This walk leads along N coast of the Mull of Oa, an area of diverse beauty, sometimes pastoral, sometimes wild, with a wonderful shoreline. In café a detailed route map has been annotated with pictures. ANY KM XCIRC XBIKE 2-B-2

1932
MAP 3
D2
✔ ✔ **THE BULLERS OF BUCHAN, nr PETERHEAD:** 8km S of Peterhead on A975 rd to/from Cruden Bay. Park and walk 100m to cottages. To rt is precarious and spectacular cliff top walk to Cruden Bay (3km), to left the walk to Longhaven Nature Reserve, a continuation of the dramatic cliffs and more sea bird city. The Bullers is at start of walk, a sheer-sided 'hole' 75m deep with an outlet to the sea thro a natural arch. Walk round the edge of it, looking down on layers of birds (who might try to dive-bomb you away from their nests); it's a wonder of nature on an awesome coast. Take gr care.

1933
MAP 2
C1
✔ ✔ **CAPE WRATH and the CLIFFS OF CLO MOR:** Britain's most NW point reached by ferry from 1km off the A838 4km S of Durness by Cape Wrath Hotel; a 10min crossing then 40min minibus ride to Cape. Ferry holds 14 and runs May-Sept (check TIC at Durness for times: 01971 511259). At 280m Clo Mor are the highest cliffs in UK; 4km round trip from Cape. MoD range – access may be restricted. In other direction, the 28km to Kinlochbervie is one of Britain's most wild and wonderful coastal walks. Beaches incl Sandwood (1524/BEACHES). While in this NW area: **SMOO CAVE** 2km E of Durness.

1934
MAP 2
C1
OLD MAN OF STORR, nr LOCHINVER: The easy, exhilarating walk to the dramatic sea stack, 3km from lighthouse off unclassified rd 14km N Lochinver. Park and follow sheep tracks; cliffs are high and steep. 1-B-2

1935
MAP 9
C3
ROCKCLIFFE TO KIPPFORD: An easy stroll along the 'Scottish Riviera' through woodland nr the shore (2km) past the 'Mote of Mark' a Dark Age hill ft with views to Rough Island. The better cliff top walk is in the other direction to Castlepoint, but Kippford has The Anchor to look forward to (1310/BEST FOOD; 1514/COASTAL VILLAGES) (1394/TEAROOMS).

1936
MAP 8
D1
ST ABBS HEAD: The most dramatic coastal scenery in S Scotland, scary in a wind, rhapsodic on a blue summer's day. Extensive wildlife reserve and trails through coastal hills and vales to cliffs. Cars can go as far as lighthouse, but best to park at visitor centre nr farm on St Abbs village rd 3km from A1107 to Eyemouth and follow route (1682/WILDLIFE). 5-10KM CIRC XBIKE 1-B-2

1937
MAP 2
B3
SINGING SANDS, ARDNAMURCHAN: Park at Arivegaig 3km Acharacle and cross wooden br, following track round side of Kentra Bay. Follow signs for Gorteneorn, and walk through forest track and woodland to beach. As you pound the sands they should 'sing' to you whilst you bathe in the the beautiful views of Rum, Eigg, Muck and Skye (and just possibly the sea). Check at TIC for directions and other walks booklet. 10KM RET XCIRC BIKE 1-B-1

1938
MAP 3
B1
EAST FROM CULLEN on the MORAY COAST: This is the same walk mentioned with reference to Sunnyside (1439/BEACHES), a golden beach with a fabulous ruined castle (Findlater) that might be your destination. There's a track E along from harbour. 2hrs return. Superb coastline. 8KM XCIRC XBIKE 1-A-1

1939
MAP 2
D2
CROMARTY, THE SOUTH SUTOR: The walk, known locally as 'The 100 Steps' although there are a few more than that, from Cromarty village (1510/COASTAL VILLAGES; 1396/TEAROOMS) round the tip of the S promontory at the narrow entrance to the Cromarty Firth. E of vill; coastal path hugs shoreline then ascends thro' woodland to headland. Good bench! Go further to top car park and viewpt panel. Return by rd. There may be dolphins out there! 5KM CIRC XBIKE 1-A-1

1940
MAP 5
C3
THE CHAIN WALK, ELIE: Unique and adventurous headland scramble at the W end of Elie (and Earlsferry), by golf course. Hand- and footholds carved into rock with chains to haul yourself up. Watch tide; don't go alone. 2-B-2

SECTION 10

Sports

SCOTLAND'S GREAT GOLF COURSES

Those listed open to non-members and available to visitors (incl women) at most times, unless otherwise stated. Handicap certificates may be required.

AYRSHIRE (MAP 1)

1941
C4 ✓ ✓ ✓ **TURNBERRY:** 01655 331000. Ailsa (championship) and Arran. Sometimes poss by application. Otherwise you must stay at hotel. (833/AYRSHIRE HOTELS.) Superb.

1942
C3 ✓ ✓ **ROYAL OLD COURSE, TROON:** V difficult to get on. No wimmen. Staying at Marine Highland Hotel (01292 314444) helps. Easier is **THE PORTLAND COURSE:** Across rd from Royal. Both 01292 311555. And 839/AYRSHIRE HOTELS for the adj Piersland House Hotel.

1943
C3 ✓ **GLASGOW GAILES/WESTERN GAILES:** 01294 311347/311649. Superb links courses next to one another, 5km S of Irvine off A78.

1944
C3 **OLD PRESTWICK:** 01292 477404. Original home of the Open and 'every challenge you'd wish to meet'. Hotels opp (eg the Golf View 01292 671234) cost less than a round. Unlikely to get on w/ends.

EAST LOTHIAN (MAP 7)

Note: There is a gr booklet available at the local TIC, entitled 'Golf in East Lothian'.

1945
B1 ✓ ✓ **GULLANE NO.1:** 01620 842255. One of 3 varied courses surrounding charming village on links and within driving distance (35km) of Edin. Muirfield is nearby, but you need intro. Gullane is okay most days except Sat/Sun. (Handicap required for no.1 only – under 24 men, 30 ladies.) No.3 best for beginners. Visitor centre acts as clubhouse for non-members on nos. 2/3. Clubhouse for members/no.1 players only.

1946
B1 ✓ ✓ **NORTH BERWICK EAST AND WEST:** E (officially the Glen Golf Club) has stunning views. A superb cliff-top course and is not too long, 01620 892726/892135. W more taxing (esp the classic 'Redan') used for Open qualifying; a v fine links. Also has 9-hole kids' course, 01620 892666.

1947
B1 **MUSSELBURGH:** The original home of golf (really: golf recorded here in 1672), but this local authority-run 9-hole links is not exactly top turf and is enclosed by Musselburgh Racecourse. Nostalgia still appeals though. 0131 665 6981. **ROYAL MUSSELBURGH** nearby compensates. It dates to 1774, fifth-oldest in Scotland. Busy early mornings and Fri-Sun, 01875 810139.

NORTH-EAST (MAPS 2 and 3)

1948
MAP 4
D3 ✓ ✓ **CARNOUSTIE:** 01241 853789. 3 good links courses; even poss (with handicap cert) to get on the championship course (though w/ends difficult). Every hole has character. Buddon Links is cheaper and often quiet. Combination tickets available. A well-managed and accessible course, increasingly a golfing must.

1949
MAP 3
D3 ✓ **MURCAR, ABERDEEN:** 01224 704354. Getting on Royal Aber Course is difficult for most people, but Murcar is a testing alternative, a seaside course 6km N of centre off Peterhead rd signed at r/bout after Exhibition Centre. Handicap cert needed. Municipal courses at Hazlehead (vary and ish conditions).

1950
MAP 3
D2 ✓ **CRUDEN BAY, nr PETERHEAD:** 01779 812285. On A975 40km N of Aber. Designed by Tom Simpson and ranked in UK top 50, a spectacular links course with the intangible aura of bygone days. Quirky holes epitomise old-fashioned style. W/ends difficult to get on.

1951
MAP 2
D2 ✓ **NAIRN:** 01667 452787. Traditional seaside links course and one of the easiest championship courses to get on. Good clubhouse, friendly folk. Nairn Dunbar on other side of town also has good links. Hand cert reqd.

1952
MAP 2
D2 ✓ **ROYAL DORNOCH:** 01862 810219. Sutherland championship course laid out by Tom Morris in 1877. Amongst top 10 courses in UK, but not busy or incessantly pounded. No poor holes. Stimulating sequences. Probably the most northerly gr golf course in the world – and not impossible to play.

1953 ✔ ✔ ✔ **ST ANDREWS:** 01334 466666. The home and Mecca of golf, v
C2 much part of the town (2257/HOLIDAY CENTRES) and probably
the largest golf complex in Europe. Old Course most central, celebrated.
Application by ballot the day before (handicap cert needed). For Jubilee
(1897, upgraded 1989) and Eden (1914, laid out by Harry S. Holt paying
homage to the Old with large, sloping greens), apply the day before. New
Course (1895, some rate the best) easiest access. Less demanding are the new
Strathtyrum and Balgove (upgraded 9-hole for beginners) courses. All 6 courses contiguous and 'in town'; the newish Dukes Course (part of Old Course
Hotel) is 3km away. Reservations (and ballot) 01334 466666. A whole lot of
golf to be had – get your money out!

1954 ✔ **LADYBANK:** 01337 830814. Best inland course in Fife; Tom Morris-
B2 designed again. V well kept and organised. Good facs. Tree-lined and picturesque.

1955 **ELIE:** Book 01333 330301. Splendid open links maintained in top condition;
C3 can be windswept. The starter has his famous periscope and may be watching you. Adj 9-hole course, often busy with kids, is fun. (01333 330955)

1956 **CRAIL:** 01333 450636. Balcomie Links originally designed by the legendary
D2 Tom Morris, or Craighead Links new sweeping course. All holes in sight of sea.
Not exp; easy to get on.

1957 **LUNDIN LINKS:** 01333 320202/ladies 320832. Challenging seaside course
C3 used as Open qualifier. Some devious contourings. There is a separate course
for women. (01333 320022)

ELSEWHERE

1958 ✔ ✔ ✔ **GLENEAGLES:** 0800 704705. Legendary golf the mainstay of
MAP 4 resort complex in perfect Perthshire (hotel 01764 662231
B3 report 1140/CO-HOUSE HOTELS). 3 courses incl PGA centenary which will host
Ryder Cup in 2014. No handicap certs reqd.

1959 ✔ ✔ **LOCH LOMOND GOLF CLUB, LUSS:** 01436 655555. On A82 1km
MAP 1 from conservation village of Luss. Exclusive American-owned club;
C2 membership only £25,000! (List closed.) We can buy a cheaper season ticket
to see the annual World Invitational tournament (early July; tickets 08705
661661); but no access to plebs to clubhouse. 18 holes of scenic golf by the
Loch. This is golfing for gold.

1960 ✔ ✔ **ROXBURGHE HOTEL GOLF COURSE nr KELSO:** 01573 450331. Only
MAP 8 championship course in the Borders. Designed by Dave Thomas
C2 along banks of R Teviot. Part of the Floors Castle estate. Open non-res.
Fairways bar/brasserie clubhouse. Details (887/BORDER HOTS).

GOOD GOLF COURSES IN GREAT PLACES

All open to women, non-members and inexpert players.

1961 ✔ **MACHRIE:** 01496 302310. Isle of Islay. 7km Pt Ellen. Worth going to Islay
MAP 1 (BA's airstrip adj course or Calmac ferry from Kennacraig nr Tarbert) just
A3 for the golf. The Machrie (Golf) Hotel does deals. Old-fashioned course to be
played by feel and instinct. Splendid, sometimes windy isolation with a warm
bar and restau at the end of it. The notorious 17th, 'Iffrin' (it means Hell), vor-
tex shaped from the dune system of marram and close-cropped grass, is one
of many gr holes. 18.

1962 ✔ **MACHRIHANISH:** 01586 810213. By Campbeltown (10km). Amongst the
MAP 1 dunes and links of the glorious 8km stretch of the Machrihanish Beach
B3 (1523/BEACHES). The Atlantic provides thunderous applause for your triumphs
over a challenging course. 9/18.

1963 ✔ **SOUTHERNESS, SOLWAY FIRTH:** 01387 880677. 25km S of Dumfries by
MAP 9 A710. A championship course on links on the silt flats of the Firth. Despite
C3 its prestige, visitors do get on. 10-12pm and 2-4pm. Under the wide Solway
sky, it's pure – southerness. 18.

1964 **ROSEMOUNT, BLAIRGOWRIE:** 01250 872622. Off A93, S of Blairgowrie.
MAP 4 ✓ An excellent, pampered and well-managed course in the middle of green
C3 Perthshire, an alternative perhaps to Gleneagles, being much easier to get on
(most days) and rather cheaper (though not at w/ends). 18.

1965 **BOAT OF GARTEN:** 01479 831282. Challenging, picturesque course in
MAP 2 ✓ town where ospreys have been known to wheel overhead. Has been called
D3 the 'Gleneagles of the North'; certainly best around, tho not for novices. 18.

1966 **GLENCRUITTEN, OBAN:** 01631 562868. Picturesque course on the edge of
MAP 1 town. Head S (A816) from Argyll Sq, bearing left at church. Course is signed.
B1 Quite tricky with many blind holes. Can get busy, so phone first. 18.

1967 **GAIRLOCH:** 01445 712407. Just as you come into town from the S on A832, it
MAP 2 looks over the bay and down to a perfect, pink, sandy beach. Small clubhouse
B2 with honesty box. Not the world's most agonising course; in fact, on a clear
day with views to Skye, you can forget agonising over anything. 9.

1968 **HARRIS GOLF CLUB, SCARISTA, ISLE OF HARRIS:** 01859 502331 (the cap-
MAP 2 tain, but no need to phone). Just turn up on the rd betw Tarbert and Rodel
A2 and leave £7 in the box. First tee commands one of the gr views in golf and
throughout this basic, but testing course, you are looking out to sea over
Scarista beach (1529/BEACHES) and bay. Sunset may put you off your swing.

1969 **NEW GALLOWAY:** Local course on S edge of this fine wee toon. Almost all on
MAP 9 a slope but affording gr views of L Ken and the Galloway Forest behind. No
B3 bunkers and only 9 short holes, but exhilarating play. Easy on, except Sun. Just
turn up. Clubs can be hired at The Smithy coffee shop in the village.

1970 **MINTO, DENHOLM:** 01450 870220. 9km E Hawick. Spacious parkland in
MAP 8 Teviot valley. Best holes 3rd, 12th & 16th. **VERTISH HILL, HAWICK:** 01450
C3 372293. A more challenging hill course. Both among the best in Borders. 18.
Best holes 2nd & 18th. An excl guide to all the courses in the Borders in avail
from TICs – 'Freedom of the Fairways'.

1971 **TAYMOUTH CASTLE, KENMORE:** 01887 830228. Spacious green acres
MAP 4 around the enigmatic empty hulk of the castle. Well-tended and organised
B3 course betw A827 to Aberfeldy and the river. Inexp, and guests at the
Kenmore Hotel (951/PERTHSHIRE HOTELS) get special rate. 18.

1972 **GIFFORD:** 01620 810591. Dinky inland course on the edge of a dinky village,
MAP 7 bypassed by the queue for the big E Lothian courses and a guarded secret
B1 among the regulars. Generally ok, but phone starter (above) for avail. 9.

1973 **STRATHPEFFER:** 01997 421011. V hilly (and we do mean hilly) course full of
MAP 2 character and with exhilarating Highland views. Small-town friendliness. You
C2 are playing up there with the gods and some other old codgers. 18.

1974 **ELGIN:** 01343 542884. 1km from town on A941 Perth rd. Many memorable
MAP 3 holes on moorland/parkland course in an area where links may lure you to
B1 the coast (Nairn, Lossiemouth). 18.

1975 **DURNESS:** 01971 511364. The most N golf course on mainland UK, on the
MAP 2 wild headland by Balnakeil Bay, looking over to Faraid Head. The last hole is
C1 'over the sea'. Only open since 1988, it's already got cult status. 2km W Durness.

1976 **ROTHESAY:** 01700 503554. Sloping course with breathtaking views of Clyde.
MAP 1 Visitors welcome. What could be finer than taking the train from Glas to
C3 Wemyss Bay for the ferry over (5/FAVOURITE JOURNEYS) and 18 holes. Finish up
with fish 'n' chips at The W End (1359/FISH AND CHIPS) on the way home.

1977 **TRAIGH, ARISAIG:** 01687 450337. A830 Ft William-Mallaig rd, 2km N Arisaig.
MAP 2 Pronounced 'try'- and you may want to. The islands are set out like stones in
B3 the sea around you and there are 9 hilly holes of fun.

BEST OF THE SKIING

*In a good yr the Scottish ski season can extend from Dec (or even Nov) till the 'lambing snow' of late April. And on a good day it can be as exhilarating as anywhere in Europe. Here's a summary (**distances in kilometres**):*

	GLENSHEE	CAIRNGORM	AONACH MOR	GLENCOE	THE LECHT
DIST/EDIN	130	215	215	165	200
DIST/GLASGOW	170	235	200	150	160
NR CENTRE	Perth 65	Inverness 45	Ft Will 10	FT Will 40	Aberdeen 95
NR TOWN	Braemar 20	Aviemore 15	Ft Will 10	Ballachulish 20	Tomintoul 11
NO OF RUNS	38	19	35	17	21
EASY	10	3	7	3	7
INTERMED	13	6	12	6	7
DIFFICULT	13	9	11	6	6
ADVANCED	2	1	5	2	1
NO OF TOWS	26	17	12	7	14
CAFÉS	3	2	3 + units	2	1 + 1 unit
GOOD FOR	*Size*	*Size*	*Uplift*	*Fewer crowds*	*Fewer crowds*
	Access from rd	*Non-skiing*	*Access*	*Nr road*	*Nr road*
	Views Glas Maol	*Views*	*Views/Sunsets*	*Views*	*Families*
	2 distinct areas	*Intermediate*	*Ski School*	*Most alpine*	*Beginners*
	Snowboarding	*Snowboarding*	*Café*		

1978 GLENSHEE
MAP 4
C2

BASE STATION: 013397 41320. **SCHOOL:** 01250 885 216 or 0870 443 0253 or 01339 741320.

WHERE TO STAY

DALMUNZIE HOUSE HOTEL: 01250 885 224. 9km S. Country house. Golf. Family-run. MED.EX

BRIDGE OF CALLY HOTEL: 01250 886231. 36km S (1197/INNS). **GLENISLA, KIRKTON OF GLENISLA:** 01575 582223. 32km SE. INX

SPITTAL OF GLENSHEE: 01250 885215. 8km S. Cheap'n'cheerful. MED.INX

WHERE TO EAT

CARGILL'S BISTRO, BLAIRGOWRIE: 01250 876735 (964/PERTHSHIRE EATS).

DALMUNZIE/BRIDGE OF CALLY HOTEL/GLENISLA: *as above.*

APRÈS-SKI

BLACKWATER INN: 17km S on main rd. A good all-round pub. Occasional live music.

SKI HIRE

BRIDGE OF CALLY SKI HIRE: Opp hotel (phone as above). On the way. **BLACKWATER SKI HIRE:** Also on main rd to slopes, but nearer. And base stn.

1979 CAIRNGORM
MAP 2
D3

BASE STATION: 01479 861261. **SCHOOL:** 01479 810296 or 01479 810656 or 01479 861261.

WHERE TO STAY

CORROUR HOUSE: 01479 810220. 11km W (1151/COUNTRY-HOUSE HOTELS). INX

COYLUMBRIDGE: 01479 810661. 10km W. Nearest and best of modern Aviemore hotels. 2 pools/sauna. Ski hire. Okay restau. Comfort when you need it. MED.EX

CAIRNGORM, AVIEMORE: 01479 810630. Main st of main town. Busy bar. Rms not unreasonably priced and lots of them.   INX

THE CROSS, KINGUSSIE: 01540 661166. (999/HIGHLANDS HOTELS) .   MED.INX

WHERE TO EAT

THE CROSS, KINGUSSIE: 01540 661166 (999/HIGHLANDS HOTELS).

HAMBLETTS, AVIEMORE: 01479 810300 (1046/HIGHLANDS RESTAUS).

THE BOATHOUSE, KINCRAIG: 01540 651394 (1047/INEXP HIGHLANDS RESTAUS).

THE OLD BRIDGE, AVIEMORE: Welcoming, good atmos (1307/BEST FOOD).

APRÈS-SKI

THE WINKING OWL, AVIEMORE: At end of main st. Owl's Nest.

SKI HIRE

COYLUMBRIDGE HOTEL: 01479 810661. Behind hotel, run by Caird Sport (major operators) and nearest to slopes. Open mornings and 4–6.30pm.

••

1980 **AONACH MOR/THE NEVIS RANGE**

MAP 2
C3   **BASE STATION:** 01397 705825. **SCHOOL:** 01397 705825.

WHERE TO EAT and STAY

See **FORT WILLIAM**, *p. 312.*

APRÈS-SKI

No pub in immediate vicinity. Nearest all-in ski centre is **NEVIS SPORT, FORT WILLIAM:** 01397 704921. Bar (side entrance) till midnight. Self-serve café all day till 5pm. Bookshop and extensive ski/outdoor shop on ground floor. Also ski hire.

SKI HIRE

As above (01397 704921), also **ELLIS BRIGHAM** (01397 706220), and base stn.

••

1981 **GLENCOE**

MAP 2
C4   **BASE STATION:** 01855 851226. **SCHOOL:** 01855 851226.

WHERE TO EAT and STAY

See **FORT WILLIAM**, *p. 312*, and also:

ISLES OF GLENCOE HOTEL, BALLACHULISH: 01855 811602. Modern development leisure centre incl pool. Good touring base (1159/KIDS).

CLACHAIG INN, GLENCOE: 01855 811 252. Famous 'outdoor inn' for walkers, climbers etc with pub (1270/BLOODY GOOD PUBS), pub food and inexp accom.

KINGSHOUSE HOTEL: 01855 851259. The classic travellers' inn 1km from A82 through Glen and nr slopes (8km). Pub with food/whisky. Inexp rms but v basic, esp bunks.

APRÈS-SKI

As above, especially Clachaig Inn and Kingshouse.

SKI HIRE

At base stn.

••

1982 **THE LECHT**

MAP 3
B3   **BASE STATION:** 019756 51440. **SCHOOL:** 019756 51412.

WHERE TO STAY

Nearest town (28km S) with big choice of hotels is Ballater.

RICHMOND ARMS HOTEL, TOMINTOUL: 01807 580777. On sq. Trad hotel, log fires. A v good prospect. 24 rms. MED.INX

DARROCH LEARG, BALLATER: 01339 755443 (971/NE HOTELS). LOTS

GLENAVON HOTEL, TOMINTOUL: 01807 580218. On sq in nearest town. CHP

WHERE TO EAT

GREEN INN, BALLATER: 01339 755701 Not gr atmos but food & service ok. For sale at TGP. MED.EXP

STATION RESTAURANT, BALLATER: 01339 755050 (991/BEST REST NE).

TOMINTOUL HOTELS above. INX

APRÈS-SKI

GLENAVON HOTEL, TOMINTOUL: 01807 580218. Good large bar for skiers, walkers (S end of Speyside Way is here) and locals.

ALLARGUE HOTEL, COCKBRIDGE: 019756 51410. On rd S to Ballater 5km from slopes and o/look Corgarff Castle and the trickle of the R Don. Rms also.

SKI HIRE

At base stn.

WEATHER AND ROAD REPORTS

Dial 09001 654 then:

655 **CAIRNGORM**; 656 **GLENSHEE**; 658 **GLENCOE**; 660 **NEVIS RANGE**; 657 **THE LECHT**; 659 **CROSS-COUNTRY SKI REPORT**

ALL CENTRES REPORT: 09001 654654.

THE BEST SLEDGING PLACES

Locals will know where the best slopes are. Here's my suggestions for EDIN/GLAS:

EDINBURGH

1983
MAP A
xC4
xA3
E3

THE BRAID HILLS: The connoisseur's choice, you sledge down friendly and not-too-challenging slopes in a crowded L S Lowry landscape that you will remember long after the thaw. Off Braid Hills Drive at the golf course. Can walk in via Blackford Glen Rd. **CORSTORPHINE HILL:** Gentle broad slope with woodland at top and trails (399/CITY WALKS) and a busy rd at the bottom. App via Clermiston Rd off Queensferry Rd. **QUEEN'S PARK:** The lesser slopes that skirt Arthur's Seat, and further in around Hunter's Bog for the more adventurous or less sociable sledger.

GLASGOW

1984
MAP B
xB1
xC1
xC5

KELVINGROVE PARK: At Park Terr side. No long runs but a winter wonderland when the rime's in the trees. **GARTNAVEL HOSPITAL GROUNDS:** In W end (Hyndland) off Gr Western Rd. You can play safe sledging into the playing field, or more adventurously through the woodlands. **QUEEN'S VIEW:** On A809 N of Bearsden 20km from centre. A v popular walk (756/BEST VIEWS) is also a gr place to sledge. Variable slopes off the main path. The Highlands can be seen on a clear day. **RUCHILL PARK:** In N of city (757/BEST VIEWS) and **QUEEN'S PARK** in S.

THE BEST LEISURE CENTRES

1985
MAP 4
C3
✓ **PERTH LEISURE POOL:** 01738 635454. A perfect example of the mega successful water-based leisure-land. Large, shaped pool with o/side section (open also in winter, when it's even more of a novelty); 2 flumes, 'wild water channel', whirlpools etc. 25m 'training' pool for lengths (sessions). Outdoor kids' area. Excellent facility. Daily 10am-10pm.

1986
MAP 2
C2
✓ **AQUADOME, INVERNESS:** 01463 667500. Inverness's all-weather attraction. Leisure waters; incl 3 flumes, wave machine and toddler area. Huge competition pool for serious swimming and luxurious health suites; massages, hydrotherapy and (ladies) that essential bikini line wax. All in all, a bigger splash. Mon-Fri 7.30am-10pm, Sat-Sun until 9pm.

1987
MAP 7
B1
✓ **DUNBAR POOL:** 01368 865456. Model of its kind, o/look old harbour (where folks used to swim on a summer's day) and castle ruins. Cool, modern design amidst the warm red sandstone. Flumes and wave machine that mimics the sea o/side; lengths just possible in betw (though it's often v crowded). Phone for opening hours.

1988
MAP 1
C3
MAGNUM CENTRE, IRVINE: 01294 278381. From Irvine's throughway system, follow signs for Harbourside, then Magnum. Big shed still unalluring and looking rather tatty but this phenomenally successful pleasuredrome provides every conceivable diversion from the monotony of my namesake o/side. From soothing bowls to frenetic skating, pools, cinema, cafés, courses, you name it. Secrete endorphins and other hormones.

1989
MAP 1
C3
VIKINGAR!, LARGS: 01475 689777. Suddenly fulfilled all the needs and gaps in this busy visitor area of the Clyde coast – a pool and sports centre, a theatre, an indoor attraction and a dab of heritage. There's something irresistible about Norse history being told in a sing-song Ayrshire accent. 'Your Viking will be with you shortly, no.' Longhouse interior, the gods and a big AV about the Battle of Largs. Phone for times (or pray to Njord and get the ferry to Cumbrae instead).

1990
MAP 1
D2
THE TIME CAPSULE, MONKLANDS: 01236 449572. They say Monklands, but where you are going is downtown Coatbridge about 15km from Glas via M8. Known rather meanly as the 'Tim Capture' (local joke – you don't want to know!). A leisure (rather than swimming) pool and ice-rink lavishly fitted out on prehistoric monster theme. Even if you haven't been swimming for yrs, this is the sort of place you force the flab into the swimsuit. Cafés and view areas. Facs of the clean-up-your-act variety (e.g. squash, health suite). 10am-9pm.

1991
MAP 1
D3
DOLLAN AQUA CENTRE, TOWN CENTRE PARK, EAST KILBRIDE: 01355 260000. An excl family leisure centre. 50m pool, fitness facs, soft play area and Scotland's first interactive flume, (aquatic pin ball machine with you as the ball!) – there had to be a twist. Mon, Wed, Fri 7.30am-9pm; Tue, Thur 8am-9pm; Sat & Sun 8am-5pm.

1992
MAP B
xA3
SCOTSTOUN LEISURE CENTRE: 0141 959 4000. Clydeside expressway then A814, rt at Victoria Park lights, first left after r/about. Danes Drive. If 'modernity is suburban' this is state of the art. 10 lane pool, sports halls, health suite, dance studio and gym. Outdoor footie and tennis – it's enormous. Call for times, but open till 10pm.

1993
MAP 5
C2
EAST SANDS LEISURE CENTRE, ST ANDREWS: 01334 476506. From S St take rd for Crail then follow signs. About 2km from centre. Bright and colourful centre o/look the E Sands, the less celebrated beach of St Andrews. Mainly a fairly conventional pool with 25m lane area as well as 50m water slide, toddlers' pool etc. Also 2 squash courts, gym with Pulsestar machines, 'remedial suite', bar and café. 7 days 7.30/8.30pm; Sat/Sun till 5pm. Times may vary.

1994
MAP 5
B4
BEACON LEISURE CENTRE, BURNTISLAND: 01592 872211. On the front of quietly-getting-on with-it Fife town nr Kirkcaldy. Family fun pool centre with 'landmark' beacon thing and external flume tubes. It does work. Loadsa kids and 'waves' do come. Latest swimming in area (9.30pm, but check). 7 days.

1995
MAP 3
D3
BEACH LEISURE CENTRE, ABERDEEN: 01224 655401. Beach Esplanade across rd from beach itself. Multisports facility with bars and cafés. 'Leisure' Pool isn't much use for swimming (Aber has many others, 2004/SWIMMING POOLS) but it's fun for kids with flumes etc. Lynx Ice Arena is adj for skating, curling, ice hockey. O/side is the long long beach and the N Sea.

THE BEST SWIMMING POOLS AND SPORTS CENTRES

For EDINBURGH, *see p. 67; for* GLASGOW, *see p. 107. And see* LEISURE CENTRES *p 259*.

1996 ✓ **STONEHAVEN OUTDOOR POOL, STONEHAVEN:** The 'Friends of
MAP 3 Stonehaven Outdoor Pool' won the day (eat your hearts out N Berwick)
C4 and they've saved a gr pool that goes from length to strength. Fabulous 1930s
Olympic-sized heated salt-water pool. There are midnight swims in midsum-
mer most Wednesdays (is that cool, or what?). June-Aug only: 11am-7.30pm
(10-6pm w/ends). Heated saltwater heaven.

1997 ✓ **GOUROCK BATHING POOL:** 01475 631561. The only other open-air
MAP 1 (proper) pool in Scotland that's still open! On coast rd S of town centre
C2 45km from central Glas. 1950s-style leisure. Heated, so it doesn't need to be a
scorcher (brilliant, but choc-a-block when it is). Open May-Sep weekdays until
8.30pm, weekends until 4.30pm.

1998 ✓ **PORTSOY OPEN-AIR POOL:** One of the most engaging of the villages on
MAP 3 this N Aberdeenshire coast 7km W of Banff with a pool flushed by the sea
C1 in an idyllic setting. Usually open Jun-Aug so take advantage of it on any
sunny day, but closed in 2001 while the council anguished about how they
could make it safe. It didn't seem to bother folk for the last 50 yrs so let's hope
it re-opens.

1999 ✓ **THE WATERFRONT, GREENOCK:** 01475 797979. Easily spotted at the
MAP 1 waterfront at Customhouse Way – vast building resembling a modernist
C2 whale carcass; a rather groovy one at that. Big leisure pool, proper swim pool,
65m flume, ice rink, gym and more. Undeniably fun, by the way. Daily AYR until
8.30pm Mon-Fri, 4.30pm Sat-Sun.

2000 ✓ **CARNEGIE CENTRE, DUNFERMLINE:** 01383 314200. Pilmuir St. Excellent
MAP 5 all-round sports centre with many courses and classes. 2 pools (ozone-
A3 treated), 25m, and kids' pool. Lane swimming lunch time and evenings.
Authentic Turkish and Aeretone Suite with men's, women's and mixed ses-
sions. Large gym with Powersport stations etc. Badminton, squash, aerobic
classes. Usually open till 9pm (including pool), but check. Keeping
Dunfermline fitter then most of us.

2001 ✓ **THE LEISUREDROME, BISHOPBRIGGS:** 0141 772 6391. 147 Balmuildy
MAP B Rd. At the N edge of Glas, best reached by car or 1km walk from stn; adj
xE1 Forth and Clyde Canal walkway (745/CITY WALKS). Large, modern, efficient with
25m pool, multi gym, sauna, games hall, café etc. Open 9am-10pm (pool hours
vary).

2002 ✓ **LINLITHGOW POOL:** 01506 846358. On edge of pleasant town off rd to
MAP 7 Lanark. Modern light and airy sports centre with sauna and steam room
A1 at the pool side and W Lothian outside the windows. Excellent community
facility, well designed and laid out. All towns should enjoy this quality of life. I
go here often for a swim and a slice of it. Mon-Sat 8.30am-9pm.

2003 **GALASHIELS POOL:** 01896 752154. An award-winning pool in the Central
MAP 8 Borders on the edge of parkland with picture windows bringing the outside
B2 in. No leisurama nonsense, just a good deck-level pool (25m) (Teviotdale
Leisure Centre). Modern pool in Hawick also good. Phone for opening hrs.

2004 **ABERDEEN BATHS:** 01224 587920. City well served with swimming pools. 3
MAP 3 in suburbs are not esp easy to find, though Hazlehead (01224 310062) is
D3 signed from inner ring road to W of centre. Bon Accord Baths are a fine exam-
ple of a municipal pool; recently refurbished, they're centrally situated behind
the W end of Union St. Annie Lennox learned to swim here. The newer Beach
Leisure Centre has just about thought of everything (1995/LEISURE CENTRES).

2005 **GOLSPIE SWIMMING POOL:** 01408 633437. A neat little pool (20m) next to
MAP 2 the High School. Nothing too high tech, but a friendly atmos and a friendly
D2 mural at one end. Hrs vary.

2006 **MACTAGGART CENTRE, BOWMORE, ISLAY:** 01496 810767. Eco-friendly pool
MAP 1 (heated by adj distillery) o/look bay. Interesting whisky cask shaped ceiling
A3 and good fitness suite. Laundry facs. Cl Mon.

THE BEST WATER SPORTS CENTRES

2007
MAP 5
C3
✓ **ELIE WATERSPORTS, ELIE:** 01333 330962/077966 84532 (day) 330942 (night). Gr beach location in totally charming wee town where there's enough going on to occupy non-watersporters. Easy lagoon for first timers and open season for non-experienced users. Wind-surfers, kayaks, water-ski. Also mt bikes and inflatable 'biscuits'. (927/930/FIFE HOTELS, 1298/PUB FOOD, 1955/GOLF).

2008
MAP 1
B1
✓ **LINNHE MARINE:** 01631 730401 or 07721 503981. Lettershuna, Port Appin. 32km N of Oban on A828 nr Portnacroish. Established, personally run business in a fine sheltered spot for learning and ploutering. They almost guarantee to get you windsurfing over to the island in 2hrs. Individual or group instruction. Wayfarers, Luggers and fishing-boats. Moorings. Castle Stalker and Lismore are just round the corner, seals & porpoises abound; the joy of sailing. May-Oct.

2009
MAP 1
C3
✓ **SCOTTISH NATIONAL WATERSPORTS CENTRE, CUMBRAE:** 01475 530757. Ferry from Largs then learn all about how to pilot things that float. You need to book – call them, then bob about 'doon the watter'.

2010
MAP 7
A1
✓ **PORT EDGAR, SOUTH QUEENSFERRY:** 0131 331 3330. At end of village, under and beyond the Forth Road Br. Major marina and water sports centre. Berth your boat, hire anything from a Wayfarer to a canoe or just use the jetty to kick off some windsurfing or jet-skiing. Big tuition programme for kids. End April-Oct.

2011
MAP 1
D3
✓ **STRATHCLYDE PARK:** 01698 266155. Major water sports centre 15km SE of Glas and easily reached from most of Central Scotland via M8 or M74 (jnct 5 or 6). 200-acre loch and centre with instruction on sailing, canoeing, windsurfing, rowing, water-skiing and hire facs for canoes, Mirrors and Wayfarers, windsurfers and trimarans. Call booking office for sessions and times.

2012
MAP 2
D3
✓ **LOCH INSH WATERSPORTS, KINCRAIG:** 01540 651272. On B970, 2km from Kincraig towards Kingussie and the A9. Marvellous loch side site launching from gently sloping dinky beach into shallow forgiving waters of L Inch. Hire of canoes, dinghies (Mirrors, Toppers, Lasers, Wayfarers) and windsurfers as well as rowing boats; river trips. An idyllic place to learn. Watch the others and the sunset from the balcony restau above (1047/INEXP HIGHLAND RESTAUS). Sports 9am-5pm, Apr-Oct.

2013
MAP 2
D3
✓ **LOCH MORLICH WATERSPORTS nr AVIEMORE:** 01479 861221. By Glenmore Forest Park, part of the plethora of outdoor activities hereabouts (skiing, walking etc). This is the loch you see from Cairngorm and just as picturesque from the woody shore. Canoes/kayaks/rowing boats and dinghies (Wayfarers, Toppers, Optimists) with instruction in everything. Evening hire poss. Good campsite adj (1228/CAMPING WITH KIDS).

2014
MAP 4
B3
✓ **CROFT-NA-CABER, nr KENMORE, LOCH TAY:** 01887 830588. S side of loch, 2km from village. Purpose-built water sports centre with instruction and hire of windsurfers, canoes, kayaks, dinghies, motor boats as well as waterskiing, river rafting (down the Tay from Aberfeldy to white water at Grandtully: pure exhilaration), archery, clay shooting, quad biking. A v good all-round activities centre in a gr setting. Timeshare chalet accom much improved (for short stays 01887 830236).

2015
MAP 2
C3
GREAT GLEN WATER PARK: 01809 501381. 3km S Invergarry on A82. On shores of tiny L Oich and L Lochy in the Gr Glen. Wonderful spot, with many other lochs nearby. Day visitors welcome with windsurfers, Wayfarers, kayaks, canoes and also mountain bikes and fishing rods for hire. Mainly, however, a chalet park with all the usual condo/timeshare facs (you can rent by the week).

2016
MAP 1
C3
CASTLE SEMPLE COUNTRY PARK, LOCHWINNOCH: 01505 842882. 30km SW Glas M8 jnct 29, A737 then A760 past Johnstone. Also 25km from Largs via A760. Loch (nr village) is 3km x 1km and at the Rangers Centre you can hire dinghies and canoes etc (also mountain bikes). Bird reserve on opp bank (1686/WILDLIFE). Peaceful place to learn.

2017
MAP 1
C2
KIP MARINA, INVERKIP: 01475 521485. Major sailing centre on Clyde coast 50km W of Glas via M8, A8 and A78 from Greenock heading S for Wemyss Bay. A yacht heaven as well as haven of Grand Prix status. Sails, charters, pub/restau, chandlers and myriad boats. Diving equipment and dinghies for hire.

2018
MAP 5
B3
LOCHORE, nr LOCHGELLY: 01592 414300. From Dunfermline-Kirkcaldy motorway take Lochgelly t/off into town and follow signs for Lochore Country Park. Small, safe loch for learning and perfecting. Canoes, dinghies and esp windsurfing. Instruction and hire. Park contains a good adventure playground.

2019
MAP 6
B2
LOCHEARNHEAD WATERSPORTS: 01567 830330. On A85 nr jnct with A84 is a water sports centre where they suggest you'll never be out of your depth. Certainly the loch is wide open and (usually) gently lapping. Kayaks, Canadian canoes and water-skiing. Café.

2020
MAP 9
B3
GALLOWAY SAILING CENTRE, LOCH KEN, nr CASTLE DOUGLAS: 01644 420626. 15km N on A713 to Ayr. Dinghies, windsurfers, canoes, kayaks, tuition. A serene loch nr Galloway Forest. Phone for times & courses.

2021
MAP 2
B2
RAASAY OUTDOOR CENTRE, nr SKYE: 01478 660266. Excl activity place! Day visits or holidays.

THE BEST DIVING SITES

Scotland's seas are primal soup, full of life and world-class sites as hard core divers already know. The E coast can be tricky if the wind is blowing from the N or E, therefore the W coast is preferable (the further N the better). Thanks to the Gulf Stream it's not cold, even without a dry suit, and once you're down it's like flying thro the Botanics (says my friend Tim Maguire). So when you see all those crazies walking into the sea, remember, they may know something that you don't know. Some day I will go down! This page due to Tim.

2022
MAP 2

WEST COAST

THE OUTER HEBRIDES: excellent with fantastic visibility esp off the W coast of **HARRIS** where you can plop in virtually anywhere.

ST KILDA: offers the best diving in the UK, but it's the hardest to get to. On the edge of the Continental Shelf and the whale migration route, it has huge drop-offs and upwellings of life. Book boat and board well in advance.

THE SUMMER ISLES: from Ullapool harbour. Wrecks, lee shores and unpolluted waters.

MAP 1
B1
OBAN: Scuba central with lots of sites in the neighbourhood and easy access to the isles. Charter a boat and search for scallops in **THE GARVELLACH** or dive the wrecks in the **SOUND OF MULL**. Somewhere off **TOBERMORY** there is reputedly, one of Scotland's most enigmatic wrecks, a Spanish galleon. Easier to find are dolphins off the coasts of **ISLAY & TIREE** and see 1681/DOLPHINS for other likely spots.

All W Coast sea lochs are good for general wildlife diving.

2023
MAP 8
D1

EAST COAST

ST ABBS HEAD: Accessible from the shore (1936/COASTAL WALKS) or by boat from **EYEMOUTH**, a marine reserve, so leave the lobsters alone. The spectacular Cathedral Rock is encrusted with green and yellow dead men's fingers and in August /Sept is a sanctuary for breeding fish (this cathedral is as beautiful as St Giles and is distinctly non-denominational). Nearby shore-based diving at **DUNBAR** is shallow, safe and simple.

MAP 5
D3
THE ISLE OF MAY: across the Forth is more advanced. Take a boat from Anstruther (1666/BIRDS). Main site is Piccadilly Circus, a central atrium fed by gullies, full of friendly seals.

SCAPA FLOW: The world-famous underwater burial site where the Germans scuttled their fleet in 1918. Think Gaudalcanal, but colder. Although the scrappies have been in, there are still dozens and cruisers down there. Most lie in 35-40m deep, so plan carefully. Majorly eerie!

DIVE OPERATORS (Don't leave home without one).

EDINBURGH: Edinburgh Diving Centre 0131 229 4838.

COLDINGHAM, BORDERS: Scoutscroft Dive Centre 01890 771669.

OBAN: Puffin Dive Centre 01631 566088. Oban Divers 01631 562755. Alchemy 01631 720337. Gannet 01631 720262.

MULL: Seafare Chandlery & Diving 01688 302277.

ULLAPOOL: Atlantic Diving Services (Achiltibuie) 01854 622261.

ORKNEY: Diving Cellar 01856 850055. European Technical Dive Centre 01856 731269. Scapa Scuba 01856 850879.

Wide network of v helpful local diving clubs around the country. Contact Scottish Sub Aqua Club 0141 425 1021.

THE BEST WINDSURFING

FOR BEGINNERS AND INSTRUCTION (*see also* WATER SPORTS).

STRATHCLYDE PARK, nr MOTHERWELL and GLASGOW: 01698 266155.

CROFT-NA-CABER, KENMORE, LOCH TAY: 01887 830588.

LINNHE MARINE, nr OBAN: 01631 730227.

LOCHORE MEADOWS, LOCHGELLY, FIFE: 01592 860264.

TIGHNABRUAICH SAILING SCHOOL, TIGHNABRUAICH: 01700 811396.

SCOTTISH NATIONAL WATERSPORTS CENTRE, CUMBRAE: 01475 530757.

STRATHCLYDE PARK, nr MOTHERWELL and GLASGOW: 1493/COUNTRY PARKS. Lots to do in this recreational zone of the conurbation. Water may not be so turquoise.

ELIE, EAST NEUK OF FIFE: 01333 330962. Small, friendly windsurfing and water sports operation on the beach (beyond the Ship Inn).

WINDSURFING SPOTS

2025 **WEST COAST**

MAP 1 **MACHRIHANISH:** Wave-sailing, fabulous long beach (1523/BEACHES). Mainly
B3 at Air Force base end.

C3 **PRESTWICK/TROON:** Town beaches.

C3 **ISLAND OF CUMBRAE:** Millport beach.

C2 **MILARROCHY BAY, LOCH LOMOND:** 8km from Drymen (45km N of Glas). W/end centre run by 7th Wave. Second beach up from Balmaha. Picturesque.

2026 **EAST COAST**

MAP 3 **FRASERBURGH:** Town beach.

MAP 4 **LUNAN BAY:** 12km N of Arbroath. Also surfing.

MAP 5 **CARNOUSTIE:** Town beach.

MAP 7 **ST ANDREWS:** W Sands.

MAP 7 **LONGNIDDRY/GULLANE:** 25/35km E of Edin via A1 and A198.

MAP 7 **PEASE BAY:** 14km S of Dunbar, 60km S of Edin via A1 (2031/SURFING).

2027 **NORTH COAST**

MAP 2 **THURSO:** Many beaches nr town and further W. (1536/BEACHES)

FOR ENTHUSIASTS

2028
MAP 1
A1

ISLAND OF TIREE: The windsurfing capital of Scotland. 40km W of Mull. Countless clean, gently sloping beaches all round island (and small inland loch) allowing surfing in all wind directions. Accom basic: Tiree Lodge Hotel (01879 220368), Kirkapol Guest House (01879 220 729) or self-catering (Oban TIC 01631 563122). Loganair fly every day except Sunday (0845 7733377) and Calmac run ferries from Oban every day except Thu & Sun (01475 650100).

INFORMATION/BOARD HIRE:

BOARDWISE, GLASGOW: 1146 Argyle St 0141 334 5559.

BOARDWISE, EDINBURGH: Lady Lawson St 0131 229 5887.

THE BEST SURFING BEACHES

A surprise for the sceptical: Scotland has some of the best surfing beaches in Europe. Forget the bronzed beachboys and lemon bleached hair, surfing in Scotland is titanium-lined, rubber and balaclavas, and you get an ice cream head even encased in the latest technology. The main season is Sept-Dec. Surfees probably don't divulge their favourite beach, but the following are good bets. Don't surf alone. This page thanks to Neil Butler.

2029 WEST COAST

MAP 2
A1, B1

ISLE OF LEWIS: Probably the best of the lot. Go N of Stornoway, N of Barvas, N of just about anywhere. Leave the A857 and your day job behind. Not the most scenic of sites, but the waves have come a long way, further than you have. Derek at Stornoway Surf and Sports (01851 705862) will tell you when and where to go.

MAP 1
B3

MACHRIHANISH: Nr Campbeltown at the foot of the Mull of Kintyre. Long strand to choose from (1523/BEACHES). Jamie at Clan Skates in Glasgow (0141 339 6523) usually has an up-to-date satellite map and a idea of both the W and (nearest to central belt) Pease Bay (*see below*).

2030 NORTH COAST

MAP 2
C1, D1

STRATHY BAY: Nr Bettyhill on the N coast halfway betw Tongue and Thurso on the A836. Go past the village, park at the graveyard. Once in the foam, paddle to the rt. From here to Cape Wrath the power and quality of the waves detonating on the shore justify comparisons with Hawaii.

MAP 2
D1

THURSO: Surf City, well not quite, but it's a good base to find your own waves. Esp to the E of town at Dunnet Bay – a 5km long beach with excellent reefs at the N end.

MAP 2
D1

WICK: On the Thurso rd at Ackergill to the S of Sinclair's Bay (1259/HOUSE PARTIES). Find the ruined castle and taking care, clamber down the gully to the beach. A monumental reef break, you are working against the backdrop of the decaying ruin drenched in history, spume and romance.

2031 EAST COAST

MAP 3
D3

NIGG BAY: Just S of Aberdeen (not to be confused with Nigg across from Cromarty) and off the vast beach at Lunan Bay (1530/BEACHES) betw Arbroath and Montrose.

MAP 7
xB1

PEASE BAY: S of Dunbar nr Cockburnspath on the A1. The nearest surfie heaven to the capital. The caravan site has parking and toilets. V consistent surf here and therefore v popular.

INFORMATION/BOARD HIRE:

GLASGOW:	**BOARDWISE:** 1146 Argyle St 0141 334 5559.
	CLAN SKATES: 45 Hyndland St 0141 330 6523.
EDINBURGH:	**BOARDWISE:** Lady Lawson St 0131 229 5887.

SECTION 11

Shopping

See also WHERE TO BUY ART, *p. 278.*

2032
MAP 4
B2
✓ **HOUSE OF BRUAR, PITLOCHRY:** Courtyard emporia and shopaholic honey pot on the A9 N of Blair Atholl esp for those who just missed Pitlochry. General Harrods in the N feel, though the food side esp good (good range of Scottish cheeses, Mackie's ice cream, Stockan and Gardens oatcakes, etc). Outdoor wear with big labels (Musto, Patagonia), golf shop & gdn centre. Falls nearby for more spiritual sustenance (1554/WATERFALLS). 7 days, till 6pm (5pm in winter). ☕

2033
MAP 3
A2
✓ **BRODIE COUNTRY FARE:** By main A96 betw Nairn and Forres, nr Brodie Castle (1694/CASTLES). Not a souvenir shoppie in the trad sense, more a drive-in one-stop shopping experience. Quality deli food, a fairly up-market boutique designer womanswear and every crafty tartanalia of note. The self-serve restau gets as busy as a motorway café. 7 days till 5.30/7pm Thurs. ☕

2034
MAP 5
D2
✓ **CRAIL POTTERY, CRAIL, FIFE:** At the foot of Rose Wynd, signposted from main st (best to walk). In a tree-shaded Mediterranean courtyard and upstairs attic is a cornucopia of brilliant, useful, irresistible things. Open 10am-5pm. Don't miss the harbour nearby, one of the most romantic neuks in the Neuk. Pity there's nowhere decent in Crail for tea.

2035
MAP 2
D2
✓ **ANTA FACTORY SHOP, FEARN, nr TAIN:** Off B9175 from Tain to the Nigg ferry, 8km through Hill of Fearn, on corner of disused airfield. Shop with adj pottery. Much tartan curtain fabric; many rugs, throws and pots. You can commission furniture to be covered in their material. Free to wander round the pottery; no organised tours. Shop. AYR daily 10am-5pm, pottery Mon-Fri only.

2036
MAP 2
C1,C2
✓ **HIGHLAND STONEWARE, LOCHINVER and ULLAPOOL:** On rd to Baddidarach as you enter Lochinver on A837; and in Mill St, Ullapool, on way N beyond centre. A modern large-scale pottery business incl a shop/warehouse and studios that you can walk round (Lochinver is more *engagé*). Similar to the 'ceramica' places you find in the Med, but not too ter-racotta – rather, painted and patterned stoneware in set styles. Gr selection, pricey – but you may have luck rummaging in the Lochinver discount section. Mail-order service. Open AYR.

2037
MAP 4
B2
✓ **MACNAUGHTON'S, PITLOCHRY:** Station Rd on corner of main st, this the best of many. A vast old-fashioned outfitter with acres of tartan attire – incl obligatory tartan pyjamas and dressing gowns! Make their own cloth, and 9m kilts prepared in 10 wks. This really is the real McCoy. 7 days till 5.30pm (4pm Sun).

2038
MAP A
xE1
✓ **KINLOCH ANDERSON, EDINBURGH:** Commercial St, Leith. A bit of a trek from uptown, but firmly on the tourist trail and rightly so. Experts in Highland dress and all things tartan; they've supplied *everybody*. They design their own tartans, have a good range of men's tweed jackets; even rugs. Mon-Sat 9am-5.30pm (5pm winter).

2039
MAP 6
A1
✓ **GREEN WELLY SHOP, TYNDRUM:** On main A82 rd W to Oban/Ft William. Adj Clifton coffee shop (1378/TEAROOMS). Outdoorwear emporium in strategic position, with racks of Goretex and other membranes. Berghaus, Barbour and the all-important midge helmet (now, there's a souvenir!). 7 days, till 5.30pm. ☕

2040
MAP 2
D3
MORTIMER'S & RITCHIE'S, GRANTOWN ON SPEY: 3 & 41-45 High St (the main st) respectively of this respectable Speyside holiday town where fishing gear is somewhat in demand (though odd to find 2 similar high quality shops adj). Mortimer's more exclusively angling for your custom, but both have a big range of flies. Outdoor clothing with all the big names betw them and every shade of olive. Ritchie's also have guns if you want to kill something. Both cl Sun.

2041
MAP 2
B2
EDINBANE POTTERY, EDINBANE, SKYE: 500m off A850 Portree (22km) – Dunvegan rd. Long-established and reputable working pottery where all the various processes are often in progress. Earthy pots of every shape and size; unusual 'lantern' plant holders. Open AYR 9am-6pm. 7 days (not w/ends wint).

2042 **SKYE SILVER, COLBOST, SKYE:** 10km Dunvegan on B884 to Glendale. Long
MAP 2 established and reputable jewellery made and sold in an old schoolhouse by
A2 the rd in distant corner of Skye, but 3 Chimneys restau nearby (2223/ISLANDS
RESTAUS). Well-made, Celtic designs, good gifts. Mar-Oct 7 days, 10am-6pm.

2043 **KILN ROOM POTTERY AND COFFEE SHOP, LAGGAN:** On main A889 route
MAP 2 to Ft William and Skye from Dalwhinnie. Simple, usable pottery made by the
C3 long wood-fired kiln method, with distinctive warm colouring. Selected
knitwear and useful things. Home-made cakes and scones; the stuff of life.
9am-6pm, 7 days. Now with hostel out back v inx incl comfy lounge with gr
vista and unique seven-person hot-tub spa (01528 544231). ☕

2044 **GLENELG CANDLES, GLENELG:** Signed from glen rd which comes over the
MAP 2 hill from Shiel Bridge (1582/SCENIC ROUTES) and hard to miss. Wooden
B3 cabin/coffee shop with multifarious candles and local art. Home-made food
that smells v tempting. Easter-Oct 9.30pm-5pm daily.

2045 **BALNAKEIL, DURNESS, SUTHERLAND:** From Durness and the main A836 rd,
MAP 2 take Balnakeil and Faraid Head rd for 2km W. Founded in the 1960s in what
C1 one imagines was a haze of hash, this craft village is still home to those seeking to 'downshift'. Varied paintings, pottery, fruit wine (01971 511354) and
weaving in the different prefab huts where the community members live and
work (the site used to be an early warning station). Lotte Glob *is* (01971
511354) v good. Some businesses seasonal, some not. Everything open in
summer season, daily 10am-6 pm (mostly).

2046 **SKYE BATIKS, PORTREE, SKYE:** In centre near TIC. V original Sri Lanka 'batiks'-
MAP 2 cotton fabrics of ancient Celtic designs in every shape and size. Mainly hand-
B2 made, majorly colourful; a unique souvenir of Skye.

2047 **ACHIN'S BOOKSHOP, LOCHINVER:** At Inverkirkaig 5km from Lochinver on
MAP 2 the 'wee mad rd' to Achiltibuie (1586/SCENIC ROUTES). Unexpected selection of
C1 books in the back of beyond providing something to read when you've
climbed everything. Outdoor wear too and gr hats. The path to Kirkaig Falls
and Suilven begins at the gate. Easter-Oct 7 days; 9.30am-6pm. Adj café 10am-
5pm. Winter, Mon-Sat 10am-5pm (unless he has to pop out on business).

2048 **KNOCKAN STUDIO, ELPHIN:** 01854 666261. Moved up from Ullapool in
MAP 2 autumn 2001. Well-crafted jewellery, nice stones, Scottish gold. (Elphin is
C2 around 23km N of Ullapool on A835.) Open AYR Mon-Sat, 9am-5pm.

2049 **IONA ABBEY SHOP:** Iona via Calmac ferry from Fionnphort on Mull. Crafts
MAP 1 and souvenirs across the way in separate building. Proceeds support a wor-
A1 thy, committed organisation. Christian literature, tapes etc, but mostly artefacts from nearby and around Scotland. Celtic crosses much in evidence, but
then this is where they came from! Mar-Oct 9.30am-5pm.

2050 **OCTOPUS CRAFTS, nr FAIRLIE, nr LARGS:** On main A78 Largs to Ardrossan
MAP 1 rd, just S of Fairlie. Smaller setup than above, but, crafts, wines and cookshop
C3 an excellent restau (1338/SEAFOOD RESTAUS) and a seafood deli. An all-round
road side experience – the sign says Fencebay Fisheries. Everything here is
hand-made and/or hand-picked. Even the wines are well chosen. Good pots.
Glass and wood. They also run courses. Cl Mon.

2051 **BALBIRNIE CRAFT CENTRE, MARKINCH:** Follow signs for Balbirnie Park from
MAP 5 Glenrothes road system, but off the A92. Farmyard courtyard of craft work-
B3 shops and retail in country park nr Balbirnie House Hotel (925/FIFE HOTELS).
Jewellery, glasswork, ceramics, leather and embroidery – bit of everything
really. Nice that something's made in Glenrothes that isn't made in millions. 7
days (Sun afternoons only).

2052 **ALDIE WATER MILL & TAIN POTTERY:** Off the A9 just S of Tain. Separate con-
MAP 2 cerns but next door to each other. Water Mill (01862 893786) spruced up since
D2 new owner took over in spring 2001. Big working pottery (01862 894112) over
the way featuring crafts by Pippa Lee and NTS tartan ceramics among others.
Mill Open 10am-5pm Apr-Sep, pottery daily in summer, Mon-Sat in wint.

2053 **BORGH POTTERY, BORVE, ISLE OF LEWIS:** On NW coast of island a wee way
MAP 2 from Stornoway, but not much of a detour from the rd to Callanish where you
B1 are probably going. Alex and Sue Blair's pleasant gallery of handthrown pots
with diff glazes; domestic and gdn wear. Some knits. Open AYR 9-6pm. Cl Sun.

2054 **ROSEHALL CRAFT SHOP, INVERNAULD, nr LAIRG:** If all else fails, follow
MAP 2 signs for Raven's Rock trail then ask someone. Otherwise, off the A837 E of the
B3 Achness Hotel. Lady Jean Gilmour's place with assistance from Lyn Park. Pop
in for home baking and a chat at least! Easter-Oct daily until 5pm.

2055 **JUST SCOTTISH, STONEHAVEN:** Main st nr square. Small selective arts/crafts
MAP 3 shop also in **ABERDEEN** nr the university. Tain Pottery, other brand leaders,
C4 and generally interesting stuff. 10am-5.30pm. Cl Sun.

2056 **GALLOWAY LODGE PRESERVES, GATEHOUSE OF FLEET:** On main st of com-
MAP 9 pact town. Packed with local jams, marmalades, chutneys and pickles. Scottish
B3 pottery by Scotia Ceramics, Highland Stoneware and Dunoon. Good presents
and jam for yourself. 10am-5pm Mon-Sat, and Sun afternoons in summer.

2057 **CRAFTS AND THINGS, nr GLENCOE VILLAGE:** On A82 betw Glencoe village
MAP 2 and Ballachulish. Eclectic mix of so many baubles that some are literally hang-
C4 ing from the rafters. Mind, body & spirit books (like this one) and reasonably
priced knit/outerwear. Good coffee shop, with local artist's work on walls. All-
round nice place. Summer season, daily until 5.30pm, wint Fri-Sun only. ☕

2058 **THOMAS CHIPPENDALE SCHOOL OF FURNITURE:** 01620 810680. B6369
MAP 7 Haddington to Gifford Rd. Anselm Fraser runs cabinet-making courses here
B1 and welcomes visitors at weekends (10am-4pm) check out the work and
commission something.

2059 **DRUMLANRIG CASTLE, nr THORNHILL, nr DUMFRIES:** A whole day out of
MAP 9 things to do (1490/COUNTRY PARKS) including the craft centre in the old sta-
C2 ble/courtyard to the side of the house. Studio-type shops with tartan, jew-
ellery and buttonholes! Hire a bike and ride while you decide.

2060 **KIRKCUDBRIGHT HIGH ST:** A run of craft shops by the Tolbooth Arts Centre.
MAP 9 Inc Jo Gallant textiles, Cranberries (general), Gill's jewellery and the High St
C3 Gallery. Browse on, then walk round to the Corner Gallery (see 2067/WOOLLIES).

WHERE TO BUY GOOD WOOLLIES

2061 ✓ ✓ **LYNDA USHER, BEAULY:** 01463 783017. Fabulous knitwear and
MAP 2 linen from a fabulous lady. V selective and based on the owner's per-
C2 sonal choice; Lynda is a big name in Scottish knitting circles. Open AYR; Mon-
Sat 9.30am-5.30pm (and some Suns in summer, till 5pm in winter).

2062 ✓ ✓ **BELINDA ROBERTSON:** 0131 225 1057. 22 Palmerston Pl, Edin.
MAP A Queen of the commissioned cashmere creations; you can only
B3 choose from the *prêt-à-porter* collection in her showroom here (or in London).
Her team of 7 girls design and process the stock which is made up in Hawick.
HILARY ROHDE's the other cashmere designer par excellence. She's too big
time even to give out a phone-number (and I promised I wouldn't).

2063 ✓ **JUDITH GLUE, KIRKWALL, ORKNEY:** Opp the cathedral. Distinctive
hand-made jumpers, the runic designs are a real winner. Also the widespread but individual Highland and Joker stoneware (jewellery and animal
clocks v popular), condiments and preserves. The landscape prints of Orkney
are by twin sister, Jane. Open AYR 7 days 9am-5.30pm (Suns only in summer).

2064 ✓ **NUMBER TWO, EDINBURGH:** St Stephen Pl. They were here on the cor-
MAP A ner of St Stephen Pl in the first 1960s flush of alternative culture, long
C1 before their trail-blazing range of Scottish machine and hand-made knitwear
could be called 'designer'. Still innovative, still filling the shop with the cardies
that Liz Taylor once admired. Open AYR 10am-5.30pm (not Sun).

2065 ✓ **HUNTER'S OF BRORA, BRORA, SUTHERLAND:** Main rd N (the A9)
MAP 2 towards Helmsdale. Certainly among the best of the larger scale mill-
D2 type emporia. Bales of their own stylish tweeds or choose from the made-up
clothing selection. Trad but unstuffy stalwarts, and some gr hats – the bow
brim is a must. Open AYR Mon-Sat, 10am-5.30pm, Sun 10am-4pm.

2066 **RAGAMUFFIN, SKYE:** On Armadale Pier, so one of the first or last things you
MAP 2 can do on Skye is rummage through the Ragamuffin store and get a nice knit.
B3 Every kind of jumper and some crafts in this Aladdin's cave within a new build;
incl tweedy things and hats.

2067 **CORNER GALLERY, KIRKCUDBRIGHT:** 75 St Mary's Street (01557 332020).
MAP 9 Anne Chaudhry's resplendent knitwear shop with some very nice gear indeed
C3 (she also has a shop at Churchgate, Moffat). Woollens not just for middle-aged
blokes on the golf course: remember – it can be designer-standard too!
Easter–Dec 10am-5pm daily. (Cl Thurs afternoon in winter, and completely
Jan-Mar.)

2068 **JOHNSTON'S CASHMERE CENTRE, ELGIN:** Large Mill Shop kind of operation
MAP 3 and full-blown visitor attraction nr the Cathedral (1716/RUINS). 'The only
B1 British mill to transform fibre to garment' (yarns spun at their factory in Elgin
and made into garments in the Borders) and though this is more British High
St than Bloomingdale's, New York, these jumpers will keep you just as warm.
Mon-Fri 9am-6pm, Sat 9am-6pm, Sun 11am-5pm. Slight variations in winter.

2069 **LOCHCARRON VISITOR CENTRE, GALASHIELS:** If you're in Galashiels (or
MAP 8 Hawick), which grew up around woollen mills, you might expect to find a
B2 good selection of woollens you can't get everywhere else; and bargains. Well,
tough! There's no stand-out place, but L Carron (incl Vivienne Westwood!) is a
big tourist attraction with mill tours (Open AYR 4 times a day), exhibits and an
okay mill shop. Hawick did invent the Y-front.

2070 **CHAS N. WHILLANS, HAWICK (PEEBLES and elsewhere):** Their main shop is
MAP 8 in Hawick (Teviotdale Mills, over the bridge at S end of main st; instead of con-
C3 tinuing on A7, turn rt and they're on the rt). They stock all the local big names
incl a good range of Pringle, Lyle & Scott and Braemar. Best to stick to the classic cuts; the 'fashion' versions are not too warm and not too cool.

HARRIS TWEED

2071 **THE REAL HARRIS TWEED, ISLE OF HARRIS:** To be awarded the Harris Tweed
MAP 2 Orb Mark, this distinctive wool cloth has to be hand-woven from yarn which
A2 has been dyed and spun in the Outer Hebrides. Much is processed industrial-
ly and finds its way into jackets etc in department stores all over the world.
The real McCoy however is still woven and worked in Harris, mainly in the S in
places on or off the Golden Road (1584/SCENIC ROUTES). The places to recommend are:

TWEEDS & KNITWEAR, 4 PLOCKROPOOL, DRINISHADDER: Organised
operators (they even cater for coach parties) with weaving demonstrations &
wool & knitwear for sale as well as tweed. Cl Sun.

JOAN McCLENNAN: NO 1, DRINISHADDER: Further down the Golden Rd. I
don't know, but I've been told, this is where you find the real golden fleece. Go
look for it.

LUSKENTYRE HARRIS TWEED: NO 6, LUSKENTYRE: 2km off W coast on
main rd S to Scarista and Rodel. Donald and Maureen Mackay's place is
notable for their bright tartan tweed. 9.30am-6pm Cl Sun.

BREANISH TWEED, 1A MELBOST, by STORNOWAY: 01851 701524 (phone
for directions & opening, though usually Mon-Fri). Lightweight, handwoven
tweed incl cashmere & made-to-measure tailoring. This is the one you want
you fashionistas!

THE BEST GARDEN CENTRES

2072
MAP 1
B1
✓ **KINLOCHLAICH HOUSE, APPIN:** On main A28 Oban-Ft William rd just N of Pt Appin t/off, the West Highlands' largest nursery/gdn centre. Set in a large walled gdn filled with plants and veg soaking up the climes of the warm Gulf stream. Donald Hutchison and daughter nurture these acres enabling you to reap what they sow; with a huge array of plants on offer it's like visiting a friend's gdn and being able to take home your fave bits. Charming cottages for let 01631 730342. 7 days: 9.30am-5.30pm (10.30am Sun). Cl Sun in winter.

2073
MAP 7
A1
✓ **DOUGAL PHILIP'S NEW HOPETOUN GARDENS, nr S QUEENSFERRY:** 01506 834433. This mega-gdn moved from quaint walled premises but great stock & 15 imaginative displays inc. Tuscan, Oriental & retreat gdns. Orangery tea-room has commanding views and tasty home-made stuff. AYR 10am-530pm.

2074
MAP 2
D3
✓ **INSHRIACH, nr KINCRAIG, nr AVIEMORE:** On B970 betw Kincraig and Inverdruie (which is on the Coylumbridge ski rd out of Aviemore), a gdn centre, nay a nursery, that puts most others in the shade. Specialising in alpines and bog plants, but with neat beds of all sorts in the grounds (and a wild gdn) of the house by the Spey and frames full of perfect specimens, this is a potterer's paradise. Mon-Fri 9am-5pm, Sat 9am-4pm. Sun 10am-4pm.

2075
MAP B
xB1
✓ **DOBBIES, MILNGAVIE, GLASGOW:** Formerly Findlay Clark's, the original home of the gdn centre chain in Campsie countryside N of city, 20km from centre via A81 or A807 (Milngavie or Kirkintilloch rds) or heading for Milngavie (pron 'Mullguy'), turn rt on Boclair Rd. Vast gdn complex and all-round visitor experience; an institution. 'Famous' coffee shop (the famous waitresses are local babes and what they turn into), saddlery with everything except horses; labels from Crabtree & Evelyn to Fisons, plus books, clothes and piles of plants; and live pets. 9am-9pm (till 7pm in winter). ☕

2076
MAP 4
C3
✓ **GLENDOICK, GLENCARSE, nr PERTH:** On A85, 10km from Perth, in the fertile Carse of the Tay. A large family-owned gdn centre notable esp for rhododendrons and azaleas, a riot of which can be viewed in the nursery behind (May only). Pagoda Garden (they practice what they preach). V popular coffee shop with superior home-baking. 7 days till 6pm. ☕

2077
MAP 6
b3
BEN LOMOND NURSERY, BALMAHA, LOCH LOMOND: Nearer Conic Hill than Ben Lomond, on the B837 just before Balmaha. Family-run, supplying the trade and gardeners in the know, as well as passing motorists, particularly with bedding plants grown in their greenhouses on the side of the loch. 9.00am-6pm, Coffee shop. 7 days.

2078
MAP 2
C2
BRIN SCHOOL FIELDS, FLICHITY, nr INVERNESS: Off A9 S of Daviot, 12km S of Inverness, then 10km SW along rd to Farr. An old school and playground dedicated to herbs, plants and all the potions and lotions that come from them. Tearoom in the school room. Mar-Oct 9.30am-6pm, Sun 2-5pm. ☕

2079
MAP 1
C2
THE TREE SHOP, CAIRNDOW, LOCH FYNE: A gdn centre specialising in trees & shrubs. Part of the Ardkinglas Estate nr (1km) the Woodland Garden (1486/GARDENS) with UK's tallest tree. The shop on the main A83 L Lomond-Inveraray rd also does houseplants & all the usual greeneries. Café. 7 days 9.30am-5pm.

2080
MAP 8
C2
FLOORS CASTLE, KELSO: 3km outside town off B6397 St Boswells rd (gdn centre has separate entrance to main visitors' gate in town). Set amongst lovely old greenhouses within walled gdns some distance from house, it has a showpiece herbaceous border all round. Nice coffee shop and patio. Centre is open AYR. 10am-5pm. (1760/COUNTRY HOUSES.) ☕

2081
MAP 4
C3
CHRISTIE'S NURSERY, KIRRIEMUIR: 01575 572977. On long straight stretch of A926 to Blairgowrie in the village of Westmuir, 3km from Kirriemuir. Looking towards the Sidlaw Hills, this is a family-run nursery specialising in hardy plants (orchids, alpines etc) with unique stocks of rare plants. This is where those in the know go for gentians, (they are world specialists), primulas and advice about the rock gdn. Mar-Oct 10am-6pm; cl Mon, Tues. Outwith these times, phone first.

2082 **CHRISTIE'S, FOCHABERS:** On A98 going into town from Buckie side. Huge
MAP 3 gdn centre and forest nursery, with tearm/restaurant. Good for shrubs, indoor
B2 plants etc and a gr place for keen and not-so-keen gardeners to browse
around. Famous floral clock strutting peacock, and aviary – an all- round shop-
ping/recreational experience. 9am-5pm, 7 days (from 10am Sun).

2083 **RAEMOIR GARDEN CENTRE, BANCHORY:** On A980 off main st 3km n of
MAP 3 town. A friendly family-run gdn centre & excl coffee-shop that keeps the fas-
C3 tidious gardeners hereabouts happy. And this is Deeside. If it's good enough
for them … 7 days 9am-5.30pm. Tearm till 5pm. ☕

2084 **KESKE NURSERIES, CLACHAN, NORTH UIST:** In the remote heart of wild and
MAP 2 watery N Uist on main rd to Benbecula S of Lochmaddy and just after Clachan
A2 Stores and the t/off for Bayhead a cottage nursery and a … bus full of plants
(tomatoes when we visited). Idiosyncratic app, but certainly the Hebridean
choice for trees, shrubs, veg and bedding plants. Go on, make a statement –
plant a tree in this treeless tract. Open AYR 1pm-late. Cl Sun.

2085 **SMEATON GARDENS, EAST LINTON:** 2km from village on N Berwick rd
MAP 7 (signed Smeaton). Up a drive in an old estate is this walled gdn going back to
B1 early 19th century. Wide range; good for fruit (and other) trees, herbaceous
etc. Nice to wander round, an additional pleasure is the 'Lake Walk' halfway
down drive through small gate in woods. 1km stroll round a secret finger lake
in magnificent mature woodland. You're only supposed to go during gdn hrs
Mon-Fri 9am-4.30pm; Sat 10am-4.30pm; Sun 11.30am-4.30pm; cl w/ends
Jan/Feb.

2086 **THE CLYDE VALLEY:** The lush valley of the mighty Clyde is gdn centre central.
MAP 1 Best reached say from Glas by M74, jnct 7, then A72 for Lanark. Betw Larkhall
D3 and Lanark there's a profusion to choose from and many have sprouted cof-
fee/craft shops. Pick your own fruit in summer and your own picnic spot to eat
it.

2087 **BINNY PLANTS, ECCLESMACHAN:** 01506 858155. Through village and up
MAP 7 driveway past Sue Ryder home. Down in dell this is run by a respected nurs-
A1 eryman, Billy Carruthers. Grasses, ferns and perennials flourishing here may
also flourish for you. thurs-Mon 10am-5pm, or call for apptmt.

2088 **DOBBIES, MONIFIETH:** 01382 530333. Big! We wouldn't call it beautiful. Daily
MAP 4 9am-6pm (until 8pm Wed & Thurs). There are other Dobbies plant supermar-
D3 kets. The one outside Edinburgh has the attraction of the Butterfly Farm adj
(1634/KIDS).

AUCTIONS AND JUNKYARDS

2089
MAP 2
D2
✓ **AULDEARN ANTIQUES, AULDEARN, nr NAIRN:** Doris and Roger Milton's cornucopia of junk, quality antiques and architectural salvage in an old manse 2km from main st (via Lethen Rd) which is 3km from main A96 Nairn-Forres rd. Serene spot for browsing through courtyard of shops and a church-ful of furniture. Kids welcome. 7 days until 5.30pm.

2090
MAP 7
B1
SAM BURNS' YARD, PRESTONPANS, nr EDINBURGH: 01875 810600. On the coast rd out of Musselburgh; if you get to Prestonpans you've missed it. By a gate in the wall you'll see cars on the kerb of a long straight stretch. The yard has piles of old bikes, assorted 'stuff' and is full of domestic and office furniture stored both outdoors and in sheds. Popular with Sunday browsers but more Vulcan's than Ali Baba's cave. 7 days until 5pm, Sun from 11am.

2091
MAP A
xD1
EASY (EDINBURGH ARCHITECTURAL SALVAGE YARD): 554 7077. Couper St off Coburg St (at N end of Gr Jnct St nr mini roundabout). Warehouseful of original house fittings and the place to go for baths, sinks, radiators, fireplaces, doors (there are rows of them) and all the other bits of Old Edin that used to be thrown out but which are now worth lots. Similar set ups at **ANGUS ARCHITECTURAL ANTIQUES**, Hill St, Montrose, in harbour area (01674 674291) and **TAYMOUTH ARCHITECTURAL**, Perth Rd, Dundee (01382 666833). All open Mon-Sat.

2092
MAP B
B3
R McTEAR and J.A. CATHCART, GLASGOW: McTear's at the Clydeway Business Centre, Elliot Pl, overlooking the SECC has sales every Fri (view Thu) and Cathcart's at 20 Anchor Lane off St. Vincent Pl near George Sq. on Wed. Mornings. See the *Herald* on Mon for details.

2093
MAP A
xE1
D1
LYON & TURNBULL, EDINBURGH: 557 8844. Broughton Pl in converted church at the end of the st. Gone are the funky Lane sales to be replaced by a more up-market operation. Fine antiques and book sales on Sats, paintings and other specialist items on Fridays. Viewing on previous Sun 2-5pm and 3 days previous, 10am-5pm (but check *The Scotsman* and *The Herald*).

2094
MAP 6
C2
ROBERTSON'S AUCTION, KINBUCK: 01786 822603. 6km N of Dunblane on B8033. Second Sat every month and alternate Fri at 10am. Viewing: Thur and Fri 9am-4pm, (and Thur 7.30-9pm). Antiques/domestic furniture-stripping.

2095
MAP 4
D2
TAYLOR'S AUCTIONS, MONTROSE: 01674 672775. Panmure Row. Auction Rooms for regular sales of household furniture and effects every second Sat. Some antique and quality stuff but all kinds incl bric-a-brac, jewellery, gdn furniture (viewing: Fri 2-5pm and 6-8pm; Sat 9am onwards). Often fascinating just to wander round; you're bound to see something you want.

2096
MAP 7
B1
LESLIE and LESLIE, HADDINGTON: 01620 822241. Market St. An outside of Edinburgh auction rm where wheelers and dealers have oft come for supplies. You can cut out the middleman here. Phone for times.

2097
MAP 5
C2
MACGREGOR AUCTIONS, ST ANDREWS: 01334 472431. 56 Largo Rd. Everything and anything – household, antiques, collectibles. Two-day sales every 2 weeks (Thurs & Fri with viewing from 9am on Wed). Specialist antiques every 2 months. Call for details.

SECTION 12

Museums, Galleries, Theatres and Music

BEST HISTORY & HERITAGE

For EDINBURGH *galleries, see p. 70;* GLASGOW, *see p. 108.*

2098
MAP 7
B1
✓ ✓ **MUSEUM OF FLIGHT, nr HADDINGTON, E LOTHIAN:** 01620 880308. 3km from A1 S of town. In the old complex of hangars and nissen huts at the side of E Fortune, an airfield dating to World War I (there's a tacky open-air market on Sundays), a large collection of planes from gliders to jets and esp wartime memorabilia has been respectly restored and preserved. Inspired and inspiring displays; not just boys' stuff. Marvel at the bravery back then and sense the unremitting passage of time. From E Fortune the airship R34 made its historic Atlantic crossings. AYR 7 days; 10.30am-5pm (till 6pm Jul-Aug). ☕

2099
MAP 5
D3
✓ ✓ **THE SECRET BUNKER, nr CRAIL/ANSTRUTHER:** 01333 310301. The nuclear bunker and regional seat of government in the event of nuclear war – a twilight labyrinth beneath a hill in rural Fife so vast, well documented and complete, it's utterly fascinating and quite chilling. Few 'museums' are as authentic or as resonant as this, even down to the 1950s records in the jukebox in the claustrophobic canteen. Makes you wonder what 300 people would have felt like incarcerated down there, what the Cold War was all about and what secrets They are cooking up these days for the wars yet to come. Apr-Oct 10am-5pm.

2100
MAP 4
C3
✓ ✓ **VERDANT WORKS, DUNDEE:** 01382 225282. West Henderson's Wynd nr Westport. Award-winning heritage museum that for once justifies the accolades. The story of jute and the city it made. Immensely effective high-tech and designer presentation of industrial & social history. Excl for kids. Almost continuous guided tour. Cafe. 7 days 10am-5pm (11am Sun); till 4pm wint. ☕

2101
MAP 2
A1
✓ ✓ **THE BLACKHOUSE VILLAGE, GEARRANNAN, nr CARLOWAY, LEWIS:** 01851 643416. At the end of the rd (3km) from A858 the W coast of Lewis, an extraordinary reconstruction of several blackhouses, the trad thatched dwelling of the Hebrides. Excl AV presentation in one of of them with café. Another is a hostel & 4 of them are self-cat accom. Gr walk starts here with viewpts. Apr-Sept 11-5.30pm. Cl Sun. Also:

2102
MAP 2
B1
✓ **THE BLACKHOUSE AT ARNOL, LEWIS:** 01851 710395. The A857 Barvas rd from Stornoway, left at jnct for 7km, then rt through township for 2km. A single blackhouse with earth floor, bed boxes and central peat fire (no chimney hole), occupied both by the family and their animals. Remarkably, this house was lived in until the 1960s. Smokists may reflect on that peaty fug. Open AYR 9.30am-6.30pm (4.30pm in wint). Cl Sun.   HS

2103
MAP 5
A3
✓ **THE ABBOT HOUSE, DUNFERMLINE:** Maygate in town centre 'historic area'. V fine conversion of ancient house demonstrating the importance of this town as a religious and trading centre from the beginning of this millennium to medieval times. Encapsulates history from Margaret and Bruce to the Beatles. One of the few tourist attractions where 'award-winning' is a reliable indicator of worth. Café and tranquil gdn; gate to the graveyard and Abbey. 7 days 10am-5pm. ☕

2104
MAP 1
B2
✓ **EASDALE ISLAND FOLK MUSEUM:** On Easdale, an island/township reached by a 5min (continuous) boat service from Seil 'island' at the end of the B844 (off the A816, 18km S of Oban). Something special about this grassy hamlet of white-washed houses on a rocky outcrop which has a pub, a tearoom and a craft shop, and this museum across the green. The history of the place (a thriving slate industry erased one stormy night in 1881, when the sea drowned the quarry) is brought to life in displays from local contributions. Easter-Sept 11am-5pm.

2105
MAP 2
D1
✓ **STRATHNAVER MUSEUM, BETTYHILL:** 01641 521418. On N coast 60km W of Thurso in a converted church which is v much part of the whole appalling saga: a graphic account of the Highland clearances told through the history of this fishing village and the Strath that lies behind it from whence its dispossessed population came; 2,500 folk were driven from their homes – it's worth going up the valley (from 2km W along the main A836) to see (esp at Achenlochy) the beautiful land they had to leave in 1812 to make way for

sheep. If interested in general Strathnaver developments, ask the fabulous Angela at Bettyhill TI office. Museum: Apr-Oct Mon-Sat 10am-5pm (cl at lunchtime).

2106
MAP 3
D1
✓ **THE MUSEUM OF SCOTTISH LIGHTHOUSES, FRASERBURGH:** At Kinnaird Head nr Harbour. A top attraction, so signed from all over. Purpose-built and v well done. Something which may appear to be of marginal interest made vital. In praise of the prism and the engineering innovation and skill that allowed Britain once to rule the seas (and the world). A gr ambition (to light the coastline) spectacularly realised. *At Scotland's Edge* by Allardyce and Hood (or its follow-up) is well worth taking home. The tour guide is like James Robertson Justice with better patter. Apr-Oct 10am-6pm (Sun afternoons); winter closes at 4pm.

2107
MAP 2
B3
✓ **GAVIN MAXWELL MUSEUM, EILEAN BAN off KYLEAKIN, SKYE:** 01599 530040. You don't have to be a Maxwell fan, *Ring of Bright Water* reader or even an otter watcher to appreciate this remarkable restoration of this fascinating man's last house on the island now under the Skye Bridge. Island itself is a natural haven & the Stevenson Lighthouse superb. Microcosm which encapsulate what's best about Scotland. 2/3 boat trips a day (12 per boat) from Vis Centr at Kyleakin (not Suns).

2108
MAP A
D3
✓ **MUSEUMS OF THE ROYAL COLLEGE OF SURGEONS, EDINBURGH:** 0131 527 1649. 18 Nicolson St. 3 separate small museums left out of the Edin section's 'attractions', but too good to miss. Displays of 'pathological anatomy' in the classic Playfair Hall in the main st (opp Festival Theatre) & the Dental Museum & Sir Jules Thom Exhibition of History of Surgery both round corner at 9 Hill Square. Extraordinary & somewhat macabre exhibits in one of the homes of medicine. Mon-Fri 2-4pm.

2109
MAP 2
C3
WEST HIGHLAND MUSEUM, FORT WILLIAM: Cameron Sq off main st, listed building next to TIC. Good refurb yet retains mood; the setting doesn't overshadow the contents. 7 rms of Jacobite memorabilia, archeology, wildlife, clans, tartans, arms etc all effectively evoke the local history. Gr oil paintings line the walls, incl a drawn battle plan of Culloden. The anamorphic painting of Charlie isn't so bonny, but a fascinating snapshot all the same. Cl Sun except July/Aug (2-5pm).

2110
MAP 1
B2
KILMARTIN HOUSE: N of Lochgilphead on the A816. 01546 510278. Centre for landscape and archeology interpretation – so much to know of the early peoples and Kilmartin Glen is littered with historic sites. Intelligent, interesting, run by a small independent trust. Excellent organic cafe (1315/VEGN RESTAUS). AYR 10am-5.30pm daily. ☕

2111
MAP 4
D2
PICTAVIA, BRECHIN: 01356 626241. S of Brechin on the Forfar rd at Brechin Castle. Centre opened summer '99 to give a multimedia interpretation of our Dark Age ancestors. Sparse on detail, high on interactivity. Listen to some music, pluck a harp and argue about the Battle of Dunnichen – was it that important? AYR Mon-Sat 9-6pm, Sun 10am-6pm (5pm winter).

2112
MAP 2
D2
CROMARTY COURTHOUSE MUSEUM, CROMARTY: 01381 600418. Church St. Housed in the 18th cent courthouse, this award-winning museum uses moving & talking models to bring to life a courtroom scene & famous Cromarty figures to paint the varied history of this important Highland town. Entrance includes multilingual taped tours of the town 7 days. 10am-5pm (winter 12-4pm). Jan & Feb – by appoint.

2113
MAP 1
D2
SUMMERLEE HERITAGE PARK, COATBRIDGE: 01236 431261 West Canal St. Follow signs. Here in the Iron Town is this tribute to the industry, ingenuity and graft that powered the Industrial Revolution and made Glas gr. Anyone with a mechanical bent or an interest in the social history of the working class will like it here; totty kids and bored teens may not. Tearoom. 7 days, 10am-5pm (Winter 10am-3.30pm). Some exhibs close earlier.

2114
MAP 2
B2
SKYE MUSEUM OF ISLAND LIFE: Kilmuir on Uig-Staffin rd, the A855, 32km N of Portree. The most authentic (or at least official) of several converted cottages on Skye where the poor crofter's life is recreated for the enrichment of ours. The small thatched township includes agricultural implements as well as domestic artefacts, many of which illustrate an improbable fascination with the royal family. Flora Macdonald's grave is nearby (1768/MONUMENTS). Cl Sun.

2115 **AUCHENDRAIN, INVERARAY:** 8km W of town on A83. A whole township
MAP 1 reconstructed to give a v fair impression of both the historical and spatial
C2 relationship betw the cottages and their various occupants. Longhouses and
byre dwellings; their furniture and their ghosts. 7 days. Apr-Sept 10am-5pm.

2116 **INVERARAY JAIL:** 'The story of Scottish crime and punishment' (sic) told in
MAP 1 'award-winning' reconstruction of courtroom with cells below, where the
C2 waxwork miscreants and their taped voices bring local history to life. Guided
tours of Peterhead can't be far off. Open AYR, 9.30am-6pm (wint 10am-5pm).

2117 **ARCTIC PENGUIN aka MARITIME HERITAGE CENTRE, INVERARAY:** 'One of
MAP 1 the world's last iron sailing ships' moored so you can't miss it at the loch side
C2 in Inveraray. More to it than would seem from the outside; displays on the history of Clydeside (the *Queens M* and *E* memorabilia etc), Highland Clearances,
the Vital Spark. Lots for kids to get a handle (or hands) on. 7 days 10am till
6pm; 5pm winter.

2118 **BONAWE IRONWORKS MUSEUM, TAYNUILT:** At its zenith, (late 17th – early
MAP 1 18th century), this ironworks was a brutal, fire-breathing monster, as 'black as
C1 the Earl of Hell's waistcoat'. But now, all is calm as the gently sloping grassy
sward carries you around from warehouse to foundry and down onto the
shores of L Etive to the pier, where the finished product was loaded on to
ships to be taken away for the purpose of empire-building (with cannonballs).
Apr-Sept daily until 6.30pm; Oct-Nov daily until 4.30pm; cl Dec-Mar.

2119 **SCOTTISH FISHERIES MUSEUM, ANSTRUTHER:** 01333 310628. In and
MAP 5 around a cobbled courtyard o/look the old fishing harbour in this busy East
D3 Neuk town. A recent stay of execution for this excellent evocation of trad
industry still alive (if not kicking). Impressive collection of models and actual
vessels incl those moored at adj quay. Crail and Pittenweem harbours nearby
for the full picture (and fresh crab/lobster). Open AYR 10am-5.30pm, Sun
11am-5pm (cl 4.30pm in winter).

2120 **ROBERT SMAIL'S PRINTING WORKS, INNERLEITHEN:** Main st. A trad print-
MAP 8 ing works till 1986 and still in use. Fascinating vignettes/instant history. Have
B2 a go at hand setting, then have a go at a Caldwell's ice-cream (1418/ICE
CREAM). May-Oct, Mon-Sat 10am-5pm, Sun 2-5pm. W/ends in Oct. (Cl 1-2pm).

2121 **MYRETON MOTOR MUSEUM, ABERLADY:** 01875 870288. On Drem rd, past
MAP 7 Luffness Mains. Ideal 'little' museum in old barn w restored vehicles dating
B1 from 1896. Even for the Luddite, engineering seems an aesthetic here. Dr
Finlay's Casebook fans prepare yourselves.

2122 **SHAMBELLIE HOUSE MUSEUM OF COSTUME, NEW ABBEY, nr DUMFRIES:**
MAP 9 Another obsession that became a museum. On 2 floors of this country house
C3 set among spectacular woodlands. Fab frocks etc from every 'period'. Apr-Oct
11am-5pm. Most accommodating tearoom staff.

2123 **ABERFELDY WATER MILL, ABERFELDY:** Mill St off main st. Excellent renova-
MAP 4 tion made all the more authentic because it was restored in 1983 by a 20th-
B3 generation miller, Tom Rodger, and once again is producing good healthy oat-
meal that you can buy for your porridge. The weight of the water in the buck-
ets turns the wheel; life goes round. The tearoom serves, amongst other
things, a v fine fly cemetery. Apr-Oct 10am-5pm (Sun 12-5pm).

2124 **WICK HERITAGE CENTRE, WICK:** 01955 605393. On Bank Row. Amazing civic
MAP 2 museum run by volunteers. Jam-packed with items about the sea, town and
D1 that hard land. Somebody should ensure these people get OBEs or some-
thing. High season only.

2125 **ABERDEEN MARITIME MUSEUM:** 01224 337700. Shiprow. Aberdeen faces
MAP 3 the sea – and this place tells you the stories. Films, exhibits, photos and paint-
D3 ings, from sail to oil. Decent cafe. Mon-Sat 10am-5pm, Sun 12-3pm.   ADM

2126 **THE SCOTTISH MARITIME MUSEUM:** Spread out over 3 sites, Irvine (01294
MAP 1 278283), Braehead (0141 886 1013) and Dumbarton (01389 763444).
C2 Dumbarton has the ship model experiment tank, Braehead (off J25A of the
MAP6 M8) has hands-on engines, while Irvine boasts a massive shed (Victorian
B4 engine shop) full of the bits that non-engineers never usually see, as well as
the hulk of an old clipper at Irvine harbour. Completely fascinating. More res-
onant than The Big Idea (1644/KID-FRIENDLY) along the road? You judge. Irvine
and Braehead open daily. AYR, Dumbarton Mon-Sat.

THE MOST INTERESTING PUBLIC GALLERIES

For EDINBURGH, see p. 70; GLASGOW, p. 108.

2127
MAP 4
C3
✓ ✓ **DUNDEE CONTEMPORARY ARTS:** Nethergate (01382 432000). State of the art (mainly cutting-edge) gallery (by award-winning architect Richard Murphy) with great café, cinema facilities, etc. which has transformed the cultural face of Dundee. People actually come from Edin/Glas for the openings & there ain't many other reasons they'd ever visit Dundee. ☕

2128
MAP 3
D3
✓ **ABERDEEN ART GALLERY:** Schoolhill. Major gallery with temp exhibits and eclectic permanent collection from Impressionists to Bellany. Large bequest from local granite merchant Alex Macdonald in 1900 contributes fascinating collection of his contemporaries: Bloomsburys, Scottish, Pre-Raphaelites. Excellent watercolour rm. An easy and rewarding gallery to visit. 10am-5pm (Sun 2-5pm).

2129
MAP 4
C3
✓ **THE FERGUSSON GALLERY, PERTH:** Marshall Pl on corner of Tay St in distinctive round tower (former waterworks). The assembled works on two floors of J D Fergusson 1874-1961. Though he spent much of his life in France, he had an influence on Scottish art and was pre-eminent amongst those now called the Colourists. It's a long way from Perth to Antibes 1913 but these pictures are a draught of the warm S. Mon-Sat 10-5pm.

2130
MAP 5
B3
✓ **KIRKCALDY MUSEUM AND ART GALLERY:** Nr railway stn, but ask for directions (it's easy to get lost). One of the best galleries in central Scotland. Splendid introduction to the history of 19th/20th-cent Scottish art. Lots of Colourists/McTaggart/Glasgow Boys. And Sickert to Redpath. Museum ain't bad. Kirkcaldy doesn't get a lot of good press, but this and the parks (1503/PARKS) are worth the journey (plus Valente's – 1347/FISH AND CHIPS). 7 days till 5pm.

2131
MAP 9
C3
✓ **HORNEL GALLERY, KIRKCUDBRIGHT:** Broughton House where he lived, now a fabulous evocation with collection of his work and atelier as was. 'Even the Queen was amazed'. The beautiful gdn stretching to the river is a real eye opener. April-Oct. 7 Days 11am-5.30pm.   NTS

2132
MAP 3
C1
✓ **DUFF HOUSE, BANFF:** Nice walk and easy to find from town centre. Important outstation of the National Gallery in meticulously restored Adam house with interesting history and spacious grounds. Ramsays, Raeburn, portraiture of mixed appeal and an El Greco. Maybe OTT for some, but major attraction in the area (go further up the Deveron, 1927/WOODLAND WALKS). Extensive prog of talks, workshops, performance. Enq TIC.

2133
MAP 9
C3
✓ **SCULPTURE AT GLENKILN RESERVOIR, nr DUMFRIES:** Take A75 to Castle Douglas and rt to Shawshead; into village, rt at T-jnct, left to Dunscore, immediate left, signed for reservoir. Follow rd along loch side and park. Not a gallery at all but sculpture scattered amongst the hills, woods and meadows around this reservoir in the Galloway Hills 16km SE of Dumfries. One or two are obvious, the others you just have to find. Epsteins and Moores. I found 3 (there are thought to be 6 in all). This is an enchanting place.

2134
THE PIER ART CENTRE, STROMNESS, ORKNEY MAINLAND: On main st (1509/COASTAL VILLAGES), a gallery on a small pier which could have come lock, stock and canvases from Cornwall. Permanent St Ives-style collection of Barbara Hepworth, Ben Nicholson, Paolozzi and others shown in a *simpatico* environment with the sea o/side. Also temporary exhibs. Cl Sun/Mon.

2135
MAP 1
C3
PAISLEY ART GALLERY AND MUSEUM: High St. Permanent collection of the world famous Paisley shawls and history of weaving techniques. Other exhibs usually have a local connection and an interactive element. Notable Greek Ionic-style building. Tues-Sat 10am-5pm, Sun 2-5pm.

2136
MAP 1
C3
MACLAURIN GALLERY, AYR: In Rozelle Park and the only art in these parts. Temporary exhibs change every month (incl local artists' work). 4 galleries and additional 5 rms featuring the Gaudi collection in Rozelle Hse; craft shop. AYR Mon-Sat 10am-5pm, Apr-Oct also Sun 2-5pm.

2137
MAP 1
B1
AN TAIRBEART ARTS CENTRE, TARBERT: 01880 821116 (Report: 1654/KIDS). Not a gallery, but Kintyre's cultural centre with temp exhibs. AYR Tues-Sat 10am-6pm.

2138 **McEWAN GALLERY nr BALLATER, DEESIDE:** A surprising place but for many
MAP 3 years this cottage gallery has been dealing in 19th/20th century, mainly
B3 Scottish art. They wrote the book! Summer exhibs, but open AYR 10am-6pm
(Sun 2-6pm). Wint hrs 01339 755429. 300m up A939 Tomintoul rd.

2139 **THE LOST GALLERY, MIDDLE OF NOWHERE, ABERDEENSHIRE:** Best
MAP 3 reached off the A944 Strathdon rd at Bellabeg, though don't follow the sign
B3 for 'Lost', the one you see in postcards. Fabulous small gallery of work by con-
temporary Scottish artists incl the owners. AYR 11am-5pm. Cl Tues.

2140 **STRATHEARN GALLERY, CRIEFF:** 32 W St (on Main St). Accessible & afford-
MAP 4 able. They know what you like. Fine and applied arts. 7 days (Thu-Sat in wint).
B3

2141 **ART-TM, INVERNESS:** 20 Bank St. 01463 712240. Excellent Scottish Arts
MAP 2 Council-backed gallery with regular arts and crafts shows. Even the staff are
C2 surprised to find something like this here. Tues-Sat 11am-6pm.

2142 **TOLQUHON GALLERY, nr ABERDEEN:** 01651 842343. Betw Ellon and
MAP 3 Oldmeldrum and nr Haddo House (1754/COUNTRY HOUSES) and Pitmedden
C2 (1483/GARDENS) – follow signs for castle, an interesting ruin for kids to clam-
ber. Real art at realistic prices. (Pron 'T'hon'.) 11am-5pm, Sun 2-5pm. Cl Thu.

2143 **JUST ART, FOCHABERS:** Main st, the A96 through Fochabers E of Elgin.
MAP 3 Changing exhibs of serious and selected mainly Scottish artists. Good ceram-
B2 ics. An interesting stop on this rd along the coast. See 1982/GARDEN CENTRES.

2144 **ST ANDREWS FINE ART:** Crowded walls of Scottish art from 1800-present.
MAP 5 Includes some good work from kent contemporaries. Peploe-Redpath and
C2 their chums. 10am-5pm. Cl Sun.

2145 **KRANENBURG & FOWLER FINE ARTS, OBAN:** Star Brae, 01631 562303. Geoff
MAP 1 and Jan source work from artists that ranges from the polite to the interest-
B1 ing. Small group of regular exhibitors and others. Cl Sun.

2146 **MORVERN GALLERY, BARVAS, ISLE OF LEWIS:** Coast rd just N of Barabhas
MAP 2 30km from Callanish and those stones. Janice Scott's excl farm steading kind
B1 of gallery with well-selected work, mainly local. Painting, tapestry, ceramics
and fab original knits. Baking. AYR 10am-5pm. Cl Sun.

2147 **GALLERY HEINZEL, ABERDEEN:** 21 Spa St. Major commercial gallery in city
MAP 3 with credibility. A showcase for NE arts with changing exhibs. Frequent atten-
D3 dees of the Glasgow Art Fair. Cl Sun/Mon.

2148 **SCOTTISH SCULPTURE WORKSHOPS, LUMSDEN nr ALFORD and HUNTLY**:
MAP 3 Main st of ribbon town on A97. Not a place to see work for sale (mainly com-
B3 missions), but work being made. They also look after the sculpture gdn at end of
st towards Alford by the school. Workshops open AYR. Mon-Fri 9am-5pm.

2149 **LOGIE STEADING nr FORRES:** Estate courtyard in beautiful countryside
MAP 3 10km S of Forres though not so obvious to find. Nr pleasant woodland walk
A2 and picnic spot. For directions, see 1915/WOODLAND WALKS. Well chosen art
and ceramics from Highland artists and workshops. Tearoom. Certainly one of
the best small galleries in N Scotland. Apr-Dec, 7 days 10.30am-5pm.

2150 **THE GLASGOW ART FAIR:** The Scottish market place for contemporary art
MAP B with mainly home-grown and London galleries with Scottish connections.
D3 Held in mid April in pavilions in George Square. 0141 552 6027 for details.
(798/ESS. CULTURE/FESTIVALS)

Prints by many contemp Scottish artists available from:

GLASGOW PRINT STUDIOS: 22 King St, Merchant City/Tron area.

EDINBURGH PRINTMAKERS WORKSHOP: 23 Union St off Leith Walk

PEACOCK VISUAL ARTS, ABERDEEN: 21 Castle St.

THE DEGREE SHOWS, EDINBURGH/GLASGOW ART SCHOOLS: Work from
final-year students. Discover the Bellanys/Howsons of the future. 2-week exhibition after manic first night (mid June).

EDINBURGH

BARS AND CLUBS

2151
MAP A
D2
✓ **NEW TOWN BAR:** 538 7775. 26 Dublin St. Basement and underground club. Tends to be watering hole for older crowd. No twinkies. Downstairs now called **KALEIDOSCOPE** open weekend nights for more shady corners and action. Open 7 days till 1am, w/ends 2am. Mixed crowd.

2152
MAP A
D2
✓ **PLANET OUT:** 524 0061. Traditionally the pre-club, pre-CCs hangout. Now has loyal following of bright-er, younger things. Handy too for the Playhouse and an unthreatening vibe. You could take your mum. 7 days till 1am.

2153
MAP A
D2
✓ **CC BLOOM'S:** 556 9331. Next to Playhouse. Bar up, disco down. Now an institution, this is where everybody eventually ends up. Busy bar with karaoke upstairs & club below. Can get pretty frenzied (478/ESSENTIAL CULTURE/CLUBS) at weekends. Don't expect miracles, although you might need one … 7 days.

2154
MAP A
C2
✓ **FRENCHIE'S:** 225 7651. Rose St Lane N nr Castle St. Intimate bar quite removed from the East End Pink Triangle. Hence more intimate but no less trashy. Fun before age (or beauty) so suits all. 7 days till 1am.

2155
MAP A
E2
✓ **STAG AND TURRET:** 478 7231. 1 Montrose Terr, Abbeyhill nr well-known cruising area. Friendly local. Pool table. 7 days till 1am.

OTHER PLACES

2156
MAP A
D2
✓ **BLUE MOON CAFÉ:** 556 2788. 36 Broughton St. Always busy, the boys and girls serve quick and cool in this all-day café. Attracts lively mixed (and earnest) crowd for food & drink and chat. Exhibitions and 'Out of the Blue' gay accessories shop downstairs. If you are arriving in Edin and don't know anybody, come here first. Food 7 days till 10ish; bar 11.30pm. (268/CAFÉS)

2157
MAP A
D1
CLAREMONT BAR & RESTAURANT: 556 5662. 133 East Claremont St. Small and cheery wee bar handy for sauna. Own crowd and occasional fetish nights. Bulkies and furries have nights too. Food 7 days till 10pm. Bar 7 days till 1am.

2158
MAP A
E1
NO. 18: 553 3222. 18 Albert Pl. Sauna for gentlemen. Discreet doorway halfway down Leith Walk. Mon–Sat 12noon-10pm. Sun 2-10pm.

2159
MAP A
D1
TOWNHOUSE HEALTH CLUB: 556 6116. 51 E Claremont St, just down from Broughton St. Move 'upmarket' and move downstairs (up & down, up & down they go) then above. The lounge is almost a lounge. New sauna, open till 11pm.

HOTELS

2160
MAP A
xE4
✓ **SOUTHSIDE GH:** 668 4422. 8 Newington Rd nr Commonwealth Pool. Not too far away and 68/EXCL LODGINGS well-appointed GH. Mixed but do advertise in *Gay Times*. No smk. 7RMS JAN-DEC X/T XPETS CC KIDS INX

2161
MAP A
xE1
✓ **ARDMOR HOUSE:** 554 4944. 74 Pilrig St. Quiet mix of contemporary & original design meet in this paean to style. Family room so straight-friendly. No smk. 5RMS JAN-DEC X/T PETS CC KIDS MED.EXP

2162
MAP A
D2
MANSFIELD HOUSE: 556 7980. 57 Dublin St. Small New Town guest house and OK gay stay. Candelabra in the hall, various other camperie. Breakfast on a tray. No public rms – you'll have to leave your door open. New Town Bar (*see above*) up the st. 5RMS JAN-DEC X/X XPETS XCC XKIDS MED.INX

2163
MAP A
B3
ST VALERY GH: 337 1893. 36 Coates Gardens, W End. Gay-friendly rather than gay GH (not gay owners). 20RMS JAN-DEC T/T XPETS CC KIDS INX

2164
MAP A
xE1
GARLANDS: 554 4205. 48 Pilrig St. Quiet st of many other GH – a stroll to the scene (but nr sauna). No smk. 6RMS JAN-DEC X/T PETS CC KIDS CHP

GLASGOW

BARS AND CLUBS

2165
MAP B
D4
✓ **DELMONICA'S:** 552 4803. 68 Virginia St. Newly refurbed stylish pub with long bar and open plan in quiet lane in Merchant City. Open-plan bar in gay quarter. Pleasant and airy during day but busy and 'sceney' at night, esp w/ends. 7 days till 12midnight.

2166
MAP B
D4
✓ **POLO LOUNGE:** 553 1221. 84 Wilson St. Great venue with stylish refurb decor, period furnishings. Something like gents' club meets Euro-lounge. Downstairs disco (Fri-Sun) with 3am licence; otherwise till 1am (one of the few pubs in town serving after midnight). (725/HIP & STYLE BARS)

2167
MAP B
C4
WATERLOO BAR: 221 7539. 306 Argyle St. Scotland's oldest gay bar and it tells. But an unpretentious down-to-earth vibe so refreshing in its way. Old-established bar and clientele. Not really for trendy young things. You might not fancy anybody but they're a friendly old bunch. 7 days till 12 midnight.

2168
MAP B
E4
CANDLE BAR: 564 1285. 20 Candleriggs. Newly refurb bar, funky design with purples and lilacs attracts the v fashion conscious younger set. Something on every night. Food till 5pm! Every day till 12 midnight.

2169
MAP B
E4
COURT BAR: 552 2463. 69 Hutcheson St, centre of Merchant City area. Long-going small bar that's fairly straight till mid-evening. 7 days till midnight.

2170
MAP B
D3
SADIE FROST'S: 332 8005. 8 W George St, in front of Queen St Stn, hence catches all the passing trade and well placed for the brief encounter. Gets jumpy nr closing time. Pool room for sporty types. 7 days till midnight.

2171
MAP B
D4
BENNET'S: 552 5761. 80 Glassford St. This was always where everyone went before the rave days! And many still do. Relentless, unashamed fun without attitude. Wed-Sun 11pm-3am, Tue is 'traditionally' straight night.

2172
MAP B
E4
REVOLVER: 553 2456. 6a John St in basement opp Italian Centre. Recent (2001) civilised subterranea. Gr juke box, pool, ale. Some uniform nights. 7 days all day to midnight.

OTHER PLACES

2173
MAP B
D4
MODA: 553 2553. Corner of Virginia St and Wilson St. Chill-out vibe in bar with mixed crowd and regular DJs. W/days till 1am and w/ends 3am.

2174
MAP B
D4
CENTURION SAUNA: 248 4485. 19 Dixon St, above Aer Lingus and St Enoch's. Till 10pm or later (some Sat all-nighters).

2175
MAP B
C4
THE LANE: 221 1802. 60 Robertson St, nr Waterloo (*see above*) opp side of Argyle St, lane on rt. You 'look for the green light'. Sauna and private club. You wouldn't call it upmarket. 7 days, afternoons till 10pm.

2176
MAP B
B1
ALBION HOTEL: 339 8620. 405 N Woodside Rd, off Gr Western Rd. Currently Glasgow's only prospect is gay-friendly (i.e. they advertise in *Gay Times*) rather than gay. From the window, prospect is of treelined River Kelvin and handy for West End living.   16RMS JAN-DEC T/T XPETS CC KIDS INX

ABERDEEN

Gay scene in Aberdeen in disarray at TGP. Only one bar/club:

2177
MAP 3
D3
BAR CASTROS: 01224 639920. 47 Netherkirkgate. Down the back of M&S. Two floors with small bar upstairs & dancefloor downstairs. They'll be pleased to see you. Most nights till 2am.

DUNDEE

2178 **CHARLIE'S BAR:** 01382 226840. 75 Seagate nr Yates Wine Lodge. Okay and
MAP 4   recently improved pub, small-city scene, but if you're in Dundee for the night,
C3   you might. 7 days till 11pm/midnight.

2179 **LIBERTY NIGHTCLUB:** 01382 200660. 124 Seagate. Along from the above so
MAP 4   follows on. Bar and dancefloor. Everybody knows everybody else, but not you.
C3   This may have its advantages. Wed-Sun till 2.30am. Also …

2180 **BAR XS:** 01382 200660. St Andrews Lane. Behind and above Liberty's. Small
MAP 4   bar, a pre-club bar on disco nights (reduced tickets avail at bar). 7 days till mid-
C3   night (11pm Sun).

HOTELS ELSEWHERE

Not many, but Auchendean more than just 'gay-friendly'.

2181 **AUCHENDEAN LODGE, DULNAIN BRIDGE:** 01479 851347. A Highland
MAP 2   retreat in an area with lots of outdoorsy things to do. Innovative cooking. (Eric
D3   and Ian well on the case 1020/INEXP HIGHLAND HOTELS). This is still the place to
take your other half away from it all. Romance and more.

           7RMS   JAN-DEC   X/T   PETS   CC   KIDS   TOS   MED.EX

THE MOST INTERESTING THEATRES AND CINEMAS

For EDINBURGH, see pp. 70-1; and GLASGOW, see pp. 109-10.

2182
MAP 1
A1
MULL LITTLE THEATRE, DERVAIG, MULL: 01688 302828. 'The smallest theatre in Britain' is still there after more than 25 years. On edge of dinky Dervaig, 10km from Tobermory. Bar and acceptable restau adj at the Druimard Country-House Hotel. Tiny auditorium, so you're almost on top of the actors. Never predictable. Its incongruity is part of its appeal. Easter-Sept. Curtain up 8.30pm. Cosy seats; cosy intervals. Box office also in Tobermory main st.

2183
MAP 1
D2
CUMBERNAULD THEATRE: 01236 732887. Nr old part of this new town on a rise o/look the ubiquitous dual carriageway (to Stirling). Follow signs for Cumbernauld House. Bar/café-restau and 258-seat theatre (in the round) with a mixed programme of one-nighters and short runs of mainly Scottish touring companies. Also concerts, drama workshops and kids' programmes. A community-based and vital theatre, one of the better reasons to 'relocate in Cumbernauld'.

2184
MAP 8
B3
BOWHILL LITTLE THEATRE, BOWHILL HOUSE, nr SELKIRK: 01750 22204. Tiny theatre off the courtyard below Bowhill House with intermittent mixed programme (must phone), but always delightful, esp with supper afterwards in Courtyard Restau (also phone to book).

2185
MAP 4
B2
PITLOCHRY THEATRE: 01796 472680. Modern rep theatre across river from main st performing usually 6 plays on different nights of the week. With a well-chosen programme of classics and popular works, the 500-seat theatre is often full. V mixed Sunday concerts and foyer fringe events. Coffee bar and recently extended restau menu. Also at all times. Portnacraig adj, by river (01796 472777), or excellent East Haugh House on rd S, 2km town centre (01796 473121).

2186
MAP 2
C2
EDEN COURT THEATRE, INVERNESS: 01463 234234. An important theatre complex making a vital contribution to the cultural life of the Highlands. Diverse programme of theatre, dance, variety, all kinds of music, opera, trad – the occasional coup. Easy to book by credit card; lots do sell out. Theatre bar and the Ness over there. Cinema programme of selected art-house/first-run movies. What would Inverness watch without it?

2187
MAP 5
C2
BYRE THEATRE, ST ANDREWS: 01334 476288. Abbey St or South St. Serious theatre in receipt of big lottery funding, so total rebuild & reopened summer 2001. Check locally. Wills bound to be there some time.

2188
MAP 8
C2
THE WYND, MELROSE: 01896 823854. 100-seater arts venue which regularly entertains locals and even Edin folk. From classic Ibsen and musicals to folk, jazz, dance and film. Intimate atmos in an intimate town.

2189
MAP 1
B3
CAMPBELTOWN PICTURE HOUSE: 01586 553657. Campbeltown, Argyll. Cinema Paradiso on the Kintyre peninsula. Lovingly preserved art deco gem; a shrine to the movies. Opened 1913, closed 1983, but such was the tide of nostalgic affection that it was refurbished and reopened resplendent in 1989. Shows mainly first-run films. To see a film here and emerge onto the esplanade of Campbeltown L is to experience the lost magic of a night at the pictures.

2190
MAP 5
C2
THE NEW PICTURE HOUSE, ST ANDREWS: 01334 473509. On North St. 'New' means 1931 and, apart from adding another screen (the small Cinema 2), it hasn't changed much, as generations of students will remember with fondness. Mainly first-run flicks and Oct-May, there's a programme of late-night cult/art movies.

2191
MAP 8
C2
THE ROXY, KELSO: 01573 224609. Horsemarket. A cinema from my youth, still remarkably here and unchanged; still the smell of hot celluloid. Few better places to watch a first-run movie or an art flick and enjoy 'real Scottish popcorn'. Sun, Tues, Wed, Sat (early) and bingo on Mon, Thur & Fri/Sat. Don't you ever close.

SECTION 13

The Islands

2192
MAP 2
B2
✔ ✔ **RAASAY:** A small car ferry (car useful, but bikes best) from Sconser betw Portree and Broadford on Skye takes you to this, the best of places. The distinctive flat top of Dun Caan presides over an island whose history and natural history is Highland Scotland in microcosm. The village with MED. INX hotel and bar (and rows of mining-type cottages) is 3km from jetty. The Outdoor Centre (01478 660226) in the big hoose (once the home of the notorious Dr No who, like others before him, allowed Raasay to go to rack and ruin) has courses galore. They'll put you up if they've got rm (mostly bunkrooms). The views from the lawn, or the viewpoint above the house, or better still from Dun Caan with the Cuillins on one side and Torridon on the other, are quite brilliant (2229/ISLAND WALKS). There's a ruined castle, a secret rhododendron-lined loch for swimming, seals, otters and eagles. Much to explore. Go quietly here. *Regular Calmac ferry from Sconser, but not Sun.*

2193
MAP 1
B2
✔ ✔ **JURA:** Small regular car ferry from Pt Askaig on Islay takes you into a different world. Jura is remote, scarcely populated and has an ineffable grandeur indifferent to the demands of tourism. Ideal for wild camping, alternatively the serviceable hotel and pub (2218/ISLAND HOTELS) in the only village (Craighouse) 15km from ferry at Feolin. Walking guides available at hotel and essential esp for the Paps, the hills that maintain such a powerful hold over the island. Easiest climb is from Three Arch Br; allow 6hrs. In May they run up all of them and back to the distillery in 3hrs. Jura House's walled gdn is a hidden jewel set above the S coastline; myriad wildflowers and Australasian trees with scenic walks to the shore. The Corryvreckan whirlpool (2236/ISLAND WALKS) is another lure, but you may need a lift in a 4-wheel drive to get close enough to walk, and its impressiveness depends upon tides. Orwell's house (Barnhill; where he wrote 1984) is not open, but there are many fascinating side tracks: the wild west coast; around L Tarbert; and the long littoral betw Craighouse and Lagg. (Also 1531/BEACHES; 1805/GRAVEYARDS.) With one rd, no st lamps and over 5,000 deer the sound of silence is everything. *Western Ferries (01496 840681) regular 7 days, 5min service from Pt Askaig.*

2194
MAP 1
A1
✔ ✔ **IONA:** Strewn with daytrippers – not so much a pilgrimage, more an invasion – but Iona still enchants (as it did the Colourists), esp if you can get away to the Bay at the Back of the Ocean (1538/BEACHES) or watch the cavalcade from the hill above the Abbey. Or stay: Argyll Hotel best (01681 700334) or B&B. Abbey shop isn't bad (2049/CRAFT SHOPS). Pilgrimage walks on Wed (10am from St John's Cross). Bike hire from Finlay Ross shop 01681 700357. Everything about Iona is benign; even the sun shines here when it's raining on Mull. *Reg 15min Calmac service from Fionnphort till 6pm (earlier in winter).*

2195
MAP 2
B3
✔ ✔ **EIGG:** After changing hands, much to-do and cause célèbre, the islanders seized the time and Eigg is finally theirs; and of course, ours. A wildlife haven for birds and sealife; otters, eagles and seal colonies. Scot Wildlife Trust warden does weekly walks around the island. July is the 'Month of Music' with lots of ceilidhs. Refurb tearoom at pier. Licenced and evening meals. Bicycle hire 01687 482469. 2 croft houses at Cleadale near Laig bay and the Singing Sands beach; contact Sue Kirk 01687 482405 (knows loads about all aspects of island). She also offers full board accom and caters for vegn and other diets. 2,000 sheep on island. Gr walk to Sgurr an Eigg – an awesome perch on a summer's day. *CalMac (from Mallaig) 01687 462403 or (better, from Arisaig) Arisaig Marine 01687 450224 every day except Thurs in summer. No car ferry; but motorbikes poss. Day trips to Rum and Muck.*

2196
MAP 2
B3
✔ ✔ **RUM:** The large island in the group S of Skye, off the coast at Mallaig. The Calmac ferry plies betw Canna, Eigg, Muck and Rum but not too conveniently and it's not easy to island-hop and make a decent visit (but *see below*). Rum the most wild and dramatic has an extraordinary time-warp mansion in Kinloch Castle which lets out 5 of its incredible rms to guests, but is mainly a museum (guided tours tie in with boat trips). Below stairs a hostel contrasts to the antique opulence above. Also a bistro, but it must be pre-booked (no lunch). Details: 2219/ISLAND HOTELS. Rum is run by Scottish Natural Heritage and there are fine trails, climbs, bird-watching spots. Coffee-shop at the Community Hall (open for day-trippers). 2 simple walks are marked for the

3hr visitors, but the island reveals its mysteries more slowly. The Doric temple mausoleum to George Bullough, the industrialist whose Highland fantasy the castle was, is a 12km (6hr) walk across the island to Harris Bay. Sighting the sea eagles may be one of the best things that ever happens to you. *Calmac ferry from Mallaig via Eigg (2hrs 15mins) or Canna at an ungodly hr. Better from Arisaig (Murdo Grant 01687 450224) Tues/Thur/Sat/Sun in summer (3hrs ashore).*

2197
MAP 1
B3
✓ **GIGHA:** Romantic small island off Kintyre coast; with classic views of its island neighbours. Easy access to mainland (20min ferry trip) contributes to an island atmos that lacks any feeling of isolation. Like Eigg, Gigha was bought by the islanders so its fragile economy is even more dependent on your visit. The island currently remains a whole estate; with gdns open at the main house (1480/GARDENS) and a hotel (2215/ISLAND HOTELS) providing comfortable surroundings, Gigha cheeses and seafood. The locals are relaxed (now) and friendly; with bike hire, B&B (CHP) and good home-cooking available courtesy of the estimable Andy & Viv at the post office on the ferry rd (01583 505251). Best Walk: Left after golf course (9 hole), through gate and follow track (signed Ardailly) past Mill L to Mill and shore; gr views to Jura (1-B-2). See: Double Beach, where the Queen once swam off the Royal Yacht; two crescents of sand on either side of the N end of the isthmus of Eilean Garbh (seen from rd but path poorly marked). *Calmac ferry from Tayinloan on A83, 27km S of Tarbert (Glas 165km). One an hour in summer, fewer in winter. Cars exp and unnecessary.*

2198
MAP 1
A1
✓ **ULVA:** Off W coast of Mull. A boat leaves Ulva Ferry on the B8073 26km S of Dervaig. Idyllic wee island with 5 well-marked walks incl to the curious basalt columns similar to Staffa, or by causeway to the smaller island of Gometra; plan routes at boathouse 'interpretive centre' and tearoom (with Ulva oysters). Meet shaggy dog Bertie, who is more than happy to be your guide to the island should you desire some 4-legged company. No accom. A charming Telford church has services 4 times a yr. Ulva is a perfect day away from the rat race of downtown Mull. *All-day 5min service in summer (not Sats) till 5pm. Ferryman: 01688 500226.*

2199
MAP 2
A3
✓ **ERISKAY:** Made famous by the sinking nearby of the SS *Politician* in 1941 and the salvaging of its cargo of whisky, immortalised by Compton Mackenzie in *Whisky Galore*, this Hebridean gem has all the 'idyllic island' ingredients: perfect beaches (1837/MARY, CHARLIE AND BOB), a hill to climb, a pub (called the Politician and telling the story round its walls; it sells decent pub food all day in summer), and a small, frequent ferry. There's only limited B & B and no hotel, but camping is ok if you're discreet. Eriskay and Barra together – the pure island experience. (Also 1789/CHURCHES *and see* THE WESTERN ISLES p. 300). *Car ferry from Ludaig, S Uist has been replaced by a causeway. Passenger boat (01851 701702) 3/4 per day acc to tides, also serves Barra. 5 per day AYR. Passenger boat (01878 720238) 3/4 per day, acc to tides, also serves Barra.*

2200
MAP 2
A3
✓ **MINGULAY:** Deserted mystical island nr the southern tip of the Outer Hebrides, the subject of one of the definitive island books, *The Road to Mingulay*. Now easily reached in summer by daily trip from Castlebay, Barra with 1.5hr journey and 3hrs ashore (enquire at TIC or Castlebay Hotel, the boat operators 01871 810223). Last inhabitants left 1912. Ruined village has the poignant air of St Kilda; similar spectacular cliffs on W side with fantastic rock formations, stacks and a huge natural arch – best viewed from boat. Mingulay was bought by NTS in '99. Only birds & sheep live here now.

2201
MAP 1
A2
✓ **COLONSAY:** Accessible to daytrippers in summer (with the ferry round trip); this island haven of wildlife, flowers and beaches (1522/BEACHES) deserves more than a few hrs exploration. Congenial hotel and pub (food not great); self-catering units nearby. Some holiday cottages, but camping discouraged. Coffee/craft/shop adj to hotel and pantry at the pier. A wild 18-hole golf course and bookshop (sic) adj. Semi-botanical gdns adj to Colonsay House and fine walks, esp to Oronsay (2232/ISLAND WALKS). Don't miss the house at Shell Beach which sells oysters and honey. *Calmac from Oban (or Islay) Sun, Wed, Fri in summer. Crossing takes just over 2hrs.*

2202
MAP 1
B1
LISMORE: Sail from Oban (car ferry) or better from Pt Appin 5km off main A828, the Oban-Ft William rd, 32km N Oban and where there's a seafood bar/restau/hotel (1345/SEAFOOD RESTAUS), to sit and wait. A rd goes down the centre of the island, but there are many hill and coastal walks and even the nr

end round Pt Ramsay feels away from it all. History, natural history and air. Bike hire on island from Mary McDougal 01631 760213 who will deliver to ferry or Port Appin Bikes 01631 730391. Tearoom (not always open) 3km S of ferry, a pleasant stroll. *Calmac service from Oban, 4 or 5 times a day (not Sun). From Pt Appin (32km N of Oban) several per day. 5mins. Last back 8.15pm 9.30 Fri & Sat, but check (6.15pm winter).*

CALMAC: 08705 650000

THE BEST ISLAND HOTELS

2203
MAP 2
A2
✓ ✓ **THE HOUSE OVER-BY at THE THREE CHIMNEYS, SKYE:** 01470 511258. At Colbost 7km W of Dunvegan by the B884 to Glendale. Eddie & Shirley Spear's quietly luxurious and tastefully decorated rms, adj or just over-by from their notable, almost legendary restau (2223/ISLAND RESTAUS). Separate dining rm for healthy buffet b/fast. Outside the sheep, the sea and the sky. Setting new standards in the Highlands, this is where to come for the pamper-yourself w/end.   6RMS JAN-DEC T/T PETS CC KIDS TOS INX

2204
MAP 2
A3
✓ **CASTLEBAY HOTEL, BARRA:** 01871 810223. Prominent position o/look bay and ferry dock. You see where you're staying long before you arrive. Exceptionally good value hotel at the centre of Barra life with nice owners who are always there. They run the boats to Mingulay, so they can sort out your days out. Good restau and bar meals (2240/WESTERN ISLES). Adj bar one of the best bars for crack and car culture in Scotland and with more than a dash of the Irish (1272/BLOODY GOOD PUBS).   12RMS JAN-DEC T/T PETS CC KIDS INX

2205
MAP 2
B3
✓ **KINLOCH LODGE, SKYE:** 01471 833333. S of Broadford in Sleat Peninsula, 18km Ryliakin, 55km Portree. The ancestral, but not overly imposing home of Lord and Lady Macdonald with new build house adj – adding 5 v well appointed rms and spacious, country drawing rm. Lady Mac is Claire Macdonald of cookery fame, so her many books for sale, cookery courses thro' yr and her hand in all the wonderful things you eat (all meals in the Lodge itself). Some Lodge rms small and less exp. See 2222/RESTAUS.
9+5RMS JAN-DEC X/T XPETS KIDS TOS LOTS

2206
MAP 1
A3
✓ **PORT CHARLOTTE HOTEL, ISLAY:** 01496 850360. The Leavey family had a choice: stay in LA or refurb a hotel in Islay. The rest is (recent) history. Modern, discreet approach in this fine whitewashed village (COASTAL VILLAGES/1513), good whisky choice, and good food for a kitchen so far-flung. Tourists in summer, hardcore twitchers in winter … and us anytime.
10RMS JAN-DEC T/T PETS CC MED.EX

2207
MAP 2
B3
✓ **EILEAN IARMAIN, SKYE:** 01471 833332. Isleornsay, Sleat. 60km S of Portree. Tucked into the bay this Gaelic inn with its gr pub and quite good food provides famously comfortable base in S of the island. 6 rms in main hotel best value (6 are in separate house). Also 4 suites over-by – nice but exp.   12RMS + 4SUITES JAN-DEC T/T PETS CC KIDS TOS EXP

2208
MAP 2
A2
✓ ✓ **ARDVOURLIE CASTLE, HARRIS:** 01859 502307. Just off main rd 45mins S Stornoway (16km N Tarbert). Not so much a castle, but a charming Victorian lodge meticulously restored by Derek Martin, a former professor at Imperial College and his sister Pamela. Huge bathrooms. Dinner by gaslight. Derek is an excellent chef. Everything home-made. They've planted 7,000 trees in gdns that stretch down to the loch. A real labour of love. Green fingers & v green-friendly. Special.   4RMS APR-OCT X/T XPETS XCC KIDS TOS EXP

2209
MAP 2
A2
✓ **SCARISTA HOUSE, SOUTH HARRIS:** 01859 550238. 21km Tarbert, 78km Stornoway. On the W coast famous for its beaches and o/look one of the best (1529/BEACHES). Tim & Patricia Martin's civilised retreat & home from home. Fixed menu meals in dining rooms o/look sea. No TVs, phones, but many books. The golf course over the rd is exquisite.
5RMS JAN-DEC X/X PETS CC KIDS TOS EXP

2210
MAP 1
A1
✓ **CALGARY FARMHOUSE, MULL:** 01688 400256. 7kms S of Dervany (30 mins Tobermory) nr beautiful Calgary Beach. Roadside bistro/restau (2227/ISLAND RESTAUS) with rms and gallery/coffee shop. Fairly basic and v sympatico. Matthew makes furniture. Family-friendly. 2 new self-cat suites above gallery. Good mod-Brit cooking. Lovely 'sculpture' work out back & to beach.   9RMS APR-OCT X/X PETS CC KIDS TOS MED.INX

2211 **KILMICHAEL, BRODICK, ARRAN:** 01770 302219. On main rd to castle/
MAP 1 Corrie, take left at bend by golf course and you're in the country. 3km down
C3 track is this delightful small country-house hotel with v individual rms and
many ornaments. Good bookcase, nice Japanese items, best hotel on the island.
And the most trad-classic cuisine.   6RMS JAN-DEC T/T PETS CC KIDS TOS EXP

2212 **HIGHLAND COTTAGE, TOBERMORY:** 01688 302030. Breadalbane St opp fire
MAP 1 stn. Trad Tobermory st above harbour (from r/bout on rd in from Craignure). 6
B1 comfy rms named after islands (all themed, one called Nantucket) not large
but all facs. Upstairs lounge with honesty bar. Big local rep for food in intimate
dining rm (open non-res, but must book). Good books, vids, vibes.
6RMS FEB T/T XPETS CC KIDS TOS MED.EXP

2213 **WESTERN ISLES HOTEL, TOBERMORY, MULL:** 01688 302012. Victorian edi-
MAP 1 fice more reminiscent of a stn hotel in town – till you see the view from your
B1 bedrm. Individual rms (rates vary but front def best) and lounges.
Conservatory also looks over the harbour and bay. Food so-so. Hotel for sale
at TGP.   26RMS JAN-DEC T/T PETS CC KIDS TOS MED.EXP

2214 **BAILE-NA-CILLE, TIMSGARRY, UIG, LEWIS:** 01851 672242. 58km W of
MAP 2 Stornoway via Garynahine and Leurbost. A far-away and long-established
A1 refuge which takes you in and restores the battered spirit. O/look sea. Easy-
going; you're one of the family and they welcome yours (1156/KIDS). Couldn't
visit this time round, but things don't change much here. No smk.
10RMS MAR-OCT X/X PETS CC KIDS MED.INX

2215 **THE GIGHA HOTEL, ISLE OF GIGHA:** 01583 505254. A short walk from the
MAP 1 ferry (or they will collect you) on an island perfectly proportioned for a short
B3 visit; easy walking and cycling. Residents' lounge peaceful with dreamy views
to Kintyre. Menu with local produce (in bar or dining-rm) gets mixed reviews.
Ask what's fresh (not frozen)! Island life without the remoteness. Also self-cat
cottages. 2197/ISLANDS.   13RMS APR-OCT T/T PETS CC KIDS TOS MED.EX

2216 **VIEWFIELD HOUSE, PORTREE, SKYE:** 01478 612217. One of the first hotels
MAP 2 you come to in Portree on the rd from S (driveway opp gas stn); you need look
B2 no further. Individual, grand but comfortable, full of antiques and memorabil-
ia, though not at all stuffy; this is also one of the best-value hotels on the
island. Log fires, communal dinner. The Macdonalds like you to eat in & in
Portree there is nowhere better. 11RMS APR-OCT X/X PETS CC KIDS TOS MED.EX

2217 **FLODIGARRY, SKYE:** 01470 552203. Staffin, 32km N of Portree. A romantic
MAP 2 country house o/look the sea, with Flora Mac's cottage in the grounds. Good
B2 food, gr crack in the bar; you'll be reeling. Report: 1150/COUNTRY-HOUSE HOTELS.
12RMS + 7COTT JAN-DEC T/X PETS CC KIDS TOS EXP

2218 **JURA HOTEL:** 01496 820243. Craighouse, 15km from Islay ferry at Feolin.
MAP 1 Serviceable, basic hotel o/look Small Isles Bay; will oblige with all
B3 walking/exploring requirements. Pub is social hub of island. Rms at front may
be small, but have the views. Keith went in 2001, got wired into a special bot-
tling of the Jura malt from over the road, and woke up next morning with
vague memories of a woman from New Zealand and notes that read, 'People
here wear weird trousers and play the Waterboys voluntarily'. Well he had a
good time – so may you.   18RMS JAN-DEC X/X PETS CC KIDS INX

2219 **KINLOCH CASTLE, RUM:** 01687 462037. The fantastic OTT edifice of a
MAP 2 Victorian entrepreneur George Bullough now mainly a museum, but 5 opu-
B3 lent rms are available. The bathrooms are from another world. Servant quar-
ters have hostel accom. Bistro dining by arrangement. Island has superb
wildlife. Run by Scottish Natural Heritage.
5RMS + HOSTEL JAN-DEC X/X X/PETS CC KIDS EXP/CHP

2220 **ISLE OF BARRA HOTEL, BARRA:** 01871 810383. The other hotel in Barra (see
MAP 2 Castlebay, above) exterior, but comfortable inside with gr setting and rms
A3 o/look fab Tangasdale Beach. Nr Seal Bay (1533/BEACHES) and other quiet
places. Bar the locals like. 3km from town (and bike hire, 2240/WESTERN ISLES).
30RMS APR-SEPT X/T PETS CC KIDS MED.INX

2221 **ARDMORY HOUSE, ROTHESAY:** 01700 502346. We've never recommended
MAP 1 anything on Bute before, so here goes: small friendly hotel up the hill
C3 (Ardmory Road) run by Muriel McGhee. Neat, unassuming, views. Nice conservatory. Mount Stuart nearby (1755/CO HOUSES) & Rothesay has its moments
(check the famous loos).   5RMS JAN-DEC T/T PETS CC XKIDS MED.EX

THE BEST RESTAURANTS IN THE ISLANDS

2222
MAP 2
B3
✓ ✓ **KINLOCH LODGE, SKYE:** 01471 833333. In S on Sleat Peninsula, 55km S of Portree signed off the 'main' Sleat rd, along a long characterful track. Lord and Lady MacDonald's family home/hotel offers a taste of the high life without hauteur; a setting and setup especially appreciated by Americans and other visitors. Lady Claire's stints at the stoves are renowned, as are the cookery books that result. Dinner almost a theatrical event, (the dining-rm: lined with oils, furnished with antiques, glinting with silver). Fixed menu. Perfect cheeses but you simply must leave rm for the puds.   EXP

2223
MAP 2
A2
✓ ✓ **THE THREE CHIMNEYS, SKYE:** 01470 511258. Colbost. 7km W Dunvegan on B884 to Glendale. Shirley and Eddie Spear's classic restau in a converted cottage on the edge of the best kind of nowhere. They shop local for everything so best ingredients. Feb-Dec. Lunch (not Sun), dinner LO 9.30pm. Check times in wint.   EXP

2224
MAP 1
C3
✓ **KILMICHAEL HOTEL, ARRAN:** 01770 302219. 3km from seafront rd in Brodick, this is the place to go for dinner. Report: 2211/HOTELS.   MED

2225
MAP 2
A1
✓ **BONAVENTURE, LEWIS:** 01851 672474. Aird Uig N of Timsgarry on B8011, about 30kms W of Stornoway via A858. This is about as far-flung as you can get and many will be the most wee westerly restau in the UK. I haven't been, but by all and many accounts it's quite brilliant. Often fully booked for dinner. Chef/prop Richard Leparoux prepares French–Scottish food from mainly local ingreds (obviously). Nautical theme in unusual ex-RAF base and poss a short hike (or car) up Forsnabhal for a spectacular panorama or sunset. Phone to book & for opening.   MED

2226
MAP 2
A3
CASTLEBAY HOTEL, CASTLEBAY: 01871 810223. V decent plain cooking in informal dining-rm or bar o/look castle and bay. Scores mainly when fresh from the bay (lobster) or off the beach (cockles in garlic butter), but their sticky toffee pudding is exactly as it ought to be. Inexpensive wines.   MED

2227
MAP 1
A1
CALGARY FARMHOUSE AND DOVECOTE RESTAU, MULL: 01688 400256. 7km from Dervaig on B8073 nr Mull's famous beach. Roadside farm setting with inexp light, piney bedrms and a bistro/wine bar restau using local produce. For Mod-Brit cuisine. Gallery/coffee shop in summer. A quiet spot for most cosmo meal on Mull.   INX

2228
MAP 2
B2
AN TUIREANN, SKYE: 01478 613306. On Struan Rd, edge of Portree (direction Uig from main rd into Portree from Sligachan). Not so much a restau, more a café-bar in an arts centre. This is where to go in Skye for interesting local and national touring exhibs and for Kate Terley's contemp mainly vegn snacks and meals. Nice soups. Best coffee. 10am-4.30pm, cl Sun.   INX

LOCHBAY SEAFOOD, SKYE: 12km N Dunvegan (2239/SKYE).   INX

CREELERS, ARRAN: 01770 302810. Edge of Brodick (2237/ARRAN).   MED

BUSTA HOUSE, SHETLAND: 01806 522506. 35km N of Lerwick (2243/SHETLAND).   MED

ARGYLL HOTEL, IONA: 01681 700334 (1185/SEASIDE INNS).   MED

FANTASTIC WALKS IN THE ISLANDS

For walk codes, see p. 11.

2229 **DUN CAAN, RAASAY:** Still one of my favourite island walks – to the flat top of
MAP 2 a magic hill (1599/VIEWS). Take ferry (2192/MAGICAL ISLANDS), ask for route from
B2 Inverarish. Go via old iron mine; looks steep when you get over the ridge, but
it's a dawdle. And amazing. 10KM XCIRC XBIKE 2-B-2

2230 **THE LOST GLEN, HARRIS:** Take B887 W from Tarbert almost to the end
MAP 2 (where at Hushinish there's a good beach,maybe a sunset), but go rt before
A1 the Big House (signed Chliostair Power Stn). Park here or further in and walk
up to dam (3km from rd). Take rt track round reservoir and the left around the
upper loch. Over the brim you arrive in a wide, wild glen; an overhang 2km
ahead is said to have the steepest angle in Europe. Go quietly; if you don't see
deer and eagles here, you're making too much noise on the gneiss.
12KM RET XCIRC XBIKE 2-B-2

2231 **CARSAIG, MULL:** In S of island, 7km from A849 Fionnphort-Craignure rd nr
MAP 1 Pennyghael. 2 walks start at pier: going left towards Lochbuie for a spectacu-
B1 lar coastal/woodland walk past Adnunan Stack (7km); or rt towards the
imposing headland where, under the cliffs, the Nuns' Cave was a shelter for
nuns evicted from Iona during the Reformation. Nearby is a quarry whose
stone was used to build Iona Abbey and much further on (9km Carsaig), at
Malcolm's Pt, the extraordinary Carsaig Arches carved by wind and sea.
15/20KM XCIRC XBIKE 2-B-2

2232 **COLONSAY:** (2201/MAGICAL ISLANDS). From hotel or the quay, walk to Colonsay
MAP 1 House and its lush, overgrown intermingling of native plants and exotics
A2 (8km round trip); or to the priory on Oronsay, the smaller island. 6km to 'the
Strand' (you might get a lift with the postman) then cross at low tide, with
enough time (at least 2hrs) to walk to the ruins. Allow longer if you want to
climb the easy peak of Ben Oronsay. Tide tables at hotel. Nice walk also from
Kiloran Beach (1522/BEACHES) to Balnahard Beach – farm track 12km ret.
12+6KM XCIRC BIKE 1-A-2

2233 **THE OLD MAN OF STORR, SKYE:** The enigmatic basalt finger visible from the
MAP 2 Portree-Staffin rd (A855). Start from car park on left, 12km from Portree.
B2 There's a well-defined path through or around the clump of woodland
towards the cliffs and a steep climb up the grassy slope to the pinnacle which
towers 165ft tall. Gr views over Raasay to the mainland. Lots of space and rabbits and birds who make the most of it. 5KM XCIRC XBIKE 2-B-2

2234 **THE QUIRANG, SKYE:** See 1597/VIEWS for directions to start pt. The strange
MAP 2 formations have names (e.g. the Table, the Needle, the Prison) and it's possible
B2 to walk round all of them. Start of the path from the car park is easy. At the first
saddle, take the second scree slope to the Table, rather than the first. When
you get to the Needle, the path to the rt betw two giant pinnacles is the easiest of the 3 options. From the top you can see the Hebrides. This place is
supernatural; anything could happen. So be careful. 6KM XCIRC XBIKE 2-B-2

2235 **HOY, ORKNEY:** There are innumerable walks on the scattered Orkney Islands
MAP 2 and on Hoy itself; on a good day you can get round the north part of the
island and see some of the most dramatic coastal scenery anywhere. A passenger ferry leaves Stromness 2 or 3 times a day and takes 30mins. Make
tracks N or S from jnct nr pier and use free Hoy brochure from TIC so as not to
miss the landmarks, the bird sanctuaries and the Old Man himself.
20/25KM CIRC MTBIKE 2-B-2

2236 **CORRYVRECKAN, JURA:** The whirlpool in the Gulf of Corryvreckan is notori-
MAP 1 ous and classified by the Royal Navy as unnavigable. Betw Jura and Scarba; to
B2 see it go to far N of Jura. From end of the rd at Ardlussa (25km Craighouse, the
village), there's a rough track to Lealt then a walk (a local may drive you) of
12km to Kinuachdrach, then a further walk of 3km. Phenomenon best seen at
certain states of tide. Consult hotel (2218/ISLAND HOTELS) and get the walk
guide. (2193/MAGICAL ISLANDS). 6/24KM XCIRC XBIKE 2-C-2

SGURR AN EIGG: Unmissable. (see 2195/MAGICAL ISLANDS)

THE BEST OF ARRAN

2237
MAP 1
C3
FERRY: Ardrossan-Brodick, 55mins. 6 per day Mon-Sat, 4 on Sun. Ardrossan-Glas, train or rd via A77/A71 1.5hr. Claonaig-Lochranza, 30mins. 9 per day (summer only). *The best way to see Arran is on a bike. See foot of page. Winter sailings – call TIC.*

WHERE TO STAY

KILMICHAEL HOUSE, BRODICK: 01770 302219. 3km from the main rd through town down a lane in real country. Attention to detail and guests. Refined atmos, some nice antique touches. All rms v individual. Still *the* place to eat on Arran, but book (2211/ISLAND HOTELS). Now also has a self-cat cottage.
6RMS JAN-DEC T/T XPETS CC KIDS TOS MED.EX

AUCHRANNIE HOUSE, BRODICK: 01770 302234. Old house enlarged but not altogether enhanced by mod cons. Some rms do look into 'the country'. Good pool, gym. Arran's other up-market hotel; conservatory restau (two AA rosettes) and busy with bar meals. Burgeoning time-share in grounds, and new leisure club.
28RMS JAN-DEC T/T XPETS CC KIDS TOS MED.EX

GRANGE HOUSE, WHITING BAY: 01770 700263. Shore rd, the esplanade. Janet and Clive Hughes planning to retire but meantime tasteful, neat, and they make a big effort with breakfast. **2002 UPDATE: HOTEL CLOSED**
9RMS APR-OCT X/T XPETS CC KIDS MED.INX

ARGENTINE HOUSE, WHITING BAY: 01770 700662. Seaside mansion on the front at Whiting Bay, a GH run by Swiss couple, the Baumgärtners. Look no further for dinner & vegns catered for.
5RMS MAR-JAN X/T PETS CC XKIDS TOS MED.INX

CORRIE HOTEL: 01770 810273. Cheap, cheerful sea- and roadside hotel in cosy Corrie. Good crack in bar. Seaview best.
18RMS APR-OCT X/X CC PETS KIDS INX

S.Y. HOSTELS: at Lochranza (01770 830631) and Whiting Bay (01770 700339). Both busy Grade 2s in picturesque areas (Mar-Oct), 25 and 15km from Brodick.

CAMPING AND CARAVAN PARKS: at Glen Rosa (01770 302380) 4km Brodick; Lamlash (01770 600251), Lochranza (01770 830273). And Glen Rosa has idyllic river side camping.

WHERE TO EAT

CREELERS, BRODICK: 01770 302810. New lease of life for the place last time we visited – enthusiastic staff and good food. Informal atmos. (1139/SEAFOOD RESTAUS). Easter-Oct. Cl Mon.
MED

BURLINGTON HOTEL, WHITING BAY: 01770 700255. Kitchen under the direction of Robin Gray who also runs an organic produce business. The sous-chefs work abroad in the winter and the food is top-notch. Nice music in the background. Easter-Oct, dinner daily.
INX

THE DISTILLERY RESTAURANT: 01770 830264. At the Distillery Visitor Centre, Lochranza. Good light menu in light even clinical rm with running water accompaniment. 11am-9pm in season (cl Wed). Phone out of season.
INX

BRODICK BAR: Best pub food in Brodick? Yes. Bar snacks, then turns into more of a bistro in the eve. Food until 10pm. Off N end of main st by Royal Mail. Bar open till midnight.
CHP

WINEPORT, CLADACH: 01770 302977. Simple bistro in developing 'centre' at start of Goat Fell walk. No frills, but you'll want that pasta and beer once you've finished. While you're there, have a look at the adj microbrewery and its pleasant Arran ales.

THE PANTRY, WHITING BAY: 01770 700489. New owners in 2000 and although not 'haute' is cheerful enough with good view. Open daily from 10.30am then lunch & dinner, in season. Out of season, call them.

WHAT TO SEE

BRODICK CASTLE: 5km walk or cycle from Brodick. Impressive museum and gdns. Tearoom. Flagship NTS property. (1700/CASTLES.)   NT

GOAT FELL: 6km/5hr gr hill walk starting from the car park at Cladach nr Castle and Brodick or sea start at Corrie. Free route leaflet at TO. (1555/HILLS.)
2-A-2

GLENASHDALE FALLS: 4km, but 2hr forest walk from Glenashdale Br at Whiting Bay. Steady, easy climb, silvan setting. (1521/WATERFALLS.)   1-B-1

CORRIE: The best village 9km N Brodick. Go by bike. Good pub. (1425/COASTAL VILLAGES.)

MACHRIE MOOR STANDING STONES: Off main coast rd 7km N of Blackwater Foot. Various assemblies of Stones, all part of an ancient landscape. We lay down there.

GLEN ROSA, GLEN SANNOX: Fine glens – Rosa nr Brodick, Sannox 11km N.
1-B-2

WHAT TO DO

GOLF: Lots of it. Brodick (01770 302513); Lochranza (01770 830273); Lamlash (01770 600296); Whiting Bay (01770 700487). Corrie and Machrie (9 holes). **TENNIS/ SWIM:** Enquiries TIC. **CYCLE HIRE:** Brodick 3 places along front, but esp Brodick Cycles (302460); also Whiting Bay (700382). 3-speed or mountain bikes. **PONY TREKKING:** Lots of opportunities – try Cairhouse Centre (860466), Brodick Trekking (302800) or North Sannox (810222).

TOURIST INFO: 01770 302140. **CALMAC:** 08705 650000.

THE BEST OF ISLAY AND JURA

2238
MAP 1
B2
FERRY: Kennacraig-Pt Askaig: 2hrs, Kennacraig-Pt Ellen: 2hrs 10 mins. Pt Askaig-Feolin, Jura: 5mins, frequent daily (01496 840681). Winter sailings – call TIC.

BY AIR: from Glas to Pt Ellen Airport in S of island. BA 08457 733377.

WHERE TO STAY

PORT CHARLOTTE HOTEL, PORT CHARLOTTE: 01496 850360. Restored Victorian inn and gdns on seafront of conservation village. Restful place, restful views. Good bistro style menu, the best around.
10RMS JAN-DEC T/T PETS CC KIDS MED.EX

HARBOUR INN, BOWMORE: 01496 810330. Nice conservatory with bay views and well crafted food by Scott Chance, one of the best on the island.
7RMS JAN-DEC T/T PETS CC KIDS MED.INX

KILMENY FARM, nr BALLYGRANT: 01496 840668. Margaret and Blair Rozga have been running this top-class GH for a surprising number of yrs. Huge attention to detail, great home-made food, house party atmos and a shared table. We'll go back.   3RMS JAN-DEC X/X XPETS XCC KIDS TOS MED.INX

THE MACHRIE, PORT ELLEN: 01496 302310. 7km N on A846. Restau and bar meals in clubhouse atmos. Restau in old byre and 15 lodges in the grounds. You'll likely be here for the golf – it seems everyone else is!
16RMS JAN-DEC T/T XPETS CC KIDS MED.INX

GLENMACHRIE, nr PORT ELLEN: 01496 302560. On A846 towards Bowmore. How did we miss it before? Multi-award-winning farmhouse with enormous care taken over food and gt meals by Rachel Whyte. Farmers with a green sensibility.   5RMS JAN-DEC X/T PETS XCC XKIDS TOS MED.INX

LOCHSIDE HOTEL, BOWMORE: 01496 810244. Probably best selection of Islay malts in the world; Alistair Birse delights in them and his 'whisky weekends'.
MED.INX

JURA HOTEL, CRAIGHOUSE: 01496 820243. The hotel for the island. Situated in front of the distillery by the bay. Front rms best. You'll have fun in the bar.

18RMS JAN-DEC X/X PETS CC KIDS INX

CAMPING, CARAVAN SITE, HOSTEL at Kintra Farm. 01496 302051. Off main rd to Pt Ellen; take Oa rd, follow Kintra signs 7km. July-August B&B in farmhouse. Grassy strand, coastal walks. **ISLAY YOUTH HOSTEL** Pt Charlotte 01496 850385.

WHERE TO EAT

HARBOUR INN, BOWMORE and **PORT CHARLOTTE HOTEL:** *see above*.

CROFT KITCHEN: Pt Charlotte. 01496 850230. Joy and Douglas Law have combined this coffee (latte, macchiato) and gift shop by day, with restau by night. March-October 10am-8.30pm. Book in season. INX

THE OLD GRANARY: Kintra Farm (as Camping, above). Good basic menu in 'barn' setting. Walk on beach after. May-Aug 5.30-11pm daily. CHP

BALLYGRANT INN: 01496 840277. S of Pt Askaig. Small, cared-for, basic pub with rms. Nice family incl a graphic designer son (he works the PC and makes the leaflets). 3RMS INX

WHAT TO SEE

ISLAY: THE DISTILLERIES esp Laphroaig and Lagavulin (classic settings) by Pt Ellen; tours by appointment. Bowmore has regular glossy tour; Ardbeg, open daily, good cafe (1458/WHISKY); **MUSEUM OF ISLAY, WILDLIFE INFO AND FIELD CENTRE** (1690/WILDLIFE): all at Pt Charlotte; **AMERICAN MONUMENT** (1766/MONUMENTS); **OA and LOCH GRUINART** (1671/BIRDS); **PORT CHARLOTTE** (1513/COASTAL VILLAGES); **KINTRA** (1931/COASTAL WALKS); **FINLAGGAN:** The romantic, sparse ruin on 'island' in L Finlaggan: last home of the Lords of the Isles. Off A846 5km S of Pt Askaig, with visitor centre Apr-Oct (daily only July-Aug).

JURA: (2193/MAGICAL ISLANDS); **THE PAPS OF JURA; CORRYVRECKAN, BARNHILL** (2236/ISLAND WALKS); **KILLCHIANAIG, KEILS** (1805/GRAVEYARDS); **LOWLANDMAN'S BAY** (1531/BEACHES); **JURA HOUSE WALLED GARDEN**; utterly magical if you catch it in the right light with no-one else around.

WHAT TO DO

GOLF at Machrie (1961/GOLF IN GREAT PLACES); **PONY-TREKKING** at Rockside Farm (01496 850231), Ballyvicar (01496 302251); **SWIMMING** at Bowmore (01496 810767); **BIKE HIRE:** Polly Taylor (01496 850488), **MARINE CHARTERS:** 01496 850436.

TOURIST INFO: 01496 810254. **CALMAC:** 08705 650000.

THE BEST OF SKYE

2239
MAP 2

THE BRIDGE: the hump (which is all it has given to a lot of the locals); unromantic but convenient; from Kyle. **THE FERRIES:** Mallaig-Armadale, 30mins. Tarbert (Harris)-Uig, 1hr 35mins (Calmac, as Mallaig). **THE BEST WAY TO SKYE** is Glenelg-Kylerhea, 5mins. Continuous Apr-Oct 01599 511302. Wint sailings: TIC.

WHERE TO STAY

HOUSE OVER-BY: 01470 571258. Reports: 2203/ISLAND HOTELS

EILEAN IARMAIN: 01471 833332. 15km S of Broadford on A851. V Gaelic inn on bay with dreamy views, good food and gr pub. Main hotel best value, but suites over rd more inex (2207/ISLAND HOTELS).

12RMS JAN-DEC T/X PETS CC KIDS EXP

FLODIGARRY: 01470 552203. 30km N Portree on A855. Far-flung N of the island; the views exceptional. Relaxed country-house ambience; local liveliness in the bar. (1150/COUNTRY-HOUSE HOTELS.)

12RMS + 7COTT JAN-DEC T/X PETS CC KIDS TOS EXP

VIEWFIELD HOUSE, PORTREE: 01478 612217. One of the oldest island houses; it's been in the MacDonald family over 200yrs. Unique and antique atmos. Gr dinner. (2216/ISLAND HOTELS.)   11RMS APR-OCT X/X PETS CC KIDS MED.EX

CUILLIN HILLS HOTEL, PORTREE: 01478 612003. On the edge of Portree (off rd N to Staffin) nr water's edge. Secluded mansion house hotel with nice conservatory. Decor slightly iffy (you may like leather-studded furniture and draped 4-posters) but gr views from most rms.

30RMS JAN-DEC T/T PETS CC KIDS MED.EX

SKEABOST: 01470 532202. 11km W of Portree on A850. Tranquil country house in lovely grounds with 9-hole golf and salmon fishing on R Snizort. New owners 2001: much improved. 26RMS MAR-DEC T/T PETS CC KIDS TOS MED.EX

TALISKER HOUSE, TALISKER: 01478 640245. Situated nr beautiful Talisker bay, this historic house was sold at TGP. New owners intend, as before, that this should be a v superior GH. Reports please.

3RMS MAR-OCT X/X XPETS XCC KIDS MED.INX

THE STEIN INN, WATERNISH: 01470 592362. Off B886, the Waternish rd which is 5km Dunvegan on the rd to Portree. Distant but v Skye location in vill row on the water & nr Lochbay (see below). Ancient inn with atmos pub (1188/SEASIDE INNS) & 5 nice rms above. An excl retreat. 5RMS JAN-DEC X/X PETS CC KIDS CHP

GRESHORNISH HOUSE HOTEL: 01470 582266. 5km from Dunvegan-Portree rd (A850) about 30km Portree & on its own peninsula along L Greshornish … so quite far away. Comfy small co house hotel – it would be nice to take over with family or mates (not exp). Billiard rm. Home-made food.

6RMS JAN-DEC X/T PETS CC KIDS MED.INX

S.Y. HOSTELS: At Kyleakin (biggest, nearest mainland), Armadale (interesting area in S), Broadford, Glen Brittle (v Cuillin), Uig (for N Skye, ferry to Hebrides). **INDEPENDENT HOSTELS** at Kyleakin and Staffin (1175/1174/HOSTELS) and many others.

WHERE TO EAT

THREE CHIMNEYS: 01470 511258. 7km W of Dunvegan on B884. Superb home cooking, best in the islands. Report: (2223/ISLAND RESTAUS).   MED

KINLOCH LODGE: 01471 833333. 13km S Broadford off A851. Classy food in almost theatrical atmos at Lady Claire's table(s). Report: (2222/ISLAND RESTAUS).

EXP

LOCHBAY SEAFOOD: 01470 592235. 12km N Dunvegan off A850. Small; simple fresh seafood in loch side setting, but closed Sat/Sun. Report: (1245/SEAFOOD RESTAUS).   INX

AN TUIREANN CAFE: 01478 613306. Nr Portree. Coffee shop/gallery. Good food and chat in a cultural caff. Report: (2228/ISLAND RESTAU; 1316/VEGN RESTAUS).

HARBOUR VIEW, PORTREE: 01478 612069. Bosville Terr on rd to Staffin and N Skye with harbour view at least from the door. Local seafood in intimate bistro dining rm (some game). Non pretentious, well-judged cooking. 7 days Easter-Oct lunch and dinner (not Sun lunch). LO 9.30pm.

CREELERS, BROADFORD: 01471 822281. Just off A87 rd from Kyleakin and bridge to Portree as you come into Broadford. Small cabin seafood restau and t/away round back, but excl local rep. 7 days in season 12-9pm.

THE OLD SCHOOL, DUNVEGAN: 01470 521421. On main rd/st in Dunvegan. Long established, serviceable bistro. Good vegn. 7 days, lunch and dinner in season. LO 9pm.

PASTA SHED, ARMADALE: no number. On the quayside at Armadale where the Mallaig ferry comes in. A real pizza hut, but best to get Alistair MacPhail to knock you up some super-fresh seafood. 7 days in season 9am-7.30pm.

ARDVASAR HOTEL: 01471 844223. Sleat in far S near Mallaig ferry. Local choice for pub grub. LO 8.30. Popular so may need to book.   MED

SLIGACHAN HOTEL: Surprisingly decent seafood in hotel dining-rm situation (The Cairidh). 7-9pm. 7 days. See also p 190.

WHAT TO SEE

THE CUILLINS (2/BIG ATTRACTIONS); **RAASAY** (2192/MAGICAL ISLANDS); (2229/ISLAND WALKS); **THE QUIRANG** (1597/VIEWS); (2234/ISLAND WALKS); **OLD MAN OF STORR** (2233/ISLAND WALKS); **DUNVEGAN** (1703/CASTLES); **EAS MOR** (1556/WATERFALLS); **ELGOL** (1601/VIEWS); **SKYE BATIKS** (2046/CRAFT SHOPS); **SKYE MUSEUM OF ISLAND LIFE** (2114/MUSEUMS); **FLORA MACDONALD'S GRAVE** (1768/MONUMENTS); **SKYE SILVER, EDINBANE POTTERY** and **CARBOST CRAFT** (2042/2041/CRAFT SHOPS); **FAIRY POOLS** (1615/PICNICS); **SLIGACHAN HOTEL** (p. 190).

WHAT TO DO

GOLF at Skeabost (*previous page*) and Sconser (01478 650351); **FISHING:** ask at hotels; Skeabost, Eilean Iarmain (*previous page*) and Greshhornish House; **SWIMMING** at Portree Pool (01478 612655); **BIKE HIRE:** Island Cycles (01478 613121); Fair Winds Bicycle Hire (01471 822270); **RIDING:** (01470 582419 or 01478 612945).

CEILIDHS: In this most Highland of islands 3 hoolies are worth mentioning, all welcoming to visitors; **SKYE SCENE CEILIDH, TIGH NA SCIRE, PORTREE** (enquire TO). Mon and Wed in season and Tues (July-Sept). Touristy, but charming. **CEOL IS CNAC** at the **AROS CENTRE** S of Portree. Most Thur/Fri in season (01478 613649) Touristy but authentic. **FLODIGARRY COUNTRY-HOUSE HOTEL:** 32km N Portree. V north, v Staffin and the stuff of a damned good shindig. Every Sat, plus other nights. Backpackers from adj hostel (1174/HOSTELS), locals and hotel guests happily get down. Till 11.30pm-ish.

TOURIST INFO: 01478 612137. **CALMAC:** 08705 650000.

THE BEST OF THE WESTERN ISLES

2240
MAP 2 **FERRIES:** Ullapool-Stornoway, 2hrs 40mins, (not Sun). Oban/Mallaig-Lochboisdale, S Uist and Castlebay, Barra; up to 6.5hrs. Uig on Skye-Tarbert, Harris (not Sun) or Lochmaddy, N Uist 1hr 40mins. Also Leverburgh, Harris-Otternish, N Uist (not Sun) 1hr 10mins. Local passenger ferry: Ludag, S Uist-Eoligarry, Barra (01851 701702). Winter sailings – call TIC.

BY AIR: BA 3 times daily (2 Sat; not Sun). Inverness/Glas/Edin. Local 01851 703240. BA Otter to Barra/Benbecula from Glas (1 a day). Linkline 08457 733377.

WHERE TO STAY

ARDVOURLIE CASTLE, N HARRIS: 01859 502307. 14km N of Tarbert on shore of L Seaforth in hills of N Harris. Victorian hunting lodge. Fab. Report: (2123/ISLAND HOTELS).

SCARISTA HOUSE, S HARRIS: 01859 550238. 20km S of Tarbert. Nr famous but often deserted beach; celebrated retreat. Also self-catering accom. Report: (2209/ISLAND HOTELS).

BAILE-NA-CILLE: 01859 672242. Nr Uig 50km W of Stornoway off A858. Welcoming old manse in far W. Report: 2214/ISLAND HOTELS.

CASTLEBAY HOTEL, CASTLEBAY, BARRA: 01871 810223. O/looks ferry terminal in main town. Excellent value. Good food. Brilliant bar (2204/ISLAND HOTELS; 1272/BLOODY GOOD PUBS).

ISLE OF BARRA HOTEL, BARRA: 01871 810383. Modern purpose-built hotel on gr beach 3km W of Castlebay. Seaviews are why we're here (2220/ISLAND HOTELS).

ROYAL HOTEL, STORNOWAY, LEWIS: 01851 702109. The best value and most central of the 3 main hotels in town. Barnacle bistro and Boatshed (probably 'best' hotel dining). All owned by same company. Some rms OK-ish, some not so see first (bedrms in the **CABARFEIDH** are better; 01851 702604).

26RMS JAN-DEC T/T PETS CC KIDS MED.INX

PARK GUEST HOUSE, STORNOWAY: 01851 702485. James St. Refurbished town house with surprisingly good menu and comfy rms tho guest-housey. A place to eat even if not staying. More accom on way at TGP.

7+2GDN RMS JAN-DEC X/T XPETS XCC XKIDS TOS CHP

LEACHIN HOUSE, TARBERT, N HARRIS: 01859 502157. 2km N on A859. Small, Victorian family house. Personal touch in furnishings, food and your excursions. Shared dinner. A Wolsey Lodge. 2RMS JAN-DEC X/T XPETS XCC KIDS INX

TETHERSTONE, S HARRIS: 01859 520357. 46 Northton nr the William MacGillvey Centre. Small v nice GH run by the Rowes. Handy to know & it's nr Scarista (above) so you can stay when it's full. Only 2 rms, but they put me up & this is a sincere name-check.

LOCHBOISDALE HOTEL, LOCHBOISDALE, S UIST: 01471 822270. In last town nr tip of Uists at ferry terminal o/look bay. Mainly fishing hotel with all rods catered for. Gr local bar. But rms vary & some ain't so great.

18RMS JAN-DEC X/T PETS CC KIDS MED.EX

POLLACHAR INN, S UIST: 01878 700215. S of Lochboisdale nr small ferry for Eriskay/Barra (2199/ISLANDS) an inn at the end of the known world. Excl value, good crack and the view/sunset across the sea to Barra. Refurb has improved.

11RMS JAN-DEC T/T PETS CC KIDS MED.INX

HOSTELS: Simple hostels within hiking distance. 2 in Lewis, 3 in Harris, 1 each in N and S Uist (Barra pending). Excellent hostelling holiday prospect (1169 & 1170/ HOSTELS).

WHERE TO EAT

BONAVENTURE, AIRD UIG: 01851 672474. 30km W of Stornaway to the end of the rd (A858 then B8011). A corner of France far from home. Report 2225/ISLAND RESTAUS.

THE THAI CAFE, STORNOWAY: 01851 701811. 27 Church St opp police stn. An unlikely find but prob the best place to eat in this town – Mrs Panida Macdonald's restau an institution here & you may have to book. Gr atmos, excl real Thai cuisine, though you couldn't be further in every respect from Bangkok. Lunch & LO 11pm. Cl Sun.

PARK GUEST HOUSE and **THE BOATSHED**, at the **ROYAL HOTEL, STORNOWAY:** (see above). The top two dining-rms in town. Park is a restau so don't be put off by guesthouse tag. V TOS (Tues-Sat). Latter slightly up-market with seafood emphasis. High teas then LO 9pm.

TIGH MEALROS, GARYNAHINE, LEWIS: 01851 621333. On A858 22km SW Stornoway. 2km S of Callanish. Unpretentious surf 'n' turf. Scallops (dived) a special. BYOB. Open AYR. LO 9pm.

COPPER KETTLE, DALBEG, LEWIS: 01851 710592. 6km N of Carloway W of Stornoway. Signed off main rd down track to lily-filled lochan. Tables on terrace in summer for tea and tiny restau with excellent plain cooking. Must book dinner.

COFFEE SHOPS at **AN LANNTAIR GALLERY, STORNOWAY**, and **CALLANISH VISITOR CENTRE, LEWIS**. The latter esp good. Daytime hrs (1734/PREHISTORIC SITES).

ARDVOURLIE and **SCARISTA HOUSE, HARRIS:** (see above). Dinner possible for non-residents. Both a drive from Stornoway. Fixed menus. Book well in advance.

FIRST FRUITS TEAROOM, TARBERT, HARRIS: Nr TO and ferry to Uig. Home-cooking that hits the spot. Good atmos. 10.30am-4.30pm Apr-Sept. For sale at TGP.

TOURIST INFO: (Stornoway) 01851 701818. **CALMAC:** 08705 650000.

2241
MAP 1
B1

FERRY: Oban-Craignure, 45mins. Main route; 6 a day. Lochaline-Fishnish, 15mins. 9-15 a day. Kilchoan-Tobermory, 35mins. 7 a day (Sun–summer only). Winter sailings – call TIC.

WHERE TO STAY

HIGHLAND COTTAGE, TOBERMORY: 01688 302030. Breadalbane St opp fire stn a street above the harbour. Report: 2212/HOTELS.

6RMS FEB-DEC T/T XPETS CC KIDS TOS MED.EX

WESTERN ISLES, TOBERMORY: 01688 302012. High above town, classic views over bay; real individuality, fire in foyer, gr conservatory. Good suites, food so-so. Report: 2213/HOTELS. 26RMS JAN-DEC T/T PETS CC KIDS TOS MED.EX

TIRORAN HOUSE: 01681 705232: In S of Mull, a treat and a retreat way down the SW of Mull nr Iona. Light, comfy house in glorious gdns with excl food & flowers. Report: 1206/GET AWAY HOTELS.

6RMS + 2COTT MAR-NOV X/X XPETS CC KIDS MED.EXP

ARGYLL HOTEL, IONA: 01681 700334. Nr ferry and on seashore o/looking Mull on rd to abbey. Laid-back, cosy accom, cottage rms, home cooking, good vegn. (1185/SEASIDE INNS) 16RMS APR-OCT X/X PETS CC KIDS MED.INX

CALGARY FARMHOUSE, CALGARY: 01688 400256. Nr Dervaig on B8073 nr Mull's famous beach. Gallery/coffee shop and good bistro/restau. Report: 2210/HOTELS. 9RMS APR-OCT X/X PETS CC KIDS MED.INX

TOBERMORY HOTEL: 01688 302091. On waterfront, cheapish/cheerful. Gr location. 16RMS JAN-DEC X/T PETS CC KIDS MED.INX

DRUIMARD COUNTRY HOUSE, DERVAIG: 01688 400345. Small, country place beside Mull Little Theatre and heart of Mull village; conservatory bar, books. Bistro style dining; see the show first.

5RMS JAN-DEC T/T PETS CC KIDS MED.EX

S.Y. HOSTEL: In Tobermory main st on bay (1171/HOSTELS).

CARAVAN PARKS: At Fishnish (all facs, nr Ferry) Craignure and Fionnphort.

CAMPING: Calgary Beach, Fishnish and at Loch Na Keal shore.

WHERE TO EAT

HIGHLAND COTTAGE: 01688 302030. As above and 2212/ISLAND HOTS. Also the local night out. Small so must book. MED

THE GLASS BARN: 2km Tobermory centre. Highly recommended (1383/TEA-ROOMS). INX

ISLAND BAKERY, TOBERMORY: 01688 302225, Main St. Bakery-deli with excl take-away pizza by Joe Reade, the son of the cheese people (and the Glass Barn above). Bottle of wine – box of pizza – sit by the sea. 7 days LO 9pm (w/end only in wint). CHP

THE ANCHORAGE, TOBERMORY: 01688 302313. Main St opp pier. Family-owned by fishing folk, so mainly seafood. Homely and friendly & not bad at all. 7 days, lunch and LO 7pm. Winter hrs will vary. INX

CALGARY FARMHOUSE: 01688 400256. Dovecote Restaurant. Local produce in v atmospheric wine-bar setting, run by mellow people (2227/ISLAND RESTAUS). Coolest dining rm on the island. INX

ARGYLL HOUSE, SALEN: 01680 300555. On main A849 half-way betw Craignure & Tobermory. Caff by day, decent pizza & pasta joint in evening but LO 8pm. INX

WHAT TO SEE

TOROSAY CASTLE: Walk or train (!) from Craignure. Fabulous gdns and fascinating insight into an endearing family's life. Teashop. (1702/CASTLES.) **DUART CASTLE:** 5km Craignure. Seat of Clan Maclean. Impressive from a distance, good view of clan history and from battlements. Teashop. (1701/CASTLES.) **EAS FORS:** Waterfall on Dervaig to Fionnphort rd. V accessible series of cataracts tumbling into the sea (1556/WATERFALLS). **THE MISHNISH:** No mission to Mull complete without a night at the Mish (1266/BLOODY GOOD PUBS), MacGochann's over the bay no contest.

WHAT TO DO

Excursions to **IONA** (from Fionnphort) and **ULVA** (from Ulva Ferry) (2194/2198/MAGICAL ISLANDS); **STAFFA** (from Fionnphort or Iona) and **THE TRESH-NISH ISLES** (Ulva Ferry or Fionnphort). Marvellous trips in summer (1665/BIRDS); walks from **CARSAIG PIER** (2231/ISLAND WALKS); or up **BEN MORE** (1887/MUNROS); **CROIG** and **QUINISH** in N, nr Dervaig and **LOCHBUIE** off the A849 at Strathcoil 9km S of Craignure: these are all serene shorelines to explore. **AROS PARK** forest walk, from Tobermory, about 7km round trip.
GOLF: Tobermory (01688 302020). Craignure (01688 302372). Both 9 holes.
FISHING: Info: 'Tackle and Books' (01688 302336).

TOURIST INFO: 01688 302182. **CALMAC:** 08705 650000.

THE BEST OF ORKNEY

2242 **FERRY:** P&O (01224 572615) Stromness: from Aber – Tue and Sat, takes 8hrs (winter: Sat o/night only); from Scrabster – 2/3 per day and 1 on Sun (winter: 2 daily, n/o Sun) takes 2hrs. From John O'Groats to Burwick (01955 611353), 40mins, up to 4 a day (May-Sept only).

BY AIR: BA (08457 733377) to Kirkwall: from Aber – 3 daily; from Edin – 2 daily; from Glas – 1 daily; from Inverness – 2 daily; from Wick – 1 daily (not w/ends). No flights on Sun.

WHERE TO STAY

FOVERAN HOTEL, ST OLA: 01856 872389. A964 Orphir rd; 4km from Kirkwall. Scandinavian style hotel is a friendly informal place serves trad food using best local ingredients; separate vegn menu. offering gr value. Comfortable light rms; gdn o/look Scapa Flow. Good restau.

8RMS   JAN-DEC   T/T   PETS   CC   KIDS   TOS   MED.INX

AYRE HOTEL, KIRKWALL: 01856 873001. Roy and Moira Dennison have spent several years refurb their family hotel in line with TIC standards; which has resulted in them having the highest grading on the mainland. Situated on the harbour front, the whole place is well tidy and well established. It's where to stay in Kirkwall.   33RMS JAN-DEC T/T PETS CC KIDS MED.EX

CLEATON HOUSE HOTEL, WESTRAY: 01857 677508. Beautifully refurbished former Victorian manse. Panoramic seascapes, relaxed atmos & wonderful food. Only other 4-star establishment.

6RMS JAN-DEC T/T PETS CC KIDS TOS MED.EX

BARONY, BIRSAY: 01856 721327. 40km from Kirkwall. Basic accom in wild corner by loch. Brown trout fishing, walks, sea air. Cabin style 'HMS Hampshire' bar.   10RMS MAY-OCT T/T PETS CC KIDS MED.INX

MERKISTER, HARRAY: 01856 771366. A fave with fishers and twitchers; handy for archaeological sites and just poss the Orkney hotel of choice. À la carte or table d'hôte in the conservatory o/look the loch.

13RMS JAN-DEC T/T PETS CC KIDS MED.INX

STROMNESS HOTEL: 01856 850298. Orkney's biggest hotel, recent refurb. Central and picturesque. We haven't stayed.

42RMS JAN-DEC T/T PETS CC KIDS MED.INX

WOODWICK HOUSE, EVIE: 01856 751330. Comfy country house and gdn, nr shore with views of islets. Managed by the Dandelion Trust charity, it's a gr retreat. Home cooking, local produce. Good value.

7RMS JAN-DEC X/T CC KIDS TOS MED.INX

S.Y. HOSTELS: At Stromness (excellent location, 01856 850589), Kirkwall (the largest, 01856 872243), Other hostels at: Hoy, N & S Ronaldsay, Stronsay. **PEED-**

IE HOSTEL, KIRKWALL: 01856 875477. Ayre Rd; by the sea. Private bedrm, own keys.

BIS GEOS HOSTEL, WESTRAY: 01857 677786. Hostel with 2 self-catering cottages. Traditional features & luxuries.

CAMPING/CARAVAN: At Kirkwall (01856 879900) and Stromness (01856 873535).

WHERE TO EAT

THE CREEL, ST MARGARET'S HOPE: 01856 831311. On S Ronaldsay, 20km S of Kirkwall. In the wild area where seals vie with the fishermen. Excl table (2 AA rosette) though fairly exp. Many sauces over meat or fish. Clootie for pud or Orkney cheeses. Popular with the islanders. Dinner only. Seal Rescue Centre nearby. Also well-appointed 3 rms, a good choice B+B.

3RMS A GOOD CHOICE B+B   MED

FOVERAN HOTEL, ST OLA: 01856 872389. 4km Kirkwall. *As above.*   MED

HAMNAVOE, STROMNESS: 01856 850606. Leslie's Close off main st. Seafood is their speciality, but they do haggis, neeps and tatties. Apr-Sept/Oct; Tue-Sat 7pm-late.   INX

THE STRYND, KIRKWALL: 01856 871552. Up lane beside TIC. New, bright sunflower tearoom; snacks, home-made cakes. Mon-Sat 9am-5pm.   CHP

THE COFFEE SHOP, STROMNESS: Nr the harbour office. Good toasties, blackboard specials. Gets busy – fill yourself up before the ferry journey! Apr-Oct; Mon-Sat 9am-6.30pm, Sun 9am-5pm.   CHP

WHAT TO SEE

SKARA BRAE: 25km W Kirkwall. Amazingly well-preserved underground labyrinth, a 5,000-year-old village (1732/PREHISTORIC SITES).

THE OLD MAN OF HOY: on Hoy; 30min ferry 2 or 3 times a day from Stromness. 3hr walk along spectacular coast (2235/ISLAND WALKS).

STANDING STONES OF STENNESS, THE RING OF BRODGAR, MAES HOWE: Around 18km W of Kirkwall on A965. Strong vibrations (1733/PREHISTORIC SITES).

YESNABY SEA STACKS: 24km W of Kirkwall. A precarious cliff top at the end of the world (1854/SPOOKY – or spiritual – PLACES).

ITALIAN CHAPEL: 8km S of Kirkwall at first causeway. A special act of faith. (1784/CHURCHES).

SKAILL HOUSE: at Skara Brae. 17th century 'mansion' built on Pictish cemetery. Set up as it was in the 1950s; with Captain Cook's crockery in the dining-rm looking remarkably unused. Apr-Sep; 7 days 9.30am-6.30pm (11.30am on Sundays) or by appointment – 01856 841501. Tearoom and visitor centre and HS link with Skara.

ST MAGNUS CATHEDRAL (1784/CHURCHES); **STROMNESS** itself (1509/COASTAL VILLAGES); **PIER ART GALLERY** (2134/INTERESTING GALLERIES); **TOMB OF THE EAGLES** (1739/PREHISTORIC SITES); **MARWICK HEAD** and many of the smaller islands (1672/BIRDS); **SCAPA FLOW** (1827/BATTLEGROUNDS; 2024/DIVING); **HIGHLAND PARK** (1464/WHISKY); **PUFFINS:** (1673/BIRDS)

WHAT TO DO

GOLF: Golf courses open to public at Kirkwall and Stromness. **SWIMMING:** Pools at Kirkwall, Stromness and Hoy. **FISHING:** Permits not required, though permission needed to fish at L of Skile. **SCUBA DIVE:** PADI training, trips, guesthouse, shop at Burray (01856 731269) and Stromness (01856 850055 or 01856 851218). **BIKE HIRE:** Kirkwall (01856 875777), Stromness (01856 850255, 01856 791225).

TOURIST INFO: 01856 872856 or 01856 850716.

THE BEST OF SHETLAND

2243 **FERRY:** P&O (01224 572615) Aber-Lerwick 14hrs (leaves 6pm arrives 8am) Mon-Fri. Also via Orkney (leaves Aber on Sat at noon and Stromness at noon on Sun; arrives 8pm; also Tue Jun-Aug).

BY AIR: BA (linkline 08457 733377, Shetland 01950 460345) sto Sumburgh: from Aber (4 a day, 2 Sat, 2 Sun). From Inverness (1 a day, not w/ends). From Glas (2 a day, 1 Sat & Sun). From Edin (1 a day, not Sun). From Wick (1 on Sat only).

WHERE TO STAY

BUSTA HOUSE: 01806 522506. Historic country house at Brae just over 30 mins from Lerwick. This is the other place to go. Elegant & tranquil. High standards, gr malt selection.   20RMS JAN-DEC T/T PETS CC KIDS MED.EX

HERRISLEA HOUSE HOTEL, TINGWALL: 01595 840208. 7km NW of Lerwick. Refurbished country house in beautiful setting. Lunch and supper till 9pm, 7 days Basic, good home cooking.   13RMS JAN-DEC T/T PETS CC KIDS MED.INX

SUMBURGH HOTEL, SUMBURGH: 01950 460201. Refurbished manor house in v S of mainland 42 km from Lerwick. Next to airport and Jarlshof excavations. Sea views as far as Fair Isle (50km S). Beaches and birds! Wide and relatively cheap menu.   32RMS JAN-DEC T/T PETS CC KIDS MED.INX

KVELDSRO HOTEL, LERWICK: 01595 692195. Pron 'Kel-ro'. Probably best proposition in Lerwick; o/look harbour. Reasonable standard at a price. Locals do eat here.   16RMS JAN-DEC T/T CC KIDS MED.EX

WESTINGS, THE INN ON THE HILL, WHITENESS: 01595 840242. 12 km from Lerwick. Breathtaking views down Whiteness Voe. Excellent base for exploring. Large selection of real ales and three different menus. Campsite alongside.   6RMS JAN-DEC T/T CC KIDS MED.INX

S.Y. HOSTEL in Lerwick, Isleburgh House: 01595 692114. Beautifully refurbished and v central. Open Apr-Sept.

CAMPING BODS (fisherman's barns). Cheap sleep in wonderful sea-shore settings. **THE SAIL LOFT** at Voe; **GRIEVE HOUSE** at Whalsay; **WIND HOUSE LODGE** at Mid Yell; **VOE HOUSE** at Walls; **BETTY MOUAT'S COTTAGE** at Dunrossness; **JOHNNIE NOTION'S** at Eashaness. Remember to take sleeping mats. Check TIC for details.

CAMPING/CARAVAN: CLICKIMIN, LERWICK 01595 741000. **LEVENWICK** 01950 422207. **THE GARTHS, FETLA** 01957 733227.

WHERE TO EAT

BUSTA HOUSE, BRAE: (*see above*). The best meal in the islands.   MED

MONTY'S BISTRO, LERWICK: 01595 696555. Mounthooley St nr TIC. Renovated building in light Med décor. Best bet in town. Good service and quality menu using Shetland's finest ingredients. Bistro: Cl Sun/Mon. Lunch and LO 9pm.   MED

SHETLAND HOTEL, LERWICK: 01595 695515. Holmsgarth Rd. Popular bistro but formal dining rm serving local produce (the real reason it's on the map). 7 days. LO 9.15pm.   MED.EXP

LERWICK HOTEL: 01595 692166 and the **KVELDSRO HOTEL:** 01595 692195 Have pub food and fairly reliable dining-rms (the Kveldsro is 'up-market' and exp).   INX/MED

Pub food also recommended at the following:

THE MID BRAE INN, BRAE: 32km N of Lerwick, 01806 522634. Lunch and supper till 9pm, 7 days. **THE MERRYFIELD HOTEL, BRESSAY:** 01595 820207. 5 mins ferry ride from Lerwick to Bressay. Better known for its excellent seafood rather than accommodation, both bar and dining rm menus worth a look. LO are for those off the 8pm ferry. Don't miss the return ferry at 10.30pm Sun-Thurs and 12.45am, Fri & Sat.   INX.MED

DA HAAF RESTAURANT, SCALLOWAY: 01595 880747. Part of the North Atlantic Fisheries College, Port Arthur. Basically a canteen but fresh Shetland seafood overlooking the harbour at reasonable prices more than makes up for the plastic trays and fluorescent lights. Lunch & LO 8pm.   INX

SCALLOWAY FISH AND CHIP SHOP: New Rd, by the castle. Quite the freshest and best fish and chips in Shetland, (if not Scotland, some say) can also sit in.

OSLA'S CAFE, LERWICK: 01595 696005. Mounthooly St, just up from Monty's. Best cafe, also supper Mon-Sat, LO 6.45pm. Incredibly good value. Cosy & very child-friendly. Art exhibitions on walls.

THE PEERIE SHOP CAFE, LERWICK: 01595 692817. A local delicacy!

WHAT TO SEE

MOUSA BROCH and **JARLSHOF** (1736/PREHISTORIC SITES), also **CLICKIMIN** broch. During July and August, recently discovered Iron Age excavations can be viewed at Old Scatness, 5 mins from airport.

ST NINIAN'S ISLE, BIGTON: 8km N of Sumburgh on W Coast. An island linked by exquisite shell-sand. Hoard of Pictish silver found in 1958 (now in Edin). Beautiful, serene spot.

SCALLOWAY: 7km W of Lerwick, a township once the ancient capital of Shetland, dominated by the atmospheric ruins of Scalloway Castle.

SHETLAND WOOLLEN COMPANY is worth a rummage.

NOUP OF NOSS, ISLE OF NOSS, off BRESSAY: 8km W of Lerwick by frequent ferry and then boat (also direct from Lerwick 01595 692577 or via TIC), May-Aug only. Excellent.

UP HELLY AA: Festival Lerwick on the last Tuesday in Jan. Ritual with hundreds of torchbearers and much fire and firewater. Norse, northern and pagan. A wild time. Permanent exhibition at St Sunniva Street, Lerwick.

SEA RACES: The Boat Race every summer from Norway. Part of the largest North Sea international annual yacht race.

BONHOGA GALLERY & WEISDALE MILL CAFE: 01595 830400. Former grain mill housing Shetland's first purpose-built gallery.

ISLAND TRAILS: Historic tours of Lerwick and the islands. Book through TIC or 01950 422408. Day trips, evening runs or short tours.

SWIMMING: at Clickimin Leisure Complex, Lerwick 01595 741000, Scalloway 01595 880745. Also at Unst, Yell, Brae, Whalsay and Sandwick. **GOLF RANGE:** at Moor Park, Gulberwick 01595 694959.

TOURIST INFO: 01595 693434.

SECTION 14

Local Centres

2244
MAP 1
C3

WHERE TO STAY

FAIRFIELD HOUSE: 01292 267461. Fairfield Rd. 1km centre on the front. Ostensibly the 'best' hotel in town. 'De luxe' facs incl pool/sauna/steam, conservatory brasserie and breakfast and notable (1 AA rosette) Fleur de Lys restau. 45RMS JAN-DEC T/T PETS CC KIDS EXP

THE IVY HOUSE: 01292 442336. 3km from centre on rd to Alloway. Small but v well-appointed establishment, more a superior restau with rms. Esp good bathrms. Serious chef. 5RMS JAN-DEC T/T PETS CC KIDS EXP

LOCHGREEN HOUSE: 01292 313343. Monktonhall Rd, Troon 12km N on way in from Ayr. White seaside mansion nr famous golf courses of Troon (1942/GREAT GOLF). Elegant setting and décor; civilised wining and dining. 15RMS (7 IN COURTYARD) JAN-DEC T/T PETS CC KIDS EXP

SAVOY PARK: 01292 266112. 16 Racecourse Rd. Period mansion run by the Hendersons for 40 yrs, but most ably assisted by Lesley Swindon – the general manager any hotel would want (1244/SCOTTISH HOTELS). 15RMS JAN-DEC T/T PETS CC KIDS MED.INX

PIERSLAND, TROON: 01292 314747. 12km N of Ayr (839/AYRSHIRE HOTELS).

BRIG O'DOON, ALLOWAY: 01292 442466. 5km S of Ayr. Romantic, many weddings, few rms. (840/AYRSHIRE HOTELS).

KYLESTROME: 01292 262474. 11 Miller Rd. Refurb *à la mode*. Nr centre. Not a lot of character, but adequate. 12RMS JAN-DEC T/T PETS CC KIDS TOS MED.EX

PARKSTONE HOTEL, PRESTWICK: 01292 477286. Modern-style down on Central Esplanade. Nice owners, nothing earth-shattering, just a good, honest, well-run hotel: decent value. 22RMS JAN-DEC T/T PETS CC KIDS TOS MED.INX

THE RICHMOND: 01292 265153. 38 Park Circus. Best of bunch in sedate terrace nr centre. John and Anne are nice folk. 6RMS JAN-DEC X/T XPETS XCC KIDS CHP

S.Y. HOSTEL: 01292 262322. Craigwiel Rd, off Racecourse Rd close to seafront, 10min walk to centre. Sleeps 86. Book ahead service (essential June, July, Aug).

WHERE TO EAT

Ayr is well served by the 5 places below which cover the range from seriously good food to trad Scottish caff cuisine. Look no further than:

FOUTERS: 01292 261391. 2 Academy St (842/AYRSHIRE RESTAUS). The best in town.

IVY HOUSE: 01292 442336. Restau of hotel above 845/AYRSHIRE RESTAUS.

THE HUNNY POT: 37 Beresford Terr. 01292 263239. Wholemeal-slanted, kid-friendly, GM-free café – good home baking and light meals. Mon-Sat 9am-10pm, Sun 10.30am-9pm.

THE STABLES: 41 Sandgate, downtown location in courtyard of shops. Coffee shop/bistro with wine bar ambience and enlightened attitude. Imaginative Scottish menu. Good teas, good beers. No smk rm. Till 5pm. Cl Sun. INX

THE TUDOR RESTAURANT: 8 Beresford St (1376/TEAROOMS). Superb caff. Till 8pm.

THE REST ...

CECCHINI'S: 01292 317171. 72 Fort St (also in Troon at 72 Fort St). Excl Italian and Med restau run by the estimable Cecchini family. Mon-Sat, lunch and LO 10pm.

PIERRINO'S: 01292 269087. Alloway Pl. The other credible Italian. LO 10pm. INX

WHAT TO SEE

CULZEAN (1695/CASTLES); **DUNURE VILLAGE** (1519/COASTAL VILLAGES) and nr (3km S on the A719) the **ELECTRIC BRAE; BURNS HERITAGE TRAIL** (1845/ LITERARY PLACES); **GAILES/TROON/PRESTWICK/TURNBERRY/BELLEISLE** (*see* GREAT GOLF, *p. 258*); **MAGNUM, IRVINE** (1988/LEISURE CENTRES); **KIDZ PLAY** (1645/KIDS).

WHAT TO DO

SWIMMING: V good pool complex at Beach Harbour Rd (01292 269793), and at Prestwick, off the road in from Ayr (01292 474015). **RIDING:** Ayrshire Equitation Centre, all standards, country setting. Book! 01292 266267. **TENNIS:** Good all-weather courts at Citadel Pl and Craigie Av near Craigie Park. Just turn up.

TOURIST OFFICE: 22 Sandgate. 01292 678100. Jan-Dec.

THE BEST OF DUMFRIES

2245

MAP 9

WHERE TO STAY

COMLONGON CASTLE, CLARENCEFIELD: 01387 870283. 14 km S via A75 t/off at Collin on B724. Turn rt at Clarencefield, signed for hotel and up 2 km avenue of trees to privately-owned castle with hotel in adj manor house. Ownership handed-on down the family, so refreshing breeze has blown through the old place. Scotland is created here for you; popular for weddings.
12RMS MAR-DEC T/T XPETS CC KIDS EXP

CAIRNDALE: 01387 254111. Surprising spa concealed within this corporate friendly old faithful; conference centre now being added. Visiting somebodies stay here. Café is popular lunch venue for all sorts.
91RMS JAN-DEC T/T PETS CC KIDS EXP

STATION HOTEL: 01387 254316. 49 Lovers' Walk. The best all-round business/ tourist hotel in town with decent upgrading of the trad stn-hotel elegance and ambience (from 1896); central and often full. 'Bistro' as well as dining-rm.
32RMS JAN-DEC T/T PETS CC KIDS MED.EX

ABBEY ARMS 01387 850489 (862/SW HOTELS). **CRIFFEL INN** 01387 850305 both in **NEW ABBEY** 12 km S of Dumfries A710. 2 gr pubs on either side of the green in this lovely wee vill where Sweetheart Abbey is the main attraction (1820/ABBEYS).
4/5RMS JAN-DEC X/T PETS CC KIDS INX

EDENBANK: 01387 252759. Reasonably priced place on Laurieknowe (main rd to Dalbeattie going SW) nr centre. Also handy for the football for those having nightmares on Terregles St.
10RMS JAN-DEC T/T PETS CC KIDS INX

No SYH, Dumfries College accom: ask at TIC.

WHERE TO EAT

PIZZERIA IL FIUME: 01387 265154. In Dock Park nr St Michael's Br, underneath Riverside pub. Usual Italian menu but gr pizzas and cosy tratt atmos. 5.30-10pm daily.
INX

BENVENUTO: 01387 259890. 42 Eastfield Rd, off Brooms Rd – follow signs for Cresswell Maternity Hospital. Sort of surreal wooden hut setting next to owner's chippy. 5pm-late. Tues-Sun.
INX

BRUNO'S: 01387 255757. 3 Balmoral Rd, off Annan Rd. Well-established Italian eaterie beside **BALMORAL** chippy (1361/FISH AND CHIP SHOPS). 6-10pm, Cl Tue.
INX

PIERRE'S: 01387 265888. 117 Queensbury St adj Tam O' Shanter Inn. Dropping Victoire from title but still safest bet for bistro food in town. 7 days. Lunch and LO 10.30pm (cl Sun even).
INX

HULLABALOO: 01387 259679. At Robert Burns Centre. Contemporary pasta/wrap/burger kind of place – good though. Opens from 11am for coffee, then lunch, then dinner. Daily in summer, Tues-Sat winter. Owners seem like nice people.   INX

SANDBAR: 01387 261122. 23 Bank St. Style bar and the style bar menu comes to Dumfries (opened 2000). Nice coffee, jolly indie/dance soundtrack, occ DJ on a Sat. Veggie option and GM-free they say. Open late daily.   INX

THE OLD BANK: 01387 253499. Snacks in converted bank. Very old school and in some contrast to Sandbar.   INX

WHAT TO SEE

ROCKCLIFFE (1514/COASTAL VILLAGES); **ROCKCLIFFE TO KIPPFORD** (1935/COASTAL WALKS); **SOUTHERNESS** (1963/GOLF IN GREAT PLACES); **SWEETHEART ABBEY** (1820/ABBEYS); **CRIFFEL** (1869/HILLS); **CAERLAVEROCK** (1664/BIRDS); **CAERLAVE-ROCK CASTLE** (1713/RUINS); **ELLISLAND FARM** (1846/LITERARY PLACES). **GARDENS** (all off A75): **CASTLE KENNEDY GARDENS** 75 acres laid out around 2 acre lily pond, 2 lochs; rare species. Apr-Sep 10am-5pm. **GLENWHAN GARDENS, DUNRAGIT** enchanting 12 acre hill side, tamed and lovingly hewn into lush over-flowing haven. Gr views and walks. Mar-Oct 10am-5pm. **THREAVE GARDEN, nr CASTLE DOUGLAS** for all seasons. AYR 9.30am-sunset.

WHAT TO DO

SWIMMING: Modern pool on river side nr Buccleuch St Br (01387 252908); **GOLF:** Southerness 25km S on A710 or Powfoot, 20km SW on B724 (01461 700327); **RIDING:** Barend at Sandyhills on 34km S on A710 (01387 780663).

TOURIST OFFICE: Whitesands. 01387 253862. Jan-Dec.

THE BEST OF DUNFERMLINE AND KIRKCALDY

2246
MAP 5

WHERE TO STAY

KEAVIL HOUSE HOTEL, CROSSFORD, DUNFERMLINE: 01383 736258. 3km W of Dunfermline on A994 towards Culross (1511/COASTAL VILLAGES) and Kincardine. Rambling mansion house in grounds within a suburban area of town, converted into modern business-type hotel with all facs incl separate leisure club (not bad pool). Best Western.
41RMS JAN-DEC T/T PETS CC KIDS TOS MED.EX

DAVAAR HOUSE HOTEL, DUNFERMLINE: 01383 736463. Grieve St which is a bugger to find; you'll have to ask. Georgian mansion in suburban st. Serviceable accom. Local reputation for food.
10RMS JAN-DEC T/T PETS CC KIDS TOS   MED.INX

DUNNIKIER HOUSE, KIRKCALDY: 01592 268393. 3 km centre in parkland area. Prob the only half-decent hotel hereabouts but not exp. We can say no more.   15RMS JAN-DEC T/T PETS CC KIDS TOS   MED.INX

STRATHEARN HOTEL, KIRKCALDY: 01592 652210. Forget the 2 'business' hotels, the Dean Park and the Parkway. This hotel on Wishart Pl opp Ravenscraig Park on coast rd and main rd E from town, about 3km from cen-tre may suffice. Ravenscraig is a beautiful coastal park for respite.
18RMS JAN-DEC T/T PETS CC KIDS INX

THE BELVEDERE, W WEMYSS, nr KIRKCALDY: 01592 654167. However, this is worth the 8km trek E of town via A955 coast rd. At beginning of neat village, a curious mixture of dereliction and conservation. Views of bay and Kirkcaldy from comfortable rms in cottages and on the seafront, all white and with red-tiled roofs. Harmless pictures, decent menu.
21RMS JAN-DEC T/T PETS CC KIDS MED.INX

No hostels (Falkland Backpackers is miles away, but good; 1177/HOSTELS*).*

WHERE TO EAT IN AND AROUND DUNFERMLINE

TOWNHOUSE: 01383 432382. 48 East Port in centre. At last a credible restau in Dunfermline by the youngest of the Brown family who run the Bouzy Rouges (555/GLAS) & the Roman Camp (872/CENTRAL HOTS), so they know what they're doing. Light, modern feel to room & menu. Open all day 12-LO9.30pm. Lunch, dinner or just grazing. Best in town no doubt.   MED

IL PESCATORE, LIMEKILNS: 01383 872999. 7km from town via B9156 or to Rosyth, then Charlestown. Local favourite and the best pasta etc around. Now has 6 inexp rms above. Good for birthdays or a stroll after dinner. 7 days, LO 11pm.   INX

TAURASIS: 01383 623798. 21 Carnegie Drive opp fire stn nr Carnegie Centre. Serviceable. Best Italian option in town.   INX

CHALMERS: 01383 724327. Chalmers St nr park entrance. Newish & rated locally at TGP. We no-say. Wed-Sun, lunch & dinner.   INX

THE NEW VICTORIA: 724175. The 'Vic' upstairs opp City Chambers on the High St since 1923. 50 main courses; an institution. 7 days till 7pm (later w/ends).

WHERE TO EAT IN AND AROUND KIRKCALDY

THE OLD RECTORY, DYSART: 01592 651211. 5km E (939/FIFE RESTAUS).

LA GONDOLA: 640085. N Harbour. The best Italian with live Enzo on Suns. INX

FEUARS ARMS: 205025. 66 Commercial St. V good pub food west of town nr high flats. Best in town for informal meal and atmos. Lunch and dinner w/ends.   INX

BAR ITZD: 01592 204257. Main St E end. Café-bar with Tex–Mex menu & accoutrements. May date rapidly (may not). 7 days. LO 9.30pm.   INX

MAXIN: 01592 263406. 5 High St at the W end. The best Chinese. 7days.   INX

VALENTE'S: 01592 205774. Not sit-in, but *absolutely the best* fish and chips (1347/FISH AND CHIPS). Take them to Ravenscraig Park nearby, walk along the coves.

WHAT TO SEE

ABBOT HOUSE, DUNFERMLINE (2103/MUSEUMS); **PITTENCRIEFF & RAVEN-SCRAIG PARKS, DUNFERMLINE** (1502/1503/TOWN PARKS) and **BEVERIDGE PARK, KIRKCALDY** (1503/TOWN PARKS); **CARNEGIE CENTRE, DUNFERMLINE** (2000/SWIMMING POOLS); **DUNFERMLINE ABBEY** (1843/MARY, CHARLIE AND BOB); **KIRKCALDY ART GALLERY** (2130/PUBLIC GALLERIES); **PILLANS, KIRK-CALDY** (1410/BAKERS); **BETTY NICOL'S** (1288/REAL ALES).

WHAT TO DO

SWIMMING/INDOOR SPORTS: *As above.* **GOLF:** Kirkcaldy is nr some of the best (see golf, p. 259). **TENNIS:** Both towns have municipal and private courts. Check TIC.

TOURIST OFFICES

DUNFERMLINE: 1 High Street. 01383 720999. Jan-Dec.

KIRKCALDY: 19 White's Causeway. 01592 267775. Jan-Dec.

THE BEST OF FORT WILLIAM

2247
MAP 2

WHERE TO STAY

INVERLOCHY CASTLE: 01397 702177. 5km out on A82 Inverness rd. One of Scotland's gr hotels. Victorian elegance recently refurb and impeccable service. (995/HIGHLANDS HOTELS).   17RMS JAN-DEC T/T XPETS CC KIDS LOTS

GLENLOY LODGE, NORTH OF BANAVIE: 01397 712700. The Haynes' rather splendid hideaway up the Caledonian Canal at Glen Loy. 1920s lodge house with cared-for grounds, occ pine martens, and sense of peace. Non-res can dine, and they do – but you'll want to stay. Pat cooks, Gordon does the cheese and wine (Dinner MED).   8RMS DEC-OCT X/X PETS CC KIDS TOS MED.EX

THE MOORINGS: 01397 772797. Banavie (follow signs), 5km out on A830 Corpach/Mallaig rd. O/look the Caledonian canal by 'Neptune's Staircase'. Good location, ok dining-rm (1 AA rosette).
                        21RMS JAN-DEC T/T PETS CC KIDS TOS MED.INX

HIGHLAND HOTEL: 01397 702291. Union Rd. High above town (best place to be), with gr views esp when you walk out the front door to the terraced lawns. Rms basic but foyer has character. Conveyor belt to the Highlands, but you may find untrendy tackiness charming. Very old school.
                        110RMS MAR-NOV X/T PETS CC KIDS MED.INX

ONICH HOTEL: 01855 821214. At Onich 16km S on A82. Loch side; good value (1011/HIGHLANDS HOTELS).

LODGE ON THE LOCH: 01855 821237. In Onich, quite stylish peace and quiet (1010/HIGHLAND HOTELS).

S.Y. HOSTEL at GLEN NEVIS: 01397 702336. 5km from town by picturesque but busy Glen Nevis rd. The Ben is above. Grade 1. Fax poss. Many other hostels in area (ask at TO for list) but esp **FW BACKPACKERS:** 01397 700711, Alma Rd.

CAMPING/CARAVAN SITE, GLEN NEVIS: 01397 702191. Nr hostel. Well-run site, mainly caravans (also for rent). Many facs incl restaus and much going on.

WHERE TO EAT

INVERLOCHY (as above): 3 AA rosettes. Best for miles.

CRANNOG: 01397 705589. On loch front. Seafood (1343/SEAFOOD RESTAUS).

THE MOORINGS: 01397 772797. 5km by A830. (*See above.*)

No 4: 01397 704222. Cameron Sq behind the TIC. At last, perhaps a restau to write home about in Ft William town. These people know their salmon and some other things about food, presentation etc so prob the poshest plate in town. À la carte and daily specials. Lunch and LO 9.30pm. Daily in season, cl Sun in winter.   MED

AN CRANN, BANAVIE: 01397 772077. 7km centre via Mallaig rd, then signed at Banavie. A local favourite, this stone barn nestles in the countryside and offers eclectic mix. V Scottish, v friendly. Easter-Oct: 5-9pm Mon-Sat, but phone first.   INX

CAFÉ BEAG, GLEN NEVIS: 01397 703601. 5km along Glen Nevis rd; past 'Braveheart' car park (!) and visitor centre. Alpine-looking cabin, cosy atmos; open fires, books, games. New managers 2001, and maybe only June-Sep from now.   INX

CAFÉ CHARDON: Coffee shop upstairs at Peter Maclennan's well-kent emporium in the main st (or access via side lane). The auld alliance continues here with pastry thingies and every kind of filled roll. Mon-Sat 9-4.30pm.   CHP

WHAT TO SEE

Most of the good things about Ft William are outside the town, but these incl some v big items esp the Ben and the Glens (Glens Nevis as well as Coe):

GLENCOE: 30km S (1581/SCENIC ROUTES; 1899/SERIOUS WALKS; 1826/BATTLE-GROUNDS); **GLEN NEVIS** (1543/GLENS); **BEN NEVIS:** 6km E on Glen Nevis rd (1900/SERIOUS WALKS); **WEST HIGHLAND WAY** (1893/LONG WALKS); **STEALL FALLS**, Glen Nevis (1559/WATERFALLS); **GLENCOE SKIING** (1981/SKIING); **AONACH MOR SKIING** (1980/SKIING) **MUSEUM** (2109/MUSEUMS). **NEVIS RANGE GONDOLA:** Aonach Mor (*see below*), open AYR, is a big attraction. Go up for the incredible view and the air and the Ben over there.

WHAT TO DO

GOLF: Ft William Golf Club (01397 704464). 5km towards Inverness on A82; **SWIMMING/SPORTS:** Lochaber Centre (01397 704 359). Beyond main st and Alexandra Hotel. Squash, sauna, 2 gyms, climbing wall, swimming (with flume). **TENNIS:** One court at Lochaber Centre, free of charge. **SKIING:** Aonach Mor (01397 705825). 12km via A82. Scotland's most modern ski resort (1980/SKIING). Gondola goes up in summer for the view. **BIKE HIRE:** Off-Beat Bikes (01397 704008). Main St and ski base stn.

TOURIST OFFICE: Cameron Square. 01397 703781. Jan-Dec.

THE BEST OF THE BORDER TOWNS

WHERE TO STAY

ROXBURGHE HOTEL, KELSO: 01573 450331 (887/BORDERS HOTELS). LOTS

BURTS, MELROSE: 01896 822285 (889/BORDERS HOTELS). MED.EX

CRINGLETIE, PEEBLES: 01721 730233 & **PHILIPBURN, SELKIRK:** 01750 20747 (888/BORDERS HOTELS). MED.EX

EDENWATER, EDNAM, nr KELSO: 01573 224070 (890/BORDERS HOTELS). MED.EX

CHURCHES, EYEMOUTH: 01890 750401 (891/BORDERS HOTELS). MED.EX

WOODLANDS, GALA: 01896 754722. Windyknowe Rd off A7 in Edin direction, A72 to Peebles. Substantial mansion above town centre with elegant hall, spacious public rms and local reputation for food and service.
10RMS JAN-DEC T/T PETS CC KID MED.EX

JEDFOREST COUNTRY HOTEL, JEDBURGH: 01835 840222 (895/BORDERS HOTELS)

EDNAM HOUSE HOTEL, KELSO: 01573 224168 (896/BORDERS HOTELS)

DRYBURGH ABBEY HOTEL nr ST BOSWELLS: 01835 822261 (893/BORDERS HOTELS)

HUNDALEE HOUSE, JEDBURGH: 01835 863011. 1km S. Jedburgh off A68. Lovely 1700 manor house in 10 acre gdn. Brilliant value, gr base, views of Cheviot hills. Nr the famously old Capon Tree.
5RMS MAR-OCT X/T XPETS XCC KIDS CHP

GLEN HOTEL and HEATHERLIE HOTEL, SELKIRK: 01750 20259/21200. Both family-run hotels in manor houses with views over town. Well-run, dependable. Selkirk makes a good touring centre.
8/7RMS JAN-DEC T/T X/T PETS/XPETS CC KIDS INX

S.Y. HOSTELS: V good in this area (1166/HOSTELS).

WHERE TO EAT

MARMIONS, MELROSE: 01896 822245 (900/BORDERS HOTELS).

CRINGLETIE, PEEBLES: 01721 730233; **PHILIPBURN, SELKIRK:** 01750 20747 (894/BORDERS HOTELS); **EDENWATER, EDNAM, nr KELSO:** 01573 224070 (890/BORDERS HOTELS).

ROXBURGHE HOTEL and FAIRWAYS: (adj brasserie in the clubhouse o/look the course (Fri/Sat only, for dinner: 01573 450331).

LAZELS, PEEBLES: 01721 720602 (1157/HOTELS THAT WELCOME KIDS).

BURT'S HOTEL, MELROSE and KING'S ARMS: (889/BORDER HOTELS) Local faves (901/BORDERS HOTELS).

AULD CROSS KEYS, DENHOLM: 01450 870305; **HORSESHOE INN, nr PEEBLES:** 01721 730225; **WHEATSHEAF, SWINTON:** 01890 860257 (1313/1312/1291 PUB FOOD). **CRAW INN, AUCHENCROW:** 01890 761253 (1194/ROADSIDE INNS).

CHAPTERS, nr MELROSE: 01896 823217 (902/BORDERS RESTAUS).

SUD ITALIA, GALASHIELS: 01896 750007. Reasonable Med option in downtown Gala nr the supermarket. Nice people. Lunch and LO 9.30/10pm. Cl Tues & Sun lunch.

BRYDONS, HAWICK: 01450 372672. 16 High St. Once Brydons were bakers, now they have this oddly funky family caff-cum-restau. Home cooking, good folk – this is a totally Hawick experience. All day and dinner Fri/Sat.

ALLANTON INN, ALLANTON, BERWICKSHIRE: 01890 818260. Main st of one-horse vill in flat shire & nr Paxton House (1762/CO HOUSES). Stone flags, real ales, surprisingly good food. Lunch & dinner LO varies.

LE BISTRO, DENHOLM: 01450 870530. Corner of the green on rd from Hawick. Pop local choice (tho Hawick is bereft), antiques & art adj. Lunch & dinner Fri/Sat.

HERGÉ'S BAR BISTRO, GALASHIELS: 01896 750400. 58 Island St on rd to Peebles. Wine-bar ambience, locals rate it. Sat night-pub only. Lunch and 6-9pm. Cl Mon.

WHAT TO SEE

THIRLESTANE CASTLE, LAUDER (1763/COUNTRY HOUSES); **TWEED FISHING** (*see below*); **PENIEL HEUGH** (1771/MONUMENTS); **MARY QUEEN OF SCOTS' HOUSE** (1832/MARY, CHARLIE AND BOB); **ANCRUM** (1809/GRAVEYARDS; 1628/PICNICS); **ABBEYS** (1817/JEDBURGH; 1818/DRYBURGH; 1821/MELROSE); **PRIORWOOD** (1481/GARDENS); **ABBOTSFORD** (1850/LITERARY PLACES); **EILDON HILLS** (1880/HILL WALKS); **RUBERSLAW** (1872/HILLS); **SCOTT'S VIEW/IRVINE'S VIEW** (1605/1606/VIEWS); **LILLIARD'S EDGE** (1828/BATTLEGROUNDS); **LOCHCARRON** and **CHAS WHILLANS** (2069/2070/WOOLLIES).

WHAT TO DO

SWIMMING: V good leisure facs both in and around Hawick and Galashiels. Galashiels Pool (01896 752154) at Livingston Pl up the hill from the one-way main st is excellent (2003/SWIMMING POOLS). Hawick's Teviotdale Leisure Centre (01450 374440) has squash courts, a gym (Universal) and a pool with fun stuff as well as length swimming. Jedburgh and Selkirk also have pools. **GOLF:** Good courses at Minto, nr Denholm (01450 870220) (18); Selkirk (01750 20621) (9); Melrose (01896 822855) (9); Hawick (01450 372293) (18); Jedburgh (01835 863587) (9). All picturesque, in fair condition, available to visitors. **RIDING:** Cowdenknowes, Earlston (01896 848020). Kailzie Stables nr Peebles. **TENNIS:** Galshiels, Abbotsford Terr; Hawick, Wilton Lodge Park; also Melrose. **CYCLE HIRE:** Galashiels, 58 High St (01896 757587); Hawick, 45 N Br St (01450 373352); Peebles, 3 High St (01721 720844). **FISHING:** There can be last-minute vacancies even on the famous Tweed. Tweed Foundation (01896 848271); J Leeming's independent agency (01573 470280). Tackle: Angler's Choice, Melrose (01896 823070); Tweedside Tackle, Kelso (01573 225306).

TOURIST INFORMATION:

JEDBURGH: Murray's Green. 01835 863435. Jan-Dec.

GALASHIELS: 01896 755551. Apr-Oct; **HAWICK:** Common Ground. 01450 372547. Apr-Oct; **MELROSE:** Adj Abbey. 01896 822555.

WHERE TO STAY – THE BEST

CULLODEN HOUSE: 01463 790461 (998/HIGHLANDS HOTELS).   LOTS

DUNAIN PARK HOTEL: 01463 230512 (1001/HIGHLANDS HOTELS).   EXP

BUNCHREW HOUSE: 01463 234917 (1007/HIGHLANDS HOTELS).   LOTS

ROYAL HIGHLAND HOTEL: 01463 231926. Academy St. Formerly the Station Hotel but big refurb since last edition – big difference so 'congrats' to owner Judith Holland. V much in the centre of things with all mod cons.

75RMS JAN-DEC T/T PETS CC KIDS EXP

THE BEST OF THE REST

MARRIOTT HOTEL: 01463 237166. Culcabock Rd. In suburban area S of centre nr A9. Modern, v well-appointed, formerly the Kingsmills, taken over in 2000. Chain hotel but dependable.   84RMS JAN-DEC T/T PETS CC KIDS EXP

GLENMORISTON: 01463 223777. Ness Bank. Scottish country house feel meets Italian influence (same people have Riva, see below). A small, smart establishment you'll be glad to find.   15RMS JAN-DEC T/T XPETS CC KIDS EXP

ARDMUIR/BRAENESS/FELSTEAD: 01463 231151/712266/231634. 3 hotels on Ness Bank, along the river opp Eden Court and v central. Felstead more a guesthouse and cheaper. All family-run, basic. Many other hotels in this st. These ones are decent value.   11/7RMS VARIES X/T PETS CC KIDS MED.INX

MOYNESS HOUSE: 01463 233836. 6 Bruce Gardens. Multi-accolade-gathering guest house in the 'burbs. Neil Gunn used to live here!   MED.INX

3 GOOD HOSTELS. S. Y. HOSTEL: 01463 231771. Victoria Drive; Large official hostel. More funky are the **STUDENT HOSTEL**: 236556. 8 Culduthel Rd, and 3 doors down **BAZPACKERS** 717663.

CAMPING AND CARAVAN PARKS: Most central (2km) at **BUGHT PARK**, 01463 236920. Well-equipped and large-scale municipal site on flat river meadow. Many facs. App via A82 Ft William rd. More picturesque at **SCANIPORT**, 01463 751351. 8km SW on B862, the scenic route to Ft Augustus. Rural.

WHERE TO EAT

DUNAIN PARK HOTEL: As above. 3 adj elegant dining-rms; drawing rm for avant/après. The country-house hotel on the L Ness edge of town where the good burghers come for Ann Nicholl's honest-to-goodness cookery and wish they'd left more rm for the puds. Excl wines; and malt list.   MED

GLEN MORISTON HOTEL: 01463 223777. Ness Bank. On rd along river. Comfortable elegant dining-rm with effective Italian menu well known as the place to eat in this town (MED). Same owners run Riva (below).

BOATH HOUSE, AULDEARN: 01667 454896. Well out of town, but worth drive. Just off A96 3km E of Nairn. 30mins from Inverness. Chef Charlie Lockely accumulating AA rosettes. Report: 996/HIGHLAND HOTELS.   MED

THE MUSTARD SEED: 01463 220220. Bank St. Brand new at TGP so we haven't sampled. Our spies send good reports, but more please. Lunch and dinner daily, AYR. V chp lunches, otherwise   INX

WOODWARD'S: 01463 709809. 99 Castle St nr castle entrance. Cosy bistro with v Scottish menu – Morayshire lamb, Dornoch venison (but 2 vegn dishes). Local rep. Dinner only LO 9.30pm.   MED

CAFÉ ONE: 01463 226200. 10 Castle St nr the Castle. Contemporary décor and cuisine in hands of good team. Reasonably priced for this standard of food and service. Castle St is becoming restau central though, so there are choices these days …   MED

RIVA: 01463 237377. 4 Ness Walk by the main br. Central, popular Italian café/restau open all day, every day (Suns from 2pm) for coffee and ice cream and full pasta/pizza range in Pazzo's adj, while Bar One+One (nachos, burgers etc) is yet another addition to the empire.   INX

RIVERHOUSE RESTAURANT: 01463 222033. Greig St, over the pedestrian bridge. Intimate but 'proper' restaurant with good trad fish dishes. Marcus in the kitchen, Colleen out front. MED

SHAPLA: 01463 241919. 2 Castle Rd on town side of br from Riva above. Indian restau with the usual menu. Roadside rm and better upstairs lounge with river views. Open late (LO 11.30pm). For yet another Italian, try **PALIO** at 26 Queensgate. Good value, straightforward. INX

THE LEMON TREE: 18 Ingle St, pedestrianised town centre st and other entrance from behind M&S. Unlikely high st location for unpretentious family-run café with home-bakes, own burgers, etc. Mon-Sat 8.30am-5.45pm. CHP

CASTLE RESTAURANT: Castle St. Excellent greasy spoon (1370/CAFÉS).

KINKELL HOUSE: off A9N. 01849 861270. Report 1025/HIGHLAND RESTAUS.

WHAT TO SEE

THE NESS ISLANDS: R Ness islands joined by iron br to both banks. A fine stroll of an evening. App via Bught Park or Ness Walk (by Eden Court) and from Dores Rd. **ART.TM**, the town's new gallery (BUY ART/2141). **LEAKEY'S BOOKSHOP:** Church St, Scotland's biggest 2nd hand bookshop in the old Gaelic kirk with good cafe. Mon-Sat 10am-5.30pm. **CULLODEN** (1824/BATTLE-GROUNDS); **CLAVA CAIRNS** (1735/PREHISTORIC SITES); **LOCH NESS** (4/BIG ATTRACTIONS); **THE PHOENIX** (1273/BLOODY GOOD PUBS); **EDEN COURT THE-ATRE** (2186/THEATRES); **SOUTH BANK, LOCH NESS** (1591/SCENIC ROUTES); **GLEN AFFRIC** (1541/GLENS); **AQUADOME** (1986/LEISURE CENTRES).

WHAT TO DO

GOLF: Inverness Golf Club (01463 239882); Torvean (on A82) (01463 711434) Championship course at Nairn (01667 452787), 25km E (1951/GREAT GOLF). **SWIMMING:** Aquadome (01463 667500) (1986/LEISURE CENTRES). **RIDING:** Highland Riding Centre (01456 450220), Drumnadrochit along L Ness. **TEN-NIS:** Inverness Tennis and Squash Club. Bishop's Rd (01463 230751). Also Municipal Courts at Bellfield Park (just turn up, 7 days). **CYCLE HIRE:** Gt Glen Cycle Hire 01397 703015. Also at Bazpackers Hostel (*above*).

TOURIST OFFICE: Castle Wynd. 01463 234353. Jan-Dec.

THE BEST OF OBAN

WHERE TO STAY

2250
MAP 1

MANOR HOUSE: 01631 562087. Gallanach Rd. On S coast rd out of town towards Kerrera ferry, o/look bay. Quiet elegance in contemp style, and a restau that serves (in an intimate dining-rm) prob the most 'fine-dining' dinner in town. Bedrms also prob the cosiest, but the competition ain't great. More delightful than de-luxe. Nice bar.   11RMS JAN-DEC T/T PETS CC KIDS TOS EXP

BARRIEMORE HOTEL: 01631 566356. Corran Esplanade. The last in a long sweep of hotels to N of centre and streets above the rest. Nice people in residence, gr view of the sea. B&B only (830/ARGYLL HOTELS).
                              13RMS MAR-OCT X/T PETS CC KIDS INX

GLENBURNIE HOTEL: 01631 562089. Corran Esplanade. And this one is also good. Run by the inimitable Strachan family, the sherry is free and the guests keep coming back.   14 RMS MAR-OCT X/T PETS CC KIDS MED.EX

COLUMBA HOTEL: 01631 562183. North Pier in the corner of the bay & centre of town. There are several Victorian/municipal gothic edifices in Oban from the days when there were many visitors. This is the one we recommend. Believe us, it's better than the others. If you get a sea view, it's not bad & the bar has good crack (& open late). Ask for a deal.   50RMS JAN-DEC T/T PETS CC KIDS MED.INX

S.Y. HOSTEL: 01631 562025. On Esplanade (i.e. on the front).

WHERE TO EAT

AIRDS HOTEL: 01631 730236. Pt Appin. 40km N by A828. A long way to go for dinner, but if you're in the area you just might want to eat at one of the best restaus in Scotland (820/ARGYLL HOTELS).   EXP

THE WATERFRONT AT THE PIER: 01631 563110. In the port, by the station, an upstairs restau that's serious about seafood. 'From pier to pan' is about right. Blackboard menu & monkfish à la carte. 2 AA rosettes are well-deserved but kill the muzak. Open L and LO 9pm ish, Mar-Dec.   MED

EE-USK, FISH CAFÉ: 01631 565666. 1004 George St, the main st E of the bay. Contemp seafood diner by the estimable Macleods who've been this way before. They have even bigger plans, but we'll wait & see. This place, meanwhile, is the best bet E of the waterfront. The name is the phonetic pron of the gaelic for 'fish'. 7 days, LO 10pm.   MED

THE MANOR HOUSE: (*see above*). The best hotel dining-rm in town. Creative sauces on fresh seafood and other good things. Booking essential.   EXP

JULIE'S COFFEE HOUSE: 01631 565952. 33 Stafford St opp Oban Whisky Vis Centre. Only 6 tables, so fills up. Nice approach to food (snacky, but hot dishes) & customers. Ice-cream from Luca's (the best, so some discernment here). 7 days 10.30am-5pm, Sun 12-4.30pm.   INX

THE STUDIO: 01631 562030. Craigard Rd off main st at Balmoral Hotel. Up the hill to find this here forever, candle-lit restau. Way beyond time for a makeover but who needs it? Surprising menu. Often have to book. Apr-Oct, 5-10pm.INX

THE KITCHEN GARDEN: 01631 566332. 14 George St. Deli-café that's often busy & you may have to queue to go upstairs to the small gallery caff. Not a bad cup of coffee & ciabatta sandwich. 7 days 9am-5.30pm (Suns 11-4pm).

CAFÉ NA LUSAN: 01631 567268. 9 Craigard Rd nr The Studio (*above*). Well it says it's 'simple, relaxed, friendly' & all this is true. Organic & internet kind of caff we like. Excl salads. 7 days 11.30am-9.30pm (till 3.30 Sun/Mon).   INX

WHAT TO SEE

DUNOLLIE CASTLE: On rd to Ganavan (1722/RUINS); **GLEN LONAN:** Gr wee glen starting 8km out of town (1548/GLENS); **SEALIFE CENTRE:** 16km N on A28 (11659/KIDS); **RARE BREEDS FARM:** 4km S from Argyll Sq (1660/KIDS); **OBAN INN:** (*see* WHISKY, *p. 167*); **McCAIG'S TOWER or FOLLY:** You can't miss it, dominating the skyline. A circular granite coliseum. Superb views of the bay. Many ways up, but a good place to start is via Stevenson St, opp Cally Hotel. Free, Open AYR (1775/MONUMENTS). **KERRERA:** The island in the Sound reached by regular ferry from coast rd to Gallanach (4km town). Ferries at set times, but several per day – check TO. A fine wee island for walking, pack your lunch but look for the tea gdn. **LISMORE:** The other, larger island (2202/MAGICAL ISLANDS). Ferry from Oban (Calmac) or Pt Appin (passengers only). **DUNSTAFFNAGE CASTLE:** Signed and visible off A85 betw Oban and Connel (7km). 13th-century. V early type of castle, more of a ft, really. Unoccupied, except for the odd Clan McDougall spectre rattling around in the dungeons. Pity about the post-industrial approach rd, but there is a chapel in the woods. **ARDCHATTAN:** 20km N via Connel. Along N shore of L Etive, a place to wander amongst ruins and gdns. Tearoom. If you're along that way, go to the end of the rd at Bonawe where the famous granite that cobbled the world was (and still is) quarried. Ironworks open as a museum is a tranquil place (2118/MUSEUMS).

WHAT TO DO

GOLF: Glencruitten (01631 562868) (1966/GOLF IN GREAT PLACES); **SWIMMING:** Atlantis Leisure Centre at Dalriach Rd (01631 566800); **PONY-TREKKING:** Achnalarig Farm, Glencruitten (01631 562745); **WINDSURFING:** Linnhe Marine (01631 730227), 32km N via A828. (2008/WATER SPORTS); **FISHING:** Plenty on lochs and R Awe and Avich – check TIC; **BIKE HIRE:** Hazelbank Cycles (01631 566476).

TOURIST INFO: Argyll Sq. 01631 563122. Jan-Dec.

WHERE TO STAY

BALLATHIE HOUSE, KINCLAVEN: 01250 883268. 20km N of Perth via Blairgowrie rd A93/left follow signs after 16km just before the famous beech hedge; or A9 and 4km N, take B9000 through Stanley. Former baronial hunting lodge beside the R Tay. Relaxed and informal atmos in definitive country house. New riverside rms. Kevin MacGillivray's award-winning food. Fishing by arrangement with Estate office.   43RMS JAN-DEC T/T PETS CC KIDS TOS LOTS

KINFAUNS CASTLE: 01738 620777. A90 main Dundee Rd, 10 mins Perth centre in lofty country setting. Magnificent building, well refurb and decent dining.   16RMS FEB-DEC T/T PETS CC KIDS LOTS

HUNTINGTOWER HOTEL: 01738 583771. Crieff rd (1km off A85, 3km W of ring route A9 signed). Elegant, modernised mansion house o/side town. Good gdns with spectacular copper beech. Subdued, panelled restau with decent menu (esp lunch) and wine list. Business-like service.

34RMS JAN-DEC T/T PETS CC KIDS TOS MED.EX

ROYAL GEORGE: 01738 624455. Tay St by the Perth Br over the Tay to the A93 rd to Blairgowrie and relatively close to Dundee rd and motorway system. Br is illuminated at night. Georgian proportions and some faded elegance which if we wait long enough will be fashionable again. Mums and farmers and visiting clergy happy here.   39RMS JAN-DEC T/T PETS CC KIDS MED.EX

S.Y. HOSTEL: 01738 623658. 107 Glasgow Rd in suburban area off main rd 1km centre. Mostly larger dorms. No café.

WHERE TO EAT

LET'S EAT: 01738 643377. 77 Kinnoull St. The place to eat (959/PERTHSHIRE RESTAUS)

63 TAY STREET: 01738 441451. 63 Tay St on riverside. Seriously good bistro. Report: (960/PERTHSHIRE EATS).

KERACHER'S: 01738 449777. Corner of South St and Scott St. Seafood corner restau run by notable local supplier. Downstairs lounge and upstairs bistro style dining. Excl ingredients and service. Cl Mon. Lunch and LO 9.30/10pm.

INX(BAR)/MED

EXCEED: 01738 621189. 65 S Methven St. Large, woody brasserie restau with varied menu, blackboard specials best. This restau changing hands & direction at TGP. Cl Tues. Lunch and LO 10pm   INX

1774: 01738 451774. 10 N Port. Fairly authentic French bistro. Intimate, intriguing. Very Perth. Cl Sun/Mon. Lunch and LO 9pm.   MED

KRUNGTHAI: 01738 633090. 161 South St. Authentic fare offered by Thai owner/chef has earned good local rep but many curries (and was that a paratha?). Lunch and till 11pm, 7 days (11.30pm w/ends).   INX

PACO'S: 01738 622290. Mill St behind M&S. A Perth city fav now gone mega with big room, café counter and terrace. Busy young atmos, food fairly uninspiring. 7 days all day.   INX

THAT BAR (THE LOFT): 01738 634523. 147 South St. Perthshire trendy, designery bar (with pool table & big TV). Predictable food upstairs. Late option (LO 11.45 at w/ends).   INX

MARCELLO'S: 143 South St. Pizza pasta pitstop. Takeaway only. Noon-11pm (midnight Fri/Sat). Good looking guys knead the dough.   INX

BETTY'S: 67 George St. Old-world parlour tearoom with gr home-baking, dish of the day and delicate soups. Opp art gallery. Licensed. 10am-5.30pm. Cl Sun.

LEMON TREE: Mill St. Innovative veggie restau above good gift shop.   INX

DELI-CIOUS: 46 Methven St. Small, cheery take-away and sit-in coffee shop. Some hot dishes. Excl sandwiches. 7.30am – evening, Suns 11am-7pm.   INX

HOLDGATE'S FISH TEAS: South St. Report: (1355/FISH 'N' CHIPS). A classic! INX

WHAT TO SEE

KINNOULL HILL (1875/HILLS); **FERGUSSON GALLERY** (2129/PUBLIC GALLERIES); **GLENDOICK** (2076/GARDEN CENTRES).

CHERRYBANK GARDENS/BRANKLYN GARDENS: Cherrybank is off Glasgow Rd, 18 acres of formal gdns around the offices of United Distillers, notable esp for heathers. Open May-Sept 10am-5pm (Suns 12-4pm). Branklyn is signed off Dundee Rd beyond Queen's Br; park and walk 100m. A tightly packed cornucopia of typical gdn flowers and shrubs. Open Mar-Oct 7 days 9.30am-dusk.

PERTH THEATRE: 01738 621031. Established 1935 and Scotland's most successful repertory theatre (Ewan MacGregor got his first break here). Bar/coffee bar and restau. Essential all-round centre even for non-theatregoers.

WHAT TO DO

SWIMMING: Excellent large leisure centre with flumes pool and 'training' pool for lengths. Part of it is outdoors. Best app via Glasgow Rd (01738 492410) (1985/LEISURE CENTRES). **SPORTS CENTRE:** The Gannochy or 'Bells' Complex for multigym (Universal), squash (5 courts), badminton etc. Hay St off Barrack St (01738 622301). **GOLF:** Interesting course on Moncreiffe Island in the middle of the Tay (01738 625170). Good courses at Murrayshall, New Scone (01738 551171). Excellent course at Blairgowrie (01250 872622) (1964/GOLF IN GREAT PLACES).

TOURIST INFO: Lower City Mills. 01738 450600. Jan-Dec.

THE BEST OF STIRLING

2252 **WHERE TO STAY**

MAP 6

STIRLING HIGHLAND: 01786 475444 (874/CENTRAL HOTELS).

BOUZY ROUGE at the SHERIFFMUIR INN: 01786 823285. 15km via Bridge of Allan & only 4 rms but an stylish stopover in empty countryside (873/CENTRAL HOTELS).

PARK LODGE: 01786 474862. 32 Park Terrace off main King's Park Rd, 500m from centre. Rather posh hotel in Georgian town (they say 'country') house nr the park and golf course. Objets and lawns. Dinner here has local rep.

10RMS JAN-DEC T/T PETS CC KIDS MED.EX

PORTCULLIS HOTEL: 01786 472290. Castle Wynd, which is no more than a cannonball's throw from the castle itself and one of the best locations in town. Pub and pub food (hearty, v popular, may be noisy) below; upstairs only 4 rms, but 3 have brilliant views of Castle/graveyard/town and plain.

4RMS JAN-DEC X/T PETS CC KIDS MED.INX

STIRLING MANAGEMENT CENTRE: 01786 451666. Not strictly speaking a hotel, but is as good as. Fully serviced rms on the univ campus (7km from centre in Br of Allan). Usually not full. Sports/entertainment facs nearby. No atmos but a business-like option. 76RMS JAN-DEC T/T XPETS CC KIDS MED.INX

THE GOLDEN LION: 01786 475351. 8 King St. V central, large, functional with very interior and not that 'great' Great Food Stop. Handy for shops/stn/Stirling stuff. 67RMS JAN-DEC T/T PETS CC KIDS MED.EX

THE GEAN HOUSE, ALLOA: 01259 219275. 12km E (879/CENTRAL HOTELS).

S.Y. HOSTEL: 01786 473442. On rd up to castle in recently renovated jail is this new-style hostel, tho still very SYH (1105/HOSTELS). The **WILLY WALLACE HOSTEL** 01786 446773 at 77 Murray Pl (corner with Friars St) is more funky. Upstairs in busy centre with many caffs & pubs nearby. Unimposing entrance but bunkrms for 56 backpackey folk.

WHERE TO EAT

HERMANN'S: 01786 450632. Mar Place House on rd up to (& v close to) Castle. Hermann Aschaber's (with Scottish wife, Kay) corner of Austria where schnitzels and strudels figure along with trad Scottish fare. 2 floor, ambient well run rms with cheery staff.   MED

THE YILL 'N' KAIL: 01786 473929. As title on rd up to Castle. Long standing restau site, this the latest version makes credible attempt at modern Scottish cuisine. Restau upstairs. Reports please. Check opening hours.   INX

SCHOLARS at the **STIRLING HIGHLAND HOTEL:** 01786 473052. The up-market, up-by-the-Castle eaterie in town, the Stirling Highland a good conversion of an old school hence the name (874/CENTRAL HOTELS). Tries to live up to reputation(EXP). **RIZZIO'S**, the Italian caff at street level, has ok buffet lunch and early evens and LO 10.30pm.   MED/INX

PIZZA EXPRESS: 01786 474950. 26 King St in middle of main shopping area The chain (but still one of the best chains) with reliably good pizza & good designery ambience. Also open later than most. 7 days 11.30/midnight.   INX

THE COTTAGE: 01786 446124. 52 Spittal St on rd up to castle. Tearm/caff with home-made aft tea-type fare but hot mains with Scottish no-nonsense approach. Upstairs and down. 7 days 10am-7pm (9pm Fri/Sat). From 12 on Suns.   CHP

PACO'S: 01786 446414. Nr TIC in town centre. Popular, big Tex-mex restau as the one in Perth. Woody ambience. LO 10.30pm.   INX

OLIVIA'S: 01786 446277. Baker St. Contemp Scottish bistro that many locals like. TOS. Lunch and dinner. LO 9.30pm. Cl Sun.   INX

THE EAST INDIA COMPANY: 01786 471330. 7 Viewfield Pl. Still proclaim to be the best Indian in town tho a bit shabby now. Good atmos in woody basement rm. Pakora bar for snacks upstairs. Open 7 days till 11pm.   INX

KAM'S GARDEN: 01786 446 445. 4 Viewfield Pl nr E India (above) so best Chinese and best Indian adj. Calm; and Kam cuisine. LO 11.30pm 7 days.   INX

ITALIA NOSTRA: 01786 473208. 25 Baker St. Gr name. The tratt to try. Busy atmos. Decent wine list. Usual pastas. 7 days. 11/12pm.   CHP

CAFÉ ALBERT at the **ALBERT HALL:** 01786 449196. Café/bistro created in a municipal hall. Hot dishes, baguettes, snacks. Newspapers and a relaxed atmos. Mon-Sat 10am-5pm.   CHP

THE BARNTON BAR AND BISTRO: 01786 461698. Barnton St opp main post office. Perenially popular. Jukebox. All-day breakfast, baked potatoes, hefty sandwiches. Newspapers. 7 days. Food till 7.45pm, then bar takes over.   CHP

ALLAN WATER CAFE, BRIDGE OF ALLAN: 8km up the rd in Br of Allan main st nr br itself. Great café, the best fish 'n' chips 'n' ice cream (1366/CAFÉS). CHP

WHAT TO SEE

STIRLING CASTLE (1692/CASTLES); **WALLACE MONUMENT/THE PINEAPPLE** (1767/1773/MONUMENTS); **BANNOCKBURN/SHERIFFMUIR** (1830/BATTLE-GROUNDS); **THE OCHILS** (1881/HILL WALKS; 1905/GLEN AND RIVER WALKS); **LOGIE OLD KIRK** (1811/GRAVEYARDS); **PARADISE** (1629/PICNICS); **DUNBLANE CATHE-DRAL** (1793/CHURCHES).

STIRLING OLD TOWN JAIL: St John's St on rd up to Castle. Guided tour and put-up job, but rather well done. Live actors. Kids will be quiet or simply tortured. Open AYR (4pm winter).

THE GHOST WALK: A stroll through old part of the town nr the castle:'a world of restless spirits and lost souls' (sound familiar?). Info: TIC or 01786 872788.

RAINBOW SLIDES: Nr Railway Stn. A leisure centre with good 25m pool and gym (Pulsestar) and for kids 3 water slides of varying thrill factors. Open 7 days (Sat and Sun till 4pm). Check times: 01786 462521.

WHAT TO DO

SWIMMING/SPORTS: (*see above*). There's also a pool at the University Sports Centre and at the Stirling Highland Hotel (with squash). **GOLF:** Stirling Golf Course v central at Queen's Rd. Quite testing and one of best in area (01786 464098). **BIKE HIRE:** Stewart Wilson Cycles, 49 Barnton St (01786 465292).

TOURIST INFO: Dumbarton Rd. 01786 475019. Jan-Dec.

THE BEST OF ULLAPOOL

WHERE TO STAY

THE CEILIDH PLACE: 01854 612103. 14 W Argyle St. Eclectic individualism; something to celebrate (1018/INEXP HIGHLAND HOTELS). Also cheap 'bunkhouse' accom. Scotland in a nutshell.   24RMS JAN-DEC T/X PETS CC KIDS EXP/CHP

MOREFIELD MOTEL: 01854 612161. Edge of town A835 heading N. Surreal location in midst of housing estate. Small motel cabins and gr seafood amongst big varied menu (1340/SEAFOOD RESTAUS).

10RMS JAN-DEC T/T PETS CC KIDS INX

S.Y. HOSTEL: 01854 612254. On Shore St (the front) converted from cottages. Grade 2. Can book by fax. Also at Achiltibuie (same number) 40km by rd, 22km by footpath. A good base for this scenic area; book in summer.

WHERE TO EAT

THE CEILIDH PLACE: *as above.*

THE MOREFIELD HOTEL: *as above.*

THE TEA STORE: Argyll St. Lauri Chilton closed her Scottish Larder which we liked & has opened this caff instead. Virtually everything is home-baked on the premises & there's an all-day b/fast if you can't face the one on the ferry. 7 days, 7.45am-5pm. Cl Sun in wint.   INX

WHAT TO SEE

CORRIESHALLOCH GORGE: 20km S (1560/WATERFALLS); **AN TEALLACH** 40km S by rd (1598/VIEWS); **ACHILTIBUIE:** 40km NW (1586/SCENIC ROUTES); **STAC POLLAIDH** (pron 'Polly', 1862/HILLS); **HIGHLAND STONEWARE** and **KNOCK-AN GALLERY** 2036/2048/CRAFT SHOPS); **HIGHLAND RARE BREEDS FARM** (1656/KIDS). **LOCH BROOM** pool/leisure centre 01854 612884.

TOURIST INFO: Argyle St. 01854 612135. Easter-Nov.

THE BEST OF WICK AND THURSO

WHERE TO STAY

FORSS HOUSE HOTEL, nr THURSO: 01847 861201. 8km W on A836. The MacGregor's family home set in 20 woodland acres by the sea is the best quality hotel for miles. Popular restau (you should book), over 210 malts in the bar comfortable spacious rms and 5 chalets in the grounds too. Breakfast in the conservatory then birds, walks, old mill and waterfall. Fishing.

13RMS JAN-DEC T/T PETS CC KIDS TOS MED.EX

PORTLAND ARMS, LYBSTER: 01593 721208. On main A9 20km S of Wick and 45km S of Thurso by A895. A coaching inn since 1851; still hospitable. Small rms are a bit, well, small but this is a hearty hotel with decent food, well managed by Marc Stevens. Feels part of the community. While in Lybster, pop down and see Waterlines (WHAT TO SEE).

22RMS JAN-DEC T/T PETS CC KIDS TOS MED.INX

BORGIE LODGE HOTEL, nr BETTYHILL: 01641 521332. A836 12km E of Tongue. Secluded trad huntin', shootin', fishin' sort of a place: 20 hill lochs and 2 rivers with salmon and trout. Shooting on the adj 12,000 acre estate and Jacqui's acclaimed cooking to come home to. Getaway people like it too though. Another MacGregor establishment – Peter's brother has Forss House (above). 7RMS AYR X/T PETS CC KIDS TOS MED.INX

ROYAL HOTEL, THURSO: 01847 893191. Trail St in town centre. Sprawling stone inn upgraded to comfortable commercialism. All mod cons but still no sign of the pool/leisure complex. Some say it can be cold here in Thurso – so take your vest. A hotel for visitors. 105RMS JAN-DEC T/T XPETS CC KIDS MED.INX

NORTHERN SANDS HOTEL, DUNNET: 01847 851270. Ask a local for a good, wee hotel and they'll point you here. Just S of Dunnet village, on the bay. Even does takeaway pizza. 12RMS JAN-DEC T/T PETS CC KIDS MED.INX

MACKAY'S HOTEL, WICK: Union Street. 01955 602323. Basic but welcoming. Business travellers during week, family-run (the Lamonts). 27RMS JAN-DEC T/T XPETS CC XKIDS MED.INX

QUAYSIDE B&B, WICK: 25 Harbour Quay. 01955 603229. Brenda Turner's great little establishment, keeping the punters happy since '96. Basic, economical and friendly – with parking (she told us to say). 6RMS (2SELF-CAT) JAN-DEC X/X XPETS CC KIDS CHP

ACKERGILL TOWER, nr WICK: 01955 603556. A rare treat (1259/HOUSEPARTIES)

S.Y. HOSTEL: 01955 611424. At Canisbay, John O'Groats (7km). Wick 25km. Regular bus service. The furthest-flung youth hostel on the mainland. Thurso now has a backpacker hostel – **SANDRA'S** at 24-26 Princes St. Cheap 'n' cheerful with snack bar adjacent. 01847 894575.

NAVIDALE HOUSE, by HELMSDALE: 01431 821258. Not stayed but we hear it's v good.

WHERE TO EAT

FORSS HOUSE HOTEL, PORTLAND ARMS, BORGIE LODGE HOTEL: (*all as above*)

LA MIRAGE, HELMSDALE: 60km S. Viva Las Vegas! (1045/INEXP HIGHLAND RESTAUS). For sale in 2001 – hope it's still there in 2002! INX

THE NORTHERN SANDS: (*see above*).

THE FERRY INN, SCRABSTER: 01847 892814. 3km W of Thurso in busy pt area o/look BP and ferry terminal for Orkney. 'Turf' (meat) on upper deck and 'surf' (fish) on top deck. Adj bar. Lunch and 6-9.30pm, 7 days. INX

DUNNET TEA-ROOM by DUNNET HEAD: 01847 851774. 15km N of Thurso by coast rd. Lunch and dinner, Easter-Sep. Cl Wed. (1054/INEXP HIGHLAND RESTAUS) CHP

OLD SMIDDY INN, THRUMSTER: 01955 651256. 7km S of Wick on A9. Bar/restau/café full of smiddyish stuff. Snacks, meals and blackboard specials. 7 days; Sun-Thur 12-2pm, 5.30-8.30pm; Fri and Sat all day. LO 9pm. CHP

QUEEN'S HOTEL: Wick town centre. Haven't tried, but popular with locals for bar food. INX

WHAT TO SEE

DUNBEATH: 32km S of Wick (1848/LITERARY PLACES; 1909/GLEN AND RIVER WALKS); **CAIRNS OF CAMSTER:** 15km S of Wick (1746/PREHISTORIC SITES); **BETTYHILL MUSEUM:** 50km W of Thurso (2105/MUSEUMS); **NORTH COAST BEACHES** (1536/BEACHES).

WICK HERITAGE CENTRE: 01955 605393. In town centre; June-Sept. Mon-Sat 10am-5pm. (INTERESTING MUSEUMS/2124). **CAITHNESS GLASS CENTRE, WICK:** 01955 602286. Home of popular gift ware; factory and visitor centre; by the airport.

WATERLINES: Lybster harbour. 01593 721520. All-new visitor centre telling Lybster's tale at its harbour. Good history – the big contrast between then and now. Plus tearoom! May-Sep, daily, 11am-5pm.

THE TRINKIE: A walk along the rocky coast E of Wick or drive through housing schemes until cliff rd appears (ask locals). Flat rocks, an open-air pool; a good spot. 2km further for the 'Brig O'Trams'.

WHALIGOE STEPS: On A9 N of Lybster; down track nr cottages and septic tank, by Cairn O' Get sign. Infamy regained after Billy Connolly's visit; 318 (Keith counted) stone cliff steps to sea where herrings used to be landed and cured. Unsignposted so ask locally for directions if lost, and go carefully.

WILDLIFE CRUISE, JOHN O' GROATS: 01955 611353. June-Aug; 90min trips to sea stacks, birds and **JOHN O' GROATS – ORKNEY:** May-Sept day trips. White water adventures and 'nature shows', try **NORTH COAST MARINE ADVENTURES**, Easter-Oct. 07867 666273.

WHAT TO DO

SWIMMING: Wick (01955 603711), Thurso (01847 893260). Both central. **GOLF:** Wick (01955 602726), Thurso (01847 893807), Reay (01847 811288). **SURFING AND WINDSURFING:** Esp round Thurso. TO have leaflet about beaches. **RIDING:** Dunnet Trekking. Glorious trekking on Dunnet Beach (01847 851689). **BIKE HIRE:** Wheels, Wick (01955 603636). **ALLSTAR FACTORY:** bowling, cinema, the whole entertainment centre idea (01847 895050).

TOURIST INFO:

WICK: Whitechapel Rd. 01955 602596. Jan-Dec.

THURSO: Riverside. 01847 892371. Apr-Oct.

HOLIDAY CENTRES

PITLOCHRY

WHERE TO STAY

KILLIECRANKIE HOTEL: 01796 473220 (950/PERTHSHIRE HOTELS).   MED.EX

PINE TREES: 01796 472121. Off Main St (959/PERTHSHIRE HOTELS).   MED.EX

DUNFALLANDY HOUSE: 01796 472648. Just out of town (2km), but away from all that. Good value country-house hotel. 8 rms.MED.INX

WHERE TO EAT

THE OLD ARMOURY: 01796 474821. (965/PERTHSHIRE EATS).   INX

KILLIECRANKIE HOTEL: Go those miles (5) to dinner; or bar meals! (*above*).
      INX

EAST HAUGH HOTEL: 01796 473121. 3km S off A9. Gr bar meals/restau. MED

PORTNACRAIG: 01796 472777. By theatre, on river. An insider choice.   INX

OLD SMITHY: 01796 472356. Main St. Coffees/restau. 7 days. LO 8.30pm. INX

PRINCE OF INDIA: 01796 472275. Off main st by McNaughton's. Unusually good Indian and good late bet.   MED

MOULIN INN: 01796 472196. Notable for pub food and atmos (1279/REAL ALE). 6km uphill. LO 9.30pm.   CHP

WHAT TO SEE

THE SALMON LADDER: From Main St and across dam to see 34-pool fish ladder (salmon leaping May-Oct, if you're lucky) and Hydro Board displays (sic);

BEN VRACKIE: Local fave with fab Trossachs views climbed from Moulin (2km from town). Rd behind Moulin Inn. Car park. 734m. Scree at top; and goats; **FASKALLY WOODS/LINN OF TUMMEL WALKS:** Well-marked woodland walks around L Faskally and Garry R. Can incl the Linn (rapids) and Pass of Killiecrankie (1829/BATTLEGROUNDS). Start: town/Garry bridge/visitor centre; **WOOLLEN SHOPS:** Many major chains and local shops in one small area/the main st. **PITLOCHRY THEATRE** (2185/THEATRES); **QUEEN'S VIEW** (1608/VIEWS); **EDRADOUR DISTILLERY** (1462/WHISKY); **MACNAUGHTON'S** (2037/OUTDOOR SHOPS); **MOULIN INN** (1279/REAL ALE).

2256
MAP 1

INVERARAY

WHERE TO STAY

GEORGE HOTEL: 01499 302111. On main st and in the Clark family for centuries (no, really – 1790). A gr value hotel – ales, good pub food, real fires. 823/ARGYLL HOTELS   CHP

LOCH FYNE HOTEL: 01499 302148. On A83 rd out of town towards W, o/look loch. Big hotel, but personally run. Good bar meals. 825/ARGYLL HOTELS. MED.INX

WHERE TO EAT

THE GEORGE/LOCH FYNE HOTELS: Bar meals esp. (*See above.*)   CHP

LOCH FYNE OYSTER BAR: 01499 600236. 14km E on A83.   INX

CREGGANS INN: 01369 860279. 32km E and S via A83/A815. On opp bank of L Fyne, but 35mins by rd. Bar meals/restau.   MED

WHAT TO SEE

INVERARAY CASTLE: Home of the Duke of Argyll and clan seat of the Campbells. Spectacular entrance hall; chronicle of Highland shenanigans unfurls in the gilded apartments. Fine walks in grounds esp to the prominent hill and folly (45mins up). Apr-Oct. **ARDKINGLAS WOODLAND:** 17km E on A83 (1486/GARDENS). **AUCHINDRAIN:** 8km S on A83; **INVERARAY JAIL** (2116/MUSEUMS); **ARGYLL WILDLIFE PARK:** 4km S on A83 (1661/KIDS)

2257
MAP 5

ST ANDREWS

WHERE TO STAY

OLD COURSE HOTEL: 01334 474371 (942/FIFE HOTELS).   LOTS

RUFFLETS: 01334 472594 (926/FIFE HOTELS).   MED.EX

RUSACKS: 01334 474321. Long-standing golfy hotel nr all courses and overlooking the 18th of the Old. Nice sun-lounge and b/fast o/looking the greens. Reliable & quite classy for a Macdonald Hotel, the recent new owners.
68RMS JAN-DEC T/T PETS CC KIDS MED.EX

INN ON NORTH STREET: 01334 474664. 127 North St. Corner of Murray park where there are numerous GH options. This a hipper, younger alternative to the stalwart, elegant but exp offerings above. Lizard bar in basement is happening place, the Cidsin on street level is quite civilised café-bar, so all corners are covered. Comfy, contemporary rms.
13RMS JAN-DEC T/T PETS CC KIDS MED.EX

GLENDERRON: 01334 477951. 9 Murray Park. A guest house with only 5 rms, but tasteful and good value. The one to choose on this st of many. INX

WHERE TO EAT

THE PEAT INN: 01334 840 206. 15km SW (934/RESTAU).   EXP

THE VINE LEAF: 01334 477497. Inauspicious entrance belies civilised St Andrews fav restau with menu that covers all bases, good vegn, good wines.

Morag & Ian Hamilton know how to look after you and what you like esp for pud. Thu-Sat dinner only. MED

THE DOLL'S HOUSE: 01334 477422. Church Sq. V central café/restau that caters well for kids (and teenagers). Eclectic range, smiley people and tables outside in summer. INX

GRANGE INN: 01334 472670. 4km E off Anstruther rd A917. V popular country pub in several rms with good local rep. Always busy. Book w/ends. INX

BROONS: 01334 478479. 117 North St. Adj to New Picture House. Locally fashionable upstairs bistro with simple contemporary menu & nice people. 7 days lunch & dinner. LO 9.30pm. INX

WESTPORT: 01334 473186. 170 South St. End of st adj 'the Arch'. Café-bar (and hotel accom pending at time of writing). Student fare but decent mod British menu. Good Sun brunch. Busy beer gdn in summer. Juices, papers. MED

BALAKA BANGLADESHI RESTAURANT: 01334 474825. 'Best Curry in Scotland' winner. Certainly as good as many in Edin or Glas. Celebrated herb & spice gdn out back which supplies other restaus in St Andrews. MED

BRAMBLES: Long-standing definitive St A coffee-shop. Cramped & cosy & usually a queue. Daytime only. (1398/TEAROOMS). CHP

OLD COURSE & RUFFLETS: Top end, top dining rms (*see above*).

INN ON NORTH ST: 01334 474664 (*see above*).

WHAT TO SEE

THE TOWN ITSELF: The lanes, cloisters, gdns and the University halls and colleges; the harbour and the botanic gdns. Perfect lawns; **THE CASTLE RUINS:** Founded in 13th cent on promontory; good for clambering over. 'Escape tunnel' to explore (if not tall). Spooky by night along this shore; **BRITISH GOLF MUSEUM:** Sophisticated audio-visual exhibition illustrating history and allure of the game. Even non-players will enjoy. **THE HIMALAYAS:** the most brilliant putting green; piles of fun, near the beach. Apr-Oct till 8pm, 7 days. Many **GOLF COURSES** (1953/GREAT GOLF); **WEST SANDS/KINSHALDY BEACH** (1534/BEACHES); **LEUCHARS CHURCH:** 9km by A91 N (1790/CHURCHES); **TENTSMUIR:** 20km by A91/A919 N (1688/WILDLIFE); **NEW PICTURE HOUSE** (2190/THEATRES); **JANETTA'S** (1417/ICE CREAM); **ST ANDREWS FINE ART**; **CATHEDRAL** (1725/RUINS); **EAST SANDS** (1993/LEISURE CENTRES).

ROYAL DEESIDE: BALLATER AND BANCHORY

WHERE TO STAY

RAEMOIR, BANCHORY: 01330 824884. Large mansion in secluded grounds 3km town by Raemoir Rd off A93. Relaxed and discreet. 9-hole golf and tennis. Growing rep for food. LOTS

DARROCH LEARG, BALLATER: 01339 755443. Town mansion above/off (at tight bend) A93 on way in from Braemar. Excellent nosh. (971/NE HOTELS.) MED

BANCHORY LODGE, BANCHORY: 01330 822625 (980/NE HOTELS). EXP

TOR-NA-COILLE, BANCHORY: 01330 822242. Town mansion above/just off main A93 on way in from Ballater. Nr golf. Antiques in tasteful/individual rms. EXP

WHERE TO EAT

DARROCH LEARG, BALLATER: 01339 755443. The other Deeside hoteliers aspire to. (*see above*).

THE OAK ROOM, BALLATER: 01339 755858. EXP

ST TROPEZ, BANCHORY: 01330 822216 (993/NE RESTAUS).   MED

THE BLACK-FACED SHEEP, ABOYNE: 01339 887311. Near main rd. Coffee shop/gift shop with excellent home-baking. Daytime hrs but supper is coming (at TGP) (1379/TEAROOMS).

MILTON RESTAURANT: 01330 844566 (990/NE RESTAUS).   MED

WHAT TO SEE

CRAIGIEVAR/DRUM (1708/1709 CASTLES); **FASQUE** (1756/COUNTRY HOUSES); **CRATHES** (1473/1765 GARDENS/COUNTRY HOUSES); **BALMORAL** (1710/CASTLES); **LOCHNAGAR** (1889/MUNROS); **ALBERT MEMORIAL** (1776/MONUMENTS); **GLEN MUICK** (1574/LOCHS); **CAMBUS O'MAY** (1630/PICNICS); **GOLF:** Well-managed/picturesque courses, open to visitors at both Ballater (013397 55567), and Banchory (01330 822447). Both 18 holes; **FISHING:** Difficult, not impossible, on Dee or on R Feugh (N bank only) – permits from Feughside Inn (01330 850225); **WALKS:** Walks down both sides of the Dee, esp Ballater to Cambus O'May, 7km; **VIEWPOINTS:** Up Craigendarroch, the Hill of the Oaks, Ballater, from Braemar Rd (45mins). Scolty Hill and Monument, Banchory. Ask for directions; **RAEMOIR GARDEN CENTRE** (2083/GARDEN CENTRES); **BURN O' VAT** (1858/SPOOKY PLACES); **MACEWAN GALLERY** (2138/WHERE TO BUY ART); **BRAEMAR–LINN OF DEE, BALLATER–TOMINTOUL** (1589/1590=/SCENIC ROUTES).

LIST OF MAPS

NOTE: The maps give general guidance on attractions in an area –
they are not exact. For more precise details, refer to the text.

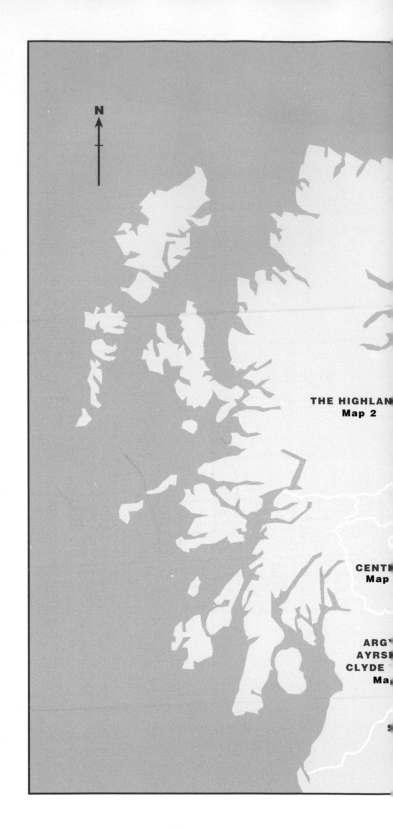

THE HIGHLAN
Map 2

CENTR
Map

ARG
AYRS
CLYDE
Ma

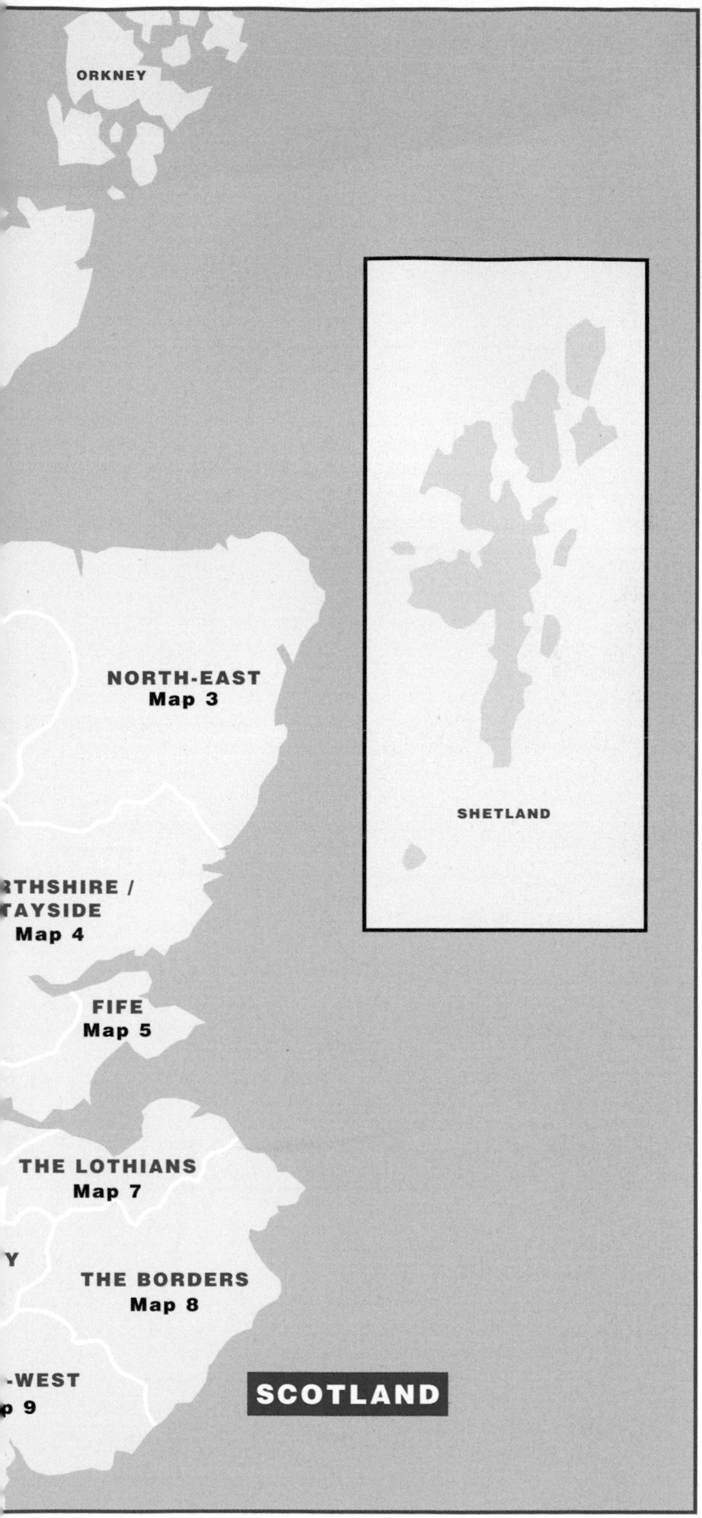

ORKNEY

NORTH-EAST
Map 3

RTHSHIRE /
TAYSIDE
Map 4

FIFE
Map 5

THE LOTHIANS
Map 7

Y

THE BORDERS
Map 8

-WEST
p 9

SHETLAND

SCOTLAND

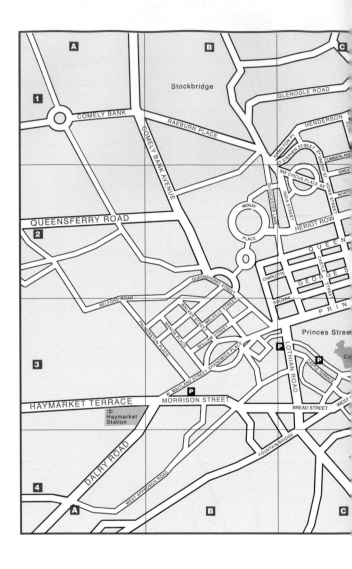

Stockbridge

GLENOGLE ROAD

COMELY BANK

RAEBURN PLACE

HENDERSON

HAMILTON PL

COMELY BANK AVENUE

ST STEPHEN STREET
ST VINCENT STREET
CUMBERLAND

NW CIRCUS PLACE
HOWE STREET
GREA

GLOUCESTER LANE

NORT

MORAY
PLACE

INDIA STREET

HERIOT ROW

QUEENSFERRY ROAD

QUEE

CASTLE STREET

QUEENSFERRY STREET

CHARLOTTE

GEORGE S

BELFORD ROAD

SQUARE

WAYNE STREET
MELVILLE STREET

PRIN

PALMERSTON PLACE

MANOR PLACE

WILLIAM STREET

SHANDWICK PLACE

Princes Stree

P

LOTHIAN ROAD

Ce

W. MAITLAND STREET

P

CASTLE TERRACE

HAYMARKET TERRACE

MORRISON STREET

BREAD STREET

WEST

Haymarket
Station

DALRY ROAD

WEST APPROACH ROAD

FOUNTAINBRIDGE

MAP A: Edinburgh City Centre

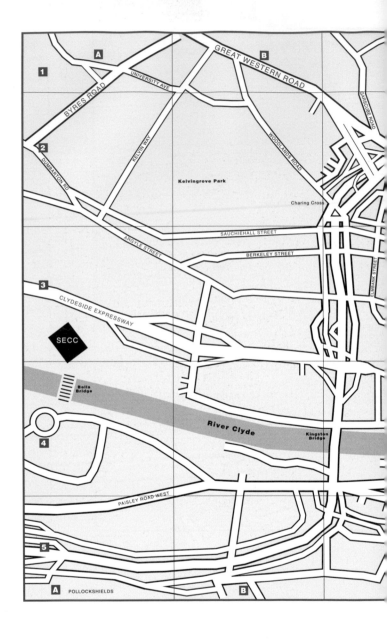

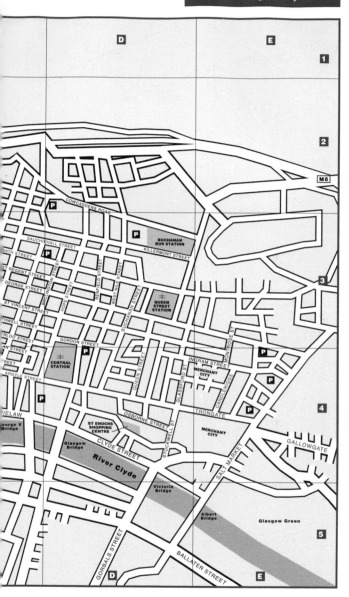

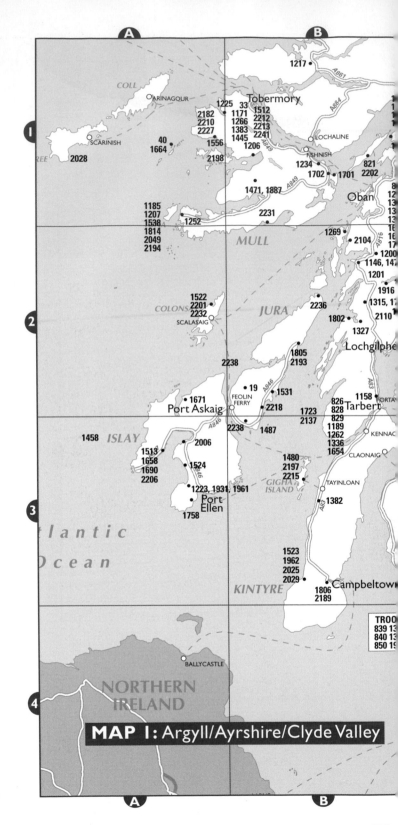

COLL

ARINAGOUR

1217

A861

Tobermory

A884

1225   33   1512
2182   1171   2212
2210   1266   1383   2213
2227   1445   2241

40   1556
1664   1206

SCARINISH

TREE

2028

2198

LOCHALINE

FISHNISH

1234

1702 • 1701

821
2202

1471, 1887

A849

A849

Oban

1185
1207
1538   1252
1814
2049
2194

2231

MULL

1269

2104

1200
1146, 147
1201

1916

1522
2201
2232

COLONS

SCALASAIG

JURA

2236

1315, 1

2110

1802

1327

2238

1805
2193

Lochgilphe

A83

19

FEOLIN
FERRY

A846

1531

826   1158
828   FORTA
829   Tarbert

1671

Port Askaig

2218

A846

2238

1487

1723
2137

1189
1262
1336
1654

KENNAC

1458   ISLAY

2006

1480
2197
2215

CLAONAIG

1513
1658
1690
2206

1524

1223, 1931, 1961

GIGHA
ISLAND

TAYINLOAN

A83

1382

Port
Ellen

1758

A t l a n t i c

O c e a n

1523
1962
2025
2029

KINTYRE

1806
2189

Campbeltow

TROO
839 13
840 13
850 19

BALLYCASTLE

NORTHERN
IRELAND

MAP 1: Argyll/Ayrshire/Clyde Valley

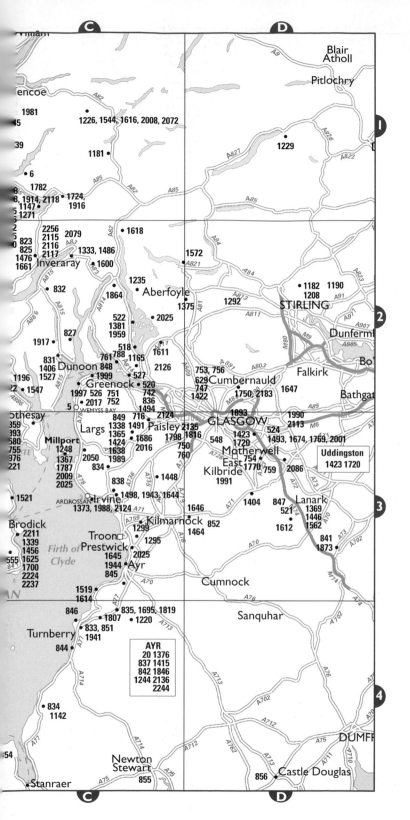

C D

William
Blair
Atholl
Pitlochry

Glencoe
1981
45
1226, 1544, 1616, 2008, 2072
39
1181
1229
6
1782
8, 1914, 2118
1147
1271
1724,
1916

2256
2115
823
2116
825
2117
1476
1661
Inveraray
1600
1618
1572
1182 1190
1208
2079
1333, 1486

832
1235
Aberfoyle
1864
1375
1292
STIRLING
522
1381
1959
2025
A811
Dunferml
518
1917
827
761
788
1165
1611
831
1406
Dunoon
848
2126
629
753, 756
747
Cumbernauld
Falkirk
Bo'
1196
1527
1999
527
520
742
836
1494
1750, 2183
1647
Bathgat
1547
1997 526 751
2017 752
5
849 716
Largs 1338 1491
1365
1686
1424
1638
2016
834
1816
750
760
548
1423
1750
524
1423
1720
1990
2113
1493, 1674, 1769, 2001
rothesay
359
393
580
755
976
221
Millport
1248
1367
1787
2009
2025
838
1498, 1943, 1644
1448
Motherwell
East
1770 759
Kilbride
1991
754
2086
Uddingston
1423 1720
1521
Brodick
2211
1339
1456
1625
1700
2224
2237
Irvine
1373, 1988, 2124
Kilmarnock
1299
1295
1646
852
1464
1404
521
1612
847
1369
1446
1562
841
1873
Firth of
Clyde
Troon
Prestwick
1645
1944
845
2025
Ayr
Cumnock
1519
1614
846
835, 1695, 1819
1807
1220
Sanquhar
Turnberry
833, 851
1941
844
AYR
20 1376
837 1415
842 1846
1244 2136
2244
834
1142
DUMFR
Stanraer
Newton
Stewart
855
856
Castle Douglas

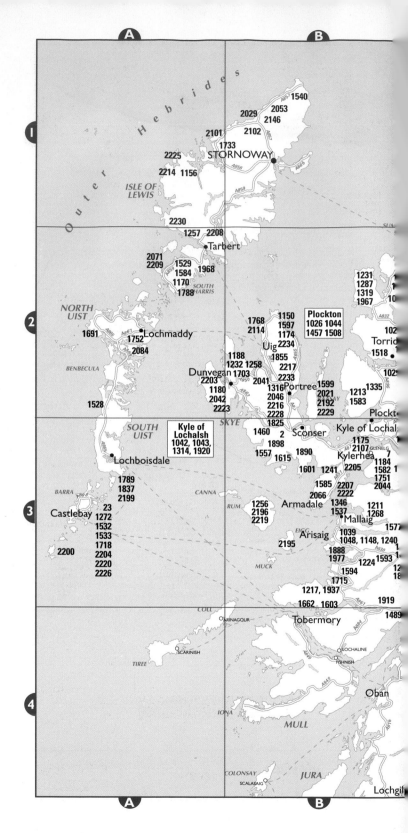

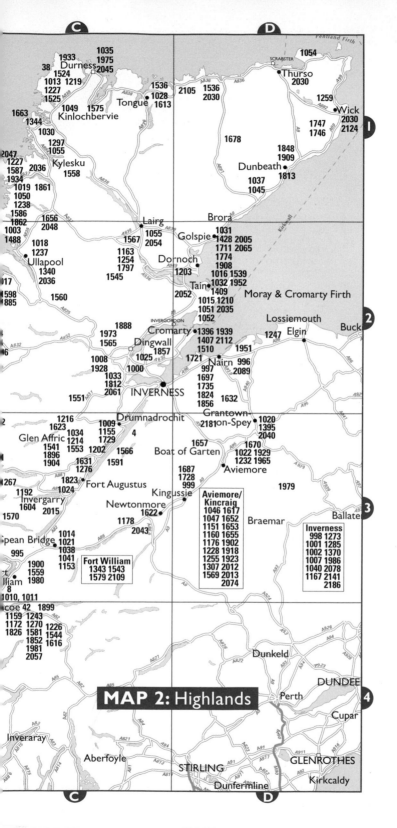

MAP 2: Highlands

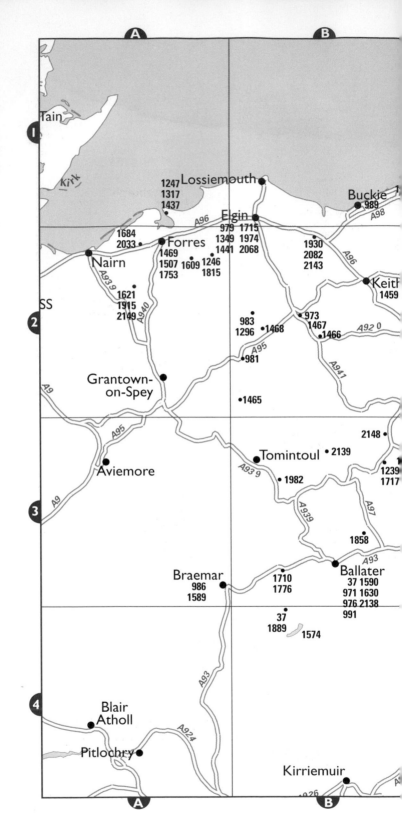

Tain

Kirk

1247 Lossiemouth
1317
1437

Buckie
989

A96 Elgin
1684   979 1715
2033   1349 1974   1930
      Forres 1441 2068 2082
1469   2143
1507 1609 1246
1753   1815

Nairn   Keith
                         1459

1621
1915
2149

SS

983   •973
1296 •1468 1467
        •1466
      •A95
      •981

Grantown-
on-Spey

•1465

                    2148 •

Tomintoul • 2139

Aviemore   1239
                   1717

A939   •1982

                    1858

            Ballater
Braemar 1710 37 1590
986   1776 971 1630
1589   976 2138
              991

        37
      1889   1574

Blair
Atholl

Pitlochry•

            Kirriemuir

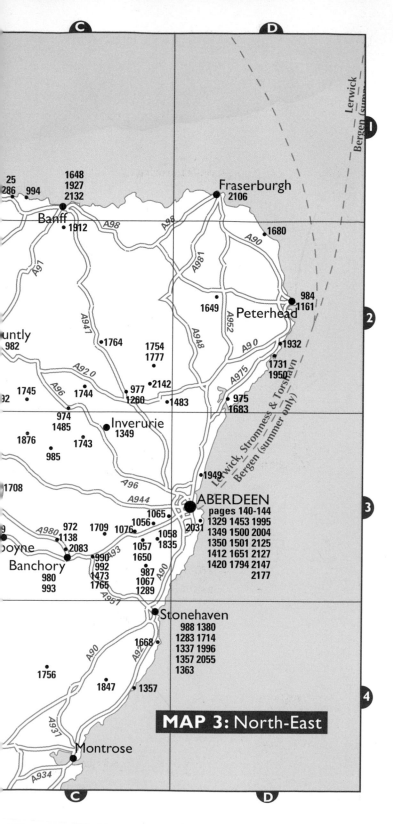

MAP 3: North-East

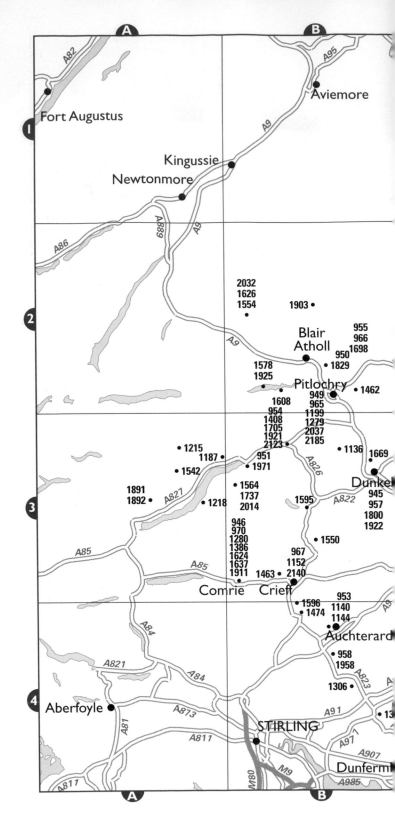

A

B

A82

A95

Aviemore

Fort Augustus

1

A9

Kingussie

Newtonmore

A889

A9

A86

2032
1626
1554

1903 •

955
966
1698

2

A9

Blair
Atholl

950
1829

1578
1925

Pitlochry

1462 •

1608
954
1408
1705
1921
2123

949
965
1199
1279
2037
2185

1136 •

1669 •

• 1215

1187 •

951
1971

A826

Dunkel

• 1542

1891
1892 •

A827

• 1218

• 1564
1737
2014

1595 •

945
957
1800
1922

A822

946
970
1280
1386
1624
1637
1911

967
1152
2140

A85

A85

1463 •

• 1550

3

Comrie

Crieff

953
1140
1144

1596
1474 •

Auchterard

958
1958 •

A823

A84

A821

1306 •

A9

4

Aberfoyle •

A873

A84

A91

• 13

A81

A811

STIRLING

A97

A907

M80

M9

Dunferm

A811

A985

A

B

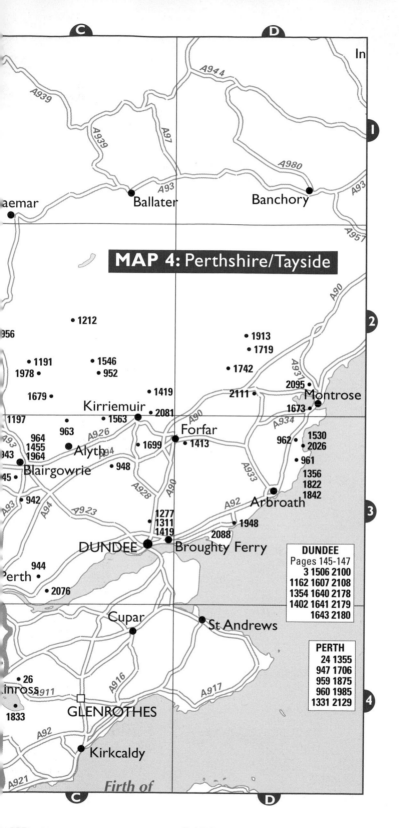

MAP 4: Perthshire/Tayside

In

Ballater
Banchory
aemar

• 1212

956

• 1191   • 1546
1978 •   • 952

1679 •
Kirriemuir • 2081

1197   • 1563
964   963
1455   • 1699
1964
• 948

943 •
45 •   Blairgowrie

• 942

944
erth •
• 2076

• 1913
• 1719
• 1742
2095 •
2111 •   Montrose
1673 •

Forfar
• 1413   962 •   1530
• 2026
• 961
1356
1822
1842
Arbroath

1277
1311
1419   • 1948
2088
DUNDEE   Broughty Ferry

Alyth

Cupar   St Andrews

• 26
inross
1833
GLENROTHES

Kirkcaldy

Firth of

DUNDEE
Pages 145-147
3 1506 2100
1162 1607 2108
1354 1640 2178
1402 1641 2179
1643 2180

PERTH
24 1355
947 1706
959 1875
960 1985
1331 2129

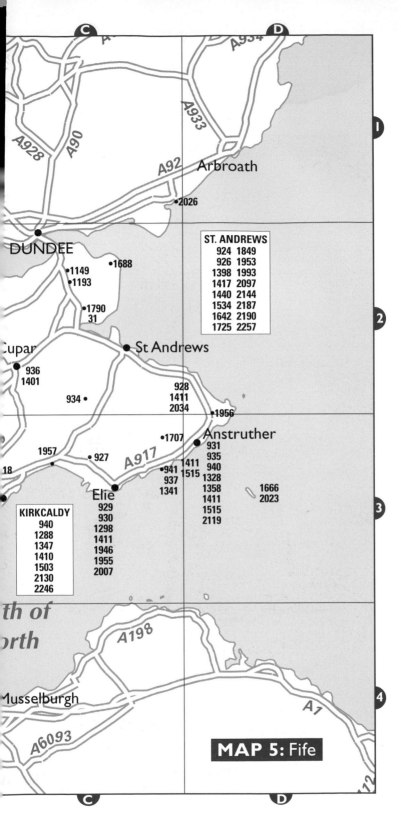

MAP 5: Fife

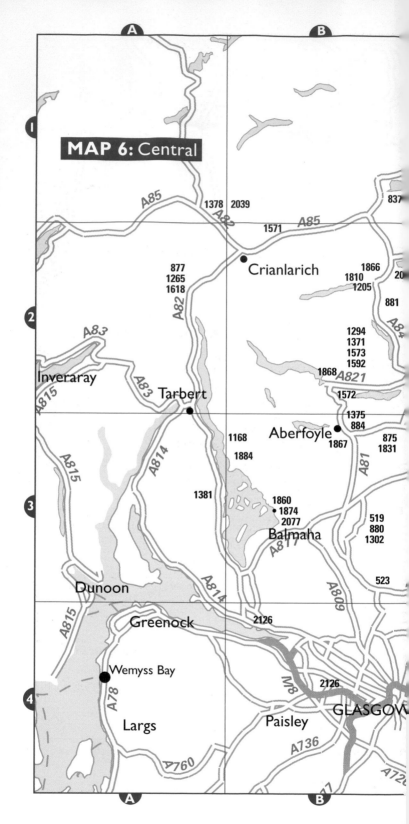

MAP 6: Central

A85 1378 2039 837

A82 1571 A85

877
1265
1618

Crianlarich

1866
1810 20
1205

881

A84

A83

1294
1371
1573
1592

Inveraray

A815

A83

Tarbert

1868 A821

1572

1375
884

Aberfoyle

1867

875
1831

A81

1168

1884

A814

A815

1381

1860
1874
2077

Balmaha

A817

519
880
1302

523

A809

Dunoon

A814

Greenock

2126

A815

Wemyss Bay

A78

M8

2126

GLASGOW

Largs

Paisley

A736

A760

A720

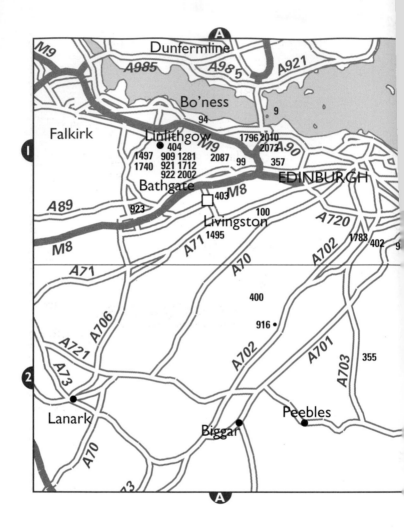

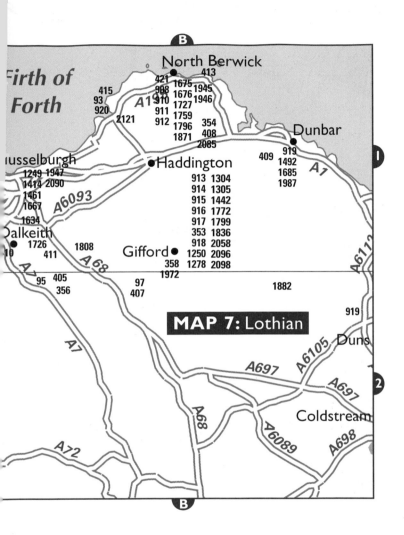

MAP 7: Lothian

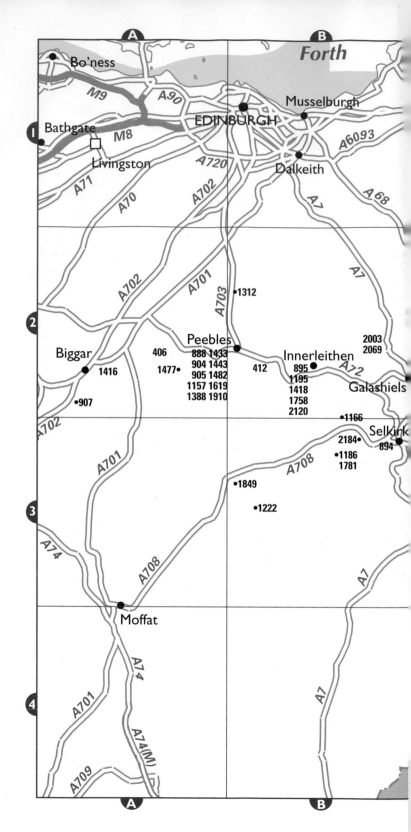

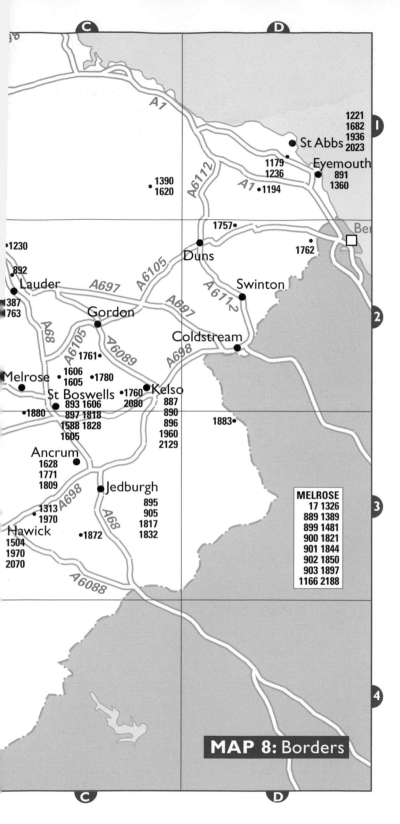

MAP 8: Borders

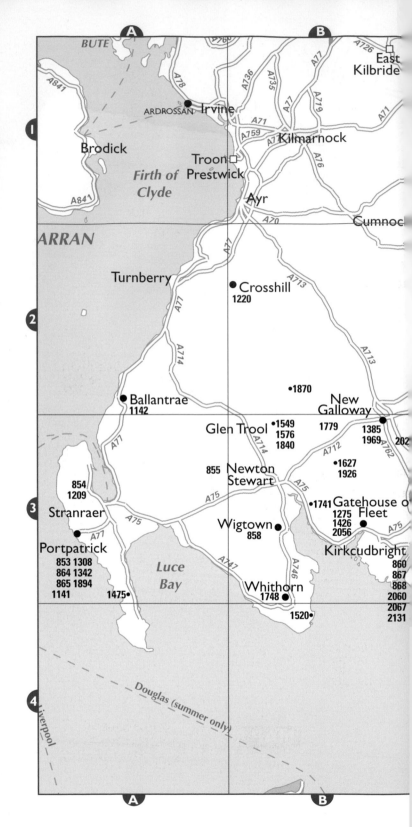

BUTE

A841

Brodick

A84¹

ARRAN

ARDROSSAN • Irvine

A78

A760

A736

A735

A77

A719

A726

East
Kilbride

A71

A71

A759

A71

Kilmarnock

Troon
Prestwick

**Firth of
Clyde**

Ayr

A76

A70

Cumnoc

Turnberry

A77

A713

• Crosshill
1220

A714

•1870

Ballantrae
1142

New
Galloway

A713

Glen Trool

•1549
1576
1840

1779

1385
1969

202

A714

A712

A762

855

Newton
Stewart

•1627
1926

854
1209

A75

A75

•1741

Gatehouse o
Fleet

1275
1426
2056

A75

Stranraer

Wigtown •

858

Kirkcudbright

A77

A77

A75

Portpatrick

853 1308
864 1342
865 1894
1141

1475•

**Luce
Bay**

A747

A746

860
867
868
2060
2067
2131

Whithorn

1748 •

1520•

Douglas (summer only)

iverpool

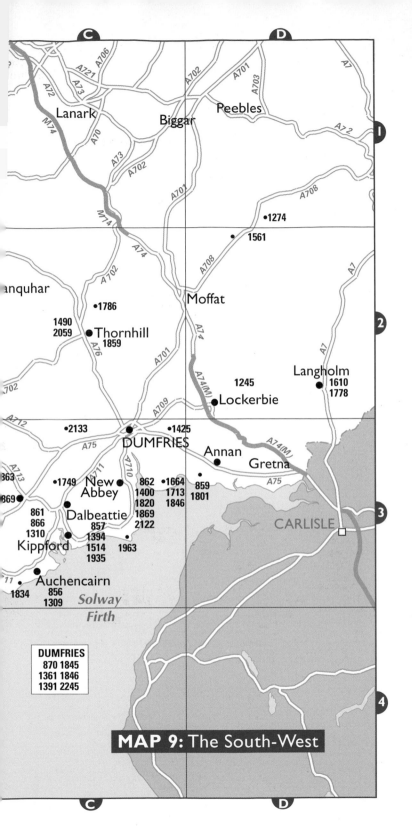

MAP 9: The South-West

INDEX